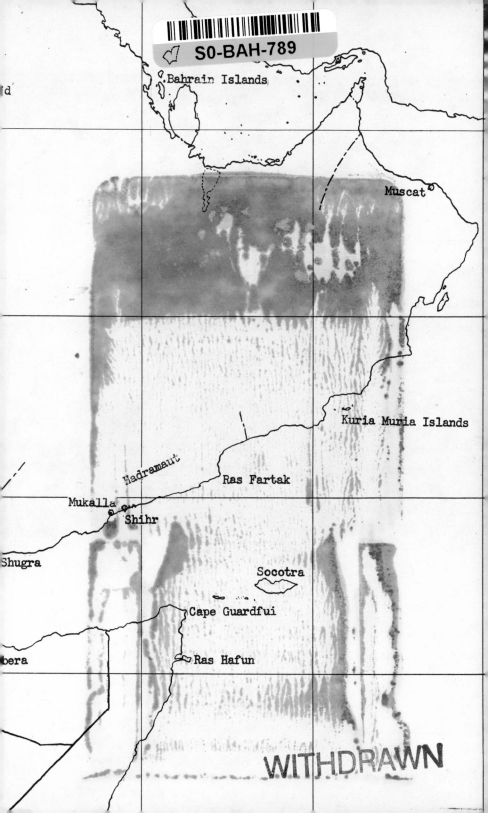

d

Bahrain Islands

Muscat

Kuria Muria Islands

Hadramaut

Ras Fartak

Mukalla

Shihr

Shugra

Socotra

Cape Guardfui

bera

Ras Hafun

Britain's Imperial Role
In The Red Sea Area
1800 - 1878

THOMAS E. MARSTON

"It seems to be a law of nature that the civilized nations shall conquer and possess the countries in a state of barbarism and by such means however unjustifiable it may appear at first sight extend the blessings of knowledge, industry and commerce among people hitherto sunk in the most gloomy depths of superstitious ignorance." — CAPTAIN JAMES MACKENZIE

THE SHOE STRING PRESS, INC.   HAMDEN, CONNECTICUT

TABLE OF CONTENTS

FOREWORD

The first half of this book in expanded form was presented
as a thesis in partial fulfillment of the requirement for a Ph. D.
degree at Harvard in 1939. Two wars and varied interests
have prevented the completion of the work until now.

During the Korean War, the author, in his position as Chief
of the Middle East-Africa Section of Army Intelligence in the
Pentagon met the late Colonel Leo J. Query, who had just returned from an assignment as Army Attaché to Ethiopia. A well-
educated and highly intelligent observer, he had traveled extensively in the area described in this book. He read a draft of the
manuscript, corrected many errors inherited from the documents, and made pertinent observations, many of which are incorporated into this volume. I owe him a great debt, not only
for the information which he supplied but also for his enthusiasm
for the project.

Another debt of gratitude is owed to Professor William L.
Langer of Harvard University, who not only directed my Ph. D.
thesis but also has continually prodded me to complete the book
when our paths have crossed in Washington and elsewhere.

I wish also to thank the Faculty of the Harvard Graduate
School for the award of a John Harvard Traveling Fellowship in
1936-1937, which helped greatly in gaining access to collections
in London.

Lastly, I would like to express my appreciation of the un-
sung heroes of the library world, the attendants at the India Office Library and the Public Records Office, whose unfailing
friendliness and cooperation provided me with a constant flow of
documents throughout a long London winter.

Thomas E. Marston
Yale University Library
New Haven, Connecticut

PLACE AND PERSONAL NAMES

In the period covered by this book, there existed no standard spellings for place and personal names in this part of the
world. For the most part, these names were transmitted orally to British and Ottoman officials, who reduced them to writing
as best they could. An effort has been made where possible to
identify places with their locations on modern maps and to reduce the variant spellings of personal names to some common
form. While these forms may offend the purists, they at least
avoid the confusion which beset the Foreign Office in London
and the Porte at Istanbul during the Yemen crisis of 1873-1875.

ABBREVIATIONS

IO: India Office documents.
FO: Foreign Office documents preserved in the Public Records
Office.
IO-BPC: India Office, Bombay Political and Secret Consulta-
tions.
IO-BSC: India Office, Bombay Secret Consultations.
IO-BSL & E: India Office, Bombay Secret Letters and Enclo-
sures
IO-BSE: India Office, Bombay Secret Enclosures.
IO-LAM: India Office, Letters from Aden and Muscat.
IO-LA: India Office, Letters from Aden.
HEIC: Honourable East India Company.
IB: India Board (ruling body of the East India Company).
JRGS: Journal of the Royal Geographical Society.
PMG: Pall Mall Gazette.

CURRENCY

During the nineteenth century the monetary unit of the Red
Sea area was the Crown, that of Abyssinia, the Maria Theresa
Thaler dated 1780. Both currencies depended for their value on
the silver content of the coin and they are of identical weight.
The documents as a rule express monetary values in dollars,

using the dollar sign. This practice has been followed in this
volume. The weight of silver in a crown or thaler is exactly
that of the American Trade Dollar and its value at any time is
exactly that of the Trade Dollar in comparison to currencies on
a gold standard. For all practical purposes the thaler is equivalent until 1851 to the American dollar. With the discovery of
the vast gold and silver resources of the American West, the
value of the thaler gradually declined until by 1878 it was worth
about sixty-five cents in American money.

THE DOCUMENTS

This volume is based largely on the documents in the
India Office and in the Foreign Office files of the Public Records
Office. Many of the interpretations and conclusions reached
are the result of the arrangement of documents in these files.
Therefore a word of explanation about the content and arrange-
ment of these files is necessary.

Both under the old East India Company and after 1858 under
the India Office the government of the Indian possessions was
carried out by committees or Boards, over which the respective
governors presided. These Boards formed a hierarchy. At the
top was the Secret Board (under the India Office, the Secret
Committee) which sat in London and had over-all direction of
Indian Affairs and the responsibility for liaison in the other government departments, such as the Foreign Office

The over all government of the Indian possessions was in
the hands of the Government of India. Many of the powers of
the Indian Government were delegated to the various Presidencies
(later Governments). Of these the Presidency (Government) of
Bombay was the one which had direct control over the Red Sea,
Persian Gulf and Indian Navy and exercised this control through
local residents.

The responsibilities and the limits of authority of these various governments do not appear to have been clearly drawn by
law, nor is any study on this subject readily available. One
gathers from the documents that the limitations imposed on any
individual government's or resident's actions depended in large
part upon personal aggressiveness, personal relationships with
superiors, and the immediate availability of military and financial resources under the government's or resident's direct
control.

In an area of vast distances and poor communications, policy direction had, of necessity, to be restricted to generalities; the responsible individuals were allowed to exercise their own judgment within very broad directives. Policy directives of this nature seemed to be very few. Most statements of policy were negative, "Thou shalt not," issued generally when some government or resident overstepped what higher authority believed to be the authority delegated, although usually only when such a move involved large and unauthorized expenditures.

The records of the Presidency (Government) of Bombay are collected in different series in the India Office. The series used as far as possible in this volume is the Secret and Political Consultations. These Consultations are arranged by date of action by the ruling Committee of the Bombay Government. The documents are copies, not originals, of all pertinent papers pertaining to a specific incident. If a bi-weekly report from Aden required no action it was simply reproduced in full. If it required action, all written opinions from members of the board were incorporated into the consultation as well as any correspondence with the Government of India or the Secret Committee in Londin, if the question was referred to them for action or advice.

The Foreign Office documents contain the original documents arranged by date of receipt, which was entered on each document. Accompanying these are Minutes by various Foreign Office officials and drafts of replies, often in several forms, including the final draft of the outgoing dispatch.

The main change in procedure which occurred after the abolition of the East India Company and the establishment of the India Office was the sending of duplicate copies of all reports direct to London, thus cutting down on the interminable delay in the Aden-Bombay-London system of communication and on the power, often exercised by the Bombay Government in Company days, of suppressing documents until the bound volumes of the Consultations arrived in London, probably a year after the documents had been acted on in Bombay.

For the historian this new procedure has one positive result. The relationship between the India Office and the Foreign Office become clear and the degree of cooperation or non-cooperation becomes evident. Relations between the Foreign Office and the Company were vague and apparently informal, and were dependent on the prestige and willingness of the various

Secretaries of the Foreign Office to cooperate; Lord Palmerston seems to have been the only Foreign Secretary who could dominate the Company in the period from 1830 to 1858. The change in 1858 from the Company to the India Office seemingly brought little improvement in cooperation except such as could be achieved by pressure within the cabinet. The personnel of the East India Company continued in the India Office and they remained independent in fact if not in theory. Except in a period of crisis when the India Office needed the help of the Foreign Office, the sole result of the changeover appeared to be that the Foreign Office received fuller information on Indian affairs than in the days of the Company.

BRITISH GOVERNMENTAL SPHERES OF INFLUENCE IN THE MIDDLE EAST

The growth of the two great trading companies in the seventeenth century, the Company of Merchants trading in the Levant (or the Levant Company) and the Honourable East India Company, led to an agreement between them delineating their respective trading areas. The Levant Company had a monopoly of trade with Egypt, the northern Red Sea as far south as Jidda and Massawa, the Hedjaz, Palestine, the Lebanon, Syria, Asia Minor, and the Ottoman Empire in Europe. The remainder of the Middle East fell into the trading area of the East India Company.

Both companies had the right to appoint ambassadors and consuls with diplomatic immunity, a right which within the Ottoman Empire was greatly broadened by the system of Capitulations. Until 1821, when the Levant Company gave up its charter, all British diplomatic officials within their trading area were appointed by the Company, although as the Company's importance dwindled in the eighteenth century the actual choice of higher officials appears to have been dictated by the Secretary of State for Foreign Affairs. After 1821, the Foreign Office inherited the appointment of diplomatic and consular officials in the Levant Company's trading area. Thus the division of interest in the nineteenth century between the Foreign Office and the East India Company and its successor, the India Office, was dictated by this early trading agreement.

<u>The Governmental Structure of the East India Company</u>
(later India Office)

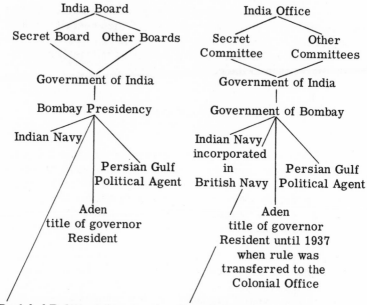

Before 1858

After 1858

The Honourable East India Co.   Secretary of State for India

India Board

Secret Board   Other Boards

Government of India

Bombay Presidency

Indian Navy

Persian Gulf
Political Agent

Aden
title of governor
Resident

Baghdad Political Agent   etc.

India Office

Secret   Other
Committee   Committees

Government of India

Government of Bombay

Indian Navy/
incorporated
in   Persian Gulf
British Navy   Political Agent

Aden
title of governor
Resident until 1937
when rule was
transferred to the
Colonial Office

Baghdad Political Agent   etc.

Apparently in practice any official could communicate directly with London under either the Company or the India Office provided he sent copies of his communication to the next higher echelon.

The East India Company was an independent agency and communication between the Secretary of State for Foreign Affairs and the India Board was private and unofficial in nature. The chief effect of the establishment of the India Office was to provide a Cabinet seat for its Secretary of State and bring the vast governmental structure which had grown up under the Company under the direct control of the British government.

RESIDENTS OF ADEN 1839-1878

Commander Stafford B. Haines, Indian Navy, 1839-1854

Colonel James Outram, Bombay Army, June-September, 1854

Brigadier William M. Coghlan, Bombay Army, 1854-1863

Colonel William Merewether, 1863-1867

Major General Edward L. Russell, 1867-1870

Major General Sir Charles W. Tremenheere, 1870-1872

Brigadier John W. Schneider, 1872-1878

The Residents had political assistants who were usually company grade officers. Haines had only one assistant, Lieutenant Cruttenden, like Haines, an officer of the Indian Navy. The remaining Residents had two or more. In the absence of the Resident the senior assistant became Acting Resident. On rare occasions when the Resident and his assistants were all away from Aden, the General Officer commanding the Aden Garrison became Acting Resident.

Britain's Imperial Role
In The Red Sea Area
1800 - 1878

I. INTRODUCTION

This study is in essence the case history of a British imperial policy, the exclusive dominance of the Red Sea, a policy which ultimately failed before the expanding economy of Western Europe.

After the expulsion of the French from India as a result of the Seven Years' War, one of the aims of East India Company policy was to protect the routes between Europe and India. Another objective was to protect their trade monopoly with the whole Indian Ocean area. As a result of these policies they became involved with the area of the Persian Gulf where continued piracy seriously threatened their communications and their trade with Persia and with Mesopotamia (modern Iraq).

The strongest power in this area was the Sultanate of Muscat, which also ruled faraway Zanzibar off the East African coast. As the trade and products of the Western Indian Ocean were negligible compared to those of India, this vast area offered little potential profit and therefore called for a minimum of expenditure. Thus Company policy developed into what might be termed a negative imperialism. This had two aspects; first the maintenance of peace in the area, including the suppression of piracy; and second, the denial of the area to any other European power.

Early interest in the Persian Gulf with its dependent interest in the Sultan of Muscat's dominions in Zanzibar served to define quite sharply the areas of the Company's direct interests in the Western Indian Ocean. The Sultan of Muscat's influence and possessions covered the southeastern shore of Arabia about as far west as the Kuria Muria Islands; the influence of his Zanzibar dependencies extended along the Arab-controlled cities of the East African coast as far north as Cape Guardafui and the island of Socotra, which was a dependency of the small Hadramaut coast Sultanate of Qishn.

It is the area between Muscat and Zanzibar with which this book is primarily concerned an area extending from the Kuria Muria Islands on the east to Socotra on the south and west, and including the Gulf of Aden, the Red Sea and the adjacent territories. Culturally, economically, and historically, this region formed a unit previous to the opening of the Suez Canal, which

was dominated by Muslim culture and governed by tribal organ-
izations. Seventy miles of desert, the isthmus of Suez, effectively cut it off from the Mediterranean economy and made it
for the western European one of the most remote parts of the
world.

A glance at any world map will show the Red Sea extending
like a long finger dividing Arabia from Africa. It is in fact a
continuation of the great geologic rift which begins with the
Jordan Valley and the Dead Sea and continues through the Wadi
Araba to the Bay of Aqaba at the head of the Red Sea. On the
north the Red Sea ends with the isthmus of Suez; on the south it
is almost closed off by the narrow strait at Bab-el-Mandeb, a
strait dominated by the island of Perim. The shores of the Red
Sea, however, constitute but a part of a larger area. The lands
along the Gulf of Aden, stretching from Cape Guardafui and
Socotra off the African Somali coast westward to Bab-el-Mandeb and thence east 600 miles along the South Arabian coast to
the Sultanate of Qishn and Ras Fartak, are part and parcel of
the Red Sea culturally, economically, and historically. To the
east of Ras Fartak the seafaring Arab tribes were responsible
for the Arab colonization of the cities of the East African coast
from Delagoa Bay to Mogadishu, north of the Juba River.

The northern end of the Red Sea is partially influenced by
the Mediterranean economy. From Suez past Q'useir on the
west coast, the country was an integral part of Egypt. On the
east the Holy Cities, Mecca and Medina, were international in
influence, but the province which they dominated was purely
tribal in organization and economy.

The area included in this economic and historical unit
therefore consists of the Hadramaut, the Yemen, the Asir
country in Arabia, the Somali coast north of Cape Guardafui,
the Dankali country, the territory around Annesley Bay
(Massawa), and Abyssinia lying west of the African side of
the Red Sea.

The Hadramaut or Hadrami Coast was scarcely known
until recent years. Barren, with few oases and a small population, it was known to both Arab and European worlds only
through the contacts made at its small ports, Mukalla and
Shihr. The sea-going Arabs from this district looked towards
India and Southeast Asia for their chief contacts. The Hadrami formed the bodyguard of the Nizam of Hyderabad and
there were large colonies of them in Singapore, Java, and

Sumatra. Since the collapse of the overland spice route of
Roman times their country has been economically unimportant,
and its chief trade has been in the necessities of life.
Historically and culturally the Yemen included what we
know today as the Aden Colony as well as the Yemen proper on
the east shore of the Red Sea, the district of Abu 'Arish and the
Farsan islands. Along the coast it consists of a low coastal
plain, hot, dry, and uninteresting, extending from thirty to
eighty miles inland and known as the Tehama. From this plain
gradually rise the spectacular mountains of the Yemen, reaching in some spots an altitude of almost 10,000 feet. The land
here is fertile with a heavy annual rainfall. Torrential rivers
hurl themselves down the mountains, watering and enriching
the foothills and the surrounding area, then being absorbed
into the ground as they reach the dry coastal plain. It was with
good reason that this upland country with its fertility and relatively mild climate was termed Arabia Felix by the ancients.
    North of Abu 'Arish lies the Asir country, an arid steppe
area. In the nineteenth century it contained the most powerful
and independent coalition of nomadic tribes of southwestern
Arabia and acted as a buffer state between the Yemen and the
Hedjaz.
    On the west coast of the Red Sea the shore line from
Q'useir southward is barren and unfriendly, until the neighborhood of Suakin is reached. Here a pleasant grassland area extends to Annesley Bay, the only natural harbor on the entire
shore of the Red Sea. The town of Massawa is situated on an
island in the bay. At this point the Abyssinian highlands come
closest to the coast, forming the main entrance to a vast
mountainous territory. This geographical situation brings
rains which, while they make the country fertile, add so much
dampness to the ever-present heat of the Red Sea that the climate along the shore is one of the most unpleasant in the world.
    From Massawa south to Zeila and Tajura stretches the
Dankali coast. Here the coastal plain widens out into another
tract of desert inhabited only by 100,000 wild tribesmen who
live either by herding their meagre flocks or by making salt
from a depression south of Massawa which was formerly an
arm of the Red Sea. There seems to be considerable rivalry
in the different areas on the Red Sea coast for the claim to the
most unpleasant climate, but the Dankali coast deserves first
place.

From the Gulf of Tajura east to Cape Guardafui extends
the Somali coast. Here the coastal plain is a fairly fertile
grassland with low hills rising in the interior. The people,
nomadic by nature, existed by raising cattle of various kinds,
which were exported principally through the port of Berbera,
the only adequate harbor east of Zeila.

To the west of the African Red Sea coast lies Abyssinia or
Ethiopia. While historically this country has had various frontiers, culturally and geographically it consists of the Abyssinian highlands, mountains sometimes 16,000 feet high, and
plateaus of an altitude of 7,000 to 10,000 feet, cut by deep river
valleys of tremendous fertility. Ethiopia is divided into four
areas by these mountains. Tigré, the northeastern area, is
the source and watershed of the Atbara River which runs
north and west, joining the Nile between Khartoum and Berber
in the Sudan. Gondar consists of the watershed around Lake
Tana, the source of the Blue Nile, and lies west and south of
Tigré, being bounded on the north and west by the plains of the
Sudan. Shoa lies to the south and east of Gondar on the watershed of the Awash River which, if it did not disappear on the
arid Dankali plain, would reach the sea at the Gulf of Tajura.
Southeast and west of Shoa lies the Galla country. This is considered part of Abyssinia by the Abyssinians, but it is Muslim
in religion. The country here is hilly rather than mountainous,
lacking the extreme fertility of the Abyssinian highlands but
far from being desert. It is the watershed and source of the
Juba River.

Along the whole coast line from Ras Fartak to Cape Guardafui, excepting of course the Egyptian area, there are only
three first-class harbors, Aden, Jibuti, and Massawa, although
the last is now shallow for modern vessels because of silting.
Poor harbors at Jidda, Berbera, Zeila, Obock, Assab Bay,
and Suakin were adequate for native trading vessels but provided only mediocre protection for nineteenth century European
merchantmen. Other ports of the area, Mocha, Hodeida,
Loheia, and Bulhar were little better than open roadsteads.
Local necessities of commerce, however, often gave these
ports a much greater importance than their physical characteristics seemed to justify, especially these ports which served
as outlets for the trade of the Yemen.

Except for Tigré, Gondar, and Shoa, the most densely
populated areas in Abyssinia, the whole area is predominantly

Sunni Muslim. The Yemen is strongly influenced by the Zaidi sect of Shi'ite Muhammadanism, which is antagonistic to the Sunni orthodoxy of the Turks. This religious antagonism does much to explain the difficulties encountered by the Ottomans in their various attempts to rule the area. Tigré, Gondar, and Shoa are partly Christian in religion, since the Ethiopian National Orthodox Church is derived from the Coptic branch of Christianity. In addition there was a Jewish minority in both the Yemen and Abyssinia. This minority, shabbily treated in the Yemen, was important in the nineteenth century, as it provided a field for European missionary activity which did not conflict with the established religions of either country. In Ethiopia the Jews were particularly respected because of the claim of Ethiopian Christianity to Hebrew background.

The only parts of the area with any real economic importance were the Yemen, which had had a brisk export trade from time immemorial in gums, frankincense and myrrh and, from the fifteenth century, in coffee, and the Somali area, where the products of southern Ethiopia and cattle provided a brisk trade.

Potentially, of course, Abyssinia had great wealth which had never been developed due to three factors: first, the lack of a suitable free port for export; second, the traditional refusal of the Abyssinian male to do agricultural work; and third, the feudal character of the government, which hampered trade by the imposition of transit dues by each small feudal unit. However, a certain small trade always existed at Zeila and Berbera, emanating from Harar and the trade routes from Central Africa which skirted the southern side of the highlands of Ethiopia.

The history of Harar is obscure. The country came under Persian influence in the seventh century during the Persian occupation of the Yemen. It was an important center of the great Adel Empire of the thirteenth century and about 1520 became the capital of that Empire when Portuguese aggressions threatened Zeila. It certainly tapped the same trade source as the Arab colonies of East Africa, in addition to trading in the products of the surrounding country which were similar to the products of the Yemen. A great variety of produce came over trade routes which centered on Harar and went thence to the coast. This gave rise to the traditional European belief in the wealth of Abyssinia and the ascription to this unknown country of many products which in reality came from the south and the

west. It should be emphasized that it was the variety and not
the volume of trade which created this impression. The most
valuable of all the exports from this area in the eighteenth and
early nineteenth centuries was similar to that in the other Arab
East African colonies, namely slaves, but in the case of Harar
it was again quality rather than quantity which counted. This
town served as the center for the export of Galla and Somali
women, highly prized in the Arab world for their beauty and
value as concubines. [Note: Somali women are generally
credited with being more attractive than Galla women. However the Somalis were regarded as nurr or free by Muslim
jurists and therefore belonged to a race unenslavable by conquest. Galla women were often enslaved by war; Somali women
were sold into slavery by their parents.]

The rest of Abyssinia, potentially wealthy though it was,
produced little or nothing for export, and what little there was
went through Metemma and the Sudan overland to Egypt.

Of the remainder of the Red Sea area, Jidda and the Holy
Cities depended entirely on the pilgrim trade for their prosperity. The Somali coast exported a considerable surplus of
cattle as well as easily-gathered products such as various
gums. Elsewhere trade was limited to the necessities of life;
some dates and rice were imported on the south Arabian shore
in return for the meagre excess of agricultural products grown
there.

Arabia Felix, or the Yemen, dominated the whole area
economically, and the prosperity of the surrounding territory
largely depended on the fortunes of this country. The Yemen
was rich and fertile, yet it was not sufficiently so to justify
Alexander's contemplated invasion, abandoned on his early
death, or Augustus' extensive expedition under Aellius Gallus,
which failed before the walls of the unknown city of Mariaba.
Both men believed the Yemen was the source of spices, unaware of the tremendous trade of the sea route from India,
which had existed from time immemorial.

Thanks to the monsoons, which in fall and winter blow
from the northeast to the southwest and in spring and summer
reverse themselves, the trip from India or from the East African coast to the south of Arabia was an easy task for the
most primitive sailing vessels. The Yemen was agriculturally
rich, but trade with the East made it important. However,
this trade might not have influenced the Yemen except for

certain other geographical facts. The Red Sea even today presents a difficult navigational problem, filled as it is with islands, reefs, and shallows. When vessels depended upon wind alone the problem was almost insuperable. The only possible solution was to transship goods from the larger sea-going vessels of the Indian Ocean to small craft capable of navigating inland waters. Two ports, Aden and Mocha, were available for this service and from the earliest times these ports became the transshipping points of the seaborne trade between the East and Egypt.

To understand the meaning of transshipment to the economy of Aden and Mocha, the process of Middle Eastern trade must be understood. A bale of Chinese silk would be sold by the manufacturer in the interior of China to a merchant who would transport it to Canton. Here it would be resold at a profit to a seagoing merchant, who usually would transport it to some port of Southwest India. Again it would be sold, to an Arab or Indian trader who would ship it to Aden or Mocha, where it would be purchased by the merchant who would move it to Suez. At each transshipment point a sale was made and it was this sale, not the handling of the commodities, that made the economy of transshipment points flourish. It was to avoid these profits, with their excessive increases in cost of the shipped goods, that the great family trading firms of the Arabs, Indians, and Chinese were formed, and it was for the same purpose that the western European trading firms, such as the East India Company and the Levant Company, were organized.

The all sea route from Asia to Europe, which was the safest, because least subject to political disturbances, channeled all trade through Aden and Mocha. In these two ports the Yemen had a natural outlet for its products more dependable and convenient than that of almost any other territory in the Indian Ocean economy. The country therefore doubly benefited from this eastern trade. How early the trade began is unknown; however, the presence of Indian products in the Eighteenth Dynasty tombs in Egypt gives some indication of its antiquity. This commerce gave birth to the tradition of the Queen of Sheba in Solomon's time. By Roman times it was flourishing, as is shown in Rostovtzeff's SOCIAL AND ECONOMIC HISTORY OF THE ROMAN EMPIRE (Oxford, Clarendon Press, 1926). In the time of Domitian it was important enough for an unknown Alexandrian merchant to write a guidebook, Periplus Maris

Erythraei, which described the Red Sea and the shores of the
Indian Ocean.

According to early tradition, the Yemen was originally
governed as one unit by the Hymaritic dynasty, which ruled
from the ancient city of Saba, probably modern Mareb, lying
about sixty miles northeast of San'a. This dynasty began about
1750 B.C. and by Roman times was already on the decline.
The best-known ruler in the days of the early Roman Empire
was Queen Balkania, or Yalkama. This name has been Euro-
peanized as Balkis. A very remarkable woman, she was the
subject of many fables, best known of which is in the traditional
association of her name with that of the Queen of Sheba (Saba).
The Yemen merchants dominated the Eastern trade at this time
and for a considerable period thereafter, gradually to be dis-
placed by Romans and East Indians.

As early as the first century, Christianity began to make
its appearance in Arabia Felix and found itself in rivalry with
both the local pagan religions and a strong Jewish colony,
which had emigrated there as a result of the Babylonian conquest of Palestine. About 342 the Byzantine Emperor Constan-
tius sent an embassy to the Yemen to foster Christianity and
trade, and about the same time the Axumite Abyssinians established some colonies there. Christianity did not make much
headway, however, until the weakened Hymaritic dynasty fell
to the expanding power of the Axumite Abyssinian Christian
monarchy. The latter captured the Yemen in 525, as a result
of a barbarous persecution of the Christians by the Jews, in
which reputedly 20,000 priests, monks, and other Christians
were killed.

Complete Abyssinian occupation was short-lived. The entire Yemen was ruled as a viceroyalty of the Negus Negusti
until 575. This period was marked by intolerable cruelty,
which led the remaining Hymarites to seek out the aid of the
Byzantine Emperor and, when this was refused, of the Persian
Emperor, Nushir-wan. According to E. G. Browne in his
HISTORY OF PERSIAN LITERATURE (Cambridge, University
Press, 1929, Vol. I, pp. 179 ff.), the Emperor decided to kill
two birds with one stone; he formed an expeditionary force of
all the convicts and malefactors in his prisons to get rid of
them and capture the Yemen at the same time. The expedition,
estimated at only 600 men, succeeded in defeating the Abyssinians, and a part of the Yemen, together with Muscat and the

Hadramaut, became a Persian dominion in 575.
The Persian rule was even shorter than the Abyssinian.
Muhammad fled from Mecca to Medina in 622 and from there
his religion, with consequent civil disturbances, spread rapidly
to the Yemen. After Muhammad's death the appearance of rival
prophets in the Yemen led to the interference of Abu Bakr, the
legally elected Calif, and to the conquest of the country, which
was incorporated in the Muslim Empire in 633.
The rise of the Abbasid Califate early in the eighth century
and the establishment of Baghdad as its capital had a profound
effect on all Middle Eastern trade. Mesopotamia (Iraq) had always been a principal land route between East and West but
now the new capital Baghdad came to dominate much of the trade
between Asia and Europe. Baghdad however, was more than
a trading center. Fantastically wealthy for its period, it was
the leading consumer area of the Middle East if not of the
world. The growth of Baghdad was accompanied by the great
spread of Arab merchants chiefly from the Persian Gulf over
the Indian Ocean area, and the consequent development of a
complex trading system of Arabic family firms. These two
factors reduced the Red Sea-India trade, which was diverted to
the Persian Gulf-Baghdad route, only the products destined for
Egypt and Palestine going now via the Yemen and the Red Sea.
From the conquest of the Yemen by the Arabs in 633 through
the Ommayed and early Abbasid period, the country was fairly
peaceful. While subject to the usual intrigues of an outlying
province of the Muslim Empire, it retained its integrity and
loyalty until 932. At this time internal weaknesses in the
Abbasid Califate led to the breakdown of central control over
the outlying provinces, and the Yemen was one of the first of
these to break away from Abbasid control. The history of the
next hundred years is obscure as the Yemen was subject to continual civil wars. By 1038 the warring factions had been reduced to two governments, one ruling the highlands from San'a,
the other ruling Aden, Lahej, and the Hadramaut. Rivalry continued between these two principalities until 1173 when Turhan
Shah, brother of Salah-ed-Din, conquered the Yemen for the
great Egyptian leader and gained control of Aden through diplomatic means. The Egyptian rule was short-lived and resulted
in chaos for the Yemen; Aden alone was able to retain a stable
government. The interior was a hotbed of tribal warfare in
which the natural independence of the tribes was aided by the

dynastic rivalries so typical of many Arab states. Not until
1477 was the country really united when one Abd-el-Wahab became Sultan of the Yemen.

Through all this chaos Aden and its environs was little influenced by the turmoil of the interior. Except for a brief period of Persian domination under the Seljukid Sultan Malikshah
about 1090, its government was stable and continuous and,
except for attacks by ambitious tribal chiefs from the interior,
peaceful.

The cause of this tranquility lay not in the strength and
wisdom of Aden's rulers but in the tremendous wealth of the
town. There were four major trade routes to the East. The
most northern route went from China through the caravan cities
of what today is Russian Turkestan, thence south of the Caspian
Sea through Persia and Asia Minor to ports on the Black Sea
and Constantinople. Another all-land route came from India
via the Khyber Pass and modern Afghanistan to Persia and
thence to Baghdad. The third route, and chief rival of the all-
sea-Aden route, came by sea from India to Hormuz Island in
the Persian Gulf and thence overland to Baghdad, piracy and
political instability around Basra often making a direct sea
trip to the mouth of the Tigris and Euphrates rivers particularly hazardous. From Baghdad the route went overland to the
Black Sea, Constantinople, Damascus and the Levant ports or
Egypt. The fourth route was the all-sea route from India to
Aden and thence up the Red Sea to Egypt. The importance of
trade to the whole Near and Middle East cannot be overestimated. When it was undisturbed the land was prosperous; when
it was cut off, the peoples of this part of the world sank to a
level of mere existence.

In order to understand the real meaning of medieval trade
to the Middle East, it is necessary to revise the present-day
concepts of this trade. Western Europeans have too often
thought of medieval trade exclusively in terms of western
Europe and particularly of that part of western Europe lying
north of the Alps. To gain any true understanding of the real
economic implications of this trade, it must be emphasized that
western European trade comprised only a part and often a very
small part of the total commerce of the trade centers of the
Middle East. Throughout medieval as well as ancient history
the Tigris and Euphrates valley and the eastern Mediterranean
constituted the great trading area, within which political events

determined the actual cities which were at any given time major trading centers.   Rome itself, the administrative center of
a great empire, was the only geographical exception to the
concentration of wealth and high standard of living otherwise
confined to the major trading and consuming area defined above.
The all-sea route from India to Egypt via Aden was used for
trade with the consumer area of Egypt, always in medieval
times a prosperous country, and for part of the trade from
India destined for the western Mediterranean and western
Europe.   When political disturbances and uncertainties upset
the other established trade routes, Aden prospered as direct
trade with the west was diverted to the all-sea route.   Trade
through Aden also increased as western Europe emerged from
the political chaos of the tenth and early eleventh centuries.
The Crusaders stimulated the demand for many Eastern luxury
products and served to increase trade direct to the West.
Meanwhile political upheavals occurring in the Middle East
served to reduce the volume of this trade considerably.   The
weakened Abbasid Califate at Baghdad was conquered by the
dynasty of the Seljuk Turks.   These disturbances, while not
disastrous to the overland trade routes, served to increase the
value and importance of the all-sea route, and Malikshah's
conquest of Aden c. 1090 was unquestionably prompted by a
desire to control this route.   The invasion of Genghis Khan in
the early thirteenth century caused such dynastic convulsions
that the overland routes were partially closed, but under the
peace enforced by his successors trade flourished.   However,
the dynasties set up by the Mongols did not have the strength
of the preceding ones and fell an easy prey to Tamurlane in
the early fifteenth century.   Each of these disturbances increased the value of the all-sea route and thus the prosperity
of Aden.
     Normally the greatest volume of trade from India went
over the sea-land route via the Persian Gulf, much of it to be
consumed by the brilliant civilization of the Abbasid Empire.
The Arabs of the Persian Gulf, having difficulty in prospering
from their semi-arid country, had always been a seafaring
people.   When there was a strong government in Persia or at
Baghdad their natural piratical tendencies were turned into the
channels of legitimate trade, but when the neighboring governments were weak with a consequent diminution of trade they reverted to piracy.   The unstable governments following the

Mongol invasions and the destruction of the wealth of Baghdad
in 1258 released the strict control over these tribes; the chaos
following Tamurlane's conquests gave them complete freedom.
It is not surprising, then, that trade on the sea route greatly
increased and that Aden reached its greatest prosperity during
the period following Tamurlane's short-lived conquests.

In 1182, at the north end of the Red Sea, occurred one of
the most fantastic episodes of history, which certainly had
much to do with the development of the policy of later Muslim
governments towards the Red Sea area. At the time Renaud de
Chatillon, one of the most romantic and flamboyant figures of
the Crusades, ruled Kerak, the great castle of the Crusaders
which controlled the road from the Sinai peninsula into what is
now Jordan. [Note: This should not be confused with the more
famous "Krak des Chevaliers," which is in Syria.]

Renaud conceived the idea of raiding the annual pilgrimage
to Mecca. For this purpose five galleys were dismantled on
the shore of the Mediterranean and their pieces transported by
camel to the Gulf of Aqaba where they were reassembled and
put to sea. Apparently the Egyptians under Salah-ed-Din had
never considered it necessary to maintain any war vessels in
the Red Sea (they had a considerable fleet in the Mediterranean)
for Renaud was able to disrupt all traffic and control the Red
Sea for some nine months while the Egyptians were assembling
a fleet to defeat him. Meanwhile one group of Renaud's men
made a cavalry raid from the coast towards the Holy City of
Medina, near which they were annihilated in an ambush.
(Schlumberger, Gustave, RENAUD DE CHATILLON, Paris,
Plon, 1898, pp. 255-283.)

The long-range result of this affair was to create in the
minds of the Mameluke Egyptian Government and its successor
the Ottoman Empire an unreasoning suspicion of the appearance
of any Europeans in the northern Red Sea. Although by the end
of the eighteenth century the Ottoman Empire could no longer
prevent European access to the area, this suspicion dominated
the actions of Turkish and native government officials in the
Red Sea who threw every obstacle in the way of Christians.

In spite of a Muslim "iron curtain" around the Red Sea and
the Aden route, its importance was understood in Italy in the
Middle Ages. Marino Sanudo, writing around 1300, fully understood the trade routes, and his remarkable pattern for economic
warfare against the Egyptians, the Secreta Fidelium Crucis,

called for a cutting of the Aden trade route by an alliance between Christian Europe and the Mongol Il-Khans of Persia, the bitter enemies of the Mamelukes. (For text of Sanudo see Bongars, GESTA DEI PER FRANCOS, Lyons, 1611, Vol. II, including Marino's maps. For discussion: Atiya, Aziz Suryal, THE CRUSADES IN THE LATER MIDDLE AGES, London, Methuen, 1938, pp. 114-127.) Although we have no direct evidence to connect Marino Sanudo's concepts to later Portuguese expansion, one cannot help but feel that this work was known to the Portuguese. Marino's plan was seriously considered by the French Government in the early eighteenth century in planning an attack on the English factories in India. There is no evidence to indicate that it was known to or used by the planners of Napoleon's invasion in Egypt in 1798, although the concept of that expedition bears a strong resemblance to Marino Sanudo's ideas.

In the fifteenth century an event occurred which contributed for a time towards a revival of the prosperity of Arabia Felix. The following story is legendary but it contains the essential facts and at least has the advantage of coming from an Arab source. In the middle of the fifteenth century there was a Kadi of Aden named Jemal-ed-din Abu Abdulla who had occasion to visit Harar, Abyssinia, where he noted his compatriots drinking a beverage made from the "berries" of a wild plant of the country and heard them praising its medicinal and stimulating effects. At the time he took little note of it but on being taken ill on his return to Aden, he sent for some of these coffee beans and tried them. Finding the beverage stimulating without any serious effect, he immediately introduced its use in Aden in an effort to replace the habit-forming chewing of the Khat leaf, a drug used at that time and still used in huge quantities for its mild stimulation. Thence the new beverage spread to the Yemen, Arabia, and Egypt, and plants were imported to the Yemen to be cultivated there (Playfair, R. L., HISTORY OF ARABIA FELIX OR YEMEN, Bombay, for the Government, 1859, p. 20). By the early sixteenth century it is certain that coffee houses had sprung up in Mecca and Egypt, for an attempt was made in 1524 by the Governor of Mecca to suppress them. It was well for the Yemen that coffee was discovered, for soon a new enemy appeared who was to kill the prosperity of Aden and would have ruined the whole Yemen except for this new product.

Until the beginning of the sixteenth century, the various countries around or bordering on the Red Sea led, on the whole, separate existences. After that time their interests were merged by the European contacts with that area.

Mention has been made of Harar, the Somali country inhabited by a people of unknown origin who were influenced by Persians driven from the Yemen reputedly in the seventh century. The fact that the religion of the people, who belonged to the Zaidee sect of the Shi'ite branch of Muhammadanism, is similar to that of the Yemen, shows its close cultural relation with that country. The empire of the Adels with its capital at Zeila grew out of this early Arab colonization, reaching its greatest power in the thirteenth and fourteenth centuries. (Anyone consulting records of early voyages in the Red Sea area should be cautioned against the confusion either in the original text or in translation between the words Aden and Adel or Adal.) In 1550 it was still a powerful empire and was able to invade and control part of Abyssinia.

The early history of Abyssinia has been adequately described in other volumes. However, a summary of it would help in understanding some of the European concepts of that country. As a civilized country it dates back to the earliest times. The original source of its culture was in the Northern Sudan, where it came in contact with the Egyptians apparently as early as the beginning of recorded Egyptian history. The history of Nubia, as the Ancients called this state, had long been inextricably bound up with that of its northern neighbor. In the eighth century B.C. Ancient Nubia reached its greatest importance when its kings ruled Egypt as the Twenty-fifth Dynasty. There are indications that this kingdom contained at least a part of Tigré if not most of the northern part of what we know as Abyssinia. In these early times, also, there was in the highlands a considerable Jewish colony driven there by the Captivity (the Assyrian domination of Palestine). Under the Ptolemies, Greek colonies were established at Annesley Bay and in Tigré, developing into the Axumite kingdom which flourished from the first to seventh centuries. It was this kingdom which was responsible for the conquest of the Yemen in 525 A.D. During the next hundred years it reached the height of its power, prosperity, and culture. This period, too, marked the real conversion of the country to the Coptic form of Christianity which had been introduced in the fourth century by Frumentius.

Then the Muslim conquest of Egypt in the seventh century cut Abyssinia off from the rest of the world. Muhammadanism spread throughout the area, along the coast, through the Sudan, in Somaliland and Harar; but the highlands of Ethiopia proved an impenetrable barrier to Muslim conquest either by sword or religion. Tigré, Gondar, and Shoa became an island of Christianity surrounded by a sea of infidels.

For centuries thereafter European knowledge of Abyssinia was based entirely on the Classical and Byzantine writers who had described Nubia and the Axumite kingdom. As both kingdoms at one time or another had controlled the Nile trade route from Central Africa, with its exports of ivory, gold, and other luxury products, Abyssinia traditionally was known as a wealthy country. In much the same manner as Alexander had attributed spices to the Yemen because of its sea trade with India, so European tradition ascribed to Abyssinia all of the ivory and gold some of which passed through this country in transit trade. In addition, the medieval myth of Prester John, the Nestorian Emperor of a Christian kingdom in the East, became fixed on Abyssinia.

After the decline of the Axumite kingdom in the seventh century the country rapidly deteriorated into the feudal chaos so well described by Plowden in the middle of the nineteenth century. Its internal feuds and politics had little influence on outside events and it is only worthwhile to note that the legitimate royal family maintained some pretensions to the throne until the time of Theodore in the nineteenth century. However the royal family only governed the country when some member of it showed unusual ability. The rest of the time the country was governed either by rebels or by feudal nobility who ruled through the legitimate emperors, much as the early Carolingians did in the France of the seventh century or the Shoguns did in Japan before Perry opened up the country to western European influence.

The fact that Christian Abyssinia was surrounded by Muslim territory gave rise to two obsessions in Ethiopia which had a profound effect on all contacts with other nations: first, an undying hatred of the Muslims, which later prevented any adequate relations between Christian Abyssinia and Muslim Egypt, a hatred which was to a lesser degree reciprocated by the Muslims; and second, a fundamental belief in the superiority of all things Abyssinian over the rest of the world, an insularity

which was incomprehensible to the chancellories of Europe in
the nineteenth century.

In one section of western Europe, the Iberian peninsula,
the crusading spirit of the twelfth and thirteenth centuries sur-
vived. Even at the time of its greatest expansion, the medieval
Muslim Empire had never conquered the northwest corner of
Spain. From the small Christian states which existed in this
area came the dynasties which were to rule modern Spain and
Portugal. The history of the Iberian peninsula in the Middle
Ages was marked by the almost continuous attempts of these
Christian rulers to add to their dominions at the expense of the
Muslim state. In effect the Spaniards and Portuguese were
carrying on a private crusade against the Muhammadans.

By 1385 the Portuguese had cleared what is now modern
Portugal of the infidels. Prevented by natural boundaries and
the growing power of the Christian Spanish states from conquests to the east, this vigorous young nation began to expand
overseas. By 1415 they had established themselves at Ceuta
on the Moroccan Atlantic coast, and gradually they explored the
west African coast.

These explorations were motivated by the usual combination of elements founds among a rapidly expanding people: national ambition, hope of plunder and economic gain, and a desire for adventure. To these elements was added the crusaders'
religious motivation which made Portuguese imperial expansion
unnecessarily destructive of existing cultures and economies
with which it came in contact.

The greatest impetus to Portuguese expansion came from
a remarkable man, Prince Henry the Navigator, a curious combination of scholar, monk, dreamer, and astute business man.
From 1415 to 1460 he directed Portuguese expansion, guided
chiefly by religious and crusading motives. The main object of
his search was the fabulous land of Prester John which by the
fifteenth century European tradition had placed in Abyssinia.
Prince Henry had developed a plan whereby, if contact could be
made with this fabulous country, Portugal and Abyssinia would
together attack the two flanks of the growing Ottoman power,
rescue the Holy Places, and crush the Turks. Fantastic as
this scheme sounds it led to further and further penetration a-
long the west African coast until, by 1462, the Guinea coast
was known.

Portuguese exploration continued unabated after Prince

Henry's death in 1460 and twenty-six years later, in 1486, Bartolomeo Diaz rounded the Cape of Good Hope. In 1497 Vasco da Gama set sail to attempt a passage to India, reaching Calicut on the Malabar coast of India on May 21, 1498. The only other voyage of exploration comparable to that of da Gama's was Columbus' discovery of the New World six years before. Da Gama brought Europe into direct contact with East Africa, Arabia, Persia, India, the Far East and Indonesia, and a new trade route was created which was to doom the age-old trade routes through the Near East and the Mediterranean. As a result, the prosperity of the Near and Middle East and the Mediterranean trading centers was dealt a fatal blow. The Persian Gulf and Red Sea, scenes of such active commerce in the fifteenth century, were gradually to become obscure backwaters of the Indian Ocean economy. The centers of Arab Muslim civilization in Egypt, Arabia, Syria, and Mesopotamia were to be deprived of regular contact with the outside world and Arab culture was to deteriorate into meaningless imitation of its ancient tradition.

Da Gama's discovery was followed up rapidly by the ambitious Portuguese. A large fleet was sent out in 1500 to establish a trading post in India. Within a few years a Portuguese empire was firmly entrenched in East Africa and India, with outposts in China, Japan, and Indonesia as far east as New Guinea. Outposts were also briefly established at Massawa and Kamaran Island in the Red Sea and at Muscat and Hormuz at the mouth of the Persian Gulf, in order to throttle trade on these two major routes. But the Portuguese did more than compete with the old trade routes; they destroyed every Muslim ship they saw, including if possible all Muslims on board. This destruction was wholly unjustified for economic reasons, but was inspired by the Portuguese version of the crusading spirit which demanded the destruction of all infidels.

Meanwhile the Portuguese had made an effort to make direct contact with Abyssinia. Acting on the traditional information about Abyssinia, in 1487 John II of Portugal sent four emissaries to report on the country. John Pedreio de Covilham alone reached it in 1490, going by way of Alexandria, Suakin and Aden to the Malabar coast, and returning via the east coast of Africa to Cairo and thence to Abyssinia. He was the first European of modern times to enter the country.

The Portuguese quickly exploited da Gama's discoveries.

In 1504 a Portuguese vessel appeared in the Red Sea for a very
short period, capturing an Arab ship. This was followed by
Albuquerque's first voyage to the Indian Ocean. After attacking Arab settlements in East Africa he touched at Socotra and
the Kuria Muria Islands and proceeded to the Persian Gulf,
where he captured the island of Hormuz which controls the entrance to the Persian Gulf and was the main trading post of
this Persian Gulf route. Then he went on to the Malabar coast
where with re-enforcements he firmly established Portuguese
power in the vicinity of Goa. By 1512 he was ready to undertake an expedition to the Red Sea.

        To the merchants who used the overseas route to India,
the incursion of the Portuguese was little better than piracy,
and certainly the treatment of Arab captives by the Portuguese
justified this opinion. Realizing that the extension of Portuguese piracy to the Red Sea would seriously affect the prosperity and trade of Egypt, the Mameluke dynasty reacted quickly
and decisively. In 1510 an Egyptian expedition captured Zeila
from the Adel Empire, which thereupon moved its capital to
Harar. With this port as a base, an Egyptian fleet patrolled
Bab-el-Mandeb to police the Red Sea. However, another power in the area, Abyssinia, holding Covilham in that country,
sent an embassy to Portugal in 1510 to obtain Christian assistance against the infidel. The Ambassador, an Ethiopian merchant by the name of Matthew, arrived in Portugal after many
delays just as Albuquerque was starting his expedition to the
Red Sea.

        The Portuguese expedition was made in force, twenty
ships manned by 2,300 men, two-thirds of whom were Portuguese. In the spring of 1513 Albuquerque attacked Aden. After
a four-day seige the Portuguese were repulsed. They proceeded thence to Mocha and then settled at Kamaran Island to
await the monsoon which would take them back to India. On
setting out on the return trip they again undertook an attack on
Aden but were again repulsed.

        As a result of this assault Kansuh-al-Ghuri, the Mameluke
Sultan of Egypt, assembled a fleet to occupy the Red Sea and
exclude the Portuguese. At the same time al-Ghuri appointed
the Sharif of Mecca as the Governor of San'a (capital of the
Yemen), and the latter immediately prepared an army to cooperate with the Egyptian fleet. In 1516, the Egyptians proceeded to attack Aden, only to be driven off by the Arabs. In

India the Portuguese viceroy Lope Soarez de Albergaria, on hearing of the actions of the Mameluke Sultan, mustered a fleet to meet him. On Soarez' arrival at Aden the Arab governor of that port, which had suffered considerable damage from the Egyptians, tendered his submission to the Portuguese, whom he could scarcely hope to drive off due to the weakened state of his defenses. Soarez then sailed into the Red Sea to attack the Egyptian fleet but was unable to catch it. Again the Portuguese were forced to remain at Kamaran awaiting the monsoon. Meanwhile they lost no time in capturing and burning Zeila, but on their return to Aden they discovered that the governor of that town, having strengthened his defenses, no longer had any idea of allowing them to land. A storm having scattered the Portuguese fleet on the way to Berbera, Soarez was forced to give up his plans and return to India.

The long years of freedom from outside interference in the Yemen had ended with the arrival of the Portuguese, but another power, as young and vigorous as the Iberians, now entered the scene. Turkish-Persian rivalry had resulted in an attempt by Shah Ismail of Persia to stir up the Shi'ite-Sunnite controversy in Turkish Asia Minor in order to weaken the Ottoman government. The Turks took effective measures against this revolutionary movement by slaughtering a reputed 40,000 Shi'ites and then, under Selim I the Grim, marched against Shah Ismail in 1514. The Mameluke dynasty of Egypt, although orthodox Sunnites, were fearful of Turkish threats to their Syrian possessions and quickly allied themselves with the Shi'ite Persians. After defeating the Persians at Chaldiran and marching to Tabriz, Selim returned rapidly to Syria to meet the Egyptian threat. On August 24, 1516, the battle of Marj-Dabik took place north of Aleppo, in which Selim through his superiority in artillery completely defeated the Mamelukes. The remnants of the Mameluke army were routed again at Gaza and completely destroyed outside of Cairo. Thus Egypt became an Ottoman province.

This change of masters, instead of altering Egyptian policy towards the Yemen, intensified it: Selim hoped to occupy that area as a base for a contemplated conquest of India. His death delayed the plan, but in 1538 a fleet was assembled at Suez for this conquest. All the Venetian sailors on ships of that state then in the harbor of Alexandria were seized to man this fleet of seventy-six vessels carrying 4,000 Janissaries and 16,000

other soldiers under Sulieman Pasha, commander of the Mameluke fleet in 1516 and now a Turkish admiral. Aden was seized
by treachery in August of 1538 and the fleet proceeded to India
where the port of Diu, a Portuguese trading post, was attacked.
The fall of this city seemed imminent when re-enforcements
from Goa, the capital of Portugal's Indian possessions, arrived.
The Turks thereupon fled from the city, arriving back at Aden
in December. After leaving a garrison there, Sulieman Pasha
went to Mocha, from which port early in 1539 the Pasha spread
his authority along the coast of the Yemen, eventually capturing
San'a and controlling the entire country.

The Portuguese retaliated against this expedition by making
preparations to attack Suez, which they did the next year. They
were repulsed by the Turks. During this expedition, in 1540,
the inhabitants of Aden delivered the city to the Portuguese,
who controlled it until 1551, when a Turkish fleet under Peri
Pash reconquered it for the Sultan.

If the Portuguese had failed to occupy any portion of the
Red Sea, they had at least achieved a slight cultural penetration
into Abyssinia. Embassies were exchanged. In 1541 Stephen
da Gama's expedition against Suez captured Massawa, which
had been occupied by the Turks in 1520. From there he sent a
force of 450 musketeers into Abyssinia to help the Negus (Emperor) against Muslim invaders under Mohammad Graneje,
ruler of the Adel kingdom of Harar, who had overrun most of
the country. A Catholic mission came into the country shortly
after da Gama's visit and tried to convince the Negus to renounce the Abyssinian church and acknowledge the Roman faith.
The mission was thereupon expelled from the country but the
Jesuits who succeeded the early missionaries remained until
1633 when they too were driven out. (See Sanceau, Elaine,
LAND OF PRESTER JOHN New York, Knopf, 1944, for the
Portuguese missions.) Plowden tells us of the unfavorable reaction which their activities created among the Abyssinians.
This antagonism was responsible for many events in Abyssinia
in the nineteenth century. After 1633 Abyssinian isolation became complete, broken only by the visit of the French doctor
C. J. Poncet in 1698, until Bruce began his extensive travels in
1770. Internal conditions remained chaotic, marked only by
the appearance of an occasional chief who managed to bring most
of the country under his control for a short period.

In the Yemen a revolt against Turkish rule took place in

1599, but it was suppressed with great cruelty by Hasan Pasha, the Turkish governor. Little by little the Indian trade declined until by 1630 it was felt that possession of the Yemen was no longer worth the expense of holding it and the Turks evacuated the province. Thus one hundred and thirty-two years after da Gama's discovery of the Cape route, European adventurers and traders had destroyed the age-old prosperity of the Near and Middle East. The ancient birthplace of European civilization, deprived of its prosperous trade between Asia and Europe, was thrown on its own resources. These were woefully meagre. Most of the area was desert, steppe country, or mountains, with Syria and the Lebanon, the Yemen and Egypt the outstanding exceptions. Under these conditions it is not surprising that the Persian and Ottoman empires should have entered a long period of decline. With this decline, Muslim civilization reached a standstill; cultural contacts with the outside world were barely kept alive, except in Muslim India, and Muhammadan culture, which ironically had preserved for Europe much of the civilization of the ancient world, lost its vitality and creative ability. Not until the nineteenth century, when new inventions stimulated the expansion of European powers in the Near and Middle East, did anything occur to alleviate the cultural stagnation of that area. By that time the ultra-conservatism of the Muslim religion, intensified by three centuries of isolation from the rest of the world, provided an almost impenetrable barrier to outside influences, a barrier so stubborn that it was not to be cracked until the upheaval resulting from the first World War.

II. THE RED SEA AREA 1632-1832

It is almost impossible to imagine the effect of the opening
of the Cape trade route on the Red Sea area. Here was a world
highway existing from time immemorial almost completely
abandoned within a hundred and fifty years. Eighty miles of
sand and rock, the Isthmus of Suez, lay between it and the
Mediterranean, one of the chief centers of European culture.
Yet the Red Sea became more remote from Europe than Java,
Sumatra or even Australia. From 1540 until 1800 few travelers
and fewer ships of European countries penetrated beyond Mocha,
some fifty-odd miles above Bab-el-Mandeb. The Red Sea had
become a backwater of the Indian Ocean economy, in some
ways the most remote civilized area in the world of the seventeenth and eighteenth centuries.

Several factors were responsible for this isolation. The
defense against the Portuguese attempts to control the area
was undertaken by the most powerful country in Europe, the
Ottoman Empire, for a twofold reason: first, to preserve the
monopoly of the Indian trade by the all-sea route; and second,
to counter a threat by a Christian country to the Holy Cities.
Christian penetration was frankly discouraged by every possible
means.

Without the transit trade, the Red Sea had little to offer
economically. Only two areas were capable of production for
export, and one of these, the Abyssinian highlands, was effectively cut off by Muslim-Christian enmity. The Yemen alone
remained an economically important area, and its trade was
easily handled by Aden and the port of Mocha, which was reputedly founded in 1430. These two ports also handled the few
exports from the Adel country coming out of the ports of Zeila
and Berbera. There was therefore little need for European
ships to penetrate further into the Red Sea.

There was also a practical factor. Mention has been made
of the dangers in navigating the Red Sea, resulting in the importance of Aden as a port where Arab sea-going vessels trans-
shipped their cargoes to smaller coastwise craft. The discoveries of the fifteenth and sixteenth centuries and the rapidly
increasing ocean trade resulting therefrom served as a great
spur to the building of larger ships. By 1600 the caravels of

Columbus were dwarfed by the merchant ships which had come into common use for ocean travel. The use of these larger vessels increased the difficulties of navigating the Red Sea and it was almost impossible for Europeans to use this natural highway until, beginning in 1794 with the cruise of the "Panther," the first modern charts began to be made.

The virtual abandonment of the all-sea route to the East via Suez did not have any immediate effect upon the Yemen. The discovery of coffee and its spread to the Near East was accompanied by the cultivation of the coffee plant which had formerly grown wild in the Adel country. The fertile valleys of the Yemen were found to be especially favorable to the cultivation of this plant, and as the use of the aromatic bean spread like wildfire throughout Europe, the Yemen, enjoying a monopoly of this product, naturally prospered.

At the beginning of the seventeenth century the great trading companies of Europe began investigating the Yemen. The British were the first to appear, in 1609, when the "Ascension" under Captain Alexander Sharpey put in at Aden and Mocha. He was followed the next year by Admiral Sir Henry Middleton, whose trip was not so successful as that of his predecessor. A third expedition in 1612 traded there very profitably but the antagonism of Muslim to Christian was a great drawback.

In 1614 the Dutch East India Company entered the picture with the arrival of a fleet under Pieter van den Broecke. He was not received with much favor, and when he returned in 1616 he was greeted with considerable unfriendliness, due largely to the fact that one of his ships had penetrated as far up the coast as Hodeida. This had made the Turkish governor, anxious to protect the Holy Cities, very suspicious of the Dutch admiral's motives.

In 1618 Captain Shilling in the "Anne Royal" obtained permission for the British East India Company to maintain a factory at Mocha, and an agreement was made on export and import duties. This factory was not permanently manned but served merely as a trading post for such British vessels as might be in port. In 1620 the Dutch also obtained a similar factory at that port, for in that year Pieter van den Broecke was appointed Governor of Surat and Mocha for the Dutch East India Company.

The most important traders in the Yemen, however, were the Banyans. We do not know when they first began to trade there, but probably it was a result of the old trade route with India. Their presence in Mocha increased the importance of that port in the seventeenth century at least for the Dutch, who obtained their supply of Indian currency for purchases in Surat from Mocha. La Roque, who was a member of de Merveille's expedition, says of them in 1709, "This...puts me in mind to say something here of the Banians in general by whom is carried on the whole trade of Arabia. They are all originally Indians, and chiefly of the Isle of Din in the kingdom of Cambaya, not far from Surat. They come into Arabia when they are young, to endeavour to make their fortunes by trading, as they spread themselves upon the same account, into several other parts of the Indies," (de la Rocque, Jean, A VOYAGE TO ARABIA THE HAPPY, London, Straham, 1726, p. 123.) When, as a result of the Anglo-French imperial conflicts of the late eighteenth century, Britain dominated India, she acquired unknowingly the control of almost the entire trade of the Red Sea area. Haines and a few other officers of the Indian Navy realized this in the 1840's, but the fact was only driven home to London and the British people by Sir Bartle Frere as a result of his Zanzibar embassy in 1873.

In 1630 the Imamate of San'a was re-established by the family of Barakat, claiming descent from Ali ibn Abu Talib, who had conquered the Yemen for Muhammad in 631 and succeeded to the Califate in 655. The ruling dynasty assumed the traditional title of Imam, which means literally "priest," and therefore enjoyed religious as well as temporal eminence. As they claimed descent from Ali they were doubly powerful among the Zaidi Yemenites. The first of these Imams of the Barakat family, Kassim by name, was largely responsible for causing the withdrawal of the Turks, as by his friendship with the mountain tribal chiefs he drove the Sunnites from the interior cities of the Yemen.

The situation of the Ottoman Empire as a whole did not justify the continued expense of fighting these mountain chiefs. A succession of weak sultans in Constantinople had allowed the Janissary corps, which had become a "palace guard" to run riot to the detriment of the central government. The Persians, ruled by Abbas the Great, had reconquered Georgia and Trans-Caucasia, Syria was in revolt, and Abasa Pasha was in Erzerum with a mutinous army, when Murad IV came to the throne in 1624. Faced with these difficulties, this able Sultan withdrew

his army from the Yemen when Kassim and his allies made the
situation too hot for the Turkish governor there.

The Imam was an absolute ruler, but a certain measure of
control was exercised by the supreme council of San'a, which
alone possessed the power of life and death. The provinces
were governed by a Dowla, or Dolas, whose powers were similar to those of a Turkish Pasha, though somewhat more limited
in extent. These Dolas were rotated from province to province
about every two years to prevent their acquiring too great
power or wealth. Assigned to each Dolas was a Baskateb or
secretary who often acted as a spy on their conduct, and a Kadi,
who was sole judge in religious and civil affairs. The cities
were ruled by a Sheik-el-Beled who acted as mayor and tax
assessor and an Emir-es-Suk who was chief of the markets.
These officials were directly responsible to the Dowla as was
the Amir-el-Bahr or Captain of the Port in the coastal towns.

In contrast to conditions in many Arab states, succession
to the Imamate in the seventeenth century appears to have been
determined by primogeniture. While this custom was sometimes violated it generally served to avoid the usual civil confusion attendant on the death of the average Arab ruler. The
ability of the Imams and the continuity of their rule can be
easily seen in the fact that from 1630 to 1707 there were but
four Imams and one civil war, a truly remarkable record
for an Arab state. This period of peace, coupled with the growing demand for coffee, provided the greatest prosperity the
Yemen had ever known.

In 1708 M. de Merveille, in command of the ships "Curieuse"
and "Diligent" of the French trading company of St. Malo,
sailed from Brest to open up trade with the Yemen. He arrived
at Mocha in January, 1709. De Merveille soon concluded a
commercial treaty with the Dowla allowing the French to have
a factory at Mocha and setting up the customs dues to be paid.
As has been mentioned, they found a Dutch factory established
there with a vessel trading yearly with Batavia in the East
Indies. This Dutch establishment was the cause of the ultimate
decline of the Yemen, for about 1712 the Dutch smuggled some
coffee plants out of the country and started their cultivation on
the island of Java. Thence they were imported to the Dutch
West Indies and gradually the cultivation of the plant spread
through both the East and West Indies and to the mainland of
South America, thus destroying the monopoly of the Yemen.

Another French expedition of the same company arrived in 1712. At the request of the Imam, several of the Frenchmen went up to "Mooab" where the Imam was then in residence. [Note: De la Rocque describes "Mooab" as being a fort and castle about a mile outside of Dhamar, which at that time was the capital of the Yemen (op. cit., pp. 183-4).]

Their arrival coincided with the arrival of an Ambassador from the Ottoman Empire. De la Rocque, a member of the French party, has preserved for us the details of this Turkish embassy, whose aim threw considerable light on the economy of the Near East and emphasized the effects of the opening of the Cape trade route on the whole area. The purpose of this embassy was to arrange to have the coffee trade carried on completely through the Red Sea and Egypt, as the direct trade from Arabia to Europe via the Cape of Good Hope had greatly decreased the revenues and commerce of the Sultan. The request was based on purely religious grounds, as a demonstration of loyalty to the Sultan as Calif, and no pretence was made of sovereignty over the Yemen. The request was of course refused. (De la Rocque, op. cit., pp. 203-5.)

French trade continued, but in 1738 a serious misunderstanding occurred between the French and the Dowla of Mocha who had been purchasing goods against the customs account. This practice had placed the Dowla $82,000 in the debt of the French company, and in 1738 a French warship accompanied the trading fleet to collect this considerable debt. The Dowla, forewarned of this, had collected an army of 20,000 men to protect the town against the possible 1,800 men the French could muster. A sharp battle resulted which ended in an anticlimax when the entire defending army fled upon the firing of an explosive mortar shell, a type of projectile the Yemeni had never before seen. The debt was rapidly settled and the Imam, displeased at this interruption of trade, removed the Dowla from office.

Before the Turkish conquest of the Yemen, Aden had been largely independent and had had a comparatively stable government. After the re-establishment of the Imamate, Aden and Lahej became an integral part of the Yemen but retained their independent traditions. It must have been due to this that the Imam had encouraged the coffee trade to go to Mocha which he could easily control, because the port there was vastly inferior to the first-class harbor at Aden. Aden, deprived of its transit trade on the all-sea route, fell into decay and by 1728 the Imam, not wishing to be bothered by the independent actions of its rulers, withdrew from any effort to maintain control over either Aden or the surrounding territory, abandoning it to the Sultan of Lahej, leader of the Abdali tribe.

The appearance of rivals in the production of coffee soon left its mark on the Yemen. By 1718 coffee had been introduced in Surinam and Jamaica. And by 1760 the power of the Imam was being threatened by rebellious tribes, a sufficient proof that the stability of this Muslim state was largely dependent on the prosperity of the country involved. Aden, the neighboring districts of Qa'taba and Ta'iz and the northern province of Abu 'Arish, were separate states when the great German traveler Karsten Niebuhr, member of a scientific expedition from Denmark, arrived in Arabia in 1762, and the Imamate was beset by continuous rebellions on its periphery.

By 1762 the French and Dutch had abandoned their factories at Mocha and the British were left in undisputed control of the export trade, the Banyans having a monopoly on internal trade.

The eighteenth century conflict between the imperial ambitions of the French and the British for the trade of the East did not affect the Red Sea. It was too far removed from the Cape route to be of strategic value in that struggle, and the domination of the northern end of the Red Sea by the Ottoman Empire dissuaded the European powers from any serious attempt to reopen the Red Sea route to the East. For in the eighteenth century Turkey was still the dominant power in Eastern Europe, with Russia as its chief antagonist. Peter the Great had formulated the general lines of Russian policy in the first quarter of the century, but the military balance between the Turks and the Russians was too even for the Slavs to do much more than occupy an occasional outlying province. While many of the forces which provided for the disintegration of the Ottoman Empire were present during this century, it required the nationalistic impetus born of the Napoleonic wars to bring them into the open. The diplomatic position of the Porte in the tangled diplomacy of the dynastic wars of the eighteenth century also helped to protect the integrity of the Empire. The Ottoman Empire was more valuable to most European countries as a potential ally than as a potential enemy, as it was always a European rather than an Eastern power.

During the eighteenth century the most important historical

event to occur in the Yemen was the expedition of which Karsten
Niebuhr was a member. Organized by King Frederick V of
Denmark, the expedition arrived in the Yemen at the end of
1762 and remained in the country for about nine months. The
publication of Niebuhr's volume BESCHREIBUNG VON ARABIEN
(Copenhagen, 1772) presented Europe with its first available
description of the area. The book was translated into other
European languages and opened to European eyes this corner
of the world which had formerly been completely unknown. The
fact that Niebuhr was a very competent observer and a good
scholar heightened the value of this work, and it had a wide
appeal which De la Rocque's excellent earlier volume had not
enjoyed.

It was Niebuhr in fact who first really brought the Yemen
to the attention of Europe. Another traveler, coming a few
years later into the area, did much the same for Abyssinia.
If the Yemen had been unknown to Europeans and its existence
forgotten by them, Abyssinia had been unknown but not forgotten, as is witnessed by Dr. Samuel Johnson's translation of
Father Lobo's history of Abyssinia and the use of the same area
as the locale of RASSELAS. In 1769 James Bruce arrived at
Massawa and spent three years in the country. The publication
of his book of travels started an immediate controversy, for
where Niebuhr's work was noted for its scholarly approach,
Bruce's work was typified by his inclusion of all the stories he
came across, whether they were based on fact or fable. However, later investigation justified many of Bruce's observations
no matter how much controversy they aroused at the time of
their publication (Bruce, James, TRAVELS TO DISCOVER THE
SOURCES OF THE NILE, 5 Vols. , London, 1790).

In the Yemen, after 1762, the power of the Imamate gradually weakened. An attack on the British factory at Mocha in
1770, resulting from the punishment of the slave of a British
sea captain, brought about the bombardment of the town by two
East India Company men-of-war in 1771. The following year
a serious rebellion, evoked by a failure of the wheat crop, almost succeeded in overthrowing the Imam and collapsed only
when the Imam, remembering the French attack of 1738, used
explosive mortar shells against the rebels.

In 1785 a new rival to the English appeared in the Red Sea:
American merchantmen. By 1800 they were the dominant factor in the coffee trade, not only bringing this product to

America, but also carrying on a direct trade from Arabia to
Europe in competition with the East India Company's route
from Arabia to Europe via Bombay. In this way they avoided
transshipping costs at Bombay and at British ports and could
undersell the British on the continent by a considerable margin.
Actually they opened an entirely new trade route, connecting
for the first time the trade of the Red Sea with that of the East
African coast, a route not exploited by the British until 1872.
The New England merchants, free of the domination of a trading company which made its profits by transshipment in India
(as in the case of the British East India Company), or in the
Mascarenes – Mauritius and Réunion islands – (as in the case
of the French companies) gave the established companies serious competition. In the early nineteenth century these New
England merchants dominated the trade of the Yemen.

The defeat of the French in the Seven Years' War ending
in 1763 cost that nation its empire in India. Some elements in
France, however, continued to plan for its recovery. France
had retained certain trading settlements in India, especially
Pondicherry and Mahé, and continued to occupy the Mascarene
islands and the Seychelles in the Indian Ocean.

After the Treaty of Paris in 1763, imperial interests in
France put forward several plans to recover the French Indian
Empire. Most of these plans involved using the Suez-Red Sea
route or the overland route to the Persian Gulf as a means of
outflanking British naval predominance in the Indian Ocean.
The British, too, considered the use of the Suez route and
actually used it twice for the transmission of dispatches, once
during the rule of Warren Hastings in India in the 1770's, and
again during the next decade at the insistence of one George
Baldwin, a British merchant in Egypt. Two factors prevented
the British exploitation of the Suez route, the opposition of the
Ottoman Empire which feared the appearance of western Christian interests so close to the Holy Cities of Arabia, and the objections of the English Levant Company which accused the East
India Company of infringing on its monopoly of trade with the
eastern Mediterranean.

The French plans were more subtle and undertaken with
greater care. As their object was the eventual reconquest of
India, they intrigued first with the Mameluke Beys of Egypt,
and in 1785 signed a secret treaty with them facilitating French
commerce. This was followed by intrigues with Muscat in the

southeast corner of Arabia. In 1790 a French consulate was
recommended for Muscat, and five years later the first French
consul appeared there.

On May 5, 1789, the Estates General of France met for
the first time in centuries to wrestle with the serious financial
and economic predicament into which that country had fallen.
The French Revolution, thus begun, unleashed forces which
were to change the aspect of the whole Near East and reopen
the Red Sea to world commerce.

In 1795 the Directory was established in France and
Napoleon began his attempt to acquire world-wide domination.
Three years later he undertook his Egyptian Expedition. As a
consequence, the British Government sent a fleet under Captain
Blanket to cruise the Red Sea in 1799, and the Government of
Bombay was ordered to occupy the island of Perim. Lieutenant
Colonel Murray with 300 men was sent to occupy the island,
which dominated the Strait of Bab-el-Mandeb. [See pp. 223-27 for
a description of this expedition.] The island was occupied for
four months, until lack of water drove Murray to retire to
Aden, where he was cordially welcomed by the Sultan of Lahej.

In 1801, as part of the plan to reconquer Egypt from the
French, General Baird was dispatched from India with a small
army to proceed up the Red Sea, landing at Qu'seir to take the
French from the rear. This marked the first use of the Red
Sea for modern military purposes. The fleet which accompanied the transports was under the command of Sir Home
Popham, who had also been given orders by the Court of Directors of the East India Company in London to use his efforts to
revive the trade in that area. Accordingly he directed Dr.
Pringle, who had come to Perim with Colonel Murray's expedition and gone on to Mocha, to undertake an embassy to the Imam.

By this time British trade with the Yemen had virtually
ceased. American competition and a revival of the trade
through Egypt now took most of the export of coffee. This was
probably due to an artificially high price maintained by the
B. E. I. C. which when its monopoly was broken by the Americans found itself in an unfavorable competitive position. The
increasing weakness of the Imamate also was reflected in a
reduced production of coffee as intertribal struggles destroyed
the crops and set up barriers to trade within the Yemen.

Dr. Pringle was courteously received by the Imam and obtained most of the concessions which the Company requested,

these being chiefly courteous treatment of British vessels and
the restoration of the freedom of trade previously allowed
them.

In 1802 Sir Home Popham, having safely escorted the transports back to India was regularly constituted Ambassador to
the States of Arabia by the Indian Government and fully authorized to enter into commercial treaties with the Imam of San'a
and the Sultan of Lahej.

He returned to Mocha the same year and planned to undertake his embassy to San'a. However sincere his motives might
have been, he committed a fundamental error by insisting on
having a guard of 100 sepoys (native Indian troops) accompany
him instead of depending for protection on the recognized government which even in its state of disorganization was quite
capable of providing an appropriate and sufficient escort. As
it transpired the sepoys were not sufficient for his protection
anyhow. The grand style in which the Ambassador traveled
excited the cupidity of the Arab just as much as the sepoy guard
aroused his suspicions. The embassy received such rough
treatment from the local sheikhs that it was forced to retire to
Mocha after being unable to get much farther than Ta'iz on the
road to San'a, less than a quarter of the distance to the capital.
Dr. Pringle and two other Englishmen, Mr. Elliot, the secretary of the Embassy, and an officer, Lieutenant Lamb, had preceded the Ambassador and had laid the groundwork for a successful conclusion of the treaty. However, Sir Home Popham's
blunder resulted in a flat rejection of any treaty by the Imam.

In 1802 a private expedition, organized and paid for by
Lord Valentia, arrived in the Red Sea for the purpose of entering into an alliance with Abyssinia if French designs on Egypt
should succeed. It explored the coast near Massawa and the
part of Abyssinia lying near the coast. The brains of this expedition was Henry Salt. While he penetrated into Tigré as far
as Adowa and Axsum, Lord Valentia (then Earl of Mountnorris)
explored the bay and the surrounding waters to which he gave
his family name, Annesley Bay. Geographically the expedition
was important, as it filled in the great gap in existing knowledge of that particular area around Massawa. The expedition
also investigated Aden, Mocha, Berbera and other minor ports,
and returned with a letter from the Emperor of Abyssinia to
George III. After his return Valentia published his travels
(Mountnorris, George [Annesley, Earl of], VOYAGES &

TRAVELS TO INDIA, CEYLON etc., 3 Vols., London, Miller, 1809, — largely written by Salt.) Valentia also made an extended report on the Red Sea area to George Canning, then Secretary for Foreign Affairs.

His report is of interest because it gives the first really accurate trade estimate of the area. Mocha was exporting about 13,000 bales of coffee yearly at $56 a bale, of which 9,000 bales were being handled by American vessels. Other exports of myrrh, gum arabic, etc., swelled the trade. The imports had been largely Indian and English cloths handled almost entirely by Banyan merchants, but in the years after the French agreement with the Imam of Muscat in 1803, the latter's privateering ventures had greatly reduced the Indian trade, with a resultant substitution of French goods via the Mascarenes and Muscat. The trade of the Yemen was further curtailed by the Wahhabiya uprising in Arabia which disturbed the whole country (vide infra), and the Sharif of Abu 'Arish, who had become the most powerful chief in the area, was willing to offer the British a trade monopoly in return for arms. Aden, Valentia found, still carried on a transshipment trade from the great fair at Berbera and was ruled by an able and friendly Sultan. In Valentia's opinion it occupied the position of greatest importance in that area. "It is the Gibraltar of the East and at trifling expense might be made impregnable," he wrote, and he urged the establishment of a factory there with a regular resident to exploit the Berbera trade. Abyssinia, he felt, did not offer the immediate profit which might come from the establishment at Aden. He commented on the chaotic condition of the country and the consequent trade hazards, yet he estimated the trade through Massawa to the interior at $400,000 annually. He also pointed out that Tigré could easily produce cotton, as the plant grew wild there. The Wahhabiya revolt indirectly had closed off trade between the interior and the coast. The town of Massawa was controlled by the Naib of Archico who was a Muslim and, owing to the weakness of the Egyptian and Turkish governments, fairly independent. However, Valentia thought that British control of Kamaran Island would provide the best control of trade with Abyssinia, and he pointed out that a French vessel had appeared while he was in Annesley Bay for the purpose of buying this island. He further recommended an alliance with the Wahhabiya to counter French advances towards Persia, and the establishment of a dispatch route via the Red Sea,

Kamaran, and Aden, to supplant the threatened overland route via Basra and the Persian Gulf.

Valentia concluded with a sentence which could easily have been written by Lord Napier sixty-five years later. "By connection with Abyssinia, a Christian country would be liberated from a most dreadful state of Anarchy, and a large extent of country would be snatched from the Mussulman's control whilst a new market would be provided for our manufacturers." Thus was born the basis of British policy towards this unknown country which continued until the events leading to the Abyssinian expedition of 1868 showed the British the true nature of the country and the difficulties involved (FO 1/1 Valentia-Canning 9/13/08).

Valentia's report was favorably received by the Foreign Office. It was decided to send Salt back again in 1809 to the Red Sea through Valentia's offices with government sanction, and to pay his expenses. He was supplied with presents for the Ras Wallad Sallassie and was ordered to proceed to Gondar to investigate the trade of the country and if possible open direct trade from England or India. Salt reached Mocha by November, 1809, where he found the price of coffee raised, thanks to American competition, to $75 a bale, a ruinous price for the B.E.I.C. with its heavy transshipping costs. It is clear that the Company, knowing of the results of Valentia's expedition, also was interested in opening up trade with Abyssinia, as Salt met Captain Rudland of the B.E.I.C. at Mocha with much the same orders as he had.

On arriving at Massawa, Salt found that the Naïb had been ousted by an Egyptian officer, Omar Aga, who refused to allow Salt any communication with the interior. A new governor, however, shortly replaced Omar Aga, a man who had had experience with the English in Syria, and he permitted Salt to proceed with two Englishmen, Pearce and Coffin, left in Abyssinia on Valentia's earlier mission. Incessant revolts made it impossible for Salt to advance beyond Tigré, and he was obliged to forward the presents and letters to the King through the Bahr Negus (governor) of that province. Salt was discouraged with the possibilities of trade because of the refusal of the Abyssinians to hold the coast line and, like travelers to become acquainted with the country later, he was doubtful of the success of any British penetration (FO 1/1 Salt-FO 3/4/11; report on his expedition). Accompanying Salt's report were copies of correspondence between Salt and the Bombay Government, including a request from Bombay for an explanation of his mission's object. Salt was in reality trespassing on their monopoly. Thus occurred the first rivalry of interest in the area between the Foreign Office and the Indian Government.

Salt also sent a report to the Indian Government on the political situation in the Red Sea, pointing out that the British could have almost anything they wished in the Yemen by giving support to the Sharif of Abu 'Arish or the Imam of San'a against the Wahhabiya. The Sharif of Abu 'Arish (or, as Salt calls him, the Sharif of Loheia) controlled the Tehama (coastal lowlands) from Loheia to Mocha, as well as Zeila on the African shore. No hostile navy existed in the Red Sea; Muhammad Ali did not have ships there at that time. It would thus be very easy for the British to consolidate any position there which they wished to take (FO 1/1 Salt-Wellesley 9/11/11). Needless to say no action was taken.

Thus ended the first interest shown in the area by the British Foreign Office. Salt returned to England. He was later made the first British Consul to Egypt.

About the middle of the eighteenth century there had arisen in the Nejd, under the leadership of Muhammad ibn Abd-el-Wahhab, a new sect which was to bring about the greatest change in the whole of Arabia since the time of Muhammad. Originating as it did in the harsh, arid country of the Nejd, it is not surprising that the Wahhabiya doctrine was extremely puritanical and severe. The members of this sect considered themselves orthodox Sunni Muslims following ibn Hanbal's school of law. However, they rejected all innovations after the third century A.H., directing their antagonism towards saint worship, which they considered polytheism.

The new doctrine spread like wildfire among the nomadic tribes of the Nejd and the northern Hedjaz and by 1803 its adherents had forcibly conquered Mecca and Medina, destroying the holy tombs and such other objects as they considered abominations.

Here mention must be made again of the Asir, a loose tribal coalition of considerable military power lying to the north of Abu 'Arish and acting as a buffer state between the Hedjaz and the Yemen. This coalition had early accepted the Wahhabiya doctrine and, after the conquest of the Holy Cities, joined with the northern Wahhabi in pushing on towards the Yemen.

The Sharif of Abu 'Arish, unable to defend himself, fled to
San'a, and the Wahhabi conquered Hodeida and Loheia in 1804,
but failed before the walls of Mocha. They then retired to the
hills, retaining control of the revenues of the Tehama, and
made incursions into the interior of the Yemen. In order to
retain control of the revenues of the Tehama they were forced
to re-establish some orderly form of government, so they returned this territory to the Sharif of Abu 'Arish, Hamad by
name, on his payment of a heavy tribute. The Imam of San'a,
Ali Mansur, was of advanced age, and his control over his
country, weakened by previous revolts, was disappearing.
However, in 1809 the Imam's eldest son Ahmad deposed his
father, who was by now almost an imbecile, and, together with
Hamad, prepared to defeat the Wahhabi. In a surprise attack
the Asir chief was killed and thus the immediate Wahhabi
danger removed.

By 1811 Muhammad Ali, an Albanian officer in the Ottoman
army, had effected his control of Egypt. He was, however,
still persona non grata in Constantinople in spite of judicious
bribery of officials of the Empire. During the previous year
the Wahhabi had penetrated Syria to the suburbs of Damascus,
and were a constant threat to Ottoman rule in the Levant. The
ambitious Egyptian Pasha saw that by recovering the Holy Cities
from the Puritans he would receive the gratitude of Constantinople and at the same time revive the prosperous transit trade
of the pilgrims through Egypt to Mecca which the Wahhabi
conquests had stopped.

In October, 1811, Egyptian troops under Toussan Bey
landed at Yanbu, the port of Medina, only to be repulsed by the
Wahhabi. This same army, heavily re-enforced, captured
Medina in November the next year and Mecca in January, 1813.

The Pasha had plans to extend his power beyond the Hedjaz.
The coffee trade of the Yemen was too tempting, and he despatched an envoy to Sharif Hamad to demand his cooperation
against the Wahhabi. Receiving evasive answers from the
Sharif, the envoy proceeded to San'a where the Imam welcomed
him with great friendliness, acceded to all his demands, and
issued instructions to the Dola of Mocha to provide a large
number of vessels for taking Muhammad Ali's troops from Suez
to Jidda. In issuing this order, the Imam was perfectly well
aware of the fact that the Dola of Mocha did not have a single
vessel under his control nor could he possibly comply with any

of the rest of the order. The Egyptian envoy proceeded to
Mocha and insisted that the order be carried out, but after interminable delays retired in disgust. The object of his mission was unquestionably to ascertain the strength and weakness
of the Yemen, which was ready to fall prey to the first invader.

In 1814 Muhammad Ali's troops with a considerable fleet
attacked al-Qunfidha, a seaport controlled by the Asir. After
an initial success, the expedition was virtually destroyed by
the Wahhabi. This defeat was avenged the next year when the
Pasha defeated the nomads at Tor, their capital in the mountains, and then proceeded to capture al-Qunfidha from the landward side. Ibrahim Pasha succeeded as commander in 1816
and in three years destroyed the Wahhabi power in the Asir
country and occupied all of the territory of Abu 'Arish which the
Wahhabi had conquered. In 1820 the Pasha returned these territories to the new Imam of San'a, el-Mehdi Abdulla, in return
for an annual tribute of coffee.

Muhammad Ali now turned his attention to more important
projects, among which was the conquest of the Sudan. In two
years, 1820-1822, Sennar and Kordofan were conquered and
the boundary of the Egyptian Empire pushed to the borders of
Abyssinia, or more correctly, the borders of the states of
Tigré and Gondar. By 1823 he controlled a large part of the
shore of both sides of the Red Sea.

At Mocha, the British factory which had continued to exist
all through the Napoleonic period was the scene of outrageous
attack. In July, 1817, Lieutenant Domincetti in command of
the "Prince of Wales" was cruelly treated by a mob who broke
into the residency while Domincetti was in bed and brought him
before the Dola of Mocha. At the same time the sepoy guard of
the residency was attacked and the building sacked. The Resident was shortly released and ordered back to India, and the
Residency temporarily abandoned. Two years elapsed in fruitless negotiations with the Imam of San'a for apology and reparation, and finally in November, 1819, William Bruce was the
bearer of an ultimatum to the Imam. He requested Salt, now
Consul at Cairo, to ascertain the relation of Mocha to Muhammad Ali. This request marked the first recognition of Egyptian interests in the area and the first use of diplomatic means
by the Company in dealing with Egypt (IO Egypt, v. 7, Bruce
(Mocha)-Salt 10/6/20).

Governor Elphinstone at Bombay made the same request of

Salt, stating that the Bombay Government intended to blockade the ports of the Yemen in case the ultimatum was rejected. The Consul was asked to ascertain the status of the Yemen in relation to Muhammad Ali and, if necessary, to ask his permission for the blockade. In any case the Pasha was to be assured that no conquest was intended (IO Egypt, v. 7, Elphinstone-Salt 6/8/20).

Salt replied to Bruce that the Pasha had given up to the Imam the provinces which Ibrahim had conquered from the Dola of Hodeida in return for a certain amount of coffee to be paid by Egypt as tribute to the Porte. Furthermore, the Pasha was aware of the intentions of the Bombay Government and hoped for an amicable settlement of the insult, offering his good offices as mediator at any time the East India Company should request it (IO Egypt v. 7 Salt-Bruce 11/19/20). The blockading squadron arrived at Mocha on December 3, 1820, and, after it was found that negotiation was impossible, bombarded the town on the twenty-sixth. By the thirtieth the two forts, main defenses of the town, were blown up and the Imam had surrendered. On January 5, 1821, a treaty was signed with the Imam of San'a giving the Company permission to have a Resident at Mocha with right to ride horseback in the town and to go through any gate of the walls, these being two restrictions on non-believers which had previously led to difficulties. The Resident had the right also to proceed inland to San'a at any time, and the Dola was required to supply an escort. The anchorage dues on British ships were abolished and the export duty reduced to a fixed two and a quarter per cent (IO Egypt, v. 7, Bruce-Salt 1/20/21).

In 1813, with the renewal of the East India Company Charter, the Company had lost its monopoly of trade with India as well as in the Red Sea. This changed the general policy of the Bombay Presidency in its actions in the Near East and reduced its dealings to a purely commercial basis, leaving the political decisions in the hands of the Secret Committee in London. In 1822 the Sultan of Lahej offered the British the right to establish a Residency at Aden in return for aid against certain rebellious tribes. Hutchinson, the agent at Mocha who received this offer on a visit to Aden, had to refuse it, telling the Sultan "from the tenor of my instructions it appears the wish of the Honorable the Governor in the Council to avoid all political arrangements with the Arab States and to maintain only commercial

relations with them" (IO Egypt, v. 7, Hutchinson-Salt 1/25/23).
    This visit to Aden and the sending of certain presents to
the Imam of San'a by the East India Company alarmed the Ottoman government, and Salt was requested by the Ambassador
to the Porte, Lord Strangford, to report on the matter. Salt
replied that the Red Sea ports were the scene of continued
minor crises due to the refusal of officials to live up to the
Capitulations (traditional extraterritorial rights of European
citizens living in the Ottoman Empire guaranteed by various
treaties). Furthermore, anchorage dues and duties combined
with various exactions, and the necessity of bribery, were
rapidly destroying what might otherwise be a profitable trade.
Since the removal of the Red Sea from the jurisdiction of the
East India Company "no enterprise can be undertaken in this
quarter [Red Sea] excepting under great responsibility, without
the consent of our Government at home, which I [Salt] conceive
would be decidedly averse to any enterprise that might compromise our tranquility with the Sublime Porte." All in all Salt
felt that in spite of these disadvantages in the Red Sea ports
under the control of the Turkish Empire, at least there was
some possibility of correcting abuses by appeals to Constantinople, while in the ports of the Yemen there was no recourse
other than to appeal to local chieftains. The Bombay Government, he thought, should be satisfied to see these ports, especially Mocha where there was constant friction, pass under
Turkish rule with some semblance of order rather than remain
as they were. He concluded, "The Indian Government has certainly, in some late proceedings in the Persian Gulf as also in
the affairs of Mocha, made war out of its limits and the same
motives may induce them perhaps to hazard as much for Aden,
rather than see it in the hands of the Turks, though I imagine
unless sanctioned by Parliament or the Government at Home
that such proceedings are not strictly legal" (IO Egypt, v. 7,
Salt-Strangford 8/16-17/22).
    During Muhammad Ali's Sudan campaign, the Pasha had
experimented with troops disciplined in the European manner
under Colonel Sèvès (Soliman Pasha), a former aide-de-camp
of Napoleon. Four thousand of these troops were sent to the
Hedjaz, much to the alarm of the people of the Yemen who
feared that he would seize the ports. While Muhammad Ali
denied any such plan, Salt advised London that some agreement
should be reached to prevent the Turks under French influence

from extending their authority in that quarter (IO Egypt, v. 7, Salt-Dart 6/9/25; copy FO 78/3185).

In 1826 another critical situation developed in Mocha when the Dola refused to settle a claim of $20,000 with some Banyan merchants, and the Imam declined to interfere. Salt was requested to solicit the influence of Muhammad Ali to obtain a peaceful settlement. In the meantime the East India Company's agent was instructed to strike his flag (FO 78/160 Bombay-Salt 10/13/26). Salt had a conference with the Pasha on January 30, 1827, in which Muhammad Ali said "The Imam is a young man lost in debauchery [this is a continually recurring phrase and refers to the daily chewing of Khat with resulting mild intoxication], the country is, in fact, without government and I believe that he has not a dollar in his treasury." His Highness went on to say that in 1820 when his troops were on the border of the Yemen, the Imam solicited him to recapture the seacoast towns (Hodeida and Loheia) from the Sharif of Abu 'Arish, in return for which the Imam promised a tribute of coffee to the Porte. This agreement had never been lived up to and the whole country was reported to be in a state of anarchy and the coffee trade non-existent; local chieftains were requesting the Pasha to take the district over. Eventually, Muhammad Ali went on to say, he felt that he would have to do this. In the meanwhile he would try to force the Imam to settle the quarrel (FO 78/160 Salt-FO 2/6/27).

Now the first great invention subsequently to change the entire system of communication was born. In 1802, William Symington applied steam propulsion to a tow boat in the Firth of Forth and in 1807 Robert Fulton built the first practical steam vessel on the Hudson River. Steam navigation was at first limited to river and coastwise vessels. The B. E. I. C. realized the possibilities of this new method of propulsion, especially as controlled propulsion made possible the safe navigation of the reef-strewn and island-studded waters of the Red Sea. The Indian navy was soon ordered to begin survey work there, and in 1829 it was planned to use the Red Sea for forwarding dispatches via the steamer "Enterprise" which was on its way to Bombay via the Cape route (FO 78/194, Bombay-Main dept. London 2/13/29). Moresby, in command of the survey work, directed Consul Barber at Alexandria to request a coaling point for this ship from Muhammad Ali, preferably at Suez (FO 78/194, Barber-FO 5/30/29). The brig "Owen

Glendower" which was bringing the coal to Suez had grounded off Jubal Island at the mouth of the Gulf of Suez and so it was planned to use Q'useir as a coaling port instead (FO 78/194, Barber FO 6/3/29). The "Enterprise," however, was a failure and the first dispatches arrived at Q'useir on a sailing vessel, the "Thetis." Survey work continued along the coast and the steamer "Hugh Lindsay" was sent out from England to continue the experiment. This vessel made the trip, arriving at Q'useir early in 1831 (FO 78/202, Barber-FO 1/17/34). The survey work is well described in Low's history of the Indian navy (Low, C.R., HISTORY OF THE INDIAN NAVY, Dondon, Bentley, 1877, Vol. II, p. 68-94), and the early voyages of the "Hugh Lindsay" in H. L. Hoskins' BRITISH ROUTES TO INDIA (New York, Longmans, 1928, pp. 108-112). It was one of the great achievements of the now almost forgotten Indian navy. Moresby, Haines, Cruttenden, Barber, Wellsted and other officers under Admiral Malcolm brought an accurate knowledge of the Red Sea to Europeans and prepared the way for its modern exploitation as a trade route.

III. MUHAMMAD ALI AND ARABIA

While the early developments in steam navigation focussed
British attention on the Red Sea, Muhammad Ali's imperial
ambitions distracted him from further expansion in Arabia.
Sultan Mahmud's failure to suppress the Greek Revolution led
him to ask for the Pasha's intervention in 1824. The manifest
weakness of the Turkish Empire after the Greek revolt and the
Russo-Turkish war of 1828 provided a temptation to the Pasha
too great to resist. On November 1, 1831, his armies, led by
Ibrahim Pasha, invaded Syria, reaching Damascus in June of
the next year. By the end of July they had captured Aleppo,
and the Sultan, realizing his inability to control his rebellious
vassal, appealed to Great Britain for aid. The resulting diplomatic crisis threatened to involve the great powers in a European war but was temporarily settled by the Treaty of Unkiar
Skelessi between the Porte and Russia and the Convention of
Kutahya between Sultan Mahmud and Muhammad Ali.

After 1823 the Pasha had been content to leave a relatively
small garrison in the Hedjaz. By 1832, after nine years of
neglect, this army was ready for mutiny. One division, stationed at Mecca, rioted in July as a result of a dispute between
Zenar Aga, its commander, and Kurshid Bey, the Egyptian
governor. As usual the dispute was caused by non-payment of
the troops, a chronic condition in both Egyptian and Turkish
armies of the nineteenth century. Among those supporting
Zenar Aga was an Albanian officer named Turchi Bilmer (or
Bilmas) [this is obviously a nickname; translated from the
Turkish it means "the ungrateful Turk"]. This officer turned
the mutiny into a revolution and, after inviting Kurshid Bey to
a meeting, captured him and established himself as governor
of the Hedjaz.

On hearing of this uprising, the Porte immediately sent a
firman to Turchi Bilmer confirming him as Turkish governor
of Hedjaz and promising him assistance against Muhammad Ali.

Muhammad Sabry in his volume L'EMPIRE EGYPTIENNE
SOUS MUHAMMAD ALI (Paris, Geunther, 1930, p. 288), states
that Turchi Bilmer's defection was instigated by the Turks and
the English to embarrass Muhammad Ali in his Syrian campaign. While the Turks certainly took advantage of it, it is

doubtful if they were responsible for its instigation and it would be interesting to find out where M. Sabry found his evidence of English intrigue. Subsequent events would indicate that Turchi Bilmer's object was to take advantage of the confusion attendant on the Syrian campaign to carve out a nice little province for himself in the Yemen.

Muhammad Ali immediately sent a force of 7,500 men under Ahmed Pasha to put down the revolt (FO 78/214 Barker-FO 9/3/32). The mutineers evacuated Jidda under the pressure of this army. But first they seized all the public property which they could lay their hands on, destroyed all the heavy cannon which they could not move easily, and seized the warships of Muhammad Ali which were in port, as well as all of his trading vessels. They then moved south into the Yemen, joined forces with the Asiri, and after capturing Hodeida laid seige to Mocha (FO 78/214; Barker-FO 12/10/32).

This port was captured in December of 1832. In February, 1833, the attempt of a small force of Turchi's army to take the port of Aden was frustrated in a night attack by the Sultan of Lahej. And in March the rebel planned to attack Jidda from the sea in conjunction with a land attack by the Asiri. But the Asiri abandoned him at the last moment and Turchi was compelled to return to Mocha. (Playfair, op. cit., p. 143.)

Muhammad Ali announced in April that he was considering an expedition against the rebels at Mocha, when the war with his Turkish suzerain was ended. Campbell, now consul general at Alexandria, wrote Palmerston that he was trying to dissuade the Pasha from this step as he considered that the conquest of the Yemen and its probable incorporation with the Pashalik of Jidda would only cause further dissensions and jealousies with the Porte (FO 78/227 Campbell-FO 4/16/33). It must be remembered that at this time negotiations were in progress between Muhammad Ali and Sultan Mahmud. After Ibrahim Pasha's victory at Konya, the Pasha claimed sovereignty over the pashaliks of Egypt, Tarsus, Syria, and Adana. Any further claims, however small, could easily upset these negotiations. This crisis was abated by the settlement of Kutahya on May 5, 1833. On June 3 Campbell was informed by Boghos Bey that the expedition against Mocha had been definitely planned and the permission of the British government was solicited. About 7,000 men and twelve field pieces were being prepared at Suez (FO 78/227 Campbell-FO 6/11/33).

Muhammad Ali did not wait to receive this permission, but immediately made preparations for attacking the rebels. Commander Moresby of the B. E. I. C. "Palinurus," surveying the Red Sea from Jidda to Suez, wrote Campbell on August 26, 1833, that the rebels were concentrated at Mocha awaiting the attack of the Egyptians. The whole Yemen was in a deplorable state. The ships of the Banyan merchants were detained in port by the rebels, and commerce had ceased. (FO 78/228 Campbell FO 10/27.) Campbell felt that the only chance for revival of trade in the district was in its occupation by Muhammad Ali. For the past few years commerce had declined; the entire coffee trade in 1832 amounted to only $1,000,000, nearly all of which was carried by American ships. He believed that Muhammad Ali's occupation of Mocha would greatly aid British commerce as he already possessed nearly all the shore of the Red Sea. Campbell added that the Pasha was delighted to receive the permission of the British government to proceed (this permission was granted in reply to his request of June 3) and regretted that he had been compelled to proceed before it arrived, due to the aggression of the rebels. Muhammad Ali had furthermore given Campbell his assurance that his possession of Mocha "should not in any way militate against our [British] interests; or against any agreements we had with the late Imaum" (FO 78/228 Campbell-FO 10/27/33 enclosing Moresby [Jiddah] -Campbell 8/26). Needless to say, Palmerston was annoyed by Muhammad Ali's action in undertaking the expedition without waiting for the permission which he had requested. Palmerston later held this against the Pasha.

After occupying Massawa on the western coast, the Egyptians hastened to capture or destroy all of the rebels' ships. These reverses led, as usual in the Near East, to desertions from Turchi's forces. By September, forsaken by his Asir allies, he had but 1,500 men left at Mocha. Facing defeat here, he was reported to have taken the fortress of Aden, a report which had no foundation. The Pasha informed Campbell that it would probably be necessary to blockade Mocha, and was warned to protect British interests there. He also evinced a desire to recover Aden from the rebels as he was afraid that Turchi Bilmer might "transfer it into a piratical stronghold" (FO 78/228 Campbell-FO 11/17 enclosing Moresby [Jiddah] -Campbell 9/12).

Muhammad Ali prepared to carry on this campaign not only

with arms, but also in two other ways almost as effective with
the Bedwin. First, a certain Wahhabi Sheik Muhammad el
Dasir, captured in the 1818-20 campaign and resident at Cairo
in partial captivity since then, was invested by the Pasha with
the pelisse of the leader of the Asir; and, second, the sum of
$60,000 was sent to buy off the neighboring tribes (FO 78/228
Campbell-FO 12/5).

Before the army despatched from Egypt under Ahmed
Pasha could arrive, Egyptian diplomacy had enlisted an army
of 25,000 Asiri under Sheikh Ali ibn Mitgal to fight for them.
As Muhammad Ali phrased it, he had "invited" the Asiri to
attack. Zebeid was captured and the Asiri refused a reputed
offer of $200,000 by Turchi Bilmer to desist. Hodeida fell and
on December 3 the Asiri approached Mocha. The rebels had
only 500 men against approximately 20,000 Asiri (Moresby's
estimate) and the town fell on December 13, 1833. About 120
Turks, including the leaders, fled to the B.E.I.C. "Tigris"
and "Benares." Mocha was plundered for three days by the
tribesmen, an event which completely destroyed any chance for
trade for the rest of the year (FO 78/245 Campbell-FO 2/22/34,
enclosing Moresby [Mocha]-Campbell 12/29/33).

The death of the Asiri leader shortly after the capture of
Mocha split the leadership of the coalition, and by May Ahmed
Pasha found himself compelled to attack the tribesmen (FO
78/246 Thurburn-FO 7/26/34, Encl. Native Agent [Jidda]-
Campbell 5/31). This attack was successful, and by October,
1834, the Egyptians were reportedly occupying the seacoast to
Mocha and receiving the submission of the Asiri (FO 78/247
Private letter, Campbell-Palmerston 11/11/34). Soon, however, this news was proved false. A letter dated November 10,
received by Clot Bey from a French doctor in the service of
the Pasha, complained of the difficulties of getting supplies in
the wild country away from the coast due to scarcity and expense, with resultant undernourishment of the army. While
Abu 'Arish and Benisher [a tribal not a place name; a branch
of this tribe inhabits a portion of the Wadi Baish, a logical
route of approach to the Asiri country] had been captured easily, this officer was of the opinion that any effective measures
against the Asiri could only be undertaken by using a small,
well-trained and highly mobile force combined with a highly
organized commissariat system. Captain Rose of the B.E.I.C.
"Coote" reported from Mocha that the Imam was ready and

willing to deal with Muhammad Ali on any terms that would re-
plenish his treasury, but that the people of San'a would resist
to the utmost any attempt at Egyptian occupation. Muhammad
Ali was incensed at the reverses suffered by Ahmed Pasha and
the report on the state of the army, and prepared to send another regiment and $40,000 more in cash to re-enforce his
troops (FO 78/257 Campbell-FO 1/3/35).

What had happened was that the tribal allies of the Egyptians, after capturing the towns of the rebels in the name of
Muhammad Ali, had thereupon refused to turn them over and
had now begun to harass the Egyptian army. Hodeida was not
actually captured until January 15, 1835, when, at the request
of the merchants, the governor of the town, well-bribed and
fearing treachery, turned it over to the Egyptians. Sheikh Husain, who had been governing Mocha since its capture by the
Asiri a year before, was requested to hold the town for Muhammad Ali. He apparently did not trust the Egyptians or was
suffering from a guilty conscience, for, on hearing of the approach of an Egyptian detachment under Muhammad Bey, he
fled to the hills on January 24 and the customs house and forts
were occupied by a few sailors from a small Egyptian ship
which happened to be in harbor (FO 78/257 Campbell-FO 2/14/
35 enclosing Denton [B. E. I. C. "Euphrates" at Mocha]-Camp-
bell 1/30/35).

The campaign dragged on, and in early June, 1835, the
Egyptians suffered a serious defeat from the Asiri. It occurred
in typical Arab fashion. A tribe of the Asir confederation, the
Rijal al-M'a, made peace with the Egyptians under Ibrahim the
younger and joined them in a campaign against the other tribes.
When the Egyptians finally caught up to the enemy deep in the
mountains, the Rijal al-M'a rebelled and attacked the Egyptians
in the rear. Ibrahim, the Sharif of Mecca and a few of the
troops fled to safety at al-Qunfidha, but the majority of the army was destroyed. Muhammad Ali immediately ordered a
fresh levy of troops, planning to raise three regiments. Kurshid Pasha was dispatched to replace Ibrahim, who had shown
neither skill nor good judgment in conducting the campaign,
and additional sums of money were supplied. Campbell commented that the campaign was exhausting the population and resources of Egypt. Great numbers of troops were lost by sickness as well as in battle, and the expense of the inadequate commissariat was enormous (FO 78/257 Campbell-FO 7/24/35).

This defeat caused a halt in active warfare. Muhammad
Ali spent a year preparing his force against any contingencies.
Eighteen thousand regular troops with a considerable amount
of artillery were sent to the Hedjaz and the seacoast towns of
the Yemen, not counting the tribal auxiliaries organized on the
spot. This army was divided into three parts. The first was
based at Yanbu under Kurshid Pasha, the second at Ta'if near
Mecca under Ahmed Pasha, and the third at Mocha under Ibrahim Pasha. Kurshid's army was to be directed against the
Wahhabi tribes of the Nejd, while Ahmed and Ibrahim were attacking the Asiri. The troops were aided by plentiful rainfall,
after three years of drought, which filled the wells and greatly
lessened the problem of transporting water by camel. The
whole number of troops was probably close to 24,000, losses
by sickness being constantly replaced. The thoroughness of the
preparations for this expedition was indicated by the fact that
Muhammad Ali ordered machinery from England so that steamers could be fabricated at Alexandria and the parts transported
overland to Suez, where they were to be assembled for transport service. Egyptian merchant ships in the Red Sea were also
mobilized for this purpose. There were thirty-two at Suez and
Tor, thirty-six at Yanbu, nine at Q'useir and twenty-four at
Jidda. As these ships ranged from 250 to 1,200 tons burden,
they comprised an impressive fleet. In addition eleven warships had been concentrated in the Red Sea, five of them of considerable size (FO 78/284. Campbell-FO 11/8/36).

Early in 1837 Muhammad Ali completed his preparations.
Ahmed Pasha and the Sharif of Mecca visited Cairo. The Sharif
was politely replaced by a candidate of Muhammad Ali's own
choosing, without any protest from the Porte (a commentary on
the weakness of the Ottoman Empire which traditionally appointed
the Sharif of Mecca). Four million dollars were reported sent
to Jidda to pay nine months' arrears in pay due the troops, and
Ahmed with the new Sharif started back to the Hedjaz on March
8 (FO 78/285 Sloane FO 3/22/36).

In the Yemen, the Imamate had continued to decline. In
1834 Imam al-Mahdi had died, to be succeeded by his son Ali
under the title of al-Mansur. Imam al-Mansur was visited in
1836 by Lieutenant Cruttenden and Assistant Surgeon Burton,
both from the "Palinurus," which was doing survey work. They
found the young Imam a weakling living in a court remarkable
chiefly for its almost continual state of drunkenness. A four-

year drought had brought the country around San'a to the point
of famine and weakened the Imam's power to an alarming extent.
   The Imam had lost control of the province of Ta'iz to the
powerful Dho Muhammad and Dho Hussein tribes. (Playfair,
op. cit., pp. 144-5.) This statement poses a serious problem
of interpretation. These tribes lived northeast of San'a far
from Ta'iz, the Dho Hussein in the oasis of Jauf. Together with
other tribes they formed a powerful coalition called the Hashid-
wa-Bekil. With their support the reigning Imam could establish
a fairly effective government in the Yemen; without their support he was little better than mayor of San'a. In the period of
this study, the Dho Muhammad and Dho Hussein are frequently
referred to in the documents. It is not apparent that the British
had any idea as to their power or location and it also seems apparent that to the British the terms Dho Muhammad and Dho
Hussein referred generically to tribes of the interior of the Yemen in contrast to the tribes in the neighborhood of Aden. It
would be tempting to interpret these references to activities of
the Hashid-wa-Bekil particularly as such an interpretation
would throw light on the otherwise obscure dealings between the
Ottoman Turks and this powerful tribal coalition in the Yemen,
but such an interpretation makes little sense. To avoid confusion therefore the term "tribes of the interior" has been used
wherever possible when the documents read "Dho Muhammad
and Dho Hussein tribes."
   In spite of the weakness of his most important opponent,
Commander Hawkins of the B. E. I. C. "Clive" reported to Consul Sloane at Alexandria that he felt Muhammad Ali's campaign
in South Arabia was bound to fail as all supplies for Arabia had
to be brought across Egypt and then across the Red Sea. With
the primitive methods of transportation available just about e-
nough food was coming in to enable the soldiers, pilgrims, and
inhabitants to exist. Furthermore, any campaign against the
Asiri had to be carried out in mountainous territory where food
was non-existent and water scarce. Even if these difficulties
could be surmounted, Hawkins believed that permanent conquest
was impossible, for the Arabs intensely disliked Egyptian rule
and even if temporarily subdued would continually make trouble.
Politically, Ahmed Pasha had stirred up bad feeling among the
Arabs by using a novel method of recruiting. He had simply
forced about 2,000 pilgrims to join his army. In addition, one
of Muhammad Ali's plans had failed when three regiments of

black Sudanese troops conscripted in Kordofan and Sennar, on the theory that they could be easily acclimated, lost half their strength, to all appearances just dying of homesickness.

After the bombardment of Mocha in 1820, the British had made a treaty with the Imam of San'a fixing the export duties at two and a quarter per cent. Muhammad Ali had pledged himself to observe this when he sought permission to attack the rebels. However, as is well known, the Egyptian Pasha had certain definite economic ideas. His system of monopolies ran directly counter to the British concept of free trade. As soon as the government of Mocha was well established in 1833, Ibrahim Pasha lost no time in setting up a coffee monopoly in the Yemen. All coffee was by compulsion sold to agents of the Pasha at a fixed price. This greatly diminished the supply, as growers refused to raise coffee on which they could not get a fair return (FO 78/3185, Captain James Mackenzie's Report on Arabia and Egypt 6/1/37). Furthermore, one-half of the reduced supply was reserved for the Pasha, who used it to pay tribute to the Porte. The remainder was sold to American merchants, who were further favored by being liable to a three per cent export duty while the British were compelled to pay seven and a quarter per cent (FO 78/318 Palmerston Campbell 1/31/37). The East India Company protested through the Foreign Office and Palmerston wrote Campbell on January 31: "I have to instruct you to express to the Pasha... the extreme astonishment with which H. M. Govt. have learnt this additional act of aggression which had been committed by the Authorities of the Pasha against British Commerce, and this fresh violation of the Rights of British Subjects.

"You will demand peremptorily of His Highness that the restrictive order... shall be immediately revoked... and the 2-1/4 % duties restored.... And you will give the Pasha plainly and distinctly to understand that Great Britain will not permit either the Pasha or his subordinates to continue this system of universal hostility to British Commerce. You will add that if such proceedings are not absolutely discontinued, H. M. 's Govt. will be compelled to take such measures as the interests and honour of Great Britain may appear to them in such case to require. P. " (FO 78/318 Palmerston-Campbell 1/3-/37).

Campbell replied that he had been informed of this state of affairs by Commander Haines, B. E. I. C. "Palinurus, " in September, and that the Pasha had sent peremptory orders to

Ibrahim to observe strictly the terms of the former treaty with
the Imam (FO 78/319 Campbell-FO 3/2/37). That Muhammad
Ali had done this is confirmed from the Bombay Records. A
dispatch from the Native Agent at Mocha in December, 1836,
reported that Ibrahim investigated the matter on his arrival
and ascertained that the proper duties were enforced. Furthermore, the Pasha had promised to do all in his power to promote British trade (BPC 1837 Native Agent-Bombay, 12/12/36).
The unsettled conditions in the Yemen (the Imam of San'a was
raising an army to attack the Egyptians, an attack which never
materialized as the Imam's army evaporated from lack of funds)
compelled Muhammad Ali temporarily to give up the idea of a
monopoly of the coffee trade and to pay the market price in order to encourage the coffee growers (BPC 1837, Campbell-
Bombay 7/26/37). Thus the cause of the economic friction was
removed for the time being, only to be replaced by more serious considerations.

During the winter of 1836-1837, one Captain James Mackenzie of the Bengal Light Cavalry, who had been travelling on
leave to England, returned via the Red Sea and Egypt. He
stopped at Mocha, Hodeida, and Jidda, and sent in a most interesting report to the Foreign Office. He was welcomed with
open arms by the few European officers in the Egyptian army
of Arabia, was an excellent observer, and was able to gain considerable information. His report covered both Arabia and
Egypt. Although the latter part of the report regarding Egypt
is outside the scope of this volume, it is worthy of passing notice here because it contains a very excellent summary of the
organization of the Egyptian army and an interesting description of Muhammad Ali's methods of recruiting and conscription.

Mackenzie, after personal observation, stated that the
Egyptian conquests in Arabia comprised only the coast for about
a mile inland, the fertile land of Ta'if near Mecca, and the Holy
City itself. The command of the seacoast however gave control
of the export trade of the Yemen and of the Hedjaz. This had
been organized on a monopolistic basis, with the Pasha buying
products at his own price from the growers, and selling to native dealers and foreign merchants at a considerable profit.
The import duty on Indian goods was ten per cent payable in
money or in kind. Once this duty was paid there was no molestation of the merchant, who could sell to whom he pleased without
bribery or exactions. Mackenzie never saw "a more liberal or

better managed customs house than the Pasha's at Jidda, and it
is the same at Mocha. There is no bribery necessary and no
annoying search after smuggled articles. ... I speak however
with reference to transactions carried on under the British
flag. " He attributed this in part to the constant presence of
two cruisers of the Indian Navy "whose guns inspire respect
and give the Turks and Arabs a favorable idea of our power."
The chief exports, coffee and senna, were raised in the territory of the Imam of San'a, "a young and weak prince who possesses a fine country which I fear will one day pass into the
hands of the grasping Pasha. "

At Jidda he had the opportunity to inspect one of three armies of Muhammad Ali which he considered very well equipped.
Here also he met several of the European officers in the Pasha's
service. These men, mostly Italian and French, were com-
missioned officers but served only as staff officers or instructors. Christians were not allowed positions of command. The
medical force was chiefly French with a few Germans. There
were no Englishmen as the pay was too low and they were not
adaptable enough. Mackenzie made a very pertinent comment
on this. "From my experience abroad I should say that the
English do not adapt themselves to the manners and customs of
a foreign country and indulge in the humours and prejudices of
the people as readily as the French and Italians — hence the preference decidedly shown, in Egypt particularly, to natives of
the above countries. " He estimated the Pasha's army in Arabia
as totalling 2,000 cavalry, 20,000 infantry and a proportionate
number of sappers and artillery, and gave the disposition of the
main forces. Each important town had a small garrison and
was administered by both a military and a civil governor of
equal power to check each other (a practice typical of the Ottoman Empire).

From discussions with responsible officers he gathered
that Muhammad Ali intended to march on Aden after conquering
or bribing the Asiri. After that it was believed that Egyptian
power would be extended to the Hadramaut and eventually to
Oman and Muscat. The conquest of Baghdad should then be
easy. Mackenzie said, "I should imagine that the British Government would never permit High Highness to extend his conquests to Muscat... on the ground of policy with reference to its
proximity to the coast of India. ... I doubt the propriety of our
permitting the Pasha to take Aden. His government is

unquestionably better than that of the lawless sheiks, but if on
the principle of humanity it is better to establish a good and
regular government which shall secure order and protection to
life and property where neither life nor property is secure –
then it is a question whether we, so intimately connected with
that part of the world in consequence of its being the best and
nearest route to India – and so much superior in knowledge
power and civilization, should not ourselves take and keep possession of Aden whose noble harbours would be of the greatest
benefit to the prosecution of our Indian Steam Navigation plans.
Besides giving us a power and consequence and commercial advantages in Arabia, Abyssinia and the north coast of Africa
which we do not at present possess, it would be the means of
extending our knowledge and religion over countries and amongst
people now immersed in the profoundest ignorance." Sooner
or later Muhammad Ali or someone else would take Aden. "It
seems to be a law of nature that the civilized nations shall conquer and possess the countries in a state of barbarism and by
such means however unjustifiable it may appear at first sight
extend the blessings of knowledge, industry and commerce a-
mong people hitherto sunk in the most gloomy depths of superstitious ignorance" (FO 78/3185 Report of Captain MacKenzie
6/1/37). Mackenzie concluded the Arabian section of his report
by predicting that Egyptian sway would not continue for very
long as the Turks were cordially hated and the Arabs were desirous of their freedom.

Up to the spring of 1837 there is little evidence to show that
Muhammad Ali was contemplating any sizeable conquests in
Arabia. His campaigns had begun because of a mutiny in his
army which threatened the whole of his power in the Holy Cities
of the Hedjaz. If such a movement was not put down, Egyptian
power in Arabia and throughout the Near East would lose prestige. He set about his campaigns in the most inexpensive way
by hiring the Asiri to fight for him. They in turn revolted,
which made it necessary to send a force to attack them. At the
same time, the rich coffee country of the Yemen was without a
master and the coffee trade was a valuable one. With very little
effort the ports of the Yemen were captured and a monopoly was
established, for, obviously, Muhammad Ali had to have some
return on the money invested in the expedition. The defeat of
the Egyptians by the Asiri in 1835 caused fresh complications
and it then became apparent that a serious campaign was
imperative.

It seems to be almost axiomatic that in countries under a
tribal organization every conquest leads on to another until a
natural frontier is reached. So it was in Arabia. If it had not
been for the prestige indispensable to holding the Holy Cities,
the Egyptians could have remained contented with the coast,
but Mecca was constantly being threatened by the Asiri and
their conquest was essential. Whether or not Muhammad Ali
intended to conquer all of Arabia is an unanswerable question,
but by the very nature of the country any serious campaign
would lead to this end as every tribe would be just as annoying
a neighbor, with just as ill-defined borders as the last. Certainly up until the defeat by the Asiri in 1835 it is probable that
Muhammad Ali was considering no great conquests. The size
of his preparations after that defeat, however, seems to indicate that a conquest of Arabia was planned, and Mackenzie's
statement was based on information which he received in Arabia.
To be sure, there is no evidence that a Pan-Arab state was in
Muhammad Ali's mind. His two appointments, the new sheikh
of the Asiri and a new Sharif of Mecca were made for local political reasons rather than for an appeal to all the Arabs. Nor
is there any indication that His Highness used religion to stir
up the tribes, even in his later intrigues against Aden, as the
Turks used it in their conquests in the Yemen in 1870-1873.
Haines' remarkable secret service organization would have reported any such moves. It is also hard to find an economic
motive for the conquest of Arabia. The richest trade, that of
Mecca via Jidda, and of the Yemen, was already under his control through the occupation of the seacoast. The planned campaign which followed in 1838-1839 could not result in much
economic profit. One can only conclude by agreeing with Dodwell (Dodwell, Henry H., THE FOUNDER OF MODERN EGYPT,
pp. 143-5) that Baghdad and Basra were the ultimate object of
the campaign after 1835. But what is most important was that
Palmerston was convinced of this and decidedly alarmed by it.
The Egyptians in Syria were entirely too close to Baghdad for
comfort, and a movement through the Nejd would threaten not
only the mouth of the Tigris and Euphrates but also British interests in the Persian Gulf, especially in Muscat and Bahrein.
Muhammad Ali's excuse for this aggression was the resurgence
of Wahhabi power after the evacuation of the Nejd in 1820. However there seems to be little evidence in British documents of
particular Wahhabi aggression near the Holy Cities after 1820.

The Egyptian campaign got under way in the early part of 1837. A large force of cavalry overran the Nejd, levied contributions from the Wahhabi and commandeered a thousand camels. A force of 10,000 men was mobilized at al-Qunfidah to attack the Asiri (FO 78/320 Campbell-FO 7/12/37).

At this time reports were current in Cairo that plans had been made for an attack on Aden. Campbell sent an inquiry to the Pasha who was at Candia, and Boghos Bey answered that Muhammad Ali flatly denied any such intention. Campbell after further investigation wrote, "I have no reason to suppose that the Pasha has any hostile intentions either on the side of Aden outside the Red Sea or to the eastward of the territory of Mocha and San'a" (FO 78/3185 Campbell-FO 9/23/37). Any precise information regarding the campaign was difficult to obtain, but on November 3, Campbell was able to inform Palmerston that the campaign was not progressing very favorably. Provisions were scarce. The coast towns, insufficiently garrisoned, were shown to be vulnerable to tribal attacks, and jealousy between Kurshid and Ahmed Pasha delayed any unified movement. Ibrahim the younger, with headquarters at Mocha, was reported as being desirous that the campaign be given up and the occupation limited to the coastal towns (FO 78/321 Campbell-FO 11/1/37).

At the same time, word reached Campbell in a private letter from Major Felix, secretary of the Bombay Government, "that the Sultan of Aden has just laid himself open by an outrage which he had committed, or allowed, on the person and property of a Madras vessel sailing under British colours, called the Duria Dowlat, and Aden has been reported to be the best situation for a coal depot between this [Bombay] and Juddah" (FO 78/321 Campbell-FO 11/1/37, quoting a private letter from Major Felix). Campbell added that the occupation of Aden by the British would prevent His Highness from extending his conquest beyond the Red Sea and would probably throw the entire coffee trade, which was largely handled by Americans at this time, into English hands.

Information on the reports of Egyptian movements in Arabia prompted Palmerston to write Campbell to warn Muhammad Ali that the movements of his troops in Syria and Arabia "seem to indicate intentions on his part to extend his authority towards the Persian Gulf and the Pashalik of Baghdad;... you will state frankly to the Pasha that the British Govt. could not see with

indifference the execution of such intentions" (FO 78/318 Palmerston-Campbell 12/8/37). Muhammad Ali protested that he
had no designs on either the Persian Gulf or Baghdad, but later
events do not show this denial to be very serious (FO 78/342
Campbell-FO 2/7/38). Campbell further used his influence to
persuade the Pasha to give up the Yemen adventure as too expensive an undertaking (FO 78/342 Campbell-FO 3/20/38).

Meanwhile an incident had occurred at Aden which transformed the whole raison d'etre of British policy in the Yemen
from a theoretical to a practical basis. The news that the
"Duria Dowlat, " an Indian buggalow sailing under British colors, had been wrecked and plundered near Aden in January,
1837, had spread over the Near East. While, as Hoskins points
out (Hoskins, op. cit. , p. 197), it was not an unusual occurence
in Arabian waters, this act of piracy was particularly notable
for the outrageous mistreatment of the vessel's passengers.
Commander Haines was ordered to investigate the matter, and
he sent back a very interesting report. Evidence seemed to
show that the ship had been wrecked purposely to recover insur-
ance on the cargo. Furthermore, the vessel had apparently
been intentionally overloaded. The participants in the plot were
the merchant who had chartered the vessel and the native authorities at Aden; the Sultan of Lahej, if not actually participating,
was at least cognizant of the whole affair (BPC Superintendent
of Indian Navy-Bombay 7/21/37, enclosing Haines-Malcolm
7/6/37 and affidavits of the survivors; also in Parl. Papers
1839 #268). The matter was made still more complicated by
the fact that the owner of the vessel was the Nawab of the Carnatic who had appealed to the Madras Government to recover
what property it could (BPC Sec'y of the Madras Govt. -Bombay
8/8/37).

The first reaction of the Bombay Government was that as
the ship was sailing under British colors and belonged to the
Nawab of the Carnatic "it will probably be required for this
government to take strong measures for exacting reparations"
(BPC Minute by Chief Secretary, 8/7/37). The Governor felt
that such measures should be taken for effectual redress, and
the papers were forwarded to the Government of India with the
request that authority should be given to enforce any demands
made (BPC Minute by Governor 8/14/37). The whole matter
was referred to the Governor General of India on September 15.

Up to this point there is no evidence that possession of

Aden had been considered by the British. In spite of the many
reports on the advantages of Aden, beginning with Valentia's
report in 1808 that it was "the Gibraltar of the East and at
trifling expense could be made impregnable" (FO 1/1 Valentia
FO 9/13/08) and evidence of other travellers and explorers,
Aden had been tried as a coaling station in 1829 and found wanting due to the lack of laborers. (Low, C.R., HISTORY OF THE
INDIAN NAVY, Vol. II, pp. 115-116.)

However, Commander Haines, who had visited there during
a survey cruise in 1835, gave a very favorable report of the
harbor. Then too the Sultan of Aden had been on the whole
friendly to Great Britain. In 1800 Aden had been a refuge for
the Indian troops who because of lack of water had been forced
to abandon Perim (FO 78/1333 India Board-FO 11/27/36 enclosing correspondence relative to Perim 1799-1800 Col. Murray-
Bombay 10/4/1799). At that time the Sultan had been anxious
to get the protection of the British. A treaty of friendship had
been made with Sir Home Popham in 1802. Again in 1822 the
Sultan had hoped for an occupation by British troops when Muhammad Ali's campaign against the Wahhabi momentarily
threatened to extend to the Yemen. Relations, then, on the
whole had been friendly, especially with Sultan Ahmad. Since
his death in 1827, there had been little intercourse with his successor, Sultan Mahsin (Muhammad Husain) but there was no
reason to believe that this Sultan would prove unfriendly.

The shipwreck incident at Aden, combined with the establishment of a monthly steam service to Suez, led Sir Robert
Grant, Governor of Bombay, to investigate the matter thoroughly. On September 23 he wrote a long Minute, in which the
rest of the Board concurred, suggesting that the British take
advantage of this affair to get possession of Aden, giving a long
description of its advantages (Parl. Papers 1839 #268, Minute
by Governor 9/23/37 pp. 18, 19, also in BSC 1837). This was
forwarded to the Governor General on September 27. The Governor General replied after a consideration of all the material
regarding the piracy and Governor Grant's Minute, "In the opinion of the Governor General in Council it would not be expedient
or proper to take possession of the town or promontory of Aden on
account of the pillage of the Ship 'Doria Dowlat' and that even if
this outrage were considered sufficient, it would be hazardous
on account of the collision it might lead us into with the Egyptian
or Arabian powers. His Lordship in Council is of the opinion

that satisfaction should in the first instance be demanded of the Sultan of Aden for this outrage. If it be granted, amicable arrangements may be made with him for the occupation of this port as a depot for coals and harbours for shelter. If it be refused, then further measures may be considered, and in the meantime information may be collected on the political state of Aden and the neighboring countries" (BPC 1837, Sec'y Govt. of India-Bombay 10/16/37).

The Bombay Government acted promptly and on the advice of Admiral Malcolm instructed Commander Haines to proceed on the next steamer to Aden to demand satisfaction for the "Doria Dowlat" outrage. If the demands for reparation were refused, Haines was to return to Bombay. He was cautioned to "use his utmost endeavor to effect an amicable settlement," and not to lose sight of the desire to establish a coal depot (BPC Minute by Board 11/29/37 and Willoughby-Malcolm 11/25/37). Haines, through Malcolm, informed the Bombay Government that he believed that there would be no difficulty in getting the Sultan to make over the furthermost point of Aden as a coal depot as it would improve his trade. He further requested proper presents to give to the Sultan (BPC 1837 Malcolm-Willoughby 11/27/37). The Government in reply advised Haines to give the presents only after satisfaction had been obtained and empowered him "to negotiate with the Sultan for the transfer to the British Government of the most isolated part of Aden" (BPC 1837. Willoughby-Malcolm 11/29/37). Further details of the negotiations are of no moment here and will be taken up in their proper place. It is sufficient to say that a formal transfer of Aden was agreed on in two documents dated January 22, 1838, although the Sultan later refused to recognize them.

News of these negotiations reached Cairo in March, 1838. Campbell was informed by Boghos Bey that British negotiations at Aden had given considerable uneasiness to the Pasha, "who evidently has some distrust of having the British as such near neighbors to Mocha." Campbell was convinced that the agents of three great powers, France, Russia, and Austria, would intrigue against the British occupation (FO 78/342 Campbell FO 3/270). Boghos Bey was requested to observe to Campbell that Muhammad Ali "qu'avait d'entreprendre de la Yemen, destinée a organizer ces contrées on avait obtenu le consentement du Gouvernement de Son Majestie Britannique" (FO 78/342 Artin

Bey-Boghos Bey 3/20/38 enclosed in Campbell-FO 3/27/38), and also to state that Aden was not autonomous, but dependent on the Imam of San'a (FO 78/342 Artin-Boghos. 3/22/38 enclosed in above). Campbell refused to make any comments until he had received Palmerston's instructions, but he did observe that, as the Sultan of Aden was capable of making a treaty with Sir Home Popham in 1802, there was little doubt of his independence (FO 78/34 Campbell-FO 4/17/38).

Meanwhile the Egyptians, fearful that this affair meant that England would force their troops out of the Yemen, proposed on March 28 that the spheres of influence be defined, England to take Aden and Egypt to retain the mountains, thus preserving the coffee trade in Egyptian hands, a fact which, as will be seen, was realized only by Haines. On the other hand, if the English only wanted a coaling station, Muhammad Ali wrote, "je puis assurer qu'après qu'on se rendre mâitre de ce pays, on y prodiguera les mêmes soins pour les affaires des Anglais, et leur procurer toutes les commodités dont ils peuvent avoir besoin comme celâ ce fait dans les autres pays soumis au gouvernement Egyptien" (FO 78/342 Muhammad Ali-Boghos 3/28/38 enclosed in Campbell FO 4/17/38). The Pasha went on to say that an Arab government in Aden could never render the services expected of it. Aden could easily be taken with a few men, and an efficient government installed. He concluded with the plea that he had obtained permission for his conquests in Arabia Felix, which statement caused Palmerston to write in the margin of Campbell's despatch "not true, he set out before he got the answer" (FO 78/342 as above).

Palmerston replied to Campbell's letter of March 27 that Her Majesty's Government as yet had received no definite information from the Governor General of India and that Boghos Bey's information was probably correct. The Government could only assume that if Aden were being occupied it was being done for sufficient reasons, adding "it is in that case also likely that the conduct of the Indian Govt. in that matter will be approved." As for the effect that the possession of Aden would have on the occupation of the Yemen by the Egyptians, it was up to the Pasha. "But Her Majesty's Govt. is not aware that any interest of Great Britain is promoted by the continuance of that occupation." Regarding Muhammad Ali's claims to having obtained permission for the expedition to the Yemen, Palmerston stated that the India Board had seen no damage to British interests in it, but as the Pasha had not waited for this permission it had had no effect in starting the expedition (FO 78/342 P Palmerston-Campbell 5/12/38).

Campbell's dispatch of April 17 brought from Palmerston in reply a very definite answer to Muhammad Ali's proposal to take Aden for the English. This document is worth quoting in full as it became the keystone of the policy of the Indian Government in dealing with Aden and the surrounding country until changing conditions in the early 1870's compelled its abandonment.

> I have to instruct you to remind Boghos Bey of the declaration already made by H. M. Govt. through you as reported in your despatch #51 of last year [vide pp. 55-6 supra] that Great Britain could not see with indifference any attempt made by Muhammad Ali to invade or conquer the country lying at and beyond the mouth of the Red Sea.
>
> With respect to the occupation of the Yemen by the Egyptian troops, you will say that the British Govt. have no desire that such occupation should continue, but, on the contrary, would be better pleased by any overt act which should show that the Pasha is engaged in improving the administration of the Provinces confided to his Govt. instead of employing the energies of his mind and the resources of the countries he governs in aggressive expeditions against neighboring districts. (FO 78/342 Palmerston-Campbell 5/24/38)

Before receiving this dispatch, Campbell was informed from Bombay that the question of the occupation of Aden was in the hands of the Government in London. When Campbell informed the Pasha of this, Muhammad Ali expressed a hope that Aden would be considered as part of the Yemen as it was known to have been at one time a part of the Turkish Empire. He requested that the Indian Government be informed that he would be delighted to allow a coal depot to be formed there as in any other part of his dominion, and pressed on Campbell the advantage of a coal depot without any expense of garrison or administration on the part of the Indian Government (FO 78/343 Campbell-FO 6/9/38).

The arrival of Palmerston's note of May 24 showed to

Muhammad Ali that the British intended no concessions. In an interview on August 7, the Pasha brought up all the same points, including his offer to establish a coaling station there for the British. To this Campbell replied that England was sufficiently powerful to take care of herself and furthermore did not wish to create an injustice in asking the Pasha to take Aden. Muhammad Ali then shifted his ground and told Campbell that his real fear was that disputes would occur between natives under Egyptian and under English influence and create misunderstandings between the two governments. He added that he would not interfere, however, and that maybe it would be best for him to evacuate the Yemen. Campbell's conclusion was that the Pasha's real fear lay in the equable rule of the British which would attract the coffee trade to Aden and break up his monopoly (FO 78/343 Campbell-FO 7/7/38).

When news of the agreement for cession of Aden was referred to the Pasha he informed Campbell that he considered Aden British territory with the mountains as boundary, and assured Campbell that neither the British government nor the East India Company would have "any cause of complaint against him respecting Aden" (FO 78/343 Campbell-FO 9/1/38).

While Muhammad Ali was being disappointed in the Yemen, his troops were highly successful in the Hedjaz and the Nejd. The Asiri had been defeated by Ahmed Pasha but had not made submission; otherwise the whole of the country had fallen to the Pasha, who considered the affair almost closed (FO 78/343 Campbell-FO 6/10/38 and 7/2/38).

Early in 1839 rumors of the Egyptian successes, especially in the Nejd, reached London from Baghdad. The Pasha's army was approaching Qatif and threatened to take Bahrein Island. Hasa was captured. Bahrein was at this time a tributary of the Nejd (FO 78/373 Campbell-FO 4/6/39 enclosing letters from Bombay) but was very close to Muscat territory, and an occupation of the island would be a decided threat to the overland route to India as well as to the predominant British influence in Muscat. Palmerston therefore wrote on November 29 that the occupation of Bahrein "could not be viewed with indifference by the British Government" (FO 78/343 Palmerston-Campbell 11/29/38). Boghos Bey denied that such an occupation was contemplated (FO 78/373 Campbell-FO 1/26/39). Reports from Vice-consul Ogilvie at Jidda seemed to indicate that Kurshid's operations had not reached the Persian Gulf in force. However,

Kurshid had captured the chief of the Wahhabi and the whole of the Nejd had submitted. Ogilvie estimated that the Egyptian army consisted of approximately 30,000 men, of whom only 5,000 were in the Nejd, and the largest number in the Hedjaz. He also gave an interesting estimate of the population of the various regions; the Nejd had an estimated population of 460,000 people with 115,000 capable of carrying arms; the Hedjaz had 480,000, of whom 400,000 were Bedwin, the remainder city dwellers — 130,000 of these were estimated as warriors; the Yemen, an area much smaller than the other two, had a population of 460,000, with 109,000 warriors.

On February 11, 1839, Campbell received a report from Commander Haines of the successful capture of Aden (FO 78/373 Campbell-FO 2/11/39 enclosing Haines-Campbell 1/28/39). At the same time, Ogilvie, British Consul at Jidda, reported that Ibrahim Pasha (the younger) was at Ta'iz, a short distance from Aden, fighting the tribes (FO 78/373 Campbell-FO 2/12/39). The details of Egyptian intrigues in the Yemen can be left to another, more appropriate, place. No crisis developed there, due to the distraction of Muhammad Ali by events in Asia Minor and Syria. In the Nejd the question of Bahrein continued to cause difficulties. Muhammad Ali undoubtedly desired the island as a base for operations against the Turks at Baghdad. Bahrein and Kuweit were both acknowledged by the Bombay Government to have been tributaries of the Wahhabi state, so that the Pasha as conqueror of that state had at least a claim to their tribute (FO 78/373 Campbell-FO 4/6/39). The situation in the Persian Gulf became critical in January, 1839. Kurshid wrote Hennel, Resident at Muscat, that he planned to seize Bahrein by force, as several Wahhabi sheikhs hostile to the Pasha had fled there and were using the island as a base for plots against the Egyptians. Hennel replied on February 28, 1839, that the Sheikh of Bahrein was in treaty relations with England and that the intentions of Kurshid would be viewed with "Deep Concern." He requested Kurshid to suspend operations until an answer came from India (FO 78/374 Campbell-FO 5/18/39 with enclosures). The answer from India was definite and to the point; they would defend Bahrein against Kurshid by force if necessary (FO 78/374 Campbell-FO 6/18/39).

The increased tension of the international crisis resulting from the obvious weakness of the Ottoman Empire restrained any forward movements of the Egyptians, and in January of

1840 Consul General Hodges, who had replaced Campbell, reported that an extraordinary meeting of the Council had decided to withdraw 4,000 troops from the Hedjaz to defend Alexandria (FO 78/404 Hodges-FO 1/4/40). This precipitated the abandonment of Arabia by Muhammad Ali, and by February 21, 1840, Hodges was assured that Kurshid had retired from the Hedjaz and Ibrahim from the Yemen and both were coming with their armies to re-enforce Alexandria. Soon the Arabian peninsula was evacuated. In the general settlement with the Sultan the administration of the Holy Cities was made over to the Porte, and Muhammad Ali was required, as a vassal of the Porte, to provide grain for the provisioning of these places (Sabry, op. cit., p. 536).

So ended the first modern attempt to establish an empire in the Arabian part of the decadent Ottoman Empire. How successful Muhammad Ali would have been if the Great Powers had not interfered is difficult to estimate. The Pasha had far more ability than Ismail, who tried to build another Egyptian empire thirty years later. However, it is doubtful if any great empire could have been sustained in the Near East until the revolution in transportation had restored in part the old trade routes which were the basic cause of its ancient wealth.

IV. CAPTURE OF ADEN

With the interest in steam navigation, Aden had by 1837 assumed a new importance in the eyes of the Indian Government. As mentioned before, the Red Sea had been dangerous for large sailing vessels, but the new vessels with steam auxiliaries seemed to provide the answer. The main drawback lay in the inefficiency of the early engines. The amount of fuel necessary for successful operation occupied a great deal of cargo space. It was impossible for a steam vessel to carry enough fuel to go from Suez to India. A coaling station in the vicinity of the mouth of the Red Sea was therefore a necessity. Aden had been investigated in 1822 and again in 1829 but had been found wanting in proper facilities. Socotra had been explored in 1835 and 1836 but the refusal of the Sultan of Qishn to cede a coaling station there ended its possible usefulness.

The investigations of Aden in 1822 and 1829 had been disappointing because Aden had deteriorated from its former prosperity into a desolate village with no facilities and no laborers, but its potentialities for greatness remained. Its site was magnificent. Built on a peninsula, formed by the crater of an extinct volcano, the town was connected with the mainland by a narrow neck of land which lent itself to very effective defense works. This peninsula and a smaller one to the west enclosed a large and deep harbor which was fully protected from all winds and seas and yet had a deep and easy channel to the Indian Ocean. On the east of the peninsula was a minor harbor which at worst provided a protected roadstead. Climatically the town was extremely hot but not unhealthy. It dominated the entrance to the Red Sea, especially the route to India, although it was a considerable distance east of Bab-el-Mandeb.

Behind the town lay a country which was not unproductive. Although without dependable rainfall, the land was fed by streams which descended from the mountains of the Yemen fifty to sixty miles from the coast. As many of these streams never reached the coast, disappearing in the sands of the desert, the coastal strip was usually quite barren.

The hinterland of Aden was in 1839, and remains today, completely tribal in organization. Even the Yemen, although at times it has had a central government, was and is basically tribal. During the period covered by this study, British officials seldom went outside the confines of the Aden settlement. They had personal contact with the chiefs of the immediate neighboring tribes and some communications with other tribes, but they had little firsthand knowledge of conditions within the tribes or of the topography of the country itself. Thus their knowledge of the tribes in the immediate vicinity of Aden, though largely obtained secondhand, was quite accurate while their knowledge of the further tribes was hazy and at times confused. One is aided in straightening out the confusion by the Handbook of Arabia compiled by the Geographical Section of the British Admiralty during World War I. As H. St. John Philby has pointed out in numerous places, this volume has its limitations, as much of the material was obtained by questioning various Arabs coming from all over the peninsula. However, these limitations are political rather than geographical, and concern chiefly the allegiance of subtribes rather than their location. Used as a background for the contemporary documents, it clarifies many points of confusion.

The most powerful tribe in the vicinity of Aden and by all odds the wealthiest, was the Abdali, whose capital was at Lahej some twenty miles inland from Aden. The sultans of this tribe were the rulers of Aden from 1728 until the British occupation in 1839. Their country was extremely rich where water flowed, and grew a large amount of agricultural produce. In addition, it controlled the main caravan routes from the hinterland to Aden. The ruling family was represented at the time of Colonel Murray's expedition to Perim in 1800 by Sultan Ahmed, who had come to power in 1792. It was he who offered Aden to Colonel Murray in return for British protection, and later in 1820 made the same offer to Haines who stopped there on his mission to the Imam. He also made a commercial treaty with Sir Home Popham in 1802 on the latter's nearly disastrous mission to those parts to counteract American domination of the export trade. Undoubtedly Sultan Ahmed hoped that an English protectorate would restore the prosperity of the port of Aden and allow it to share the trade which flourished in Mocha where a Residency of the East India Company was established. In 1827 the old man died, to be succeeded by his grandnephew Muhammad Hussain (M'Hussein, Mohsin, Mahsin — variant spellings in the documents) ibn Fadhl. By this time the great economic decline of the Yemen was well started, and the general policy of this ruler was marked by a desire to be left alone. He was the Sultan with whom the English had their dealings in 1830 and, under his rule, Aden reached the nadir of its career. By the time of the English occupation the shrine of the Sayyid Hydroose was the only stone building left intact from the former greatness of the city.

A subdivision of the Abdali tribe, the Aqrabi (Agrabi) lived at and around Bir Ahmed, a miserable little port on the landward side of the outer harbor of Aden. A very small group, with not more than 250 fighting men, their only source of income was the transit duties on the small amount of trade that came to their port, augmented by judicious banditry. Formerly under the sovereignty of the Abdali tribe, they had revolted in 1770 and rebuilt a medieval fort at Bir Ahmed. Their sheikh was Hyder ibn Maidee who ruled from 1833 to 1858, when he resigned in favor of his son Abd Allah. One of the chief ambitions of the Abdali Sultans was to regain their sovereignty over this group who were notorious disturbers of the peace.

To the east of Aden lay the Fadhli tribe whose estimated population in 1878 was about 20,000. Their land was very poor, lying along the barren seacoast, and their chief settlement was a small port named Shuqra. From this place they fished and also carried on a slight trade, chiefly importing dates, which were the staple food of the Fadhli tribesman during the dry season. Their origins were lost in tradition; they were ruled from 1828 to 1870 by Ahmed ibn Abd Allah, a chief who was noteworthy for his fanatical antagonism towards the British.

The Haushabi tribe lived in the foothills of the Yemen massif north and west of the Abdali. This tribe resulted from the breakdown of the rule of the Imam of San'a. Their ruler was Sultan Mani ibn Salah who died in 1858. They were always friendly to the British.

To the east and north of the Fadhli lay the 'Aulaqi country. The tribal group was divided into two parts, the Upper 'Aulaqi in the north and the Lower 'Aulaqi on the seacoast. For a while these tribes had been united under a Vakeel of the Imam of San'a, but their separation apparently took place in antiquity. The British had no dealings with them until Coghlan began to search for an ally at the rear of the Fadhli in 1854. The Lower 'Aulaqi had relations with the Nizam of Hyderabad as he had a number of these tribesmen in his bodyguard.

The Alawi tribe lived in the Haushabi country, next to the

Abdali, and recognized the Haushabi Sultan as their sovereign.
In the mountains to the north of the Haushabi lay the territory
of the Amir of Dhala, with whom Aden had slight relations.
The Yafa tribe lay to the east of the Haushabi and had no direct
relations with the British except through commerce.

To the west of the Abdali and Aqrabi, the country as far as
Bab-el-Mandeb was very barren and wild. It was occupied by
a group of small independent nomadic tribes collectively called
the Subahi, which were in no way organized and were thus impossible to deal with. They were the chief raiders of caravans
and the most turbulent element in the district. As they were
hated by all the other tribes, the British were little bothered
by them; the agricultural Arabs successfully quarantined the
marauders from themselves and the trade routes. (The above
is based on Hunter, Major F. M. , and Sealey, Captain C. W. H. ,
AN ACCOUNT OF THE ARAB TRIBES IN THE VICINITY OF
ADEN, compiled under the Order of the Government, Government Central Press, Bombay, 1886.)

The focal point of tribal disturbances was Sheikh 'Othman,
a crossroad which lay at the landward end of the peninsula of
Aden, with a supply of water which supplemented the tanks of
Aden. Here the territories of the Abdali, the Aqrabi and the
Fadhli met. Here also all the trade routes to Aden converged.
Any one of the three tribes could thus effectively shut off trade
with Aden even if the other two remained neutral. Within very
easy raiding distance of Bir Ahmed, it was the center of the
Abdali-Aqrabi feud, and thus this intertribal feud was a matter
of extreme importance for the ruler of Aden.

The incidents leading up to the decision of the Bombay Government to occupy Aden have already been discussed. Commander Haines was ordered to go to Aden on the "Bernice" on
November 25, 1837, to demand redress for the piracy committed on the "Doria Dowlat" and the restoration of its cargo
or an indemnity equal to its value. At Aden, Haines was received by the Sultan Muhammad Hussain with whom he began
negotiations for a treaty allowing the British to occupy Aden and
use it as a coaling depot. The Sultan implied that he would a-
gree to such a treaty if the British would accept him as an ally,
i. e. , make an offensive and defensive alliance with him. Such
a demand was of course outside Haines' power to decide, and
he referred the Sultan to Bombay for an answer. However, a
tentative agreement was drawn up whereby, in payment for an

undetermined sum, the peninsula of Aden to Khor Maksar, a creek at the neck of the peninsula including all the cape and the islands of the bay and Sira Island, were to become the property of the East India Company. All Muslims were to be protected and the Sultan allowed free access to Aden (BSC 1838, Haines [Aden]-Bombay 1/20/38). Apparently these terms were satisfactory and, after considerable wrangling, the Sultan reduced his demand for a yearly stipend of 50,000 crowns to 8,700 crowns (crown = thaler or dollar). Haines, landing for a final signing of the treaty, was warned by his interpreter that there was a plot to kidnap him. Luckily the plot misfired and Haines sailed for Mocha (BSC 1838, Haines [Mocha Roads]-Bombay, 2/3/38).

The Governor of Bombay on receipt of this information felt that the attempted kidnapping of Haines was a matter of small consequence, important only as an indication that if Aden was to be at all useful to the British, it had to be completely in their hands. He requested that measures be taken to find out the strength of a force necessary to capture Aden (BSC 1838, Minute by Governor 3/26/38).

The Secret Committee in London, on being informed of these events, instructed the Bombay Government to occupy Aden without delay, using force if necessary (BSC 1838, Secret Committee-Bombay 5/30/38). Haines was ordered to return to Aden on the schooner "Coote" to resume negotiations, and to use all methods of persuasion to get the Sultan to cede Aden peacefully. He was given an escort of thirty European troops and instructed to exceed the agreed stipend of 8,700 crowns if it would ease negotiations (BSC 1838, Bombay-Indian Navy (9/5/38).

The Bombay Government reported these orders to the Governor General of India, explaining their action in ordering such a move by the statement "the Home Authorities attach much importance to the possession of Aden, and it has occurred to this Government that any delay in our endeavours to obtain possession may be productive of future difficulties" (BSC 1838, Bombay Government of India 9/5/38). To which Lord Auckland replied "his Lordship is glad to find that in the present crisis of our affairs the Governor in Council has resolved to resort to other than peaceful means for the attainment of the object in view" (BSC 1838, Government of India-Bombay 13/4/38).

To the natives of Aden, Haines' appearance in the unimpressive "Coote" was a sign of weakness, and they refused to surrender Aden. Haines requested that military and naval forces be dispatched, after the Sultan had ordered that there was to be no intercourse between the natives and the "Coote" (BSC 1838, Haines-Bombay 11/6/38). Haines was informed by the Bombay Government that a force of 650 infantry and 100 artillery was being sent to occupy the town with orders to do as little damage as possible in its occupation (BSC 1838, Bombay-Haines 12/2/38). Meanwhile the natives fired on the "Coote" whenever possible. The British retaliated by fitting a long gun on the ship's pinnace, which then blockaded Aden by preventing caravans from crossing the peninsula (BSC 1839, Haines-Bombay 12/12/38). After final negotiations proved fruitless, the town was occupied on January 16, 1839, by a combined naval and army force.

The morality of the occupation of the Aden has been attacked many times. It is interesting to note that, at the time, little was thought about this aspect of the occupation. The earliest violent attack on the occupation is in Blackwoods Magazine for April, 1843. After comparing the occupation of Aden with the Afghan affair, it attributes them both to "a system we have so long pursued — of taking the previous owner's consent for granted, whenever it suited our views to possess ourselves of a fortress, island or tract of territory belonging to any nation not sufficiently civilized to have representatives at the Congress of Vienna" (Anonymous, "The Occupation of Aden," Blackwoods Magazine, April, 1843, Vol. LIII, p. 485). The date of this article (1843) is interesting. As 1836-1837 ushered in an economic depression in England after the wild speculation of the middle thirties in stocks of the first railroad companies, so the denouement of the Afghan campaign in 1840 ushered in a reaction against the land-grabbing of the same period. The depression in Imperialism, however, lasted much longer than the business depression.

Regardless of the morality of this occupation, subsequent events show that the British provided the only secure spot in an area which was characterized by the breakdown and feebleness of all other governing bodies, and preserved what little trade there was left in a land whose economy the Europeans had so unwittingly begun to destroy three hundred years before.

Immediately upon the occupation of the Peninsula, Commander Haines assumed political control of the new British possession. He found himself faced with a two-fold problem:

first, to restore the town itself so that it could function as a
port; second, to make the settlement secure from its turbulent
neighbors.

The solution to the first aspect of the problem was largely
a question of patience and time. The Bombay Government had
instructed the Political Officer to use as much of the local government of the Abdali Sultan as was practicable and to retain
the existing laws and taxes excepting only such provisions as
might be considered inhumane to the British standards of the
time. As Muslim law is based on a high standard of morality
and was the basis of the law of Aden, the customs of the people
were little changed. The laws were applied with justice in civil
cases so seldom found in Muslim courts when no strong central
government acted as a check on arbitrary conduct. Therefore
there was no great problem in the establishment of an effective
local government which was easily understood by the inhabitants
of the town (BSC 1839, Minute by Governor 2/21/39).

Information on the other internal affairs of the Settlement
during its first five years is difficult to find. However a certain amount of information appears in the Bombay Secret Proceedings in the India Office.

In March, 1840, Haines reported that trade was increasing
steadily despite tribal difficulties around Aden (BSC 1840, Haines
-Bombay 2/2/40). It was apparent then that some definite plan
for rebuilding the town must be formulated as the only building
of any permanence there was the Mosque of Hydroose. Haines
proposed that all the land should be revalued and reallotted.
This problem was complicated by the undefined limits of
Haines' authority as well as by the constant friction between the
Political Officer and the military, especially in the bazaars
which the military had put under martial law without Haines'
consent. The population of Aden had already increased to
4,600, showing a gain of 1,715 persons since September, 1839
(BSC 1840, Haines-Bombay 3/31/40). The Government of
Bombay agreed with the Resident that provision should be made
for rebuilding the town, and advocated the payment of a ground
rent to the Aden government by real estate owners, a rent
which should be moderate "so as to encourage new settlers"
(BSC 1840, Minute by Board 4/15/40). It also agreed that the
government would give land for the building of any new mosques
provided the inhabitants of Aden would erect them. At the same
time, the powers of the civil and military authorities were

more adequately defined with the purpose of preventing either
authority from becoming predominant (BSC 1840, Minute by
Board 4/15/40, 134-3-4).

It is of no importance to go into the details of the lengthy
controversy which ensued over the construction of defenses at
Aden. On the landward side, where there was no controversy,
temporary fieldworks were replaced by permanent fortifications
as rapidly as possible. The coastal defenses, however, were
an entirely different problem. Soon after its occupation, Aden
had been protected by two small batteries and a gunboat, a perfectly satisfactory defense against an attack by any local tribe
or group of pirates. These batteries, however, were no defense against any European fleet and various plans were put forward to develop more adequate coastal defense. The question
soon became involved in the larger problem of coastal defenses
of the whole Bombay Presidency. There are many pages of
reports on this in the Secret Proceedings for the years 1840-
1844. The whole matter was dropped in 1844 because of disagreement among the authorities and lack of funds; Aden as
well as the rest of the Bombay Presidency remained for years
with a minimum of coastal defenses.

All during this period there was continual agitation from
the military at Aden for a troop of horse to be used primarily
for policing the Settlement, but which could also make short
forays into the hinterland if necessary. Their requests were
constantly refused by the Presidency since Indian horses were
unable to stand the climate and properly acclimated Arabian
horses were difficult to obtain.

The tyranny of Sharif Husain at Mocha (see Chapter VI)
considerably helped Aden, not only in driving the trade of Mocha
to Aden but also in providing immigrants, chiefly the better
class of Mocha merchants and craftsmen. In November, 1842,
Haines wrote, "I am happy to report that the populace of Aden
have commenced building permanent shops and houses" (BSC
1842, Haines-Bombay 11/2/42).

On the receipt of this letter the Board requested a report
on the population (BSC 1842, Minute by Board 11/19/42).
Haines complied with this request on December 29, 1842. It
is interesting to compare the figures with those of 1839. In
March, 1839, the population consisted of 276 Arab males, 341
Arab females, 257 Jewish males, 301 females, 26 Somali
males, 37 females, 4 Egyptians, and a floating population of

about 150 Somalis, a total of 1,297 (BSC 1839, Haines-Bombay
3/5/39). In December, 1842, the town had a population of
16,454 people exclusive of 3,484 troops and camp followers, a
grand total of 19,938 people of whom 857 were Europeans.
This figure cannot be taken as final as many Muslims would not
acknowledge the number of females in their houses and there
was an additional floating population of about 1,000 Somalis
(BSC 1843, Haines-Bombay 12/29/42). Shortly before this,
Haines, in explaining the importation of hay from the Hadramaut coast, gave the following census of the animal population
of Aden, compared with that of 1839:

	1839	1842
Horses	2	80
Camels	11	70
Donkeys	18	4,000-5,000
Cows	40	200-300

The increase in population placed a serious strain on the
water supply, at best none too good. It was collected in rain
water catch basins. This situation was to continue until the
acquisition of new water supplies in 1855. Luckily during the
first few years of the Settlement's growth, rain was fairly plentiful and no serious crisis arose.

One incident occurred shortly after the capture of Aden
which is of marked interest as showing the general policy of
the Bombay Government towards missionaries. In January,
1840, a certain Mr. Samuel arrived in Aden. He represented
himself to Haines as a missionary to the Jews and proposed
that Haines should issue a proclamation beseeching the Jews of
the Yemen (who were numerous) to come to Aden and work as
laborers for the Government on a promise of pay, food and
lodging to be paid by the Government while they were away from
home. As Samuel had no official introduction to the Resident
and Haines had no orders, and since the idea seemed impudent
anyway, Haines refused. Samuel thereupon asked the Resident's
assistance in forming a school to educate Jewish children, the
school to be financed by donations. Haines consulted the leaders of the local Jews and found them unanimously opposed to
the idea. Moreover the school would have been in violation of
a governmental order which forbade interference of any kind
with the religion of the people of Aden, so Haines rebuffed

Samuel again but wished that the Government of Bombay would substantiate his refusal (BSC 1840, Haines-Bombay 1/20/40). The Board approved Haines' conduct and advised him that he should not encourage the school nor s hould he obstruct it, "but if Capt. Haines should find it likely to create a commotion, he will use his discretion in suppressing it" (BSC 1840, Minute by Board 2/15/40).

In three years Aden grew from a mud village to a thriving town. The population figures given in this chapter are from the Bombay documents and do not agree with Colonel Jacob's figures of 25,000 given in KINGS OF ARABIA (Jacob, Harold F., London, Mills & Boon, 1923, p. 45), although he had obviously based his estimate on some official source. Haines' policies of encouragement of trade and protection of the merchant were directly responsible for this growth, and here we have an outstanding example of the way trade will seek a place of security. This growth was not to continue at the same rate, however, because of the limited water supply and because the Government of India gradually lost interest in Aden as a trading center. In the next few years, the Government's apathy became obvious as one after another of Haines' recommendations was vetoed.

However, as long as Aden itself continued as an island of security in a sea of governmental chaos, the town prospered in spite of all discouragement. The continuous turmoil existing around Aden and in the Yemen was almost unbelievable. While it destroyed what little was left of the prosperity of Arabia Felix, at the same time it enabled the British with very meagre resources to hold their position at Aden and establish a firm foundation for its future prosperity.

V. ADEN AND THE TRIBES 1839-1843

Much of the history of the British settlement of Aden re-
volves around its relationship with the neighboring tribes.
"Tribe" is a familiar enough term, yet its meaning as a governmental institution is not well known. Many of the problems
facing the British were a normal result of the conflict between
tribal habit and organization and a government operated on
western concepts. This fact was fully realized at Aden but not
always understood either in Bombay or London, or later in
Constantinople.

There are many indications of tribal influence in Middle
Eastern culture and much of the Middle East even today is under tribal local rule. This is especially true of the Arabian
peninsula where modern government, where it exists, is simply superimposed on traditional tribal self-government, the
central government arrogating to itself certain tribal functions
whether by consent or by threat of force.

To understand the basis of conflict between western ideas
of government and tribal rule it is necessary to have some
knowledge of the composition and organization of the tribe itself. Throughout the Middle East where tribal organization
persists it may influence all types of people, the city and town
dweller, the settled agriculturalist, the semi-nomad based on
a permanent agricultural area, and the nomad completely dependent on finding pasturage for his herd during interminable
wanderings.

The basic unit in tribal life is the family, first in its smaller size of immediate relatives (i.e., wife, children, grandpar-
ents), and then in its larger form of close consanguinity. Several families form clans (to borrow a Scotch expression) all of
whose members have more or less tenuous blood relationships
to each other. The tribe is formed of groups of clans, although
often these clans are grouped together into subtribes, a group
of which form the tribe. In spite of the pretences of consanguinity maintained by the great tribes of Arabia such as the Anizah,
the Awamir, etc., membership by clan within a tribe is largely
a matter of political convenience. Many tribes wax and wane in
size according to the ability and success of their leadership,
and clans attach and detach themselves according to convenience.

Such changes, however, are not lightly made, and the deterioration of a tribe may take several generations to be openly shown.

The tribe is not necessarily the highest form of tribal life. There exist in the Middle East several very important tribal confederacies. Those in Iran are of ancient origin and have shown a remarkable resilience to many attempts by medieval and modern governments to break them up. In Arabia the only outstanding tribal confederacy in the early nineteenth century was that of the Asiri. In addition the two Imamates of Southern Arabia, that of San'a (the present day Yemen) and that of Oman, though with the superficial appearance of organized governments, were and still are essentially tribal confederations. They show the tendency to return to tribal rivalries under weak leadership, a centrifugal tendency which is the basic weakness of tribal government.

In most of the Middle East lack of water and a rigorous climate make life marginal at best and subject to natural disasters. Too much rain at one time may be just as damaging as a prolonged period of drought; three days of the hot winds from the desert at the wrong time may destroy an apparently ample crop; and locusts are an ever present danger. This factor, as much as the concept of predestination which Muslim theologians have often read into the teachings of Muhammad, have led the Middle Easterner to adopt a completely fatalistic attitude towards the vicissitudes of life. At the same time this fatalistic attitude has served to make the Middle Easterner an extreme individualist and a sharp competitor for what necessities of life can be obtained from an unfavorable environment. The loyalties of the individual tribesman may best be summed up in an Iranian saying:

> Myself and my tribe against the government
> Myself and my brother against the tribe
> Myself against my brother.

In other words, corporative or cooperative action outside of the immediate family is totally alien to the individual tribesman unless such action clearly will benefit him personally.

If unrestrained, this individualism would lead to anarchy, and therefore out of necessity the individual has had to concede many of his personal rights to a larger group, the clan or the tribe, for his own self-protection. Out of these concessions has

grown in Arabia an elaborate code of tribal custom much of
which has little basis in the Muslim religion and some of which
runs counter to the teachings of Muhammad. It should be
pointed out that many of Muhammad's moral teachings were designed to counteract abuses and excesses in the tribal code of
his day.

In order to organize for self-protection, the family placed
the responsibility for its relationship with other families in the
hand of one individual, usually the father; the clan placed its
responsibility in the hands of the leader of one of its families,
and the tribe in the leader of one of its clans. In both the clan
and the tribe, this authority tended to become hereditary in one
family, descending from member to member picked for his
ability rather than for immediate consanguinity. Therefore,
leadership often passed not from father to son but to an uncle or
a nephew if such an individual showed the necessary capacity for
responsibility and leadership.

In establishing this delegation of authority to a leader, the
individuals delegate responsibility from themselves as individuals to the unit as a whole whether it be family, clan, or tribe.
It is this principle of collective responsibility which has led to
the greatest stumbling block in relations between tribal organization and governments operating under regular concepts of
government whether they be westerners such as the British in
Aden or governments operating under Muslim law such as the
Ottoman Empire, as both western and Muslim law hold the individual responsible for his actions and his property. Many of
the irritations between the British at Aden and the neighboring
tribes lay in this clash between the concepts of individual and
collective responsibility, and there are indications in the documents that Ottoman officials in the Red Sea area were often con-
fronted and baffled by the same conflict.

The tribal leader who might assume the title of Sheikh,
Sultan, or Amir, was the executive authority for the tribe and
handled all relationships of the tribe with other tribes or governments. He also was the final authority for settling intratribal disputes if such settlement was possible. For handling
the tribes' business, he usually received a small annual tribute
from the various members of the tribe. The tribal treasury,
particularly around Aden, was further augmented by the collection of transit dues on caravans which passed through tribal territory. Out of these funds the tribal leader maintained a small

staff. Usually a man learned in tribal custom acted as judge
in minor disputes and legal adviser in major ones which would
have to be decided finally by the tribal leader. While many of
these men had some training in Muslim law it would hardly be
proper to describe them by the classic legal title of Kadi although they fulfilled many of the functions of that office. As a
rule they were much better acquainted with the complexities of
tribal custom than with Muslim jurisprudence. Other employ-
ees of the tribal leader were a secretary to handle official letters (often also serving as legal adviser), and a treasurer to
handle the tribal and personal accounts of the tribal leader.
There is no indication that the tribal and personal accounts
were kept separately.

The position of treasurer always was a delicate one among
the Arabs. A treasurer had to be trusted or else subject to
some means of control. Often personal slaves were used for
treasurers and accountants. In the Aden area, however, Ye-
menese Jews filled these positions as they held a very inferior
place in the social structure of southwest Arabia, were outside
of the control of Muslim law and therefore subject to effective
personal control by the tribal leader. The British at Aden took
full advantage of this fact in setting up a very effective intelligence system within tribal councils (see p. 82).

A tribal leader was far from being an absolute ruler of his
tribe. He was usually advised by a tribal council composed of
relatives, of subtribe or clan leaders, and often of individuals
whose judgment was respected. These councils were informal,
their meetings were often protracted, and agreement was often
impossible. Even if agreement was reached, there was no assurance that a subtribe or clan would back such an agreement
if it ran counter to their own interests. This tendency to demur
was most marked when a tribal action was unsuccessful or resulted in a stalemate.

It was this lack of internal cohesion within the tribes and
conflicts of interests between the tribes which made it possible
for the British to establish some measure of stable relations
between the newly occupied port of Aden and the hinterland on
which it had to depend for trade and some of its essential supplies. To stabilize these relations was the second task of Commander Haines while reorganizing the internal government of
Aden itself. On February 5, 1839, Haines wrote to the Government (BSC 1839, Haines-Bombay 2/5/39) stating his views on

establishing relations with the tribes. He thought it would be prudent to pension the Sultan of Lahej, his son Ahmed, and also his son-in-law Mahsin West, who was a very influential contact with the Haushabi and Yafa tribes. He felt that the tribes would seek British protection in preference to Egyptian occupation, and, unaware of Muhammad Ali's agreement of September, 1838, suggested the establishment line running from Bab-el-Mandeb along the meridian (44 degrees east) to separate the Egyptian and British spheres of influence. Such a line would preserve San'a and the rich coffee-growing country for the British.

The question of pensions, or rather subsidies, was complicated, as before the occupation Sultan Mahsin of Lahej paid each tribe a portion of the customs dues of Aden, partly to encourage their use of the port and partly as a payment to secure the roads from attack. As one of the Sultan's main sources of income had been these customs dues, Haines felt it only fair to give him trade preferences. His suggestions were a subsidy of $3,000 a year to the Sultan, $1,200 to his son Ahmed, a similar amount to Mahsin West, and $2,000 to various other tribes to protect the roads, as well as certain pensions to individuals who had suffered unduly in the attack on the city.

By subsidizing these men, Haines hoped to establish a method of reward and punishment by which he could control their actions and prevent interference with the growth of agriculture and trade. The expense could be born by the customs duties as trade developed, Haines believed. And last, but not least, the threat of loss of the subsidy would keep the tribes in check until they realized that the safety of the roads was conducive to their own welfare (BSC 1839, Haines-Bombay 2/5/39).

The Bombay Government agreed in the main with Haines' ideas, but felt that the total of the subsidies should on no account be more than the total subsidy agreed on in the first treaty, and that it should be clearly understood that it was to be granted only during the good behavior of the tribes (BSC 1839, Minute by Governor 2/18/39). The whole matter was sent to the Governor General of India for his approval.

Relations with the various local tribes at first improved. Visits were paid by local chieftains, the roads were kept open, stolen kafilas (caravans) were returned to their owners, and wheat and jowaree (Indian millet) entered Aden in "apparent safety" (BSC 1839, Haines-Bombay 2/28/39). However, work on the field works and defenses of Aden continued to be pushed and Haines felt that a strong garrison would be needed for some time. Soon Aden received its first tests of the results of inter-tribal warfare. On March 7, 1839, the roads were almost closed, the kafilas arriving under a heavy guard, while Sultans Mahsin and Ahmed, and Mahsin West, pled inability to control the minor clans around them. Under these circumstances the Government advised Haines to warn the various chiefs that they would be held personally responsible for the actions of their tribesmen (BSC 1839, Bombay-Haines 3/22/39).

Haines immediately began to negotiate treaties with the various chiefs. These were merely treaties of peace, to in-sure both sides against molestation, as no authority had as yet been received from the Government of India to sanction the pay-ment of subsidies. These were arranged with the minor tribes first, the Aqrabi and some of the lesser clans of the Subahi. It soon became obvious that some action would have to be taken on the question of subsidies as the time was approaching when it was customary for the local chiefs to receive their annual subsidy from the customs duties of Aden. A refusal of this pay-ment would undoubtedly make trouble, a state to be carefully avoided until the outer defenses were in a condition to resist attack (BSC 1839, Haines-Bombay 3/7/39).

All action in Aden temporarily ceased, however, while Haines went to Bombay on leave, the last leave which he took until his removal from office in March, 1854. He had much to discuss with the Government. Aden was but a small town at the time of its capture; the first census, taken in February, showed a population of 1,297 in about 200 houses (BSC 1839, Haines-Bombay 3/5/39), a decline from a population of 30,000 at the end of the seventeenth century, estimated by Playfair on the evidence of the capacity of the water tanks discovered in 1855 (Playfair, R. L. , A MEMOIR ON THE ANCIENT RESER-VOIRS LATELY DISCOVERED. . . AT ADEN, Aden, Jail Press, 1857, p. 7). Questions of administration and of customs duties had to be discussed as Haines had been trying to get along with as small modifications of the former government as possible, and customs dues had been levied according to the pre-occupa-tion rates. Haines felt the need of a competent officer to handle the accounts, as accomplishment for which his training as a naval officer had not fitted him (BSC 1839, Haines-Bombay 4/10/39). He also wished to rebuild the town, destroying old

houses near the walls which would make excellent cover for
attacking tribesmen, and cleaning up the town itself which was
the usual mélange of buildings and shacks to be found in most
small Arab settlements (BSC 1839, Haines-Bombay 2/5/39).

Haines firmly believed that Aden could become the main
outlet for trade in the Yemen and could regain its former commercial greatness. To this end he worked continually during
his fifteen-year tenure of office. That he understood the problem thoroughly is shown, for example, by his recommendations
regarding the customs duties. In the first place, a reduction
in duties was necessary. The custom receipts which in April,
1839, had been $402, in May had been but $89 (exclusive of
transit dues). A reduction of duties would discourage smug-
gling. With the consent of the government, he proposed that
the average duty should be retained at five per cent ad valorem
but that the customary additional handling charge of four and
one-half per cent should be abolished. Secondly and more important, Aden should be made a free port, doing away with the
export duty of five per cent and all transit duties both to and
from the interior. Horses, sheep, bullocks, and asses were
to be free of duty. In connection with the customs regulations,
slavery was to be outlawed and all import and export of firearms and explosives forbidden without the express permission
of the Political Agent. A curious case arose in connection with
the customs duties. A certain holy man Sayud Zine ibn Alowi
Hydroose was a descendant and keeper of the tomb of a local
saint named Hydroose. The holy man had enjoyed the right to
receive gifts from passing mariners free of duty in return for
his blessings on their voyage. It was decided that such a tradition would be entirely too confusing to the customs administration, and shortly a pension was granted him in lieu of this
privilege (BSC 1839, Haines-Bombay 6/9/39). It was an excellent investment. Sayud ibn Hydroose, as he was commonly
called, remained a good friend of the British for twenty-five
years until Colonel Merewether discovered, in negotiating for
the purchase of Little Aden in 1864, that he had the not uncom-
mon habit of taking pay from both sides.

The Bombay Government approved of Haines' proposals,
but wanted a report on the duties levied at Mocha before giving
a decision. However, it refused to pay the expenses of a European official to superintend the customs house and keep the accounts, a decision that led to Haines' downfall in 1854 and his

subsequent disgrace (BSC 1839, Bombay-Haines 8/10/39).

Haines was confirmed as Political Agent in September, 1839. Governor Carnac recommended him as "the fittest person for the duties...for I deem it highly desirable that we should strengthen his authority by any means in our power" (BSC 1839, Minute by Carnac 9/9/39). Trade prospered through the summer and a census taken in September showed a population of 1,615 (excluding the garrison), a total which already was beginning to tax Aden's small water supply (BSC 1839, Haines-Bombay 9/13/39). The first coasting vessels from Shihr and Mukalla on the Hadramaut coast were beginning to arrive. But this peaceful growth was soon threatened by troubles with Aden's neighbors, the Arab tribes, troubles which took an acute form for the next two years and intermittently plagued successive Residents.

When Haines returned from Bombay in the beginning of June, 1839, he found tribal affairs comparatively quiet. This breathing spell was a godsend to the British as they had found the defenses of Aden in a state of collapse and the town open to attack on all sides. Contemporaries estimated the military strength of the tribes at about 100,000 fighting men. These estimates, however, seem way out of line with those given in the able description of the tribes in Hunter and Sealey's report in 1886 which estimates the total population of the tribes at a little over 200,000 people (op. cit.). It is possible that the larger estimate included the fighting men of other tribes of the interior. Even discounting these tribes, the total of the fighting men of the neighboring chieftains was enough to overwhelm a settlement which lacked adequate defenses and was garrisoned by only about 1,800 to 2,000 men. And the Arab tribesmen were fairly good fighters, armed with matchlocks. They, of course, had no artillery but they were excellent cameleers and able raiders. Haines found out during the next stormy years their greatest military weakness, their inability to keep a force together for more than a few days. The constant dissatisfaction with the bargains made between the tribes averted many a potential attack, as did intertribal jealousies. In relations with the British, tribal leaders showed two main interests, money and prestige.

The subsidy plan was a partial answer to the first interest. As Haines was consistently forbidden to use any but defensive tactics against the tribes, he was compelled to augment this first weapon by blockades of the small Arab ports where dates were imported, the standard food of Arabs during the hot season. Thus he hoped to show the tribesmen that their pocket-book was better served by peaceful pursuits, the raising of vegetables and grain for sale in the Aden market, than by raiding caravans and travellers for what booty they could gather.

As a weapon against the secondary interest, Haines could only use his own ingenuity and uncanny ability to outwit the chiefs. In this he was aided by a secret service system which was remarkably efficient and worthy of description. In 1845 after an amazingly accurate description of what was happening in San'a, Haines was asked by the Bombay Government how he obtained his information. He replied "through the Jews." They were the only accurate and reliable observers and were employed by Haines through two Jews resident in Aden, Menhakain and Shumadiel by name. These two men received letters in Hebrew, incomprehensible to the Arabs, from San'a, Qa'taba, Lahej, etc., from men who were employed by the local chiefs of those towns as accountants or cashiers. These men were interested in the welfare of Aden as their families lived there, and they were further spurred on by infrequent presents. The information which they provided was then checked against reports of merchants from these places, and in cases of emergency as many as four express messengers, unknown to each other, were sent out to check the information. By this secret service system Haines found that bazaar rumors and estimates were to be discounted by about fifty per cent (BSC 1845, Haines-Bombay 4/28/45). Thus Haines was able to keep as well or better informed than his Arab opponents and fight intrigue with intrigue, much to the discomfiture of the chiefs.

The period from the capture of Aden until the first attack by the tribes in November, 1839, was one in which the chiefs tried out the British to find out how much could be obtained from them, for Haines had returned from Bombay with authority to negotiate subsidies to a total of $8,000 a year.

On June 6 Haines had his first interview with Sultan Mahsin of Lahej. It took him three days to convince the Abdali chief that the granting of stipends was a generous act on the part of the British and that such a grant in fact made the Sultan answerable for the safety of the roads. His arguments had little influence, for in mid-August a report came to Haines' notice that the Fadhli Sultan and Sheikh Maidi of the Aqrabi were discussing a night attack on Aden, or at least an effort to block off trade. The Fadhli Sultan was ostensibly annoyed at the loss of trade at his port of Shuqra, but Haines very properly considered that Sultan Mahsin of Lahej was at the bottom of the trouble. The Resident advised the Government that he was ready to resist, and suggested stoppage of stipends and blockades of the ports, especially Shuqra, if trouble should begin (BSC 1839, Haines-Bombay 8/23/39). The Government approved, but warned Haines to take only defensive measures. These would not prevent him from discontinuing the stipends and blockading ports (BSC 1839, Minute by Board 9/9/39).

When Haines had met the Sultan of Lahej in June, 1839, he had exacted a bond of good behavior from him and a guarantee that a guard of twenty men be kept at Sheikh 'Othman (a few miles outside the walls) to prevent disturbances on the caravan route. In August a murder was committed there which caused Haines to admonish the old Sultan and threaten him with a loss of stipend if any more breaches of the peace occurred (BSC 1839, Haines-Bombay 9/13/39). This resulted in a withdrawal of the guard in October, ostensibly due to a quarrel between the old Sultan and his son. However, Haines discovered that at the same time Sultan Mahsin was beginning to use his not inconsiderable wealth to organize a coalition against Aden. Haines sent Mahsin West and Qatif (steward to the Sultan of Lahej, and British Agent there) inland to prevent the Haushabi, Yafa, A-miri, Alawi and Raftan tribes (all living in the foothills of the High Yemen north of Lahej) from joining the Abdali. (What the "Raftan" tribe refers to is not clear.) This they succeeded in doing. He also worked to obtain documentary proof to enable him to stop Sultan Mahsin's subsidy.

As a result of this incident, he suggested to the Government that a troop of irregular horse would be a useful addition to the garrison, a request often made by future residents. With them he could capture Sultan Mahsin's family and hold them as hostages for his good behavior (BSC 1839, Haines-Bombay 10/20/39).

The Governor approved Haines' measures, but felt that a troop of irregular horse would only complicate matters in the interior. Haines was informed that he should refer to Bombay for instructions "except in a case of great emergency when... he should be left to act on his own responsibility" (BSC 1839, Minute by Board 11/19/39).

The Abdali Sultan continued his plans and a date was fixed
for the attack. The wily Mahsin abdicated, turning the Sultanate over to his son Ahmed, thus clearing himself from any possible violation of his bond. November 3, 1839, was the date
agreed upon and the roads were closed from the first to the
third. But when the Arabs discovered that the garrison was on
the alert, the attack was delayed in hopes that the British would
relax their vigilance. The tribes had planned to drive camels
and bullocks before the main body so that they would receive
the "first and as they [the Arabs] suppose the only destructive
fire." The inhabitants of Aden, convinced that the attack would
be successful, buried their valuables or left town altogether.
Early in the morning of the eleventh the attack commenced.
Five thousand Arabs stormed the outposts and succeeded in
forcing the walls in one spot. Here they were caught between
two fires, and at seven in the morning were compelled to retire
leaving fifty dead. The British troops behaved excellently and
the defensive plans worked to perfection. Thus Aden weathered
its first attack (BSC 1839, Haines-Bombay 11/12/39).

Three days after the attack, supplies began to re-enter
Aden. Sultan Mahsin of the Abdali protested his innocence in
the matter, simultaneously deputing Sultan Ahmed, his son, to
persuade the 'Aulaqi and Yafas to join the coalition against A-
den, and thus increase the Arab forces to twenty- or twenty-
five thousand men. These tribes however declined to break
faith with the British. Haines countered this move by trying to
induce the various coast chieftains to send their ships to Aden
instead of to Shuqra on the Fadhli coast. Also he investigated
other sources of supply for cattle, grass, and firewood so as
to make Aden independent of the interior. The question of
banning the hostile tribesmen from Aden was considered, but
the advantages of their trade so outweighed the disadvantages of
their gaining information about the defenses of the settlement
that the idea was dropped.

No open attack was projected by the tribes until after the
month of Ramadan was over (December 9, 1839), but a plan
constantly to annoy the British and terrorize the roads was instituted. To this end the Arabs began erection of a tower at
Bir Ahmed, a junction of the caravan routes outside the settlement, from which raiding parties could blockade Aden at will.

Haines' reaction to this Arab plotting was a desire to execute a short quick march into the interior, capture Lahej, and

remove Sultan Mahsin from power. The expenses, Haines believed, could be paid by a fine on the Sultan for his breach of
contract, for he had considerable wealth, and peace could be
made conditional on the surrender of two hostages for the good
behavior of the Abdalis, and the establishment of a native agent
in Lahej to further commercial interests and advise the Arab
government there. Haines was afraid that unless some action
was taken there would be danger of disturbances against the
British throughout southern Arabia, as the natives, "who do
not appear to be entirely satisfied with my determined silence,
attribute it to an incomprehensible want of courage or rather
as they term it 'cold-heatedness'; so contrary to their own max-
im of revenging every insult among themselves" (BSC 1840,
Haines-Bombay 12/11/39 and Haines-Bombay 12/15/39).

On December 17, 1839, Haines sent the "Euphrates" to
Shuqra with instructions to allow no vessel to leave or enter
that port. Immediately following this blockade the roads were
opened and kafilas allowed to enter Aden (BSC 1840, Haines-
Bombay 12/30/39).

The Government of Bombay then asked for further information as to the strength required for an expedition inland (BSC
1840, Minute by Board 1/13/40), and Haines told them in a letter of February 1, 1840. As there was no prospect of an apology from either the Fadhli or Abdali Sultans, nor any offer of
security for the future, Haines felt that Aden could never flourish as a trading post until the tribes had been compelled "to
respect our strength and courage." Trade had been completely
stopped except for supplies, and the coffee kafilas from the
mountains had been turned back. The Resident believed that
the march inland would be necessary in order to impress the
chiefs. Two or three troops of cavalry and six or eight pieces
of mountain artillery were essential, as well as three thousand
infantry for the expedition and an additional five or six hundred
to garrison Aden. With such a force Lahej could be captured
easily and Sultan Mahsin brought to terms (BSC 1840, Haines-
Bombay 2/1/40).

This dispatch upset the Bombay Government considerably.
Aside from the question of expense, the troops in India were
more than occupied in the disastrous Afghan campaign. Haines
was warned not to expect any sanction for such an expedition.
He was ordered to confine himself to the occupation of Aden and
not to undertake any offensive operations without permission.

These instructions concluded, "If Aden cannot be made a valuable acquisition without entering into aggressive warfare with
the Arab chiefs in the interior, the sooner it is abandoned or
surrendered for a consideration the better. Commander Haines
has ample means to defend himself" (BSC 1840, Minute by
Board 2/15/40).

Meanwhile changes took place in the Abdali tribe. Sultan
Mahsin, after a long conference with the other sheikhs, abdicated in fact to his son Ahmed. The feelings of the tribesmen
were divided; the poorer members and the agriculturists desired friendship with the British, while the few wealthy and influential members claimed that the only courage of the English
was their walls. For a short while the tribe showed a conciliatory spirit, but on February 1, 1840, information reached A-
den that emissaries from Ibrahim Pasha had arrived in the Yemen, whereupon the entire attitude of the tribe changed suddenly. The British Agent at Mocha, Abdul Russool, reported that
Sultan Mahsin's emissaries had been at that port to ask for
guns and men, and Ibrahim Pasha had given them encouragement (BSC 1840, Haines-Bombay 2/1/40).

The temporary peace of the district was broken shortly
after the first of February. The Fadhli Sultan again closed the
roads and was reported to be endeavoring to stir up a religious
war. Furthermore, a report was current in the interior that
England was at war with Egypt, a rumor originating undoubtedly from increased tension in the Near East, the stiffening of
Palmerston's policy towards Muhammad Ali, and the antagonistic attitude of Colonel Hodges, the new English Consul General, toward the Pasha. Nature, too, encouraged the tribes,
for with the ending of the monsoon they considered it impossible
for the garrison to receive re-enforcements (BSC 1840, Haines
-Bombay 3/2/40). [Note: Arab vessels depended entirely on
the monsoon winds for travelling between India and Aden. The
tribesmen could not comprehend the ability of British sailing
vessels to sail close-hauled into the wind nor could they understand the ability of the steamship to disregard the wind entirely.]

As a result of these factors, Haines wrote the Secret Committee in London complaining of the difficulty of dealing with
the Arabs who had such an exaggerated idea of the power of
Muhammad Ali. As long as this concept remained there could
be no chance for a real peace as they continually expected his
intervention. There was also a prevalent belief that the

Christian powers had no influence with the Muslim states. Haines added "Since 1835, I have been fully aware that Muhammad Ali looked forward to the conquest of Aden as a certain and desirable event, for in reply to my official report that the British had been successful on this point [Haines refers to his letter to Muhammad Ali reporting the conquest of Aden] he wrote, 'I have been striving for years for the possession of the Yemen but you, in one day, have taken its eye, and rendered it useless to me!'" Haines also feared that a blockade of Alexandria would lead to the sending of the whole Egyptian force in the Yemen against Aden, or at least the use of the Viceroy's troops to re-enforce the tribes (BSC 1840, Haines-Secret Committee 2/7/40). Haines failed to consider one other point which led the tribes to believe in the weakness of the English. There were close connections between the tribes of the south coast of Arabia and India, not only through Arab merchants at Indian ports, but also through the Arabs who were members of the bodyguards of the Indian princes, especially of the Nizam of Hyderabad who drew most of his picked guards from the Hadramaut. The Muslim world was more closely knit than is commonly realized, and news in an exaggerated form spread quickly through the bazaars, sometimes as quickly as through the official news sources. Unquestionably British prestige was considerably lowered throughout the east by the disastrous Afghan expedition.

The rapidity of this spread of news through native sources was well-illustrated in March, 1840. Rumors of a battle and massacre at Shuqra reached Bombay before the dispatch from Aden which explained the incident. The "Elphinstone" had been sent to Shuqra, with the stopping of the monsoon, to renew the blockade and cause the Fadhli Sultan to withdraw his forces from the suburbs of Aden. A slight skirmish took place when the "Elphinstone" was forced to fire a broadside at Shuqra (which consisted of a fort and a customs house) in reply to musket fire from the shore. Two Arabs were killed. By the time the bazaar rumors reached Bombay, eighty were reported killed and many wounded. The Government was much relieved by the official version of this affair which had compelled the Fadhli Sultan to retire from the walls of Aden and open the roads (BSC 1840, Haines-Bombay 3/25/40 and Minute by Board 4/11/40).

The use of force having failed, the chiefs now turned to

another method of intimidating the British. Two plots to murder Haines were planned. The first was very simple. Haines
was to be requested to come outside the walls to conclude a
final treaty of peace, and he was to be murdered during the
conference. This plan was foiled by Haines' demand for a full
apology before the treaty could be signed. The Fadhli Sultan's
plan was similar except that the conference was to be held in
Aden. The Arabs believed Aden would be an easy prize with
Haines out of the way. (This is a most interesting commentary
on tribal psychology. Realizing their own inability to remain
unified except through the personal respect for and domination
by some s trong and successful leader, they applied the same
principle to the British. They thought that by removing Haines
from the scene, British unity would dissolve and Aden could
be reconquered with ease. It should be noted that in the Muslim world assassination had been regarded for centuries as a
legitimate political weapon.) At the same time both the Abdali
and the Fadhli Sultans were intriguing with other tribes for a
grand concerted attack on the settlement. Haines remarked
that the Arabs were so busy intriguing that trade was flourishing and no attempt was being made to hinder the caravans (BSC
1840, Haines-Bombay 3/31/40).

The Egyptian evacuation of the Yemen was ordered in late
February, 1840, and relieved Aden of danger from that quarter,
but the tribes were not discouraged. An attack was planned for
May and the British spy system was alerted so that Aden would
receive ample warning (BSC 1840, Haines-Bombay 4/28/40).

The attack took place early in the morning of May 21. Two
thousand Fadhli, supported by two or three thousand Abdali
tribesmen, attacked at the harbor end of the old Turkish wall.
The engagement lasted for nearly two hours during which time
the Bedwin captured a certain amount of loot, evidence to them
that they had achieved a victory. After the attack, the Abdalis
tried to murder Haines' two agents in Lahej, Hassan Abdallah
Kateef and Mahsin West, but fortunately both escaped. A few
days later, however, Kateef was shot and killed outside a
mosque in Lahej while under the promise of safe conduct. This
outrage, in addition to the two attacks on the settlement, Haines
felt, was an insult demanding direct action against Sultan Mahsin. The Government of Bombay was sympathetic but felt that
it would be unwise to take action without an overwhelming force
which at the moment would be "very difficult and costly to

provide" (BSC 1840, Haines-Bombay 6/2/40 and Minute by Board 6/24/40).

A second attack was projected for June, but heavy rains compelled the tribes to postpone it in order to save their crops. However, a small party raided the outposts on June 20 leaving two dead. The real attack came on July 7 early in the morning. The Arabs were decisively defeated with no English casualties (BSC 1840, Haines-Bombay 7/9/40).

The tribes, undaunted by this last failure, again began maneuvering for a coalition against Aden. On August 4 the Fadhli and Abdali launched an assault against Bir Ahmed, the small fortified town near the walls owned by the Aqrabi tribe who had been faithful to the English, and they were repulsed. Haines was informed that the Fadhli Sultan had given up the idea of capturing Aden, but planned to drive the British out by wearing them down with continual annoyances on the roads, and minor forays against the outworks, by bodies of about 500 men. These plans were upset by a sudden coalition of the Haushabi, Alawi, Amiri and Raftan tribes against the Fadhli and Abdali over an intertribal dispute. The cause of this trouble was the diversion of a mountain stream near Zaylah, a hamlet on the border of the Abdali territory (BSC 1840, Haines-Bombay 8/13/40). While of no importance at the moment except that it relieved the pressure on the settlement, this dispute continued to be a source of intertribal friction, at times violence, until thirty-three years later it became the focal point for Turkish penetration in that area, and is still today (1958) a point of argument between the British and the Yemen.

In India, meanwhile, a discussion was going on between the Indian Government and that of Bombay regarding the advisability of an expedition against the tribes. When news of the attack of May 21, 1840, reached the Governor General, he wrote to Bombay strongly pressing for the necessity of an expedition against Lahej and suggesting that it take place in December when the relief was sent for the garrison (BSC 1840, Govt. of India-Bombay 7/6/40). The Bombay Government, its resources of men and money strained to the utmost by the Afghan campaign and other troubles in India, felt that it was impossible to equip an adequate force, as suggested by Haines, and discouraged the idea (BSC 1840, Bombay-Govt. of India 10/19/40). The lapse of time in making this decision showed the difficulties with which the successive Residents at Aden were faced. By

the time the consent of the Indian Government for an expedition
had reached Bombay, the attack of July 7 had taken place and
been successfully beaten off, and the immediate necessity for
an expedition had disappeared.

After the attack of July 7, 1840, Aden was peaceful. Although intrigue continued, the roads were open to trade in provisions from the immediate neighborhood and to a certain a-
mount of coffee trade, although this was hindered by duties
levied by the Sultan of Lahej and by the uncertainty of his actions. In November came disquieting news. A certain fanatic
Sheikh Fuki Said had conquered Ta'iz, several days' journey
from Aden, and was attempting to rouse the country against the
British (BSC 1840, Haines-Bombay 11/9/40).

By the end of November the new enemy's influence began
to be felt. Although on the surface all remained quiet, the
Sheikh had advanced to the small town of Denwah. He assumed
the titles of Mahdi al-Montither and Sultan and attracted the
superstitious devotion of the local chieftains. While stirring
up religious enthusiasm to drive the infidels from the Yemen,
he kept his followers together by allowing them to plunder a
few small hill forts. Besides appealing to the tribes' religious
fanaticism, he attracted them by a promise of freedom from
taxation, and by convincing them that all true believers under
his care were invulnerable to sword or bullet. The Sheikh
wrote to the Sharif at Mocha and demanded that Mocha, Hodeida,
and Zabid be turned over to him as "regenerator of the faith."
The Sharif seized this opportunity to turn him against Aden by
replying that he could not very well refuse this demand, but
suggesting that the Sheikh first regenerate the faith by driving
the infidels from Aden. By the first of December, the fanatic
had assembled an army of 12,000 men but was restrained from
approaching the settlement by the appearance of the Imam of
San'a with an army of 20,000. The Arabs believed that the I-
mam was coming to join the forces of the fanatical Sheikh, but
Haines was very doubtful of this as the Sheikh was of the Shafai
(Orthodox Sunni) sect, a usurper and a rebel, while the Imam
was a Zaidi (moderate Shi'ite) and legal ruler of the country
(BSC 1840, Haines-Bombay 11/28/40 and 12/4/40).

On December 16 Sheikh Fuki sent some Yemeni tribesmen
who had joined him to assault the Imam's troops near Yerim.
On approaching the camp of the Imam this force, in true tribal
fashion, declared themselves his subjects and promptly joined

with him in a night attack on the Sheikh. This attack was successful and was followed by two other engagements. The Sheikh
was finally defeated in a terrible slaughter at Denwah (presumably near Yerim) on December 25, 1840. Thus another enemy
was removed from the vicinity of Aden, and a serious setback
was administered to the plans of Sultan Mahsin, who had
counted heavily on Sheikh Fuki's aid against the settlement
(BSC 1841, Haines-Bombay 12/29/40).

The harvest season followed shortly after this defeat, and
the country settled into quiet. Overtures of peace were made
in March, 1841, by Sultan Mahsin through Mahsin West. Haines
demanded that the Sultan come to meet him at Aden prepared to
leave two hostages as a guarantee of good conduct. At the same
time several outrages occurred on the roads by the orders of
Sultan Mahsin. But by now the immense profit which the tribesmen gained by their trade with Aden made many of them resentful of the tyranny of their Sultan (BSC 1841, Haines-Bombay 3/4/41 and Haines-Secret Committee 2/10/41). As evidence of this state of affairs, when Sultan Mahsin ordered the
roads closed and all trade directed to Bir Ahmed the roads remained open and trade flourished in Aden (BSC 1841, Haines-
Bombay 4/1/41). The Sultan then tried to achieve his ends by
levying extremely heavy transit duties on goods going to Aden,
at the same time imprisoning the Jews at Lahej, forty-one in
all, until they paid an amount equal to his annual stipend from
Aden. But a violent quarrel between the Fadhli and Abdali
chiefs prevented any more drastic measures being taken by Sultan Mahsin, and the country remained relatively calm (BSC
1841, Haines-Bombay 4/30/41).

Sultan Mahsin, unable to settle his quarrel with the Fadhli,
entered a treaty of friendship with Sheikh Hyder ibn Maidi of
the Aqrabi whereby trade was to go to Bir Ahmed across the
bay from Aden and thence in small boats to Mukalla and Shihr.
This strategem was successful in diverting trade from Aden,
although supplies continued to be plentiful. On May 28, 1841,
Haines asked the permission of the Government to blockade
Bir Ahmed and stop this diversion (BSC 1841, Haines-Bombay
5/28/41). The Government of India felt that a blockade, accompanied or preceded by strong representations, might be justifi-
able "in order to counteract the hostile contrivances of the Chief
of Lahej, " and offered no objection to its adoption, as it appeared to be the only possible way of averting damage to Aden's

trade. His Lordship in Council feared that an attack on Lahej itself might be only a temporary measure as the Sultan might force a permanent occupation of the territory after the retirement of the expedition "and be in that manner the source of much embarrassment." Haines was advised to await the effect of the blockade and at the same time cultivate the friendship of the other tribes in favor of the British against the Chief of Lahej (BSC 1841, Govt. of India-Bombay 7/19/41).

Sultan Mahsin continued his attempts to form a coalition against the British, but succeeded only in stirring up intertribal strife (BSC 1841, Haines-Bombay 6/29/41 and 7/28/41). As September approached conditions in the interior became chaotic. Haines' policy of the encouragement of trade, with its resulting increase in the prosperity of the Arab agriculturist, began to bear fruit in continual rebellion, and agitation against the blockade and consequent closing of a rich market. A large kafila finally came through under heavy guard on September 5. This so exasperated the Abdali Sultan that he decided to attack. Six days later a suspiciously large Abdali kafila appeared at Aden. It was only with the greatest difficulty that Haines and the military were able to get them outside the walls by nightfall, and firing began immediately on the outworks (BSC 1841, Haines-Bombay 9/9/41 and 9/11/41).

The Abdali Sultan was discouraged by the failure of this plot and the Fadhli Sultan was diverted from further intrigues by the sending of the "Euphrates" to blockade his port of Shuqra. The roads remained closed for a time, but pressure on Aden was removed by the change in the monsoon, which opened trade with Mukalla and Shihr on the Hadramaut coast, and which signalled the beginning of the annual fair at Berbera on the Somali coast (BSC 1841, Haines-Bombay 10/2/41).

However, the situation had been so acute that Haines ordered a military demonstration outside the walls. A small force (500 men) marched to Sheikh 'Othman on October 5, 1841, destroyed a small mud fort there, and quickly returned to the settlement without casualties (Anonymous, "Officer in the Queen's Army," HISTORICAL & STATISTICAL SKETCHES OF ADEN, Madras, Twigg, 1848, p. 63). As a further demonstration, the "Elphinstone" was ordered not only to blockade Shuqra but also to destroy the fishing boats of the Fadhli there, since Haines was aware that the Fadhli Sultan had ordered "that his boats were now and then to appear at night off Aden Front Bay and secure any small fishing and trading boats which they could" (BSC 1841, Haines-Bombay 11/18/41).

By the end of November, 1841, rumors that the tribes desired peace began to reach Aden. This development was largely due to the pressure of the blockades at Shuqra and Bir Ahmed, which had cut off the absolutely necessary date trade. Dates were the standard food with which the tribes eked out their existence after the harvests were used up. The Bombay Government was relieved that economic measures had been effective, and advised the political agent "to persevere in his efforts to come to an amicable settlement [with the tribes], ... provided he is satisfied of their sincerity and that there is a likelihood of their fulfilling any engagement which they may enter into" (BSC 1841, Haines-Bombay 11/28/41 and Minute by the Board 12/10/41).

The Abdali and Fadhli Sultans both attempted to feel out the attitude of the British on making peace. They arranged to meet Haines in Aden together, but the Abdali Sultan doublecrossed his ally by appearing four days before the specified date, on December 2, 1841. Haines presented him with peace terms. First, the Sultan of Lahej should publicly ask pardon for his insulting actions against the British. Second, he should leave two of his children in Aden as hostages for future good behavior. Third, he should restore all money, household, and landed property seized from the family of Kateef, the late British representative at Lahej. Fourth, he should restore all property plundered in the attacks on Aden. The Sultan of Lahej tried to get Haines to relax the second point without success. The discussions lasted until December 13 when the Abdali left Aden. In the meantime, the Fadhli Sultan had approached but had been frightened away by the report that Sultan Mahsin had been made a prisoner. The only result of the conference was the discovery that Mahsin West, whom Haines had been using as an agent with the Haushabi and other more distant tribes, had been hand in glove with the Lahej Sultan, and had connived at Kateef's murder so as to increase his own influence with Haines and with Sultan Mahsin. He was summarily dismissed from the government service. The discussions revealed to Haines the obstacles to be faced in relations with local chieftains who were so practiced in dissimulation and lacking in the idea of "Honour" that the only way to deal with them was to punish them for their misdemeanors and try to demonstrate that

their comfort and wealth would be increased by tranquillity.
"Fear alone will control them for a while. . . . Such a measure
alone [referring to a punitive expedition], is required to make
this settlement answer more than the expectations of the government, and produce a fourfold return" (BSC 1842, Haines-
Secret Committee 12/10/41 enclosed in Haines-Bombay 1/4/42).

The Abdali Sultan, thwarted in his peace efforts, sought to
organize still another attack on Aden. But the Fadhli tribe was
impatient for peace. They were a tribe of little wealth and few
resources, and the blockade at Shuqra had cut off fishing and
the date trade, two of the main sources of their food supply.
The Fadhli Sultan bluntly refused to cooperate in spite of efforts
by Sultan Mahsin to hire his fighting men. Attempts to tamper
with the Haushabi chief also failed, thanks to the profit he
gained from his trade with Aden, and the threat of his more
powerful neighbor, the Imam of San'a, to hold him responsible
for any interference with the coffee kafilas from the mountains
(BSC 1842, Haines-Bombay 1/31/32 and 3/4/42).

In view of Sultan Mahsin's failure to arrange another coalition, Haines requested in February, 1842, that he be empowered to restore stipends to all the chiefs who had broken their
bond, except the Sultan of Lahej, and thus display evidence of
good faith on the part of the British. This the Government of
Bombay agreed to, but recommended that the arrears of stipend not be paid (BSC 1842, Haines-Bombay 2/7/42 and Minute
by the Board N. D.). Negotiations continued with the Fadhli
Sultan, and the country enjoyed peace and quiet for some time
while Sultan Mahsin of Lahej was engrossed in getting three of
his sons married.

The Sultan, however, still continued half-heartedly his intrigues against the English. Not strong enough to attack Aden
alone, his plans necessitated a coalition with some other tribe.
Fortunately for the peace of Aden, he could find no allies. But
he caused considerable annoyance by enforcing an exorbitant
tax on supplies entering the settlement. Haines explained well
the Sultan's insolent behavior in a letter to Bombay of May 31:

> Thus it is evident their [the Arab chieftains'] ignorant
> minds cannot comprehend the powers of British India
> though so close to Arabia, and nothing but ocular demon-
> stration (in the trifling way requisite) will convince them
> that it is the lenity and consideration of a strong power

for their ignorance, not weakness, that has prevented
a well merited chastisement being inflicted. (BSC 1842,
Haines-Bombay 5/31/42.)

British prestige was raised at the end of 1842 by reports
of victories in China and Afghanistan, which, in the exaggerated
form of bazaar rumors, had a very beneficial effect (BSC 1842,
Haines-Secret Committee 11/11/42). By January, 1843, the
Lahej Sultan appeared ready to listen to reason, which gratified
the Bombay Government who "hoped that the result will be
honorable and lasting peace" (BSC 1843, Haines-Bombay 2/3/
43 and Minute by Board 2/15/43). On January 29 the old Sultan
finally arrived at Aden and conversations began. On February
28, Haines was able to report that peace had been concluded
with Sultan Mahsin, subject to ratification by the Indian Government. Several questions had been left open, especially that of
the stipend. The old chief had to return to Lahej on a litter,
exhausted by the pomp of the negotiations (BSC 1843, Haines-
Bombay 2/28/43). Tranquillity reigned at Aden and by July the
Bombay Government believed that the garrison at Aden could
be safely reduced (BSC 1843, Minute by Board 7/12/43). During the same month Lieutenant Cruttenden was sent to Lahej at
the request of the Sultan for the first British visit to the interi-
or (BSC 1843, Haines-Bombay 7/29).
        The question of the stipend was finally settled. In early
February, 1844, Sultan Mahsin swore an oath to observe the
treaty, and his stipend was paid (BSC 1844, Haines-Bombay
3/3/44). Thus ended the first phase of the establishment of A-
den as a British settlement.
        Hampered by a lack of authority to take offensive measures,
Haines successfully weathered the storm of tribal attacks by
using purely defensive weapons, the most important of which
was intrigue, basing it on the principle of "divide and rule."
His handling of the various tribes was masterful, and thanks to
his shrewdness in taking advantage of intertribal dissension it
was very effective. Space forbids a more detailed mention of
tribal diplomacy, or rather duplicity, which Haines so fully expounded in his monthly reports. Unquestionably the tribes, by
acting quickly after the capture of Aden in 1839, could easily
have driven the British out of the Yemen, but their delay allowed
temporary field works to be established, and every passing day
strengthened the British settlement. In the later attacks, more

cohesion and unity of purpose amongst all the tribes might well
have brought success, but the tribal temperament precluded
any unified action for more than about forty-eight hours. Haines'
dispatches are filled with descriptions of tribal alliances which
lasted for a day or two only to dissolve, often in bloodshed, after a long conference.

It has been obvious that little aid was received from the
Bombay Government. Except shortly after the first attack, re-
enforcements were not sent nor was the garrison strengthened.
This is not strange, as the resources of the Indian and Bombay
Governments were considerably strained by the disastrous Af-
ghan campaign, troubles in the Sind, and various difficulties
throughout India. Even in the matter of ships Aden was limited.
As will be seen, this period from 1839 to 1842 was one of naval
activity and rivalry with the French, at the mouth of the Red
Sea. Yet there were always too few ships stationed at Aden.
In spite of this, Haines was able to influence the tribes proba-
bly as much by blockading the two small ports of Shuqra and
Bir Ahmed as by any other means.

One other factor must be considered in judging Haines' success. That is the question of armaments. The Arabs were
armed with matchlock muskets, the British with flintlocks. However, the margin of difference between Arab armaments and
those of the British soldiers was nowhere near as great as it
was to be in 1858, when Coghlan with a small force could, with
safety, march to Sheikh 'Othman, or in 1865, when Merewether
could march all over the countryside and defeat the Arab lines
with no loss and little difficulty.

While Haines was dealing successfully with the local tribes,
there were other interests at work in the Yemen and Red Sea
which threatened to make the British position at Aden untenable.

VI. RELATIONS BETWEEN ADEN AND THE YEMEN 1839-1843

Immediately after the capture of Aden, the British were too busy consolidating their position at the settlement to be much involved with affairs outside the immediate vicinity. The Egyptian forces, although as close to Aden as Ta'iz about sixty miles away, were locked in a struggle with the tribes and with Sheikh Sherzebee of the Hajariya district, lying across the Mocha-Ta'iz road, who had applied to Haines for a treaty of friendship and commerce. If successful with the Hajariya, the Egyptians still would be faced by inland tribes as well as by the Imam of San'a before they could completely control the Yemen. However, Haines was apprehensive lest a decisive victory over any of these enemies leave the way open for Ibrahim to use bribery and thus gain the whole coffee country for Muhammad Ali (FO 78/373, Campbell-FO 2/28/30 enclosing Haines -Campbell 2/28/39. BSC 1839, Haines-Bombay 2/25/39).

The agreement as to a division between Egyptian and British spheres of influence suggested by Muhammad Ali in March, 1838, yet not yet been communicated to Haines, who nevertheless appeared to be the one English official having any real knowledge of the hinterland around Aden. Haines therefore suggested, on February 5, 1839, that the boundary be drawn along the forty-fourth meridian from Bab-el-Mandeb, thus giving the Egyptians the coast and placing the coffee country in the British sphere of influence (BSC 1839, Haines-Bombay 2/5/39).

A little later he was informed of the agreement with the Pasha, and wrote in protest to the Bombay Government that such a boundary, i.e., the mountain chain, not only deprived Aden of all hope of trade but gave the Egyptians full control of the coffee country (BSC 1839, Haines-Bombay 3/7/39). This information was a distinct shock to the Governor General of India, as the only mountain range which he could find on his map was one running north and south about fifty miles from the west coast. Using this range as a boundary he had figured that the coffee country would be outside the Egyptian sphere. No range of mountains running east and west was shown in the government maps. The Governor General wrote to Bombay, "That officer [Haines] should be called on for an explanation, as to the mountains he alludes to, and the divisions of the country which

lie northwards from it. For there is probably some omission
or inaccuracy in the map which is the only means the Governor
General possesses of understanding the question. " He added
that it was most necessary that this point be cleared up as the
British could not interfere beyond the agreed boundary (BSC
1839, Government of India-Bombay 4/25/39). Haines' reply
painted a rather gloomy description of the results of Muhammad Ali's boundary. The Tehama (lowlands), he remarked,
was a sandy plain producing a sparse crop of grain and vegetables, while the wealth of the Yemen lay in the rich mountain
valleys which the Egyptians had connected by roads to Mocha
and Hodeida thereby gaining a monopoly of the coffee trade.
Haines felt that neither the Egyptians nor the British had any
right to interfere in the tribal affairs of the mountains, though
the Egyptians continually did so. However, they had been compelled to withdraw to a certain extent in late May, 1839. Under
the circumstances Haines thought it was inadvisable to proceed
with further permanent fortifications for Aden until its use as
a commercial center could be proved (BSC 1839, Haines-Bombay 6/9/39).

In London, meanwhile, the Secret Committee had requested
Palmerston's permission to negotiate treaties with the local
chiefs. Palmerston, his attitude toward Muhammad Ali stiff-
ened by remembrance of the affairs in Syria, replied, "I am
not aware of any reason which should prevent the Indian Govt.
from directing their agent at Aden to contract treaties of friendship and commerce with those chiefs whose independence is
threatened by Muhammad Ali, or to afford those chiefs any assistance which the Indian Govt. may think proper to offer in
order to help them to defend themselves and if it should be determined eventually to pursue such a course, a communication
to Muhammad Ali might perhaps restrain him from any further
aggressions in that quarter" (FO 78/3185, Palmerston-Sir John
Hobhouse 5/10/39; the underlined passages were changes, made
by Palmerston himself, which considerably strengthened the
tone of the original draft).

It was unnecessary, however, to take advantage of this permission. By July, 1839, the Egyptians in the Yemen were in
sore straits. The customs house officials had become fractious
at Mocha and Hodeida and minor mutinies were breaking out in
the army. The reason was obvious, for all officials were at
least twenty months in arrears of pay (BSC 1839, Haines-Bombay

7/11/39). Deserters began flocking into Aden, willing to work as coolies to avoid being returned to Egyptian territory. Ibrahim requested them to be returned, but Haines did not feel any necessity for compliance (BSC 1839, Haines-Bombay 8/2/39). Mutinies continued to flare up in the Egyptian army, which, in the Yemen, had been reduced to about 3,000 men (BSC 1839, Haines-Bombay 8/11/39). In August, 1839, letters arrived from the Hajayria Sheikh, Cassim Sherzebee, offering the British his country if they would help rid the district of the Egyptians (BSC 1839, two letters Sheikh Sherzebee-Haines without date — approximately 9/9/39). In a Minute by Carnac, the Governor of Bombay, approved by the Bombay Government, Haines was advised to keep on good terms with the chief but to "avoid committing the government to any engagement direct or implied by which we could be called upon to mix ourselves with their internal disputes or interfere with the adjustment of their differences with the Egyptian officials.

"In a word I consider that it would at least be premature, if ever it can be found expedient to extend our political connections beyond those to which we may already be committed by our possession of Aden" (BSC 1839, Minute by Carnac 9/19/39). (Hajayria country lies in an area which has always been a part of the Yemen.) However, Haines was asked to report any violation of the sphere-of-influence agreement by the Egyptian army.

In November, 1839, Haines was informed from Mocha that Muhammad Ali was negotiating with the Imam of San'a. This information was forwarded by Abdul Russool, the Company's native agent at Mocha, who added that he had gotten the facts direct from Sherifdeen, the Pasha's ambassador. The Imam was to be provided with arms, ammunition, and money to remove the British from Aden, and if successful, was to rule the Yemen for the Pasha and pay him an annual tribute. To do this the Imam chiefly needed money, as his treasury was empty. Haines thought that the scheme would fall through as money was also the Egyptians' greatest need (BSC 1840, Haines-Bombay 11/19/39). The negotiations were left to one Said Hussein who returned with the answer that the Imam did not wish to drive the British out of Aden even if he was able to do so. However, he offered San'a to the Pasha for a life pension, retaining the real and personal property of his family and the leadership of his tribe. The Ambassador bore this request to his master in Cairo. Meanwhile the situation of the Egyptians deteriorated,

the arrears of pay increased, and the country became openly
rebellious. By February, 1840, all roads to Mocha were closed
and caravans near Hodeida and Abu 'Arish were plundered
(BSC 1840, Haines-Bombay 2/1/40). After two interviews with
Muhammad Ali, Consul Hodges at Alexandria got the information from him that he had been negotiating with the Imam but
that these negotiations had now ceased (FO 78/404. Hodges-
FO 2/22/40 and 3/31/40). Dodwell (op. cit. , p. 152) evidently
believes this whole incident to be merely a rumor which Hodges
took literally. But since the reports which Abdul Russool forwarded in regard to other happenings in and near Mocha were
reliable and quite accurate, why should this be doubted?

Because of the critical international situation, Muhammad
Ali decided to retire from the Yemen. The evacuation began in
April, 1840. The country was in a state of demoralization.
The army was concentrated at Mocha; the infantry was evacuated by ships while the cavalry retired overland. The Pasha
was reported to be turning over the seacoast towns to the Sharif of Mecca, Muhammad Ibn 'Aun, who did not have the power
to protect them. Haines predicted, "They will be plundered of
everything by the Bedwin on his taking possession and the towns
will dwindle into insignificance" (BSC 1840, Haines-Bombay
4/28/40). To protect British interests the B. E. I. C. "Elphinstone" was sent to Jidda, and the "Euphrates" to Mocha (BSC
1840, Haines-Secret Committee 4/9/40).

The seacoast towns were not turned over to the Sharif of
Mecca after all, but to Sharif Husain of Abu 'Arish (BSC 1840,
Haines-Bombay 6/2/40). This gentleman had been secretary to
Muhammad Amir Bey, Muhammad Ali's governor of Mocha in
1836. When the troops of the Pasha were evacuated, Muhammad Ali sold the seacoast towns to the highest bidder. The I-
mam of San'a was too impoverished to bid and the struggle
rested between Ali Homeida, a powerful chief of the Tehama,
and this Sharif Husain whose only claim to fame was holy character and descent. He was backed by Hajji Yusuf, a wealthy
merchant of Hodeida, who promised a yearly tribute of $90,000
to Muhammad Ali and made a large down payment to the Pasha's
treasury (FO 78/3185, IB-FO 6/27/48 enclosing Haines-Secret
Committee 5/25/48). Sharif Husain was a Muslim of the most
bigoted type, called by the merchants at Mocha "a tyrannous
miserly extortioner" (BSC 1840, Haines-Bombay 6/2/40). At
the moment he had the support of the Asiri, but how long this

arrangement would last no one knew (BSC 1840, Haines-Bombay 6/2/40).

Trouble began in Mocha almost immediately. Haines wrote Hodges, British Consul General in Egypt, on August 9, 1840, "I fear he must have received his governments under the advice or direction to him to place every impediment in the way of British commerce" (FO 78/3185, Hodges-FO 9/22/40). Abdul Russool, British Agent at Mocha, complained that his property had been confiscated and that numerous violations of the Commercial Treaty of 1821 had occurred. Captain Moresby and the "Euphrates" were ordered to Mocha again to investigate and re-open trade, using judicious bribery if necessary. Moresby met the Sharif on August 28 and persuaded him to sign a new treaty on the same terms as the earlier one. The Sharif complained about Russool's actions but allowed his family to leave Mocha, and requested that an Englishman replace him. When the treaty was signed, salutes were fired and the British flag raised over Russool's house. Three times the Sharif requested that the flag be taken down. Meeting with refusal, he then had it cut down. This caused an immediate crisis but Captain Moresby was mollified by a partial apology from the Sharif, and sailed the next day (FO 78/3185, Haines-Secret Committee 9/14/40, enclosing Moresby-Haines 9/4/40).

Meanwhile the Imam of San'a had sent his nephew to Aden to ratify a treaty of peace and commerce with the British and also, he hoped, to get aid against the Sharif, who was occupying the seacoast towns which were by all rights his property (BSC 1840, Haines-Bombay 8/13/40). The Bombay Government warned Haines not to "involve us in any clash on Mocha" (BSC 1840, Minute by Carnac 9/18/40). With this in mind, Haines advised the Bombay Government not to reestablish an agency at Mocha, the post having been left vacant when Russool was compelled to flee (BPC 1840, Haines-Bombay 11/10/40). Abdul Russool, however, shortly returned to Mocha, where he lived for many years and acted as an unofficial agent for the Aden residency, continuing in his friendship for the British and providing them with valuable information.

At Hodeida, the evacuation of the Egyptians was carried on quietly, beginning at the end of April, 1840. This port, as well as Mocha, was left to the tender mercies of Sharif Husain, but as the port of Abu 'Arish, his home, it was not subject to the difficulties that existed at Mocha (BSC 1840, Haines-Bombay 6/2/40).

On top of the affront to the British flag at Mocha, the Sharif followed up in September, 1840, with a letter to Haines of the most insulting nature. After calling Russool a "two-faced liar" among the milder epithets, the Sharif accused the English of acting contrary to decent custom in taking Aden "that belongs to Mussulmans" (FO 78/3185, Haines-Secret Committee 9/14/40). The Sharif was not able to maintain peace for very long. At best, his authority was only enforced in the towns. The roads were unsafe and his caravans continually raided. The Imam of San'a had assembled a force to attack Mocha and for a while it appeared that he would be successful. Ta'iz was captured and the army then continued towards Mocha. The "Clive," Captain Saunders commanding, was dispatched to that port to observe and protect British interests there (BSC 1841, Haines -Bombay 12/26/40). Faced by the threat of the Imam, the Sharif, or rather his brother Hamud who was the immediate governor, levied a "donation" of 5,000 crowns on the merchants of the place (BSC 1841, Haines-Bombay 12/29/40). The Imam, having stopped to defeat the fanatic Fuki Said, drew closer to Mocha, while in the north the Asiri had surrounded Zabid, where Sharif Husain was residing at the moment, and demanded an annual tribute from him. This confusion effectually stopped all trade in the Yemen and the merchants in Mocha, anxious to leave for Aden, were prevented from doing so by Sharif Hamud.

As conditions at Mocha grew worse, the Sharif developed new methods of extortion, including the time-honored method of placing the merchants in jail and exacting a ransom. This, however, was found to be too slow so he hit on a most ingenious scheme. A large number of carpenters were hired to build a granary. On its completion the merchants were assembled to inspect it. After inducing twenty-five of the wealthiest to enter, they were locked in, the price of emission being a tenth of their wealth (BSC 1841, Haines-Bombay 2/2/41).

By March 1, 1841, refugees began arriving from Mocha to settle at Aden. These were on the whole artisans and people of the lower classes, as the merchants at both Mocha and Hodeida were virtual prisoners. The Imam, with true Arab initiative, had merely waited in the hinterland near Mocha and aside from closing the roads had taken no offensive measures (BSC 1841, Haines-Bombay 2/4/41). From the north it was reported that Jidda, the Holy Cities, and the Hedjaz were quiet, having been peacefully transferred to a Bey sent from the Porte, who was to share the administration with the grand Sharif Ibn 'Aun under the sovereignty of Sultan Abdul Medjid (BSC 1841, Haines-Bombay 4/1/41).

The delays of the Imam had enabled the Sharif at Mocha to bring his defenses to such a state of efficiency that the capture of the city could only be accomplished by treachery or by outside aid. The Imam dispatched his vizier to Aden to obtain British aid in blockading the port, promising to arrange a final settlement of the sovereignty of Zeila, a port on the African coast, which was dependent on Mocha (BSC 1841, Haines-Bombay 4/30/41). This small port was of considerable importance, as it controlled the route to Shoa and southern Abyssinia. The government of Bombay was sympathetic to the Imam's offer; Zeila would be an important acquisition and the Sharif of Mocha deserved punishment (BSC 1841, Govt. of Bombay-Govt. of India 5/20/41).

At Mocha the Sharif continued to heap insults on the British. The Banyan merchants were imprisoned for a ransom of 2,500 crowns each and, with true Arab delicacy, all sick Hajjis and other beggars were ordered sent to Aden (BSC 1841, Haines-Bombay 7/25-). Captain Harris, already on his expedition to Shoa, (vide pp. 128-35), urged forcefully on the Bombay Government the desirability for the acquisition of Zeila from the authorities at Mocha, but the Government felt that they were unable to act until the situation at Mocha improved (BSC 1841, Harris-Haines 7/20/41, Minute by Board 10/8-).

From Massawa, Lieutenant Christopher of the "Constance" reported that troops from the Pashalik of Jidda were being mobilized for the occupation of Mocha (BSC 1841, Christopher-Haines N.D.) and word from Mocha seemed to substantiate this, as the Sharif had begun removing guns and valuables to Abu 'Arish (BSC 1841, Haines-Bombay 10/2). At the same time the flow of laborers and skilled artisans from Mocha increased, 383 immigrants coming to Aden within a week.

The ambassador from the Imam finally arrived at Aden on November 27, 1841, requesting definite information as to the intentions of the British regarding the insults suffered at Mocha. Haines, having no definite information, could only politely put him off, and the chance to lend aid to the Imam was lost (BSC 1841, Haines-Bombay 11/28). The Imam, dispirited, retired from Mocha to Ta'iz. Four months later he again sent an envoy

to Haines asking for help in capturing Mocha, which had by this
time been put in an excellent state of defense. Again Haines
could offer nothing, but he did achieve something since he was
able to influence the Imam to export his coffee to Aden instead
of to its rival. All this time the tyrannical actions of the Sharif were sending a steady stream of immigrants to Aden, an
important factor in the growth and prosperity of the settlement
(BSC 1842, Haines-Bombay 3/4/42).

In London, the outrages at Mocha had been brought to the
attention of the Foreign Office by the India Board. The Foreign
Office, knowing next to nothing of the actual situation in the Red
Sea, and assuming that all of Muhammad Ali's conquests in
Arabia had been turned over to the Ottoman Sultan, immediately
lodged a protest at Constantinople (BSC 1842, Government of
India-Bombay 2/28/42, enclosing Aberdeen-Fitzgerald 12/22/
41). A certain Eshref Bey was ordered to go to Mocha to settle
the grievance of the English and passed through Egypt on his
way thither in March, 1842 (FO 78/502, Barnett-FO 3/20/42).
This was officially reported to Haines in May with the additional
information that Eshref had been instructed to depose the Sharif (BSC 1842, Govt. of India-Bombay 5/16/42).

Haines, on hearing of this action by the Foreign Office, expressed surprise that the British should thus recognize the sovereignty of the Ottoman Empire over the Red Sea ports. As he
explained in a dispatch of June 27, Mocha had always been a dependency of the Imam of San'a. In the earlier years of the nineteenth century when the British had a Resident there, all dealings had been with the Imam's government until the forcible
occupation of the port by Muhammad Ali's troops (BSC 1842,
Haines-Bombay 6/27/42).

The Bombay Government promptly protested to the government of India about the action of the Foreign Office. This complaint led to the first inquiry into the question of sovereignty
which was to become so important in 1873. The Foreign Office
made investigation both in Constantinople and at home, and decided finally that the less said about the matter the better. As
a result, the question was studiously avoided; Turkish officials
were recognized as having de facto authority on the spot but
their de jure rights were conscientiously ignored. This avoid-
ance of the question of sovereignty was largely responsible, at
a later date, for the inability of the British to control the slave
trade in the Red Sea. If they recognized the authority of firmans

sent from Constantinople to Turkish officials in southern Arabia to suppress this trade, they automatically recognized the
sovereignty of the Porte in the area. Fortunately for the British, the files of the Turkish Foreign Ministry were in such
chaotic condition that the record of this incident was not discovered in 1873 and was not used as an argument to support
Ottoman claims.

The struggle between the Imam and the Sharif persisted,
though without any major operations. On April 10, 1842, Haines
transmitted to the Secret Committee another and more impressive offer of the Imam, this time to give the English the Tehama in return for a blockade of Mocha (BSC 1842, Haines-
Secret Committee 4/10/42). Next Sharif Husain dealt the British another blow by inducing a Mr. Webb, master of the American brig "Rattler," to export coffee from Mocha instead of Aden
by cutting the export duty to three per cent and waiving all anchorage dues (BSC 1842, Haines-Bombay 5/31/42).

Eshref Bey was reported at Mocha in June. The "Clive"
under Captain Saunders was ordered to Mocha to explain to the
Turkish commissioner the offenses of Sharif Husain against the
British. These offenses are worth setting down in full. First,
the British flag had been cut down. Second, the property of the
British agent had been confiscated by an armed force. Third,
money had been extorted from British subjects (Banyan merchants) by force and threat. Fourth, vessels from Aden had
not been allowed to purchase provisions at Mocha except by
bribery. Fifth, the government of Aden had not been allowed
to buy supplies at Mocha for government purposes. Sixth, the
British agent had been intentionally hindered in performing his
duties. Seventh, the English had been subject to daily insult
and abuse (BSC 1842, Haines-Saunders [about 6/10/42] enclosed
in Haines-Bombay 6/27/42). In enclosing the above order,
Haines remarked that Osman Pasha at Jidda had just barely
enough troops to protect himself. In the event of the Sharif's
refusal to take orders from the Porte, Osman would have to
call on either Egypt or Constantinople for aid or else bribe the
Asiri to do the work of enforcement. Saunders reported from
Mocha on June 12 that Eshref had not yet arrived but that the
Sharif had evacuated everything of value from the town (BSC
1842, Saunders-Haines 6/12/42, enc. in Haines-Bombay 6/27).

The meeting never took place. Eshref decided to remain in
Jidda, and no developments occurred until October, 1842, when

the Sharif refused to recognize the firman from the Porte ordering his removal (BSC 1842, Haines-Bombay 10/2/42). Nevertheless, Husain had taken the precaution of extorting as much
as possible from the merchants and removing this money, together with the daily customs receipts, to Abu 'Arish (BSC 1842,
Haines-Bombay 7/29/42). At the same time tribal outbreaks
near Jidda and Mecca emphasized the weakness of the force at
the disposal of Osman Pasha. At the end of October Haines received a note from Eshref reporting his arrival at Hodeida.
This time the "Clive" was sent with Lieutenant Cruttenden, deputy Political Agent at Aden, aboard to meet the Commissioner,
and to present the following demands: first, the removal from
office of Husain and members of his family who were ruling the
seaport towns rightly belonging to the Imam; second, the reim-
bursement of the British Agent for his lost property; third, a
satisfactory settlement of the question of the seaport towns between the Imam and the Porte. Cruttenden was further to inform Eshref that the Aden Squadron and the forces of the Imam
would back up any such arrangement but that this would be con-
ditioned by the Imam's approval of the person replacing Sharif
Husain. The letter from Eshref intimated that the Sharif had
explained that his troubles with the English were based on a
misunderstanding caused by his governor of Mocha and implied
his willingness to rehoist the British flag (BSC 1842, Eshref
Bey-Haines, N.D., and Haines-Cruttenden 10/29/42, enc.
Haines-Bombay 11/1/42).

Cruttenden reported from Mocha on November 1 that Eshref had left Hodeida for Jidda. What arrangements he had made
with the Sharif were at that time unknown although the English
flag was flying over the Residency at Mocha. He further dis-
closed that the Imam of San'a, who had given such promise, had
retired to his capital and was "buried in indolence and sensual-
ity," and that trade at Mocha was very trivial (BSC 1842, Cruttenden [Mocha]-Haines 11/1/42, enc. in Haines-Bombay 11/16/4).

Cruttenden then sailed for Jidda, arriving there on November 19 only to find that Eshref had gone to Mecca. However,
he found out that the Sharif of Abu 'Arish had subjected himself
to the Porte after he had given a handsome present to Eshref,
half of which was to go to Osman Pasha, "to at least delay" any
measures against him with the assurance that the "gift" would
be trebled if a favorable decision was received from the Porte.
Eshref was afraid to leave Mecca until the "Clive" had left Jidda,

and refused to communicate with any British official. Muhammad Aga Bey, the temporary governor of Jidda, had helped Cruttenden get the information that the Porte planned to reconquer the Tehama, but he said he failed to see how it could be done until the present arrangements for the Pashalik of Jidda were changed. The Pasha paid a fixed annual sum to run the Pashalik, out of which troops and official expenses were paid, all receipts over and above this sum being retained by the Pasha as his own. Muhammad Aga Bey also informed Cruttenden that a return of Muhammad Ali's troops would be a blessing to the country and that a re-occupation of the port of Mocha by the Turks or Egyptians would nip the commerce of Aden "in the bud" and that English "hopes of reestablishing free trade with the coffee country and thus making Aden the Emporium" would be effectively blocked. In the Pashalik of Jidda the situation was now extremely tense because of jealousy between the Turkish officials and those remaining from the regime of Muhammad Ali (BSC 1843, Cruttenden-Haines, N.D., enc. in Haines-Bombay 12/29/42). Governor Arthur commented on this dispatch, "I do not see any further measures can be adopted without orders from home. The mission has been quite abortive" (BSC 1843, Minute by Gov. Arthur N.D.).

The Sharif must have received a favorable reply from Constantinople because in May, 1843, Haines reported that he had ventured to offer to pay a handsome tribute if the Porte would grant him all of San'a and Lower Arabia (BSC 1843, Haines-Bombay 5/19/43). Meanwhile conditions at Jidda, especially the consistent violation of the commercial treaty of 1838 by the Turkish officials, and the fact that Banyan merchants were British subjects, compelled Haines to send a ship there during the trading and pilgrimage season (BSC 1843, Haines-Bombay 5/19/43).

The Foreign Office had protested about the Eshref affair at Constantinople, and in June, 1843, copies of firmans and orders to the governor of Jidda were received in Bombay (BSC 1843, Minute by Board N.D. [approx. June 10]). In July Haines reported the arrival at Hodeida of a new commissioner who was to exact satisfaction for the British and compel Husain to pay an annual tribute of 70,000 crowns to the Porte for his possession of the seaports that belonged to the Imam. By this time Haines was of the opinion that it would be just as well to let the whole matter drop, as he felt that the Porte's only object in making a

settlement with the English was to try to revive the trade of
Mocha (BSC 1843, Haines-Bombay 7/4/43). In this the government of Bombay concurred (BSC 1843, Minute 7/24/43). Three
weeks later, the Sharif was proclaimed a Pasha and ruler of
the seaports, the Tehama, Ta'iz and the adjacent country
(BSC 1843, Haines-Bombay 7/29/43).

In Zeila, a tributary of Mocha, Shermarkee Ali, friend of
the British and a powerful sheikh, had seized the town and imprisoned the Sharif's garrison (thirty men) (BSC 1843, Haines-
Bombay 5/29/43). Shermarkee arrived in Aden on August 27,
1843, and expressed his willingness to place the town under
British protection, suppress slavery, open the road to Harar,
and cut duties to five per cent (BSC 1843, Haines-Bombay 8/31/
43). This offer was passed on to the government of India which
replied on October 7 (BSC, 1843 Govt. of India-Bombay 10/7/43):

> "His Lordship in Council wishes to impress upon the
> Governor in Council of Bombay the extreme inexpediency
> of interfering in any manner in the disputes of the chiefs
> of Africa and Arabia.
>
> "Our relations with those chiefs are and must con-
> tinue to be commercially of very minute importance and
> politically of no importance at all. Intervention in a
> single case might lead to much future interference,
> necessarily productive of much expense and certainly
> of no profit, while the rumour of our interference, ex-
> aggerated in its details and misrepresented as to its
> object, would excite the attention and jealousy of more
> than one European Power.
>
> "The British Govt. only retains Aden for the purpose
> of protecting our depot of coal, not for that of promoting
> intervention in the affairs of the neighboring chiefs of
> Africa and Arabia and of generally extending its posses-
> sions in that quarter.
>
> "The Governor General in Council deeply regrets the
> enormous cost at which a mere depot of coals is now
> protected and he would learn with pleasure that the means
> had been found of restricting our Post at Aden so as to
> render it more nearly in proportion to the sole unambi-
> tious purpose for which it is held there.
>
> "His Lordship in Council will be led to question the
> expediency of having an officer nominally charged with

what are termed Political functions at Aden, should he
find that in practice the delegation of such functions
where there is so little occasion for their legitimate
exercise has a tendency to create a disposition to meddle
in matters where in we have really no interest, no right
of interference and in which the most ample and unequiv-
ocal success would hardly compensate for the charge of
the officers salary for one year.

"The Governor General in Council will recognize
de facto rulers be they who they may, will regard with
friendship all who are friendly and will most deeply re-
gret the necessity should it ever arise for the adoption
of measures of coercion for the protection of our interests in the Arabian and Persian Gulphs and more especially in the Red Sea.

J. Thomason

Sec'y to Govt. of India"

This letter was forwarded to Haines immediately with orders to conform carefully to the line of policy which was indicated in it. (It was also sent to Major Rawlinson, Political
Agent at Baghdad, and Captain Hennel at Muscat; [BSC 1843,
Minute by Governor Arthur N. D.]).

In the light of the above dispatch, the advice of Stratford
Canning (British Ambassador at Constantinople) to the India
Board is very interesting. In February the India Board forwarded to the Bombay Government a letter of Canning's which
said in part, "I venture to submit whether it might not be better
for the Indian government to employ in certain cases a more
active influence for the protection of British subjects and British Commerce on the banks of the Hijaz and the Yemen as well
as in neighboring seas. " Upon which the India Board commented
"It will be right for you to be very cautious as to any instructions which you may think fit to issue in compliance with the
suggestion conveyed in the dispatch from Sir Stratford Canning."
These dispatches had been forwarded to the government of India.
The Governor General replied on May 27 in almost the precise
terms of the dispatch quoted above, that if the de facto ruler of
Mocha insulted British subjects "his Lordship would much re-
gret the circumstances and would confine the interference for
redress within the strictest limits of necessity" and added that

the British government did not have sufficient interests in the
Red Sea "to make it prudent to attract the attention of European
powers and to excite their jealousies with respect to our proceedings in that quarter." (All quotations from BSC 1843,
Minute 10/21/43.)

These dispatches clearly illustrate, first, the difficulties
involved in any diplomatic action in remote districts due to the
slow means of communication, and second, the differing viewpoints of the Foreign Office and the India Board. Haines had
reported the failure of Eshref to live up to his orders on December 29, 1842, not only to Bombay but direct to London. By
February 5, 1843, the India Board was able to send to Bombay
the letter containing Stratford Canning's advice, but not until
April 28 could they forward his report on what had happened,
which was that the "Porte, conscious of her weakness in this
remote part of the Empire," had allowed Eshref's disobedience
to pass unheeded (BSC 1843, Minute 10/21/43). All this information had to be forwarded from Bombay to the government of
India for advice, thereby incurring often a delay of a month,
depending on where the Governor General was residing at the
moment. Then the reply must be discussed and orders prepared
for Haines' guidance. In this particular case the matter took
almost a year. As to the second point, Canning's advice for the
government of India to "employ...a more active influence" was
very well taken, for if such measures had been employed at the
beginning the whole Mocha affair could well have been avoided.
The Indian Government, however, was controlled by the fact
that the incident was too small a matter for the expenses involved and by a very real fear that any interference in the Red
Sea would stimulate foreign rivalries which Aden was ill-equipped
to meet. For a long period Aden could easily have been taken
by any foreign force. Furthermore it must be remembered that
while the East India Company was the governmental body which
controlled a large Empire, it still was a trading company and
its post at Aden was causing a large deficit each year. The expenses of the ill-fated Afghan campaign and the troubles in the
Sind had badly depleted the treasury. Aden was to the Company
"a mere depot of coals" and the Red Sea just a highway.

To the Bombay Government, Aden was a more important
unit, a part of that system of control of the routes to the East
which insured a rapid communication of mails and, in cases of
necessity, of officials, and an important base for the Indian

navy. The letter of October 7 annoyed them, especially the
content of the second paragraph. The government of Bombay
protested on October 31 that it had always laid all letters involving questions of interference before the Indian Government,
and was resentful that "from the tone of your letter it should be
imagined that this Government has been favourably disposed to
an aggressive or intermeddling policy either in the Red Sea or
Persian Gulf or in an other Quarter" (BSC 1843, Bombay-Govt.
of India 10/31/43). The Bombay Government controlled and
directed the Indian navy and through this force came in contact
with outlying countries in a totally different manner from the
government of India. Of necessity its viewpoint was colored
by this fact. Its ships were on their own from the time they
left port, and the instructions given to their officers could be
only general in character. Therefore, both governments were
often faced by faits accomplis which the Bombay Government
could understand but the government of India often could not.
Unquestionably many of the "interventions in the affairs of...
chiefs" were routine naval matters.

In Aden, meanwhile, Eshref Bey arrived in September to
meet a Mr. Smith who had been appointed Consul at Mocha
(BSC 1843, Haines-Bombay 7/22/42). Haines reported that
Eshref had asked if a consular firman had arrived, the first
notice to Haines or the government of Bombay that a consul had
been appointed to that port. And on November 16 Haines ordered the "Bernice," Lieutenant Johnstone commanding, to go
to Jidda to protect British trade there (BSC 1843, Haines-Bombay 11/25/43). The government of India meanwhile postponed
all action regarding Mocha pending Consul Smith's arrival (BSC
1843, Govt. of India-Bombay 12/8/43). Apparently Mr. Smith
was recalled because there is nothing in the documents to indicate that he ever even left England, nor are there any documents to indicate that any such appointment was even considered.

The Imam of San'a died on January 8 and the Yemen was
immediately threatened with a civil war (BSC 1844, Haines-
Bombay 3/2/44). This broke out soon after and continued spo-
radically for the next few years, impoverishing the whole of
the Yemen and causing disturbances in the Tehama. The port
of Mocha, ruined by the policies of Sharif Husain of Abu 'Arish,
disappeared from the scene as a rival of Aden, and gradually
deteriorated into a mud village. Thus ended the immediate
dangers to Aden from the hinterland of Arabia.

The letter of the Governor General of India of October 7, 1843, effectively stopped all further interest in the lands of the Red Sea until British interest in Abyssinia was aroused from a different quarter, the Foreign Office under the leadership of Palmerston. A further curtailment of the Aden Squadron prevented much more first-hand information from reaching Haines and continual civil wars prevented the growth of any de facto government strong enough to threaten Aden or give much aid to the tribes immediately surrounding the town. In a very real sense the orders of the Governor General closed an era of interest and penetration in the Red Sea and left Aden to carry on its existence as a trading post and "mere depot of coals."

VII. SHOA 1840-1843

By the occupation of Aden, the British dominated not only the entrance to the Red Sea but also the African shore stretching from Cape Guardafui, the easternmost point of Africa, to the strait of Bab-el-Mandeb at the entrance to the Red Sea. Events on both coasts thus became of vital importance to the settlement at Aden.

The northeast coast of Africa can be conveniently divided into three sections. The first section, stretching from Cape Guardafui west past the port of Berbera, is familiar to us today as British Somaliland and was then known as the Somali coast. It was of great economic importance to the settlement of Aden. Its chief port, Berbera, was the only good harbor on the coast. Here, for six months out of the year, a few nomadic shepherds grazed their flocks, but from September to April during the northeast monsoon, it became the site of a great fair, drawing as many as 25,000 people from as far as the interior of Africa. Caravans from Harar, on the trade routes across Africa, brought down slaves and other products and returned laden with Indian goods paid for in gold dust. Berbera was also the source of supply for certain essential edibles. In the 1840's refrigeration was of course unknown, and the rich grazing country of the Somali coast supplied the garrison and wealthy inhabitants of Aden with fresh meat in the form of live sheep. It was also the main source of ghee, clarified butter. The interest of any European country in this district would be small unless it had a settlement nearby dependent on it for provisions. The immediate hinterland was lacking in both minerals and agricultural produce, and the tribes were notoriously savage although quite amenable to reason. To the British at Aden, the independence of this district, especially the port of Berbera, was a vital necessity, and their policy towards the Somali coast was that of a policeman, to give reasonable protection to the Banyan merchants trading there and to prevent intertribal disputes from cutting off essential supplies. Although at one time there was talk of establishing a British protectorate over the tribes to prevent any other nation from establishing itself on this coast, it was not until the Egyptian expansion in 1870 that the pre-eminent influence of the British was threatened.

The second section of the coast, to the west and north, was dominated by two small ports, Zeila and Tajura. (Present day Jibuti, terminus of the Addis Ababa Railway and port of French Somaliland, lies approximately halfway between them.) These two ports, both fair harbors for native craft, were also outlets for the trade of Shoa and Harar, two of the chief feudal divisions of Abyssinia and, to all intents and purposes, independent governments in 1840. Disputes among the tribes of the interior had cut off most of the trade with the seacoast but a flourishing, though small, trade in slaves continued. The sovereignty of these two ports was a puzzling question. Zeila had undeniably been under the rule of the Dowla of Mocha under the Imam of San'a, and, under Muhammad Ali and the Sharif, the governor of the town continued to be appointed from Mocha, and the town was garrisoned with soldiers from the Yemen. The ruler of Tajura, however, claimed complete independence although he paid a small yearly tribute to Zeila for certain services.

The significance of these ports to a European power was two-fold. First, they controlled one of the two routes to Abyssinia, and their possession by a commercial power might lead to the development of trade with the interior. Second, they were of considerable strategic value in controlling the mouth of the Red Sea, and, in the hands of a rival power, might threaten the British at Aden.

The third portion of the coast, from Tajura along the western shore of the Red Sea to Suakin (close to the modern Port Sudan), was an inhospitable and unfriendly shore, containing only one important harbor, controlled by the island of Massawa. This harbor, at that time the best in the Red Sea, was the end of the second route from the coast to Abyssinia, the route to its two richest provinces, Tigré and Gondar, both of which were, de facto, independent kingdoms. Massawa was and had been for years occupied by a Turkish force, and was a part of the Pashalik of Jidda, its governor responsible to the Pasha of that port. While there was no question as to the authority of the Turks on the island of Massawa itself, their claims to the sovereignty of the coastal plain were purely theoretical.

It is important to point out again the divided interest in this area within the British Government itself. The East India Company's interest was directed towards southern Abyssinia (Shoa and Harar), taking in the coast as far north as Bab-el-Mandeb on the western shore, and Hodeida on the Arabian coast of the

Red Sea. While originally the East India Company had appointed the consul at Jidda, by 1850 the responsibility apparently rested entirely with the Foreign Office, the consul reporting in duplicate to the government of Bombay and the Consul General at Constantinople (and, in cases of emergency, to Alexandria). The interest of the Foreign Office, on the other hand, was directed toward northern Abyssinia (Tigré and Gondar). With the appointment of Plowden as Consul to Abyssinia in the winter of 1847-1848, the Indian navy reduced its calls at Massawa, where a number of Banyan merchants resided, and the Bombay Government received no information from there, except through rumors reaching Aden, or an occasional private letter to the Resident forwarded by him to Bombay.

Before 1839, there is little evidence in the documents of any particular intentions of the British or Indian Governments to intervene in the affairs of the African coast or Abyssinia. In 1827 Ras Suporguardias, of Tigré, sent a certain William Coffin with a letter to George IV. Coffin had been on Salt's expedition of 1809-1810, and had decided to remain in Ethiopia. The Ras sent King George some minor presents and requested some horsemen, doctors, painters, and other craftsmen to teach the Ethiopians new methods of civilization. These requests were of course ignored, as the British had similar requests from every semi-civilized ruler throughout the East (FO 1/2, Ras Suporguardias-George IV 4/24/27). Coffin, who had brought the letter to England, was delayed there for five years, penniless except for the kindness of Lord Valentia whose faith in the value of opening up Abyssinia never weakened. The cause of Coffin's delay lay in a quarrel between the Foreign Office and the Colonial Office, which had previously handled all African affairs, as to which office was to answer the letter.

After a considerable length of time, Valentia, who had become Lord Mountnorris, interested the East India Company in Coffin's plight. They agreed to supply the customary return presents, and Palmerston, who had by now replaced Lord Aberdeen as Foreign Minister, prepared a letter of greeting to the Ras (FO 1/2, Palmerston-Ras Suporguardias 2/6/32). For some unknown reason the presents, which were to be dispatched from Bombay to Mocha, were never sent; Coffin, finding himself in disgrace with the Ras, was compelled to flee for his life from Tigré to Massawa. In 1838 these presents were reported to be still reposing in the government warehouse at Bombay (BPC 1838, 6/14/38).

When Coffin had left for his return trip to Abyssinia, Campbell, British Consul General at Alexandria, was instructed to
sound out Muhammad Ali on his ambitions in that area. The
Pasha stated that he had no intention of interfering with Abyssinia but would be glad to be of service to the British Government if they were interested in the country (FO 1/3, Campbell-
FO 10/23/33).

In 1837 a sharp encounter between the Egyptian troops and
the Abyssinians took place in the Sennar province of the Sudan.
The cause of this affair is obscure but appeared to be jealousy
between two local chiefs who were brothers. After several
raids which disturbed the frontier, Kurshid Pasha, at that time
in command of the province, intervened to restore order. After
a severe skirmish in which the Egyptians were defeated with a
loss of 850 men, the Abyssinians threatened war on a large
scale if there was any more interference (FO 1/3, Campbell-
FO 10/23/37). Muhammad Ali assured Campbell that he intended no reprisals and would be satisfied with an apology, and
so the matter ended (FO 1/3, Campbell-FO 12/14/37).

It is impossible to understand thoroughly the development
of later events in Abyssinia without a knowledge of the activities
of the early travelers, especially the missionaries. The only
coherent account of the early missionary activity exists in the
history of the French Catholic missions (Poilet, J.B., Editor,
LES MISSIONS CATHOLIQUES FRANCAIS AUX XIX SIECLE,
Paris, Libraire Armand Colin, N.D.; Vol. II, Abyssinie, Inde,
Indo-Chine, N.D. [c. 1900]). This version is not, however,
completely accurate. On page sixteen the statement is made
"Pendant qu'une Mission Anglicane, introduite en Ethiopie à
la suite des ambassades d'Annesley et de Salt (1800-1810) était
expulsée par l'ordre du dedjaz Oubie alors roi de Tigré. "
The first expedition of Valentia and Salt left two Englishmen in
Tigré, Nathaniel Pearce and William Coffin. The first gentleman was an undisciplined young Englishman whom Lord Valentia had picked up in Mocha, the second was a rather pathetic
individual who tried to become a merchant in Abyssinia. Neither
man bore the remotest resemblance to a missionary, although
Pearce notes that Salt sent him some printed Ethiopic psalters
to try to exchange for manuscripts. (Pearce, Nathaniel, LIFE
AND ADVENTURES OF NATHANIEL PEARCE, edited by
J.J.Halls, London, Colburn & Bentley, 1831, Vol. II, pp. 127ff.)

In 1829, when William Coffin was still in London after having

brought the letter to George IV in 1827, he was approached by
the Church Missionary Society to take a missionary back with
him. He refused, stating "the persons employed by the Missionary Society may let their zeal get the better of their pru-
dence, and if they do, the fate of the Jesuits (17th Century)
awaits them, Death or Banishment" (FO 1/2, Mountnorris
[Valentia]-Aberdeen 11/29/29, and Aberdeen-Mountnorris
9/26/29).

Undiscouraged by this rebuff, the Church Missionary Society decided to send Samuel Gobat, a graduate of the Missionary
Institute at Basle, into Abyssinia in 1830 accompanied by two
other missionaries named Kugler and Achinger. According to
Guillaume Lejean, writing much later, these men were personally admired by the Abyssinians, but their Protestant teaching,
with its disregard for the traditional worship of the Virgin
Mary, antagonized the Ethiopian hierarchy and the feudal nobility. (Lejean, Guillaume, THEODORE II, LE NOUVEL EM-
PEREUR D'ABYSSINIE, Paris, Amyot, N.D. [c. 1865], pp. 37-
38.) When Ras Oubie came into power in Tigré in 1832, Gobat
was expelled. He returned in 1835, but almost continuous illness prevented him from being active, and he shortly left the
country. He later became the first Protestant Bishop of Jerusalem under the joint protection of the English and Prussian
governments.

Gobat was followed by J. Lewis Krapf who with two com-
panions named Isenberg and Blumhardt arrived at Adowa in
Tigré early in January, 1838. (These men, employed by the
Church Missionary Society, are probably the "Frêres Moraves"
mentioned by Lejean [op. cit., p. 38].) They had been preceded
by two adventurous young French brothers, A. Thomson and
Arnauld d'Abbadie and a companion, a Lazarist, Father Sapeto.
(Poilet, op. cit., p. 16; also d'Abbadie, Arnauld, DOUZE ANS
DANS LE HAUTE ETHIOPIE, Paris, Hachette, 1862, Vol. I,
pp. 536-7.) The Catholic priest, claiming to be of the same religion as the Abyssinians, won the confidence of the feudal nobility, and Krapf and his companions were ordered out of Abyssinia by Oubie in March, 1838. Krapf said the nobility disliked
the Protestant Mission "partly from bigotry, partly from unsat-
isfied greed" (Krapf, J. Lewis, TRAVELS, RESEARCHES AND
MISSIONARY LABOURS, London, Trubner, 1860, p. 18).

Finding the field favorable for Catholic missionary activity,
A. Thomson d'Abbadie returned to Rome. There the Propaganda

determined on the establishment of an organized mission. Cardinal Franzoni, Prefect of the Propaganda, thereupon appointed Justin de Jacobis head of this mission and assigned a M. Montouri to accompany him. Both men were natives of Naples. (Poilet, op. cit., pp. 18-19.)

This missionary activity of the Propaganda naturally would fall under the general protection of Catholics which the French Government exercised throughout the Near East. However, A. Thomson d'Abbadie, in order to insure the success of the mission, made a move which gave rise to international complications. The mother of the d'Abbadie brothers was an Irish woman and the sons were born in Dublin. For this reason, they had a claim to British protection. In 1839, before returning to Abyssinia with de Jacobis and Montouri, d'Abbadie appealed through Darcel O'Connell, M.P., for British protection against the exactions of the Naïb of Arkiko and the difficulties which he had experienced previously with Muhammad Ali's governor of Massawa. In the letter d'Abbadie frankly stated that he was taking three missionaries with him, but did not indicate what sect they represented. He then emphasized the importance of opening up Abyssinia to British trade. "It is needless perhaps to remark that in establishing a European mission in Abyssinia I am paving the way for future commercial intercourse with that country" (FO 1/3, A. Thomson d'Abbadie-Darcel O'Connell, M.P., N.D. [spring of 1839]).

O'Connell forwarded this letter to Palmerston with the suggestion that the d'Abbadie mission might provide an instrument in suppressing the slave trade as well as opening up British commerce with Abyssinia (FO 1/3, O'Connell-Palmerston 6/12/39). Palmerston accepted the whole affair at its face value, requested the India Board for a cruiser of the Indian navy to cover d'Abbadie's entrance into Abyssinia at Massawa, and ordered Campbell in Egypt to obtain passage for the mission through Egyptian territory from Muhammad Ali (FO 1/3, FO-IB 6/12/39, IB-FO 6/14/39, FO-Campbell 6/17/39). He also prepared a letter to Ras Oubie in reply to a letter which d'Abbadie had brought out, stating that Britain would "use her good offices and friendly aid" to terminate the border difficulties between the Egyptians and the Abyssinians (FO 1/3, Palmerston-King of Abyssinia 6/17/39). Thus with British protection, d'Abbadie and the Catholic missionaries entered Abyssinia late in 1839, joining M. Sapeto at Adowa. Here they split up,

de Jacobis remaining in Tigré, Sapeto going to Gondar and
Montouri to Khartoum. (Poilet, op. cit., p. 19.) Palmerston's
letter to the king was never delivered, but was later used unsuccessfully by d'Abbadie in order to influence Haines in Aden
to facilitate his entry into Shoa (IO-BSC 1840, Haines-Bombay
12/29/40).
    The first nineteenth century travelers to Abyssinia had
been British, a natural enough consequence of the East India
Company's interests in Mocha. Not until 1835 had any French
travelers appeared. In that year two young Frenchmen, Combes
and Tamisier, entered the country via Massawa and penetrated
into Gondar, the Galla country, and as far as Shoa. As far as
can be discovered from their book (Combes, Edward, and
Tamisier, M., UN VOYAGE EN ABYSSINIE, Paris, Dessart,
4 Vols., 1838), this trip was undertaken on their own initiative.
This is corroborated by the anonymous reviewer of their volume in the Nouvelles Annales des Voyages who, to judge from
the nature of the review, apparently knew them personally
(1838, Vol. 78, pp. 293ff.; reference to their motives for undertaking the trip, p. 320).
    The trip made by Combes and Tamisier had one concrete
result – it brought Sahle Selassie, King of Shoa, into contact
with Europeans and opened the way for future travelers to that
country, not because the King was progressive, but because he
believed all Europeans to be omniscient and fine craftsmen who
could make weapons for him (op. cit., Vol. 2, pp. 347-353).
For this reason the Frenchmen had had difficulty in obtaining
permission to leave Shoa.
    The report of Combes and Tamisier on their travels seems
to have had two other results. First, the French Ministry of
Marine sent an official expedition under Lieutenant Charlemagne
Theophile Lefebvre to explore Abyssinia and the Red Sea coast.
This expedition appears to have been largely scientific in character, although it was instructed to report on the possibilities
of colonization in Abyssinia. There is no evidence of any kind
that its members became involved in the internal politics of the
country. The results of this expedition, which lasted from 1839
to 1843, were published in 1848 (Lefebvre, Charlemagne Theophile, VOYAGE EN ABYSSINIE ... 1839-1843, Paris, Bertrand,
6 Vols and atlas). Second, a young adventurer, Charles E.
Rochet d'Hericourt set out on his own to cross Africa by foot
from Shoa to the mouth of the Niger River.

Meanwhile, Krapf and Isenberg, who had been driven out
of Tigré by Oubie, had returned to Cairo where they filed an
interesting report on Abyssinia with Campbell, the British Consul General, though the report contained little of commercial
or political value. Bidwell in the Foreign Office commented
"It affords useful hints for deciding on the course which it might
be expedient for Great Britain to pursue with respect to future
intercourse" (FO 78/343-Campbell-FO 10/22/38). Soon these
two missionaries were on their way to Shoa by invitation of
Sahle Selassie. Isenberg remained but a few months, leaving
Krapf alone in Shoa. (Isenberg, W., and Krapf, J. Lewis,
JOURNALS, London, Seeley, Burnside & Seeley, 1843; con-
densed account in Krapf, J. Lewis, TRAVELS, RESEARCHES
AND MISSIONARY LABOURS, London, Trubner, 1860, pp. 13-
107.) The presence of Krapf in Shoa provided the English
with a check on the activities of Rochet d'Hericourt who,
as the missionary relates, was a man of an "intriguing
disposition."

D'Hericourt arrived in Shoa in the fall of 1839 and immediately won the confidence of Sahle Selassie by presenting him
with a mill for making gunpowder. He soon influenced the king
in favor of France. When he left Shoa for France he bore presents and a letter to Louis Philippe.

As the diplomatic crisis in Europe over the Egyptian question deepened, the Foreign Office and the India Board became
increasingly suspicious of French interests in Abyssinia. They
had good reason to be. The French Ministry of Marine had already sent the Lefebvre expedition into Abyssinia, and on October 21, 1839, two young captains in the engineering corps of
the French army, Ferret and Galinier, left Marseilles to explore Tigré and Gondar under the patronage of the Duc de Dal-
matie (Marshal Soult), then Premier and Minister of Foreign
Affairs. Their trip was apparently financed privately from sub-
scription among the various members of the Cabinet and ostensibly was a scientific expedition under the general supervision
of the Academy of Sciences. They spent the winter in Egypt
and did not proceed down the Red Sea until August of 1840. On
September 18, at Wajh (on the Arabian coast) they met Rochet
d'Hericourt returning from his first trip to Shoa (Ferret, Pierre
Victoire, and Galinier, Joseph-Germaine, VOYAGE EN ABYS-
SINIE, 2 vols., Paris, Paulin, 1847, dedicated to the Duc de
Nemours, Vol. I, p. 307). By January, 1841, they were at

Adowa where they met de Jacobis and Montouri. They reported
the great success of de Jacobis' labors in Tigré and the tremendous influence which he had developed with Ras Oubie who had
offered him the position of Abuna or head of the Abyssinian
Church (ibid., Vol. I, pp. 480-5).

The Ferret-Galinier expedition had had little publicity,
but on May 23, 1840, the Journal des Débats announced a new
expedition of Combes and Tamisier backed by a large mercantile firm. The avowed object of this expedition was not Massawa and northern Abyssinia, but Zeila and the approaches to
Shoa (BSC 1840, Secret Committee-Haines 7/2/40 and enclosures).

While the India Board might distrust French intrigues in
northern Abyssinia, this area was of relatively little concern
to them and properly fell under the jurisdiction of the Foreign
Office to whom it was important in relation to the whole Egyptian question. Zeila, however, lay directly in the sphere of
influences of Aden, being outside the straits of Bab-el-Mandeb,
and was a matter of serious concern.

On July 2, 1840, the Secret Committee in London therefore
advised Haines of the new expedition of Combes and Tamisier
and requested him to send an officer to Zeila to counteract any
French influence there, authorizing him to spend a reasonable
sum of money to accomplish this object, and especially to purchase some station which would control the harbor of Tajura.
"How that object will be secured, you will best be able to judge
.... we have so much confidence in your zeal and ability, that
we willingly give you entire discretion... except that we desire
that no compulsory means may be resorted to, or any attempt
made to obtain a footing on the points in question, by threats of
armed force or intimidation of any kind. We are inclined to
believe with the writer of the enclosed letters that your agent
might be able to take such steps, quietly as would secure for
Great Britain a preference either in a commercial or political
point of view, or both, amongst that part of the African coast
which is opposite to Aden and we concur in the opinion that the
settlement of any other European commercial agency or military
station on that coast would be highly detrimental to British interests" (BSC 1840, Secret Committee-Haines 7/2/40).

As the tribes had been discouraged by the failure of their
attack of July 7, 1840, Aden was comparatively peaceful, and
Haines was able to turn his energies wholeheartedly to the new
project. Captain Moresby in the "Sesostris" and Lieutenant

Barker in the "Euphrates" were despatched to Tajura immediately. On August 24, Moresby returned, informing Haines that he had succeeded in purchasing the Musa islands at the head of the bay of Tajura (presumably two tiny islands in the Ghoubat Kharab at present nameless) for 1,100 crowns from the local chief. He also had signed a treaty of friendship and commerce with the tribe. Sheikh Ali Shermarkee had acted as interpreter for him most successfully. This man was a Somali from Berbera who had great influence along the coast. He had first come to the notice of the British government in 1829, when he had saved several lives in a shipwreck, and for the rest of his life proved a firm friend of the British Government.

Meanwhile Lieutenant Barker in the "Euphrates" was surveying the bay and investigating political conditions around Tajura. The Sultan's territory extended inland to the salt lake of Assal, two days' journey away. Barker was informed that normally the trip to Shoa was very easy and one could travel there with little expense, but at the moment an inter-tribal feud had closed all the roads. The town of Tajura itself had about 2,000 inhabitants whose main source of income was exporting slaves, chiefly Galla women. The Sultan claimed to be completely independent, although he paid 1,200-1,300 crowns head money a year to Zeila. Rumors of coal in abundance near the harbor were reported but Lieutenant Barker was unable to get definite information. The only reasonable anchorage was at the Musa islands, since the harbor at Tajura was fit only for small native vessels. The village was the seat of a fair for three months of the year, October through December. While slaves were the chief export, gums, skins, ivory, senna, gold dust, myrrh, frankincense, and ostrich feathers were also sold, besides innumerable cattle of all kinds. Mocha was the customary market for the export of these products, as it was for the products of the whole coast from Suakin to Berbera (FO 78/3185, Haines-India Board 9/14/40, enclosing reports by Moresby 8/24/40 and Barker 8/17/40).

The government of Tajura is worthy of notice for its practical simplicity. The district was ruled by a sultan who was succeeded at his death by his vizier, the man judged best fitted to rule since he had been in closer contact with affairs of state than any other person (FO 78/3185, Haines-IB 9/14/40, report of Barker 8/17/40, also BSC 1840; also Rochet d'Hericourt, Charles E., VOYAGE SUR LA COTE ORIENTALE DE LA MER

ROUGE..., Paris, Bertrand, 1841, p. 43).

Both Barker and Moresby agreed that little could be done about obtaining a foothold at Zeila where the governor of Mocha was both titular and actual sovereign. Both felt that the possibilities of trade through these ports were great, but that the natives were so used to trading with Mocha that considerable advantages would have to be offered by the English to break this monopoly established by tradition. The French were unknown there, and it was dubious that they could very easily establish influence, unless it was done through the Sharif at Mocha (FO 78/3185, Haines-IB 9/14/40, enclosing reports of Moresby and Barker).

Meanwhile Haines wrote Consul General Hodges in Alexandria, "French ships begin to make their appearance in these seas, we have now lying here a vessel pierced for 18 guns and a frigate is daily expected. There is a French brig at Mocha and a transport laden with guns and arms is at Massawa, they are do doubt wishing to gain a footing in Abyssinia" (FO 78/3185, Hodges-FO 9/22/40 quoting a private letter from Haines). This same dispatch also enclosed a letter from Haines which listed the French ships shortly expected in the Red Sea, one 44-gun frigate, one 30-gun frigate, the "Dordine," the 18-gun corvette "Caroline." The "Ankobar," which had been reported at Mocha, had sailed to Massawa after trying to purchase land at Assab Bay or Edd (FO 78/3185, Hodges-FO 9/22/40. Enc. Haines-Hodges 9/10/40).

The "Ankobar" was an armed merchantman which had been sent out from Bordeaux to support the second expedition of Combes and Tamisier. The "Dordine" is probably the "Dordogne," a frigate of the French navy stationed at Bourbon which was used the next year under the command of Captain Guillain to transport the French troops which occupied the island of Nossi-Bé north of Madagascar (Guillain, M., DOCUMENTS SUR L'HISTOIRE... DE MADAGASCAR, Paris, Imprimerie Royale, 1845, p. 151). It is interesting to speculate on French naval activities and intents but it is very difficult to find out anything about them from printed material. The islands of Bourbon (now Réunion) were the French naval base for the Indian Ocean. In 1840 Rear Admiral de Hell was appointed commander of the station and appears almost immediately to have instituted an aggressive policy. Coupland in his work EAST AFRICA AND ITS INVADERS (Oxford, Clarendon Press, 1938,

pp. 438-445), describes French activity at Zanzibar, and there
is considerable material in books on Madagascar on the occupation of Nossi-Bé in 1841 (ibid., pp. 445ff.; Guillain, op. cit.,
for first hand account of the occupation pp. 151-178). In view
of the international crisis over Muhammad Ali, it is safe to assume that French activity in the Red Sea area was largely for
the purposes of intelligence, i.e., observation of British activity in the Aden area. How far the French would have been prepared to go to back up one of their adventurous countrymen in
Abyssinia is a moot point. The fears of the East India Company were probably exaggerated, although the French might
have pressed any claims until there was danger of an actual conflict, especially after the formation of the Thiers Ministry in
France on March 1, 1840.

Under these circumstances Haines ordered Moresby and
Barker to purchase a small island at the end of Ghoubet Khareb
(the bay at the end of the Gulf of Tajura), also the island of
Eibat (Sa'ad Din) which controlled the harbor of Zeila, and to
make a treaty of friendship with Eibat. Possession of the Musa
islands, purchased in August, was to be officially signified by
the raising of the British flag (FO 78/3185, Haines-IB 9/14/40,
enclosing Haines-Bombay 8/28/40).

The "Elphinstone," Lieutenant Ethersey commanding, was
sent to Massawa to observe the actions of the French, and another vessel was requested from Bombay so that the British
squadron would be on an equal footing with their rivals.

Barker had no difficulty in persuading the Sultan to sell the
island at the mouth of Ghoubet Kharab for 200 dollars and a
barrel of cannon powder. The Sultan also offered the island of
Jibuti to the English, but on investigation Barker found that the
Sultan did not own it.

At the same time, Moresby succeeded in purchasing the
island of Eibat from Sayud Muhammad Bar, the governor of
Zeila, by a treaty signed on September 3 (FO 78/3185, IB-FO
11/21/40, enclosing reports from Haines 9/25/40).

The treaties with Tajura and Zeila were very similar in
tone. A reciprocal import duty of five per cent was established,
and the chiefs pledged themselves not to enter into treaty relations with any other power without first informing the British.
Usual clauses of friendship were included, but the Sultan of Tajura further pledged himself to do everything in his power to
open up trade with the interior (Aitchison, D.V., A COLLECTION

OF TREATIES, ENGAGEMENTS AND SUNNUDS RELATING TO
INDIA AND NEIGHBORING COUNTRIES, Calcutta, Foreign
Office Press, 1876, Vol. VII, Nos. LXXVII and LXXVIII, pp.
177-9; see also bibliography for publication 1929-1933). Subsequently the British Government desired to change the clauses
of an exclusive nature which might be directed against the trade
of another nation, but unsettled conditions in the Yemen and a
lack of interest in East Africa prevented any modification
(Aitchison, op. cit., Vol. VII, p. 174).

With these treaties in hand, Haines appointed J. Hatchatoor,
a Banyan merchant, as agent in Tajura (BSC 1840, Haines-Bombay 9/25/40), but his power was limited by order of the government of India to ascertaining the resources of the country,
especially coal, and the supervision of trade (BSC 1840, Govt.
of India-Govt. of Bombay 11/9/40). British interests in Zeila
were taken care of by Sheikh Ali Shermarkee who was also very
influential in Berbera. The status of this man is hard to determine. He certainly had no official appointment and apparently
was not under British protection, although the Political Agent
at Aden, with the consent of the Indian Government, had been
able to extract him from difficulties with the Sharif of Mocha.

The French ships continued their activity in the Red Sea.
Haines received a letter from the Chief of Edd reporting that
the French wished to buy his harbor, which was only a roadstead (BSC 1840, Haines-Bombay 9/25/40). Lieutenant Ethersey in command of the brig "Elphinstone" confirmed this on
his return from Massawa where he had found the "Ankobar."
The activities of the French were not easy to discover. However, investigation showed that they had negotiated for the purchase of Anfile, a port on the mainland across from Massawa.
The Naïb of Arkiko, an independent chief who controlled the
land around Annesley Bay, was reported to have sold them this
port for 2,000 crowns, 400 of which had been paid as a deposit.

Lieutenant Ethersey also gave a very good description of
the state of Massawa, the first since that of Valentia and Salt.
The island of Massawa commanded Annesley Bay, the one fine
harbor on the African coast between Suakin and Tajura. The
island itself also had excellent harbors but lacked drinking water which had to be accumulated in large tanks from rainfalls
or else brought over from the mainland. Massawa was the residence of a Turkish officer called a Kaimakam and about 150
troops. The main part of the Kaimakam's duties was to collect

customs and port dues, since Massawa controlled the trade at
Annesley Bay. Out of this money the Naïb of Arkiko was paid
his salary of 12,000 crowns a year. The Naïb was ruler of the
town of Arkiko and, roughly, of the land surrounding Annesley
Bay. While the position of Naïb was more or less hereditary,
the man occupying the position was approved by the Pasha of
Jidda. In return, the Naïb kept the country at peace and protected merchants. Anfile, nearby, had a good harbor and was
the nearest port to Abyssinia; Gondar was fifteen days' journey,
Adowa six days', Axum seven, and Adigrat five days' journey
away (FO 78/3185, IB-FO 11/21/40 enclosing Haines-Bombay
10/2/40).

From this description it would appear that despite Turkish
claims to sovereignty over all Abyssinia the Turks actually
controlled only the island of Massawa itself. While the Naïb
was approved by the Pasha of Jidda, he was paid a subsidy only
to keep the roads clear and was perfectly justified in claiming
complete independence.

In December, 1840, an incident happened at Aden which
deepened Haines' suspicion of French activity. A. Thomson
d'Abbadie had left his brother in Abyssinia and arrived at Aden
preparatory to returning to Europe for "reasons of health."
While in Aden, he showed great interest in all phases of the settlement and British activity in the area. D'Abbadie had come
to Abyssinia with recommendations from Palmerston, a letter
from Palmerston to the King of Abyssinia and a commission to
do some research for the London Athenaeum Society. The letter to the King had not been delivered, and he now gave it to
Haines for delivery. He stayed in Aden a short time and took
his departure for Suez, but quickly returned, stating that he
was on his way to Shoa. On his second arrival at Aden there
were awaiting him several letters from the French Ministry of
Foreign Affairs which further aroused Haines' suspicions, and
on his departure to Shoa, Haines, through Shermarkee, placed
all sorts of difficulties in his way at Zeila and Tajura (BSC 1841,
Haines-Bombay 12/29/40).

A. Thomson d'Abbadie was soon joined by his brother Arnauld who had been ejected from Tigré by Ras Oubie after an
argument over a matter of Abyssinian etiquette. Arnauld d'Abbadie arrived at Massawa to find the "Ankobar" at anchor. This
vessel had found trade at Massawa very poor and was preparing
to depart for Aden, so Arnauld took passage on it. The vessel

stopped at Edd which the captain claimed had been purchased
by himself and an agent of the French Government (presumably
M. Combes). No claim was advanced at that time by the captain of any purchase at Anfile as Ethersey had reported. After
stopping at Mocha and Aden, Arnauld repaired to Berbera where
he met his brother Thomson. From here they intended to go
first to Harar and then to Shoa, but were prevented by the intrigues of Shermarkee. On January 15 they gave up this plan
and moved to Zeila hoping to go directly to Shoa. Here they
were again detained. They finally gave up and on May 12, 1841,
began their journey back to Europe (d'Abbadie, op. cit., pp.
568-607).

In Shoa, J. Lewis Krapf had observed Rochet d'Hericourt's
intrigues with great suspicion. After the departure of this
traveler for France on March 1, 1840, Krapf became deeply
disturbed when Rochet's influence over Sahle Selassie seemed
to increase with his absence. On July 3, 1840, the missionary
wrote to Consul General Campbell in Alexandria details which
showed that M. Rochet was not personally disinterested in promoting friendship with France. According to Krapf, he had
concocted a rather clever scheme. He had advised Sahle Selassie that if he wished to conquer all of Abyssinia he should
organize his troops on the French model and that he, personally, would obtain a treaty from Louis Philippe and arrange for
a supply of arms and ammunition from the French Government.
Rochet had talked freely of his plan to Krapf and told him that
he planned to become ruler of Abyssinia by training a thousand
men in the European manner and then forcing the king to obey
him, adding that if there was a British India, why should there
not be a French Abyssinia. Krapf, although he declares in his
book "I kept aloof from all political relations," (TRAVELS,
RESEARCHES AND MISSIONARY LABORS DURING AN EIGHT-
EEN YEARS RESIDENCE IN EASTERN AFRICA, Boston, Tick-
nor and Fields, 1860, p. 26), obviously was well-informed for
he was able to state that the King of Shoa was well-disposed
towards England. Krapf stated his belief that if English influence were introduced there it would spread all over east and
central Africa, as many of the trade routes across Africa converged on Ankobar (capital of Shoa). He expounded on the re-
spectable character of the King and his desire to civilize his
people. The chief danger, to Krapf's mind, was delaying until
Rochet returned and was able to influence the King again. If

the Frenchman's plans succeeded and if the Galla (Muhammadan) tribesmen rallied to his side as he hoped, he could easily make Abyssinia completely French and actually become a threat to Muhammad Ali (FO 1/3, Krapf-Campbell, 7/3/40).

On July 6, Sahle Selassie wrote to the Indian Government. Influenced by Krapf and further swayed by reports of the successes of the British against the Arabs at Aden, which were greatly exaggerated by the time they reached Ankobar (FO 1/3, Krapf-Haines, August 1840), the King of Shoa wrote to the Indian Government via Haines, requesting friendship. The King naively went on to say "but arts and sciences are not yet come into my country as they are in yours. Therefore you may please assist me in this respect. The thing in which you may assist me is in sending guns, cannon and other things which are not to be got in my country" (FO 78/3185, IO-FO 11/21/40, enclosing letter from King of Shoa to Haines). Accompanying this message was the present of three horses, one mule ("indifferent beasts" remarked Haines) (BSC 1840, Haines-Bombay 9/25/40) and a "gassela hide" for Haines' wife. A covering letter was sent by Krapf recommending that the British consolidate their influence in Shoa, as the country lay on the trade routes across Africa and the slave trade could be fairly easily suppressed while spreading English influence over central and east Africa. He concluded his letter with an appeal from Sahle Selassie for medicines to cure "1. Anaphrodism or impotency; 2. Sickness of the eyes; 3. Venery; 4. Small pox; 5. Epistasis or hemorrage from the nose; 6. Remedies against Rheumatism in the feet and pains in the shoulder blades; 7. Against sickness of the heart; 8. Against the egression of the straight gut on going to stool" (FO 78/3185, IO-FO 11/21/40 enclosing Krapf-Haines 7/1/40).

The government of Bombay meanwhile decided to ask the consent of the government of India for an expedition to Shoa to conclude a treaty of peace and friendship, and requested the Resident at Aden to ascertain the best route, type of presents to be sent, etc. (BSC 1840, Minute by Board 10/12/40).

Thus when Krapf's letter to Campbell in Alexandria was forwarded to the India Board by the Foreign Office on December 2 with the suggestion that the Indian Government might be the best means of getting in touch with Sahle Selassie, the India Board could reply that an expedition had already been planned to counteract French intrigues there (FO 1/3, FO-IB 12/2/40, and IB-FO 12/14/40).

In India, the government readily consented to the expedition to Shoa and left the details up to the Bombay Government (BSC 1840, India-Bombay 11/1/40).

At the same time French shipping activity continued in the Red Sea area. While the Bombay Government refused to send a war vessel to re-enforce the squadron at Aden, the government at home took a different view of the situation and ordered a vessel of the Royal Navy to the Red Sea (FO 1/3, IB-FO 1/31/41 enclosing London-Bombay 10/26/40). Lieutenant Barker charted the bay of Tajura, and investigated the question of routes for an expedition. It is interesting to note the tension between France and England as reflected at Aden. The "Ankobar" lay at anchor in Aden's harbor from December 15 to January 4, prepared to depart at a moment's notice should war break out (BSC 1841, Haines-Secret Committee 1/10/41).

In Aden three travelers had appeared, all bent on exploring Shoa and east Africa. M. Combes in the "Ankobar" returned to Aden from Massawa preparatory to setting out to investigate Berbera and the hinterland; M. d'Abbadie suddenly returned from Suez, receiving packages from the French Foreign Ministry; and a certain Dr. Beke arrived from England to explore Shoa. The first two men landed on the African shore January, 1841, carefully observed by Indian navy vessels, to be successfully blocked by the influence of the British with the native rulers. The third gentleman had made his way inland shortly before.

While in Aden, Combes talked quite freely to Haines of the purchase of Edd for which he had been awarded the "Legion d'Honneur." The purchase consisted of a strip of land thirty-eight miles long and ten miles deep along the shore. Combes confessed that Tajura was a much more desirable situation but that the English had forestalled him (BSC 1841, Haines-Bombay 1/1/41).

The route to Shoa was being carefully studied by Haines, who acquired all possible information. Although Krapf had advised Haines that an intertribal struggle over the salt lakes of Assal had made the safety of the road uncertain, the Tajura caravan route was judged the best. The expedition, Haines thought, should consist of a commissioner, an engineering officer to map the country, a cavalry or infantry officer to report on the state of the people, a medical officer, a native assistant, and guides and guards. The latter, Haines advised, should be

natives, as the appearance of Indian soldiers would excite suspicion and possibly cause trouble with the unfriendly tribes.
Camels and a few horses for transport could be obtained at Tajura. (FO 1/3, IB-FO 1/13/41, enclosing Haines-Bombay
11/20/40.)

On January 11, 1841, the Indian Government advised Bombay that the expedition could start whenever the time was considered propitious, leaving the details as to the assignment of
officers, size of expedition, etc., to the discretion of the Bombay Government (BSC 1841, India-Bombay 1/11/41). Captain
W. Cornwallis Harris of the B. E. I. C. Engineers, who had had
considerable game hunting experience in the south of Africa,
was chosen as its leader. He was allowed to pick his own officers and supervise the preparations. The list of these men
appears in Captain Harris' book THE HIGHLANDS OF ETHIO-
PIA (second ed., London, Longmans, 1844, 2 vols., p. xiv).
The expedition comprised, besides Captain Harris, five other
officers, including two doctors, three civilians, J. Hatchatoor,
the British Agent at Tajura, seventeen non-commissioned and
enlisted men as guards (against Haines' advice) and a carpenter, a smith, and two servants (ibid., Vol. I, p. xxiv).

On April 24, 1841, Harris received his orders. After advising him on certain points, especially the usefulness of Krapf
and Beke after his arrival in Shoa, the orders read:

> 1. To endeavour to enter into a convention with the
> King of Shoa for securing a free and unrestricted com-
> mercial intercourse with the territories described to
> be under his authority. [This is the only paragraph
> quoted in the Blue Book together with the treaty–1844.
> Accounts and Papers V. 5 East Indies.]
> 2. To endeavour to form similar conventions...
> with the chiefs of the country on the line of the road
> from Tedjoura... also with the rulers of the countries
> adjacent to and beyond Shoa.
> 3. To prosecute such scientific researches and ob-
> tain such a geographical knowledge... as may be found
> practicable.
> 4. To describe the prevailing systems of govern-
> ment, administration of justice, etc.,... together with
> an accurate account of the productions and capabilities
> of the soil, the climate and seasons. In short to explore

the country, to report on its agriculture and to ascertain in what manner and to what extent commercial
intercourse may be established with the interior.

5. To search diligently for coal more especially in
such locations as may be made available for steam
navigation in the Red Sea. . . .

6. To report the probable advantages which the
British government is likely to receive from the continued cultivation of friendly relations with Shoa and
the neighboring countries.

7. To obtain specimens of any interesting natural
or artificial products. . . more especially those which
are likely to be sought after as articles of British
commerce.

8. To ascertain to what extent British and Indian
manufactures are likely to find a ready sale.

9. Lastly to ascertain to what extent slavery and
the slave trade exists in these countries. . . and to endeavour if possible to strike at the root of this de-
testable traffic in human flesh by persuading the king
of Shoa. . . to prohibit it under the severest penalties. . . .

The Governor in Council has been led to suppose
that ultimately an extensive field for commercial
enterprise may be opened by British merchants in this
part of Africa.

The governor stated that he had been informed that the country
was populous and produced gold and coffee of a superior quality
(BSC 1841, Bombay-Harris 4/24/41).

The orders then went on to summarize French activity in
Shoa. The incidents of 1840 were recapitulated with the comment that Tigré and Amhara were too busy with their own affairs to be very open to French intrigue, which was additionally
weakened by the fact that d'Abbadie, one French explorer, was
an adherent of the Bourbons, while Lefebvre, another Frenchman in Tigré, was an Orléanist. The governor showed that he
was much agitated by Krapf's reports of Rochet d'Hericourt's
activities in Shoa. "It is considered that the establishment of
a French influence in Abyssinia will prove prejudicial to British
interests more especially in the Red Sea. It will therefore be
your duty by all the legitimate means in your power to endeavour to counteract the schemes of aggrandizement reputed to

M. Rochet.... In carrying these instructions into effect however, you will be careful to avoid coming into hostile collision with M. Rochet or any other French emissaries who you may find in Abyssinia. " The orders concluded with administrative details of the expedition (BSC 1841, Bombay-Harris 4/24/41).

The expedition sailed from Bombay on April 26, 1841. The military escort of volunteers was picked up at Aden and the party arrived at Tajura on May 18. From then on the expedition was in continual difficulties. The Sultan of Tajura tried to demand an increase in his subsidy which Haines flatly refused. (BSC 1841, Haines-Bombay 7/25/41.) At Goongoontah (not on modern maps; on Harris' map it is shown about four miles west of the west end of Lake Assal) two non-commissioned officers were murdered in their sleep by Dankali tribesmen (Harris, op. cit., pp. 119ff). Harris wrote Haines that the hardships of the route could be considerably lessened by an accord with the native chief of Haheita (in the interior behind Zeila) and the possibilities of the discovery of a route through to Zeila in order to avoid "the avaricious and imbecile Sultan of Tejourra" (BSC 1841, Haines-Bombay Sept. 1841). As Haines pointed out to the Bombay Government, Zeila was controlled by Mocha, and unless aid were given to the Imam of San'a in gaining Mocha, there was little hope for the development of this route (BSC 1841, Haines-Bombay N.D. [approx. Sept. 1841]). The Government took the matter under advisement but did not wish to get involved in the Mocha affair (BSC 1841, Minute by Board 10/8/41). The expedition reached Ankobar in Shoa on July 18, 1841. Harris found a rather unpromising situation there with French influence very powerful in memory, although no Frenchmen were there at that time (BSC 1841, Haines-Secret Committee 9/15/41). Lieutenant Barker of the Indian navy meanwhile volunteered to return via the Harar-Zeila route. He started out, but soon became ill with fever, and was taken down to Tajura though the kindness of some natives (Barker, Lieutenant W., "Narrative of a journey to Shoa," in Forrest, George W., ed., SELECTIONS FROM THE TRAVELS AND JOURNALS PRESERVED IN THE BOMBAY SECRETARIAT, Bombay, Government Central Press, 1906).

By November the expedition, still in Shoa, was awkwardly short of money; Maria Theresa dollars were then, and indeed up to 1935, the only acceptable currency. Troubles on the road kept dispatches and supplies from traveling freely (BSC 1841,

Haines-Bombay 11/26, Harris-Haines 10/8/41). Harris wrote
Haines the "opinions and promises of M. Rochet had apparently
gained great influence" with the king (BSC 1841, Harris-Haines
10/15/41). This was almost the last dispatch to come from the
expedition for a considerable period of time as the route was
soon after completely closed by intertribal dissension. In Shoa,
the expedition met with much politeness and little success. In
India, it was practically forgotten.

Finally, by dint of much persuasion, Harris convinced the
King to sign a treaty of commerce and friendship on November
16, 1841. As the treaty never was effective its provisions are
not worth mentioning, except for an agreement for a reciprocal
duty of five per cent. The remaining articles were couched in
the vaguest terms. (Aitchison, C. V., op. cit., Vol. VII, pp.
185-7.) The expedition remained in Shoa throughout the year
1842. At the end of November, Rochet d'Hericourt arrived on
his second trip. He found the expedition in bad straits due to
lack of money with which to pay their way out of Shoa. By collecting from Sahle Selassie the amount of money which he had
spent for the king in France, M. Rochet was able to lend Harris
7,000 francs in Abyssinian money which was later repaid to
Rochet at Aden. (Rochet d'Hericourt, Charles E., SECOND
VOYAGE..., Paris, Bertrand, 1846, pp. 161-2.) The expedition left in January, 1843, for the coast.

In Shoa, d'Hericourt succeeded in convincing Sahle Selassie
to sign a treaty of friendship and commerce similar to the one
which had been signed with the English. Both treaties were
completely meaningless, however, as tribal feuds cut off all
chances of commerce. These disputes were an intensification
of the troubles which Harris had met with on his journey to
Shoa. At last, Sahle Selassie forbade the appearance of any
more Europeans in the country, and from 1843 Shoa became a
country again unknown to Europeans, until in the late 1870's
rumors of a remarkable young king of Shoa, Menelik by name,
began to be heard.

It might be well to review the events leading up to the expensive and abortive Harris expedition, for the facts behind it
are obscure and contradictory. The decision to undertake the
Shoa exploration was arrived at by the government of Bombay
on October 12, 1840. One week later, October 19, this same
Government refused Haines' request for an expedition to Lahej
to pacify the tribes and thus firmly establish the safety of the

settlement at Aden, as there was not sufficient money for such an undertaking. Not more than a month earlier, on hearing of the insults to the British flag at Mocha, Haines had been warned not to "involve us in any clash on Mocha. " Why then should such an expensive expedition be decided on? Nothing was known of Shoa except wild rumors and the few facts obtained from Krapf. Of the French explorers, only Combes and Tamisier had published the results of their travels, and this work had little information on Shoa.

The reason unquestionably lies in Anglo-French rivalry in the Indian Ocean. The stakes were very high, the domination of the southern waters of the world from the Cape of Good Hope to the South Pacific islands, and the game was played in the Foreign Offices of Paris and London as a grand chess game played on a map. It was the last appearance of the old imperialism of the eighteenth century which, essentially mercantilist in character, depended on the establishment of a line of bases from which effective raids could be made on the shipping lanes of the potential enemy. The main French base for this plan was the island of Bourbon (present day Réunion) returned to France by England after the Napoleonic wars. France had had renewed relations with Zanzibar in the summer of 1840, the small island of Nossi-Bé off the northeast coast of Madagascar was occupied in 1841, and French intrigues began in the Comorro Islands.

French intrigues in Tahiti also contributed to the uneasiness of the Bombay Government. These indications of French imperial expansion in a vast area of ocean dominated since 1815 by the British, combined with French imperial schemes nearer home, the Algerian campaigns and the diplomatic crisis over Muhammad Ali, created an apparent clash of interests, considered more seriously by London than by Bombay. In the vast area of the Indian Ocean, both British and French forces were spread very thin. The presence of one small vessel or, often, of one official, meant the predominance of national influence over a considerable area of land or ocean. Haines' manipulation of the tiny naval force at his disposal in the acquisition of the islands off Zeila and Tajura successfully forestalled the French in that area. Hamerton's appointment as political agent at Zanzibar early in 1840 successfully countered French influence there. But in Tahiti, the absence of Pritchard, the British agent in 1841, lost that island group to the French. Thus was the game played; ships and officials were the pawns.

In Abyssinia, both north and south, the alarums and excur-
sions of the various travelers and explorers had only one concrete result, the establishment of a Roman Catholic mission in
Tigré. This mission, established entirely by the adventure-
some spirit of two Frenchmen, was to play a large part in directing the policy of the French and British governments in
events which were to follow. Otherwise, these travels had no
results, not even the obvious one of showing to the British and
French Foreign Ministries the xenophobic nature of the Abyssinian ruling class. If they had only learned this lesson much
later effort and money would not have been wasted.

VIII. ADEN AND ARABIA 1843-1854

After the agreement to pay subsidies to the chiefs of the hinterland of Aden, in February, 1842, there continued to be minor manifestations of tribal hostility to the British. In a dispatch of May 31, 1842, Haines tried to analyze the basic difficulties in treating with the tribes. He explained that the Arabian petty chiefs were in constant communication with India, and that Sultan Mahsin of Lahej was convinced from private letters that the Bombay Government was powerless to punish him. Haines felt that the tribes interpreted the "apparent quietness to which the British submit to insults" as a sign of weakness and that "their ignorant minds cannot comprehend the power of British India though so close to Arabia, and nothing but ocular demonstration (in the trifling way requisite) will convince them that it is the lenity and consideration of a strong power for their ignorance, not weakness, that prevents a well merited chastisement being inflicted" (BSC 1842, Haines-Bombay 5/31/42). This quotation represents the attitude of Haines for the next few years. However, the Bombay Government would at no time sanction any sorties outside the walls of the settlement. As a result of this prohibition on active punitive measures, British prestige at Aden gradually declined as insult after insult went unpunished.

The greatest loss of prestige was incurred by the weakness of British policy towards the Sharif of Mocha. This, plus the restrictions imposed on the Resident by the order of the Indian Government on October 7, 1843, reduced the sphere of Haines' activity and caused the British to adopt a dangerous passivity in a land where "face" was a most important element in the maintenance of peaceful relations with the tribes. It is strange that the governments in India, an oriental country where "face" also was of foremost concern, could not see that the keeping of "face" was important in Arabia.

Haines therefore was forced to consolidate the gains which had been made in Aden by the use of imagination, diplomacy, and bluff. On January 29, 1843, the Sultan of Lahej had come in person to Aden to make peace, and negotiations were opened (BSC 1843, Haines-Bombay 2/3/43). A peace was made, subject to the approval of the Bombay Government. The stipend was to be restored and an indemnity paid to the heirs of Kateef, the former British Agent at Lahej (BSC 1843, Haines-Bombay 2/28/43). This information was forwarded by the Bombay Government to the government of India on March 16 (BSC 1843, Minute 3/16/43). Seven months later on October 27 the Bombay Government was still awaiting an answer. The tribes became restive in November, as no reply about the stipends was forthcoming, and threatened a concerted attack (BSC 1843, Haines-Bombay 11/29/43). However, this coalition did not last and the peace remained unbroken for the next two and a half years.

On December 15, 1844, the French war steamer "Crocodile," Captain Robin commanding, arrived at Aden from Mayotte, Bourbon, and Zanzibar with only five tons of coal. Captain Robin applied officially for 185 tons of coal in order to return to Mayotte, a request which Haines granted. The French commander, asked the reason for his trip to Aden, said that it was to investigate the Red Sea, since it was completely unknown to the French navy; he claimed that previous French ships which had appeared in the Red Sea had all been privately owned. Haines suspected, however, that a site for a naval base was being considered, especially as Captain Robin reported that the French commander in chief at Bourbon expected to visit Aden in February or March (BSC 1845 Haines-Bombay 12/20/44).

Haines' action in supplying coal was severely criticized by Governor Arthur of the Bombay Government, who wrote "we are not bound to aid these voyages of discovery on the part of a rival though friendly nation, " especially as the coal supply at Aden was limited and barely sufficient for the use of the Indian Government (BSC 1845, Minute by Governor Arthur 1/13/45). The rest of the board agreed with the Governor except for General MacMahon, who felt that Haines could not very well have refused this request although he should be instructed to refuse similar requests in the future (BSC 1845, Minute by MacMahon N. D.). The board agreed that it was a dangerous precedent, and that if similar demands were made by other ships the coal supply would be depleted, as it all had to be shipped by sail from England around the Cape of Good Hope and was thus very expensive. To make matters worse, the "Crocodile" was later seen along the south Arabian coast, near Mukalla, by H. M. brig "Serpent, " well away from the return course to Mayotte (BSC 1845, Haines-Bombay 12/30/44). It was fairly obvious then that a stop for coal at Aden was intentional and not fortuitous as Captain Robin had claimed.

The government of India on reviewing the incident instructed the Bombay Government that Haines should politely refuse other requests by French ships for coal as the supply was limited, but should make exceptions in the case of French ships driven to Aden by stress of weather or in actual danger due to lack of coal (BSC 1845, India-Bombay 2/8/45).

In March, 1845, the small French sloop of war "Zelée" arrived and its commander asked Haines, in the name of the governor of Bourbon, if French ships could always obtain coal at Aden. If this was impossible, he requested permission for the French to establish a coal depot there as it was the only good harbor at all seasons of the year. To this Haines replied that all the coal was owned by the government of India or the P. & O. Steamship Line, and added that he lacked the power to decide the question of the establishment of a French coal depot (BSC 1845, Haines-Secret Committee 3/11/45, and Haines-Bombay 3/12/45). Meanwhile Commodore Blackwood of H. M. S. "Fox" had reported to Bombay the presence of four French warships in the Red Sea and the intention of the French to make a geographical tour of the area (BSC 1845, Commodore Blackwood-Bombay 3/31/45). The government of India on receipt of this information felt that Haines was unwise to let the conversation get around to the matter of a coal depot, and requested him "not to enter upon such topics of conversation as are calculated to lead to inconvenient references to his own government" (BSC 1845, Govt. of India-Bombay 4/25/45). Haines was almost immediately placed in the same embarrassing position on April 19, 1845, by the arrival of the French steamer "Archimede" from China for Suez. The Captain demanded 285 tons of coal to get to Suez as he was carrying dispatches for the French Government. Haines refused, but was able to find some privately owned coal which the "Archimede" could purchase (BSC 1845, Haines-Bombay 4/20/45, and BSC 1845, Haines-Commodore Blackwood 7/28/45). The appearance of the "Archimede" at Aden was of considerable importance as she was the first French steamship officially to use the Suez route for communications with the East. As Haines had indicated in other reports, the route was used for travelers to Bourbon and was also unquestionably used by Frenchmen traveling to India on British vessels, but this was the first official use of the Red Sea route by any other nation than the English.

Reports filtered in from Egypt of French attempts to purchase either Massawa or Mocha from the Porte for bases in
the Red Sea, but these apparently had no foundation (BSC 1845,
Haines-Bombay 8/25/45, Haines-Bombay 11/26/45). In August,
1845, the Secret Committee in London wrote the government of
India regarding a French coal depot at Aden, "we are inclined
to think that the project should not meet with discouragement.
We see no objection to it (an opinion in which the Secretary of
State for Foreign Affairs coincides) and we should regard it as
an additional security for the tranquility of the Red Sea. It
may prevent the French from seeking to form a settlement elsewhere while it would place under our control the supply of fuel
for the steam vessels employed by them in those parts" (BSC
1845, India-Bombay 11/19/45 enclosing Secret Committee-In-
dia 8/15/45). The Governor General did not concur in this
opinion, believing that the refusal of a coal depot at Aden would
discourage any intention of the French to keep steamers for the
navigation of the Red Sea as the expense of operating their own
base would be immense (BSC 1845, India-Bombay 11/19/45,
enc. India Secret Committee 11/18/45). Haines was informed
that he was not to act on this letter of the Secret Committee
without orders from the Governor General (BSC 1845, Minute
12/15/45). In England, however, an agreement was made between the French Government and the Peninsular and Oriental
Steamship Company to supply coal (BSC 1846, Haines-Bombay
12/26/45). Upon receipt of this news the government of Bombay commented sourly "In effect by this arrangement, a coal
depot is given to the French at Aden" (BSC 1846, Minute 1/9/46).
        While Aden was flourishing (Haines reported that the new
town and fortifications were almost finished), (BSC 1845, Haines
-Secret Committee 11/10/45) news from other parts of the Red
Sea was not encouraging.
        In 1844, in the Yemen, Imam al-Hadi of San'a had died,
and was succeeded by the former Imam, Ali al-Mansur. The
new Imam's first action was to reconquer some of his territory
which had rebelled. He marched to Qa'taba and retired only
when revolution threatened at San'a. Sharif Husain of Abu
'Arish meanwhile prepared to attack the forces of the Imam.
(Playfair, R. L. , op. cit. , pp. 150-51.)   With fifteen to twenty
thousand troops he approached Ta'iz and proclaimed to the
tribes near Aden that he was authorized by the Porte to reconquer the southern Yemen. The defenses of Aden immediately

were put in readiness (BSC 1845, Haines-Bombay 1/31/45, Haines-Secret Committee 1/10/45 and 1/28/45), and the annual relief troops were dispatched from India before schedule as reinforcements (BSC 1845, Minutes by Board, 2/14/45 and 2/19/45). The threat to Aden evaporated after a few minor clashes inland, and the entire country from Ibb to San'a was left in a state of anarchy as the Sharif retired to Abu 'Arish (BSC 1845, Haines-Bombay 6/14/45). From this chaos, a new Imam was chosen at the end of 1845, one Sidi Cassim ibn Metwakeel, who was able to restore a semblance of government in the highlands (BSC 1845, Haines-Bombay 11/16/45).

Nor was the province of the Hedjaz more fortunate. On June 25, 1845, the Turkish governor, Osman Pasha, died suddenly. Under the governmental system of this Turkish province, the Pasha paid the expenses of his army from his own pocket out of the taxes he had collected. His sudden death removed any chance for the troops to collect their pay which was several years in arrears. The troops, therefore, resorted to looting. No caravans were safe and the province was reported to be in a state of anarchy (BSC 1845, Haines-Bombay 8/14/45).

To add to the troubles of southern Arabia, torrential rains visited the area early in May, 1846, followed by a vicious cholera epidemic throughout the Yemen and the Hadramaut. The rains caused severe damage in Aden, and the cholera epidemic, which at its height cost 100 lives in three days, brought death to 20 Europeans and 480 natives in the settlement (BSC 1846, Haines-Bombay, 5/8, 5/13, 5/31 and 6/15/46).

The cholera epidemic, the first in Arabia for ten years, brought Europe face to face with one of the most vexing problems presented by the use of the Red Sea route. All of the Mediterranean countries were rightfully terrified of this scourge which was constantly threatening the Far East and especially India. The use of the Cape route to India had successfully isolated Europe from contamination from the Far East, for the voyage was so long that the danger of epidemic was over long before a ship reached its first European landfall. The same situation was true on the run from Aden to India in 1846, where because of the inefficiency of the steam engine, sail was used as the chief means of propulsion. The trip from Aden to Suez was, however, usually made under power and was relatively brief, so that ships infected at Aden were still contagious on their arrival at Suez. As a result the Egyptian Government

forbade the debarkation of either passengers or freight at Suez
and for a considerable period the Suez-Indian service was discontinued.

This epidemic began a forty-six year period of negotiations
between all the European countries and Egypt and the Ottoman
Empire which finally resulted in the agreement in 1892 called
the Venice Convention, which established international quarantine restrictions for the Red Sea, by then Suez Canal, route.

The cholera epidemic had scarcely subsided when the whole
of the southwest corner of Arabia was disturbed in the summer
of 1846 by the appearance of a fanatic from Mecca named Sayud
Ismail. He had left the Holy City alone, preaching a "Holy
War" against the "Ferenghis, " and had acquired a group of dis-
ciples and dervishes on frequent stops on his way south. He
had received support from Sharif Husain of Abu 'Arish, who
was only too glad to help anyone dislodge the British. The first
news of this fanatic reached Aden on August 2. On the eighth,
Haines was informed that the Sayud was approaching Lahej with
a fighting force of 3,000 men, many of whom came from the
Asiri. On the eleventh, Sultan Mahsin of Lahej submitted to
the Sayud, and three days later abdicated in his favor. In the
face of this news, many of the Arab inhabitants of Aden fled to
the hinterland for fear of an attack (BSC 1846, Haines-Bombay
8/15/46). On August 15 caravans from the interior stopped arriving at Aden, and two days later an attack was made on the
British outposts which cost the Arabs six killed and seventeen
wounded (BSC 1846, Haines-Bombay 8/17/46).

Early in the morning of August 26 a force of 2,000 Arabs
attacked the walls of the settlement. After a sharp battle they
were driven off, with the loss of twenty-three killed and wounded.
The Sayud then announced his intention of besieging Aden. As
Aden with its dependence on provisions from the hinterland was
ill-prepared to withstand an extended siege, Haines requested
permission to conduct a campaign outside the walls when the
annual relief forces arrived and at the same time to conduct a
blockade of the Fadhli ports (BSC 1846, Haines-Bombay 8/30/
46). The Bombay Government sanctioned the blockade but informed Haines that, although they were in sympathy with an offensive beyond the walls, permission must be obtained from the
government of India for such an action (BSC 1846, Minute 9/9/46).

On August 28 the Arabs held a large meeting before the walls
of the town at which it was decided to launch an assault on

September 1. But, in typical tribal fashion, this threat suddenly evaporated. The Sayud and Sheikh Hyder ibn Maidi of Bir
Ahmed became embroiled in a violent argument as to the division of the loot which they had yet to gain. On September 1,
instead of an attack, caravans again came to the settlement
and the whole tribal army disappeared (BSC 1846, Haines-Bombay 9/15/46).

While this ended the immediate threat to Aden, it did not
restore friendly relations with the chiefs who had broken their
agreements with the British. Haines determined to punish the
Fadhli Sultan by blockading his port of Shuqra, as he had been
the leader in inducing the other chiefs to join the Sayud. On
October 4, after the tribes again had closed the roads, the
"Constance" was sent to blockade this tiny port. The roads
were reopened almost immediately and the Aqrabi chief quickly
came to terms (BSC 1846, Haines-Bombay 10/15/46). Eco-
nomics had proved a more potent force than fanaticism, for in
a month over 200,000 rupees worth of exports, mostly fresh
produce, had been held up in Lahej by the blockade, and the
chiefs, especially the Sultan of Lahej, were beginning to get repercussions from the landowners. On November 4 the Fadhli
Sultan asked for a truce and ten days later peace was made with
him (BSC 1846, Haines-Bombay 11/15/46). On the twenty-third
Mahsin of Lahej asked for peace terms and agreed to a truce
(BSC 1846, Haines-Bombay 11/25/46).

As the Sultan of Lahej controlled most of the caravan routes
into Aden, his defection was a very serious matter and suitable
punishment had to be determined. The government of India decided to withhold his pension until a period of good behavior had
passed (BSC 1847, Govt. of India-Bombay 1/25/47). The pension was restored in November, 1847, but the aged Sultan died
on the twenty-ninth of that month and the question remained
open until a successor could be appointed (BSC 1847, Haines-
Bombay 11/30/47).

Sayud Ismail, having lost his hold on the tribes around
Aden, now looked to other sources for aid against the British.
He appealed to the Imam of San'a for support without success.
The Imam, who was friendly to the British and completely penniless, dismissed the Sayud's petition by asking him "why a
man possessed of supernatural power should rely on earthly
assistance so entirely" (BSC 1847, Haines-Bombay 12/18/46).
With this answer the Sayud vanished quietly into the obscurity
of central Arabia.

This incident marked clearly the existence of certain essential trends in south Arabia. First and most obviously it showed the unstable nature of the existing tribal governments and the ability of any mountebank to stir up a religious war which would at the same time provide plenty of booty. Second, and more important, it emphasized the rivalry between the Sharif of Abu 'Arish and the Imam of San'a, the anti-British convictions of the former and the pro-British sentiments of the latter. The motives behind both men were similar; they were economic. If the Sharif controlled Aden, he controlled all outlets of the profitable coffee trade. If the British controlled Aden, the Imam had available a free port to export his most valuable product.

After a long period of argument regarding the defenses of Aden, some conclusions emerged in 1846 in a Minute by the Governor General of India dated September 30. This report, inspired by Sayud Ismail's threat to the settlement, envisaged the establishment of Aden as a fortified town. The Governor General, Lord Hardinge, advocated a garrison of 1,700 men, 200 of whom were to be detailed for coastal defense work. He suggested that it might be advisable to limit the population, now upward of 20,000, to the available water supply, and completely reorient the town, concentrating the buildings in one place and abolishing the western suburban trading center, thus making a clearing 1,000 feet wide between the walls and the town. The question of limiting the population of the town was difficult, but the Governor General felt that the desertion of the town by many of the Arabs at the approach of the Fakir Sayud Ismail showed that the people were untrustworthy from the military point of view. On the other hand, his Lordship believed that the plan of some of the extremists for seaward fortifications employing 2,000 gunners and an additional garrison of 2,000 more was ridiculous as it would make the total garrison 5,700, larger than the English force needed to defend the whole island of Ceylon (BSC 1846, Minute by Governor General 9/30/46).

The more extreme policies were not carried out for lack of funds. The garrison was established at a maximum of 1,700, but it is manifest that no definite policy had been arrived at as to the future disposition of Aden. As his dispatches testify, Haines was thoroughly convinced that Aden's future lay in its re-establishment as the pre-eminent trading port in that part of the world, a position which Aden had occupied until the opening of the Cape route to India in the sixteenth century. As we have seen, some officials in India looked upon it as a coal depot, others as a fortified spot to protect the route via Suez. As a result of these conflicting viewpoints no really sustained effort was made to direct the growth of Aden in any direction for many years, and it was not until the Abyssinian campaign of 1868 and the encroachment of the Turks and Egyptians into Aden's sphere of influence that any consistent policy was assumed.

The tribes remained friendly towards the settlement throughout 1847, though disturbances between the Urgli and Abdali occasionally threatened to upset the hinterland. In February, 1847, Haines felt it necessary to send his assistant, Lieutenant Cruttenden, to the Somali coast to settle the differences which for two years had caused the annual Berbera fair to be split between Berbera and Bulhar, an open roadstead about thirty miles to the west. This discord was a serious threat to Aden as the Berbera fair supplied Aden with its meat during the hot season in the form of live sheep. Also the Banyan merchants conducted a huge trade at the fair and any disturbance usually meant indiscriminate piracy by the disgruntled parties. In addition to visiting Berbera, Cruttenden was instructed to inspect the whole Hadramaut coast and the island of Socotra, which the French were reported to have surveyed very accurately (BSC 1847, Haines-Bombay 2/9/47).

Cruttenden returned on April 20 with the gratifying news that he had been able to settle the difference between the tribes at Berbera, and he hoped that a permanent peace would be established. In exploring along the coast Cruttenden had found but one suitable harbor for a coaling station, at Ras Hafun, about 150 miles south of Cape Guardafui. Socotra was found to be almost deserted. Fever had killed many people and most of those remaining had died during a severe famine in 1844. All evidences of the short British occupation in 1835 had disappeared except for about 100 tons of coal. On the other hand the whole district of the Somali coast was prospering due to the temporary abolition of the slave trade in Zanzibar which forced the traders to come to Tajura and Berbera with their human commodities. Cruttenden also reported that a French survey of the Somali coast and Socotra had been made early in 1847, in connection with Captain Guillain's intrigues on the east African coast during which he had attempted to undermine Britain's predominant position at Zanzibar. The Hadramaut coast also was peaceful and the British had been well received at both Mu-kalla and Shihr (BSC 1847, Cruttenden-Haines 4/20/47 encl. in Haines-Bombay 4/27/47).

Meanwhile, in Bombay, discussions continued as to the future status of Aden. In February, 1847, Haines was requested to make an accurate census of the population and to investigate ways of increasing the water supply. Further rules were laid down for the guidance of the Resident: No persons other than subjects of His Majesty or the B. E. I. C. or residents of Aden were to be allowed in the town without the permission of the Resident who was given authority to expel any one who had not obtained that permission, proper indulgence being used in cases where bona fide trade was an object. No aliens were to be allowed in the police force except unusually talented individuals and the police were forbidden to participate in trade. The Political Agent was to have charge of all licensing and to give preference to British subjects if possible. The Assistant Political Agent was to try all minor suits, enforce public health regulations, and inspect tenements (his duties already included Postmaster, tax collector, judge and a few other rather important positions) (BSC 1847, Minute enclosed in India-Bombay 2/11/47). Haines replied in April that he had been trying to get an accurate census of the population but that the natives moved around so much it was almost impossible (BSC 1847, Haines-Bombay 4/15/47).

In July, 1847, further discussions as to the future of Aden took place in Bombay. The Governor, Sir George Clerk, wrote on July 10 that it would be an excellent idea to put Aden under a governor. "It would tend to render our dominion in that important position secure, to improve our means of availing ourselves of the resources of the neighbouring countries, whether dependent upon them as now in a small degree or as may hereafter happen, requiring their cooperation to a greater extent, and restore to that port the considerable trade of which it was formerly the emporium.

"I conclude that the occasion would be taken. . . . to declare the Peninsula of Aden to be a British Possession" (BSC 1847, Minute by Governor 7/10/47). Secretary Reid concurred and pointed out that the powers of the present Resident were limited and constant delays were incurred by the necessity of referring to India for authority to act (BSC 1847, Minute by Mr. Reid 7/20/47). Mr. Willoughby brought up the dissension which had

arisen between Haines and the military in relation to the new
fortifications. He felt that Haines was "a zealous and in some
respects able officer" and did not wish to see measures taken
which would "bear hard on a meritorious officer" and "deprive
the Government of his great local experience and knowledge."
A governorship was deemed too important for Aden and any
such position would mean a higher salary than its importance
warranted. Any change, he felt, should be made with a minimum of publicity, "our possession of that settlement being
viewed by France and probably by other European powers with
the eye of jealousy and envy." However, Willoughby felt that
it was most important that, whatever was decided, the official
in charge of the settlement should have his powers more accurately defined (BSC 1847, Minute by Willoughby 7/22/47).

The Board agreed on July 23 that, in any case, Aden should
be declared a British possession (BSC 1847, Minute by Board
7/23/47). There is no evidence to show that any of the various
suggestions ever reached Aden. The entire matter was apparently sidetracked and no more mention is made of any plans for
the development of the settlement.

In Aden, after a series of discussions beginning in February, 1848, a treaty was arranged with the new Sultan of Lahej,
Ahmed Mahsin. He arrived in Aden on February 29 and remained there until March 8. Haines could not convince him to
lower his transit duties, but the Sultan readily accepted an
article of treaty designed to promote the growth of vegetables.
The Sultan requested the inclusion of five other articles. First
he wished to build a house in Aden. As the Political Office, and
certain other buildings used officially, had formerly belonged
to the Sultan of Lahej, Haines suggested that the government
might build one for him at a cost of not more than 10,000 rupees.
Second, the Sultan requested the loan of native surveyors by the
Aden government to build a small fort at Lahej, the Sultan to
pay all expenses. Third, the Sultan requested that all stipend
money except that for the Fadhli chief be given to him to distribute as it would give him more power to keep the roads open.
Haines recommended this. Fourth, the Sultan desired six
twelve-pounders with shot and powder. Fifth, the Sultan wished
to place himself under the protection of the British Government.
This amounted virtually to an offensive and defensive alliance.
The remainder of the treaty was the normal one of friendship
and commerce (BSC 1848, Haines-Bombay 3/12/48).

Sir George Clerk thought the proposed treaty very satisfactory. He accepted the first three extra articles, felt that
the fourth should be declined and that the fifth should wait for
a further promise of good behavior (BSC 1848, Minute by Governor 4/4/48). Mr. Willoughby objected to the first article,
felt the third gave too much power to the Sultan of Lahej and
made a very sage comment on article five, "our relations at
Aden seem to me to depend as much on contingencies in Europe
as in India" (BSC 1848, Minute by Mr. Willoughby 4/7/48). The
Indian Government approved the main body of the treaty and disposed of the requests of the Sultan by accepting the second and
third articles, refusing the first and fourth, and referring the
fifth to the Home Authorities (BSC 1848, Govt. of India-Bombay
5/6/48).

The treaty was put in force immediately. The third request of Sultan Ahmed, which was accepted by the Indian Government and incorporated into the new treaty, marked a new
method in dealing with the tribes. It was requested by Ahmed
probably to increase his own prestige but it simplified many of
the Resident's problems. By giving Ahmed the right to distribute the stipend money to all the chiefs but the Fadhli, Haines
was able to place the responsibility for keeping the roads open
on one man. While this was a change in British policy, it was
not new to the tribes, for this method had been used by the
Sultans of Lahej before the British occupation.

Trouble on the Somali coast recommenced, upsetting the
Berbera fair and Aden's all-important food supply. Cruttenden
was sent over to Berbera again in the fall of 1847. Two tribes
owned the fair grounds equally, the Ayal Ahmeds and the Ayal
Yunis. At some previous time the Ayal Ahmeds had built a fortified tower on the site of the fair (which was uninhabited except
during the fair period). Possession of this tower naturally gave
the Ayal Ahmeds mastery of the fair grounds and caused friction between the tribes. Cruttenden settled the argument by ordering the tower razed, and this time it was hoped that the
source of the trouble had been found and corrected. The continual tribal strife had damaged trade and it was feared that the
usual supply of meat for Aden might not be forthcoming. A
serious situation had also arisen due to the seizure of slave
ships belonging to tribes which did not have slave trade treaties
with the English. This amounted to piracy on the part of the
British ships (BSC 1848, Cruttenden-Haines 11/24/47, encl. in
Haines-Bombay 11/27/47).

Haines sent Cruttenden for the third time to Berbera on
January 4, 1848, to observe conditions at the fair and to report
on the state of the Somali coast (BSC 1848, Haines-Bombay
1/5/48). Cruttenden, after forwarding a report from Berbera
cautioning the Banyan traders against using the open roadstead
at Bulhar because of tribal raids, filed his full report on his
return in April. He found the fair progressing very well except
that a prolonged drought had made ghee almost unobtainable.
He also reported that chaotic conditions inland had prevented
any caravans from Shoa from getting through to the coast. Leaving Berbera on January 19, he sailed eastwards and stopped at
Las Khoreh, about 350 miles east of Berbera, a capital of the
Al Ursugli tribe. Cruttenden found this tribe more civilized
than the others on the Somali coast. After exploring a considerable part of the country and a mountain range two days' inland (the Al Mountains) he left on February 7 for Ras Hafun,
where he learned that a French offer to purchase the port had
been rejected. The offer had amounted to $6,000, and after its
refusal the French had been forced away only by the threat of
an attack. Cruttenden was skeptical of all the details as "the
Somalis are impressed with the idea that a bitter and endless
feud exists between the English and the French nations and thus
by way of ingratiating themselves, do not scruple to (at least)
highly exaggerate the proceedings of these surveying vessels."
He, however, satisfied himself that an offer actually had been
made and rejected. At Ras Hafun, Cruttenden found that the
water on the promontory was fit for drinking but that the prices
of provisions were exorbitant. The anchorage was fair, but not
the best, especially during the southwest monsoon. The trade
consisted of bartering ostrich feathers, ivory, ambergris, and
gums for dates and rice. The place had one very real disad-
vantage, a penetrating stench caused by rotting vegetable matter thrown up on the shore. Returning to Berbera, he found
the fair still going very well. The loss of two boats in a storm
at Bulhar had caused the few dissenting members of the tribes
to return to Berbera, and caravans had finally come from
Harar and Shoa after fighting their way through the Dankali
tribes above Tajura, the same tribes with which Captain Harris
had had so much trouble. At Berbera, Cruttenden heard of the
details of the death of Sahle Selassie and the revolt which followed. Conditions in Shoa were reportedly chaotic (BSC 1848,
Cruttenden-Haines 4/4/48, enc. in Haines-Bombay 4/5/48).

In June, 1847, word reached Aden that the Ottoman Government was about to take over Mocha and Hodeida, and that Massawa had changed hands. Reports of Turkish interference in the Yemen induced the Imam of San'a to attack his old enemy Sharif Husain early in 1848. For a year a desultory campaign ensued which impoverished both adversaries and dealt the death blow to the trade from the interior through Mocha. The absence of any strong force in the Yemen provided an irresistible invitation to the outsider and the Turkish Government was soon to take advantage of this chaos.

In April, 1849, reports of a definite Ottoman re-occupation of the seaport towns reached Aden. On April 19 three ships and several buggalows loaded with Turkish troops reached Hodeida simultaneously with the appearance of an Arab force of Sharif Ibn 'Aun of Mecca on the landward side of the town. The town refused to yield and some skirmishes occurred. However, no concerted attack took place because Sharif Abdallah al Siraf, son of Ibn 'Aun, in command of the Arabs from Mecca, claimed that the Porte had appointed him Governor of Hodeida while Teufik Pasha, commander of the Turkish ships, claimed that he was the appointed representative of the Porte. Sharif Ibn 'Aun was able to settle the difficulty by obtaining an agreement whereby Teufik Pasha took control of Hodeida, Beit Faqi and Sanif while Sharif Abdallah took Mocha, Zabid, Hes and Musa. Teufik Pasha was reportedly a former secretary of the late Osman Pasha of Jidda. He had obtained his influence in Constantinople by efficient espionage on his master, and had been sent "to arrange the affairs of the Yemen and to punish Sharif Husain" (BSC 1849, Haines-Bombay 6/13/49, also in FO 1/5).

Both Teufik and Sharif Abdallah agreed to pay 100,000 crowns a year to the Porte in return for which they were to be given 1,000 infantry and 300 cavalry whose expenses were to be met out of remaining revenues. Haines estimated their expenses as follows: 100,000 crowns tribute; salary of infantry 1,000 men at 5 crowns a month, 60,000 crowns; 300 cavalry at 10 crowns per month for men and horses, 36,000 crowns; 2,000 Arab matchlock men at 4 crowns per month, 96,000 crowns; 3,750 crowns per month to Sharif Husain to pay him for evacuating the towns, 45,000 crowns per year; expenses of private and public establishments of the government, 80,000 crowns; a grand total of 417,000 crowns per year. In previous years, this figure might have been met. Hodeida under Husain's special protection had 100,000 crowns yearly in customs dues alone, but the various exactions of Husain's regime had ruined the trade of the towns. In Mocha but one merchant remained and four-fifths of the houses were in a state of ruin. Haines estimated the present revenue of all of the towns of the Tehama at not more than 200,000 crowns a year, leaving an annual deficit of 217,000 crowns. He predicted that first the new governors would let the tribute to the Porte go into arrears, then the pay of the troops. Levies in the form of forced loans would be made on the merchants with promises to allow deductions from the duties to stop complaints. The customs would be farmed out to remove the odium of taxes from the government, and between the exactions of the tax farmers and the bribes to get complaints tried in the Turkish Civil Courts the merchants would be ruined. As an indication, complaints already were reaching Aden that the five per cent duties, mandatory under the British-Ottoman Commercial Treaty of 1838, were not being adhered to and that the pre-treaty scale of duties was being enforced. If the protests, which Haines had already forwarded to the Consul General in Egypt, were heeded, he predicted that the duties would be reduced but that other exactions such as tonnage dues, etc., would be added as at Jidda, thus actually doubling the revenue. The hill tribes, now under the Imam of San'a, would thus be forced to send their trade through Aden.

Haines' predictions were soon realized. The duties levied at the port of Hodeida were raised to ten per cent ad valorem on cloth, twenty-five per cent on tobacco, twelve per cent on iron, sixteen per cent on lead, fifteen per cent on spices and one-half crown per bag of rice. At Mocha the duties were about half of this, but all merchants were compelled to pay additional duties on goods shipped from port to port; thus a merchant might have to pay duties both at Mocha and Hodeida on the same goods (BSC 1849, Haines-Bombay 6/13/49; and FO 1/5 IB-FO 7/31/49 encl. Haines-Bombay 6/13/49).

This state of affairs caused Governor Falkland to call the special attention of the Secret Committee "to the declining state of British commerce in the Ports of the Red Sea, and its probable utter ruin, if measures are not speedily adopted to secure that only those duties which are stipulated for in our treaty with the Porte are levied" (BSC 1849, Minute by Governor 7/5/49).

That the Turks were not going to be content to limit themselves to the seaport towns was indicated by immediate demands on the Imam of San'a, the mountain tribes, and the ports of Mukalla and Shihr in the Hadramaut to yield to Turkish power. These orders were refused.

A month later, reliable information reached Aden that the Imam of San'a had been offered a monthly salary if he would turn over his territory to the Porte (BSC 1849, Haines-Bombay 7/17/49). On August 21, 1849, the Imam went to Hodeida with Teufik Pasha and Ibn 'Aun, who had gone to meet him, and was presented the next day with the Order of the Crescent in diamonds, a dress of honor, a rich sword and dagger, and three horses. An agreement was soon reached. First, the country of the Imam was to stay under his rule, but was to be considered a territory of the Porte. Second, the resources were divided, one-half to go to the Imam personally, one-half to be used to rule the country aided by 1,000 Turkish infantry. Third, the Imam should receive 3,700 crowns a month for personal expenses, this payment having precedence over any claim of the Porte. Haines believed that Teufik was just asking for trouble, for Ibrahim Pasha with 10,000 trained men had been unable to control the tribes of the Yemen. There was also a considerable religious barrier as the mountain tribes were of the Zaidee sect (moderate Shi'ites) while the Turks were, of course, Sunnites. Furthermore each tribe had its own leader and was a political entity, and while subject to the general control of the Imam, considered itself an independent unit which had to be consulted in making such an agreement. Haines was convinced that the Imam took this course only to get a 25,000 crown bribe, 17,000 crowns of which was levied on the merchants to be repaid from the customs accounts. The Turks had no effective way to enforce any agreements and their plans to concentrate the trade of the interior at Mocha and Hodeida, Haines felt, was bound to be resisted with force (BSC 1849, Haines-Bombay 7/27/49 and FO 78/3185, IB-FO 8/31/49). In July, 1849, Teufik marched with 200 men to San'a, and on the first Friday he was there ordered Turkish forms of prayer to be used (Orthodox Sunni) in the mosques, and Sultan Abdul Mejid's name to be introduced into the service. This was too much for the Zaidees, who massacred all the Turks except for Teufik and a few men who were saved by the Imam. Sharif Ibn 'Aun immediately started to march on San'a but departed with neither a full treasury nor a good commissariat, and was apparently headed for disaster (BSC 1849, Haines-Bombay 8/27/49).

However, this warlike move was unnecessary as Teufik was
freed by the Imam after paying 24,000 crowns ransom (BSC
1849, Haines-Bombay 9/18/49).

In spite of the disturbances in the Yemen, the surroundings
of Aden were peaceful during the year of 1849. In December,
1848, a serious epidemic of smallpox had broken out in the
hinterland, which attacked, among others, the Sultan of Lahej
and three of his brothers (BSC 1849, Haines-Bombay 12/47/48).
The Sultan died almost immediately and his brother Ali-ibn
Mahsin was elected. He was a young man of twenty-nine and a
great favorite with the tribe (BSC 1849, Haines-Bombay 1/28/
49). The British speedily made a new treaty with him in the
identical terms of the one with his brother, and he was paid his
subsidy. The epidemic allowed the British to show their friendliness, as Surgeon Vaughan at his own expense went inland and
was able to vaccinate a few of the Arabs. At the same time,
through the local merchants, arrangements were made with
Sultan Ali of Lahej to supply water for the town (BSC 1849,
Haines-Bombay 5/25/49).

In the Yemen the Imam of San'a did not enjoy his independence for long. Early in December, 1849, he was murdered by
his guards after ordering the execution of his uncle and his
nephew, heir to the Imamate. This resulted in the country a-
round San'a being thrown into an uproar. The roads to Hodeida
and Mocha were closed by the mountain tribes with the usual
object of gaining booty (BSC 1850, Haines-Bombay 12/27/49,
1/15/50, 4/14/50).

The ports under Turkish control suffered at the same time
by the death of Teufik Pasha at the end of March, 1850. Shortly
before his death he had made heavy levies on Mocha and the
interior villages, which resulted in an increase in transit duties
at these places to meet his demands (BSC 1850, Haines-Bombay 4/14/50). In Mocha alone the transit dues from the interior
were raised to twelve per cent ad valorem, which, of course,
resulted in the diversion of more trade to Aden (BSC 1850,
Haines-Bombay 4/28/50).

Sharif Abdallah Pasha, former governor of Mocha, was appointed the new governor of Hodeida, and immediately organized
a force to capture Mukalla and Shihr. This force consisted of
300 regulars and 400 to 500 other armed men to be transported
in an antique warship, two war Zebehs, and four buggalows.
Haines reported that the Arabs of the Hadramaut had dropped

their differences to unite against this danger, and predicted
disaster for the Turks (BSC 1850, Haines-Bombay 5/13/50).
Abdallah's force passed Aden on July 8 and was defeated about
a month later in a sea battle; most of the survivors were massacred at the town of Rhaima (Ras Rahmat?) by the inhabitants
(BSC 1850, Haines-Bombay 8/15/50). A few Turks regained
their ships and the remnants of the expedition returned to
Mocha after losing all its guns, ammunition, and supplies.

At Aden the tranquility was broken on May 29, 1850, by
news of a murder at Bir Ahmed. An unarmed boat from the
"Auckland" had been fired on without provocation by the tribesmen, killing a sailor and wounding a boy. Haines felt that
Sheikh Hyder ibn Maidi should be removed from office for this
offence, but decided to turn the matter over to his overlord the
Sultan of Lahej (BSC 1850, Haines-Bombay 6/12/50). The
Sultan promised to produce the criminal and prepared a force
to seize Bir Ahmed. By the end of the year nothing had been
done, but finally on January 4, 1851, a force of 3,000 men under Sultan Ali of Lahej attacked Bir Ahmed and as preparations
were being made to bombard the fortified castle there, the
Sheikh surrendered. Sultan Ali then requested Haines' advice.
Haines told him to allow the mercantile and other unoffending
elements to return home after swearing allegiance to Sultan
Ali, to destroy the castle, to prohibit the erection of any fortified spot there, and to keep Sheikh Hyder captive at Lahej until
the murderer of the sailor had been apprehended. Sultan Ali
replied on January 12 that he would try to comply with these
wishes (BSC 1851, Haines-Bombay 1/14/51).

Intrigue and then a serious illness of Sultan Ali prevented
the murderer of the sailor from being turned over to the English. At the end of February, 1851, Sultan Ali requested the
presence of Lieutenant Cruttenden. At the same time the Lieutenant gave a group of officers permission to go bustard shoot-
ing near Lahej. They left for that town on February 28. In
Lahej, Cruttenden discussed the question of the murder with the
sick Sultan and was informed by him that the only chance of producing the murderer of the British sailor was by blockading
Bir Ahmed (BSC 1851, Haines-Bombay 3/10/51 and Cruttenden-Haines 3/5/51).

On March 3, Cruttenden returned to Aden, leaving the
other officers to their hunting. Almost immediately after Cruttenden's arrival at Aden a messenger appeared requesting a

doctor for the party of hunters. After leaving Cruttenden on
March 2, the group of officers with their guards had gone to
Wahut, where they were given a house as guests of the Sultan.
Captain J. D. Milne retired early, after giving some money to
the children of the house. The rest of the party, having been
received very kindly, dismissed their personal guards and sat
up talking. About one o'clock they heard some shrieks from
Milne and saw his assassin rush out. This gentleman was a
holy man, Sayud Muhammad Husain by name. On the arrival
of the British officers he had objected violently to having infidels staying so close to his home, but his anger had appeared
momentary and nothing more had been thought about it. The
assassin, after inflicting slight wounds on two other officers,
escaped to the Haushabi country. Here the chief forced him to
leave and he received sanctuary in the country of the Fadhlis,
barely escaping a posse sent out by Sultan Ali to intercept him.
Sultan Ali secured Sayud Muhammad Husain's relatives as hostages and sent twelve Sayuds to the Fadhli country to try to
catch the fugitive.

Haines felt that the question of punishment was difficult.
Any measures against the Fadhlis if they persisted in giving
sanctuary to the assassin would only serve to stop the caravans
and tie up trade. Sultan Ali of Lahej was certainly blameless
as this breach of Arab hospitality was a disgrace to his tribe.
Haines suggested that the castle at Bir Ahmed be destroyed
and every house at Wahut — a small village — be torn down except for the Mosque, as an example to the fanatics who "only
understand brute courage and force of arms" (BSC 1851, Haines
-Bombay 3/13/41). Such a punishment could easily be carried
out by the forces of the garrison in about twelve hours.

Cruttenden, who left for Bombay immediately after the
murder of Captain Milne, discussed the outrage with the Bombay Government. In a memorandum of March 31, he acquitted
Sultan Ali of any blame in the matter, but recommended that
steps should be taken to prevent a recurrence of such lawless-
ness. He advised that all stipends should be stopped until the
murderers of both the sailor and Captain Milne were surrendered and that the Sultan destroy Wahut and the castle at Bir
Ahmed (BSC 1851, Memo by Cruttenden 3/31/51). Governor
Falkland felt that Haines had not been remiss in allowing the
officers to go inland, but that they had been unwise in dismissing their guards. Furthermore, he did not wish to sanction an

expedition inland and thus give the matter a political complexion which he felt it did not have (BSC 1851, Minute by Falkland 3/30/51).

Another assassination was attempted, this time inside Aden. Mr. Lessus, an officer, succeeded in killing his assailant, however, and the body was hung from the gate at Aden in chains (BSC 1851, Haines-Bombay 3/27/51).

The Governor General of India advised the Bombay Government that the Sultan of Lahej should seize and execute the murderer of Captain Milne. If this was not done within a reasonable time, then all friendly intercourse should cease and further measures could then be considered (BSC 1851, Govt. of India-Bombay 4/21/41).

On the basis of these assassinations, Haines pressed again for the establishment of a mounted police force inside Aden. At the same time, steps were taken to examine all people entering Aden; examinations were conducted at the Barrier Gate and again at the Main Gate. Passes were issued requiring the entering Arab to leave by three o'clock in the afternoon, and the carrying of arms was prohibited except by Sultan Ali, his family, or his official agents (BSC 1851, Haines-Bombay 4/6/51).

The tribes remained quiet, however, and supplies continued plentiful. Haines believed that the only result of stopping Sultan Ali's stipend would be to close the roads. The Fadhli Sultan, who was shielding Captain Milne's murderer, gave evidence of wishing his stipend stopped as he could then plunder the caravans. In such event, Haines suggested that Shuqra, Asala and Gab Walleh, his three villages, be destroyed (BSC 1851, Haines-Bombay 5/9/51). The Bombay Government ordered the Fadhli Sultan's stipend stopped regardless of the consequences (BSC 1851, Minute 5/29/51).

Sultan Ali meanwhile sent one of Sayud Muhammad Husain's relatives to Aden as a hostage on May 12 and reported that he was trying to get hold of one of the family of Boghi, assassin of the sailor, for the same purpose (BSC 1851, Haines-Bombay 5/15/51).

The government of India on June 10 sanctioned the use of force if the assassin was not produced (BSC 1851, Govt. of India-Bombay 6/10/51). Haines was instructed to use his own judgment but was advised that he could get no re-inforcements for at least two months (BSC 1851, Bombay-Haines 6/28/51). Unseasonably hot weather prevented any expedition's being undertaken immediately, though Sultan Ali advised Haines that war was the only way in which the assassin could be brought to justice (BSC 1851, Haines-Bombay 7/24/51).

The wreck of the "Sons of Commerce," a coal brig, near Aden, resulted in another outrage, the death of two sailors and a subsequent plundering of the hulk. The "Elphinstone's" cutter was fired on when she went to rescue the survivors but luckily no one was injured (BSC 1851, Haines-Bombay 7/19/51).

Inside the tribes the political situation rising from Captain Milne's murder had become so intense that Sultan Ali informed Haines on August 10 that he could not trust his tribe to aid the English in a punitive expedition against the Fadhli. Further internal dissensions prevented Haines from using the pressure of the outlying tribes, the Yaffai and Urglis, against the Fadhli. Haines suggested that a punitive expedition go out to destroy the fort at Bir Ahmed and the assassin's house at Wahut, carefully avoiding any damage to the crops which were essential to Aden's welfare (BSC 1851, Haines-Bombay 8/11/51).

Governor Falkland then wavered in his desire for an expedition as he did not feel that "diplomatic means had been exhausted" (BSC 1851, Minute by Falkland 8/26/51). He did, however, advocate an increase in the Aden garrison, but was overruled on this point by the commander in chief of the Bombay forces.

Haines meanwhile considered delivering an ultimatum to Sultan Ali to produce the murderers, although he doubted if Captain Milne's assassin would ever be given up as he was of too high a caste (BSC 1851, Haines-Bombay 8/25).

All plans for an expedition were halted by orders from the Secret Committee in London which decreed that no measure more severe than stoppage of stipends was to be undertaken except under "circumstances of extreme necessity." The Governor General considered from the tone of the letter of the Secret Committee "that they do not consider the Chief's refusal to give up or punish the murderer of a British officer to constitute the necessity which would justify hostilities." The Governor General went on to say, "His Lordship apprehends that the stoppage of the chief's stipend will be just sufficient punishment to exasperate him to further violence rather than deter him from future offenses.... Nevertheless the orders of the Honourable the Secret Committee are to be obeyed" (BSC 1851, Govt. of India-Bombay 9/29/51).

One of the murderers of the seamen of the "Sons of Commerce" was seized by Sultan Ali and publicly executed in Lahej
on October 20, 1851. The Sheikh at Bir Ahmed exultantly
seized two of Boghi's innocent relatives and was about to execute them when Haines intervened (BSC 1851, Haines-Bombay
10/27/51). The countryside remained quiet for the rest of the
year and Haines, restricted by the orders of the Secret Committee, could do little towards bringing the assassins to justice.
    In Arabia, the Turks continued to try to expand their influ-
ence. Sanif, inland from Hodeida, was captured in January,
1851 (BSC 1851, Haines-Bombay 1/27/51), and further advances
were made in February with the object of forcing trade from
the coffee country to the ports of Mocha and Hodeida rather than
Aden. Haines felt that the Turks would run into difficulties as
they were dealing with a "crafty and deceitful population" of a
different sect, and pointed out as an example the death of the
self-styled "Governor of the Yemen," Mustafa Subri Pasha, who
died suddenly while he was guest of Sheikh Ali Homieda under
rather suspicious circumstances; the Arabs said "The coffee
disagreed with him" (BSC 1851, Haines-Bombay 2/14/51). Suspicion also surrounded the death of the Sharif of Abu 'Arish,
Husain bin Ali Hydra, the life-long foe of the British, who "died
suddenly" at Mocha in March on his way to see the Turkish
Pasha to protest the non-payment of his monthly salary (BSC
1851, Haines-Bombay 3/15/51).
    Reports came to Aden from Jidda of a serious incident
there. Mr. Ogilvie was the consul at this port, appointed by
the East India Company with the consent of the Foreign Office
but responsible to the Consul General at Constantinople, a curious arrangement surviving from the days when the Red Sea was
the trading monopoly of the East India Company. From 1845
to November, 1849, no British war vessel had appeared at Jidda,
and Ogilvie was left to his own devices. Ogilvie had many complaints about the government of Jidda, which was being ruled by
a servant of Hasyb Pasha. The Pasha himself spent most of
his time at Mecca and was to all intents and purposes inaccessible, leaving Jidda to the kind ministrations of his servant who
was responsible to no one, much less the Porte. Ogilvie complained of excessive duties, but the chief issue at the moment
was the indemnity for the seizure of the buggalow "Scythia" by
the Turks two years before. Saunders, in command of the "Elphinstone" which had investigated the seizure, could see no

reason why Ogilvie had made no effort to collect the amount
from the Turkish government, as they had admitted the claim
(FO 78/840, #15 Gilbert [acting Consul General Alexandria]-
FO 5/31/50, encl. Ogilvie-Saunders 3/15/50, Saunders-Ogil-
vie 3/19/50). Other charges of extortion were mentioned showing violations of the commercial treaty, excessive valuations,
large sums of money owed to merchants by the Turkish government which had been withheld, the usual forced loans, etc.

Palmerston sent instructions for Canning, British Ambassador at Constantinople, to make a protest, saying "That H. M.
Govt. cannot any longer tolerate the continuance of these vexa-
tious Abuses & that if the Porte cannot apply a corrective Remedy the British Govt. must take such steps as the Circumstances of the Case may require in order to protect British Subjects from further Vexation and to obtain for them just Redress
for the Injuries which they have hitherto received. " He added,
"I understand Mr. Ogilvie to be a Person appointed by the East
India Company & therefore if they are dissatisfied with him they
have the Remedy in their own Hands" (FO 78/840, Minute by
Palmerston on Gilbert-FO 5/31/50).

As nothing was done about these complaints, Palmerston
became annoyed, but there was little he could do as Ogilvie was
not responsible to him. The Turks reshuffled all the officials
in the Red Sea; Aga Pasha replaced Hasyb and was immediately
marooned by an outbreak of the plague at Mecca. Haines
summed the matter up in three points: first, that the Turkish
authorities in the Hedjaz needed money so badly that they would
not obey orders; second, the British Vice-Consul had not the
power and respect he should have had, nor did he appear to try
to enforce justice; third, the Vice-Consul had made no real effort to see that the treaty was observed (FO 78/840 Gilbert-
FO 9/16/50, encl. Haines-Bombay 4/14/50; also in BSC 1850).

Consul General Murray, at Alexandria, got to the bottom
of the whole trouble very quickly. He found that Mr. Ogilvie
was subject to delirium tremens and had had such a bad attack
that Haines was compelled to send a ship to take him to Aden
(FO 78/875 #3 Murray-FO 2/18/51).

In the Hedjaz, early in 1851, the Turks removed Sharif Muhammad Ibn 'Aun and his sons Abdallah and Ali from power and
shipped them off to Egypt, leaving the country in a state of uneasiness (BSC 1851, Haines-Bombay 6/13/51). Turkish advances received a severe blow in September when an army of

1,000 men was annihilated by the Asiri near Hodeida (BSC 1851, Haines-Bombay 10/27/51).

This abruptly ended Turkish movements in Arabia. In April, 1852, another complete shake-up of Turkish officials took place; all officers were again withdrawn and replaced by new men (BSC 1852, Haines-Bombay 5/3/52). This shake-up was immediately followed by the detention of several vessels from Aden at Mocha; the object was to compel all shipments to be made in Arab vessels which paid an export duty of twelve per cent in contrast to the five per cent paid by vessels registered from Aden (BSC 1852, Haines-Bombay 6/9/52). At the same time Mustafa Pasha, the new governor of Hodeida, wrote requesting that duty be levied on all merchandise entering Aden, as the Porte felt that the free passage of merchandise was injurious to the trade of the Yemen. Actually, the increase in coffee trade at Aden had reduced the revenues of Mocha and Hodeida to a dangerously low point. In forwarding the Pasha's request to Bombay, Haines forcefully pointed out the advantages of keeping Aden a free port, and in this he was backed by the Bombay Government (BSC 1852, Minute 6/25/52).

Making Aden a free port had drawn trade there, for ships not only avoided the duties levied by the Turks — five per cent for ships of British registry, twelve per cent on others plus an export tax of twelve and a half crowns per bale of coffee — but also avoided a tedious and sometimes dangerous voyage in the Red Sea. Haines felt that the Turks' desire to conquer the Yemen was almost entirely prompted by a wish to control the trade of that comparatively rich district and force it to go through the ports of Mocha and Hodeida. The Turks had been unsuccessful because of lack of funds and of men. What little trade was left at Mocha and Hodeida was being rapidly destroyed by two typical Turkish practices: first, the demand that the merchants advance money without interest to be paid back by allowing deductions from the customs dues of the next year; and second, the demand for forced loans. As the governors were changed every two or three years, and the new governor consistently refused to recognize his predecessor's obligations, the money advanced was to all intents and purposes confiscated. That the trade at Aden was increasing is shown by an interesting set of figures (BSC 1852, Haines-Bombay 5/29/52):

Bales Of Coffee Passing Through Aden

		Value in Rupees
1849-50	6,558	96,847
1850-51	13,037	1,57,874
1851-52	28,550	3,65,780

These figures, joined with those from a report made at Aden of the previous year on the payment of pilot fees, make an interesting comment on trade in that area (BSC 1851, Haines -Bombay 6/11/51):

Ships

1848-49

British*		American		French		Dutch		Russian	
No.	Tons	No.	Tons	No.	Tons	No.	Tons	No.	Tons
79	33,640	8	1,875	3	468	-	-	-	-

1849-50

| 71 | 34,051| 11 | 2,793 | 2 | 202 | - | - | - | - |

1850-51

| 61 | 27,440| 9 | 2,161 | 7 | 2,015 | 2 | 1,258| 1 | 330 |

These figures, of course, represent only merchant ships which requested pilots; the local and Arab coasting vessels did not use them. They give evidence of the growing importance of Aden as a port for the Yemen, and account for the consequent deterioration of Hodeida and Mocha.

A reappearance of the French in Red Sea waters caused some uneasiness in India. The French (frigate "Eurydice") had unsuccessfully attempted to purchase Kamaran Island in 1851, but the frigate remained in Red Sea waters. She was re-ported to have left consular agents at Mocha and Hodeida (BSC 1852, Haines-Bombay 4/24/52, also in FO 78/3185). The Foreign Office received assurances from Constantinople that there was no immediate danger of the cession of any land in the Red

---

*These figures presumably include the vessels on the regular Suez-India run.

Sea to the French, and that any consular agent who had been left had not been given letters of recommendation by the Porte (FO 78/3185, Rose-FO 7/4/52).

The fair in Berbera was disrupted anew by the ancient enmity of the tribes, stirred up by the ambitions of Shermarkee Ali who had asked to be put under Turkish protection so as to use Turkish force to control the Somali coast. The famous tower still remained standing, and the fair was moved to Bander Kabrit to be out of range of it (BSC 1852, Haines-Bombay 12/25/51). The fort finally was destroyed by tribesmen, but Shermarkee next made the blunder of attacking and robbing a vessel from Aden. The S.S. "Victoria" was dispatched immediately to demand indemnity from Shermarkee to the amount of the plundered property plus the cost of sending the "Victoria" across the Gulf. Fortunately, two of Shermarkee's vessels were in the Aden harbor, and were held by the English until the indemnity was paid (BSC 1852, Haines-Bombay 4/9/52). The fair had been larger than ever, seventy-six vessels and twelve to fifteen thousand people. Shermarkee finally came to Aden in September and paid his indemnity, but the incident broke his power at Berbera (BSC 1852, Haines-Bombay 9/25/52).

At Aden the question of the murderers remained unresolved. There were several refusals to produce the Sayud Muhammad Husain, and then he was reported to have died of poison in November, 1852. Boghi remained at large, and very much alive (BSC 1852, Haines-Bombay 11/14/52). However, intertribal relations were strained and towards the end of the year disturbances caused delays and trouble for the kafilas entering town.

In April, 1853, Sultan Ali again requested the help of the English in destroying the fort at Bir Ahmed (BSC 1853, Haines-Bombay 4/17/53). Heretofore, Sultan Ali's antagonism to Bir Ahmed had appeared to be due to the Aqrabi troubles with the English. Such was not the case; the antagonism lay much deeper. The Aqrabi tribe which held Bir Ahmed was a very small tribe which had thrown off the yoke of the Abdalis in 1770. The main object and desire of the Abdali Sultan was to bring this tribe back under his sovereignty. (Hunter, Major F.M. & Sealey, Captain C.W.H., AN ACCOUNT OF THE ARAB TRIBES IN THE VICINITY OF ADEN, Bombay, Government Central Press, 1886, pp. 15-16.) This rivalry had been ably used by Captain Haines in preserving the peace around Aden, as the Aqrabi and Abdali rivalry prevented any dangerous coalition.

The present difficulties with the Aqrabi were due to the influence of the Fadhli Sultan, as the Aqrabi would join anyone who was antagonistic to the Abdali. Haines refused the Lahej Sultan's request on several valid grounds, the most realistic of which was Haines' doubts as to Sultan Ali's integrity (BSC 1853, Haines-Bombay 4/17/53). The Fadhli Sultan was prevented from disturbing the roads only by the alertness of the caravan guards supplied by the Abdalis. On May 17 the Fadhlis attacked a new fort at Sheikh 'Othman built by Sultan Ali, and threatened to capture the springs at Hiswah supplying the water boats which with the growth of Aden had become an essential part of the town's water supply. The "Mahi," a schooner, and two cutters were sent to cover the attack from the sea, and their fire prevented the capture of the fort until re-inforcements arrived from Sultan Ali. The "Mahi" then stood by to protect the water supply (BSC 1853, Haines-Bombay 5/24).

This disturbance produced at least one good result; it impressed the Arabs with the importance of Aden to their wellbeing. Haines, quoting the Arabs, wrote that "Aden is the head, the near neighborhood the body and one cannot exist without the other" (BSC 1853, Haines-Bombay 6/11/53). In August, 1853, a twelve-month truce between the Abdali and Fadhli was agreed on (BSC 1853, Haines-Bombay 8/13/53).

The Turks now quickened their attempts to re-establish authority over the Yemen and Hedjaz. The usual complaints of violations of the commercial treaty of 1838 were received. These extortions were causing a renewed migration to Aden from Mocha. In May, Haines wrote "Mocha is now a ruined and deserted town, it has very little trade and its revenue is trifling and many of the few remaining inhabitants would come to Aden if permitted" (BSC 1853, Haines-Bombay 5/26/53). In February, 1853, it was reported that the Turks under Muhammad Pasha were about to make a new attempt to capture the Yemen (BSC 1853, Haines-Bombay 2/11/53). Slight skirmishes stopped trade completely in the Tehama. This state of affairs continued until April when the tribes were bought off and partial peace restored (BSC 1853, Haines-Bombay 4/16/53).

In July, 1853, the Imam of San'a sent a delegation to Constantinople to purchase the government of the seaports. This met with little success, although unquestionably it would have made for peace in the much-disturbed Yemen.

Reports began to seep in of the deplorable state of Turkish

arms in the Hedjaz. Cole, the new Vice-Consul at Jidda, had
been left there by the "Elphinstone" on April 26, 1853. The
ship brought back reports that the Turkish governor was 65,000
crowns in debt and that 8,000 of his troops were more than a
year in arrears of pay. Although all was quiet on the surface,
trouble was brewing (BSC 1853, Haines-Bombay 5/26/53).

As the year progressed and the difficulties between Russia
and Turkey which preceded the Crimean War became more and
more threatening, Haines laid plans to evacuate the few Christians in the Hedjaz. In December Haines sent the "Elphinstone"
to Jidda to protect British interests, and at almost the same
time the tribes there took the opportunity offered by the outbreak of the Russo-Turkish war to revolt, the unpaid and under-
fed Turkish army joining them (BSC 1853, Haines-Bombay 12/
10/53, and BSC 1854, Haines-Bombay 12/27/53).

At the beginning of 1854 the Bombay Government decided
to audit the Aden accounts, an action which Haines had requested
yearly. The audit discovered a deficiency of L28,000. Haines,
Cruttenden, and all the other civil officials were instantly removed. Haines offered to make this good from his private fortune which amounted to L10,000, assigning his pension to the
Bombay Government, and making deductions from his future
salary. However, the Bombay Government was so furious at
its own lack of attention to detail that Haines was made the
scapegoat. He was placed under arrest and twice tried on criminal charges, and was acquitted both times by different juries.
The government then brought civil suit against him, rejected
his offer of settlement, and imprisoned him for debt. In 1855,
he was released under guard at his home in Bombay because of
health, but was ordered returned to prison as the Advocate General felt that his release under bond would require another civil
suit to collect the sum involved (BSC 1855, Howard [Advocate
General]-Bombay 8/2/55 and 8/21/55). The Court of Directors
in London decided that, as Haines had withdrawn his offer of
the payment of his fortune as he considered the government's
terms were too hard, the offer had been made in bad faith and
ordered his return to prison as Haines had the right to gain his
release by going through bankruptcy proceedings. The Board
added "under the circumstances of this case, his not making
such application admits of none but a discreditable interpretation" (BSC 1855, Resolution N.D. [about 11/1/55]). Haines remained in jail until Sir George Clerk became governor under

the newly-organized India Office and pardoned Haines early in
1860 (above information from Allens Indian Mail, August 6,
1860, reprinted in full in Low, Charles R., HISTORY OF THE
INDIAN NAVY 1613-1863, London, Bentley, 1877, Vol. II,
pp. 527-28).

There is little need to comment on the actions of the Bombay Government. The smallness and peculiarly limited percep-
tion of the Indian official in dealing with the personal affairs of
his brother officers is well-known. The morale of the Honorable East India Company was rapidly breaking down, and, above
all, it is to be remembered that Haines was a naval officer. It
is difficult to estimate the rivalry between the Army and Navy
in India or their relative social status, but there is other evidence besides this isolated case to show that there was no love
lost between the services. Haines suffered throughout his career as Political Agent by being a naval officer, as shown in
the rather patronizing tone of many of the official Minutes. His
removal and the housecleaning that followed marked the close
of the first period of Aden's occupation.

One cannot help but admire Haines' abilities and his real
greatness. His conception of Aden was a broad one, the establishment of a commercial city in the Red Sea area and the re-
establishment of Arabian trade to its former greatness. Working under serious handicaps he achieved wonders, and one must
agree with the article in Allens Indian Mail at the time of his
death: "A dark chapter in the history of the Bombay government
has at length come to a conclusion.... A mere debtor — if indeed he were that — has been for nearly six years confined to
jail in a deadly climate at the suit of the government which he
had served with preeminent zeal and ability" (ibid.).

IX. ABYSSINIA 1840-1848

To the European of the mid-nineteenth century, Abyssinia meant only the northern section of modern Ethiopia, the provinces of Gondar and Tigré. This territory was the Abyssinia of most of the early travelers, Bruce, Valentia, and before them the Portuguese. The reason is very simple. Gondar and Tigré were the richest agricultural provinces and supported the largest and most civilized population. Furthermore, there were but four roads into Abyssinia: (1) the route used by Harris to Shoa; (2) the route from Zeila via Harar to the interior, now the right-of-way to the Jibuti-Addis Ababa railway; (3) the route from Massawa to Adowa and thence inland to Lake Tana and other parts of Gondar; and (4) the route into Gondar overland from Egypt, through the Sudan following the Blue Nile and then overland to Lake Tana.

To follow the first of these routes meant not only dealing with numerous hostile tribes, suspicious of the stranger and at feud with each other, but also a passage through some of the most unpleasant country in the world, lacking in water, viciously hot and extremely rough. As a trade route, it was only used by caravans going to the Berbera fair; other inland traffic either went north to the Adowa-Massawa road or branched off on the second route before reaching Shoa and went via Harar to Zeila or Berbera and the coast – a route just as unpleasant as the one from Shoa to Tajura but much shorter.

The Nile route was the important overland trade route to Egypt from Central Africa. Khartoum, of course, was the chief mercantile center of this route, and much traffic came from Central Africa to Khartoum and then continued down the Nile to Egypt or branched off overland to Suakin on the Red Sea. However, Abyssinia did not lie directly on the road, and the passage across the desert from the Nile to Gondar was not the pleasantest possible trip. Furthermore, the Sudan was the home of some of the more fanatical Muslim tribes who, although not dangerous to the infidel, were not friendly. In addition to this, the first half of the nineteenth century witnessed the application of Muahmmad Ali's economic idea of monopoly to its fullest extent in the Sudan, a policy which was not conducive to the expansion of European trade there.

There remained then the route from Massawa. After leaving Arkiko, a village on the mainland at the end of Annesley Bay, the traveler went through about sixty miles of arid, hot country until he reached the beginning of the great Abyssinian plateau. This plateau, itself rather bleak, was cut by tremendous valleys, the bottoms of which were extremely rich, almost tropically luxuriant in their growth. The religious centers of Adowa and Axum were but a hundred and fifty miles away from Massawa, and from there routes led to various centers in the interior of Abyssinia.

Many travelers have described this country but there is one description far superior to any other. Consul Plowden, in 1854, forwarded to the Foreign Office a "Memorandum on Abyssinia." This remarkable document deserves to be better known. It was reprinted in one of the Blue Books on Abyssinia, but is far more accessible in a little volume edited by John Camden Hotten called ABYSSINIA AND ITS PEOPLE OR LIFE IN THE LAND OF PRESTER JOHN, where it is reprinted in its entirety along with other enclosures from Plowden regarding the life and customs of Abyssinia (London, John Camden Hotten, 1868, pp. 111-245; also FO 1/8 Plowden-Granville 7/9/54).

Abyssinia was to all intents and purposes a medieval feudal kingdom. As is usually the case in such a government, the authority of the emperor depended on his own abilities. The eighteenth century witnessed a decline in the ability of the emperors until by 1800 they had become puppets totally devoid of authority, as a rule protected by some local governor for the political symbolism which still attached itself to the title. In the early nineteenth century the real power in Abyssinia was the local provincial governor or "Ras." This man was in fact an independent ruler, and often made a pretence of kingship as Sahle Selassie had in Shoa. These Ras usually came from the military leaders of the province, gaining their position by intrigue, revolution, or both, usually claiming for legalistic purposes some descent, collateral or fictitious, from old ruling provincial families. Under the Ras, the province was divided among "Dejazmatches," local lords who had entire control of all sources of revenue, and the power of life and death which in theory belonged to the Ras alone. Dejazmatches were the curse of trade and commerce in Abyssinia, as they depended for their revenue on tolls taken from all merchants passing through their districts. The Ras controlled his Dejazmatches purely and simply by

superior force, compelling them to pay him tribute and to provide troops in time of war. Under the Dejazmatch were local
chieftains who might control one or more villages and were the
main source of the Dejazmatch's fighting force, having any-
where from five to five hundred fighting men under them according to their means. Each Dejazmatch and Ras had of course
his own private army of matchlock men and personal guards
besides the feudal levies which he could raise by his authority,
which usually depended on the power of his purse and on his
persuasive ability. The pattern is not strange. The Abyssinian
Empire was organized much as Egypt had been in the chaotic
period between the Sixth and Twelfth Dynasties, or China in the
days of the warlords, or medieval Europe stripped of the fol-
derol of feudal theory. It is the pattern common to any country
lacking a strong central government, cursed with difficult communications, and having a large uneducated populace.

Abyssinia was of course a Christian country. At the head
of the church was the "Abuna," a man of considerable importance both religiously and politically. The Abyssinian church
was closely related to the Coptic church of Egypt, as the country had been converted to Christianity by the Egyptian church,
and the appointment of the Abuna originally was made by the
Patriarch of Alexandria with the consent of the Emperor. But
by the nineteenth century it was almost impossible to tell which
man initiated the appointment and which one gave his consent.
Aside from the appointment of the Abuna, the Abyssinian church
was, in practice, independent of the Coptic church, as it was
divided from it by the great expanse of the Muslim Sudan. The
policy of the clergy was not exactly progressive; in fact they
represented the most conservative force in an ultraconservative
country, keeping education to themselves and violently resent-
ing missionary efforts. Above all, the Abyssinian clergy feared
and hated the efforts of the Roman Catholics to enroll the church
under their leadership, a fact which probably did more than
any other one thing to prevent French influence from spreading
into the country.

Besides the Christians, Abyssinia also contained a colony
of Jews, the Falashas, who had preserved their religion in its
ancient form and were considered an inferior people, but not
persecuted, and also a large Muslim population. This minority,
called the Gallas, lived by themselves to the south and east of
Gondar, separating it from Shoa, and acting as an ethnological

and religious barrier between the two great Christian sections
of Abyssinia. The Gallas were famous throughout the Near
East for their beauty and notorious for their propensity for selling their children into slavery; the combination made their
country the leading area for slave traders in North Eastern Africa. The people were an independent lot and rather poor,
their country not especially fertile, so they augmented their in-
comes by raids into the territories of Gondar and Shoa. As the
Gallas commanded a high price in the slave market because of
their beauty, the local governors in Christian territory found
war against them not only a pleasant vengeance but also profitable.

In dealing with the Abyssinian people, especially the upper
class, the European found two characteristics which hindered
negotiations. The first was an extremely complicated and sym-
bolic ceremonial which attended all social and business activities and required a great deal of tact, patience, and knowledge,
as an accident movement at the wrong time might mortally offend an Abyssinian and spoil a year's negotiations. (Such an
incident played a large part in the imprisonment of the missionaries in 1863.) The second characteristic was a profound and
complacent confidence in the pre-eminence of Ethiopian civilization in the world and the great superiority of the Abyssinian
above all of his fellow men in way of life, method of thought,
and general intelligence. Any outsider was considered an
immensely inferior person who had come to Abyssinia to see
and enjoy its greatness. An individual might be convinced that
the outside world had something to give, as Sahle Selassie had
been in Shoa, or Theodore in Gondar, but his openness to progress was usually blocked by his advisers. Theodore is an excellent example of this. While two Englishmen, Bell and Plowden, had his ear, he made serious efforts towards progress.
On their deaths, he returned to the ultraconservatism of his
countrymen. Understanding this fact, the success of Menelik II
in the last years of the nineteenth century seems all the more
remarkable and gives him a just claim to a better position in
history than he at present occupies. (Based on Plowden's reports. FO 1/4 Plowden Memo on Trade 8/20/47, FO 1/7
Plowden London – Memo on the Social System of Abyssinia
6/20/52, FO 1/7 Plowden-London – Report on Relations with
North Abyssinia, 3/23/83, FO 1/8 Plowden-London – Memo on
Abyssinia 7/9/54, FO 1/9 Plowden-London – Memo on King
Theodore 6/25/55.)

Northern Abyssinia and its port Massawa fell in the sphere of the Foreign Office, who had expressed little or no concern with the country since Lord Annesley's second expedition of 1811, headed by Henry Salt. However, with the establishment of Aden as a British possession and the consequent development of regular steamship travel in the Red Sea, the port of Massawa came under the observation of the Aden government particularly as rumors of French activity near Massawa constantly reached Aden.

As a result, a ship of the Indian navy stationed at Aden was sent to Massawa of often as practicable. The object of these visits was twofold, to observe French activity, and to check on the treatment of the Banyan merchants, the chief traders in northern Abyssinia, who as British Indian subjects were under British protection.

The Ottoman Empire made pretentions of sovereignty over Abyssinia and did, in fact, control the island of Massawa, and through subsidies exercised some influence on the tribes in the immediate area of Annesley Bay. Massawa was traditionally a part of the Pashalik of Jidda, and consequently had come under the control of Muhammad Ali when he obtained control of the Hedjaz. In 1851, with the general settlement of the Near Eastern Question, the Hedjaz and Massawa reverted to Ottoman control.

Due to a lack of ships at the Aden station and the continued demands of affairs at Aden and on the Somali coast it was not until August, 1841, that a ship from Aden called at Massawa, the "Constance," under the command of Lieutenant Christopher. A new revolving gun had just been installed on the ship, and as Christopher chose the time of his arrival to test his new acquisition, the first appearance of a ship from Aden not only made a strong impression but also created a minor panic. He found a French Vice-Consul, who had been established there only five months, already in difficulties due to the refusal of the garrison to give a salute to the French flag. Christopher also heard the first reports of the French acquisition of Edd, a God-forsaken roadstead two hundred miles south of Massawa.

Christopher considered that the Turks along the coast were in an anomalous position. They claimed, according to the governor, the entire coast of the Red Sea on both sides from Suez to Bab-el-Mandeb, yet the Naïb of Arkiko, the ruler of a village at the end of Annesley Bay, claimed to be completely independent

and was, in fact, nominated and elected by the village without
any reference to the governor of Massawa. The complexities
of Abyssinian politics were expounded to Christopher, who
learned that Ras Suporguardias of Tigré, who called himself
king and who had inscribed a letter to George IV in 1827, had
been murdered about six years previously by a coalition between
the Ras of Gondar and one of Suporguardias' former Dejazmatches, Oubie by name. Oubie, setting himself up as Ras of
Tigré, was reported to have obtained an Abuna at his court
which upset this coalition, as the Abuna customarily resided
with the Ras of Gondar. The result was imminent war in the
interior (BSC 1841, Haines-Bombay 9/9/41, encl. Christopher
-Haines N.D.).

The rumored appointment of an Abuna at the court of Ras
Oubie focused attention on the activities of the Catholic missionaries in Abyssinia. The Abuna, or head of the Abyssinian
church, usually resided in Gondar. In 1840 the office was vacant, the previous incumbent having died, and tense Abyssinian
-Egyptian rivalry in the border provinces prevented any negotiations with the Coptic Patriarch in Alexandria for the appointment of a new Abuna. To build up his prestige in his rivalry
with Ras Ali of Gondar, Oubie endeavored to obtain the appointment of the new Abuna to his court in Tigré rather than the traditional place of residence at Gondar where Ras Ali ruled.

M. de Jacobis, head of the Catholic mission, was a man
whose character and integrity were universally admired even
by his opponents. However, some of his most ardent support-
ers deplored his talent for becoming inextricably involved in
local Abyssinian politics. He had become a close friend of Ras
Oubie and the Ras suggested that the new Abuna be appointed by
Rome rather than by the Coptic church. This must have been
a tempting offer to the missionary for in effect it would have
placed the Abyssinian church in Tigré under the authority of the
Papacy. The offer was filled with political dynamite and was
rejected by de Jacobis, who did, however, agree to intercede
with the Patriarch at Alexandria for the appointment of the new
Abuna to Ras Oubie's court rather than to that of Ras Ali. De
Jacobis' intercession was without effect and a young Copt named
Salama was appointed as Abuna to reside at Gondar. (Lejean,
op. cit., pp. 39-42.)

By his ill-considered interference in local politics de Jacobis brought upon himself the hatred of the new Abuna, lost any

influence which he might have gained in Gondar, and in effect
committed future French intrigues to the support of Ras Oubie
of Tigré.

Activity of French warships in the winter of 1841-1842 compelled Haines to send the "Constance" in February, 1842, to
Massawa to check on French intrigue in that quarter, to inspect
Edd and then proceed to Q'useir below Suez to see if Muhammad
Ali was fortifying the port (BSC 1842, Haines-Bombay 2/6/42).
These orders were followed up by later orders issued after the
arrival of the French ship "Prévoyante" at Aden with a mission
to Oubie — "to watch the progress of the insurrection and British trade at Massawa" (BSC 1842, Haines-Bombay 3/30/42
encl. Haines-Saunders 3/30/42).

Christopher could find no certain intelligence on conditions
in the interior on his arrival at Massawa so he sent messengers
inland. He did find out that the insurrection was over and the
Abuna properly installed at Gondar. In a "terrific" battle which
had taken place with 70,000 participants, there had been only
fifty deaths. Oubie, captured by Ras Ali of Gondar, had purchased his freedom and returned to his government in Tigré
where he was reported to be unfriendly to foreigners. The
French were very active although they seemed to be accomplishing little. M. Lefebvre, the French Vice-Consul, was exploring
the route from Anfile, 110 miles south of Massawa, inland, a
route which turned out to be far more difficult than the Massawa
road, and various French intrigues were reported in Abyssinia
proper. Regarding English trade, Christopher found various
violations of the Treaty of 1838 at Massawa but, not having a
copy of the treaty, could do little to enforce it. In his opinion,
these violations were due to the tyranny of petty officials rather
than any intentional policy of the Turks (BSC 1842, Haines-
Bombay 5/30/42 encl. Christopher-Saunders 5/4/42).

In October, 1842, Christopher was able to report that
northern Abyssinia was quiet. All reports indicated the complete failure of French intrigues in the country. Ras Oubie had
been demoted from Ras of Tigré; the position was now held by
Arrah Selassie, son of Welad Selassie, the old friend of Valentia and Salt. Oubie became the Ras of Semen, a province between Tigré and Gondar, close under the eyes of Ras Ali (BSC
1842, Haines-Bombay 10/24/42).

In Shoa, Captain Harris was able to get considerable information about north Abyssinia. Hearing of Harris' presence,

the new Abuna sent him a messenger to convince him that an
English Agent should be sent to Gondar. Harris, disillusioned
about the wealth of Shoa which did not live up to the advance
notice given by the Jesuits in Portuguese days, felt that north
Abyssinia, whose people, he said, "were basically traders,"
should be opened up to British commerce.

In June and July, 1843, the "Constance" again visited the
Abyssinian coast. Christopher found the governor of Massawa
adamant against enforcing the Treaty of 1838; he said that he
had direct orders from Osman Pasha, governor of Jidda, to
disregard it. French influence was apparently at a low point.
M. de Jacobis, head of the Catholic mission at Adowa, was the
only politically active Frenchman in the interior; the others,
Lefebvre, Dillon, and the d'Abbadies were engaged in researches that were obviously purely scientific. Trade at Massawa was almost non-existent; the four-months report from the
customs listed 206 slaves, 392 teeth of ivory, 89 horns of civet,
with total receipts of only 1,530 crowns. Christopher stopped
at Anfile and Edd and found them miserable villages. The natives at Edd asked when the French settlers were coming, in
the hope that their tiny income might be increased (BSC 1843,
Haines-Bombay 7/23/43 encl. Christopher [at Zeila]-Haines
7/9/42).

The "Constance" was at Massawa again at the end of November, 1843. This time Christopher found considerable news
from the interior. The nominal Emperor of Abyssinia, Tekla
Georgis, had died without issue at Ras Ali's capital in Gondar,
ending the legitimate succession and by the place of his death
giving Ras Ali a claim on the emperorship. Ras Oubie remained Ali's only rival, but he was momentarily in eclipse. In
Christopher's opinion, Ras Ali was entitled to English support
as the legitimate ruler of the country (BSC 1844, Haines-Bombay 3/18/44, encl. Christopher-Senior Naval Officer 12/15/43).
The "Constance" had started back to Aden but was almost immediately recalled to Massawa by the appearance of Ras Oubie and
an army in the mountain passes fifty miles from Annesley Bay.
He extorted $1,200 from the Naïb of Arkiko for protection and
stopped all commerce. The Turks, threatened with ejection,
tried to make some feeble concessions but with little success.
Christopher felt that the intrigues of the French priest de Jacobis was behind this attempt to seize Massawa and gain a port
on the coast free from Turkish monopolistic practices and

domination (BSC 1844, Haines-Bombay 3/18/44, encl. Christopher N.D. and Christopher-Haines 2/18/44).

Late in 1844, a brother of the Abuna appeared in Aden with a letter of friendship and presents to the Queen which were forwarded to London. The letter requested a consul at Massawa in order to cut down slave trade and help commerce (BSC 1844, Haines-Secret Committee 7/5/44). There is no evidence to show that this communication ever reached the Foreign Office.

Lieutenant Christopher's reports show the policy to which the English and the French soon became committed in Abyssinia. They also show that the powers were led into these policies by the tactics of the Abyssinian rulers rather than by their own desires. Aside from any legitimistic claims which either Ras Ali or Ras Oubie might have made, they were rulers in fact and probably of equally humble origin. The French, having first penetrated into northern Abyssinia, chose to support Ras Oubie. This was a practical step as his territories lay nearest the coast, were the most easily accessible, and controlled the most commerce. They were able to convince him to allow the establishment of a Roman Catholic mission at Adowa, the sacred city of Abyssinia. From this, French influence could easily emanate. Furthermore, the traditional protection of the Catholic church provided a first-class motive for later attempts at interference in Abyssinian affairs. Faced by this situation, the English were forced to take sides with Ras Ali or any other ruler of Gondar. Gondar was the traditional center of Abyssinian life, and the ruler could claim a few legalistic trappings to his title. This gave the English the chance to refer to Ras Oubie as a "rebel" and Ras Ali, and later Theodore, as the legitimate ruler of the country. However, this policy had the drawback that Ras Oubie controlled the roads to Gondar so that any British official must, to save his own skin, appear impartial. The policy of Ras Oubie and Ras Ali is perfectly obvious; they considered Europeans inferior and were merely using the English or the French in whatever way would accrue to the advantage of the respective Ras in Abyssinia.

The "Elphinstone" was sent in April, 1845, to make a routine inspection of Massawa and also to carry 1,000 rupees in crowns for Mr. Coffin from the Foreign Office (BSC 1845, Haines-Bombay 4/19/45). William Coffin had arrived in Aden in June, 1841, with letters and certain presents from Ras Oubie to the Queen. He was sent to Egypt and his letters and presents

forwarded to England (FO 1/3, Haines-Barnett [Alexandria]
6/22/41, and Barnett-FO 9/19/41, and FO-Barnett 9/30/41).
On the advice of the India Board, who could see no object in
dealing with Ras Oubie until the results of Harris' expedition
to Shoa were known, nothing was done about the matter (FO 1/3
-IB-FO 10/23/41), and Coffin returned to Abyssinia only to be
expelled in disgrace by Ras Oubie for failing to get an answer
to his letter. In 1844 Coffin was reported living in poverty in
Massawa (BSC 1844, Haines-Bombay 3/18/44). The gift of
1,000 crowns to Mr. Coffin was merely a belated attempt by the
Foreign Office to make up for the difficulties they had caused.

Lack of vessels at the Aden Station prevented Haines from
checking on Massawa for a considerable length of time. In 1847,
information reached Aden that the French were trying to export
200 free laborers from Massawa for plantations on Bourbon.
(See Coupland, R., EAST AFRICA AND ITS INVADERS, pp.
429ff. for a discussion of this problem.) Haines could not see
how the French could do this unless they dealt through the regular slave trade channels. Furthermore, he considered that
the Abyssinians would make poor laborers, as it was beneath
their dignity to till the soil (BSC 1847, Haines-Bombay 8/25/
47). The absence of British ships at Massawa resulted in louder and louder complaints by the Banyan merchants against the
violations of the Treaty of 1838 which, together with a continued
half-hearted war between Ras Ali and Ras Oubie, had practically
caused all commerce to cease (BSC 1847, Haines-Bombay 8/25/
47 encl. Lieutenant Rennie-Haines 8/17/47; Rennie obtained
this information in Jidda).

Such desultory reports were not to continue however. At
the Foreign Office in London plans were being made to establish
a consulate at Massawa. Apparently the subject was initiated
by a letter from Dr. Beke to Palmerston dated November 9,
1846, bringing to the Foreign Minister's attention a report from
the French newspapers of Rochet's return from Shoa. Beke referred to former letters of his which are missing from the Foreign Office files, written before Palmerston became Foreign
Minister in the Russell Cabinet in July, 1846.

Dr. Charles T. Beke has had the reputation of a great authority on Abyssinia, a reputation he enjoyed during the eighteen-
fifties and -sixties, and it is interesting to see what basis there
was for it. Charles T. Beek — he changed his name to Beke "in
anticipation of my coming to live at Bekesborough" (THE BRITISH

CAPTIVES IN ABYSSINIA, second ed., London, Longmans, 1867, Preface p. v) – had spent but two and a half years, 1840-1843, in Shoa. He had never explored Gondar or Tigré, knew nothing, except by hearsay, of the coast near Massawa, and based most of his remarkable information entirely on rumor. The man was undeniably brilliant yet he never made one move, so far as can be shown by the documents, which was inspired by any motive except to inflate his reputation or his finances. There is no need to detail his actions. Two letters from him to the Foreign Office in the Abyssinian files (FO 1/26) bring charges of such an obscene nature against certain responsible officials in the British Government that they act as a sufficient condemnation of the man.

At the same time that Beke forwarded his letter to the Foreign Office, another arrived forwarded from the Colonial Office. This letter was from David Barclay of the Colonial Office writing on behalf of the "Mauritius Association" on the subject of importing Abyssinian labor for the Mauritius plantations, and proposing the establishment of a consulate at Massawa. Beke obtained an interview with David Barclay, and told him that a rich trade could be opened up with Abyssinia in mules, cattle, grain, gold, ivory, gums, coffee, myrrh, ginger, butter, honey wax, etc., and that Massawa could be easily purchased from the Porte (FO 1/4 Barclay [CO]-FO 10/22/46). Beke's knowledge of northern Abyssinia was certainly rudimentary to believe that myrrh and ginger came from there. He merely ascribed to Gondar and Tigré the products sold in Shoa.

Palmerston, commenting on the above documents, wrote "1. Where exactly is Massawa? 2. Who and What is Dr. Beke, I remember his name and have some vague impression not quite in his favour" (FO 1/4 Minute by Palmerston 12/11/46). Investigation proved that Beke, while professor of English at Leipzig University, had been employed as secretary by Consul Hart and in the Consul's absence in 1838 had been Acting Consul. While Acting Consul, he had brought charges against Mr. Hart with the object of getting his position. An investigation at the India Board would also have shown that Dr. Beke, in the process of collecting a just debt, had "shaken down" the Bombay Government for an additional Ł100 in payment of "services" rendered to the Harris Expedition at Shoa, the "services" being the transportation of a letter from Harris to the coast on one of Beke's regular trips and the payment being made merely to stop the flood of unpleasant letters from Beke's pen. Bidwell, a Foreign Office official, wrote "Dr. Beke is a clever man but 'pushing.'" Upon which Palmerston commented "I am inclined to think it would be a good thing to appt. a consul at Massawa & perhaps Dr. Beke would be a good man for it. Query as to Salary."

"I remember now that I thought it not quite right of him to send representations to the disparagement of his superior at Leipzig & with a view apparently to get his place." (FO 1/4, Minute 12/11/46, Palmerston's note dated 12/15/46.)

At the same time the Foreign Office received a letter from Massawa written by Walter Plowden, who was the son of a Bengal Civil Service official formerly in the employ of a mercantile firm in Calcutta. Plowden had been four years in northern Abyssinia and on his trip out of that country had been requested by Ras Ali to take presents from the Ras to England. These presents were of no pecuniary value, he said, and he was remaining in Massawa until word reached him as to whether or not to proceed to England. He requested that a mission of some kind be sent as Ras Oubie's recent break with the French Catholic mission combined with a rejection of Ras Ali's overtures might well close the country completely.* The Foreign Office immediately instructed him to come to England, supplying funds for his journey from Alexandria (FO 1/4 Palmerston-Plowden 12/10/46 and Palmerston-Murray 12/10/46).

Plowden arrived in England in August and delivered a report to the Foreign Office. He explained that Ras Ali's presents were intended only as an exchange of courtesies and indicated a desire on the part of the Ras to protect English travelers. He explained that the chiefs, of a military caste, had only the vaguest ideas of the value of commerce and that any treaty would be observed only as long as it was convenient for them to do so. Ras Ali he described as reflective and humane, always amenable to reason from his friends. A friendly reply to the Ras might well lead to results which the Ras could appreciate

---

*The cause of de Jacobis' fall from grace in 1845 is obscure. Lejean ascribes it to intrigues of the Abuna (Lejean, G. , op. cit. , p. 43) as does the Catholic history of the mission (Poilet, J.B. , op. cit. , pp. 21-22). Oubie expelled the mission from Tigré but allowed them to settle in the border province at Halai (FO 1/4 Plowden [Massawa]-Palmerston 10/15/46).

but only if commercial relations were based not so much on treaties as on mutual interest. Massawa, the only port, was a miserable place, without water, but a good trade could be built up through that town by a well regulated system of imports. Plowden felt that the introduction of manufactured goods to the country might stimulate the Abyssinian to "new wants and luxuries that... would speedily incite a spirit to, and a necessity for, labour that would divert their attention from that lust of war and ambition, sprung from idleness, that now devastates the land, and call into existence a class of labourers and artificers that would counterbalance the military, and force their chiefs into a system of government better adapted to the security of their new pursuits" (FO 1/4, Plowden-Remarks 8/13/47). The independent tribes on the coast were no obstacle to trade due to their fear of Abyssinia's military strength. Plowden suggested that a reply to the Ras "lay more emphasis on superiority in arts and sciences and less on war" as the counsellors of the Ras "have the undefined jealousy on that point [superiority of arms] of most savage natives which render them irritable and might defeat in a moment or retard our views" (FO 1/4, Plowden-Remarks 8/13/47).

Chief of Clerks Hammond who interviewed Plowden was impressed by him. He noted that Plowden's uncle had reported him as an "enterprising youth too erratic for the mercantile business" who had gone into Abyssinia on his own. Hammond added "I think he might be well employed in Abyssinia" (FO 1/4 Memo by Mr. Hammond 8/18/47, attached to Plowden-Remarks 8/13/47).

To this Palmerston replied "I will appoint Mr. Plowden Consul at Massawa and instructions should be prepared for him accordingly.

"I do not think it expedient to endeavor to obtain Possession of any territory in that Quarter, our object ought rather to be to encourage and secure the Independence of the Native Rulers, a draft of Treaty with the Sovereigns of Abyssinia should be prepared and sh^d be sent out by Mr. Plowden who should go up to Gondar to propose it. It should be as... [unreadable words] consistent with our purpose and I should suppose from what Mr. Plowden says that it ought either to be with the Emperor or to be signed in his name by the Ras or to be with the Emperor & the Ras jointly. Mr. Plowden's residence sh^d be Massawa but he should go up from Time to Time to Gondar to keep up

personal Relations with the Ras, and to settle with him any
questions which may arise" (FO 1/4 Minute by Palmerston 8/
22/47, attached to Plowden-Remarks 8/13/47).

Plowden also filed a long and interesting report on the possibilities of Abyssinian trade. He said that slave caravans
were conducted only by Muslims; the gold was not of a fine quality; the coffee was as fine as that of the Yemen; musk, wax,
and a very few spices were produced. Gum trees abounded
everywhere but no trade in gums had ever been developed.
Cattle were cheap and a good trade in hides was possible. The
land near Massawa was ideal for cotton and indigo. Hippo
tusks, saltpetre, and sulphur were common; gold and copper
ore were found in Gondar; and last but most highly developed
was the trade in mules for Mauritius and Bourbon. The total
trade brought Massawa a total of about $70,000 a year in cus-
toms duties. For return goods, Plowden recommended the
usual stock handled by Banyan merchants – calico, scarlet cloth,
silks, carpets of brilliant colors, Indian piece goods, velvet
and muslin, European sword blades and guns (matchlocks were
the only type in demand in Gondar, but in Tigré there was a
growing demand for flintlocks and even percussion muskets).
At present the goods chiefly in demand were German sword
blades, matchlocks from Syria, Persian carpets, looking
glasses, copper in any shape, frankincense bottles, and beads
of all descriptions. The only monetary unit was the Maria
Theresa Thaler – the crown or dollar of the Red Sea district.
British protection, Plowden felt, would encourage the Abyssinian merchant who was an enterprising man and dealings should
take place with the Naïb of Arkiko who was virtually independent rather than with the Porte. The Naïb's jealousy of the Turkish governor would make him fairly easy to bargain with and
Arkiko had a tolerably good harbor if difficulties with the Turks
made necessary a port other than Massawa (FO 1/4, Plowden,
Memo on Trade 8/20/47).

Plowden also filed a report on the sovereignty of Massawa.
Originally sovereignty unquestionably resided with the Emperor,
who used to appoint a "ruler of the sea" who lived at Dixan.
This power had lapsed so long before the nineteenth century that
any claims to it would have been ridiculous. The real question
of sovereignty lay between the Turks and the Naïb of Arkiko.
The coast had been conquered in the sixteenth century by Selim I,
and at that time an arrangement had been made whereby the Naïb

ruled in the name of the Sultan and paid a yearly tribute. When the conquest was abandoned, the Naïb continued to rule Massawa and the surrounding districts as an independent chief. A family quarrel in the early nineteenth century resulted in an appeal to the Pasha of Jidda to settle the argument. The Turks thereupon occupied the island of Massawa, paying a tribute of $1,000 a month to the Naïb for abandoning to them the import and export duties. For some time the Naïbs had ceased to require a firman confirming their authority, and were considered de facto rulers of the mainland as the Turks were of the island. On the mainland, the Naïb made peace and war at his own pleasure, received tribute and sold land. He refused to allow the French consular agent to cross his territory without his permission. In all probability, Plowden believed, the Pasha of Egypt (Massawa had been transferred to the Pashalik of Egypt from the Pashalik of Jidda early in 1847) would seize Arkiko and build a fort there, thus depriving the Naïb of his power. Plowden suggested that, as Constantinople was not yet aware of the importance of Massawa, a reasonable agreement might be made with them (FO 1/4, Plowden-Memo on Sovereignty of Massawa 8/28/47).

Palmerston, on perusing this document, came to the conclusion that Plowden should be accredited to the Turkish Government as consular agent at Massawa where he should hoist his flag, his purpose there to protect Banyan merchants and investigate trade conditions (FO 1/4, Plowden-Memo on Sovereignty 8/28/47, notes by Palmerston). On further consideration the Foreign Minister wrote that Plowden should do as the French consul had done regarding Turkish sovereignty, use Massawa as a base and go up to Gondar once a year. He went on, "I do not see any advantage in our getting possession of Lands in these quarters, all we want is Trade and Land is not necessary for Trade.... Possession of land involves civil and military Establishments, Expenses & Responsibility & the Red Sea is not a good place for a settlement to be made by the Govt. But Mr. Plowden might communicate with Mr. Macqueen's African Colonization Society" (FO 1/4, Minute by Palmerston 8/30/47).

Much to his annoyance, Plowden was kept waiting in London for various formalities. But on January 3, 1848, he received his instructions. They were as follows: Plowden was to proceed to Massawa and to ascertain trade conditions there and the

sovereign rights of the Naïb and the Turks. If the Turks had
rights only to the island, his consulate should be placed at Arkiko; if they had rights on both island and mainland, he was to
raise his flag at Massawa. He was then to proceed to Tigré
(sic) with the presents and impress on Ras Ali (Ali was Ras of
Gondar) the desire of the English to have friendly relations with
him indicating that these friendly relations could best be shown
by encouraging commercial dealings. If the Ras was favorable,
Plowden was to present him with a draft treaty of Friendship
and Commerce in the usual form, specifying a five per cent
import duty and no export duty, with a most-favored-nation
clause including a trial before the British Consul for a British
subject, and a promise on the part of the British Government
to try to keep the routes to the seacoast open. This treaty was
to be signed in the name of the Ras and the Emperor. Plowden
was to acquire all possible political and commercial knowledge
especially relating to the stability of the local chiefs, in pursuit of which he was empowered to go to Gondar or even to Shoa
if necessary (FO 1/5, #1 to Plowden 1/3/48). He was further
instructed to send all his communications to the Consul General
of Egypt for his perusal, although Plowden was responsible only
to the Foreign Office (FO 1/5, #2 to Plowden 1/4/48). On receiving these instructions Plowden left immediately for his post.
　　Palmerston's purpose in sending a consul to Abyssinia is
perfectly clear. It was to provide a check on any French actions in that quarter. A secondary purpose, and one almost as
important, was to open up the country to British commerce.
Even taking the most pessimistic view of the matter, Abyssinia
was a potentially rich country and its trade could be of considerable value. In commenting on the revival of monopolies by
Muhammad Ali in the Sennar in 1847, Consul General Murray
wrote, "It is not only the encroachment of Egypt but also the
intrigues of France that require to be closely watched on that
coast (Suakin to Massawa), for if the independence of Abyssinia
and the free egress of its produce be duly secured it will afford
a gradually increasing field for the extension of British Commerce" (FO 78/708, Murray-FO 10/2/47).

X. ABYSSINIA 1848-1854

Plowden embarked from Aden on the "Tigris" and arrived at Massawa on August 5, 1848. During the voyage the "Tigris" put in at Anfile, which owed allegiance to the Naïb of Arkiko, and Plowden found it a tolerable harbor with a small village of Dankali and Taltals eking out a living in a hot and dry country. He also investigated reports of the French purchase of Edd which appeared to be well-grounded (FO 1/5, #5 Plowden-FO 8/16/48).

At Massawa itself Plowden found a considerable change in the relations between the Naïb of Arkiko and the governor. After a dispute between two claimants to the position of Naïb, Egyptian troops had been called in. They captured and burned Arkiko and placed a certain Muhammad in the position of Naïb. This gentleman, under pressure, immediately resigned his position in favor of the Egyptians, who had begun fortifying the village. The neighboring tribes refused to recognize the Egyptians as rulers of Arkiko, and as the governor had only 500 Nubian troops there was little that he could do to enforce his authority. Ibrahim Pasha, acting Viceroy of Egypt, had ordered an export duty of twelve per cent levied on all mules whether passing through Massawa or not, and laid claim to the entire coast. It was reported that he wished to reconquer all the land conquered by Selim I, and that he had planned an expedition against the province of Hamasein, which lay fifty miles to the northwest of Massawa. Hamasein was inhabited by Christians and was a recognized part of the old Abyssinian empire. This plan was delayed, however, by the illness of Ibrahim Pasha. Plowden felt that if commerce was to be developed with Abyssinia the boundaries of Abyssinia and the Turkish Empire would have to be defined. He considered Turkish claims to the entire coast preposterous (FO 1/5, #7 Plowden-FO 8/17/48).

Consul General Murray, in Alexandria, after investigating the acquisition of Suakin and Massawa by the Pasha of Egypt, discovered that they had been acquired through bribery with the sole purpose of extending Muhammad Ali's monopolies to the province of Sennar and to the Abyssinian trade. He stated that these territories were not contiguous with the other territories of the Pashalik of Egypt, which in the case of Massawa certainly was true, the province of Hamasein lying between the Sudan and that port (FO 78/757, #27 Murray-FO 6/6/46). There was every indication that the aged Pasha was planning an economic penetration to the south if not an actual occupation.

The Egyptian governor of Massawa was living up to the Treaty of Commerce of 1838 in his dealings with the British-protected Banyan merchants, but excessively high duties, sometimes thirty per cent, with very irregular additional fees, were being levied on imports from Abyssinia (FO 1/5, #2 Consular Plowden-FO 10/29/48). This excessive duty considerably cut down trade with the interior especially as the Egyptians had extended their import controls to the mainland. In Abyssinia itself Ras Ali had consolidated his position as the dominant chief and was receiving tribute from all quarters although, as Plowden stated, "his government could not be called stable" (FO 1/5, #6 Plowden-FO 8/16/48). In October the consul received a letter from Ras Oubie welcoming him and offering to forward him safely to Ras Ali (FO 1/5, #12 Plowden-FO 10/29/48). After getting himself a house at Moncullo, a village on the mainland, he left for the interior at the end of December, 1848. Before leaving, he filed several reports on the trade at Massawa. They are extremely enlightening as to the methods pursued by Muhammad Ali. Taking Abyssinian ghee as an example, of which large quantities were shipped to Arabia, a twenty per cent ad valorem duty was levied on the Abyssinian merchant. In addition, five per cent more went to the governor, and other officials exacted a further five per cent in fees. The official weigher at the Customs house who paid $700 a year for his position, charged another five per cent for weighing the butter. This resulted in a net profit of about $40,000 a year of which the Egyptian Government collected probably one-half.

Under these circumstances, Plowden could only recommend that an attempt be made to open up Anfile as an alternate route to Tigré. However, the tribes around this port were independent, so there was no responsible government which could guarantee to keep this route open (FO 1/5, #14 Plowden-FO 12/10/48). Otherwise, Plowden suggested, the only way in which the English Government could possibly live up to the clause in the proposed treaty in which they guaranteed to keep the route to Abyssinia open would be to place Abyssinian merchants under British protection at Massawa, enrolling them of their own free will. If this should be impossible, a definition of the boundaries

of Abyssinia and a published code of duties would be an aid to
commerce (FO 1/5, #15 Plowden-FO 12/10/48). Hammond
attached a Minute to this report stating that it was possible to
grant protection to Abyssinian merchants if Abyssinia were totally independent of the Turkish Empire, but that to do so, a
consul to Massawa must be accredited by the Ottoman Empire
(Plowden was not so accredited) to which Palmerston added
that such protection must be unofficial (FO 1/5, Minute attached to #15 Plowden-FO 12/10/48).

In early January, 1849, Ras Oubie had ordered a levy of
revenue on the coast, and with eight to twelve thousand men
raided the territory claimed by the Turks, burned Moncullo,
destroyed the houses of Plowden and the French consul, and
also a Roman Catholic chapel there, slaughtered about 500 people and captured 500 more. On January 12 the Ras settled down
on the mainland across from the island of Massawa (BSC 1849,
Haines-Bombay 1/28/49), remaining until the Egyptian governor
paid him 12,000 crowns to go away (BSC 1849, Haines-Bombay
2/21/49). Plowden in Adowa was informed of the raid by the
Ras who disclaimed any connection with the burning of Plowden's house (FO 1/5, #4 Plowden [at Adowa]-Fo 1/27/49).

In March, 1849, following the illness of Muhammad Ali,
Murray, at Alexandria, reported the return of Massawa and
Suakin to the Porte and their re-attachment to the Pashalik of
Jidda. Murray believed that Muhammad Ali had been unable
effectively to enforce his monopolies in the Sennar. Therefore
he was more than willing to give up these ports, which were not
profitable to him (FO 1/5 #14 Murray-FO 3/18/49). Abbas,
who had succeeded Ibrahim as acting Viceroy of Egypt, had begun a policy of retrenchment immediately on his assumption of
office. It was probably this, rather than inability to enforce
monopolies, which caused the return of Massawa to the Pashalik of Jidda.

Plowden was well received at Adowa by Ras Oubie, who
asked him to forward a letter to Palmerston requesting artisans
to build a church and aid in pressing his claims to the coastal
area. This was quite a change for the Ras, who hitherto had
treated all Europeans except de Jacobis with contempt. The
Ras promised to treat the workmen well and pay them liberally,
a promise which Plowden felt he would keep, as the Ras, whatever his other qualities, had never been known to go back on his
word. Plowden suggested that an architect, four masons, and

a carpenter be sent (FO 1/5, #5 Plowden [at Debra Tabor]-
FO 3/3/49).

These letters brought replies from Palmerston. To Oubie's
request for English aid in pressing his coastal claims, Palmerston replied that he could not do so as the sovereign of Turkey
was also a friend of the Queen (FO 1/5, #2 FO-Plowden 7/3/49).
Palmerston, however, noted that "Sir S. Canning might be instructed to inquire as to the matter in dispute" (FO 1/5, #2
FO-Plowden 7/3/49 Minute on draft). To the request for workmen, the Foreign Office asked for more precise information
as to the conditions existing in Tigré and advised Plowden to
try to divert Ras Oubie's thoughts from the subject (FO 1/5
#4 FO-Plowden 7/3/49).

These answers to Oubie were presented to him in March
of 1850. The Ras was annoyed at the refusal to aid him against
the Turks. He was polite to Plowden but disgusted at the refusal of the "Franks" to help him. Plowden tried to convince him
of the political reasons for this refusal, but the Abyssinian's
mind could not grasp the fact that a Christian power could be
friendly with the Muslim, who, he believed, was the natural
enemy of all Christians (FO 1/6, #8 Plowden [Massawa]-FO
4/2/50). Oubie was also annoyed that no workmen had arrived,
pointing out that many Armenians and Greeks lived in his dominion in perfect safety. Plowden suggested to the Foreign
Office that some workers might come from India who would be
skilled enough for the Ras, be able to stand the climate, and
cost less (FO 1/6, #9 Plowden [Massawa]-FO 4/2/50).

At Debra Tabor, the capital of Gondar, or, more properly,
the capital of Ras Ali (each Ras chose his own capital), Plowden was well received by the Ras, who was delighted with the
presents brought to him (FO 1/5, #6 Plowden [Debra Tabor]-
FO 3/3/49). Plowden stayed with Ras Ali for about nine months,
finally convincing him to sign the Treaty of Friendship and
Commerce on November 2, 1849 (FO 1/6, Plowden [Debra Ta-
bor]-FO 1/2/50). The ratification was delivered to the Ras on
March 1, 1852. On signing the treaty the Ras said that possibly
in ten years an English merchant might appear but not until
some protection could be arranged to the coast (FO 1/6, #7
Plowden [Massawa]-FO 4/5/50). The Ras also wrote asking
for presents of gold, cloth, and guns, and announcing that he
was sending presents by Plowden. The Foreign Office decided
to send him presents to the value of £250 (FO 1/6, #3 Plowden
[Debra Tabor]-FO 1/2/50 and Minute).

Plowden returned to Massawa in April, 1850. Many changes had taken place. The port had been returned to the Pashalik of Jidda. In May of 1849 the "Constance" had visited the place and found Selim Effendi the new governor of the island. The Egyptian troops were still there but were soon to be relieved by a garrison from Jidda. M. Bolanger had replaced M. de Goutier as French Vice-Consul and apparently all was quiet. It was rumored from the interior that one of Ras Ali's Dejazmatches was contemplating a revolt, but no other disturbances were reported.

In England, a gentleman by the name of Mr. Savary appeared, presenting himself as an authority on Abyssinia. He proclaimed great possibilities in the establishment of an empire there, and made such a profound impression that Palmerston was willing to grant him a hearing after checking up on the man. In a letter to Palmerston Mr. Savary presented letters of recommendation from the Mayor of Plymouth. Palmerston smelled a rat when he read Mr. Savary's letter; he wrote entirely too good an English style for one who claimed to be a stranger to England, born of a French father and Italian mother. Palmerston, realizing he was an adventurer, was nevertheless interested in the man as he showed an intimate knowledge of Abyssinia, and resolved to have a detective investigate him before granting an interview. The police discovered Mr. Savary to be a fake who had never been outside England, but who was making an excellent living lecturing on Abyssinia (FO 1/5, series of letters and reports from various individuals to Palmerston dated from 9/28/49 to 11/13/49).

This small anecdote is illustrative of a common occurrence which one finds in Abyssinian files of the Foreign Office. While representing a most extreme case, it shows the fascination which Abyssinia apparently had for crooks, crack-pots, and sentimentalists who continually wrote in to the Secretary for Foreign Affairs. Some, like Beke, were looking for their own advancement; others, like Kirwen Joyce, to be mentioned later, might be called adventurers, although the term is too polite. During the eighteen-fifties and -sixties, Abyssinia seemed to attract about the least admirable group of men that one could find. Whatever a man might be in Europe, his character seemed to leave him in Abyssinia. There are but five Englishmen for whom one can have any admiration during this period. The five who deserve to be mentioned are Plowden and his friend John

Bell, an adviser to King Theodore; the Reverend Mr. Flaad, a
missionary who acted as messenger between the captives and
London in 1865-1868, and Dr. Henry Blanc and Lieutenant Prideaux of the Indian Army who went with Rassam on his mission
to Theodore. (Rassam was not an Englishman but a Mesopota-
mian Christian, therefore the above remarks do not apply to
him.) The documents of the period are not pleasant reading,
and exhibit a pettiness that is often beyond understanding. If,
at some distant date in the future, an archeologist should discover the Abyssinian files of the Foreign Office he would be
justified in claiming that the Abyssinian chieftains were of a
much higher civilization than many of the English with whom
they dealt.

In 1849, a letter came from the young King of Shoa via E-
gypt asking to open communications with the British. He wanted
gold and men to build him a palace, to paint pictures, to make
a crown and to show him how to manufacture cannon. He sent
twenty-six elephant tusks and thirty-one kobos (antelope) horns
as presents (FO 1/5, #32 Murray-FO 5/21/49). The Foreign
Office forwarded him a complimentary letter, 1,500 crowns in
gold, and told him that workmen would come if any could be
found who were willing (FO 1/5, FO-King of Shoa 7/4/49).
When the gold finally arrived at Shoa it was refused by the King,
who said that 300 sovereigns was too little and that Captain
Harris had brought his father presents on 150 camels. Furthermore, the King accused the British of sending him brass coins,
not real gold; they were green gold instead of the red gold the
King was used to. On the return of the box to Aden, two of the
sovereigns were found sawed in two and several showed teeth
marks where they had been bitten (FO 1/7, IB-FO 4/21/52
encl. Haines-Bombay 3/22/51; also in BSC 1852).

A curious incident occurred about this time in the offer of
Edd to the English Government by the former French Consul at
Massawa, M. de Goutier. As Palmerston commented, "It
might be a desirable acquisition of the E.I.C. but why should
an ex-French Consul want to sell it to the English Govt?" (FO
1/6 #10 Murray-FO 4/15/50). The matter was not followed up
but the answer is fairly simple. M. de Goutier represented
the government of Louis Philippe; his replacement in 1849 would
correspond to the change in government in France. The French
government took no "official" measures in the Red Sea waters
and the legal title to Edd may well have been vested in the

individual who was French Consul at Massawa.

Plowden was faced with considerable difficulties on his return to the coast. He had not been accredited to the Porte, and the consulate had been established so secretly that it gave rise to rumors in Constantinople that the English had occupied Massawa. This had caused Stratford Canning to do some difficult explaining during which time he admitted freely the rights of the Turks to Massawa and Suakin (FO 78/3185, Canning-FO 9/27/48). This suspicion of the intent of the British Government must certainly have communicated itself to Massawa, for Plowden found all of his packing cases impounded at the customs house despite his diplomatic passport. Furthermore, all possible insults were offered him. No men were allowed to work for him and the presents to Ras Ali from the Queen were seized.

In addition to this, Ras Oubie threatened to come down to Massawa to collect his "tribute" from the Turks, who of course blamed Plowden for this event. In January, 1850, a messenger from Oubie had come demanding 1,000 crowns tribute; he left after the Turks had given him a small present. About the tenth of March another messenger appeared, demanding four years' tribute or 4,000 crowns. This was refused, but as Oubie was only sixty miles away with a reported army of 20,000 men, refugees flocked from the coast flooding the island. Plowden reported that Oubie had given strict orders not to attack Massawa as he claimed tribute only from the coastal lands. The French Consul, completely disgusted with the Ottoman authorities, had struck his flag and left the port (FO 1/6, IB-FO 5/27/50 encl. Haines-Bombay 4/18/50; also in BSC 1850). Under these circumstances Plowden wrote to Haines requesting a warship for his protection, as the head of the customs house was at present the only official of any rank in Massawa. He considered himself responsible to no one; he detained all of Plowden's packages and even his mail. The commander of the troops, a very young officer, was friendly, but powerless to do anything, and Massawa was practically without a government (FO 1/6, IB-FO 8/27/50, encl. Plowden-Haines 4/6/50; also in BSC 1850). The Foreign Office immediately lodged a protest with the Porte against such treatment and applied for a vizierial letter appointing Plowden as Consul to Massawa (FO 1/6, #165 FO Canning 6/7/50).

When Plowden was in Gondar he had recommended a group of Abyssinian pilgrims who were going to Jerusalem to Finn,

the British Consul there. On arrival at Jerusalem the Abyssinians had had trouble with the Turkish governor because of a
row between the Abyssinian and Armenian churches. It seems
that at one time the Abyssinians had had a flourishing church
at Jerusalem with a large library attached, but in 1838 the
plague had driven them out of the city and the Turks, at the instigation of the Armenians, had burnt all their books and papers
on the pretext of infection. The Armenian church promptly
seized the Abyssinian convent and church, allowing the Abyssinians to worship there only infrequently. Samual Gobat, the
English bishop who had tried to intervene in the case and had
explored the Armenian claims, characterized these gentle Christians as "clever liars" but was unable to get them to allow a
neutral party to keep the key to the church (FO 1/6, #24 Finn-
FO 11/30/50). A further investigation proved that the Armenians, Copts, and Abyssinians were organized in one inter-
communion under the Turkish "millet" system, and that the
Armenians, the wealthiest, dominated the Abyssinians, whom
they beat at pleasure and even placed in iron collars equipped
with screws to tighten the grip of this yoke. In December, 1850,
the British Consul and the Bishop managed to scare the Patriarch of the Armenians into stopping these practices by assuming an unofficial protectorate over the Abyssinians. The Patriarch, fearful that the Abyssinians might turn Anglican,
thereupon allowed the key to the church to be kept in a public
place (FO 1/6, #25 Finn-FO 12/9/50). Thus began the fiction
of British protection of Abyssinians in Jerusalem which was to
become an element in the background of the Abyssinian campaign of 1867-1868.

The death of Muhammad Ali in 1849 had made considerable
changes in the economy of the Sudan. The system of monopolies,
which the old Pasha had tried to enforce in Sennar, was abandoned with a resultant influx of European merchants. In 1849
the Austrians appointed a consul at Khartoum and in January,
1850, Murray recommended that Britain do the same. He submitted the name of John Petherick as the best man for the post,
which was to be entirely of a commercial nature. Petherick
had expressed his willingness to assume the position without
salary if allowed Ł25 a year for a Turkish Janissary as a consulate guard (FO 78/840, #2 Murray-FO 1/5/50). This appointment was made. While unimportant politically, the step is indicative of Palmerston's policy of expansion of British trade in
that section of the world.

Plowden, after going up to Tigré for a few months to avoid the summer heat, returned to Massawa in the fall of 1850. He had investigated the possibilities of Anfile as a port, and found it in no way comparable to Massawa except that it was free of Turkish domination. A French group exploring near there approached him claiming to be under British protection. Plowden did not encourage these advances (FO 1/6 #15 Plowden-FO 10/28/50).

In February, 1851, the "Mahi" arrived at Massawa from Aden much to Plowden's relief as he had been receiving more insults from the Turkish officials, who had ordered any men working for Plowden to be flogged, and who had detained Ras Ali's presents to the Queen in violation of an order from the Porte. The "Mahi" brought additional presents for Ras Ali from the Queen which were seized when landed; the customs officials refused to return them to the ship. As Plowden had had no reply to his appeals to the Pasha of Jidda against the actions of the customs officials, he went across to that port in the "Mahi" to find Ogilvie, the English Consul, nearly dead from delirium tremens and all of Plowden's mail on his desk. Plowden had several interviews with Aga Pasha and reached an agreement with him which resulted in the immediate handing over of all the goods held in the Massawa customs house. Plowden felt this could be only a temporary arrangement "as it is evident from the hostility existing between the Turks and the Abyssinians that the former must always regard with jealousy my influence and friendship with the latter" (FO 1/6, #1 Plowden-FO 3/15/51). Plowden explained that he had never tried to give offense to the Turks; first, the ground which he rented on which to build a one-room house was obtained from a poor landlord and did not contain a habitable residence; second, Plowden had never traded, although he had that privilege; third, he had imported no firearms into Abyssinia except a few sent as official presents and those for his own use; and fourth, his house on the mainland had only a garden and a shed for mules (FO 1/6, #2 Plowden-FO 3/16/51). In other words, he had done nothing to arouse any jealousy of his position as consul.

Palmerston, upon receipt of this in May, 1851, wrote a stiff note for Canning to present to the Porte. He said that any more complaints from Plowden would cause a warship to be dispatched to Massawa with instructions "to adopt such measures as seem necessary to Protect Mr. Plowden in the full enjoyment

of those liberties and privileges which of right belong to him
and to obtain redress and satisfaction for all past grievances"
(FO 1/6, FO-Canning 5/27/51).

Plowden, having received the ratification of the treaty with
Ras Ali, started out in the spring of 1851 to present it personally to him. At Adowa he had a great deal of difficulty persuad-
ing Ras Oubie to let him pass into Gondar, as Oubie was about
to rebel against Ali. Plowden therefore warned the Foreign Of-
five that he might be cut off for a while (FO 1/6, #9 Plowden
[Adowa]-FO 5/18/51). June 23, just outside of the camp of Ras
Ali at Bichana, Plowden was robbed and the ratification and
Plowden's private papers were stolen, apparently by spies of
Ras Oubie (FO 1/6, #10 Plowden-FO 6/24/51). A second ratification was forwarded to Plowden which he delivered to the
Ras. An unusual rainy season, combined with the uncertain
policies of Ras Oubie, kept Plowden in Gondar until February,
1852, when he began his return journey, arriving at Massawa
in April, 1852.

On his return to the coast, Plowden found that a French
frigate, the "Eurydice," had been in the Red Sea for a considerable time after delivering Rochet d'Hericourt as French
Consul at Jidda. Its commander when at Jidda showed the Pasha there a firman purportedly granting the French the right
to build forts on the African coast, and he had indicated a desire to purchase some land from the Pasha for that purpose.
Plowden did not feel that this report was wholly correct, but he
felt sure that the French intended to take up some position on
the coast and were collecting information (FO 1/7, #4 Plowden-
FO 4/10/52). This report was forwarded to Lord Cowley at
Paris, who brought the matter up to Thouvenal the French Foreign Minister. Thouvenal said that the ship was at Jidda to
prosecute some claims against the Imam of Muscat [actually
the only French activity at this time near Muscat was an attempt
to acquire the Kuria Muria Islands; these were never the property of the Sultan of Muscat, nor did the Ottoman Empire at
this time claim sovereignty in that part of Arabia]; and to investigate the treatment of French missionaries in the Red Sea
area. He added that as far as he knew there were no plans for
occupation of any territory in that area, but that he was not con-
versant with the affairs of the Ministry of Marine (FO 1/7,
#295 Cowley-FO 6/3/52). The ignorance of the French and Brit-
ish Foreign Offices of the state of affairs in the Red Sea was

shown by a statement from Murray in Alexandria regarding the
French warship which had left a Consul at Massawa, "a port
where the French have hitherto never had any establishment"
(FO 1/7, Murray-FO 5/18/52). A statement concerning which
the India Board expressed considerable doubt.

The question of the protection of Abyssinian pilgrims again
was raised when Bishop Gobat, bishop of Jerusalem and one of
the first missionaries to Abyssinia in 1830-1832 wrote to the
Foreign Office that he had received identical letters from Ras
Oubie and Ras Ali requesting protection for their pilgrims.
The Prussian envoy in London also suggested that protection be
given as Prussia and England had equal interests in the Protestant Bishopric of Jerusalem (FO 1/7, Gobat-Malmesbury 6/29/
52 and Bunsen-FO 7/5/52). Malmesbury, now Secretary for
Foreign Affairs, recommended that the British Consul be instructed to use his good offices on behalf of the Abyssinians as
Christians who lacked temporal protection in Jerusalem; but he
could not understand why Ras Ali went over the head of the British Consul. Furthermore he felt the British must guard against
any controversy with the Porte on this matter (FO 1/7, Minute
by Malmesbury 7/7/52). Bishop Gobat and Consul Finn were
advised of this decision, and Bishop Gobat was warned against
getting involved in political affairs (FO 1/7, FO-Gobat 7/10/52,
FO-Finn 7/10/52).

The long visit of Plowden to Gondar bore fruit in some extremely interesting reports on Abyssinian conditions. The first
of these, "A Memorandum on the Social System of Abyssinia,"
was forwarded on June 20, 1852. In it, Plowden explained the
futility of some of the articles in the Treaty of Friendship. Regarding protection of British subjects, Ras Ali could only guarantee their protection in his own camp. Duties were levied by
every local chief and a merchant had to pay them in practically
every pass in the mountains. These taxes were based on the
bargaining ability of the merchant rather than on a fixed rate.
The chief articles in demand in Abyssinia were powder and guns,
both of which were forbidden by the Turks to pass Massawa.
In fact, Plowden could not see how either Ras Ali or the British
could attempt to live up to the commercial treaty while the
Turks controlled all access by sea. The only possible means
of making the treaty work would be to establish a British port
in the Red Sea which would act as a trading base. Plowden saw
no necessity under the circumstances for his remaining as consul,

as there was little he could do and all communications with Ras Ali could easily be carried on by a vice-consul at Massawa at considerably less expense (FO 1/7, #6 Plowden-FO 6/20/52).

Plowden went into the higher country north of Annesley Bay during the hot weather of 1852, but was back in Massawa in November. He discovered that the French had gotten a firman from the Porte for the establishment of a Roman Catholic mission at Massawa. However, the population was so indignant that the governor had delayed the execution of the order (FO #24, Plowden-FO 11/5/52).

In Sennar, difficulties between the Abyssinians and the Egyptians had begun in 1851 with a raid from the Abyssinian side of the border which destroyed about 100 villages. This led to a greatly increased Egyptian garrison there which revolted in the fall of 1852 (FO 78/875, #22 Murray-FO 8/6/51 and FO 1/7, #25 Plowden-FO 12/14/52). The revolt caused a great amount of unrest in Massawa. The Pasha, uncertain of his troops, lacked authority, and Ras Oubie, an astute gentleman, threatened an invasion. Plowden was put in a difficult position. Such an invasion would probably result in Plowden's house being destroyed. If it should be spared, the Turkish governor would accuse him of being in league with the Abyssinians. Furthermore, if he should get information from Ras Oubie of an attempted invasion, was he obligated to warn the Turkish governor? Plowden's anomalous position was responsible for his dilemma. He had to reside in Massawa to communicate with Europe yet he was Consul to Abyssinia and not accredited to the Porte.

In January, 1853, a Roman Catholic mission was established on the mainland at Moncullo. The former residence of a Roman Catholic missionary was transformed into a chapel by erecting a cross on it, and became the abode of a bishop with the title of Vicar Apostolic of Abyssinia; de Jacobis was consecrated as the bishop. The Abuna, who had the same title and considered his claim valid, forbade the Catholic priests to enter Abyssinia unless they promised not to say mass and ordain priests and deacons in the Abuna's bishopric. The Catholics thereupon raised a great outcry against "their cruel persecution" (FO 1/7, #2 Plowden-FO 1/24/53).

This mission turned out to be larger than was at first indicated. A bishop to the Gallas was appointed with several assistants who were to go into the Galla country south of Gojjam. Plowden compared this vigorous step with the quarrels of the

Protestant missionaries who were accomplishing nothing. The
Catholic mission consisted of two bishops and twelve priests.
It had the backing of the wealth of the church and was not inac-
tive in secular affairs "being... supported by the strong arm of
France" (FO 1/7, #4 Plowden-FO 2/12/53). There is good
reason to infer that private mercantile interests in France,
having been completely unsuccessful in political missions to
Abyssinia, were backing a religious method of penetration.

The presence of the Roman Catholic missionaries and their
subsequent quarrels with the Abuna threatened to have serious
complications. It is important to remember that the Abyssinian
church had reason to be antagonistic to the Catholics, and jealousy was not the only motive. The Portuguese had brought the
Jesuits with them into Abyssinia in the sixteenth century. In
1633 the Jesuits were forcibly expelled from Abyssinia after
they had tried to supplant the Abyssinian priesthood, and the
tradition of their actions and their expulsion was still alive in
Abyssinia throughout the nineteenth century. An incident occurred in 1852 which caused considerable additional friction between the Abuna and the French. A Coptic merchant, a friend
of the Abuna, going on a mission for him to the Patriarch of
Alexandria, was seized by the French Consul at Jidda on the
complaint of one of the lay brothers of the Catholic mission.
In return, the Abuna had nine mules belonging to the French
Vice-Consul at Massawa seized until the Copt and his property
should be released. The situation threatened to become a serious crisis, and did result in the banning of all Europeans from
Abyssinia until Plowden and the French Consul at Massawa ar-
bitrated the matter (FO 1/7, #9 Plowden-FO 2/15/53).

In March, Plowden forwarded a remarkable document entitled "Report on Relations with Northern Abyssinia." It was
really a continuation of his memorandum mentioned above, and
discussed in greater detail the impossible situation caused by
the Turkish occupation of Massawa. It was published with political deletions in the Journal of the Royal Geographical Society,
Volume XXV ("Memorandum on Abyssinia, Communicated from
the Foreign Office," pp. 315 ff.). The deleted section was
naturally the most interesting. Plowden admitted that he had
great influence with both Ras Oubie and Ras Ali but that it was
purely a personal relationship and not a substantial foundation
for the establishment of sound commercial relations. He described the commercial situation as chaotic, remarking that the

native merchants travelled with armed guards and, if the duties
in a small place were too high, fought it out in pitched battles
with the customs officials. As there was no conception of the
value of human life in Abyssinia, the Consul could not act in any
regular and well-understood manner but had to adapt himself
to the idiosyncrasies and customs of a dozen different local chiefs,
all completely ignorant of European traditions. Stolen property
was sometimes recovered after long and difficult negotiations
but if a murderer was brought to justice and executed it might
well start a long and dangerous blood feud. Plowden admitted
that he had had little trouble, but he felt that the government
should be "forewarned of the possibility of accidents even their
probability should a stranger be appointed Consul," truly prophetic words. The chiefs, while friendly, were quite undependable, and the only influence which could be exercised was through
personal interviews. Ras Ali and Ras Oubie, Plowden thought,
were the only two chiefs who had any conception of the position
of the Europeans in the world. The rest of the chiefs, and all
the populace, looked on them as mere curiosities, regarding
them with indifference except when they could profit from them.
A European could only gain esteem by a personal character
which the Abyssinian could appreciate, "as we can aid the Abyssinian in no way or harm them, our wealth is the only reason
that the chiefs should consider us." Reports from India had
raised a fear of the English among the Abyssinians, especially
in Shoa, and given intriguers a basis for attacking English influence. Plowden, therefore, requested instructions be given
him as to his future policies. With the Turks at Massawa
claiming sovereignty fifty miles inland, there was little he could
do to encourage trade. Plowden's position in Massawa was dubious as the Turks were jealous of all intercourse between the
British Government and Abyssinia for fear of stopping the flow
of slaves from the Galla country, and because of mutual distrust
between the Abyssinians and the Turks (FO 1/7, #10 Plowden-
FO 3/23/53).

Ras Oubie became seriously ill in March, 1853, and his
illness prompted Plowden to comment that if he died his successor would probably be Plowden's enemy, as the death of any
chief usually meant the imprisonment of all the dead chieftain's
friends. He remarked that this showed the futility of building up
relations based on personal friendship alone (FO 1/7, #15
Plowden-FO 4/2/53).

The matter was discussed at the Foreign Office. Lord
Clarendon, then Foreign Minister, did not wish to give up the
advantages which the British had already gained by their treaty
with Ras Ali. He suggested the possible establishment of a
British post on the Red Sea or an arrangement with the Turkish
Government about trade at Massawa. Hammond replied that the
situation could be remedied by appointing Plowden as Consul to
the Ottoman Empire at Massawa except for the fact that there
were serious questions of Turkish rights of sovereignty in that
quarter. A compromise was finally reached, and Plowden was
advised to seek a residence on the coast from which he could
communicate with Europe so that his influence in Abyssinia
would not be wasted (FO 1/7, Minute 8/20/53 by Hammond with
notations by Clarendon dated 9/1/53, 9/28/53 and 9/29/53).
This information was embodied in a dispatch to Plowden which
advised him that the government did not wish to abandon what
little they had gained, and instructed him to try to find a place
of residence away from Massawa with a safe means of communication (FO 1/7, #1 to Plowden 10/3/53).

The Minute of Hammond brings up an essential point of
British policy which was consistently maintained. The titles of
the Sultan, it is well-known, were very far-reaching. On the
basis of these titles it was possible for the Porte to make a legalistic claim to almost any piece of territory in the Near and
Middle East. As British influence and interests grew in this
section of the world, it became apparent to the Foreign Office
that one question to be avoided at all costs was a discussion of
sovereignty. This policy was not definitely put into words until
1871 when Egyptian occupation of Berbera and Turkish aggressions in the Yemen threatened Aden's existence, but it was
slowly taking shape, this note being the first concrete information of its presence, although there are earlier inferential
references to it.

Plowden had filed his trade reports for Massawa three
months late, as he had had difficulty getting the figures. He
attributed this to a policy of the Turks of teaching the inhabitants
of Massawa to be fanatics and to have nothing to do with Europeans. This was so marked that all officials and merchants
were deterred by threats from having any communications with
Plowden (FO 1/7, #11 Plowden-FO 3/24/53).

Plowden spent the summer at Halai, thirty miles from
Annesley Bay, near Dixan. Here reports reached him of the

successful revolt of Kassai or Kassa, a minor chief in Gondar.
He was reported to have completely defeated Ras Ali, and all
indications made Plowden believe that he might be the man who
could civilize Abyssinia, as he had already abolished "some
disgusting practices" (FO 1/7, #24 Plowden-FO 7/28/53). The
news of this victory was confirmed in August and the whole
country was reported in arms (FO 1/7, #25 Plowden-FO 8/27/53).
    Meanwhile the Abuna had pled with Plowden to get English
protection for Abyssinians going to Egypt via Massawa and
Jidda, in return for which he agreed to use his influence, which
was considerable, in favor of the English (FO 1/7, #24 Plowden-
FO 7/28/53). Plowden was advised by Clarendon to give all the
aid and advice to the Abuna and Abyssinian pilgrims that he
could without committing himself or the Government, the same
instructions being sent to Cole, the new Consul at Jidda (FO
1/7, #2 to Plowden 11/4/53).
    Ras Ali was again defeated by Kassai in August, 1853, and
fled to the Galla country, leaving Kassai in control of Gondar.
Oubie by this time had left Ali to his fate and declared his neutrality, but besought Plowden to get him arms and ammunition
for which he was willing to pay (FO 1/7, #30 Plowden-FO 9/28/
53, #31 Plowden-FO 9/28/53, #35 Plowden-FO 10/15/53).
    As Kassai's campaign progressed, Abyssinia was thrown
into a state of complete confusion. Ras Ali, reduced to the
position of a rebel chieftain, attacked Tigré; and Ras Oubie,
his erstwhile ally, retired into Gondar, leaving the province in
chaos (FO 1/8, #37 Plowden-FO 12/21/53). The confusion became so great that it was difficult to make out who was fighting
whom. Plowden was worried lest Ras Ali apply to him for aid,
and asked $200 for presents to be given to the Ras if by some
twist of fate he should be victorious. The Foreign Office unofficially granted this request (FO 1/8, #3 Plowden-FO 1/25/54,
separate letter Clarendon-Plowden 4/15/54). Kassai began to
get the upper hand in February by defeating Buro Goscho, one
of Ras Ali's allies, and causing the Ras to seek sanctuary. The
Shiho tribes along the coast took advantage of the confusion to
raid close to Massawa but refrained from burning the villages
as they did not wish to hurt Plowden. The Pasha looked on in
silence. "When the Shihos retire, having done all the mischief
they can, the Pasha will send a lieutenant and some troops to
demand revenue from such Bedwin as are not quite ruined, and
this is called government" (FO 1/8, #8 Plowden-FO 3/14/54).

The continued presence of the "Caiman," a French war vessel, in the Red Sea during the winter of 1853-1854 (BSC 1854, Haines-Bombay 2/28/53) caused the Foreign Office to lodge a protest in Paris. Lord Cowley, the British Ambassador, received a denial from Druyn de Lhuys, the French Foreign Minister, that the French had intentions of acquiring any settlement in those parts and, on Cowley's insistence, produced assurances from the Ministry of Marine that it had issued no such authorization to the admiral in command (FO 1/8, #326 FO-Cowley 4/11/54, #589 Cowley-FO 5/2/54). The presence of this French vessel complicated the quarrel between the Abuna and the Catholic mission. The Abuna, who had warned the Catholics against appointing priests, holding masses, etc., found that they were doing so, and threatened to eject them forcibly from Abyssinia. The French Vice-Consul at Massawa threatened reprisals in the form of seizing all Abyssinian property at that port. Plowden pointed out that the English Government had not felt reprisals necessary after the ejection of a Protestant mission a few years before, and thought that the French Consul was demanding entirely too much. He added "the establishment of a Papal Authority in a country which had been Christian for 1500 years does not seem sound" (FO 1/8, #2 Plowden-FO 1/9/54).

Clarendon lodged a protest at Paris, advising the French Government that reprisals would put all foreigners in Abyssinia in danger and achieve no results (FO 1/8, #358 FO-Cowley 4/17/54). Clarendon also instructed Lord Lyons at Rome, through the Minister at Florence, to inform Cardinal Antonelli, Papal Secretary of State, that a persistent conflict between the Catholic Church and the Abuna might compel the British Government to put the Abuna under its protection (FO 1/8, #38 FO-Scarlett [Florence] 4/20/54). The Cardinal, after investigating at the Propaganda, reported that it was believed the matter had been settled (FO 1/8, #33 Lyons-FO 6/13/54).

In March, 1854, it was reported to Plowden that the governor of Taka, an Egyptian outpost in Sennar, had raided Senhait and Bogos [called Mogos in Plowden's dispatches], about 120 miles northwest of Massawa, and carried off 300 inhabitants into slavery. The inhabitants were Christians by faith, had never paid tribute to Egypt, being a part of the Province of Tigré, and were under the rule of Oubie, although he, due to affairs in Abyssinia, was unable to protect them. The Bey of Taka had further threatened to continue these raids until the

people became Muslim and recognized the Pasha of Egypt as
their ruler. The native chiefs had asked Plowden to intervene
for them, professing a willingness to pay ransom for the captives if the sum demanded was not too great (FO 1/8, #9 Plowden-FO 3/15/54).

Plowden protested this aggression to Consul General Bruce
at Alexandria, and went to investigate the situation. On his arrival in Bogos, Plowden found the churches burned and the villages destroyed, with daily messages from the Bey offering the
tribes the choice of the Koran or the sword. Plowden was satisfied that the land was a part of Tigré; only five years before
Halhal, a neighboring district, had submitted to the Pasha of
Egypt after the use of similar tactics. Plowden, annoyed by
these aggressions, proceeded to Kassala to see the Bey (FO
#11, Plowden [Bogos]-FO 3/30/54). At Kassala, Plowden dis-
covered that the Bey was reputedly a fanatic whose one ambition
was to propagate the faith by the sword, and who believed that
Abyssinia was the property of the Pasha of Egypt, although, as
Plowden remarked, "the Abyssinians have more right to the
Yemen which they once possessed than the Turks to Abyssinia
where they have never set foot" (FO 1/8, #73 Plowden [Kassala]
4/18/54). The Bey claimed that the populace of Bogos and Senhait were idolaters, not Christians. However, Plowden had
seen several churches and met many professing Christians
there. The Bey had taken the choicest girl captives into his
harem and was disposing of the rest at the slave market as fast
as possible. He refused to give up any of the captives except
on orders from Cairo, and answered to Plowden that these people had no religion, that he had plundered them before, and had
every right to plunder them again. The Consul remarked that
this attitude would undoubtedly get him a promotion from Cairo
(FO 1/8, #14 Plowden-FO N.D., #15 Plowden-FO 4/20/54).

Bruce, Consul General at Alexandria, brought the matter
to the attention of the Viceroy of Egypt, who promised an investigation, informing Bruce that a new governor had just been dispatched to Kassala. Bruce was suspicious of the Pasha's actions, as he felt that Egyptian power might be extended into
Abyssinia "for which the present disturbed state of the country
offers great facilities" (FO 78/1035, #23A Bruce-FO 5/31/54).
In London, Clarendon informed Bruce that he should tell the
Viceroy of Egypt that "Her Majesty's Government cannot remain
indifferent to the fate of these Christians" and that the Bey must

release the captives. He added that he thoroughly approved
Plowden's actions (FO 1/8, #1 FO-Plowden 6/26/54).

More pressure by Bruce compelled the Viceroy to send an
officer to investigate the raid together with Plowden, and to
order the release of the captives even before Clarendon's orders
had reached Alexandria (FO 1/8, #29 Bruce-FO 6/16/54).
Clarendon replied that he was pleased that the Viceroy had
shown a disposition to help in this affair for "H. M. Government
will not acquiesce in any assumption either on the part of the
Porte or on that of himself of any authority over the independent
territory of Abyssinia. " The Bey of Taka had not only committed
an outrage on a Christian people but had insulted the British
Government by interfering with Plowden's dispatches (mentioned
by Plowden in #16 Plowden-FO 4/26/54). Under these circumstances Clarendon demanded the removal of the Bey as an apology. If the Viceroy did not agree to this, the matter would have
to be taken up with the Porte (FO 1/8, #37 FO-Bruce 6/30/54).

In Kassala, Plowden had further troubles with the Bey.
Orders from Cairo had stopped the sale of the captives but they
were being tortured to make them become Muslims. The governor said to Plowden's dragoman "I would rather be put to
death by my master than deliver up these slaves to become
again Christians and moreover it is very far from Kassala to
Cairo" (FO 1/8, #18 Plowden-FO 6/3/54, and #17 Plowden-
FO 6/2/54). As delay followed delay in Cairo and the officer
who was to arbitrate the dispute did not arrive, Plowden returned to Massawa. Vigorous representations by the Consul
General caused 203 prisoners to be returned in October, and
comparative peace reigned at Bogos (FO 1/9, #4 Plowden-FO
11/3/54).

In Cairo, the election of a new patriarch of the Coptic church
had caused considerable commotion and intrigue. In 1852 an
election was voided by the Viceroy, who insisted that Abyssinia
had been involved in the intrigues affecting its results. At this
point the French had stepped in and offered to take the Copts
under their protection, an offer which was refused due to the
fear by the Copts that such a move would open their church to
the proselytizing of the Catholic church. In June, 1854, a new
patriarch was elected who was acceptable to both the Pasha and
the church (FO 1/8, #26 Bruce-FO 6/7/54). At the same time
Bruce received letters from the Abuna requesting to be taken
under British protection because of his persecution by the Roman

Catholic missionaries. He declared that they had seized three
churches, brought in a bishop, and made converts in violation
of the restrictions attached to permission to travel in Abyssinia.
Furthermore, when Ras Oubie drove them out of Tigré, they
proceeded to seize the Abuna's property at Massawa and Jidda
(FO 1/8, #37 Bruce-FO 6/30/54). This was a further reper-
cussion of the affair which Cardinal Antonelli had reported as
settled.

Clarendon ordered Bruce to tell the Abuna to keep the British Government informed on religious affairs (FO 1/8, #40 FO-
Bruce 7/22/54), and then instructed Lord Bulwer, British Ambassador at Florence, to inform Cardinal Antonelli of these
complaints. Antonelli was requested to inform the Government
what measures were to be taken to prevent the recurrence of
such incidents, as upon his advice depended the measures which
the British Government might find necessary to use to protect
non-Catholic Christians (FO 1/8, #4 FO-Bulwer 7/26/54). The
Cardinal evaded responsibility for the incident, and placed the
blame entirely on the French Consul at Jidda who was responsible only to the French Government (FO 1/8, #21 Bulwer-FO
8/16/54). However, pressure on Antonelli forced him to investigate the matter, and he finally admitted the incident and showed
Lyons at Rome a copy of the rebuke which he had sent to Father
Felicissimo at Massawa (FO 1/8, #48 Bulwer-FO 10/17/54 encl.
#62 Lyons-Bulwer 10/13/54).

The continued activity of the French vessels in the Red Sea,
the "Caiman," a steamer, and the frigate "Jeanne d'Arc,"
caused another protest to be made at Paris. The interest of
the French in Kamaran Island had compelled the Pasha of Hodeida to place a small garrison there. The appearance of the
"Caiman," the first steamer ever seen in many Red Sea ports
[since the vessels which the Indian Navy used to visit these ports
were all sailing ships] made a tremendous impression on the
natives which was soon dispelled by the parsimonious dealings
of the French in purchasing supplies. On the evidence of French
aims put forward by the India Board (FO 1/8, IB-FO 10/4/54
encl. Outram-Bombay 7/18/54, also in BSC 1854), Cowley was
ordered in October, 1854, to find out how this checked with the
official French statements of April (FO 1/8, #989 FO-Cowley
10/5/54). De Lhuys again denied any intention by the French to
acquire territory in the Red Sea and showed Lyons the official
orders to the Admiral of the China Station (Bourbon). These

orders, however, were so indefinite that it was obvious he could do almost anything he wished (FO 1/8, #1269 Cowley-FO 10/22/54).

In Abyssinia, Kassai was increasing his power. Ras Ali had given up the fight and was living in sanctuary with Kassai's permission. Oubie in Tigré also gave up the battle and sent tribute to Kassai as his overlord, and the country was tolerably quiet (FO 1/8, #19 Plowden-FO 6/29/54). Kassai requested the Abuna to come to Gondar, but this the Abuna refused to do until the Catholic Bishop de Jacobis had been expelled from Gondar. In June, 1854, Kassai destroyed the army of the remaining rebel in Gondar, Dejazmatch Buro Goscho, and became the ruler of North Abyssinia with Ras Oubie as his only possible rival. Plowden hoped that Kassai would try to organize Abyssinia, although he felt that it would mean little without a seaport (FO 1/8, #28 Plowden-FO 7/10/54).

In Massawa things went from bad to worse. The governor informed Ras Oubie in June, 1854, that the salt plains a hundred miles south of Massawa, the chief source of salt for all Abyssinia, were the property of the Porte, a ridiculous claim (FO-1/8, #21 Plowden-FO 6/30/54). It was only Plowden's influence which prevented the Ras from raiding the port in retaliation and doing considerable damage. The Shiho tribes also declared their independence, as they always did when the Turkish governor was in trouble, and their raids through the countryside stopped all commerce (FO 1/8, #31 Plowden-FO 8/28/54). The governor kept up his petty tyrannies and vexations. Plowden was refused a hundred pounds of lead sent him with the permission of the Viceroy of Egypt. The governor further refused to allow Plowden to have his stove fixed without express orders from Constantinople. Plowden commented on the disorder apparent as soon as he crossed into Turkish territory after his trip to Kassala. Constant incendiary fires occurred at Massawa and the local police force had ceased to exist. The governor insulted all Christians and told the populace that French and English aid in the Crimean War was commanded by the Porte (FO 1/8, #22 Plowden-FO 6/25/54, #24 Plowden-FO 7/2/54). These reports were confirmed to Consul General Bruce by Mr. Barroni, a merchant at Massawa and a friend of Plowden's, who acted as Plowden's agent when the Consul was in the interior (FO 1/8, #46 Bruce-FO 11/24/54).

Plowden sent in his classic "Memorandum on Abyssinia"

early in July, 1854 (FO 1/8, #27 Plowden-FO; Memorandum on
Abyssinia 7/9/54 reprinted in full in Hotten, J. C. , op. cit. ,
pp. 126-246). It is a remarkable document not only for its content but for its excellent style. While the whole report is of
tremendous value to anyone interested in Abyssinia, the historically important section is the one which contains Plowden's
conclusions. After discussing the possible ports of Abyssinia,
of which Massawa was the only feasible one, Plowden remarked
that the Egyptians ruled the Sudan with some semblance of order
and tranquillity, but that the Turkish rule of Massawa was nothing more nor less than a blockade of Abyssinia without any effort to govern the town. The governor in charge who had to
send in his yearly paper that his "20 provinces" were tranquil
always managed to choose the most disturbed time to file the
report. Plowden could see only three possible solutions. The
first, that Egypt and Abyssinia be under the same government,
was manifestly impossible. The second, that the Turks recognize Abyssinia as a separate country and protect the trade there,
was possible only if boundaries were defined, the roads made
safe, and Abyssinian merchants put under British protection
with consulates established at Adowa and Gondar. The third,
that England take possession of a route to Abyssinia, meant the
British occupation of Massawa (FO 1/8, #27 Plowden-FO 7/9/54).

In September, 1854, Plowden had gone to Adowa to see
Oubie. Here he found that a pitched battle between Oubie and
Kassai was scheduled to take place early in November, 1854.
A victory for Kassai would mean hope for the improvement of
Abyssinia (FO 1/9, #32 Plowden [Adowa]-FO 9/25/54). This
battle never took place. Oubie sued for peace, paid tribute,
and kept the title of Ras, while acknowledging Kassai as Emper-
or of Abyssinia. Kassai meanwhile had written Plowden expressing his esteem for England and advising Plowden that the
slave trade had been forbidden in Abyssinia (FO 1/9, #36 Plowden-FO 11/6/54 and #38 Plowden-FO 11/28/54).

In November Plowden and the French Vice-Consul were
forced to present a joint protest to the governor of Massawa.
The Naïb of Arkiko, by now a tool of the governor, had marched
into Hamasein province, a part of Tigré, with 150 Turkish soldiers, and burned villages and churches on the pretext that the
chief of the Hamasein had raided some Shiho herds. If this action by the tribes had occurred, the governor should have protested to Ras Oubie or asked his government for orders and in

any case should have informed the consuls of his intentions. Plowden felt it very inconvenient that the governor should have the power to provoke war at his pleasure and meditate the conquest of Christian provinces while he was totally unable to govern his own territory. Plowden thought that while, in this case, the Abyssinians were quite able to take care of themselves, the final result would only lead to bloodshed and banditry (FO 1/9, #39 Plowden-FO 11/28/54).

Shortly afterwards Plowden had to protest again as the troops of the governor ravaged the province of Mensa, northwest of Massawa, for no apparent good reason. These protests caused de Redcliffe [Stratford Canning had been elevated to the peerage in 1852 and had assumed the title Stratford de Redcliffe] to inform the Porte in a very stiff note that the situation had to be changed at Massawa and that another vizierial letter was useless (FO 1/9, #182 de Redcliffe-FO 3/12/55). In April de Redcliffe was shown the instructions to the new governor of Massawa. These were not completely satisfactory, but he felt that any improvement was a gain, and if necessary more vigorous measures could be taken (FO 1/9, #281 de Redcliffe-FO 4/12/55).

After news of the attack on Mensa, Plowden, who had received no word from the Foreign Office for a year, went up to Senhait at the end of 1854 to prevent, if possible, new raids in that district. He found that such raids had been planned to convert all the tribes on the Abyssinian border, but that Omar Bey, the new Egyptian governor, had ordered them stopped (FO 1/9, #4 Plowden-FO 1/9/55).

News from Abyssinia showed Kassai's continually increasing power. He had consolidated his position by defeating Ras Oubie in February, 1855, taking his rival a prisoner during the battle. In view of this, Plowden requested that his leave be postponed so that he could visit Kassai, the way having been opened by Kassai's letter to him regarding the slave trade.

The period from 1848 to 1855 covers of course the Crimean War. Although, to the naive, the alliance of the French, English, and the Porte might seem to stop their rivalries, the converse is true. Certainly, both in Arabia and on the African coast of the Red Sea, Muslim antagonism to the Christian was intensified. Whether or not the Pashas in this district were acting under orders is an interesting question but quite impossible to answer. It is certain that the Porte regarded the Red Sea as a Turkish lake and resented any European activities in

it, especially those which came close to the Holy Cities. Plowden's comment that the governor of Massawa had told the people
that the French and English were allies of the Turks at the command of the Porte was certainly believed by most Muslims.

French and English rivalries also continued. The most interesting aspect of this is the British tendency to protect the
non-Catholic Christians against the aggressions of French-pro-
tected Catholicism. While the French never made political
gains in this part of the world through their traditional protectorate of the Roman Church, they were a constant irritant and
a danger to British interests. As for French colonial aims at
this period, there is no basis for claiming that there were any
definite projects in mind. On the other hand, they would unquestionably have accepted anything which by chance came their
way. It is interesting to note that the revolution of 1848 made
little difference in the continuity of French interests.

XI. ADEN AND ARABIA 1854-1857

When Haines was recalled to India, Brigadier Clarke,
commander in chief of the garrison, became acting Political
Agent. Probably otherwise an able officer, he showed himself
surprisingly naive in his dealings with the Arabs. These wily
gentlemen, assuming that by the removal of Haines all their
past sins were forgotten, immediately descended on Brigadier
Clarke with a vast quantity of preposterous claims. Sultan Ali
carried this to its extremity by producing a document with
Haines' name forged to it promising to give the Abdali military
support in the reconquest of Bir Ahmed (BSC 1854, Clarke-
Bombay 3/31/54). The question was referred to Haines, at
Bombay, who stated that he had never signed any documents
with the Arabs unless absolutely necessary, and denied any such
agreement. Haines took the opportunity to describe his policy
with the Arabs. He stated, "My opinion is that much correspondence with Arabs is disadvantageous, it prolongs disputes
and in the end will even prove of no avail. More will be done
in a personal conference of a few hours than in a month's correspondence. Good will, kindness and respect will also do
more than even the bayonet can in Arabia. " Clarke, Haines
felt, had misinterpreted his actions. Haines had had no communication with the Abdali chief since the chief's pension had
been stopped. Further, Haines thought that the Aqrabi would
never be peaceful until reunited with the Abdali. Clarke had
written to the various chiefs and tried to deal with each one
separately, while Haines had made one chief alone responsible
for the roads. Clarke "expresses his feelings as an Englishman that justice and equal good will should be open and shown
to all. I agree with Brigadier Clarke had he Europeans to deal
with, but he has Arabs who are most difficult to control and
manage and I may add almost impossible to deal with (as the
Turks have found in the Hejaz and Yemen to their cost after 50
years' experience). " By entering into correspondence with the
Fadhli, Clarke insulted Sultan Ali of the Abdali, an action which
might cause serious trouble. "Our European ideas of equity
and politics will not be comprehensible to the Arabs. "
    "Long experience with the Arabs (upwards of 30 years) has
taught me that they must be defeated with their own weapons,

by quietly letting them know you perceive their intentions, before they are prepared to carry them out, and let them feel you
are their superior in tact, intellect, judgment and activity of
purpose, that their secret thoughts are known to you, that your
information is sure, secret and correct and that you are prepared to counteract their designs; this united with frankness,
firmness, decision and consistency will secure an Englishman
his point and he will have moral power over them and be respected
and feared and they will afterwards give him little trouble. Had
I remained in power another month, I should, through Sultan
Ali M'Hussein's power influence and money, have I think secured a permanent peace and the order of the government to pay
the Foutheli [Fadhli] his stipend with the Chief of Lahej's concurrence. " In treating directly with the Fadhli, Clarke would
be inviting this chief to try to dictate his own terms, Haines
thought. "He is a snake in the grass that will bite as opportunity offers and his acquaintance is by no means desirable.... I
only hope and trust for the prosperity of Aden that the new line
of policy pursued may prove advantageous but I fear it will not. "
Haines concluded by stating that bayonets and arms would be
useless in Arabia unless backed up by moral force and respect
(BSC 1854, Haines [in Bombay]-Bombay 4/13/54). The Bombay Government forwarded this letter to the acting Political
Agent for his guidance (BSC 1854, Resolution 4/25/54).

Clarke also wished to break up Aden's monopoly of trade
and encourage other ports to compete, feeling that the fifteen
years of occupation had shown no results (BSC 1854, Clarke-
Bombay 4/27/54). He was curtly reminded that a letter governing his policy had been forwarded to him (BSC 1854, Minute
5/7/54).

Meanwhile discussions were taking place regarding the new
officials for Aden. Referring to certain papers of 1847 which
recommended combining the offices of Political Resident and
Commander in Chief, Lord Elphinstone, the Governor of Bombay, felt that the time was ripe for such a change especially
with the threat of the Crimean War. "At such a crisis," he
wrote, "it is certainly most desirable that all authority both
military and political at such an important isolated point should
be centered in able and vigourous hands. " He suggested Colonel
James Outram as the logical man for the post, dependent, of
course, on the consent of the government of India. Outram had
shown his willingness to accept, giving up his then post as

Resident at Baroda, without asking about the salary. Elphinstone suggested giving him the combined salaries of the two
posts, i. e. , 2,000 rupees per month for Resident and 1,832
rupees per month for Commander in Chief, a total of 3,832 rupees, and granting him the title of "Political Resident and Commandant at Aden. " Outram had asked for Lieutenant Playfair
of the Madras Artillery as an assistant. In 1839, when Aden
was established, the government of India had laid down a rule
that as Aden was primarily a naval base, the assistant should
be a naval officer, but Elphinstone thought this "an unpolitic
restriction" (BSC 1854, Minute by Elphinstone 4/17/54, concurred in by the rest of the Board).

Outram arrived in June and took over the Residency from
Clarke. He found little change in the situation from that at
Haines' recall in March, although the tone of Outram's report
indicates that things were in rather a mess (BSC 1854, Outram-
Bombay 6/26/54 and 7/12/54). Outram, suspicious of the
French in spite of their alliance with the British in the Crimean
War, decided that Haines and other officials had underestimated
the seriousness of their actions and believed that they were
threatening to occupy immediately some position in the Red Sea
(BSC 1854, Outram-Bombay 7/18/54). He also sent in a long
report on the tribes, aided by information given by the Reverend
George Percy Badger, a missionary at Aden and a very able
man who had helped Haines and was to be invaluable to later
residents. Mr. Badger was extremely learned in Arabic customs and Muslim law, and his English-Arabic dictionary is still
a standard reference book. Outram, after damning the policy
of the government by the word "vacillating, " stated that he
would handle the matter of a murder by force if necessary. He
thoroughly agreed with Haines' policy in all details and requested
such power to act against the tribes as might be necessary
(BSC 1854, Outram-Bombay 8/10/54).

Elphinstone in a long Minute pointed out the specific instructions of the Court of Directors in London against any change in
policy. He commented on the expenditure of Ł75,000 annually
to support the garrison and the consistent refusal of London to
allow this force to be used. He hoped permission would be given
to Outram to use his discretion (BSC 1854, Minute by Elphinstone 9/6/54 and Outram-Bombay 9/13/54).

At the end of September, 1854, Outram became ill and was
compelled to return to Bombay for his health. His place was

taken by his Chief of Staff Lieutenant Colonel William M. Coghlan. Thus, by luck, Aden acquired another extremely able, if
not brilliant, Resident. Coghlan showed such marked abilities
that when Outram's health definitely prevented his return,
Coghlan was appointed as regular Resident.

Meanwhile Outram's dispatches caused the Governor General of India considerable surprise, and convinced him that
Clarke's reports to London had resulted in a misconception of
the facts of the situation at Aden. As the Secret Committee had
issued certain orders they had to be obeyed, but he felt that the
Resident should be informed that he should aid the Sultan of Lahej
if he believed it necessary (BSC 1854, Govt. of India-Bombay
10/18/54). The interior however remained calm, and Coghlan
had no need to exercise the discretion granted to him which he
understood applied only in case of atrocities or a coalition a-
gainst Aden (BSC 1854, Coghlan-Bombay 11/28/54).

By December, 1854, the damage to British influence caused
by Clarke's policies began to show itself. Although peace reigned
it was obvious that it was due largely to false promises made
by Sultan Ali to the Aqrabi and Fadhli. These tribes were already demanding that Bir Ahmed be reopened as a port. It had
been closed by agreement with Sultan Ali who had promised
certain advantages which were not forthcoming. Normally under such circumstances Sultan Ali would have demanded British
aid to get him out of his mess. With Haines' relief by Clarke,
the guiding hand had been removed, and Clarke's treatment of
Sultan Ali and the Fadhli Sultan had not only allowed them both
a free hand but had also antagonized Sultan Ali. With these facts
before him, Coghlan felt it better to preserve the fort at Bir
Ahmed and make it over to Sultan Ali than to destroy it. He also started to negotiate with the 'Aulaqi tribe, a powerful inland
tribe who had never opposed the British and yet had never had
any negotiations with them. This tribe lay to the east and north
of the Fadhli country and was in an excellent position to bring
pressure on the other tribes. In case of trouble and the consequent cutting off of supplies, Coghlan felt that the capture of
Bir Ahmed was the best means of retaliation (BSC 1855, Coghlan
-Bombay 12/4/54).

Meanwhile, the Secret Committee wrote new instructions to
Coghlan, informing him that there were no treaty obligations to
support the Sultan of Lahej as the Bombay Government had
thought. It ended with a specific declaration, "You will clearly

understand that neither on the present nor on any future occasion
are you to engage in any inland military operations without specific orders from that Government [Bombay]" (BSC 1855, Secret
Committee-Coghlan 12/9/54).

As the year 1855 wore on, the interior became more and
more disturbed. In January, Coghlan was forced to forbid any
Europeans to go outside the walls or land on the Arabian shore
(BSC 1855, Coghlan-Bombay 1/12/55).

The Governor General of India, having digested the orders
of the Secret Committee, suggested in February that further
outrages could not be disregarded. As "inland military operations" were discouraged, his Lordship suggested that sudden
surprise night attacks be made on the coastal villages (BSC 1855,
Govt. of India-Bombay 2/8/55).

The truce between the Fadhli and the Abdali was due to ex-
pire on March 19, and Coghlan was convinced that this would be
the occasion for trouble. He was certain that the only obstacle
in the way of peace with the Fadhli tribe was the intransigence
of the old Sultan. However, Coghlan had been able to detach the
'Aulaqi from their alliance with the Fadhli and also had started
trade with them by sea (BSC 1855, Coghlan-Bombay 3/14/55
and 3/15/55). As the Resident had predicted, trouble started
as soon as the truce ended. As the Fadhli began blocking the
road, Coghlan blockaded Shuqra; the "Mahi" and the "Elphinstone" took turns at Shuqra and Bir Ahmed (BSC 1855, Coghlan-
Bombay 3/27/55 and 3/28/55). Negotiations with the 'Aulaqi
continued with the visit of the heir apparent of the Upper 'Aulaqi
to Aden and the return visit of an interpreter of the Residency,
Hormudz Rassam (BSC 1855, Coghlan-Bombay 4/21/55 and
5/12/55). Hormudz Rassam was a very able Christian from
Baghdad who had been a protégé of Sir Henry Layard in his exploration of ancient Nineveh. Rassam's father had been interpreter at the Baghdad Residency, and young Rassam had wanted
to go into the government service. He was sent to Aden as an
interpreter and rose to the office of first political assistant at
the time of the Abyssinian troubles. His mission to effect the
release of King Theodore's captives is his greatest claim to
fame, but he also was a very important member of the Coghlan
mission to settle the Muscat-Zanzibar dynastic claims in 1860,
and for a short time he was in charge of the Residency at Muscat. In Rassam and the Reverend Mr. Badger, Coghlan had two
very able advisers on Arab affairs and the importance of these

two men, as well as Captain Playfair, later Sir Robert Playfair, cannot be overestimated. Haines' success in dealing with the Arabs was due almost entirely to his own uncanny ability to understand the Arab mind; Coghlan's success was due unquestionably to his intelligent use of able advisers.

On May 27, Sheikh 'Othman was attacked and supplies were cut off completely (BSC 1855, Coghlan-Bombay 5/27/55). Governor Elphinstone commented that the Resident was drifting entirely too much into Arab affairs contrary to the orders of the Secret Committee (BSC 1855, Minute by Elphinstone 6/27/55). However, the coming of Ramadan, the Muslim month of fasting, lifted pressure on the town and all was peaceful.

By July matters became very difficult. The kafilas were continually plundered. As a result of Clarke's lack of diplomacy, Coghlan found it impossible to deal with the Fadhli or the Abdali, as both insisted on dictating their terms for peace. The only way that the Resident could see to restore peace was for a combined attack by the British and the 'Aulaqi, the British on Bir Ahmed and the 'Aulaqi on the rear of the tribes (BSC 1855, Coghlan-Bombay 7/7/55).

Elphinstone approved these ideas although they were contrary to the orders of the Secret Committee, but consoled himself by the fact that both Shuqra and Bir Ahmed were on the seacoast and thus any such moves would not be "inland military operations." A dispatch on these lines was prepared for the approval of the Governor General of India (BSC 1855, Minute by Elphinstone 7/25/55).

By the end of July the roads had been entirely closed and the water supply at Sheikh 'Othman captured by the Fadhli (BSC 1855, Coghlan-Bombay 7/30/55). The Governor General, after reading Elphinstone's Minute of July 25, sent it on to London with the urgent request that Coghlan be allowed to act (BSC 1855, Govt. of India-Bombay 8/6/55). Elphinstone suggested that Coghlan not be informed of all this "as it is best he did not know that the Governor General and the Secret Committee do not agree" (BSC 1855, Minute by Elphinstone 8/19/55).

Coghlan in Aden prepared for siege. The roads were open for five days, from the first of August to the fifth, but were then closed. Supplies in the town were plentiful except for firewood, forage, and reeds which could not be supplied from other Red Sea ports (BSC 1855, Coghlan-Bombay 8/12/55).

The Fadhli were unable to keep the roads closed for very

long, and in September Coghlan felt that the situation was stable
enough for him to take a trip in the Gulf of Aden as far as Mukalla and possibly to the Kuria Muria Islands, acquired by England in 1854 from the Imam of Muscat, to see if any places
were suitable for cable sites (BSC 1855, Coghlan-Bombay 9/12/
55). Before leaving Aden Coghlan suggested as peace terms to
the Fadhli, a restoration of the stipend, expulsion of the criminal Boghi in return for the lifting of the blockade at Bir Ahmed
and Shuqra. These were accepted by the Fadhli, thanks to the
influence of Sultan Ali, and a sort of peace was patched up in
September. However, the arrears of his stipend were not
granted to the Fadhli Sultan (BSC 1855, Coghlan-Bombay 9/21/55).

    This uneasy situation was made more complicated in Octo-
ber by the discovery that the Sayud Muhammad Husain, the murderer of Captain Milne, had not been poisoned as reported but
was quite healthy and acting as one of the Fadhli chieftain's
principal advisers (BSC 1855, Minute by Elphinstone 11/9/55
quoting private letter from Coghlan). The Bombay Government
then decided to direct Coghlan, who had returned from the Gulf
of Aden, to order the delivery of the murderers, Sayud Muhammad Husain and Boghi, by the Fadhli Sultan within seven days
or else face a restoration of the blockade and the loss of his stipend for the rest of his life (BSC 1855, Resolution 11/14/55).
As a blockade of Berbera was being considered at this time, the
result of the murder of Lieutenant Stroyan (vide infra), Coghlan
requested the Bombay Government to consider the withdrawal
of this action on the Somali coast as such a blockade, occurring
simultaneously with a cessation of supplies from the interior,
would have a very serious effect on Aden's food supply (BSC
1855, Coghlan-Bombay 10/28/55). It was decided to forego the
ultimatum to the Fadhli temporarily, as a great many incidents
were suddenly occurring in the Red Sea area which were dis-
tracting the attention of the authorities at Aden and Bombay away
from the immediate environs of the town, and made no naval
vessels available for action against the tribes.

    Several times, in the years after the British occupation of
Aden, Berbera had been forcibly brought to the attention of the
Political Agent by the ambitions of Ali Shermarkee. As has
been mentioned before, Berbera was one of the chief sources of
supply for Aden, especially of meat. In the days before refrigeration, the best way to keep meat fresh was to keep it on the
hoof, and in a town whose civilian population was predominantly

Arabic and whose military population was predominantly Sepoy,
lamb and sheep were about the only non-controversial sources
of meat. Sheep were plentiful in the Somali country and non-
existent in the Arabian hinterland near Aden. Berbera was also
the outlet for the trade of Shoa which the Harris expedition and
Rochet d'Hericourt's trips had so vainly tried to open up. Another reputedly rich country was Harar, a Muslim section of
Abyssinia. Berbera was also Harar's chief seaport. While the
Harris expedition had fairly well exploded the idea of the wealth
of Shoa, Harar had never been visited, due largely to the fanatical nature of the people and the difficulties of the road which
passed through a country in a constant state of turmoil, stem-
ming from the same tribal rivalries which had cut off communications with Shoa after the return of Harris and Rochet d'Hericourt.

    In the middle of 1854, a young officer of the Indian Army,
Richard Burton, received a leave of absence from his regimental duties to join an expedition to discover the sources of the
Nile with other army officers, John Speke, Herne, and a Lieutenant Stroyan of the Indian Navy. Before starting on their expedition the officers split up to do some preliminary explorations, and Burton decided to try to penetrate to Harar. After
spending some time with Shermarkee in Zeila, he left on foot
for Harar on November 27, 1854 (BSC 1855 Coghlan-Bombay
12/28/54). His trip is fully described in the best Burton style
in his book FIRST FOOTSTEPS IN EAST AFRICA (London,
Longmans, 1856). Of much more interest to the historian is his
report to the Bombay Government (BSC 1855, Coghlan-Bombay
2/22/55, encl. Burton-Coghlan 2/22/55). In commenting on
Zeila, Burton stated that Shermarkee's chief desire was to see
Zeila and Tajura become British possessions, and that the antagonism of Harar towards Shermarkee was due to his attempts
to get the Harar caravans to go to Zeila rather than to Berbera
which actually was farther away. Harar, Burton found, was
purely a commercial city whose fanatical tendencies were exaggerated. Its importance and wealth were due to its being on the
main road to the coast from Central Africa, not to any particular wealth of the land around it.

    But Berbera interested Burton the most. He found upon in-
vestigation that the constant tribal quarrels had caused a decline
of the fair. Other factors contributing to this decline was a
growing system of "protectors" whom Burton would undoubtedly

have called racketeers were he writing today, and also a fear
among the natives that some foreign power would seize Berbera.
Burton's comment on this shows that his historical knowledge
did not equal his linguistic abilities. "The Turks would have
done so before now if not prevented by our Government." Burton noted that Berbera, Tajura, and Zeila were the only ports
for the export of slaves from the Galla country, and attributed
part of the decline of trade in the Berbera district to this increase in slave traffic "which is easier and more profitable than
raising cotton or coffee." To restore Berbera to its former
greatness Burton put forth three alternatives. The first was the
establishment of a consul or vice-consul at Berbera, the second,
to give it over to Shermarkee, the third, to establish a commercial agency there under one of the Political Assistants to the
Resident of Aden. Burton felt that the first plan would soon be
imitated by other nations and would have no weight with the nomadic peoples. The second plan had its points but Shermarkee
was a Turkish official, as ruler of Zeila which was subject to
Mocha, and also was at feud with the Somalis at Berbera. The
third plan Burton thought was the best, as the Somalis admired
the British, and commercial relations were important both to
Aden and the fair. Such a move would decrease Aden's dependence on her hinterland and help increase supplies to a town
which had grown from 16,500 in 1842 to over 25,000 in 1854.
Burton felt that such an agency would be the basis for a new
town on once wealthy land. Water was reported to be plentiful
about fifteen or twenty feet below the surface, and the high
ground near Berbera healthy. Furthermore, it would be an excellent site as a base for slave trade suppression from Jidda to
Mombasa (BSC 1855, Coghlan-Bombay 2/22/55 encl. Burton-
Coghlan 2/22/55).

One immediate result of Burton's trip to Harar was a request from the Amir of Harar for a doctor who knew about consumption. Coghlan sent a Sayud who had a certain amount of
contemporary medical knowledge (BSC 1855, Coghlan-Bombay
3/14/55).

Burton returned to Berbera early in March, 1855, rejoin-
ing his fellow officers, and the expedition planned to leave at
the end of April for the interior of Africa. Burton discovered
a fine supply of good water at Berbera near the site he suggested
for an agency, and thus answered one objection which had been
raised to his plan (BSC 1855, Coghlan-Bombay 4/20/55). On

April 19 the officers, having been in Berbera for a month or
more and having been well-received all the time, dismissed
their guards. As they were asleep some assassins crept in
their tents and murdered Lieutenant Stroyan. Speke and Burton
were seriously injured, only Herne escaping unharmed. At the
time the motive was hard to establish. Coghlan guessed it was
due either to Burton's known friendship with Shermarkee or his
plans for English occupation. Actually, later investigation
proved it was merely robbery. The criminals were known to
be of either the Essa Musa or Ayal Ahmed tribes as the fair had
been over for a month and these were the only natives around.
Coghlan was at a loss to know what punishment to prescribe in
the event of the assassins not being produced and an indemnity
paid, as the nomadic tribes had no property to destroy. He
could only suggest a blockade to prevent the fair being held the
next year (BSC 1855, Coghlan-Bombay 4/23/55).

This news greatly disturbed Governor Elphinstone, who was
keenly disappointed in the check which had been given to exploration and the opening of commerce. The governor felt that the
officers themselves were largely to blame, for in dismissing
their guards they had gone against the advice of their hosts.
He regretted that Coghlan had demanded a large indemnity,
15,000 rupees, with his demand for the assassins; furthermore
he believed a blockade would ruin the Aden market (BSC 1855,
Minute by Elphinstone 4/22/55).

Investigation proved that the Habr Owuls, a subtribe of the
Ayal Ahmuds, were the sole offenders (BSC 1855, Coghlan-
Bombay 6/24/55). The Indian Government thought that Coghlan's
terms were entirely too hard and decreed that at least one of
the murderers should be put to death, the rest banished, and
the indemnity be greatly reduced. At the same time, the Governor General of India indicated that he was strongly averse to
the establishment of an agency at Berbera (BSC 1855, Govt. of
India-Bombay 6/29/55).

A blockade was enforced as soon as the fair opened and
managed to cut off the trade to a certain extent. In February,
1856, a prisoner was produced by the Somalis, but Coghlan
did not believe him to be one of the murderers (BSC 1856, Coghlan-Bombay 2/23/56). A deposition of the Somali elders claimed
this man was the chief offender, although Coghlan had found out
that the true culprit's name was On Ali, a man of very good family (BSC 1856, Coghlan-Bombay 3/16/56). The Bombay

Government decided that the blockade should continue until On
Ali was produced (BSC 1856, Minute 4/1/56). By May, 1856,
Coghlan suggested that the blockade be lifted, as the loss of the
fair had been a serious punishment to the Somalis. Furthermore, it appeared impossible to have the murderer produced,
the Somalis having shown their good faith in producing one of
the culprits (BSC 1856, Coghlan-Bombay 5/22/56). This course
was approved by the Bombay Government (BSC 1856, Resolution
6/7/56).

Coghlan heard rumors at the same time that the Turks
threatened to occupy Berbera when the blockade was withdrawn,
since the insurrections at Mecca and Massawa (see below) had
been put down. Such an occupation, Coghlan believed, would
divert a rich trade and stimulate slave traffic. He suggested
including a clause in the treaty which was proposed to close the
Burton incident, guaranteeing the independence of Berbera.
He added, "I need not point out how exceedingly embarrassing
it would be to Aden were Berbera in the hands of a foreign
power" (BSC 1856, Coghlan-Bombay 5/29/56).

This course was not approved by the Governor General, who
felt such a clause amounted to a practical guarantee of protection. As for Turkish aggression, his Lordship said "that authority still is, and his Lordship in Council believes always will
be, too feeble and too far from any center of support to bear extension to a spot so isolated and inaccessible to the resources
of Turkey as Berbera. As regards France, it would be the
height of rashness to attempt to prophesy what may be, as time
goes on, the policy of that Power in the East....

"... The Governor General... deprecates a counter policy
on the part of India which shall hinder its government with the
obligation to defend... a nook of Africa at a distance of 1,600
miles from its resources."

He considered that the Somalis were independent de facto
as the government of India had dealt with them as independent
chiefs and made engagements with them. "It is easy for an unscrupulous state bent on aggrandizing itself at the expense of a
rude people, to find a plausible ground of quarrel, which shall
leave it free to seek such satisfaction as may best suit its purpose. A recognition in words of the independence of Berbera by
another state without the engagement to defend it, would be no
obstacle to such designs." As the British Government had the
right to oppose any designs of conquest on the Somali coast

anyway, the Governor General felt that there was no need of any guarantee of independence (BSC 1856, Govt. of India-Bombay 7/28/56). A treaty was signed in November, 1856, closing the incident (BSC 1856, Coghlan-Bombay 11/10/56).

In the fall of 1855, Coghlan had made a trip around the Gulf of Aden on the "Semiramis." He visited the 'Aulaqi chieftain first and signed a treaty with him abolishing the slave trade. The "Semiramis" then crossed the Gulf of Aden to Burnt Island [Mait Island on modern maps] sixty miles west of Las Khoreh, which he found to have considerable new guano deposits since the original deposits had been exhausted by the Somalis. (It is interesting to note that the natives of the Red Sea and Persian Gulf had known the fertilizing value of guano long before it was known in Europe.) Coghlan then steamed along the coast arranging slave trade treaties with the local tribes, and discovered that the blockade of Berbera had greatly stimulated trade in the other ports. Then he visited Berbera, which impressed him greatly as a market place. He could not agree with Burton that the Somalis could settle down to agriculture. Briefly, he considered that Berbera "had no neighborhood." He wrote in further detail of a possible English agency there, a plan which he approved in part, but of course he did not know that the government of India had already decided against any such plan (BSC 1855, Coghlan-Bombay 11/8/55). While the only results of this trip were some minor anti-slave trade treaties which were unenforceable at the moment, it gave Coghlan a chance to see the district and understand more fully the problems of Aden.

Since the beginning of the crisis which led up to the Crimean War, the Hedjaz, the most fanatical portion of the Turkish empire, had been in continual turmoil. Towards the end of 1854 a rebellion, begun in June of that year, had quieted down to the extent of an armed truce. But on October 29, 1855, a firman of the Porte prohibiting the slave trade at Mecca caused rebellion to burst out anew. According to an account forwarded to Coghlan by a Banyan merchant in Hodeida, the Kadi who read the firman was almost mobbed when he ruled that the order must be obeyed. The mob was led by ulema who claimed that the Sultan's order did not agree with the order of God and that it should be defied. The poor Kadi was rescued by a detachment of Turkish troops. During this disturbance, a muezzin was ascending the minaret of a neighboring mosque to call the faithful to prayer and was killed by a wild shot from one of the

soldier's guns. This aroused the entire population. The army
in the citadel was besieged after a bloody fight in which eighty
people were killed. The Sharif Abdul Muttalib came quickly
from Ta'if to quell the disturbance and was greeted at Mecca
with an order from the Porte demanding his seizure and deposition. The Sharif promptly declared himself a rebel and joined
the mob closing all the roads. He then demanded from the
Pasha at Jidda that the order be rescinded, that slavery remain,
and that the flags of the English and French consulates at Jidda
be taken down. The Pasha replied that slavery was of no moment, but taking down the flags was impossible, and proceeded
to place a heavy guard on the consulates. (BSC 1855, Coghlan-
Bombay 12/11/55 encl. letters from an unnamed merchant under British protection at Hodeida, from Abdul Russool at Mocha
and Consul West at Suez, all corroborating each other in full
detail.)

Letters from Consul Page, who had replaced Cole at Jidda,
confirmed the above report, giving more detail of the rioting in
Mecca, which had turned into a looting-fest. Consul Page attributed the whole matter to the replacement of Sharif Abdul
Muttalib by Abdallah ibn Nasser; he believed the reading of the
slave trade firman was just an excuse (BSC 1856, Page-Bombay
11/13/56). In this crisis, the Bombay Government found it impossible to send a ship to Jidda. Admiral Leeke, commander
in chief of the Indian Navy, wrote, "Your Lordship is aware
that the most of the vessels of the Indian Navy are worn out by
incessant employ and it is only by dint of management and per-
severance, to say but little of the heavy responsibility, that I
am enabled to keep them afloat." The "Queen" which the governor had requested, a ship that three and a half years before
had been condemned, was under repair. "Moreover," to quote
Admiral Leeke, "she is so full of vermin and the stench on
board is so great that the Surgeon has reported that some steps
must be taken to purify her" (BSC 1856, Admiral Leeke-Bom-
bay 1/8/56). The "Queen," however, was sent.

The riots in Mecca provoked revolt throughout Arabia.
The Sharif of Abu 'Arish marched on Mocha, and the Yemen,
even, became disturbed (BSC 1856, Coghlan-Bombay 12/26/55).
At the same time an insurrection occurred at Massawa. But
the Turks regained control of Mecca by the early days of 1856
and the situation was apparently under control (BSC 1856,
Coghlan-Bombay 1/12/56).

At this stage the ever-threatening Asiri rose, blocked the roads near Jidda, and started to march on the Yemen (BSC 1856, Coghlan-Bombay 1/25/56). The Asiri, not wanting to face the Turkish entrenchments at Hodeida, suddenly turned southwards. A wild fanatic Moplah Sayud Fadhl was reported in their camp preaching a holy war against Aden and Lahej, which threw the country around Aden into terror. Coghlan was not too alarmed by this as he felt the Asiri would find the Yemen easy to plunder and they would thus be distracted from the Aden hinterland (BSC 1856, Coghlan-Bombay 2/13/56).

The "Queen" arrived at Hodeida on January 28 and immediately was put at the disposal of the Pasha. While the ship had too great a draft to be brought close in shore, two of her guns were mounted on small boats to guard the seaward flanks of the town's walls (BSC 1856, Coghlan-Bombay 2/13/56). The "Elphinstone's" appearance off Jidda restored confidence there and matters apparently quieted down as Sharif Muttalib's men began to desert him (BSC 1856, Page-Bombay 1/15/56). In February, an outbreak of cholera near Mocha caused the Asiri to retire, and peace appeared to settle over the Yemen (BSC 1856, Coghlan-Bombay 2/25/56). Sharif Ibn 'Aun arrived at Jidda on April 13 to replace Muttalib. (What happened to Sharif Abdallah ibn Nasser is not clear.) This was a signal for Muttalib to attack Mecca, which he almost succeeded in occupying, but, finally unsuccessful, he retired to Ta'if. Page considered that the only reason the Turks still held the Hedjaz was due to the appearance of the "Elphinstone" and the "Queen" (BSC 1856, Page-Bombay 4/19/56).

On May 19 Ta'if was besieged by the Turks; on May 22 the town surrendered and Muttalib was shipped off to Constantinople under guard (BSC 1856, Page-Bombay 5/24/56). The fanatic Moplah Sayud Fadhl, one of the leaders of this revolt, was extremely dangerous to the English; he was an Indian Muslim who had been expelled from India by the Government for his violent fanaticism. Page informed the Bombay Government that the Moplah had been granted refuge by the Turkish government and there was little that could be done about it. At the same time Page commented on the dual nature of the government of the Holy Places which was the fundamental cause of much of the trouble. The Pasha of the Hedjaz theoretically was the civil ruler of the country and shared equal power with the Grand Sharif, the spiritual ruler who must be descended from the family of

the prophet. Because of the religious nature of Muslim law
there was no clear-cut definition of authority between these two
men, and as each had his own separate and overlapping set of
officials, continuous bickering and jealousy resulted in Mecca,
Medina and Ta'if; Jidda was completely under Turkish control.
Page further commented on the blindness of the Turkish government in not breaking the power of the Asiri when the death of
their leader, Amir Hyder, which had occured early in 1855,
provided an easy opportunity. They were the sole remaining
powerful tribal group in western Arabia, and any measures tak-
en to break their influence would certainly have been helpful in
making the country really peaceful and stable (BSC 1856, Page-
Bombay 7/2/56).

The slave trade began to interest the Indian Government in
the 1850's and as time went on held their attention to an increasing extent. Slavery in Muslim countries was of ancient origin
and was sanctioned by the Koran. The lot of the slave in the
Muslim world was a not unhappy one. As Consul West at Suez
reported in 1873, the slave was better off than the peasant as
he had a master to take care of him if he was in trouble, and
he was well-treated because he had certain rights provided for
his protection by the Koran (FO 84/1371, West [Suez]-Cairo,
7/28/73).

The real inhumanity of Muslim slavery was in the trade
which brought these slaves to market. The general history of
the suppression of the slave trade is well-known, but there is
not general realization of the fact that the successful blockades
of the west and southeast coasts of Africa caused the slave trade
to increase tremendously from Mombasa northwards. While
this section of the coast remained open, it increased the inhumanity of the trade because the poor slaves were compelled to
march longer and longer distances to the seacoast. As the British anti-slave trade squadron could only stop vessels registered
from countries which had anti-slave trade treaties with Great
Britain, it was obvious that treaties must be negotiated with all
of the Muslim countries of the Middle East. The religious nature of slavery in this section of the world made negotiation of
such treaties extremely difficult, especially with the Ottoman
Empire. Furthermore, the enormous pretensions of sovereignty implied by the Sultan's title made the legal aspects of negotiations with independent chiefs in the Persian Gulf and Red Sea
areas extremely involved. Coupled with these legal difficulties,

the deplorable state of the ships of the Indian Navy made any actual patrolling of the area impossible. For this reason Aden had never been the base of any anti-slave trade patrol, nor had any attempts been made to establish such an organization. In 1855, the Porte issued, or was reported to have issued, a firman suppressing the slave trade. By an opinion of the Advocate General of the Bombay Government this firman applied only to the Persian Gulf and to ships in the Persian Gulf belonging to the territories of independent chiefs with whom treaties had been made. Coghlan had made such treaties with minor chiefs throughout the Gulf of Aden district and plans were on foot to close Zeila and Tajura, the chief ports of the trade, by giving Shermarkee Ali a pension in lieu of the income he received from this traffic. This plan was completely upset by Shermarkee, who had a sudden feud with Abu Bakr, the Turkish governor of Zeila, who had replaced him in 1855. Shermarkee blockaded the port of Zeila after Abu Bakr had refused to let him remove some property which Shermarkee claimed was his. While the pros and cons of this argument are not important, merely the usual record of bribery and greed, Shermarkee was apparently in the right. However, his actions made him persona non grata with the Turkish government and completely ruined his usefulness to the English (BSC 1856, Coghlan-Bombay 4/9/56).

M. Henri Lambert, French Consul at Aden, had made a trip through the area in the spring of 1856 and found the slave trade in full swing. According to his findings, 8,650 slaves had been imported through the Red Sea ports of the Arabian peninsula in the year of 1855. The Hadramaut ports accounted for about 7,500 more and the Persian Gulf ports another 15,000, making a total of 31,150, which Lambert said was about half the number estimated by the Arabs. Coghlan, on the basis of this finding, requested two small steamers based at Perim to put down the traffic (BSC 1856, Coghlan-Bombay 5/22/56). However, it was apparent that these anti-slave trade firmans of the Porte were for European consumption alone when the government at Bombay received the following brief note from the Foreign Office via the Secret Committee: "I am directed by Lord Clarendon to state to you for the information of the Commissioners for the affairs of India that he is not aware of the existence of any Secret treaty between Great Britain and the Porte authorizing officers of the Indian Navy to search vessels under the Ottoman Flag" (BSC 1856, Secret Committee-Bombay 10/4/

56). Thus ended the first attempts to suppress the slave trade in Red Sea waters.

From the establishment of a temporary peace with the Fadhli in September, 1855, the country around Aden remained quiet. The threatened approach of the Asiri did much to dispel any friction among the tribes, and peace reigned. A serious lack of rain in the year 1856 did not help the crops, but the discovery of some old reservoirs on the peninsula helped relieve the water supply. While the Crimean War did not affect the actions of the Aden government in any way outside the town, it filled the Aden jails. At the outbreak of the war, most of the best sailors in the British Merchant Marine joined the Navy, and the Aden coal ships were "manned by scum" (Playfair, Sir Robert Lambert, "Reminiscences," Chambers Journal, sixth series, Vol. II #56, December 24, 1898, p. 49). Many of these men were arrested for disturbances at Aden and put to work on public work projects. With these men Captain Playfair, having discovered what apparently were ancient reservoirs, dug out the remains, cleaned them up, and made them serviceable. He considered them of great antiquity, and from debris found in them dated their construction at about 600 A.D. By January 1, 1857, reservoirs of a capacity of 3,538,715 gallons had been repaired and were in use, leaving thirty-two more to be repaired varying in capacity from 8,000 to 4,800,000 gallons. The cost of repairs in two years had been only 11,542 rupees. (Playfair, Captain Robert L., A MEMOIR ON THE ANCIENT RESERVOIRS LATELY DISCOVERED... AT ADEN, Aden, Jail Press, 1857, pp. 7 and 21.) According to Playfair their discovery was accidental. He had turned out men from the jail into the crater to move earth, so as to keep them busy and out of the sun ("Reminiscences," vide supra, p. 50). Such a discovery gave the town a greater feeling of security, and increased the possibilities of future growth, previously limited by the water supply.

The three years, then, after Haines' disgrace were marked by a renewed interest in the Red Sea area by the Indian Government. The year 1856 marked the beginning of an interest in Perim which resulted in its occupation (vide infra). It is difficult to judge how much of this activity was caused by French diplomacy in Egypt. With the exception of the occupation of Perim, no mention is made of negotiations for the construction of a Suez Canal. The affairs of the Somali coast were forced upon the attention of the Resident by the actions of a single officer

with a desire for exploration, and those of the Hedjaz by a serious threat to British-protected subjects. The Crimean War
passed Aden by unnoticed, its only evidence in the active assistance offered the Turks at Hodeida and Jidda during Muttalib's
revolt. It is certainly apparent that the Secret Committee had
had no change of heart towards Aden and were perfectly willing
to let the settlement drift along. The interest of the Bombay
Government soon waned after the Haines affair was settled, and
Outram, a personal friend of Lord Elphinstone, was no longer
Resident. Aden still remained but a coaling station in the eyes
of the government and was due to remain so until the Abyssinian
campaign and the opening of the Suez Canal showed its importance as a strategic military and naval base.

XII. PERIM

"On sait l'histoire, L'Occupation d'Aden par les Anglais
(1839) avait secoué l'apathie du gouvernement de Julliet. En
1840, il envoy a prendre Perim; seulement son envoyé vint
mouiller sa Fregate devant Aden, ou, naïvement, à table, il
raconta à ses hôtes, les officiers anglais, le but de sa mission!
Les anglais ne protestérent pas, toastérent à la gloire de la
France, mais le lendemain quand nôtre bâtiment atterrit a Perim, le pavillon anglais flottait depuis quelques heures sur l'îlot
'Perim était à prendre,' nous repondit-on 'puisque vous veniez
pour le prendre: nous 'avons pris!'"

The above quotation was written by Paul Bonnetain of the
French Colonial Service in 1885 for "La France Coloniale," a
history of the French Empire published under the editorship of
Alfred Rambaud, the distinguished French historian (LA FRANCE
COLONIALE, Paris, Armand Colin et Cie. , seventh ed. , 1895,
p. 435). Aside from being inaccurate history, it gave rise to
a legend about the British occupation of Perim which had continued until today. The facts are quite different.

The interest in the occupation of the island of Perim began
with the Bombay Government, although there had been some
agitation in shipping circles for the establishment of a lighthouse
there. On May 30, 1856, the Government wrote Coghlan requesting information about the island and the possibility of a
settlement there (BSC 1856, Bombay-Coghlan 5/30/56). The
"Elphinstone" was sent to Perim and returned after a short investigation to report that the island lacked water but that there
remained from the expedition of 1799 a large tank to hold water
which was in good repair. The island contained an excellent,
well-protected harbor four to six fathoms deep. As for provisions, firewood, and water, the island was only one and a half
miles from Bab-el-Mandeb and eleven miles from the other
shore, both shores capable of supplying a sufficiency of provisions. Coghlan felt that it had tremendous strategic importance
commanding the mouth of the Red Sea and that in the event of a
Suez Canal it would be doubly important. Furthermore, it was
a very strategic point to suppress the slave trade, situated as
it was directly on the route from Zeila, Tajura, and Zanzibar
to all the Red Sea ports. Aside from these considerations, it

was becoming increasingly necessary to have a lighthouse there.
The P. & O. boats were making two to three trips a month to
India, an Australian line was about to be established, and the
Mauritius Company planned to extend its service from Aden to
Suez. Coghlan estimated that 90,000 tons of steam traffic a
year entered the Red Sea. As to territorial claims, Coghlan
felt that while the island was unoccupied, the Porte would claim
it if the matter were brought to their attention. The last occu-
pants had been the Indian army in 1799, so that England had a
satisfactory claim (FO 78/1333, IB-FO 11/3/56 encl. Coghlan-
Bombay 8/27/56, also in BSC 1856).

However, the Governor of Bombay was not satisfied by this
report and felt that the objections raised by the experience of
the occupation of 1799 had not been answered, especially the
lack of water. He added that the idea of an occupation was "not
to render it [Perim] a Cronstadt but to prevent others from making it one." He further felt that a simple occupation of the island was sufficient as it had already been officially taken possession of in 1799 by the East India Company (FO 78/1333, IB-FO
11/3/56 encl. Minute by Elphinstone 10/1/56; also in BSC 1856).
Others of the Board of Government believed that the occupation
was so necessary that Coghlan should immediately be ordered
to take possession and place a small body of men there with a
boat at their disposal. The two possible objections, lack of water and French jealousy, should be discounted, the first because
other means of providing water could be found, and the second
because the French had no essential interests in the Red Sea
(FO 78/1333, IB-FO 11/3/56, encl. Minute by Malet 10/2/56;
also in BSC 1856). However, Elphinstone did not share this
feeling of urgency and proposed to get the consent of the Home
Government (FO 78/1333, IB-FO 11/3/56, encl. Minute by Elphinstone 10/3/56; also in BSC 1856).

In London the question was turned over to the Foreign Office which agreed with the Bombay Government that no time
should be lost in taking possession of the island and erecting an
excellent lighthouse there (FO 78/1333, FO-IB 11/9/56).

Coghlan had been furnished with a copy of all the papers
which related to the occupation of the island in 1799. The Bombay Government had received orders dated November 18, 1798,
from London to occupy Perim in order to close the mouth of the
Red Sea against possible dangers resulting from Napoleon's invasion of Egypt. Acting on these orders, Colonel J. Murray with

his regiment took possession of the island on May 3, 1799, in
the name of the East India Company. Colonel Murray described
the island as completely barren, lacking in water, but with an
excellent harbor. His batteries could command the Eastern
passage (Arabian side) but not the western. Mocha was a dependable source of supply, but during the northern monsoon it
was necessary to cross to the Abyssinian side for water. In a
month the lack of water was acute and Murray decided to leave
in August for Socotra as there was no other place which was
suitable for defense. On September 21, Murray gave up and
left for Aden. Here the Sultan cordially received him and offered Aden to the British if he could have British protection for
his territories. Murray's description of Aden was enthusiastic
and he felt it had excellent possibilities. However, on February 26, 1800, Murray was ordered to return to Bombay and to
decline the offer of Aden. (FO 78/1333, IB-FO 11/27/56, encl.
copies of the documents; also copies in BSC 1856, originals in
Bombay Political and Secret Proceedings 1798, 1799, 1800.)

Coghlan pointed out to the Bombay Government that the situation in 1856 was quiet different from that of 1799. Murray had
called Perim indefensible without a large force. Coghlan agreed
that this had been true when Perim was a lonely outpost with
Bombay the closest British settlement. But in 1856 Perim was
only a short distance from Aden and was strategically very important when supported by a maritime power (FO 78/1333, IB-
FO 11/27/56, encl. Coghlan-Bombay 10/27/58; also in BSC
1856). Mr. Lumsden of the Bombay Government, in London on
sick leave, filed a very interesting report on the necessity of
a lighthouse in the Red Sea. He advocated four lights, one at
Suez roadstead, one at Shadwan at the entrance to the Sea of
Suez, a very narrow channel, one at Dadalus Shoal which rises
in the center of the Red Sea, in the middle of the steamer lane,
and probably the most important one at Perim. He said that the
island was surrounded by very deceptive currents which were
dangerous for sailing vessels and large steamships and that,
because of this, steamships were delayed because to avoid danger they had to pass Perim in the daytime (FO 78/1333, Memo
by Mr. Lumsden Jan. 1857).

In accordance with Lord Clarendon's consent, Perim was
occupied as soon as possible; Coghlan issued the orders to Lieutenant Grey to re-occupy the island for the purpose of erecting
certain works there. He was to take thirty sappers, a few

artificers, and three months' provisions and immediately to construct a reservoir. Captain Playfair was to go with Grey to Perim and then proceed to Mocha to arrange for provisions. Grey was advised to act with caution, not to antagonize any one or make any show of arms, and above all to reply to questions about the occupation by saying that its purpose was to construct a lighthouse (FO 78/1333, IB-FO 2/18/57 encl. Coghlan-Bombay 12/29/56; also in BSC 1857). These instructions were forwarded to London with the remark that a light was to be sent immediately to Lieutenant Grey "so that the ostensible object of the British Government may form a prominent feature in Lt. Grey's proceedings" (FO 78/1333, IB-FO 2/18/57 encl. Resolution 1/13/57; also in BSC 1857).

Coghlan reported to the Bombay Government in February that as arrangements had been made to get water and supplies from Sheikh Said, he was dispatching forty Sepoys as a permanent garrison, and that on the arrival of the light sent from India it would be installed (FO 78/1333, IB-FO 4/8/57, encl. Coghlan-Bombay 2/4/57; also in BSC 1857). The light arrived but was never put up because of an interminable wrangle between the various military authorities in Bombay about its position and the necessity for preserving the best sites for the batteries. Finally it was agreed that the top of the island was the best site. Then the battle of words began over the best type of light to be used. After a long and sometimes acid correspondence, the matter was forgotten until 1859, when protests from the Peninsular and Oriental steamship lines led to the establishment of the proposed four lights in the Red Sea which were completed in 1862-1863 (see FO 78/1785).

The story of the occupation of Perim has had many versions. The favorite one is that a French ship arrived at Aden with the object of occupying Perim and that Coghlan invited all the officers to a large dinner while dispatching the "Mahi" to occupy the island. That a French brig arrived at Aden at the time the "Mahi" was dispatched probably was the basis of the tale. Coghlan gives a rather guarded and garbled version of the occupation in Low's history (Low, Charles R., HISTORY OF THE INDIAN NAVY, Vol. II, pp. 384-386). Playfair completely denies the truth of any of the details of Coghlan's story. His comment on French actions in the Red Sea is interesting. "At the time of which I write [1857], their reports and recommendations rarely got beyond the <u>cartons</u> of the Ministers to whom they were addressed, the favourable opportunity was always neglected, and sometimes we stepped in and acted while they were considering the advisability of action" (Playfair, Sir Robert L., "Reminiscences," Chambers Journal, Vol. II #59, January 14, 1899, p. 98).

The motives for the occupation are obvious. Primarily it was a strategic step; ostensibly it was to aid steam commerce. It was successfully carried out and its secrecy resulted in the rise of romantic stories.

XIII. ABYSSINIA 1855-1860

As Plowden was preparing in March of 1855 to go up to
Gondar to meet Kassa, the new ruler of Abyssinia, the Bombay
Government received a proposal from Dr. Beke for the opening
up of Abyssinia. The worthy Doctor, having been unsuccessful
in interesting the Foreign Office in any of his schemes, chief
of which was the financing of an expedition of a Dr. Bialloblotzky
to discover the sources of the Nile (FO 1/5 Beke-Palmerston
8/2/48), had become a merchant in Mauritius. Having met
Coghlan on board ship in 1853, he approached him with a new
plan which on the surface appeared very sensible. Beke complained of the discontinuance of the shipping line to Mauritius
from London via the Cape of Good Hope and the fact that the island was dependent on a French service to Bourbon for its mail
and imports. He proposed that in connection with a new mail
line from Suez to Mauritius, arrangements be made to open up
the Abyssinian trade at Massawa with a system of native ships
bringing goods from Massawa to Aden where transshipment
could be made to ocean-going vessels for Mauritius and India
(BSC 1855, Coghlan-Bombay 3/3/55 encl. Beke-Coghlan 2/8/55).
The Bombay Government showed an interest in this idea
and requested further particulars so that it could be considered
along with Burton's plan for a proposed agency at Berbera, as
the Government felt that the uncertainty of Aden's relations with
the tribes of the Yemen made it advisable to consider increasing
Aden's supplies from the west shore of the Red Sea (BSC 1855,
Minute 3/27/55). Beke's proposal reached Coghlan in November and on investigation proved preposterous. Beke proposed
that a factory be established on the tablelands of Abyssinia near
the coast, that Massawa be occupied by the English, and that a
fleet of native vessels be organized to trade between Massawa
and Aden. The factory was to be subsidized by a grant of a
mere Ł50,000 from the government, and as Coghlan remarked,
"Though not stated in words it is an easy deduction, that the
proposer, Dr. Beke, be appointed to the charge of this factory
on a guaranteed salary of Ł5,000 per year for ten years without
any guaranteed return" (BSC 1855, Coghlan-Bombay 11/8/55).
Mr. Lumsden of the Bombay Government remarked, "Dr. Beke's
scheme appears to me to be more visionary than the views

attributed by Lieutenant Col. Coghlan to Lieutenant Burton"
(BSC 1855, Minute by Mr. Lumsden 12/3/55).

While it may seem ridiculous to discuss such a proposal,
it must be remembered that Dr. Beke was a fairly prolific
pamphleteer, and a popular speaker in England with considerable influence there. Thus he received a hearing from a large
audience while the Foreign Office could say little. The influence
of Dr. Beke in the events in England leading up to the Abyssinian
campaign cannot be overestimated.

Plowden began his trip to Gondar to visit Kassa, the new
ruler of Abyssinia, in March of 1855 and at Adowa he heard
that Kassa had taken the throne name "Theodore," to fulfill an
ancient prophecy predicting that a king of this name would reform Abyssinia. Theodore had ordered that all Muhammadans
in the kingdom become converted to Christianity within a year
and contemplated two campaigns, first against the Gallas and
then against Shoa. He was reported to have dreams of turning
the course of the Nile and reducing Egypt to submission. Theodore was believed to be preparing to suppress feudalism and
replace it with an organized government. He had already tried
to suppress bribery in the courts and to discourage polygamy.
On the basis of Theodore's reputation, Plowden felt that he was
capable of a great deal of good or a great deal of evil depending
on his advisers, an uncannily accurate prediction (FO 1/8, #16
Plowden [Adowa]-FO 4/7/55).

Reaching Gondar early in June, Plowden forwarded to the
Foreign Office a long and interesting report on Theodore. In
his youth, Plowden reported, Kassa had always believed himself destined to be the ruler of Ethiopia. Rising to the position
of Dejazmatch under Ras Ali, he had disciplined his army in a
manner unknown in Abyssinia and had welded it into a unit by
making war on the Shangallas and Arabs. In 1852 he withdrew
his allegiance to the ruling Ras and revolted, conquering everything before him but showing surprising clemency in dealing
with his defeated foes. He was a vigorous, energetic man with
a great many good qualities unusual in an Abyssinian leader:
he was direct in his dealings, usually in control of himself, generous to a fault, and free of cupidity. His worst faults were
his sudden temper, an unfailing pride in his position, and his
fanatical zeal. He had promulgated several reforms in the short
period of his power by abolishing the slave trade among his
Christian subjects, abolishing the custom of turning over

murderers to the tender mercies of the family of the deceased, and had partially broken the feudal system by replacing the old chiefs with his own men, and forbidding them the power of life and death over their subjects. He had replaced the feudal levy with a standing army which was paid regularly. Tolerant in allowing anyone to practice his own religion, he was fanatically opposed to the propagation of any faith but that of the Abyssinian Church. Theodore informed Plowden that he wished to send an embassy to England, but refused to renew the treaty of friendship and commerce with England as he objected to the extraterritorial clause; he believed that all people in Abyssinia should come under his jurisdiction.

Plowden believed that Theodore was perfectly capable of attacking Massawa and capturing it from the Turks, but that he was incapable of carrying on a war with the Egyptians as he wanted to do. Under the circumstances Plowden felt there were three courses open: first, to withdraw the Consul because of Theodore's refusal to renew the treaty; second, to wait before receiving his embassy until the results of his attacks on Massawa and Egypt were known; third, to accept his embassy in the best possible manner hoping that Theodore would make Massawa impossible for the Turks to retain (FO 1/9, #18 Plowden-FO [Memo on Theodore] 6/25/55).

Clarendon on receipt of this dispatch suggested that a message be sent congratulating Theodore on his accession, and that Plowden be authorized to defray the expenses of an embassy. Hammond suggested that such a course might be unwise because Said Pasha, Viceroy of Egypt, knowing Theodore's anti-Egyptian views, might be offended by the reception of such an embassy by the British (FO 1/9, Minute N.D. on #18 Plowden-FO 6/25/55). Finally Plowden was informed that the British would be delighted to receive an embassy if Theodore would renounce his intentions of attacking Egypt and Massawa, as Said Pasha had stopped all attacks on Abyssinian territory (FO 1/8, #10 FO-Plowden 11/27/55).

The Catholic Bishop de Jacobis, who had escaped to Egyptian territory during the chaos resulting from Kassa's revolt, returned to Gondar as Theodore campaigned against the Gallas, threatening to bring down the wrath of the French Government on Theodore as a result of his expulsion. Plowden remarked to him that if the French wished to support a mission in Gondar they would make a treaty providing for it. He added that it was

far better "for the cause of progress that neither this or any
other mission should at present set foot in Abyssinia, " and that
those who wished to preach the Gospel should respect the established church and pass on to teach the pagan tribes. "But these
humble and far more dangerous labours, " Plowden remarked,
"might not be hailed with the shout of worldly triumph that would
accompany the prostration of the Abyssinian Church at the foot-
stool of the Chair of St. Peter. " Plowden had proof that de Jacobis had tried to supplant the Abuna himself and have Roman
Catholicism recognized as the state religion (FO 1/9 #19, Plowden-FO 6/27/55). (Plowden referred undoubtedly to de Jacobis'
intrigues of 1842.)

In the Hedjaz, Muttalib's revolt against the Turks had brok-
en out. At Massawa, the tribes followed suit. Barroni, Plowden's agent, appealed to Coghlan on December 12, 1855, for a
ship to save the Europeans and Banyans from the almost certain
destruction of the town. The basis of the trouble was the governor's attempt to rule the mainland, supplanting the Naïb with
his own officials. The Shihos had risen, burned all the towns
including Moncullo, and were threatening Massawa itself (BSC
1856, Coghlan-Bombay 1/12/56, encl. Barroni-Coghlan 12/20/
55). However, the governor with the aid of some Egyptian
troops put down the revolt. At the same time Bruce, British
Consul in Cairo, heard various rumors about Massawa, the
chief of which was that the French contemplated seizing the port
as a reprisal for the indignities suffered by the Catholic mission there. In the light of these reports and the negotiations
progressing in Egypt about the proposed Suez Canal, Bruce
wished de Redcliffe's advice on having the Porte cede Massawa
to Theodore if the Home Government did not wish a pretext to
seize it for themselves (FO 1/9, #3 Bruce-de Redcliffe 2/17/56).

The Foreign Office in reply informed Bruce that it had requested de Redcliffe to advise the Porte to cede Massawa to
Abyssinia as it was of no use to Turkey (FO 1/9, #4 FO-Bruce
3/7/56). Of course this advice was not heeded.

In Massawa, the governor, having successfully repressed
the revolt, was using the Egyptian troops to raid the Christian
provinces in Hamasein. After a few minor raids, whose chief
purpose was to get some slaves, the Egyptian commander refused to attack the provinces of Mensa, Bogos and Senhait as
ordered by the governor. Such raids, Bruce felt, would surely
result in reprisals by Theodore and indefinitely delay peace

between Egypt and Abyssinia (FO 1/9   #30 Bruce-FO 6/20/56, and #4 Plowden [Gondar]-FO 4/22/56).

In October, 1856, Plowden, still in Gondar, recorded the appearance of a rival to Theodore in Tigré. This rebel was called Dejazmatch Negussie and apparently controlled about one-third of the province. De Jacobis, after conferring with Negussie, received permission to preach in his territory in return for de Jacobis' promise to obtain French arms for the rebel. The French Vice-Consul in Massawa was reported to have said that Negussie should be supported by France in every possible way because of his reception of the Catholic mission, that he had reported in those terms to his ministry and expected to receive a satisfactory answer (FO 1/10, #8 Plowden [Gondar]-FO 10/5/56).

Plowden received his dispatches from England, after over a year's delay, in November. In answer to the British request for the establishment of peace between Abyssinia and Egypt, Theodore showed Plowden the draft of a letter which Theodore was writing to England in which the King reserved the right to demand certain territories but promised to take no hostile steps until he should receive a reply to his embassy to England which he hoped he could soon send. The King claimed the Arab country to the village of Sennar, and the territory to and including Massawa. However, the King refused to send an embassy until Tigré had been completely subdued (FO 1/10, #14 Plowden-FO 11/12/56).

Plowden also commented on the supposed religious persecution by Theodore. He pointed out that the King's antagonism to the Muslims was as much dynastic as religious, as the rulers of Gondar from 1790 onwards had been from a Galla-Muslim family; Ras Ali, the last of the line, had adopted the Christian faith only after he had become Ras. The Roman Catholics had put themselves in a difficult position with their open support of the rebel Negussie. In Plowden's opinion, Theodore would never again consent to their presence. Some German Protestant missionaries in the country were allowed to wander as they wished and distribute their pamphlets and books so long as they did not preach. Theodore remarked about them, "I do not know that they are doing much good or any harm" (FO 1/10, #13 Plowden [Gondar]-FO 11/11/56).

On the receipt of these dispatches, the Foreign Office instructed Plowden to try to induce Theodore to accept a new

treaty proposing any modifications which he might desire. Plowden was also to impress on the King that the British could not
aid him in any way with armed forces, but wished to know in
what manner they could aid his reforms (FO 1/10, #2 FO-Plowden 3/3/57, and #3 FO-Plowden 3/4/57).

In Egypt, Bruce reported that the Viceroy, Said Pasha,
planned to make an inspection trip through the Sudan and Red
Sea to Suakin. The Pasha had proposed a steamship line in the
Red Sea touching at Suakin and Massawa, both of which Said was
anxious to regain for the Pashalik of Egypt. He was also contemplating the reorganization of Sennar and the Sudan under the
government of native princes with Turkish viziers in command
of the troops, since the system of putting the provinces under
Turkish commanders had ruined their prosperity. While he was
apparently desirous for peace with Abyssinia, reports from the
camp of Theodore were not encouraging; an epidemic of cholera
had so reduced the garrisons in the Sudan that it was felt Theodore would take the opportunity to attack (FO 78/1222, #52
Bruce-FO 11/4/56).

Meanwhile the Foreign Office had ordered Lord Cowley,
British Ambassador at Paris, to investigate French interference
in Abyssinia. Count Walewski, the French Foreign Minister,
was asked if the Catholic missionaries were justified in making
such a liberal use of the name of the Imperial Government, and
replied that he knew nothing of Abyssinia, but that the French
claimed protection of all the Roman Catholics in the East (FO
1/10, #410 Cowley-FO 3/13/56). Under pressure, he presented
Cowley with a memorandum supposedly giving a summary of the
latest intelligence received by the French Foreign Office from
Abyssinia. The memorandum either indicated intentional evasion or abysmal ignorance of what was going on, but Cowley did
not feel that he could press for more information (FO 1/10,
#446 Cowley-FO 3/20/57).

The Coptic Patriarch of Alexandria visited Abyssinia in
December of 1856. While not bearing official letters from Said
Pasha, he had had several conferences with him before leaving
Cairo (FO 78/1222, #52 Bruce-FO 11/4/56). The visit of the
Patriarch was neither well-timed nor advisable. Theodore and
the Abuna were mutually distrustful, and the Abuna's desire to
have certain political prisoners set free accentuated the natural
dislike between two men of imperious and unbending personal-
ities. The Patriarch made a poor impression on Theodore, who

expected to meet a very holy man. The Patriarch brought, among
other presents, a diamond cross apparently significant of some
Turkish Order and this, together with his constant derogatory
remarks on Abyssinia, convinced Theodore that the man had become half Muslim, and was in reality an emissary from the
Viceroy of Egypt, whose object was to get Abyssinia to submit
to its Muslim neighbor. The Abuna and the Patriarch confirmed
Theodore's suspicion by presenting him with the draft of a letter to be sent to Said Pasha in which the Viceroy was addressed
as a superior of Theodore. The letter stated "that the king was
to send 40 mules for the Viceroy's artillery and prayed the
Viceroy to send all the Coptic soldiers in his service, three
Turkish officers to discipline the troops, regimental bands,
pioneers, mappers, engineers, bakers, doctors, and medicines,
cannons and muskets" (FO 1/10, #2 Plowden [Debra Tabor]-
FO 1/15/57). At the same time rumors from the border indicated that the Egyptian troops were advancing and that the Patriarch was an emissary of the Pasha. The combination of
events caused Theodore to explode, although there is no reason
to believe from other evidence that the proposals from Said
were any more than a sincere attempt to help Theodore civilize
Abyssinia in return for a stabilized boundary, and probably the
exclusion of Europeans from Abyssinia. The Abuna and the Patriarch were placed under guard in their tents. Luckily Plowden and his friend Bell remained in Theodore's good graces and
arranged for a partial reconciliation. Plowden believed that the
object of the Patriarch's mission was a sincere desire to aid in
the civilization of Abyssinia with the eventual hope that the
Abyssinian church could be brought in closer contact with
the Coptic church of Egypt (FO 1/10, #2 Plowden-FO
1/15/57).

Continued reports came in to Gondar of increasing troop
re-enforcements in the Sennar. These rumors disturbed Theodore, who was convinced that a move was being made to attack
the Arab provinces on the border, which were tributary to him,
at the same time as the Gallas were to attack his rear. The
King therefore decided to inform the English Government that
he would not be able to keep his promise not to attack Egyptian
territory, and indefinitely postponed his embassy to England.
Plowden pointed out that any aggression against the Arab tribes
by Said would be aggression against Abyssinia, as Theodore
was the rightful ruler of this territory, and informed the Foreign

Office that any reports of aggressive action on the part of the tribes against their Sudanese neighbors was not a "casus belli," as intertribal raiding was a common occurrence (FO 1/10, #4 Plowden-FO 2/5/57). There is no evidence to prove hostile intentions on Said's part, nor to show that these troop movements were any more than routine re-enforcements brought up to fill depletions created by the cholera epidemic (FO 1/10, #26 Bruce-FO 4/29/57).

Plowden persisted in trying to obtain a treaty with Theodore, but was convinced by September, 1857, that it was impossible to get a favorable answer (FO 1/10, #13 Plowden-FO 9/7/57 ("Duplicate"); FO 1/10, #7 Plowden-FO 4/2/57, #10 Plowden-FO 5/20/57).

On finally receiving a copy of Cowley's letter from Paris regarding French denials of any knowledge of the political actions of the Catholic mission, Plowden replied that the French Foreign Office apparently knew nothing of what had gone on since 1854. Plowden had very good evidence that the mission had supplied the rebel Negussie with firearms and that certain of the priests had positions of importance in Negussie's government.

French Catholic influence on the coast continued to grow, and in October Plowden's dispatches were seized and opened, and his messenger imprisoned, by order of a high official of Negussie, a Roman Catholic convert and servant of de Jacobis (FO 1/10, #20 Plowden [Debra Tabor]-FO 11/18/57). This incident was indicative of the growing French influence with Negussie in Tigré and corresponded with increased French activity in the Red Sea.

Coghlan in Aden reported that the French had repurchased Edd for 50,000 francs in June, 1857 (FO 1/10, IB-FO 8/5/57 encl. Coghlan-Bombay 7/4/57; also in BSC 1857). The first group to try to settle this village was refused possession by the Dankali and returned to Suez, where it was reported that M. Pastré, a French merchant, was arranging for forcible occupation of the village (FO 1/10, IB-FO 10/20/57 encl. Coghlan-Bombay 9/15/57; also in BSC 1857). Cowley, in April, 1858, was unable to get a positive answer from Walewski about French intentions at Edd, and, as the French were quite upset by the occupation of Perim, he did not think it advisable to press the matter (FO 1/10, #235 Cowley-FO 4/6/58). Plowden also reported the purchase, and said that Combes and Tamisier had first purchased the place but that no effort had ever been made to occupy it. M. de Goutier, the former French Vice-Consul at Massawa, had claimed title to it (he had tried to dispose of it to the British), and had finally sold it to M. Pastré of Cairo (FO 1/10, #7 Plowden [Dembea]-FO 9/18/57). This is apparently the whole story of the transaction. Yet in 1872 the Foreign Office considered Edd to be a possession of the French Government, although there is no evidence to show that it was ever more than the project of some companies of merchants. Comte Stanislaus Russel confirms this in his book UNE MISSION EN ABYSSINIE (Paris, Plon, 1884, p. 191).

At Massawa, the usual complaints were forthcoming. Barroni wrote Coghlan that the new governor took some wise measures at first but soon lapsed into the traditional Turkish misrule, deciding all civil cases by bribery, especially those involving the payment of debts, and pretending to be entitled to five per cent of all debts which were placed before him for judgment. He further aided and abetted the slave trade, which was becoming a major industry at that port (FO 1/10, IB-FO 11/19/ 57 encl. Barroni-Coghlan 9/1/57; also BSC 1857 in Coghlan-Bombay 9/17/57).

More serious were the intrigues of the French Catholics with Negussie. On September 18, Barroni reported that Mr. Bullard, the French Consul, had gone to Tigré to present fifteen guns to Negussie which he had obtained from a German firm under British protection. Bullard was accompanied by some additional Catholic priests, newly landed from Europe, and some officials of the Turkish government (FO 1/10, IB-FO 11/19/57 encl. Barroni-Coghlan 9/18/57; also in BSC 1857 Coghlan-Bombay 9/24). Under these circumstances Plowden vainly pled for a British ship in the Red Sea to keep up British influence there (FO 1/10, #24 Plowden [Debra Tabor]-FO 11/20/57).

In November, 1857, the Patriarch of Alexandria parted from Theodore on fairly friendly terms, taking with him a present of ivory for Said Pasha. The Patriarch and Abuna, Plowden reported, had unsuccessfully tried to get Theodore to close all of Abyssinia to the Europeans and allow the Copts alone to have access to the country (FO 1/10, #22 Plowden [Debra Tabor]-FO 11/22/57). Theodore still contemplated his campaign against Negussie, whose position had been strengthened by the announcement of the Roman Catholic mission that he was the supreme and lawful authority in Abyssinia, and that as the defender of the

Catholic faith he would receive the support of France (FO 1/10, #19 Plowden [Debra Tabor]-FO 11/15/57).

At the end of November, 1857, Plowden forwarded a letter from Theodore to the Queen announcing his intention of sending an embassy to London. The Consul decided to wait in Gondar to accompany the envoys. The King, Plowden felt, would fulfill his obligations to protect travelers, but his pride would never allow him to receive a consul, nor allow a foreign flag to be raised in his country. Despite his difficulties, Theodore requested no aid from the English. Plowden suggested that two or three hundred old percussion muskets for his soldiers, and a handsome piece for his own use, with a proportionate number of caps, would make a very agreeable present for him, especially as the French had re-armed Negussie, who was getting three cannon sent to him from Massawa and to whom the French contemplated sending a military mission of fifty infantry and artillerymen (FO 1/10, #23 Plowden [Debra Tabor]-FO 11/25/ 57). The War Office refused to issue any arms to be sent to Theodore so the matter was dropped (FO 1/10, WO-FO 5/25/59 and #1 FO-Plowden 5/31/59).

Plowden, half sick from fever and prevented by a rebellion of Negussie from returning to Massawa by the direct route, decided to remain in Gondar until he felt well enough to try the arduous, roundabout trip to the coast through Sennar. In June, 1858, he reported that Theodore's generals had been successful in some minor battles with Negussie while Theodore was campaigning against the Gallas. The embassy, Plowden thought, was far in the future (FO 1/10, #2 Plowden [Gondar]-FO 6/5/58 and #4 Plowden [Gondar]-FO 7/5/58).

A revolution was attempted in Massawa on July 24, not only against the infidel but also against the Turk. The Hadrami group in Massawa saw an insult in some casual remark of a Christian servant of M. Rizzo, a merchant in Massawa. They proceeded to riot and attack the Christian houses and the government buildings. The Governor, evidently forewarned, quickly threw a guard around all the threatened buildings, and after a few serious hours the rising was put down with only a few minor injuries resulting. This action weakened the already weak governor, and Barroni, fearful of another uprising, requested that a British vessel visit the port (FO 78/1402, #161 Green-FO 9/11/58 encl. Barroni-Green 7/24/58). Needless to say no vessel appeared.

As a result of the riots a new governor was appointed at
Massawa. He apparently was a great deal more conciliatory to
the mercantile element than his predecessor. But in May, 1859,
disturbing news came to Coghlan from Barroni. A native of
Savoy, Leon des Avanchers, who was also a Roman Catholic
priest, had returned from visiting Negussie's camp. This priest
had been traveling for two years in the Red Sea district and had
come to the rebel's camp with a message from the Sardinian
Government requesting Negussie to allow the Sardinians to col-
onize the province of Hamasein, in return for which they would
send troops to help Negussie. The rebel agreed to this and letters were sent to the Sardinian Consul General via Father Juvenal of the Catholic mission at Aden. In April, several Europeans arrived at Massawa. One, named Gerhard, had seventy-
two cases of muskets with him which he landed after paying a
600-crown bribe. Another was an Englishman by the name of
Kerwin Joyce, formerly of the Indian Army in Bombay and the
Crimea, and lately a member of the secret police in Alexandria.
Also there were two Frenchmen who were taking service with
Negussie and a Mr. Matteo Wagner who proceeded to sell Gerhard's muskets for nine crowns apiece to the rebels, as well as
two cannon and a great deal of ammunition, and promised them
further arms. Barroni believed that this group, of whom Kerwin Joyce was the leader, was a semi-religious organization
having relations with Rome, Sardinia, France, and Ireland.
They had promised to send Negussie a large staff of engineers
and teachers. A few days later a vessel arrived, ostensibly to
purchase mules for Mauritius, but bearing a considerable number of Europeans, and two more small vessels were reported
as coming (FO 1/10, IO-FO 6/7/59, encl. Coghlan-Bombay 5/
3/59; also in BSL & E 1859).

Coghlan considered Barroni's fears exaggerated, but felt
that the move was being organized by Catholic sympathizers.
He rejected the Bombay Government's suggestion that the local
priest in Aden, who was admittedly a go-between, be removed,
as his successor would probably follow the same course. "It
would be vain to exact from any of them a pledge of non-interference in secular affairs," he added. Coghlan met Joyce, who
was in Aden at the time, and felt that the whole affair was more
likely to be a gun-running scheme in which the runners had the
sanction of the Catholic church (BSLE 1859, Coghlan-Bombay
6/21/59). This was borne out by the receipt of a letter from

Father Juvenal, Roman Catholic chaplain at Aden, enclosing a
letter given to him by a priest in Tigré and addressed to Cavour.
Father Juvenal enclosed it with the remark that it had been sent
to him to forward but that he wished to have nothing to do with
this affair (BSLE 1859, Coghlan-Bombay 6/23/59). Further reports indicated that fourteen more cases of muskets and five
thousand boxes of percussion caps had been landed at Massawa,
and twenty thousand muskets were reported in the Red Sea waters (BSLE 1859, Coghlan-Bombay 7/1/59).

Plowden, still held in Gondar by illness, received these reports and commented that if any of the Europeans were killed
by Theodore while "peacefully transporting arms...there will
not be wanting eloquent pens to depict him as a blood-thirsty
tyrant and homicide and to excite Europe against him." Plowden thought that Theodore would be thoroughly justified in ex-
pelling any members of the Catholic mission on political grounds,
and advised the Foreign Office to protest to France if they
wished to support Theodore. "If however Her Majesty's Government does not consider that the nation has any interest in the
matter and is disposed to acquiesce in the king's downfall, and
to leave the future government of Abyssinia virtually in the
hands of France, I do not see what use I can be here" (FO 1/10,
#10 Plowden [Gondar]-FO 6/1/59). He added that he was leav-
ing for the coast as soon as his health would allow.

Plowden had every right to be discouraged. There is no
evidence to prove that either the Earl of Malmesbury or Lord
John Russell had the least interest in Abyssinia, or the Red Sea
area, for, from 1858 until 1860, they failed to answer any of
Plowden's correspondence and made no comments on reports
forwarded from the India Office. As for the group under the
leadership of Joyce, later evidence shows that Coghlan's belief
that the expedition was a privately organized gun-running exploit
was probably correct. At the time of the Abyssinian campaign,
an investigation showed Kerwin Joyce to be an unscrupulous
rogue with a most unsavory reputation. Unquestionably this
group planned to back Negussie and then exploit him.

Plowden recovered enough in September, 1859, to start his
return to Massawa and immediately was thrown from his horse
and broke a leg (FO 1/11, #13 Plowden [Gondar]-FO 9/20/59,
and #2 Plowden [Gondar] 2/2/60). Not until January 18, 1860,
did the Foreign Office finally send the Consul new instructions,
ordering him to return to Massawa and stay there as "the

interests of that port are intimately connected with British interests in India and with judicious care and encouragement it may become the outlet for a large trade between Abyssinia and H. M. dominions.

"The proceedings of other foreign nations should carefully be watched, in order to prevent or counteract efforts to establish paramount influence in that quarter.

"Attempts of such powers to form Naval Stations should be inquired into (with due caution) and... should be reported to H. M. Government and should also be given to the Senior Naval Officer of H. M. ships with whom you may be able to communicate" (FO 1/11, #1 FO-Plowden 1/18/60).

These were the first instructions sent to Plowden since 1857. He never received them. In February, 1860, he started for the coast. Near Gondar he was attacked and wounded by a minor rebel chief. He was ransomed by the authorities in Gondar on March 4 and taken to that town, where he died of his wounds on March 13. Thus at a critical moment the British were deprived of the services of their able consul.

Meanwhile, French intrigues at Massawa increased in intensity. At the end of 1859, M. Barroni, Plowden's agent at Massawa, had reported, to both Consul General Colquhoun at Alexandria and Coghlan at Aden, the appearance of a French vessel at Zula, the "Yemen," owned by Pastré Freres. Presents to the Ras of Tigré from the French Emperor had been landed together with a group of priests who were reported to constitute an embassy to the Ras (FO 1/11, Barroni-Colquhoun N. D. encl. in Colquhoun-FO 2/6/60).

Coghlan, in Aden, convinced that the French contemplated the establishment of a naval base at Massawa, proceeded to that port to investigate (BSC 1860, Coghlan-Bombay 12/17/59). His first investigations proved that Kerwin Joyce and his friends were indulging in gun-running, having received eight field pieces from France which they were about to sell to Negussie for $1,100 and the promise of "a province." While gun-running was forbidden by Turkish law, the Turkish governor was completely helpless on the mainland. He therefore asked Coghlan's aid in suppressing this traffic and Coghlan suggested to the Bombay Government that Joyce be refused British protection if he persisted in this trade, a suggestion which was approved by the Bombay Government (BSC 1860, Coghlan-Playfair, in Playfair-Bombay 1/17/60 and Resolution by Bombay Govt. 2/13/60).

Coghlan then turned his attention to the reports of the French embassy. These reports were apparently true; the embassy was instructed first to go to the Ras of Tigré and thence to Theodore in Gondar. They had been instructed to negotiate four points with Theodore: first, that he recognize the independence of Negussie; second, that he agree to definite boundaries between Negussie and himself; third, that Theodore establish perfect religious tolerance; and, fourth, that Theodore open Gondar to the Roman Catholic mission. The mission had landed fifty-five cases of freight, twenty-one of which were said to contain arms, a present from the French Emperor to Negussie. The remainder were reported to be the private property of M. Eurichy, a French adventurer, and were also reported to contain firearms. The mission had landed on the mainland and had had no communications with the Turkish authorities at Massawa.

Coghlan then proceeded around Annesley Bay, and landed at Dissei Island to investigate reports of the French purchase of the island. He was informed by the natives that the French had spent a few days there and had told them that the island was now French, having been given to them, they claimed, by Negussie the Ras of Tigré. Coghlan found survey marks indicating a very recent mapping of the island. This island, Coghlan reported, had a good harbor, excellent water supply, a comparatively pleasant climate, and it dominated the entrance to Annesley Bay. The inhabitants claimed to be independent but the Naïb of Arkiko had a shadowy claim. Negussie had no title to the island, and the Turks on Massawa, thirty miles to the north, hardly knew of its existence. The French, Coghlan discovered, had also claimed the area around Zula (Adulis) on the mainland as French territory. He commented, "confining the more immediate results (of these claims) to the Red Sea and the overland route, I cannot refrain from expressing my opinion that they portend disagreeable implications," especially as in June, 1860, the French planned to open a bimonthly steamship route from Suez to China, and any insult to their mission in Abyssinia would provide a pretext for the use of force. In conclusion, Coghlan suggested that the British forestall the French by buying Dissei as a telegraph station for the projected Suez-to-India cable (BSC 1860, Coghlan-Bombay 2/13/60, also in FO 1/11, IO-FO 3/20/60).

A copy of Coghlan's report was forwarded to the Foreign Office by the India Office, and arrived there at just about the

same time as Plowden's last dispatch from Abyssinia which confirmed the presence of the French mission which was stalled at
Halai by warfare between Theodore and Negussie. Further confirmation came from Colquhoun in Alexandria (FO 1/11, Colquhoun-FO 3/31/60). Palmerston commented on these dispatches,
"If the French were to make good their possession of Abyssinia
they could without difficulty and whenever it might suit them
drop down on Egypt and thus get possession of the whole southern shore of the Mediterranean area" (FO 1/11, Palmerston's
Minute attached to #4 Plowden-FO 2/5/60). In view of this,
Lord Cowley, British Ambassador in Paris, was instructed to
inquire of Thouvenal, the French Foreign Minister, the extent
of French intentions in the Red Sea (FO 1/11, FO-Cowley [Paris]
4/16/60).

Actually the facts of the French mission were quite different from the rumors reported to Coghlan. Comte Stanislaus Russel, who was killed a few years later in the French intrigues in
Mexico, left a journal of this mission which, together with his
instructions and official reports, was published in 1884 as a
piece of anti-British propaganda at the time of the crisis over
the British occupation of Egypt (Russel, Stanislaus, op. cit.,
introduction by Gabriel Charmes). Russel (Roussel in the British documents) was descended from a branch of the family of
the Duke of Bedford which had fled to France after the execution
of Charles I and for a long time had participated in the Stuart
movement in France. By 1859 Russel was a captain in the
French Navy, and on October 13 of that year he was instructed
by Chasseloup-Laubat, Minister for Algeria and the Colonies,
to proceed to Abyssinia to explore the African shore from Massawa to Bab-el-Mandeb and investigate the advantages of certain
places offered to the French Government for settlement.

His instructions read in part:

> Cette mission doit âvoir pour object d'explorer le
> littoral africain de cette mer [Red Sea], sour tout la
> partie qui se prolonge depuis Massowah jusqu'au Goobat-
> Kharah [in the Bay of Tajura], en dehors du détroit de
> Bab-el-Mandeb, et de recueiller des renseignements
> précis sur les avantages politiques, maritimes et
> commerciaux qui peuvent présenter les divers points
> placés sur ce littoral, soit pour un établissment
> commercial, soit pour assurer nos relations avec

l'Abyssinie. Plusieurs points ont été signalés ou offerts
au gouvernement de l'Empereur.
   Le roi de Tigré, l'un des principaux chefs de l'Abyssinie, a réclamé, par l'intermediare de Mgr. de Jacobis
...le protectorate de la France. D'une autre côté...
la province d'Edd acquisi par MM. Pastré freres, de
Marseilles, a été gratuitement offerte à la France par
ces négociants. Enfin le chef About-Baker-Ibrahim
offré de ceder a la France les territoires de Ras-Ali et
Aouana,*... en dehors de la Mer Rouge et en régard
d'Aden. Je n'entends pas limiter a ces points l'exploration qui vous est confiée; je desire, au contraire, que
vous vous consideriez comme parfaitment autorisé
a l'entendre en dehors ce circle.

Russel was warned against acquiring any territory over which
the Ottoman Sultan or the Pasha of Egypt had any claim, and
was requested to find out possible British intentions of exploit-
ing their ownership of the Musa Islands which dominate the Bay
of Tajura.
   Russel was warned, "vous eviterez avec soin tout acte et
toute démarche de nature à engager, a quelque degré que ce
soit, le gouvernement qui doit rester enterement maître de ses
determinations."
   The captain was instructed to inform no one of the nature
of his mission except that in an emergency he could inform
French consular officials. The whole mission was to be disguised as a hydrographic survey of the Ministry of Marine, and
a ship, the "Yemen," was provided for Russel's use by Pastré
Freres, the Marseilles mercantile house which had title to Edd.
(Russel, Stanislaus, op. cit., p. 273.)
   These instructions throw light on certain rumors current
in Abyssinia. First, they clearly prove that Negussie, through
the influence of the Lazarist mission of Mgr. de Jacobis, had
asked to be placed under French protection and had offered the
French two places for settlement, Zula (Adulis) and Ras Domer-
iah, opposite Perim on the African shore. Negussie's claim to

---

*Ras Ali is the promontory and small harbor just east of Ta-
jura. Aouana seems very difficult to identify, no such place is
mentioned on modern maps nor is there any place with a reasonably similar name.

either of these places was very dubious. Second, the offer of
Abu Bekr throws light on the activities of the former French
consul at Aden, M. Lambert; it indicated that he had been meddling in the Somali coast politics, taking the part of Abu Bekr
against the friend of the British, Ali Shermarkee.

Russel first went to Rome where he interviewed the Pope
and made arrangements for Father Sapeto, a colleague of de
Jacobis, to accompany him as interpreter. On December 1,
1859, he left Suez on the "Yemen" accompanied by Father Sapeto, four naval officers (one a doctor), and ten French marines
to serve as guards. The "Yemen" arrived at Massawa on the
eleventh. Russel immediately wrote to Negussie and then explored Zula and Dissie Island. On December 28, Russel, five
companions, six marines, and two servants set out for the interior. They reached Halai on the edges of the Abyssinian highlands and there settled down to await a reply from the Ras.

Almost immediately Russel was joined by Mgr. de Jacobis
and his troubles began. Rumors spread through Abyssinia that
Russel had been sent to mediate between Theodore and Negussie,
fix the boundaries of their territories, etc. These rumors did
not help Russel. Halai, while ostensibly in Negussie's territory, was not overly friendly to the Ras and the people were offended at the guard of French marines which Captain Russel had
brought along. In addition to a growing unfriendliness on the part
of the people, de Jacobis continually and persistently pressed
Russel to intervene in Abyssinian politics on the side of Negussie.

Shortly Negussie informed Russel that it was impossible for
the French to get to his court as Theodore's army lay between
the Ras and the coast. Meanwhile, M. Gilbert, the French
consul in Massawa, was urging Russel to return to the coast before he got into serious trouble as conditions around Halai were
deteriorating rapidly. After a month at Halai the party returned
to Massawa, on one occasion having to fight its way out.
Russel placed de Jacobis and the Catholics under French protection, but this was as far as he felt he was able to go. His
sole achievement was a questionable arrangement with local
chiefs to recruit labor for Mayotte and Réunion at a monthly
wage of $5.00.

Russel left Massawa for Aden on February 17, 1860, and
arrived at the Indian Ocean port on the twenty-seventh. Here
he met Admiral de Lingle and "La Cordelière," sent to investigate the death of the French consul at Aden, M. Lambert (vide

infra p. 255).   He then proceeded to Berbera and Tajura and
returned northward stopping at Perim, Raheita, Assab, (Edd)
Massawa, and Jidda.   (All this information from Russel, op.
cit., various citations.) Actually Russel accomplished nothing
although his reports on the Bay of Tajura probably had some influence on the French purchase of Obock two years later.   He
had made the same mistake Sir Home Popham made in the Yemen in 1802 and Major Harris in Shoa in 1841; he brought foreign soldiers as guards instead of depending on natives.   All
three expeditions nearly ended in disaster for this reason.

Meanwhile in Paris, Lord Cowley pressed Thouvenal, the
French Foreign Minister, for information on French intentions
in the Red Sea.   Thouvenal replied by stating that the establishment of a packet and mercantile service from Suez to the East
had long been contemplated by the French Government and that
an embassy had been sent to gain some place on the Abyssinian
coast as a coaling station.   (Russel had the title Ambassador.)
The embassy had reported that the best spot was in the territory of the Ras of Tigré (Dissie) but as yet no decision had been
reached.   He added that the whole question of sovereignty was
very difficult as had been shown by the previous difficulties of
the Roman Catholic mission and suggested that to avoid complications a joint commission might be established to decide any
questions involved (FO 1/11, Cowley-FO 4/19/60).

In Paris, the Russel mission continued to have repercussions.   On May 25 Lord Cowley reported an illuminating occurrence at a French cabinet meeting.   Thouvenal had seen a report in the French newspapers that Russel had taken possession
of the island of Dissie and demanded an explanation as to how
this could be done without consulting the Foreign Office.   The
Minister of Marine admitted the accuracy of the report. (Russel's
book does not confirm this face; he merely reported it as being
the most suitable place for a coaling station.) Thouvenal then
stated that there was no trace of any correspondence on this
subject with the Foreign Office and that the matter was an im-
politic demonstration against a friendly power, England, and an
infringement on the sovereignty of the Porte.   The Emperor
then said that the subject was not worth discussion and the argument stopped.   Thouvenal, telling Cowley of the incident, added
that he was still completely in the dark on the question and could
only assume that a coaling station was wanted (FO 78/3186,
Cowley-FO 5/25/60).

News of Plowden's death reached England in June of 1860.
On receiving the news at Aden, Playfair, the acting Resident,
appointed M. Barroni as temporary British agent at Massawa,
an appointment which was approved by the Foreign Office (FO
1/11, Colquhoun-FO 5/29/60, IO-FO 6/8/60 and FO-IO 6/15/
60). This was followed by the arrival of news from Colquhoun
of the results of Playfair's investigation of the death of M. Lambert, the French consul at Aden. Colquhoun had transmitted a
copy of Playfair's findings to M. Sabatier, the French Consul
General in Alexandria, and instructed Consul Walne at Cairo to
investigate French actions concerning Lambert's death. Walne's
report was not encouraging, for he said that Count Russel was
"only too anxious to get up a good atrocity as a pretext for intervention in one neighborhood," and had reported the affair to
Paris which had ordered Admiral de Lingle, Commandant at
Bourbon, to investigate (FO 1/11, Colquhoun-FO 8/4/60). This
latter information appears to be distorted; the Russel mission
seems to have been wholly separate from the de Lingle investigation as it was started by a different French ministry. However, Russel's remarks about the Lambert affair in particular
and British actions in general are extremely intemperate. He
refused to visit Zeila because he believed that the first appearance of a French vessel there should be to avenge the murder
of the French consul (Russel, op. cit. , pp. 196-7, 217).

In December, Lord Cowley was again instructed to ascertain the views of the French Government on Abyssinia. These
instructions had been delayed, according to a note appended to
the document, "this inquiry should have been made 5 months
ago but your Lordship's minute was overlooked" (FO 1/11, FO-
Cowley 12/5/60). Cowley replied that Thouvenal was very ignorant on the subject of Abyssinia, that he personally took no
interest in the area. Cowley believed that the French Foreign
Office had no policy except their traditional protection of the
Roman Catholic faith in the Near East. In respect to this policy
he felt that they would do anything, right or wrong. He added
that a line of French postal steamers was to begin operations
from Suez to the East in March of 1861 (FO 1/11, Cowley-FO
12/10/60).

Meanwhile the whole political situation in Abyssinia had
changed, through events which were unknown to both London
and Paris for a considerable time. Plowden's murder had led
Theodore to attack Negussie, for Garrad, the minor chief who

was responsible for Plowden's fatal injuries, was an ally of the Ras of Tigré. He caught up with Garrad in October, 1860. Plowden's friend Bell killed the rebel with his own hands, but was himself slain later in the battle (FO 78/1590, Colquhoun-FO 2/2/61). Bishop de Jacobis, head of the Roman Catholic mission, had died of natural causes in August of 1860 (BSE 1860, Playfair-Bombay 8/22/60), and on January 3, 1861, Theodore met Negussie in battle near Axum. The Ras of Tigré's army was routed and the Ras himself, who escaped from the battle field, was shortly captured and put to death by Theodore (FO 78/1590, Colquhoun-FO 2/18/61; copy in FO 1/11 and in IO-FO 4/12/61). However, a glance at the references will show that the Foreign Office was not fully informed of the situation. The dispatch from Colquhoun containing the news of Bell's death was buried in the Egyptian files although it had to do only with Abyssinia. That from Playfair was never transmitted from the India Office to the Foreign Office although news of de Jacobis' death was of primary political importance in the Abyssinian situation.

The death of Bell, following that of Plowden, removed the last westernizing and moderating influence on Theodore's actions. From that time on he relapsed into traditional Abyssinian despotism. De Jacobis' decease removed the spearhead of the effective unofficial French intrigues in Tigré, and Negussie's execution removed any possibility of the restoration of French influence in northern Abyssinia. Possibly this full information would have made the Foreign Office more cautious in the next steps which they took in the area, steps which were to lead directly to the military expedition of 1867-1868.

In December, 1856, Coghlan was invited by Sultan Ali to visit Lahej. He departed on December 16 with Playfair, Rassam, eight officers, and sixteen men of the newly formed Aden irregular horse on the first state visit made by a Resident to the interior. After spending the night at Sheikh 'Othman, which Coghlan found had a plentiful supply of water, the party arrived at Lahej on the seventeenth. Coghlan described Lahej as a neat town in the center of a rich agricultural country. After greetings by the Sultan, he met the Sultan's family who impressed him greatly with their intelligence. Coghlan expressed the wish that they might be given a European education, as that course might greatly improve the whole situation. On Coghlan's return the party stopped with the Aqrabi chief who received them well (BSC 1857, Coghlan-Bombay 12/25/56).

At the end of March the Fadhli Sultan paid a visit to Bir Ahmed and communicated with Coghlan through Sayud Alowi ibn Hydroose; pride prevented his entering Aden. He sent a sworn certificate that the murderer of Captain Milne had been expelled from his tribe, and his stipend was paid to him from the date of the certificate (BSC 1857, Coghlan-Bombay 4/10/57).

A continued drought became a serious matter and, by May, Aden was dependent on the interior for water, the ancient reservoirs useless unless rain fell to fill them (BSC 1857, Coghlan-Bombay 5/8/57). This situation aroused Sultan Ali's cupidity and he placed a tax on water from Sheikh 'Othman although he did not own the wells. Coghlan promptly stopped the Sultan's stipend, so the Sultan raised the tax on water to six and a half annas (13 cents) a load, a tax of twenty-five per cent (BSC 1857, Coghlan-Bombay 6/26/57). This placed Coghlan in a very difficult position as the Aden garrison was below strength due to the withdrawal of part of the troops to India to put down the Mutiny and the use of part of the remainder to occupy Perim (BSC 1857, Coghlan-Bombay 6/9/57). Therefore, if Sultan Ali cut off the water supply, it was impossible for Coghlan to take Sheikh 'Othman by force without the aid of allies. The use of an ally at this time was inadvisable as the local situation made it extremely dangerous to set one tribe against another. However, Rassam conferred with Sultan Ali at Sheikh 'Othman and, through diplomacy and bluff, succeeded in reducing the tax to one anna a load (BSC 1857, Coghlan-Bombay 7/9/57).

In September Coghlan received an invitation from the Fadhli Sultan to visit him in Shuqra. This gentleman especially requested to see a steamer, which put Coghlan in a difficult position as he had only two sailing vessels stationed at Aden. As the Sultan knew two to twelve steamers visited Aden each month, all of which he assumed belonged to the British Government, Coghlan felt it necessary to request a steamer from the Government. Furthermore, requests for information from England about guano deposits and telegraph stations indicated that a survey of the whole Gulf of Aden had to be made, for which a sailing vessel was entirely too undependable (BSC 1857, Coghlan-Bombay 9/17/57). A vessel was finally supplied by the end of 1857.

In Aden, the drought continued. Coghlan finally was compelled to get some old boilers from Bombay and set up a temporary condenser system to distill sea water for human consumption (BSC 1857, Coghlan-Bombay 9/27/57). H.M.S. "Encounter" reached Aden in October from England, dispatched after reports of the weakness of the garrison had been received in London. She arrived in bad condition and was suitable only for harbor defense. Meanwhile certain intertribal friction continued but lack of water prevented any crisis (BSC 1857, Coghlan-Bombay 10/24/57). Rain fell about the first of November, 1857, ending the drought and filling the reservoirs (BSC 1857, Coghlan-Bombay 10/11/57).

The arrival of rain released the tribal jealousies held in check by the prolonged drought. On December 28, 1857, the Fadhli Sultan occupied part of the town of Lahej after a feeble resistance by Sultan Ali. The Fadhli retreated after collecting some booty, stopped at Sheikh 'Othman, and retired to his own country. Sultan Ali then attacked Bir Ahmed on the third of January, 1858, but was repulsed. Meanwhile Sultan Ali's correspondence with Coghlan became more and more insulting and objectionable, presenting unfounded complaints, refusing reasonable explanations, and threatening to close the roads. Coghlan stated that Sultan Ali's motives were obvious. He resented peace having been made with the Fadhli Sultan in 1857 without his aid and wished to stir up the English against the tribes so he could act as arbiter (BSLE 1858, Coghlan-Bombay 1/12/58).

If Aden had not been dependent on the countryside for supplies, Coghlan would have paid no attention to Sultan Ali's

increasing offensiveness. However, his offenses against the
English since 1857 had been serious. First, he had sowed dissension among the Aqrabi, whose chief was responsible for the
final establishment of peace between the Fadhli and the British.
Second, he had been difficult about the water question. Third,
he had instigated a raid by a Subahi tribe against a kafila so that
he could repel it. Fourth, some plundering had occurred in November and December, 1857. Fifth, Sultan Ali had written a
circular letter to the tribes charging Coghlan with disregarding
the treaty with the Abdali and had threatened to keep his people
from entering Aden and to close the country "until the Government shall come to its senses." Sixth, he had intentionally delayed an ambassador from San'a. Seventh, he had openly enter-
tained the murderers Boghi and the Sayud of Wahut. Eighth, he
had caused trouble with other tribes friendly to the English who
had appealed to Coghlan for aid against the Abdali. In view of
all this, Coghlan suggested that, if the Abdali closed the roads,
a military demonstration should be made and Sheikh 'Othman
occupied until Sultan Ali came to his senses. The occupation of
Sheikh 'Othman, junction of all the caravan routes into Aden,
would keep the roads open. Such a course was safe, as the remainder of the tribes were friendly to the British and as there
was internal dissension in the Abdali tribe. By allowing the Abdali people access to Aden, Coghlan could indicate that such a
demonstration was directed at Sultan Ali rather than the Abdali.
Coghlan felt that such a course was extremely necessary to preserve for Aden the gains which had been made (BSLE 1858,
Coghlan-Bombay 2/24/58).

     Sultan Ali's stipend was stopped again on March 1 because
of his entertainment of the murderers and his seizure of 6,000
rupees worth of coffee (BSLE 1858, Coghlan-Bombay 3/6/58).
Sultan Ali thereupon occupied Sheikh 'Othman with 500 men, cut
off water and supplies, and threatened to stop the entire caravan
traffic. As there was no hope of reconciliation, Coghlan said
he would make a demonstration unless Bombay forbade him to
do so in their reply to his letter of February 24 (BSLE 1858,
Coghlan-Bombay 3/16/58).

     As no reply was received in the mail from Bombay, a dem-
onstration was made on March 17. Coghlan felt that such action
"was tacitly recognized by the absence of any expressed inhibi-
tion." With 500 infantry, 50 artillery men, 40 seamen and 11
of the Aden troop, Coghlan marched the two miles to Sheikh

'Othman and ordered the Arabs to evacuate before he was compelled to open fire. The Arabs replied with a volley and put up
a stubborn resistance for an hour. Forty Arabs were killed,
which Coghlan remarked "would put Sultan Ali in an embarrassing position with his people." Finding Sheikh 'Othman not easy
to defend with a small garrison, Coghlan destroyed the fort and
retired to Aden where he was loudly welcomed by the Arab residents (BSLE 1858, Coghlan-Bombay 3/18/58). That Coghlan
had been correct in assuming the tacit approval of the Government was emphasized by a letter from Bombay. "The Right
Honorable the Governor in Council after full consideration was
with reluctance about to sanction the adoption of measures of
coercion suggested by you when the receipt of your subsequent
letter, informing the Government of the movement you had been
compelled to make against Sheikh 'Othman only rendered it necessary for the Government to record its full approval of your
proceedings" (BSLE 1858, Anderson-Coghlan 4/7/58).

Supplies began coming in immediately although there was
a temporary stoppage due to arguments between the Abdali chiefs.
Coghlan requested permission to make peace with the Abdali
and this was granted, although he was instructed not to occupy
Sheikh 'Othman as it was easy to get into the Lahej country without using this place as an outpost (BSLE 1858, Coghlan-Bombay
3/20/58 and Bombay-Coghlan 4/7/58).

Negotiations were begun on March 21, Sultan Ali suggesting
Sayud Alowi ibn Hydroose as his ambassador. The Abdali Sultan
had returned the coffee which he had confiscated, but still kept
Boghi in the country (BSLE 1858, Coghlan-Bombay 4/3/58).
By April 30, negotiations had progressed to the point where the
Sultan had given promises of good conduct (BSLE 1858, Coghlan-
Bombay 4/30/58). On the first of July Coghlan had a meeting
with Sultan Ali, when a settlement of differences was made.

The demonstration brought up again the question of an Aden
troop. One had been established in 1856 by volunteers from
"Jacob's Horse" but most of them were removed in 1857 to join
the Persian expedition in the short-lived Anglo-Persian War.
The Government's suggestion of providing a native camel corps
did not meet with Coghlan's approval as the Arabs were excellent cameleers and it would have been difficult to gain any superiority over them (BSLE 1858, Coghlan-Bombay 9/30/58).
Thus the question stood, a subject of continual debate, until
1867 when a new and permanent troop was formed.

The year 1859 opened with another drought. By April the
situation was becoming acute, with provisions scarcer and
scarcer (BSLE 1859, Coghlan-Bombay 4/3/59). However, this
was broken on April 30 by a copious downpour which filled all
the ancient reservoirs; 10 million gallons were collected in two
hours. This rain unfortunately was followed by a cloudburst on
May 1 at eleven at night which caused the main pass to be closed
by a landslide; there were at least eleven deaths and thirty people missing (BSLE 1859, Coghlan-Bombay 5/1/59). These two
storms, however, saved the crops of the district, which were
abundant later in the year. Aden and the hinterland remained
quiet for a considerable time.

The efficacy of Coghlan's military demonstration in quieting
the country was obvious from the calm which descended on the
tribes, and its result was a justification of Haines' desires
which he had never been permitted to carry out. The tribes
could understand force and, until it was used, would do nothing
but cause trouble.

On April 16, 1860, the Bombay Government appointed Brigadier Coghlan, Hormudz Rassam, and the Reverend G. P. Badger to investigate the disputes between Zanzibar and Muscat and
between Muscat and Sohar which were causing a considerable
amount of trouble in the northwestern part of the Indian Ocean
area. Rassam at the same time was appointed temporary British Resident at Muscat. These troubles were dynastic in origin,
and interfered seriously with British efforts to suppress the
slave trade and piracy in the Persian Gulf. (BSE Resolution-
Bombay Govt. 4/16/40; for details of the mission see Coupland,
Reginald, EXPLOITATION OF EAST AFRICA, pp. 26-31.)

Captain Playfair was left in charge as Acting Resident at
Aden. In August, 1860, the Fadhli caused the first tribal disturbance near Aden since 1858, when some camels were stolen
in a raid and one Somali was killed. These camels were being
used to draw water to Aden where a prolonged dry spell had
exhausted the reservoirs (BSE 1860, Playfair-Bombay 8/17/60).
The Bombay Government instructed Playfair to get compensation
for the family of the Somali (BSE 1860, Resolution 9/4/60).
Playfair, however, demurred as the camels had been restored
and the Somali was not a British subject (BSE 1860, Playfair-
Bombay 9/22/60).

The year 1861 was quiet around Aden. At the end of the year
Brigadier Robertson was sent as Acting Resident in Coghlan's

absence, but he died, almost immediately, in January, 1862 (FO 78/1675, Colquhoun-FO 1/17/62). He was replaced by Major General R. W. Honner C. B. in May, 1862. In October the surrounding countryside was disturbed by attacks on the kafilas. These disturbances, as well as rumors that the French were intriguing with the tribes to obtain a site near Aden, led Honner to investigate a report that the Chief of Bir Ahmed would be willing to sell Jebel Ihsan or Little Aden to the British for $30,000 (BSE 1862, Honner-Bombay 11/18/62). The Government in Council vetoed the idea, but suggested subsidizing the Chief of Bir Ahmed as protection against French intrigue (BSE 1862, Minute by Governor 12/6/62).

Coghlan returned to Aden in January, 1863. He immediately reached an agreement with the Chief of Bir Ahmed on Jebel Ihsan, reserving for the English the right to purchase the peninsula, which the chief was unable to sell at the time. In May, the chief arranged certain claims on the land so that he appeared to be in a position to sell the peninsula to the British. The price was $3,000 and a stipend of $30 a month until the total sum of about $18,000 had been paid (BSE 1863 Coghlan-Bombay 5/18/63). The continued presence of French war vessels in Aden waters and their surveys of the surrounding territories led the Secretary of State for India, Sir Charles Wood, to authorize Coghlan to conclude the purchase: "Her Majesty's Government ... are of the opinion that its acquisition is most desirable and they therefore authorize you to enter into negotiations... for the purchase of the territory to which you refer and to conclude an arrangement for its cession on the most advantageous terms on which it can be obtained" (BSE Sir C. Wood-Coghlan 12/24/63). Coghlan made tentative arrangements on January 28, 1864, on the terms described above, at the same time reporting that the French had probably bought Ras Imran, an island fifteen miles west of Aden Harbor, a completely worthless piece of land except for its proximity to Aden (BSE Coghlan-Bombay 1/23/64). Jebel Ihsan or Little Aden was a high promontory with a small anchorage, valuable only because of its protection of Aden harbor. Its purchase was motivated simply by a desire to prevent its acquisition by anybody else. However, conflicting property claims held up final negotiations until 1870.

It has been obvious that there is little readily available statistical data about Aden. However, as a result of considerable controversy in India over the trade figures of 1859 which

were published there, Captain Playfair wrote a short pamphlet
on the trade of Aden in the year 1859. The figures which he
gives are as follows (money expressed in rupees):

	Imports		Exports	
	1857-58	1858-59	1857-58	1858-59
United Kingdom	14,66,277	16,14,195	2,08,042	54,273
Bombay	8,92,786	10,65,847	5,87,696	3,16,484
Dutch etc.	3,39,783	3,60,599	14,259	27,068
Ports in Red Sea	8,17,084	2,72,418	6,31,649	4,51,488
Ports in Africa (except Red Sea)	5,45,058	2,65,974	4,18,440	3,31,570
Ports in Arabia (except Red Sea)	1,26,635	1,51,473	83,835	1,10,779
U.S.A.	1,83,220	2,13,188	2,58,721	2,59,267
France	13,878	7,950	5,21,144	67,883
Totals (1858-59)		59,46,356		31,22,688

The decline in trade figures in 1858-1859 Playfair estimated
were caused first by the Jidda massacre (vide infra), second,
by disturbances in the Yemen, third, by a famine in the Yemen,
and fourth, by a serious cholera epidemic which broke out in
Arabia from Muscat to Jidda (Playfair, Captain Robert L.,
MEMORANDUM ON THE TRADE OF ADEN FOR 1858-9, Bombay, Jail Press, 1859). These figures total about Ł1,250,000
combined exports and imports, which indicated a tremendous
growth in trade since the occupation in 1839. The policy of
Haines in making Aden a free port, which was continued by his
successors, had borne considerable fruit.
    The Somali coast was relatively quiet between 1857 and
1860. The treaty with the Habr Owul tribe, settling all details
remaining from the death of Lieutenant Stroyan, was finally
officially signed and sealed on March 3, 1857; at that time
Frushard, in command of the "Elphinstone," reported the fair
at Berbera progressing with 10,000 people in attendance and
forty-one ships at anchor, fifteen of large size (BSC 1857

Coghlan-Bombay 3/12/57). In April, 1857, Coghlan reported
that Boo Bekr (Abu Bakr), the ruler of Zeila, had been deposed
by the Pasha of Hodeida, and Shermarkee restored to power
(BSC 1857, Coghlan-Bombay 4/24/57). Meanwhile, at the request of the Secret Committee, Coghlan had been investigating
various islands for guano, but had found very little; the natives
had used up the supply in past years (BSC 1857, Coghlan-Bombay 5/11/57). In September, 1857, reports arrived at Aden that
"Baron" Heughlin, Austrian Consul at Khartoum, was exploring
the Arabian coast and that Austria was preparing to occupy Socotra (BSC 1857, Coghlan-Bombay 9/28/57). This gentleman
was actually Dr. Von Heughlin, an eminent ornithologist. With
an officer of the Austrian Navy he had been on a scientific expedition on the Somali coast and was kidnapped near Cape Guardafui and held for ransom. This ended the expedition and both
gentlemen returned to Europe (BSC 1857, Coghlan-Bombay
12/12/57).

Much to the surprise of everyone, including the officers of
the schooner, the "Mahi" captured two slave ships from Zanzibar in January, 1858. This marked the first capture of a slave
ship in Aden waters, and was the more surprising because the
"Mahi" and the "Elphinstone," the only two boats stationed at
Aden, were so well-known (BSLE 1858, Coghlan-Bombay 3/13/
58). The lack of a suitable steamer prevented much action on
the Somali and African coasts during these years, especially as
troubles in Aden and the Hedjaz kept all ships busy. An act of
piracy on the brig "Telegraph" on the Somali coast in August
brought swift retribution with a bombardment of the town involved
(BSLE 1858, Coghlan-Bombay 9/7/58). Continual reports of
the slave trade filtered in but nothing could be done about it.
However, in October rumors flew that the Turks were about to
take Berbera. These did not materialize, luckily for Aden, but
Coghlan had the "Lady Canning" in readiness and sent it there
to prevent an occupation (BSLE 1858, Coghlan-Bombay 10/2/58).
At the same time Captain Playfair, sent to the Somali coast to
investigate further the "Telegraph" affair, arrived at Berbera
to find a Turkish war buggalow approaching the harbor. It turned
away when it sighted the "Lady Canning" and was not seen again
(BSLE 1858, Coghlan-Bombay 10/11/58).

In June, 1859, M. Henri Lambert, the Vice-Consul of
France at Aden, made one of his many journeys to the African
coast. He left Mocha on June 3 for Tajura to purchase mules for

Mauritius, since he was a merchant as well as Consul. Off Ras
Ali near Tajura his ship met a heavy sea and fog and was
wrecked on the Musa Islands. M. Lambert, instead of staying
on the wreck, ordered a raft to be made and he, his servant,
and one sailor tried to make the shore, but were drowned.
Playfair left Aden immediately on the H. M. S. "Furious" to investigate, as M. Lambert's inquiries into the slave trade and
his activities against it had made him very unpopular in certain
quarters. Playfair found the wreck untouched and under guard
of Shermarkee's men; upon investigation he could see no reason
to suspect foul play (FO 78/1467, Walne-FO 7/7/59 encl. Cogh-
lan-Walne 6/16/59 and 6/18/59).

      While to the British Playfair's investigation closed the in-
cident, the French in one of their moments of imperial expansion tried to use it as a cause for aggression. Almost immediately the French warship "La Cordeliere" arrived at Aden
carrying Admiral de Lingle, who, with Captain Russel, made
an investigation and sailed away. (Russel, op. cit. , pp. 195-6.)

      Early in 1861 de Lingle returned with two French naval
vessels, the "Cordeliere" and "La Somme." The admiral proceeded to Hodeida and soon wrote an insulting letter to Ahmed
Pasha, the Turkish governor, demanding (1) that Ali Shermarkee be made a prisoner; (2) that his property be confiscated
and an indemnity of $25,000 given to the family of M. Lambert;
(3) that the Nakoda and crew of the boat on which Lambert lost
his life be imprisoned except for a sailor who had given evidence
against Shermarkee and the crew. The "Lady Canning" was
sent to Hodeida to observe the investigation. The commanding
officer reported that the Pasha stated that he believed Shermarkee innocent but that he was under considerable pressure from
the French, and felt that the affair should be referred to Constantinople for settlement. Meanwhile, de Lingle took matters
into his own hands. He sailed to Zeila to get witnesses, and
seized three buggalows belonging to Shermarkee and took twenty
prisoners. He apparently thought better of this last incident,
and released the prisoners before stopping at Aden, where he
informed Playfair that he would give him full information and
presented him with copies of the deposition which he had obtained.
In spite of these, Playfair commented, "I have not yet heard a
single circumstance which makes me doubt that M. Lambert's
death was not accidental. " Playfair's conclusions can hardly
have been biased. The reports from Aden indicate that Lambert

was a close personal friend of the Acting Resident and that if he could have found any reason to believe that the French Consul's death was murder he would have left nothing undone to bring the murderer to trial (BSE 1851, Playfair-Bombay 4/20/61).

De Lingle, on returning to Hodeida, badly mistreated his voluntary witnesses to force them to change their stories, and also tried bribery (BSE 1861 Playfair-Bombay 5/20/61). Playfair shortly received a letter of protest from Ahmed Pasha against the "arbitrary and insulting conduct of the French" who, he said, had appointed a new governor of Zeila (Abu Bakr) without consulting him, and had refused him any of the evidence so that he could not conduct a trial of the individuals as he was obliged to do (BSE 1861, Playfair-Bombay 5/29/61). Enclosed was a copy of a letter from de Lingle to Ahmed Pasha in which the French Commodore said, "The English were averse to any French Consuls being in these parts and would conceal this murder if possible and make others afraid to be killed" (BSE 1861, de Lingle-Ahmed Pasha 5/7/61 encl. in Playfair-Bombay 5/29/61).

De Lingle refused to give up the further prisoners he had seized, chief of whom was Shermarkee, and proceeded to Jidda where he tried to get Ali Pasha to try the men. Ali refused as he felt that the evidence was obtained by torture and believed that the whole affair should be discussed in Constantinople. Shermarkee died in Jidda, on May 24, 1861, "of a broken heart" at eighty-five years of age. In Aden, Playfair refused de Lingle's demand for the seizure and surrender of Shermarkee's property. De Lingle, due to engine trouble on "La Somme," decided to return to France instead of proceeding to Suez (BSE 1861, Playfair-Bombay 6/8/61). On his way he stopped at Zeila to obtain more evidence from Abu Bakr, his self-appointed governor, and sailed for France with his prisoners (BSC 1861, Playfair-Bombay 7/12/61). One of the prisoners died on the way, and another died at the prison in Brest where all were incarcerated. Whatever became of the rest of the prisoners no one knows (BSE 1862, Playfair-Bombay 1/12/62). The whole incident was an outrageous abuse of international law and the laws of the countries involved.

In the spring of 1862 the French naval vessel "Curieux" appeared in the Red Sea bearing a M. Schiffer (sic: proper spelling, Schaeffer), whose title appeared to be Premier Secretaire Interprété de l'Empereur, and some Dankali natives whom

de Lingle had taken to Hodeida as witnesses. This ship visited
the whole coast from Bab-el-Mandeb to Zeila and finally selected the Bander of Obock as a settlement, purchasing it for
$3,000 from the Dankali chieftain. This harbor was relatively
unknown to Aden; the older officers who had been in the Indian
Navy knew it only as a spot where small craft sometimes anchored at night. The natives reported it as a possible good harbor but with no back country to supply it; the few tribesmen
there were dependent on the Arab coast for supplies. Aside
from prestige value and the very dubious strategic value of having a settlement in this locality, the only possible point of the
acquisition was perhaps a means of controlling the trade of
south Abyssinia which largely went through Zeila. But this trade
was small unless the slave trade could be developed. Further,
the legality of the purchase was highly dubious as the coast was
part of the Pashalik of the Yemen, as the English had long since
found out in their efforts to suppress the slave trade there.
Coupled with the rumored purchase of Edd by Pastré Freres, a
large commercial concern, and the acquisition of Dissei, it
would appear that the French were aiming at dominance of the
Abyssinian trade (BSE 1862, Honner-Bombay 5/23/62).

Captain Cruttenden, accompanied by General Honner, was
sent on H.M.S. "Zenobia" to investigate Obock after the "Curieux" had left. They found the harbor relatively useless as it
was exposed to the land winds. The natives were much upset
by the purchase, not for patriotic motives, but because the chief
of Raheita, a neighboring district, had received all the money
for the place and refused to split with the local chiefs. An expedition had been planned by the natives to drive the French out,
but the "Curieux" had left just before the attackers arrived at
the beach. The site provided no natural defenses, the only food
was goat mutton, and wood and fresh water were the only articles
in abundance (BSE 1862, Honner-Bombay 6/2/62, also FO 78/
1675, encl. in Saunders-FO 7/15/62). When Lord Cowley requested further information from Thouvenal in Paris regarding
the affair, Thouvenal admitted that M. Schaeffer, the chief dragoman of the Imperial Embassy at Constantinople, had gone to the
Red Sea to purchase a coaling station but that no conquest was
planned. He advised Cowley that formal possession had been
taken after the place had been bought for $10,000 (FO 78/3187,
Confidential Memo printed for use of Foreign Office 3/10/74).
Actually a treaty was entered into between the French Government

and Abu Bakr and other chiefs which was signed on March 11,
1862. It gave to the French Government the port of Obock, and
a virtual protectorate over all of what is now French Somaliland. Included was a provision which granted them Ghoubat
Kharab, the innermost bay of the Gulf of Tajura, if Obock should
not be satisfactory. (Text of treaty in Angoulvant, G., and
Vigneras, Sylvain, DJIBOUTI, MER ROUGE ET ABYSSINIE,
Paris, Libraire Africaine et Coloniale, 1902, pp. 9-11.)

Meanwhile an incident occurred on the Somali coast in
which the conduct of the British stands in marked contrast to
de Lingle's handling of the Lambert affair. In the fall of 1862,
fourteen sailors from H. M. S. "Penguin" were killed in an attack on one of the ship's boats at Bereda, just west of Cape
Guardafui. Playfair left on the "Semiramis" to investigate.
The "Penguin" had been on slave trade patrol off the Juba River
and one of her small boats had been separated by a storm and
driven north, finally seeking shelter around the Cape about
September 26. The sailors had landed first just south of the
Cape for water, and had had to flee after a misunderstanding
with the natives. Apparently the murders occurred due to a
similar misunderstanding, or else for robbery. The Sultan of
the tribe who controlled this area Playfair found to be completely blameless. The Sultan produced as many of the criminals as
could be found and after a trial had them executed. Thus the
matter was settled, a far different procedure from that adopted
by Lingle (BSE 1862, Playfair-Honner 11/1/62).

Rumors that the French were about to purchase the island
of Socotra, combined with French involvements in Abyssinia
and the Franco-Austrian War in Europe, led the government in
India to consider defense preparations for the Red Sea, Egypt,
and Aden against the French. Lieutenant General Sir James
Outram, onetime resident at Aden, considered that in view of
the international situation and the strength of the French fleet
in the Mediterranean, any defense of Egypt would be left up to
the Indian Government. He recommended heavily re-enforcing
Aden and laying up supplies there in order to seize Q'useir and
Suez if necessary. The increase in the slave trade and the disturbances would justify the presence of a strong naval force in
the Red Sea (BSE 1859, Govt. of India-IO 7/13/59, Minute of
Sir James Outram 6/13/59).

The Governor General, Canning, concurred with Outram,
saying that French actions in the Red Sea, Burma, and Cochin

China seemed to be too concerted to be just the work of adventurers. However, he felt that there was no need for re-enforcements at Aden but that the naval force in the Red Sea should be augmented by a large vessel from the Indian Navy (it possessed only three) and some ships from the Royal Navy (BSE 1859, Govt. of India-IO 7/13/59, Minute by Canning 6/23/59). These orders were put into effect on August 5 but were cancelled ten days later when word was received that the war in Italy had ceased. The vessels were diverted to China. (BSE 1859, Minutes by Elphinstone 8/5/59 and 8/15/59.)

The suppression of Muttalib's revolt in the Hedjaz did not
bring peace to Arabia. Many earlier reports from the Yemen
and the Hedjaz indicated the chaotic conditions prevalent in
Arabia Felix, but it was not until 1856 that any English eyewit-
nesses penetrated the interior. In the fall of 1856, the Reverend H.A. Stern, a missionary to the Jews, later imprisoned by
King Theodore, went into the Yemen and visited San'a disguised
as a dervish. An account of his trip is published in the Jewish
Intelligence. Unfortunately this account is entirely too sentimental to be useful; his only really important contribution was
an estimate of the population of San'a which he puts at 40,000,
of whom 18,000 were Jews. (Stern, Henry A., "Journal of the
Rev. H.A. Stern," in the Missionary Intelligence section of
Jewish Intelligence, Vol. XXIII, 1857: April, pp. 101 ff.; May,
pp. 139 ff.; August, pp. 258 ff.) On his return to Aden, in December, Coghlan pumped him for information and was able to
obtain a considerable amount of information about the district.
Stern reported that the Yemen was in complete anarchy and
the Imam held a title devoid of power. The present incumbent,
Ghalib ibn Muhammad ibn Yahya (otherwise known as Ghalib
el-Hadi), son of Muhammad ibn Yahya murdered in 1849, was
residing at Bilad Ans, forty miles south of San'a. He had neither the money nor the influence to restore his power, had succeeded in completely alienating his subjects and was spending
his days in a life of dissipation and drunkenness (from Khat),
apparently a common characteristic of all the early nineteenth
century Imams. San'a was ruled by Haji el Khaima, a merchant elected by his fellows as governor of the city, but his influence was felt only in the city proper. Of the three Banyan
merchants who had resided there, two had been murdered and
the third had become a Muslim to save his own life. The Jews
who resided in San'a, although large in number, were an op-
pressed minority, plundered of all their possessions and living
in abject poverty. Stern described the country as extremely
beautiful and apparently very rich, but in such a complete state
of chaos that no life was safe. He felt that San'a was the prey
of any small, well-disciplined force which wished to take the
city (BSC 1857, Coghlan-Bombay 12/11/56). Stern's description

of the Yemen explains the ease and the difficulty which faced
the Turks in their attempts to conquer the Yemen. It is not
hard to see the temptation which this rich land, without any organized defense, offered to an official with a small organized
army. Military progress was easily made with a very small
force against such disorganization, but when a certain point was
reached, and the fanaticism of the Zaidi populace became aroused
against the Sunnite Turks, the small force requisite for military
conquest was little protection to the conquerors.

   To a large extent, the same conditions were true in the
Hedjaz. The Turks merely tried here to hold the sacred places,
Mecca and Medina, and Ta'if, their military headquarters, and
to keep the roads open from Jidda. Under ordinary circumstances this was comparatively easy to do with a small force.
In the Hedjaz, the Turks did not have to deal with the fanaticism
of another sect, but they did have to deal with a population which
had been for countless generations tribal in organization and
completely independent in action. While the rise of the Wahhabis
in the eighteenth century had split these ancient tribal organiza-
tions, and the conquests and diplomacy of Muhammad Ali had
succeeded in breaking their power except for the Asiri, the desire for independent action and the hatred of outside interference remained. The revolt of Sharif Muttalib in 1856 renewed
this spirit and, although the revolt was successfully repressed,
the populace remained unsettled. Furthermore, the Indian
Mutiny stirred up the entire Muslim world against the infidel
although in very few places outside of India did this fanaticism
take active form. The Crimean War also had made a profound
impression in the Hedjaz and to the fanatical tribesman had
aroused a hatred of the Europeans. To him all "ifrangi" were
infidels, and the Russian "ifrangi" had attacked the Turkish
Empire, the defender of the Muslim faith and the seat of the
calif, although that title had not been propagandized as it was
to be a few years later. This was quite comprehensible to the
people. But that the French "ifrangi" and the English "ifrangi"
were allies of the Porte was completely beyond understanding,
for were not all "ifrangi" infidels, and were not "ifrangi" attacking the Muslim Empire? A combination of these factors,
the taste of independence under Muttalib and the religious situation resulting from the Crimean War and the Indian Mutiny,
made the population of the Hedjaz extremely restive.

   The "Elphinstone" had been at Jidda off and on after

Muttalib's revolt, and finally left on April 15, 1857. Immediately Mahmud Pasha, the governor, made a very insulting remark about Consul Page to the French Consul, and Consul Page struck his flag on April 16. This verbal insult, Page said, was the culmination of a series of events. His primary charge against the Pasha was extortion; Page estimated that he had obtained a fortune of 20,000 to 30,000 purses (Ł100,000-Ł150,000) out of his position as governor. Specifically, Page charged a continual violation, in fact a complete disregard, of the Commercial Treaty of 1838, a complete disregard of the Capitulations, compelling defendents under British protection to stand trial in Turkish courts, and other more minor incidents. Page felt that only the presence of the British at Aden prevented more serious violations of the treaties. His business was turned over to the French Consul who did not suffer from these various treaty infractions, as French interests at Jidda were limited to helping Algerians make the pilgrimage to Mecca (BSC 1857, Page-Bombay 4/22/57, encl. Page-de Redcliffe 4/16/57).

In October, Coghlan reported that Namek Pasha had arrived as Governor of the Hedjaz and that Page had renewed his official relations (BSC 1857, Coghlan-Bombay 10/24/57). Page reported the incident on October 19, saying that Namek had arrived on October 13 and had immediately had a consultation with Page, and that the consular flag had been rehoisted the next day. Namek, in speaking of Mahmud, said that he was an excellent soldier but completely unversed in civil government. Even the Hadramis, the most fanatical and intolerant section of Jidda's population, had praise for Page's handling of the argument. Page felt that the break in relations had had a good effect as it prevented an anti-foreign party from being formed, since the Arabs were convinced of the justice of Page's attitude, and it also put a stop to some of the worst financial abuses by bringing the government of Jidda under the scrutiny of the Porte. Apparently due to the Crimean War, the Consuls at Jidda had positions of considerably more influence than before, and this fact caused a certain amount of jealousy in the port, both among the officials, for the Consuls acted as a check on their extortion, and among the population, as the Consuls were agents of Christian powers in the Muslim Holy Land. The appointment of Namek Pasha, who had been on a mission to England to negotiate a loan, also brought with it a reorganization of the province. He had directly

under him the Seriasker of the Hedjaz, commander in chief,
and the Governor of the Yemen, both formerly independent officials. Furthermore the various credits made to the government of the Hedjaz had been increased and codified. Direct payment of Ł10,000 per month was made from Constantinople, in
addition to grain from Egypt, a part of that Pashalik's tribute
to the Porte, and the expenses of the annual pilgrimage were
reimbursed to the governor, the total amounting to Ł360,000 a
year, "the annual cost to the Sublime Porte for the honour of
the possession of the Hejaz." The one unfortunate part of the
new arrangement was that the Pasha had to make Mecca and
Ta'if his chief seats of Residence and leave the government of
Jidda to a deputy (BSC 1857, Page-Bombay 10/19/57).

Page reported later the abolition of some of the taxes which
had caused his complaints (the boatloading tax, etc.), and a
general attempt to keep duties in line with the treaty of 1838.
The only apparent danger lay in the replacement of the Turkish
regulars of the garrison by Bashi Bazooks, irregular troops
(BSC 1857, Page-Bombay 10/28/57).

The Hedjaz was disturbed almost immediately, however,
by the death of Sharif Ibn 'Aun on March 28, 1858, and the appointment of Sharif 'Ali as his successor. The country immediately rebelled and the situation became exceedingly dangerous.
However, Page's fears were allayed by the appearance of the
H. M. S. "Cyclops," Captain Pullen commanding, on March 21
(BSLE 1858, Page-Bombay 3/31/58).

The Bombay Government had been agitated by reports, at
the time of Muttalib's revolt, of the presence of one of the Moplah chiefs in Mecca. This sect from the Malabar coast was the
source of continual trouble to the Madras government, their
fierce fanaticism usually exhibited in massacring Hindus, a
habit which was evident as late as 1921-1922. Considerable difficulties had caused the expulsion of the leaders of this movement from India, and several found sanctuary in the Holy Cities.
As it was impossible to get the Turkish government to expel
them, it was felt wise to keep a watch on them. Page, however,
found it absolutely impossible to do this without an unofficial
agent in Mecca, but he was able to assure the Bombay Government that they could not leave Arabia without his knowledge
(BSLE 1858, Page-Bombay 12/4/57).

Early in June a long discussion took place over the ownership of a ship, the "Eranee," which the Consul finally awarded

to two British subjects on the basis of the ship's papers filed
with him. This caused considerable feeling in Jidda but apparently was to have no serious consequences.

On June 15, the officers of the "Cyclops" returned to their
ship as usual at 6 P.M. , having spent the day in Jidda which had
seemed peaceful. At 9:30 P.M. , two naked Greeks swam out
to the vessel and reported a massacre of all the Christians in
town. Captain Pullen, in the expectation that the garrison would
protect the Consulates, did nothing until next morning when the
consular flags did not appear. Putting over two armed boats he
went ashore, but was compelled to return because of the hostility of the populace. Page was reported to have been cut to
pieces and M. Eveillard, the French Consul, shot, his wife
stabbed to death and his daughter and her maid wounded. In all,
twenty-one Christians were massacred. The rising occurred
so suddenly that the Kaimakam was taken unawares. He acted
as promptly as he could and immediately marched on to the
Consulates where he was able to rescue Mlle. Eveillard and her
maid along with several other Christians, and secrete them in
his harem. The rising apparently started among the Hadrami
class (the leading merchants and also most fanatical element of
the population), and Pullen was convinced that it was designed
to drive the Christians from the Holy Land. After collecting
the twenty-six survivors on board the "Cyclops," Pullen awaited
the arrival of Namek Pasha from Mecca.

Namek Pasha arrived on June 20 and immediately wished
to send all the suspects to Constantinople until he discovered
that one of the chief witnesses was Feruji Yusum, his personal
banker. He then tried to make it appear that the seizure of the
"Eranee" was the cause of the trouble. Pullen, seeing that he
could get nowhere with him, sailed with the survivors for Suez,
having obtained the names of some of the culprits. (FO 78/1402,
Green-London 7/6/58 encl. Pullen-Admiralty 6/25/58.)

Coghlan heard the news in three weeks but was unable to
send a ship as he had none at Aden (BSLE 1858, Coghlan-Bombay 7/4/58). The Resident was unable to arrive at any satisfactory conclusions on the basis of reports which had reached him,
although he had been informed for quite some time that the inhabitants of Jidda had planned an uprising to expel the infidel.
News from other Red Sea ports was not encouraging and he was
afraid similar outbreaks might occur elsewhere (BSLE 1858,
Coghlan-Bomb ay 7/10/58). In Egypt like fears were expressed,

and reports from Cairo and Suez indicated a great uneasiness
among the Arabs (FO 78/1402, Green-London 7/7/58). Walne
at Cairo felt that the situation there was dangerous as the populace, already aroused by the Indian Mutiny, was considerably
stirred by the news from Jidda (FO 78/1402, Walne-Green
7/5/58).

Coghlan finally was able to send the "Elphinstone" into the
Red Sea to guard the Christian population of Hodeida and Mocha,
and at the same time he obtained a confidential list of the chief
instigators of the massacre, which he forwarded to London
(BSLE 1858, Coghlan-Bombay 2/28/58). These culprits were
listed as Ibrahim Aga, the Kaimakam, Sheikh Baghafur, the
head of the merchants who led the attack on Thomas Sava and
Co. (a Greek firm under British protection and the leading mercantile establishment of the Red Sea), Abdullah el Fera el Moh-
tessib, an employee of the Porte and native of Upper Egypt who
led the attack on the English Consulate, and Salem Sultan, a
merchant (FO 78/1402, Green-London 7/29/58). In the meantime, Ismail Pasha had been dispatched with 494 men to Jidda
by the Khedive of Egypt to restore order (FO 78/1402, Green-
London 7/23/58 via ship and cable). However, the Pasha merely seized a great many innocent people and then left for Mecca,
as he was afraid to molest the powerful Hadrami merchants
(FO 78/1402, Green-London 8/4/58).

Authorities in London had ordered Pullen to return to Jidda
and demand the arrest of the culprits under threat of bombardment. He arrived on July 23 and delivered this ultimatum with
a thirty-six hour period of grace. After waiting forty hours
without reply, he started to bombard the town on the twenty-
fifth, destroying fifteen buggalows. At 11 A.M. he received a
letter from the Pasha which was unsatisfactory, and so continued bombarding at four-hour intervals. On the twenty-ninth
the troops arrived from the interior, but Namek Pasha could
give no satisfaction as he did not have full power to act, and
yet insisted on convicting the guilty ones in the local court. As
this course had achieved no results by the fourth of August,
Pullen began his bombardment again. In Consul Calvert's words,
the bombardment was designed "to inspire a wholesome dread
among the natives. In this we perfectly succeeded for Jidda
was in a short time quite deserted and the inhabitants were seen
flying in all directions to the neighboring villages." The bombardment occurred at an opportune moment as a large group of

pilgrims arrived back from Mecca just in time to be fully impressed. On August 5, Ismail Pasha arrived with full power
to act (i. e., the power of life and death which Namek Pasha did
not have), and seized and executed eleven people. None of these
was a ringleader, however, and Pullen left dissatisfied with the
results (FO 78/1402, Green-London 8/16/58 encl. Calvert-
Green 8/8/58). Coghlan from Aden reported that the bombardment had had a beneficial effect, and had not aroused any feeling
against the English in the Hedjaz nor had it been considered an
attack on the Holy Cities (BSLE 1858, Coghlan-Bombay 9/25/58).

The actions of the Pasha did not satisfy either the British
or the French Governments and, after lodging a protest at Constantinople, it was decided that a three-power commission was
to investigate the matter. Pullen was appointed as the English
commissioner and ordered to work with his French colleague to
get the necessary information, but the Porte was to enforce the
findings of the commission by its own means. With M. Sabatier,
the French Consul General in Egypt, as the French commissioner, and a Turkish official, the commission was to investigate
Namek Pasha's conduct, the conduct of the local officials, obtain the dismissal of the Kaimakan, and demand a contribution
levied on the inhabitants of the town (FO 78/1488, FO-Pullen
#1, 8/25/58). Pullen was further warned to seek only justice,
and to try to reduce the French indemnity demands which the
Foreign Office considered unduly high. Furthermore, he should
not use force unless absolutely necessary and then only with
governmental permission (FO 78/1488, FO-Pullen #3, 9/2/58
and #4, 9/17/58). Pullen first consulted Ismail Pasha who had
brought back thirty-six prisoners, but met with obstacles immediately as Ismail had "no authority" to talk or to let the prisoners be interviewed (FO 78/1488, Pullen-Bulwer 9/22/58).

Pullen and M. Sabatier arrived in Jidda on October 12 and
began investigations, although no Turkish commissioner had
appeared. They found that the executions and arrests had removed most of the lower class witnesses who might possibly
testify against the wealthy and prominent citizens involved (FO
78/1488, Pullen-Bulwer 11/3/58). Pullen's services were required by the Admiralty, and he was replaced by Consul Walne
on November 8 (FO 78/1488, FO-Pullen 11/8/58).

The details of the various evasions and subterfuges of the
Turks are of no particular importance. An attempt was made
to blame the whole matter on the Moplah Sayud Fayzul but the

charges did not hold water. The damages were estimated at at least 3,000,000 piasters. On the first of January, 1859, the commission reached its conclusions, and decided that the whole motive for the massacre was not religious in any way but was the very natural and ordinary one of robbery. Abdallah el Moh-tessib and one Sheikh Amudi, both prominent Hadramaut mer-chants, planned the whole uprising as a means of getting gold in the amount of Ł10,000 which Consul Page kept in the consul-ate. These two men had aroused the mob, and under the cover of the riot seized this gold and all the currency in the French Consulate and the mercantile establishments. Both were pub-licly executed at Jidda on January 12 and a large number of the prominent merchants sentenced to life imprisonment. The ac-tions of the Kaimakan were peculiar and inexplicable. Hearsay testimony hitched him to the plot but the saving of the lives of two Christians at the very acute peril of his own made any accu-sations very difficult (FO 78/1488, Walne-FO 1/2/59 and 1/14/59). After futile attempts to get the claims properly settled, the commission moved to Constantinople and finished its work there.

In the Yemen the Turks had had difficulties. In June, 1858, the Imam of San'a, Ghalib el-Hadi, having reached another cri-sis in his financial affairs, sold Ta'iz to the Turks. Ahmed Pasha thereupon marched to take the town, joined by the Imam and a few hundred irregulars. As usual, the tribes rose, the Arab irregulars deserted, and the Turkish troops had to buy their way out, having lost half their number in casualties. This damage to Turkish prestige had the usual result. The tribes, always ready to take advantage of a weak adversary, threatened Mocha and Yerim and had to be bought off (BSLE 1858, Coghlan-Bombay 9/25/58).

In January, 1859, the Imam of San'a sent an ambassador to Aden to beseech English aid in reorganizing his country, of-fering to place it under English protection. Coghlan told him that when the offer had been made before, at a time when such an arrangement would have been practical, the government had refused, and that such an idea was completely impractical in 1859 because of the complete anarchy of the country, and Turk-ish possession of the seaports (BSLE 1859, Coghlan-Bombay 1/16/59). In the Yemen, Ahmed Pasha spent a year in 1859 and 1860 in the interior, and succeeded in adding the hill district of Hafash to his dominion while a strong force remained there.

But when a small garrison was left, the inhabitants rose and killed part of it. Ahmed Pasha returned and destroyed thirty villages and all the coffee trees, the whole riches of this district. All this was done by the Pasha on his own, without the consent and contrary to the orders of the Porte (BSE 1860, Playfair-Bombay 7/17/60). The continuing disturbances led to another visit to Aden by the Hajariya chiefs to improve trade relations. This hill tribe occupied one of the richest of the coffee sections of the Yemen, and the continued exactions of the Turks had hurt their trade (BSE 1860, Playfair-Bombay 8/1/60).

The state of Turkish government in the province is well-illustrated by an incident which occurred in April, 1860. A quarrel broke out between two tribes near Mocha. Ahmed Pasha, governor of the Yemen, sent for the chiefs and fined them $3,000 and $10,000 respectively and sent them back to Mocha in the care of Suffer Aga and 130 soldiers. There they were jailed pending payment of the fines, which they claimed they could not pay. Suffer Aga was presented with $1,000 and the chiefs asked for time to collect the rest. The Turkish officer told them that if the remainder was not paid the next day, they would be flogged to death. That night the chiefs were released by a party of 220 Arabs who did no other violence. Suffer Aga attacked this Arab party and suffered a severe defeat, upon which the Arabs blockaded Mocha. A similar episode occurred near Beit el Faqih above Mocha. Playfair remarked that if this continued much longer there was every possibility that Mocha, already a ruin, would be completely deserted (BSE 1860, Playfair-Bombay 8/17/60). Such actions resulted in visits from the chiefs of the Yafa and Hashad wa Bakeel* tribes early in 1861 who came to further amicable trade relations (BSE 1860, Playfair-Bombay 3/2/61 and 3/18/61).

Ahmed Pasha meanwhile continued his excesses. In March of 1861 he exacted a forced loan of $20,000 from the merchants of Hodeida and allowed only six hours for payment (BSE Playfair-Bombay 4/2/61). Continued rumors came to Aden that the Turkish officials were profiting from the suppression of the slave trade off the Zanzibar coast by encouraging its growth

---

*These tribes reside north and west of San'a. They normally would have no relations with Aden unless the Turkish occupation of Hodeida, their normal port, forced them to use the long overland route to Aden.

through the Red Sea area. As no slave trade treaty existed with
the Porte, the British were powerless to mitigate this evil. The
Yemen remained quiet though misgoverned. In April of 1863,
Brigadier Coghlan visited Mocha. His comments are interesting. "The dilapidated condition of this once populous city is
deplorable; bad government and exorbitant taxation by means of
farmed revenues have diverted its commerce to other channels,
Aden probably receiving the greatest of it as well as of its population which is now fallen to less than 2,000 of all ages; in a
few years, Mocha will be abandoned, its handsome houses, imposing forts and picturesque minarets may for a while remain
monuments to its former greatness, but these will all too speedily decay as the greater portion of the city is already decayed
and their remains will attest the feebleness and corruption of a
government which has already converted a fine city, the emporium of a large trade into a state of desolation which must be
seen to be understood" (BSE 1863, Coghlan-Bombay 4/29/63).

In the Jidda area, quiet continued, the bombardment having
served as an excellent lesson. The Turkish governors had apparently gotten the local tribes under some kind of control.

The establishment of the cable from Suez to Aden has been
mentioned. In 1858, Coghlan received a copy of a firman from
the Porte authorizing the Pasha of the Yemen to allow the landing of the cable at one or two points on the Arabian coast. Coghlan wrote Green at Alexandria that he assumed that this meant
only as far as Bab-el-Mandeb and warned him that care must
be exercised in dealing with the Porte on this matter as the
Turks might claim the cable points east of Aden on the Hadrami
and Muscat coast (FO 78/3186, Green-London 1/8/59). His
advice was acted upon. The India Office informed the Foreign
Office that it had ordered its residents at Bushire and Zanzibar
(which included Muscat) to disregard this firman (FO 78/3186,
IO-FO 3/31/59).

XVI. ABYSSINIA, THE IMPRISONMENT OF CAMERON

Immediately upon receiving news of Plowden's death, the
Foreign Office began looking for a replacement. On June 30,
1860, Captain C. D. Cameron, formerly of the Indian Army,
was appointed at a salary of Ł 600 a year plus Ł300 for expenses
(FO 1/11, Minute 6/30/60). Because of indecisions, instructions to Cameron were not issued until February 2, 1861. He
was then instructed to make his headquarters at Massawa, to
familiarize himself with the affairs of Abyssinia, and watch the
slave trade. He was cautioned against becoming too partisan
or getting involved in intrigues to set up exclusive British influence in Abyssinia, and he was especially instructed to watch
all "proceedings which may tend to alter the state of possession
either on the seacoast or in the interior of the country" (FO 1/11.
Instructions to Cameron [Political] 2/2/61). Dr. Beke, hearing
of Cameron's appointment, wrote to Lord John Russell on March
5: "as Capt. Cameron is still in England, I would most res-
pectfully represent to your Lordship the expediency of appointing that officer to some other post. . . . and nominating myself
Consul in Abyssinia on account of my peculiar qualifications for
that difficult position under existing circumstances" (FO 1/11,
Beke-Russell 3/5/61). Beke had had an interview with Lord
John Russell on February 19 in which he did not make a very
favorable impression.

Meanwhile an apparently minor incident occurred which was
to lead later to very serious consequences. On January 28,
1861, Barroni, acting agent in Massawa, forwarded via Colquhoun at Alexandria a letter from Theodore stating that he wished
to send an embassy to England and requesting Barroni to come
to Adowa to accompany the embassy. This was forwarded by
Colquhoun on February 28, 1861, as an enclosure in Colquhoun's
dispatch #23 of that date. This letter was apparently lost, since
on receipt of Barroni's dispatch of September 8, 1861, requesting a reply to Theodore's letter, neither Theodore's nor Barroni's letters could be found (FO 1/11, note on Barroni-Russell
9/9/61). It was the failure to answer this letter which Theodore later considered a mortal insult and was the basis of his
antagonism to the British. The letters are at present filed in
FO 1/11 in their proper place, but when they were found is not
indicated.

Barroni was advised by Colquhoun on March 10, 1861, to dissuade Theodore from sending an embassy until instructions were received from London (FO 78/1590, Colquhoun-Barroni 3/10/61), and this delay was not helpful in preparing the way for Cameron when he arrived in Abyssinia.

Cameron remained in England to see the Reverend Stern, the missionary of the Jews Society in Abyssinia who had returned to England on leave. At Stern's suggestion, a letter was prepared thanking Theodore for his aid at the time of Plowden's death which was to be sent to the Emperor together with a present of a gun and a brace of pistols (FO 1/11, Cameron-Russell 8/17/61).

Not until the last day of 1861 was Cameron at Cairo preparing to go to Massawa (FO 1/11 Cameron [Cairo] FO 12/31/61). Cameron was at Aden on January 13, 1862, and took over the archives at Massawa on February 10, at which time Mr. Barroni retired from any further connection with the consulate (FO 1/12, Cameron-FO 2/9/62 & 2/10/62). Cameron found that the Turks were planning an extension of their power along the coast line to Bab-el-Mandeb, having already raised their flag at Adulis (Zula), Dissei and Edd. They also intended to plant military colonies along the frontiers in order to strengthen their hold on the sea coast. Theodore was watching this carefully because it threatened the salt mines at Taltal which supplied salt for all North Abyssinia and the sulphur mines nearby, which were essential to the Abyssinians for making gun powder (FO 1/12, Cameron-FO 3/29/62).

Cameron left for the interior in April, 1862, with a hunting party of the Duke of Saxe-Coburg which penetrated only into the territory around Adowa (FO 1/12, Cameron-FO 4/20/62). He remained there for a while and then, on Theodore's invitation, went to Gondar to meet the Emperor. He found that Theodore had pacified almost the entire country, including Shoa, and was proceeding against the Gallas. Theodore had also apparently broken the feudal system of much of its power (FO 1/12, Cameron-FO 7/22/62).

Cameron's report on Turkish plans for the extension of their power on the coast, coupled with a recurrence of the disputes in Jerusalem over the Abyssinian church, caused Lord John Russell to warn the Porte not to permit any proceedings which would bring them into conflict with the King of Abyssinia (FO 1/12, Finn [Jerusalem]-FO 3/13/62, 5/7/62, 6/3/62, and

FO-Bulwer 8/2/62). Finn, British Consul at Jerusalem, clearly
expressed the Turkish attitude towards the Abyssinians. As
they were closely allied to the Coptic church, they were considered as Copts, their territory was considered as part of the
Pashalik of Jidda and all firmans regarding them were forwarded
through Jidda.

It is interesting to note the conflict in policy between the
Foreign Office and the India Office in these incidents. The Turkish occupation of Dissei was welcomed by the India Office as a
relief from the danger of French occupation. The Foreign Office, while having somewhat the same attitude, was fearful that
Turkish expansion in this area would lead to conflict between
Abyssinia and the Porte which might well give the French undue
opportunity for interference.

The trip of Mr. Schaeffer to purchase Obock was carefully
watched by Colquhoun (FO 1/12, Colquhoun-FO 5/10/62). Cowley in Paris questioned Thouvenal regarding this trip. Why
Schaeffer had travelled under the assumed name of Captain
Mansfeldt was unknown to Thouvenal except that he was travelling on a mission from the Ministry of Marine and wished to escape observation. In discussing the matter, Thouvenal stated
that France had no desire to interfere in Abyssinia or to acquire
any land on the Red Sea coast except Obock which they wished to
use as a coaling station. However, they had lately named a
young Vice-consul M. Lejean to Abyssinia to study its resources
and trade (FO 1/12, Cowley-FO 6/6/62).

Reports of coal near Aden caused a considerable flurry of
excitement in London, the location of the deposits being sometimes in Arabia and sometimes on the Abyssinian coast. The
geologic structure of the area did not give any evidence of coal
formations, but rumors constantly reappeared. They all proved
groundless. If coal deposits of good quality had been found in
the Red Sea area, their possession would have been of the greatest value to the British.

Private reports reaching London in the summer of 1862 led
Hammond to write in July "Capt. Cameron had already given
much trouble & his notions of doing business are remarkable
and require to be carefully watched" (FO 1/12, Hammond, on
Humberston M. P.-Lord John Russell 7/31/62). These remarks
were prophetic. On October 7 Cameron was received by Theodore at Gojjam. The Emperor broke into a tirade on the encroachment of the Turks. Two days later, Cameron was again

received and gave the Emperor the presents with which he was
greatly pleased. A few days later, he had another audience
during which Theodore told him of his plans to attack Egypt, as
it was a wealthy country, and asked if the British would prevent
French interference on the coast and hold off a Turkish fleet.
The Emperor also asked about sending an embassy to London.
The object of this embassy was to appeal to all Christians to
help him in his coming expedition against the Muslims. Cameron stayed a few more days, and was then ordered by Theodore
to return to the coast and get an answer as soon as possible regarding the Emperor's embassy to England. Cameron pressed
for a renewal of the treaty and offered to go to Metemma to settle a border dispute. Theodore refused to consider the treaty
and told Cameron not to go to Metemma, that there was an epidemic of fever there. On October 31, Theodore presented him
with $1,000 and told him to go to Massawa, giving him a request
for aid against the Muslims addressed to Holland (Theodore had
already sent similar requests to France and Russia). In spite
of Theodore's advice, Cameron decided to proceed on his own
to Metemma and settle the border dispute (FO 1/12, Cameron-
FO 10/31/62). This dispatch was received in London on February 12, 1863, forwarded to the India Office on May 5 and returned from the India Office a year later (May 11, 1864) without
comment. Again Theodore was insulted by having his offer of
an embassy completely ignored.

Cameron followed this report with others, suggesting various methods of spreading British influence in Abyssinia. This
series of reports resulted in a discussion of the Abyssinian situation at the Foreign Office. The general tenor of this conference was that Cameron was meddling too much in the internal
affairs of Abyssinia. The results are well summed up by Lord
John Russell, "Our Consul seems disposed to meddle a great
deal too much. He should have gone away when the King told
him. But he must keep us informed about the French proceedings" (FO 1/13, Minute on Cameron-FO 11/10/62). This information was forwarded to Cameron on April 22, 1863, in the
form of new instructions to him ordering him to remain in
Massawa (FO 1/13, FO-Cameron 4/22/63). At the same time
Hertslet at the Foreign Office prepared a memorandum on Abyssinia summarizing British relations with that country from Valentia's trip. Hertslet pointed out how Coffin's failure in 1843
to return from England to Ras Oubie without a present from the

Queen nearly cost him his life. Hertslet concluded with the information that Cameron's whereabouts was unknown at that time
(FO 1/13, Memo by Hertslet 5/16/63). All this is sufficient
evidence that the Foreign Office was concerned about conditions
inside Abyssinia and worried lest Cameron get into trouble from
which it would be difficult to extricate him.

Cameron had been attacked by robbers on his way down to
Massawa and was forced to seek sanctuary at Axum where he
remained for a considerable time (FO 1/13, Cameron-FO 1/1/
63). At this time he also reported that messages from the
French Emperor had reached Theodore.

He was next heard from in May in the Gedaref Sudan where
he reported that the slave trade was flourishing. A Minute attached to this memo reads in part: "Mr. Cameron is supposed
to be at Massawa" (FO 1/13, #9 Cameron-FO 5/18/63 & Minute
attached). The Consul had left Axum with an escort across
Tigré and gone into the province of Bogos. Here the usual disputes between Muslims and Christians were going on. Cameron
settled some of the disputes and wrote to Theodore asking him
to establish a regular government there, a rather unwise move
as the territory claimed its independence and was a no man's
land between Egyptian territory, the Pashalik of Jidda and Abyssinia, all three powers collecting some sort of tribute from the
area (FO 1/13, #10 Cameron-FO 3/31/63). Cameron then turned
south into the Hamasein province (definitely part of Abyssinia)
and settled some feuds between local chiefs, calling himself in
his dispatch an "envoy." Minutes attached state "That Capt.
Cameron be informed that he had been ordered to return to and
remain at Massawa.... Remind him of his proper position.
He is a mere Consul and not an Envoy" (FO 1/13, #6, Cameron-
FO 3/31/63). He then proceeded to Kassala and advised the
Pasha of the Sudan that Bogos was under British protection (FO
1/13, #13 Cameron-FO 5/30/63). Having directed a survey of
trade to be made at Suakin by a Greek merchant (FO 1/13, #14
Cameron-FO 5/20/63), Cameron then started his return to Lon-
dar via Metemma to ascertain the situation in Abyssinia (FO
1/13, #13 Cameron-FO 5/20/63).

Cameron's actions brought repercussions. He had employed
as an assistant a Mr. Speedy, who acted as messenger and agent
for him. This man, who had no official position, had addressed
the Pasha of the Sudan in official tones regarding the British
protection of Bogos. Colquhoun had to disavow these actions and

was backed in this by the Foreign Office (FO 1/13, Colquhoun-
FO 8/17/63; FO-Colquhoun 9/8/63). At Constantinople, Bulwer
received a complaint from the Porte that the Consul would not
recognize the district of Habab as a dependency of the Sanjak
of Massawa and was encouraging Abyssinia to claim the district
(FO 1/13 Bulwer-FO 9/19/63). This district lay on the coast
north of Massawa, and while Turkish claims to it might be de-
batable, Abyssinian claims were extremely shadowy, if they
existed at all.

The Foreign Office ordered Cameron on August 13 to stay
at Massawa and informed him "You hold no representative character in Abyssinia" (FO 1/13, FO-Cameron 8/13/63), repeating
the order on September 8 after receiving Colquhoun's dispatch
of August 17 regarding the alleged British protection of the
province of Bogos (FO 1/13, FO-Cameron 9/8/63).

It would seem that Cameron was an incompetent meddler.
Such was not the case. He based his actions on his interpretation of Plowden's dispatches of which he had copies. However,
where Plowden used tact, understanding of the people, and personal prestige to accomplish his ends without compromising the
British Government, Cameron used his official position, thereby putting his actions in a totally different light. A review of
Plowden's dispatches will show that he never committed his
home government on anything but acted simply on his own. Cameron, on the other hand, was creating new policies for the home
government to back up. It is fair to Cameron to say that his intentions were of the best and were based on an honest misunderstanding of the import of his predecessor's actions. In general
his basic idea was correct, as Colquhoun so adequately remarked
in a dispatch of August 14 when he stated that only if the Turkish government would give back the coast to Abyssinia could
commerce be opened up and the slave trade checked (FO 78/
1755, Colquhoun-FO 8/14/63).

The first intimation of real trouble in Gondar came from
Colquhoun in September, 1863, when Mr. Epperle, a German
missionary, wrote to him that Cameron was at Metemma and
that Theodore had imprisoned the French Consul. He added that
the Abyssinians were raiding across the border into the Sudan
(FO 1/13, Colquhoun-FO 9/25/63). In October the French Embassy in London asked the Foreign Office for any information
that they might have on M. Lejean's imprisonment and requested
the good offices of the British Consul to have him released.

The first details came in letters from the Reverend Mr. Stern to Colquhoun. In April, 1863, the French Consul M. Guillaume Lejean arrived and insisted on an audience with Theodore although the Emperor was in a bad mood. The Emperor, annoyed, had put him in chains for twenty-four hours. Stern also suggested that the British take notice of the Emperor's request for an embassy, which was not wholly unreasonable and might have some beneficial results on Theodore's growing tyranny and capriciousness (FO 1/13, Stern-Colquhoun 4/21/63 and 5/26/63 encl. in Colquhoun-FO 9/30/63). Colquhoun commented that the French would probably make the most of M. Lejean's arrest and felt that some understanding should be reached with the French as "passions are so much roused out here, that it is most desirable that calm and dispassionate action at home should take their place" (FO 1/13, Colquhoun-FO 9/30/63).

Lejean in his book (THEODORE II, LE NOUVEL EMPEREUR D'ABYSSINIE, Paris, Amyot, N.D. (1873?), pp. 151-2) described these events. He stated that he himself had no idea why he was put in chains for a few hours and then released on parole to live in Debra Tabor; further, that he did not bring a letter from Napoleon III but that it arrived after his imprisonment. The section of the letter regarding toleration of the Roman Catholic mission so enraged Theodore that on September 28, 1863, he ordered Lejean expelled from the country as an insult to the French Emperor (ibid., pp. 159 ff.). Theodore then changed his mind and ordered Lejean returned to imprisonment at his capital. Luckily for the French Consul he had already passed into the territory of a rebellious tribal chief who refused to return him to the officer of the Emperor who had been ordered to bring him back (ibid., pp. 161-2).

In November Lord Cowley asked the Foreign Office if he should find out the French intentions on the Lejean affair. On being told to investigate, he talked to Drouyn de Lhuys, the French Foreign Minister, who said that "if he knew how satisfaction could be obtained, he would take measures for requiring it, but he was afraid that nothing effective could be done" (FO 1/13, Cowley-FO 11/14/63). This was a very accurate statement of the situation, as the British were soon to find out.

In October, 1863, a fantastic episode began in the story of Egyptian, Abyssinian, and British relations. A certain Count de Bisson, who was apparently a Belgian but who called himself a French General, arrived in Egypt on a reported scientific

expedition to the Abyssinian border. He had sixty uniformed
soldiers with him, four small field pieces, and a thousand rifles.
On close questioning he admitted that he was going to found a
military colony and said that "he was acting with the knowledge
of his government." Khedive Ismail asked Nubar Pasha, then
Egyptian Minister in Paris, to investigate this. He replied that
the French Government had no knowledge of the expedition. De
Bisson was thereupon sent up to Khartoum at the expense of the
Egyptian Government and the Pasha there was instructed to
treat him civilly and to help him, but to order all porters, camels, and mules withdrawn when de Bisson reached the Abyssinian frontier. The Khedive felt that de Bisson might ally himself with a rebel chief on the border and help stop the small
raids which Theodore was conducting, causing the Egyptians to
keep an army of 2,200 men on the border. Colquhoun warned
the Khedive that a "free corps" on the border would only cause
trouble, to which the Khedive replied that Cameron's actions
were not exactly peaceful (FO 1/13, Colquhoun-FO 11/11/63
encl. Colquhoun-Bulwer 11/8/63). English enquiries at Paris
confirmed the lack of knowledge of de Bisson's expedition (FO
1/14, Cowley-FO 2/23/64).

De Bisson's arrival in Khartoum was reported by Consul
Petherick, who added that de Bisson expected about 100 more
soldiers to join him. Colquhoun again took the matter up with
the Khedive who said that de Bisson offered "to assist his [the
Khedive's] Governor General in protecting his Abyssinia frontier" but that Mussa Pasha had refused the offer. The Count
had then told the Pasha that the province of Bogos had been
ceded to him [!] and proposed to go there to take possession
and protect the inhabitants against the incursions of the Abyssinians (FO 1/14, Colquhoun-FO 1/11/64). In March, 1864,
de Bisson was reported to be proceeding to Bogos, the men of
the expedition suffering severely from fever (FO 1/14, Colquhoun-FO 3/17/64). Letters from Aden reported the appearance
of the remnants of this expedition near Massawa (FO 1/14, Colquhoun-FO 4/28/64). In December, 1864, Rassam, then at
Massawa on his mission to Abyssinia, ran across information
about the expedition. De Bisson had apparently run out on his
men, leaving them stranded in Bogos, after having been unable
to accomplish anything, and had returned to Egypt to bring
some exorbitant fiscal claims against the Khedive (FO 1/14.
Rassam-Merewether [Aden] 12/2/64 in IO-FO 12/25/64). Thus

came to an end an expedition which seems to have been purely
a private one by a soldier of fortune.

Cameron returned to Gondar in September, 1863 (without
having received his instructions to remain at Massawa) and reported more fully on the Lejean affair. The French Consul had
been chained because he had insisted on an audience with the
Emperor without the usual formalities and had appeared before
him wearing his sword, a serious breach of Abyssinian etiquette.
This had caused Theodore to be critical of Napoleon's letter to
him, which he claimed addressed him as a servant and had no
official seal. Lejean answered moderately and the rest of the
Europeans interceded and brought about at least an outward reconciliation. The Emperor had then ordered Lejean to leave his
presence. The Consul insisted that the matter of an embassy
to France be brought up but the Emperor refused to discuss the
matter as Napoleon had rejected his friendship. Cameron enclosed a copy of Napoleon's letter, which was very conciliatory
and friendly, but which asked for protection of the Roman Catholics, and the latter was probably what enraged Theodore (FO
1/14, Cameron-FO 10/2/63).

In January Colquhoun talked with a Frenchman, M. Labarre,
who had been with Lejean. Labarre reported that Cameron was
in Gondar "not exactly a prisoner" and that Lejean had been
sent out of Abyssinia to Kassala under guard. Cameron had not
offended the King, but Theodore had become extremely suspicious of all Europeans around him (FO 1/14, Colquhoun-FO
1/23/64).

The first word from Cameron regarding serious trouble
came in an indirect manner. The Reverend C. F. Haussman, a
missionary stopping at Gallabat on his way to Europe, visited
Consul Petherick at Khartoum. He stated that he had come at
Cameron's request, as the Consul was forbidden to send any
written communications. His report to Petherick was forwarded
to Colquhoun.

In October, 1863, the Reverend Stern, on his way out to return to Europe, had passed the King's camp at Woggera. He
had stopped to pay his respects to the King, normally the courteous thing to do. In this instance it was most unwise: Stern's
interpreter did a very poor job and the king ordered him beaten.
Stern, unable to stand the sight, turned away, biting his thumb.
Unfortunately the use of this gesture in Abyssinia meant that
Stern would seek vengeance on the King, so he was seized and

beaten also. Stern's servant died of the beating but Stern recovered.

Cameron immediately applied for an interview, but, unable
to get one, wrote to Theodore in the name of friendship between
England and Abyssinia. Theodore replied "Where are the signs
of that friendship?" (meaning where was the answer to his letters to the English Government). Stern's papers were seized,
and as the Emperor thought that there were some remarks derogatory to him, he had Stern's feet chained. On November 11,
1863, a military force appeared at Jenda, where all the Euro-
peons had been sent, and made them all prisoners, although
Rosenthal, another missionary, was the only one chained. A
couple of days later letters arrived from England, having been
first read by Theodore's men. As there was no answer to Theodore's letter, Cameron was placed in a very awkward position,
and it was rumored in Abyssinia that two Egyptian armies were
approaching. Haussmann was allowed by the King to leave on
November 26, 1863; Stern and Rosenthal were in chains and the
remainder of the Europeans were at the King's camp at Woggera.
While not actually prisoners, they were greatly restricted in
their movements. Haussmann concluded, "It is not at all likely
that the King will set the prisoners free or let the English Consul go until the answers of the English Govt. to the letters of
the King will have arrived. Further I allow myself the remark
that any forcible means to get the liberty of the prisoners... will
in my opinion and that of every European in Abyssinia... prove
highly dangerous for the surety and even the lives of them" (FO
1/14, Haussmann-Petherick 1/4/64 in Colquhoun-FO 2/24/64).
Petherick in a covering letter offered his services for a mission (FO 1/14, Petherick-Colquhoun 1/4/64), but Colquhoun felt
that Merewether, now Resident at Aden, was in a much better
position to communicate with Abyssinia, as the cable from Egypt
to Aden was temporarily in operation (FO 1/14, Colquhoun-FO
2/2/64).

On receipt of this report the Foreign Office cabled Colquhoun to wire Merewether to use any means of obtaining the release of the Consul and other British subjects and to warn Theodore that his refusal to comply "will produce a very unfavorable
impression on the British government which may result in serious consequences to himself" (FO 1/14, FO-Colquhoun (cable)
3/9/64).

Colquhoun reported to London that Merewether was unable

to do anything as he had no ship at his disposal at Aden. However he felt that sending a threatening letter to the Emperor by
ship would do little good. Mr. Speedy, Cameron's agent at
Massawa, had been in Aden in February and knew nothing of
Cameron's difficulties with the King, although he had received
some communications from the Consul (FO 1/14, Colquhoun-
FO 4/11/64, encl. Merewether-Colquhoun 3/21/64). Colquhoun
added that Merewether had written Bombay for orders.

The governmental vacuum existing in this area of course
had a direct bearing on the slowness of communications. In the
present day of modern mail service, telegraph, cable, and
radio, it is difficult for us to conceive of the great delays involved. Yet these delays do much to explain the events which
follow. On April 10, 1864, the Foreign Office received some
minor dispatches sent by Cameron from Gondar on August 15,
1863; the time of transmission was eight months. Haussmann
remarked on English mail arriving in Abyssinia in November
of 1863. This mail contained the instructions of the Foreign
Office of April 22, 1863, for Cameron to remain at Massawa,
again a transmission time of eight months. Haussman left
Woggera on November 26 and reached Khartoum on January 4,
thirty-nine days of travel to cover about four hundred miles as
the crow flies. Petherick's letter of January 4 from Khartoum
arrived at Alexandria on February 24 — fifty-one days in transmission. Communication from Alexandria to London was about
twelve days by mail. Therefore under favorable circumstances
it took about three and a half months' transmission time from
Abyssinia to Gondar via Khartoum. Under the most favorable
circumstances Plowden's dispatches had taken three months in
transmission from the interior to London via Massawa. At best
then there was a six months' lapse between the time an incident
happened in Abyssinia and instructions could be returned there
from the Foreign Office. There was only one way to improve
this situation, and that was by communicating with Aden and
from thence to Massawa.

However, there was a further complication, as the Foreign
Office found out. It had no authority over the Resident at Aden.
While the Resident kept the Consul General at Alexandria informed of developments, it was purely a private cooperative
arrangement. The Resident was responsible to the Government
of Bombay, which in major policies was responsible to the Government of India, which was responsible to the India Office in

London, although in less important policies the India Office often dealt directly with the Bombay Government and, in an emergency, directly with the Resident at Aden. Therefore the Foreign Office cable to Colquhoun of March 9 reappeared at the Foreign Office on June 4, having been referred by Merewether to the Bombay Government, which referred it to London for action.

It should also be remembered that before the opening of the Suez Canal the Red Sea area was a very minor section of the Indian Ocean economy. All military forces and virtually all naval forces were at the disposition of the Indian Government and the India Office. The ninety-mile-wide isthmus of Suez made it more efficient to deal with affairs in Abyssinia through Bombay than through Alexandria, all maps to the contrary notwithstanding. It is only by remembering these conditions that we can understand and interpret the events in Abyssinia which subjected the Foreign Office to much criticism from people in England who depended on their maps alone for information.

On receiving the Foreign Office cable to Colquhoun of March 9, Merivale in the India Office wrote to the Foreign Office on June 4 describing the method of transmission. He stated that the government of India had no relations with the King of Abyssinia and that "Sir Charles Wood is extremely desirous to avoid all interference from the trade of India with the states bordering on the Red Sea." But Merivale suggested that if Lord Russell had communicated immediately with Sir Charles Wood, instructions would have been sent to the Bombay Government to take action in concert with the Admiral of the Naval Station there. Merivale concluded "Sir Charles Wood will be happy to forward to Bombay or to Aden any orders which Lord Russell may consider best adapted to meet the emergencies of the case" (FO 1/14, Merivale [IO]-FO 6/4/64).

Thus began the first real collaborative effort between the Foreign Office and the India Office in the area which had long been divided into separate spheres of action, the Foreign Office having consuls at Jidda and in Abyssinia, the Indian Government controlling policies in the southern part of the area. Previous collaboration had been in very slight incidents, protests by the Foreign Office at Constantinople or Paris on incidents occurring in the Red Sea reported through the Indian Government or aid given to the Consul by the Resident at Aden. During this collaboration, first in the Abyssinian affair and later in the questions

of Turkish sovereignty in the Yemen and Somali coast, sharp
differences of policy were bound to appear. These differences
of policy had to be compromised, and serve to explain much of
what happened.

The next information from Abyssinia came in April, 1864,
via Merewether at Aden in a private letter to Colquhoun, informing him of Petherick's sudden retirement because of health;
this closed Khartoum as a source of information. (Petherick
was a merchant in Khartoum who acted as British Consul without any compensation.) Merewether told the Consul General
of his helplessness in Aden. The Indian Navy had ceased to
exist, its vessels replaced by one frigate and two or three small
sloops of the British Navy, none of which was stationed permanently at Aden. Thus British sea power in the western Indian Ocean was at its lowest ebb. Merewether had information
from the governor of Massawa that the Europeans had all been
placed in chains for about ten days, but a later letter without
date addressed to a Roman Catholic priest near Massawa reported that their chains had been removed, although they were
still prisoners. The prisoners had forwarded the information
that there would be no release until a "civil answer to the king's
letter arrives" (FO 1/14, Colquhoun-FO 4/28/64 encl. private
letters, Merewether-Colquhoun 4/21/64).

On May 11, 1864, the India Office returned to the Foreign Office without comment Theodore's letter and other information which had been sent to them May 5, 1863. Written
on the back of the King's letter is a note "To go by, nothing to
be done on this. M. Murray." This would indicate that the
Foreign Office had deliberately as a matter of policy refused
to answer the letter (FO 1/14, IO-FO 5/11/64). Four days
later Lord Shaftesbury, chairman of the Jews Society, wrote
to Lord Russell enclosing a letter from Mrs. Stern (whose husband was a missionary of that society), and asking for an investigation of the situation (FO 1/14, Shaftesbury-Russell 5/15/
64). The investigation proved that on February 12, 1863, it
was decided to order Cameron to return to Massawa and await
further orders and that "no notice beyond this was to be taken
of his dispatches" (FO 1/14, Minute-5/16/64). These instructions had been issued in the Foreign Office on receipt of Theodore's letter. However, this information and his new instructions had not been sent to Cameron until April 22, 1863.

Lord Russell reviewed the situation in a Minute to J. Murray

of the Foreign Office on May 18. He admitted that he was at a
loss to know how to rescue Cameron and the other British subjects. He did not place any blame on Cameron for he doubted
if he had received the relevant order from the Foreign Office.
However, he did not feel that Cameron could be left to his fate.
He suggested asking the India Office for some of their agents
at Aden or elsewhere who might know the country and might be
authorized to spend some money to effect a rescue. Force, of
course, was out of the question, he felt, and the condition imposed by the King, that an embassy be received, had been objected to and "could scarcely be countenanced seeing that we
should have to pay the whole of their expenses." He suggested
that Beke, who had offered his services, might go, but added
a rather curious statement "would it be right to risk the detention of additional Europeans?" Which would certainly imply
that if a non-European were to be sent, Lord Russell wouldn't
particularly care what happened to him (FO 1/14, Minute Rus-
sell-Murray 5/18/64).

The next day, in another Minute, Russell stated, "I believe
the best chance will be to send a letter of the Queen in very general terms, desiring friendship & a letter from me saying we
can hold no intercourse with King nor deliver the Queen's letter unless he liberates Capt. Cameron, Mr. Stern and any other
British subjects he has in custody. Perhaps Dr. Beke might be
charged with this business. He must omit promising any assistance against the Turks. R." (FO 1/14, Minute, Russell,
5/19/64).

It would be well to consider how and why this unfortunate and almost insoluble situation came about. It would be
easy to blame Cameron, but an examination of his original instructions shows that he followed them to the letter in his dealings with Theodore. Furthermore, except in his first meeting
with the Emperor when he was too insistent on getting his business done, he seemed to have acted with discretion and tact.
The fundamental blame seems to lie in the Foreign Office. Desiring to have some check on French intrigues in the area, they
appointed a consul as rapidly as possible after news of Plowden's death. On receiving Theodore's second letter (through
Cameron) asking for an embassy, they felt they were getting in
too deep, as they did not wish to spend the money on such an
embassy. However, as the India Office had the predominate
interests in this area, the matter was turned over to them without

comment so that they could take advantage of it if, in their opinion, that would be wise. Fearing trouble in Abyssinia, the Foreign Office instructed Cameron to return to Massawa and stay
there. Here, however, some error was made. The instructions were decided upon on February 12, but the letter to Cameron was not sent until April 22. This two-month delay in issuance of the instructions was fatal. If Cameron had received
the new instructions two months earlier he could probably have
gotten out. Also, there is little excuse for the Foreign Office
in not at least acknowledging Theodore's letter. He was a supposedly friendly monarch who had sent not one, but two letters
asking for an embassy. (The first had been forwarded by Mr.
Barroni in January, 1861.) Theodore was quite properly insulted by this lack of courtesy and acted as he had done previously with the Patriarch of Alexandria in 1857 and with Lejean
the French Vice-consul in 1863. Probably the real answer to
the lack of attention to this matter by the Foreign Office can
best be explained by the fact that interest in the Empire was at
a low point in England, due to the American Civil War and interest in home affairs, and the Emperor of Abyssinia just did
not seem important.

However, Cameron and the missionaries were prisoners
and something had to be done. Colquhoun reported that old
Mr. Barroni, who knew more about Abyssinia than almost anyone else, had died, removing the last hope of any help from
near the border of Abyssinia, and that Theodore "would appear
to have become subject to fits of rage which almost deprive him
of his reason & would render all approach dangerous" (FO 1/14,
Colquhoun-FO 5/10/64). However, in Aden, there was a Christian Persian, Hormudz Rassam by name. This man had been
discovered by Sir Henry Layard during his archeological studies
in Persia and had become an official of the Indian Government.
He had been appointed as a political officer at Aden, had accompanied Brigadier Coghlan on his mission to Zanzibar in 1861,
and for a time had been Acting Resident at Muscat. He had
written to his old patron, Sir Henry Layard, now Under Secretary for Foreign Affairs, suggesting that the Abuna be used as
an intermediary (FO 1/14, Rassam-Layard [private letter]
5/24/64). G. P. Badger, of Aden, who was in England at the
time, wrote to Layard a few days later suggesting that Rassam
take the letters to the Abuna, but he warned Layard that such
letters must be official letters from the Queen, not letters or

communications from the Foreign Office. However, such a course was not practicable unless a ship could be assigned to this mission (FO 1/14, Badger-Layard [private] 6/4/64). Badger had a conference with Murray at the Foreign Office on June 6, at which time it was decided to send Rassam on the mission (FO 1/14, Murray-Layard 6/6/64). Lord Russell commented "but the India Office must not object to our Consul at Cairo writing to Aden according to circumstances, it would be too hard to have to send from Cairo and from Aden to England when a man's life and liberty are at stake. R." (FO 1/14, Minute by Russell 6/9/64).

On June 17 the Foreign Office issued instructions to Rassam. It informed him that Theodore's chief complaint was the lack of a letter from the Queen, which he was now to bear. This letter was in Egypt, being correctly translated into Amharic. Further he was to be provided if possible with letters of recommendation from the Patriarch at Alexandria to the Abuna and the Emperor. Rassam was to be conveyed to Massawa by warship and to forward from there a letter to the King stating that he had the Queen's reply and also to forward his letters of recommendation from the Patriarch of the Copts. "He should then await at Massawa King Theodore's reply, before deciding upon the question of the necessity either of proceeding in person to Gondar to deliver the Queen's letter or of sending it for delivery to Captain Cameron, and on receiving the reply he should be guided as to the course to be pursued, always bearing in mind that the release of the above prisoners is the important object to which alone he had to look." The instructions concluded, "The above instructions should however not be held so binding upon Mr. Rassam as to prevent his adopting any other course...; and he should be specially careful not to place himself in a position which may cause further embarrassment to H. M. G." (FO 1/14, FO-IO 6/17/64 encl. instructions to Rassam).

Reade, the Consul in Alexandria, was meanwhile having difficulties. He could find no one to translate the Queen's letter into Amharic although an Arabic translation had been made. He further felt, after consultation with other officials, that Theodore's offer of an embassy should be accepted because of the danger of French influence (FO 1/14, Reade-FO 7/3/64 [telegram]). He also had had trouble in getting the Patriarch of the Copts to give assistance but finally obtained the letters of introduction (FO 1/14, Reade-FO 6/30/64). The Foreign Office decided to change the Queen's letter to accept the embassy, but it was too late – the letter was finally on its way to Aden (FO 1/14, Reade-FO 7/11/64). Rassam left Aden and arrived at Massawa on August 23, 1864. He had difficulty getting anyone to act as messenger to the King because of fear of what Theodore might do, but he finally obtained some men willing to go. From all reports he could get, it was obvious that Theodore would not allow any Europeans to penetrate the interior without his permission (FO 1/14, IO-FO 9/24/64, encl. Aden-Bombay 9/6/64).

XVII. THE RASSAM MISSION

In September, 1864, Ayrton, Consul at Cairo, received the first direct word from Abyssinia since January in a letter from Mr. Haussmann at Gallabat. He informed the Consul that Cameron had received his orders on November 23, 1863, and had showed them to the King who simply said that there was no letter for him. Cameron was imprisoned January 2, 1864, and together with Stern was tortured in May. Haussmann was afraid that if the correspondence with Theodore was published, the King would soon hear about it as he had two competent translators with him, both Abyssinians who had studied in Europe. Theodore had been having difficulties with his lesser chiefs and his temper was not improved by the constant necessity of being forced to put down revolts (FO 1/14, Ayrton [Cairo]-FO 9/16/64).

In December, 1864, Rassam at Massawa was able to report that one of his messengers had returned with letters from Cameron to Munzinger, a Swiss who lived at that port. Rassam felt that the de Bisson affair in Hamasein had not helped Theodore to be more friendly to Europeans. The messenger reported that the Abuna had been imprisoned for intervening in favor of Cameron early in 1864 and had never been released but was still in disgrace, his property confiscated. Rassam's first two messengers had been imprisoned without an opportunity to deliver the letter to Theodore. Now the envoy was sending three independent messengers. Rassam stated, "There is no doubt that the Emperor has been crazy for the last two years and for the safety and ultimate return of Capt. Cameron and the other European prisoners, precautionary measures have to be adopted for realizing our wishes" (FO 1/14, IO-FO 12/23/64, encl. Rassam-Merewether 12/2/64). This belief (that Theodore was crazy) appears in many statements of Europeans, but there is no evidence to show that he was. The few conversations reported show him to be perfectly sane. He was, however, overly suspicious of everyone, a not unnatural reaction of a ruler who was constantly threatened by revolts by his subordinates, and whose recent experience with the French and English Governments had done nothing to dispel his suspicions of their integrity. The French had given his rival, Negussie, arms and other aid against him in 1859. They had insisted on his

tolerating a Roman Catholic mission in his country and had sent
to him, in Lejean, an envoy who had not been exactly tactful.
The English had refused to answer two letters offering friendship, certainly not a gracious thing to do after the way he had
acted at the time of Plowden's death. The missionaries were
harmless enough, but apparently had been overly critical of
him in their writings. All in all, Theodore had plenty of justification for his actions.

A very real and pertinent criticism of the actions of the
Foreign Office appeared in the Bombay Gazette of January 3,
1865 (present in FO 1/15). It gives a thorough summary of the
situation reporting among other things the untruth of a rumor
that Theodore wished to marry Victoria. The author of the
article did not believe that Rassam and Dr. Blanc (an army surgeon who had accompanied him) could effect the release of the
prisoners and felt that an expeditionary force was impractical
except possibly from Egypt. The author concludes, "It is ridiculous to send as ambassadors to a potentate who resents nothing
so much as an insult to his dignity two subordinate officers
from Aden to plead for the release of the English prisoners.
England has nothing to lose in prestige by flattering the barbar-
ians pride with a costly Embassy and rich presents.... At any
rate it is clear that no good end can be gained by the further
stay of Mr. Rassam and his colleague at Massawa: where they
are not in a position to employ either force or persuasion"
(Bombay Gazette, 1/3/65).

Rassam apparently felt much the same way, for in a private
letter to Layard he suggested that such an embassy headed by
Brigadier Coghlan should be sent after the release of the captives (FO 1/15, Rassam-Layard [private] 1/20/65). At the
same time Rassam reported to Badger at Aden that a certain
Menelik, grandson of Sahle Selassie of Shoa had revolted against
Theodore in alliance with the Wallos tribe of the Gallas, the
first mention of this great king-to-be (FO 1/15, Rassam-Bad-
ger 1/20/65).

Colquhoun, Consul General at Alexandria, had conversations with Baron Heughlin, the Austrian naturalist, who had
done considerable exploration work in Abyssinia and who was a
great admirer of Theodore. He believed that the Emperor had
plenty of provocation for his actions. Knowing Theodore as he
did, he felt that Rassam had acted properly in waiting at Massawa as one "could not force the King." He offered to go, if

necessary, on a mission to Theodore. Lord Russell, ready to
grasp at any straw, noted, "If Mr. Rassam fails, Baron Heughlin should be asked to go to Abyssinia. R. " (FO 1/15, Colquhoun-FO 1/27/65).

The Foreign Office then consulted Coghlan, now retired
and living in England. He felt that the letter of the Queen which
Rassam carried should be cancelled and that an embassy with
a considerable retinue and a supply of presents should go bearing a letter from the Queen which should not mention the captives, leaving that part of the problem up to the envoys. He
believed that the alternative, the use of Egyptian troops against
Theodore, would certainly lead the King to murder the prisoners (FO 1/15, Memo by Coghlan 2/8/65). Colquhoun was instructed to inform Rassam that the Queen's letter had been cancelled and a new letter being prepared, but not to wait for it if
he had an opportunity to go to Gondar (FO 1/15, FO-Colquhoun
[cable] 2/13/65). Rassam was also informed that the Foreign
Office was sending 100 muskets as a present to the King (FO
1/15, FO-Rassam 2/17/65). A new letter from the Queen was
prepared saying that an embassy from Theodore would be well
received and adding that the Queen believed that the Emperor's
withdrawal of favor from Cameron was malicious gossip (FO
1/15, FO-IO 2/17/65, encl. draft of letter from Queen Victoria
to Theodore).

Colquhoun in Alexandria interviewed a Coptic priest, Abd-
al-Melak, who had just come from Gondar. This man reported
that the Abuna had obtained from Theodore a promise to release the prisoners if the Abuna could assure the King that the
British would exact no retributions, such a promise to be contained in a letter from the Consul General at Alexandria. As
Colquhoun could make no such assurances without higher authority he requested orders (FO 1/15, Colquhoun-FO 2/12/65).
This permission was granted by the Foreign Office immediately
(FO 1/15, FO-Colquhoun 2/27/65). Then what was virtually a
copy of Colquhoun's dispatch appeared in the Pall Mall Gazette
of February 23, 1865, and the Foreign Office wished to know
where the leak occurred (FO 1/15, FO-Colquhoun 2/27/65).
Colquhoun was unable to find any leak in Egypt (FO 78/1871,
Colquhoun-FO 3/6/65). Later events showed the leak must have
been in London. The priest Abd-al-Melak left for Abyssinia
on March 27 and that was the last heard of him (FO 78/1871,
Colquhoun-FO 3/24/65). There was apparently no question of

this man's authenticity or sincerity as Colquhoun was able to check on him from many sources.

At Massawa, Rassam still awaited his messengers' return. It was not indecision on Theodore's part that was holding them up but rather the fact that Theodore's tenuous rule over the local chiefs had broken down and all of Tigré province was in revolt. In February, 1865, Rassam did receive letters from the prisoners, who reported that they were all well. Flaad and Schimper, two missionaries, both emphasized that the basic trouble lay in the lack of an answer to Theodore's letter (FO 1/15, Aden-Bombay 3/5/65). Rassam was also informed that eight prisoners were at Magdala, Theodore's mountain stronghold: Cameron and his four servants, the missionaries Stern and Rosenthal, and a Frenchman, M. Bardel. At the same time the amended letter from the Queen reached Aden and was forwarded to Rassam who was joined by Lieutenant Prideaux of the Indian army (FO 1/15, Merewether-Rassam 3/26/65).

Meanwhile Rassam was able to obtain the services of an influential Abyssinian, Ibrahim by name, as a messenger. This man told Rassam that the revolts prevented the King from accepting Rassam's mission; Theodore, afraid of a repetition of the Plowden tragedy, did not feel he could guarantee safe conduct into Gondar. He also reported that all of Rassam's other messengers were held up by the revolts. He then departed with a third letter to the King (FO 1/15, Rassam-Merewether 4/10/65). Rassam continued to cool his heels at Massawa. He received occasional intelligence from the interior and letters from the captives. Flaad wrote on March 16, 1865, that the captives were in despair and felt that they had been forgotten by Europe (FO 1/15, in Rassam-Merewether 4/28/65). Occasional letters from Cameron containing wild rumors served to becloud the whole issue.

In June Rassam became thoroughly discouraged. He had been in Massawa almost a year, and felt that he would get no results (FO 1/15, Rassam-Merewether 6/28/65). Revolts had cut off practically all communication with the interior. Suddenly, in August, all of Rassam's messengers returned with the report that Cameron had been released from chains and that Theodore had asked Rassam to come to Gondar, via the Sudan and Metemma to avoid the revolts in Tigré. To do this, Rassam had to go through the Egyptian Sudan, so he went to Egypt to obtain permission, arriving at Suez on September 5, 1865 (FO 1/16, [cable] Stanton-FO 9/5/65).

Of course this whole affair could not be kept quiet in England, especially as at the time of Rassam's arrival at Massawa, the captives felt that it was again safe to write letters. Nearly every one of Rassam's dispatches contained references to receiving and transmitting private letters from the captives to London. Many of these letters are in the files of the Foreign Office, including copies of many personal ones. Some of the missionaries had been sent out by the London Society for Promoting Christianity among the Jews, and of course they had relatives in England. Of these missionaries, probably the worst treated had been Mr. Stern, whose wife was living in London. After August, 1864, she was receiving letters from her husband. The ubiquitous Dr. Beke, back in England after his experience as a merchant at Mauritius, was in constant communication with the Foreign Office, offering his services (for a price), and his advice, which always managed to come around to the fact that a large trading firm should be set up in Tigré for the purpose of encouraging the growth of cotton. (It must be remembered that at this time the American Civil War had cut off almost all importation of cotton to England, resulting in the virtual shutdown of one of England's leading industries, the cotton mills of Lancashire.) Unfortunately for Dr. Beke, the Foreign Office was well aware of his character, so that he was forced to capitalize on the plight of the poor captives to achieve his purposes. As a geographer of good repute he had access to the more serious journals. Now he combined his resources with those of a Mr. Purday and put on a publicity campaign for the captives.

The leaks in information mentioned above continued. In April, copies of the Queen's new letter to Theodore (which had not yet left Egypt) appeared in the European press. On investigation Colquhoun was able to inform the Foreign Office that information often got into the Bombay papers and that the French and German missionaries in Tigré were often active correspondents of European journals.

The first real attack on the Foreign Office came in the April 1 issue of the Pall Mall Gazette. It reprinted a letter from Mr. Stern to his wife, dated January 17, 1865. The letter was a simple narration of what had happened to the missionaries, ending with the wish that some aid would soon arrive. The Pall Mall Gazette added, "This letter Mr. Layard may as well extract and lay by with other documents relating to the matter

which have reached him from time to time since 1863. Probably he sees the letter here for the first time. It is at least true
that its publication has been prohibited by certain persons.
What reasons they had for the prohibition... we must leave to
our readers to guess, at present" (FO 1/15, encl. in Desbor-
ough-Hammond 4/5/65). There is no evidence that the Foreign
Office ever prohibited or officially advised against the publication of this letter, but some member of the Foreign Office staff,
having knowledge of Colquhoun's fear for the safety of the prisoners if too much appeared in the European press, may well
have advised privately against its publication. The newspaper
campaign continued and naturally resulted in questions in Parliament. On May 23, the Foreign Office ordered Letters and
Papers relation to the Imprisonment of British Subjects to be
prepared for presentation to Parliament (commonly known as
Abyssinia, Blue Book #1). It was to contain (1) the instructions
to Cameron; (2) Cameron's letter on the proposed embassy to
England and the reply of the Foreign Office; (3) letter of the
King; (4) report of Cameron from Bogos; (5) orders to Cameron
to return to Massawa; (6) date of answer by Queen to Theodore's
letter; (7) list of presents to be sent to Theodore; (8) all offers
of assistance made to the Foreign Office (FO 11/5, Order for
the Presentation to Parl. etc. 5/23/65).

Apparently after a cabinet meeting at which the matter was
discussed, Lord Russell wrote the following memorandum
dated June 8 (FO 1/15, Memo by Russell 6/8/65):

> "I cannot think it would be wise to send a military
> expedition to attack the King of Abyssinia. I know not
> how we could reach him in that way. But Mr. Rassam
> & Lieut. Ridgeway [apparently an error; Lord Russell
> must mean Lieutenant Prideaux] with the Queen's letter
> might produce a good effect & if they are willing to go
> I should be disposed to send them.
> "I should send with them ten or twelve servants as
> escort with a few presents and no threats."

It is interesting to note that Lord Russell still maintained
that a messenger should be sent to the King, instead of a full-
fledged embassy as so many who were acquainted with the area
and with the East advised. While he had already agreed to certain points, such as willingness to accept Theodore's embassy,

he was not yet ready to put on the big show of a full-fledged embassy with rich gifts. If he had done this, the results might have been far different. The Foreign Office could not seem to understand the importance of "face" in dealing with Abyssinia.

Dr. Beke, meanwhile, having sold the idea to the relatives of the missionaries, the Jews Society, and others that he could get the captives released by a personal expedition, applied to the government for help in going to Abyssinia in the role of a private traveller to "reason with the King." Lord Russell noted "Make the reply to Beke civil but firm and openly disclaim any connection between him and H. M. G." (FO 1/15, Beke-Russell 7/7/65 & Minute by Russell). On July 13 Beke was so informed, with the warning that the government could not hold themselves responsible for anything that might happen and instructing him that he had "no authority whatever to deal with the political affairs of that country" (FO 1/15, FO-Beke 7/13/65). Beke cheerfully replied that he had no desire to be connected with the government as he was convinced anyone so connected would get into trouble (FO 1/16, Beke-Russell 7/21/65). Russell received almost immediately a petition from the friends and relatives of the captives stating that they had appealed to Beke to undertake this mission but did not wish to interfere with the government, on which Russell commented "acknowledge and advise them not to print letters in the newspapers which may prove injurious to Mr. Stern" (FO 1/16, Petition to Russell 7/30/65 & Minute). Mr. Charles H. Purday, Beke's associate who claimed to represent the relatives of the captives, replied sarcastically thanking Russell for his advice on withholding publication of the letters and suggesting the members of the government in debate in Parliament might do the same, on which letter Russell commented "Dr Beke probably caused this mischief" (FO 1/16, Purday-Russell 8/17/65).

When news came from Rassam that Cameron had been released, the Jews Society withdrew their financial support of Beke's expedition. This caused Beke to write to Russell to inform him that Beke's mission would not interfere with the government. On this Lord Shaftesbury, President of the British and Foreign Bible Society and the leading organizer of missionary and philanthropic activities of his time, commented to Lord Russell "Public opinion will demand from us some endeavor to rescue the prisoners" (i. e. , the missionaries), (FO 1/16, Beke-Russell 10/13/65, Shaftesbury-Russell 10/14/65). Beke persisted in his efforts and on December 13 his arrival in Egypt was reported by Colonel Stanton, the new Consul General at Alexandria (FO 1/16, Stanton-Layard 12/13/65).

As if Beke's private trip did not add confusion enough, Lord Russell proceeded to complicate the situation further by taking advantage of the offer of William Gifford Palgrave, at that time a semi-official British agent in the Near East, to undertake a mission to Theodore. This gentleman, son of the historian Sir Francis Palgrave and brother of Francis Turner Palgrave of "Golden Treasury" fame, is chiefly known to us through his NARRATIVE OF A YEAR'S JOURNEY THROUGH CENTRAL AND EASTERN ARABIA. He was a brilliant and able man (of Jewish extraction) who had been an officer in the Indian Army and then a Jesuit priest. He was instructed on July 21, 1865, to proceed to Egypt and place himself under the orders of Consul General Stanton at Alexandria (FO 1/16, FO-Palgrave 7/21/65). Stanton was told to instruct Aden to recall Rassam from Massawa when Palgrave left for the interior (he was to go to Abyssinia via the Nile and Metemma), or if Rassam had already started to Gondar, to hold Palgrave in Egypt (FO 1/16, FO-Stanton 7/21/65). Similar instructions were sent to the India Office (FO 1/16, FO-IO 7/24/65). Palgrave was to go as a private citizen with a guard of four armed Nubians, and his mission was limited to freeing the prisoners. He was not to make any agreements with the King, but he was to inform Theodore that he could expect no relations with England unless the prisoners were released (FO 1/16, addition to FO-Stanton 7/21/65). What motivated this decision is not shown in the documents. Probably Rassam's lack of success and Beke's constant letters stating that a person not an official of the government would be more likely to succeed had much to do with it. Is it possible that Lord Russell was afraid that Beke might be successful, so that he tried to forestall him by using the same tactics? This may be the answer. It was certainly the other extreme from sending a full-fledged embassy as those acquainted with the area had recommended. Undoubtedly public opinion forced Lord Russell to act.

Rassam's sudden appearance at Suez on September 5 with word of Theodore's acceptance of his mission and the release of Cameron from chains left Stanton with two emissaries on his hands. Of the two, he personally preferred Palgrave (FO 1/16, [cable] Stanton-FO 9/6/65). He was instructed by the Foreign

Office "Do not take any steps until you hear further from Lord
Russell. Keep Rassam and do not let Palgrave go" (FO 1/16
[cable] FO-Stanton 9/7/65). Two days later Stanton was further instructed that Rassam should go at once to Theodore by
Egypt and Metemma, accompanied, if possible, by the officer
who was with him at Massawa. Palgrave was to remain in
Egypt (FO 1/16, [cable] FO-Stanton 9/9/65). Such instructions
should have been sufficient, but the Palgrave mission had become mixed up with the Egyptian government and the Viceroy
was amazed at the upset in plans (FO 1/16, [cable] Stanton-FO
9/11/65). The Foreign Office replied that Rassam was to go
as soon as possible and was to try to get the missionaries released. He was also instructed to inform Theodore that the
present consul at Jerusalem was to use his good offices for the
protection of the Abyssinian Christians in the same way that
his predecessor had (FO 1/16 [cable] FO-Stanton 9/11/65).
Rassam's reports reached London shortly; the King's letter to
him was not signed and was very curt, charging Cameron with
interfering in internal affairs.

Russell commented "Last of King's letter to Rassam explains whole story & confirms what we all along said namely
that Capt. Cameron's interference in the internal affairs of
Abyssinia & in the disputes between Theodore and the Egyptians
was the real cause of the King's displeasure and of the treatment Cameron has met with" (FO 1/16 Rassam-Russell N.D.).
By this statement Russell established the policy of putting the
blame on Cameron and refusing to recognize the responsibility
of the Foreign Office in its inexplicable refusal to answer Theodore's letter (FO 1/16, Minute by Russell 9/5/65). At the
same time Consul Moore at Jerusalem was instructed to follow
Lord Malmesbury's orders of July, 1852, and to use his influence to protect the Abyssinian monks from the perennial beat-
ings they took at the hands of their fellow Christians, the Armenians, thus removing one possible cause of Theodore's displeasure (FO 1/16, FO-Moore [Jerusalem] 9/27/65). This
question seems to have appeared far more important in the eyes
of the Foreign Office than it really was. There was no evidence
from Abyssinia that Theodore was ever particularly concerned
about his subjects at the Holy City as Russell finally admitted
in a memo of September 23 (FO 1/16, Minute by Russell 9/23/65).

Stanton still wished to have Palgrave at least go to the Sudan to investigate the slave trade, and wired on September 16

that the Viceroy had a steamer ready for him at Cairo and all preparations were made (FO 78/1871, [cable] Stanton-FO 9/16/ 65). Rassam left for Aden where he arrived on September 25 to receive information that the news of Cameron's release from chains had been false. He also found letters from Cameron requesting him to come up to Gondar immediately (FO 1/16, Rassam-Layard 9/29/65 and Merewether-Layard 9/10/65). Rassam left for Massawa on October 5 (FO 1/16, Merewether-Layard 10/6/65) on which Lord Russell commented "I have long had my fears that Rassam would be too easily detered by difficulties.

"My opinion is that if he fails or delays on the coast, Palgrave should be sent at once by the Nile. Write this in a private letter to Col. Stanton" (FO 1/16, Minute by Russell 10/24/65).

Meanwhile, wishing to familiarize Stanton with the British policy towards Abyssinia, Lord Russell sent a long memorandum to him on October 5, 1865. This memorandum was seen and approved by both the Queen and Palmerston.

It began by telling the past history of British and Abyssinian relations, citing the treaty with Ras Ali of November 2, 1849, and Theodore's refusal to recognize this treaty. The memorandum goes on,

> It may be argued that H. M. Govt. should have insisted on the validity of the treaty on the one hand & protected the Emperor of Abyssinia from the Turks on the other. But considering the short term of power of the Abyssinian Kings whatever be their title, the difficulty of reaching with a regular British force the seat of their Empire, the little value of a victory gained at Gondar or Shoa, the risk of failure and certainty of expense, it has seemed to the British Government a preferable course to withdraw as much as possible from Abyssinian engagements, Abyssinian alliances and British interference in Abyssinia.
>
> This course however has not been taken without giving rise to groundless reproaches, many unfounded allegations and some embarrassing & painful occurrences. [A critical reference to Dr. Beke present in the first draft was crossed out in the final version.] There is reason to believe that the Emperor holds Capt. Cameron as a hostage for the recognition by England already made

in 1849 of the independence of Abyssinia, for the suppression of Egyptian aggressions along the frontier and for
restitution of the Church & Convent at Jerusalem, torn
from him and his people by the Copts, Armenians and
Turks.

The memorandum mentions Plowden's settlement of border
affairs: "England has from time to time used her influence to
prevent aggressions on the Egyptian frontier but could not consent to guarantee the integrity of the Abyssinian territory.

"Such a guarantee would be in the opinion of H. M. Govt. an
unwise engagement impractical in execution."

In explanation of British actions regarding the Abyssinians
and their church at Jerusalem, Lord Russell stated, "Anyone
who follows with attention the proceedures of the Turkish Government in the various provinces under its direct rule must be
aware that the Xtian sects, subjects of the Ottoman Porte, frequently persecute one another, and that the Sultan is often appealed to to rescue individuals and communities from the
maltreatment or cruelty of their fellow Xtians.

"H. M. Ambassador at the sublime Porte uses his good offices on such occasions, and generally w. success." The
memorandum then discusses the Jerusalem affair of 1852 and
quotes Malmesbury's letter to Bishop Gobat.

Lord Russell then went into considerable detail about the
incident leading up to Cameron's imprisonment, playing down
the lack of answer to Theodore's letter and emphasizing rather
Cameron's interference in Bogos and the border states, "for
which he incurred the displeasure of his own Govt."

The memorandum concludes, "The policy of the Br. Govt.
has been founded entirely on the desire to promote trade and
intercourse w. Abyssinia.

"I am well aware that there are persons who wish H. M. G.
to interfere on behalf of Abyssinia as a Xtian country against
Turkey & Egypt as Mohamadan Countries.

"But this policy has never been adopted by the British Govt.
and, I trust never will be.

"If we were to make ourselves the protectors of the Emper-
or Theodore against the Sultan and his Viceroy of Egypt we
should become responsible for his acts, and be entangled in
his quarrels with all his neighbors and rivals.

"The obligations of the Br. Govt. are various enough and

many enough without undertaking so costly, hazardous & un-
profitable a Protectorate." (FO 78/1870, FO-Stanton 10/5/65
contains the corrected first draft. FO 1/16 contains the second
draft of this letter.) At first glance, there is nothing in this
statement of policy to which any one could take exception. On
second thought, one wonders how, in the light of Plowden's very
informative dispatches, the British Government could expect to
have normal governmental relations with a country feudal in
character, with a central government completely dependent on
force for authority and with rulers who were interested only in
what the British could do for them. After the years of Plowden's
consulship it certainly should have been apparent that England
could have no regular trade relation with Abyssinia if that country controlled no port of entry on the coast. At the time of
Plowden's death, instead of examining closely the advisability
of having a consul in Abyssinia, the government rushed ahead
to appoint a new man and get him out as soon as possible in
order to check on French intrigues. Plowden's appointment was
certainly "founded entirely on the desire to promote trade and
intercourse with Abyssinia," but Cameron's appointment was
inspired by Anglo-French rivalry, a fact admitted at the time
but soon lost sight of.

In Alexandria, Stanton had Palgrave on his hands and on
October 7 was instructed to keep him there for two more months
(FO 1/16, FO-Stanton 10/7/65). Rassam left Massawa as soon
as possible and started the long trip to Metemma on October 15
(FO 1/16 [cable] Stanton-FO 11/4/65) leaving Munzinger as his
agent on the coast. Beke arrived in Egypt on December 13 and
planned to go on to Massawa shortly, although Stanton tried to
dissuade him (FO 1/16, Stanton-Layard 12/13/65).

Beke, in Cairo, looked up Palgrave, who, he said, had told
him that Rassam's instructions were limited to getting the release of Cameron, that the missionaries were to be left to their
fate, and that he had offered information to the Pall Mall Gazette
on the whole Abyssinian question if his name was not used (FO
1/17, Beke-Mr. Purday, encl. in Herstlet-Layard 1/11/66).
Palgrave denied making any such remarks to Dr. Beke. He had
in fact stated that Rassam was instructed to get the release of
all the prisoners "but the first and most imperative step was
the release of Captain Cameron for obvious reasons," and he
denied other statements attributed to him by Beke (FO 1/17, Pal-
grave-Stanton 1/31/66 in Stanton-FO 2/1/66). Beke's intent in

distorting Palgrave's remarks obviously was to justify his own mission. Beke does not mention this discussion in his book (Beke, Charles T. , THE BRITISH CAPTIVES IN ABYSSINIA, London, Longmans, 1867, second ed.), but persists in accusing the Foreign Office of instructing Rassam to release only the English subjects and to leave the missionaries alone. This incident would probably not be worth mentioning except that the rumor (probably circulated by Beke when he was in Massawa) reached Theodore at a critical point in the Rassam mission, and unquestionably had an unfortunate influence on the result of that mission.

Upon Palmerston's death in November, 1865, Lord John Russell took over the premiership and was succeeded by Lord Clarendon as Secretary of Foreign Affairs. One of the new Foreign Minister's first steps was to ask Hertslet to prepare a memo on the Abyssinian question. Hertslet absolved Cameron of any blame in exceeding his instructions in his dealings with Theodore and blamed the Foreign Office for not answering Theodore's letter, attributing this decision to the advice of Brigadier Coghlan, stating however that he was informed of this by hearsay only. [There is actually nothing to indicate that Coghlan was consulted. He was at Aden at the time the letter was received. While there is nothing in the India Office records to indicate that his advice was sought, he might have been questioned by private letter. Such advice was certainly at variance with his memo of February 8, 1865.] Hertslet expressed his opinion that Mr. Rassam was incapable of performing this mission and that a "British gentleman" should have been sent, not an oriental (FO 1/17, Hertslet-Clarendon 1/13/66; Confidential Memo).

Rassam had reached Metemma on November 21, 1865. On receiving that information from Stanton, the Foreign Office released the news to the papers on February 14, 1866, adding that as of October 17 the prisoners were in good health (FO 1/16, Newspaper release 2/14/66 based on cable Stanton-FO 2/12/66). Beke reached Aden on January 10 (FO 1/16 Merewether-Layard 1/21/66). At Aden, Merewether tried to dissuade Beke from going inland from Massawa. In a most courteous letter dated February 8 the Resident gave Beke the latest information regarding the captives and the status of the Rassam mission and requested him not to proceed as his mission might easily upset the delicate situation in the interior (Rassam, Hormudz,

NARRATIVE OF THE BRITISH MISSION TO THEODORE, London, John Murray, 1869, Vol. II, pp. 46-49; FO 1/17, Merewether-FO 2/8/66). As Rassam states, the letter should have caused any reasonable man at least to halt his mission temporarily, "But Dr. Beke's overweening estimate of his own abilities and of his knowledge of the customs of the country...led him to persist at all risks – not to himself but to the captives generally and the members of the Mission – in his most injudicious scheme" (ibid., Vol. II, pp. 49-50).

Rassam at Metemma received a messenger from Theodore on December 26 informing him that an escort was being sent to meet him and take him to the King whom he expected to meet at Lake Demba (Lake Tana), (FO 1/17 cable Stanton-FO 3/8/66). In forwarding Rassam's dispatch Stanton said, "There appears from the courteous tone of the King's letter to Mr. Rassam reason to hope that the mission of that gentleman may be successful and that the captives will ere this be liberated" (FO 1/17, Stanton-FO 3/7/66). On January 27, Rassam's party reached the King's camp at Ashfa in the province of Damot about fifty miles south, southwest of Lake Tana. The next day he was received by the King with all honors. On January 29, Rassam received a letter from the King releasing to him "Cammeron and all other Europeans about whom your Majesty has written" (ibid., Vol. I, p. 266). Stanton cabled this news to England on April 5 (FO 1/17, cable Stanton-FO 4/5/66) and it was released to the press on April 28 on confirmation from Aden (FO 1/17, Rassam-Merewether private letter, N.D. & news release of 4/28/66). At the same time the Foreign Office informed Palgrave he was no longer needed and ordered him to return to England from Egypt (FO 1/17, FO-Stanton 4/26/66).

Beke meanwhile completely disregarded Merewether's letter; in fact he did not even reply to it. He soon moved inland from Massawa to Halai from whence he sent a letter to Theodore. Merewether commented that as Rassam was already with the King he might be able to undo the bad effects of a second mission and explain "the real nature and object of Dr. Beke's proceedings" (FO 1/17, Stanton-FO 3/16/66, encl. Merewether-FO 3/3/66). At Halai, Beke was held up by one of the omnipresent revolts and wrote a second letter to the King asking safe conduct (Beke, op. cit., p. 394). Beke's letters are rather strange for one who claimed to know the customs of the country so well. He heads his letters "from the Englishman," which,

as Rassam comments, is "a style which is neither English nor
Oriental and must have seemed as strange to an Abyssinian as
it would be to a European" (Rassam, op. cit., Vol. II, p. 46).
The King at first advised him to come to Metemma but, on receiving his second letter, chided him for going to Halai without
the royal permission and told him to return to Massawa. However, illness forced Beke to return to the coast and thence to
England, where he arrived in June, 1866. According to his
own accounts, he had spent £1,818/4/5 on the expedition aside
from personal equipment for himself and his wife, this money
having been received from the Jews Society and the relatives of
the captives (Beke, op. cit., p. 247).

Just what had been happening in Abyssinia since Plowden's
death in 1860 that had caused all this trouble? It is very difficult to establish the real facts. We have very little evidence
of other than a hearsay character. Aside from Cameron's
early dispatches which are perfectly frank, all communications
are very guarded, except for a few smuggled out from Stern
and Rosenthal. There is no question but that Theodore had all
letters read and translated for him, especially after the arrests
of Stern and Rosenthal. The information in Dr. Blanc's book
(Blanc, Henry, A NARRATIVE OF CAPTIVITY IN ABYSSINIA,
London, Smith, 1868) as well as Rassam's work (op. cit.) are
based on recollections by the captives of events which had happened several years before. Mr. Flaad's report (FO 1/17,
Memorandum by Mr. Flaad, 7/10/66) is based on his recollec-
tion of events three and four years old. Cameron was unable
to make a report until 1868 (FO 1/26, Cameron-Stanley 9/28/
68). Lejean, the French Consul, published his THEODORE II
about 1865, and gives a first hand account only of his own experience (op. cit.). His later book (VOYAGE EN ABYSSINIE,
Paris, c. 1873) contained chiefly a description of the country.
The one available Abyssinian source, Alaqa Walda Maryam's
CHRONICLES OF THEODORE, throws no light on the subject;
it deals chiefly with tribal revolts and mentions the captives
only in passing. (Mondon-Vidailhet, C., CHRONIQUE DE
THEODORE II, Paris, 1904, gives a French translation of the
whole Chronicle; Weld-Blundell, H., "History of King Theodore," in the Journal of the African Society, London, 1907,
Vol. 6, pp. 12 ff., gives an English translation of the latter
part of the Chronicle from the imprisonment of Cameron to the
death of Theodore.) One can only assess all this evidence

together with other available information, to reach certain tentative conclusions.

There is no question but that the captives were largely victims of circumstances beyond their control. In addition, they seemed to have thoroughly misunderstood the character of the rulers with whom they were dealing. In 1853, Plowden, in a report on relations with Abyssinia (FO 1/7, Plowden-FO 3/23/53), stated that a consul could not act in a well-understood manner "but must adapt himself and his procedure to the exigencies of a dozen semi-savage chieftains ignorant of all European traditions." He went on to state that the chiefs believed in the superiority of the Abyssinian above all other races and regarded the white man as a curiosity. He said "Thus a European only gains esteem from his personal character which the Abyssinian fully appreciates." In an earlier dispatch he had described the feudal and lawless character of the country and its chaotic condition (FO 1/7, Plowden-FO 6/20/52, Memo on the Social System of Abyssinia). In his great Memorandum on Abyssinia of July 9, 1854, Plowden stated that up until the time of Bruce (c. 1790) white men were welcomed in Abyssinia but there was a marked reluctance to let them depart. "The great difficulty for an European is to steer between too much decision and too much facility. The former will confer on him the appellation 'brute' and general dislike, the latter 'coward' and general disrespect" (FO 1/8, Plowden-FO 7/9/54). Plowden's admiration for Theodore was based on his character, which was in great contrast to the average chief (FO 1/9, Plowden-FO 6/25/55, Memo on Theodore, quoted in entirety in Rassam, op. cit., Vol. I, pp. 282-7, and Beke, op. cit., pp. 30-38). After remarking on his generosity, lack of cupidity, his honesty and personal decency Plowden said, "The worst points of his character are, his violent anger at times, his unyielding pride as regards his kingly and divine right and his fanatical religious zeal." He also recorded Theodore's ambitions for reform, abolition of the slave trade, abolition of private justice with the substitution of state justice, the breaking of the power of the great feudal chief and the substitution of non-hereditary governors, regular payment of his army with a consequent ban on plundering the countryside, and his fanatical desire to abolish Muhammadanism from his country by first conquering the Gallas and then compelling all Muslims to become Christian or leave the country. In all this, he was dependent entirely on his army "regarding nothing with pleasure or desire except for munitions of war for his soldiers."

At the time of Plowden's death, Theodore had reached the height of his power. He had subdued his greatest rival in northern Abyssinia, Ras Oubie, and controlled all of the Christian part of the country, including Shoa. The sole remaining rival, Negussie, a relative of Oubie, was conquered in January, 1861. However much Theodore may have wished to build up the administration of his country where he was now without a rival, he was essentially a warrior. After 1861 he turned his attention to the Galla tribes to the south. He had considerable success in several campaigns, but each time he was away from northern Abyssinia revolts broke out. In a country organized in such a haphazard manner as Abyssinia and controllable only by force, the proverb "When the cat's away, the mice will play" is highly applicable. Theodore told Rassam at their first meeting in 1866 "If I go south, my people rebel in the north; and when I go to the west, they rebel in the east. I have pardoned the rebels over and over again; nevertheless, they persist in their disobedience and defy me" (Rassam, op. cit., Vol. I, p. 251). It is not surprising therefore that Theodore should become suspicious of everyone, suspicious to the point of being accused by many of having hallucinations. Nor is it surprising that these experiences should increase his violent angers almost to the point of insanity and make him unduly sensitive regarding his kingly rights. Theodore's attitude had repercussions on his government also as he turned loose his formerly partially disciplined soldiery to live off the country and to plunder, and took unduly harsh revenge on the rebels with the usual result of driving more and more chiefs to revolt instead of terrifying them into loyalty. Rassam gives an excellent description of Theodore's court with its intrigues, aura of suspicion, and feeling of insecurity due to the King's rages. It was in this atmosphere that a large number of Europeans lived and worked, some of whom were out-and-out adventurers, but most of whom were simple missionaries and lay readers.

Dr. Beke's volume, while an apology for his viewpoint and a political attack on the policies of the Palmerston and Russell governments, has certain excellent portions. He gives an excellent summary of the missionary activity in Abyssinia from 1855 to 1863 (op. cit., pp. 108-113). Aside from the Jesuit mission, alluded to previously in relation to the French intrigues

with Ras Oubie and virtually without influence in the country
after de Jacobis' death in 1860, there was a mission supported
by the British and Foreign Bible Society, a mission of the London Society for Promoting Christianity among the Jews, and a
Scottish mission. The British and Foreign Bible Society mission, under the leadership of the Reverend Mr. Flaad (sometimes spelled Flad), consisted of a group of lay artisans who
followed their usual vocations while doing their missionary
work. They had settled near Gaffat where Theodore "regarding
nothing with pleasure or desire except minitions of war for his
soldiery" (FO 1/9, Plowden-FO 6/25/56) had pretty well succeeded in turning the mission into a small arsenal for his army.
They were high in Theodore's favor and were subjected to little
interference. The mission of the Jews Society consisted of the
Reverend Mr. Stern, Mr. Rosenthal, and the latter's wife. As
their work was only among the Falashas (Abyssinian Jews),
Theodore interfered little with them until Stern's unfortunate
encounter with him. The third mission consisted of two Germans, Messrs. Stieger and Brandeis, who were also little interfered with until all Europeans came under Theodore's displeasure.

The adventurers were no concern of the British Government except insofar as they might make trouble, but some of
them apparently had attached themselves to Consul Cameron.
When Cameron was appointed as Consul he was granted a liberal salary and expense account, yet the records are full of his
rather peculiar monetary transactions and continual requests
for funds. He apparently acquired a curious and expensive entourage. He had an agent at Massawa, first a Mr. Walker to
be succeeded by a Mr. Speedy whom Theodore regarded as an
enemy, probably because the gentleman was not very tactful.
Cameron had with him, besides several Abyssinian servants,
a Mr. Makerer and a Mr. Bardel and an Italian Mr. Pietro.
These men might all be classed as adventurers, and Mr. Bardel
was certainly responsible for much of Cameron's trouble. With
this entourage it is not surprising that Cameron was constantly
in need of funds.

Consul Cameron was unquestionably the first of the Europeans to get into trouble. When Theodore wrote his letter to
the Queen he had told Cameron to return to Massawa and await
a reply. Cameron had taken some Abyssinian servants to Kassala on the way into Abyssinia and one of these, feeling that the
Consul had cheated him, went back to the King and reported

that the Consul had been dealing with the Egyptians against Theo-
dore. Cameron's return to Gondar without the answer to the
King's letter confirmed this suspicion in Theodore's mind. Why
Cameron returned against Theodore's wish is not clear. At
the time he stated that he wished to determine conditions in
Abyssinia (FO 1/13, Cameron-FO 5/20/63), for he had been at
Bogos only a short distance from Massawa. In 1868 in his final
report he states that he wanted to investigate Beke's opinions
on commerce in the area and especially the growth of cotton
(FO 1/26 Cameron-Stanley 9/28/68). As there is no evidence
of any instructions from the Foreign Office to do this and as
none of Beke's letters was ever forwarded to Cameron one can
only conclude that he was investigating for the ambitious doctor
at Beke's private request. In 1868 he also disclaimed any connection with Bardel and the others, although Rassam continually
mentions them as in Cameron's employ. While the King was
previously suspicious of Cameron, he really fell from grace
when he appealed to the King for Stern's release at the time of
the missionary's torture and imprisonment. Cameron's action
in this matter was certainly correct, but from his own evidence
in 1868 he apparently acted against Flaad's advice by going in
to the King when he was in one of his rages. After this Cameron
was virtually a prisoner, but he was not chained until he asked
the King for permission to proceed to the coast in accordance
with his orders. His chief difficulty with the King seems to
have been, first, a too forceful approach to Theodore and an
insistence on getting his business done, and second, an unfortunate ability to choose just the wrong time to appear at the
court. These procedures made him an easy prey to the intrigues
of his enemies.

Stern's imprisonment was sheer mischance (see pp.279-80).
He had received permission to leave Abyssinia and simply
stopped to take his leave of the King as a matter of courtesy.
After having Stern tortured, the King had Stern's and Rosenthal's private papers translated, and, finding some unflattering
remarks in Rosenthal's papers about his ancestry, put them
both in chains. These events, as well as Napoleon's letter which
arrived while Consul Lejean was at his court, made the King
so suspicious of Europeans that thereafter none of them was
safe unless, like the Bible Society artisans, they were useful.

During this period conditions in Theodore's empire had
gone from bad to worse. Revolts increased, Tigré was

completely out of the King's control, and he was virtually without authority in Shoa.   In Gondar, the King's authority existed
only in the places occupied by his army.   His cruelties continually made matters worse so that, by the time of Rassam's
arrival, the Rassam party had to take the long circuitous route
from the coast by the Sudan and Metemma and then be accompanied to Theodore's court by an armed escort of considerable
size.

XVIII. THE FAILURE OF THE RASSAM MISSION

Although Theodore had promised to release the prisoners
on January 28, 1866, they were not, in fact, released at that
time. On February 4, Rassam had another interview with the
King during which Theodore again ranted against the captives.
These rantings and subsequent inquiries led Rassam to believe
that Mr. Bardel was the prime intriguer against the Europeans;
he was the person who had translated Stern's and Rosenthal's
writings for the King. After the interview Theodore presented
Rassam with $5,000 as a present to be used in any way "except
in a manner unpleasing to God" (Rassam, op. cit., Vol. I,
p. 306). The envoy was criticized later for accepting this gift
but under the circumstances he could not have done otherwise;
he quite properly credited this sum to the account of the British
Government.

The entire party, the court, the Emperor and Rassam's
mission moved to Korata where on February 28 they were joined
by the artisans from Gaffat. Rassam was shortly informed that
the captives at Magdala had been released on February 24 and
were traveling slowly to join him. On March 4, Rassam received the first intimation that there might be difficulties when
Theodore, writing as King rather than friend, asked the envoy
to "consult" with him (Rassam, op. cit., Vol. II, p. 21). Rassam attributed this change in attitude to the news of Beke's arrival at Massawa.

Theodore informed Rassam that he had decided to have the
Magdala captives tried before him again. Rassam was worried
by this because of Theodore's intense hatred of Cameron, Stern,
and Rosenthal. On March 12 the captives arrived. On March 15
a trial was held at Rassam's tent, with Rassam acting as judge.
The King had presented formal charges against Cameron and
Bardel with an inference that the King might wish a substantial
indemnity. After an argument with Bardel, who wished to con-
test the charges against him, Rassam had all of them admit that
they had done wrong and ask forgiveness. While this farce of
a trial was going on, Rassam was informed of the King's intention to keep him and his party as hostages in Abyssinia until artisans could come from England. Further complications were
added the same day by the arrival of Dr. Beke's first letter to

Theodore. Rassam attributed much of his later difficulties to this letter and especially the petition from the families of the missionaries which was enclosed. Rassam said:

> It is by no means improbable, however, that when he [Theodore] read the petition, where in the petitioners 'humbly, at the feet of your Majesty, plead for mercy and pardon for the wretched Europeans, ' and understood from Dr. Beke himself 'the Englishman' that he was commissioned on the part of the petitioners to 'supplicate your majesty in their names for their [the captives'] pardon and release' — in fact that the said 'Englishman' proposed to come up to him with a verdict of guilty in his hand against those whom the king designated his 'enemies' — that his Majesty began to think he had let the captives off too cheaply and was more than ever disposed to exact satisfaction in some shape or other" (Rassam, op. cit. , Vol. II, pp. 22-2).

Rassam, however, missed one of the most important points in Theodore's calculations. He mentions "Four brass cannon which had been made at Gaffat by the King's European artisans" (ibid. , Vol II, p. 24). These artisans had always been well-treated by the King and were never at any time subject to imprisonment, being only forbidden to leave the country and restricted to the immediate area of Gaffat. As Plowden said, Theodore regarded "nothing with pleasure or desire except munitions of war for his soldiery" (FO 1/19, Plowden-FO 6/25/55). It is not surprising, then, that as the time approached for the Europeans to leave the country the King should begin to worry about how he was to replace these valuable men.

On March 25, Rassam's party and the artisans went to Zagé across Lake Tana at Theodore's request. Rassam had a very friendly interview with the King who, the next day, called a meeting of his counsellors to discuss the departure of the Europeans. All advised him to let the Europeans go. However, Theodore felt that he had no surety for the future. He then called for Rassam, who, on his appearance at the royal tent found that the King was not in the best of moods. After the usual recriminations against the Europeans including, this time, M. Lejean the former French Consul, he also attacked the Egyptian government and the Patriarch of the Copts. He condemned

the ingratitude of many of the Europeans who had been in Abyssinia and concluded by saying, "You see how I have been treated
by people who ought to have requited me differently. How am
I to know that you will act differently? You may not abuse me
when you leave my country, but still you may forget me. "
Rassam pled with Theodore to believe him and the King finally
said, "Very well, I will try you; and may you reach your country safely"Rassam, op. cit., Vol. II, p. 63). In dismissal Theodore asked Rassam to visit him to say good-bye before leaving.

Rassam returned to Korata to find considerable difficulties
there. There are strong indications in the published letters of
the various prisoners that there was considerable jealousy and
bad feeling among those who had been imprisoned in Abyssinia.
Considering their varied backgrounds and the long imprisonment together, such ill feeling is not at all surprising. Mutual
distrust was increased by a rumor that Rassam had been sent
to obtain only the release of Cameron, a rumor which can be
traced directly to Dr. Beke. It took all of Rassam's considerable tact to keep the prisoners from getting into trouble by
making statements which might be reported to Theodore and
cause new complications. In addition, the exodus was delayed
because Theodore had decided to create a new decoration for
Rassam's party and to have presents made for them, refusing
to allow the party to proceed until these were finished.

On April 8, 1866, Rassam received a verbal message to
bring the captives with him to the King's camp at Zagé. This
was exactly what he had been trying to avoid as he was afraid
that the appearance of these people would send the King into
one of his rages. Rassam decided to go to Zagé without the
captives, as all preparations for departure had been made and
arrangements for transport were complete. On April 12 Theodore, in a fearful rage, ordered the captives to be rearrested
on their departure from Korata and ordered Rassam and his
party to go to Zagé. On arrival at Zagé the next day, Friday,
April 13, the whole party was immediately arrested. When the
King had calmed down he ordered the release of the Rassam
mission, but decided that all the prisoners should be tried
again. This farce was held on April 16 and 17, ending in a formal reconciliation. Immediately Theodore prepared a letter to
Queen Victoria stating that the prisoners had been made over
to Rassam and that Theodore was keeping Rassam with him for
advice. Later this was misconstrued to indicate that Rassam

refused to remain without the prisoners and thereby prevented
their repatriation. However, in all his correspondence, after
Rassam's arrival Theodore never considered the prisoners except as part of Rassam's mission. When he stated that he was
going to keep Rassam, he meant to keep the whole group. He
also requested Rassam to draw up a letter asking for artisans,
which the envoy did, bearing in mind that the King was going to
read it. Theodore's message read in part: "My desire is that
you should send to her Majesty, The Queen, and obtain for me
a man who can make cannons and muskets, and one who can
smelt iron; also an instructor of artillery. I want these people
to come here with their implements and everything necessary
for their work, and then they shall teach us and return" (Rassam, op. cit. , Vol. II, pp. 101-2 and FO 1/17 encl. in Rassam
-Clarendon, 4/18/66). Rassam's letter was very flattering,
and Theodore, much to Rassam's relief, chose Mr. Flaad as
messenger. Flaad was to inform the government as to the restraint under which Rassam wrote the letter. On April 2, 1866,
Mr. Flaad departed for England.

Until June 25, 1866, Rassam and his party enjoyed freedom, traveling with the King's court to Korata and thence to
Gaffat. On the twenty-fifth they were summoned to court by
the King and faced with two rumors, first that a railroad had
been built to Kassala for the purpose of bringing English, French
and Turkish troops to attack Theodore; second, that a report
had come from Jerusalem that as soon as Rassam and his party
were safely out of Abyssinia, the English were going to attack
Theodore. Rassam suspected the latter rumor to be a trumped-
up story, but felt that Beke's sudden disappearance from Halai
and Massawa had made the King suspicious, especially as he
had interceded with the rebels in Tigré to protect Beke, but they on
receipt of Theodore's request could find no sign of the doctor.
Shortly, Theodore decided to send the Europeans, except for
those in his service, to Magdala. They arrived there on July 12,
1866. The party consisted of Rassam, Dr. Blanc, Lieutenant
Prideaux, Cameron, Stern, Rosenthal, Kerans and Pietro,
the other Europeans having gone into the King's service. On
the sixteenth the prisoners were fettered by order of the Chief
of Magdala. They were to remain thus until April 11, 1868.
(All the material relative to the events of the Rassam mission
may be found in Rassam's book, op. cit. , Vol. I, pp. 243-320,
Vol. II, pp. 1-161; they are also confirmed in FO 1/17, Flaad

– Memo. 7/10/66 and the encl. in Stanton-FO 5/19/66 of part of a journal of events by Rassam.)

The Foreign Office in London awaited word of Rassam's return to the coast with the prisoners. Stanton was able to report on May 19 that Rassam was preparing to take his leave of the King, but the Consul General was worried by the news that Theodore had just received a letter from Beke (FO 1/17, Stanton-FO 5/19/66). Three days later Stanton enclosed the draft of a letter from Merewether to Theodore inviting the King to send an embassy to England together with a few of his people who should receive an English education (FO 1/17, Stanton-FO 5/22/66 enclosure). This letter was apparently never sent to Theodore as Flaad appeared at Massawa before the final draft could be prepared.

Flaad arrived at Alexandria on June 29, a little over two months after leaving the King's court. He reported Theodore's desire for a guarantee of good disposition towards him by England before allowing the prisoners to leave the country. Flaad added that Rassam had done very well and that Bardel's intrigues were at the bottom of his troubles (FO 1/17, Stanton-FO 6/29/66). Flaad was rushed straight to London, appearing at the Foreign Office on July 10. Here he gave a full report on the detention of Rassam and the prisoners, praising Rassam's actions and stating that Rassam was "calm, prudent, cautious and sincere." He concluded by saying that his report should not be made public because of possible repercussions in Abyssinia (FO 1/17, Flaad report on Rassam's detention 7/10/66). At the same time he gave a full report on the origins of the imprisonment of Cameron and the others. He ascribed the imprisonment to: first, the indiscretions of Cameron; second, the negligence of the Foreign Office; and third, the conduct of certain Europeans that aroused the King's suspicions. Of the latter he chiefly blamed Bardel whom, he stated, Cameron had brought to Abyssinia as his secretary. (Cameron denied this in 1868 but all evidence points to the truth of this statement.) Bardel, "a man of equivocal character," quarreled with Cameron, then entered Theodore's service and went to France in 1862 with a letter to Napoleon, returning with the answer after the arrival of Consul Lejean and Dr. Layard. Bardel had told the King that the English would not send an answer to him because they liked Egypt better than Theodore, informing Flaad privately that he had heard this rumor in Alexandria. Flaad

commented, "I must say, the Govt. as well as the daily newspapers and societies like that who sent Dr. Beke acted very im-
prudently since our captivity began. " Flaad added that it was
essential that no articles appear in the press about the captives,
as Bardel, now in favor with the King, was in direct communication with Father Delmonte, the head of the Lazarist mission
at Massawa, adding, "Mr. Bardel is a man, who would not care
much, if all our people would be killed in one day." He reviewed
the story of the imprisonment of Cameron and the rest. Flaad
suggested the sending of presents and artisans as requested by
Theodore, but not the use of force, as he felt that the lives of
the Europeans, who with their families totalled sixty-one souls,
would be imperiled by the use of force (FO 1/17, Flaad – Memo
on the origins of the captivity, 7/10/66).

The Conservative Derby government replaced Lord Russell's Liberal cabinet in July, 1866, and Lord Clarendon was succeeded by Lord Stanley as Foreign Minister. The new Foreign
Minister had an interview with Flaad on July 16. Stanley's
first reaction was to suggest that someone such as Palgrave
should be sent to Theodore with presents which were not to be
delivered until the captives were released (FO 1/17, Memo by
Stanley 7/13/66). Or to put it in simpler language, to ransom
the prisoners, for that is what it amounted to. Rumors from
two different sources came to the Foreign Office that Egypt was
about to attack Abyssinia and that French arms and officers
were being sent to Alexandria from Algiers for this purpose
(FO 1/18, Merewether [at London]-FO 7/18/66). Lord Cowley
in Paris and Colonel Stanton at Alexandria were instructed to
investigate, as such action would have been fatal to the prisoners (FO 1/18, FO-Cowley 7/18/66, FO-Stanton 7/18/66). The
rumors were proved to be false although the situation at Bogos
was tense with continued Muslim raids against the Christian
population (FO 1/18, Stanton-FO 7/10/66, 7/29/66, 8/25/66).
Meanwhile an additional letter arrived from Theodore to Flaad
detailing the King's wishes: two gunsmiths, an artillery officer,
an ironfounder who could erect a furnace and foundry, one or
two boat builders, a cartwright and wheelwright, a small steam
engine for the foundry, a turning bench and tools, a still, machinery for making percussion caps with necessary copper plate
etc. , a good telescope, a gunpowder mill, a supply of powder
and caps, carpets, silks, sporting guns, goblets and European
curiosities (FO 1/18, Theodore-Flaad, N. D.). Flaad replied

to the King that he was trying to get artisans and hoped to arrive
in Massawa at the end of September (FO 1/18, Flaad-Theodore
7/18/66). Flaad, however, refused the responsibility of selecting the artisans (FO 1/18, Memo by Murray 7/28/66).

Merewether, the Resident at Aden then on leave in London,
reported that he had gotten a group of artisans together, but in
late July, when Dr. Beke published a letter on Abyssinia in the
press, the entire party got frightened and refused to go (FO 1/
18, Memo by Murray 8/1/66). Merewether soon met with more
success obtaining the services of an Irish engineer named Tal-
bot. The Resident suggested that the contracts for the artisans
require employment for three years at a high salary, to be paid,
of course, by Theodore. At the same time he recommended a
list of machinery and gifts to be sent to the King, the total cost
of which would be Ł3,500 (FO 1/18, Memo by Merewether 8/13/
66). Flaad meanwhile had an interview with the Queen on August 14, and a letter was prepared from her to Theodore (FO
1/18, Memo by Hammond, N. D.). Flaad forwarded this information to Theodore on September 1, adding that he had been delayed a month but hoped to bring the artisans with him (FO 1/18,
Flaad-Theodore 9/1/66).

While these plans were going ahead and Merewether was
obtaining the machinery for the artisans, word arrived from
Goodfellow, acting Resident at Aden, of the King's mistreatment
and imprisonment of the Rassam party. On receipt of this information Flaad wrote Merewether that he saw no point in sending the artisans; he felt that Theodore would only demand more
and more. He thought that the government must now use stronger methods (FO 1/18, Flaad-Merewether [London] 9/19/66).
On receipt of this, Merewether noted that the British policy
should be changed. That Flaad should go to Massawa with the
artisans he felt was absolutely essential for the safety of the
prisoners, but he also felt that Flaad should send up to Theodore
a letter informing the King that the artisans would proceed only
on the release of the prisoners. If they were not released,
Merewether recommended that a punitive force should be sent
to rescue the prisoners. He advised the Foreign Office that
about 10,000 troops would be needed who, he said, would be
greatly aided by the revolts in Tigre and elsewhere (FO 1/18,
Memo, Merewether 9/25/66). A cabinet meeting rejected this
plan much to Merewether's disappointment as he felt it was the
only course open, especially as the incident was damaging

British prestige throughout the East (FO 1/18, Merewether-Murray N.D. [approx. Sept 28]).

The letter from the Queen was prepared for Flaad to take with him saying in part "We find it difficult to reconcile your assurances with the obstacles which were still opposed to the departure of our servants and the other Europeans." It went on to say that Flaad would not bear the presents with him but would leave them at Massawa together with the artisans to await the fulfillment of Theodore's promises (FO 1/18, Victoria-Theodore, 10/4/66). Flaad was instructed to tell the King that the confidence of Her Majesty's government in Theodore was weakened by the detention of Rassam and that the King was to be informed that the British did not wish the Egyptians to disturb him (FO 1/18, Instructions to Flaad 10/8/66). Flaad arrived at Alexandria on October 18 (FO 1/18, Stanley-FO 10/19/66) and proceeded to Massawa. Merewether was at the same time preparing to return to Aden. The Foreign Office left the question of forwarding the presents and the artisans completely in the Resident's hands, suggesting merely that the artisans remain in healthy Aden rather than in hot and fever-ridden Massawa (FO 1/18, Hammond-Merewether 10/31/66). Merewether decided that he had best remain at Massawa until the captives were released and then bring up the presents and possibly the artisans if conditions justified it to Metemma (FO 1/18, Merewether-Hammond 11/3/66).

Flaad, on his arrival at Massawa, found letters from the captives, all of whom were depressed and felt that a military expedition was their only hope of release. Flaad pointed out that if such a step was taken, it must be begun at once as the rainy season would soon prevent any such steps until September, 1867. He believed that the prisoners would be safe enough if British troops were used but feared for the captives if Egyptians were employed (FO 1/18, Flaad-Herstlet 11/5/66). Merewether arrived at the Red Sea port a month later to find a letter from Rassam stating that he thought coercive force would be the only way in which they could be released (FO 1/19, Rassam-Merewether 11/5/66 in Merewether-FO 12/10/66). The next reports from Massawa indicated that neither Flaad's nor Merewether's messengers had been able to proceed beyond Adowa due to rebellions in the interior. Merewether was worried by Rassam's request for seeds and the information that 400 political prisoners had been sent to Magdala, resulting in a shortage

of provisions. Theodore apparently had but 15,000 men left in
his army and his position was desperate, as he held only a portion of Amhara (FO 1/19, Merewether-FO 1/15/67).

Victoria's letter was received by Theodore about December 28, 1866; he forwarded it to Rassam at Magdala on that date.
On January 7, 1867, he requested Rassam to do his best to get
the artisans to come up to the interior. This letter was very
disconcerting as it brought up again all the charges against the
prisoners. It concluded "I wish you to get them [the skillful
artisans] via Metemma in order that they may teach me wisdom
and show me clever arts. When this is done, I shall make you
glad, and send you away, by the power of God" (Rassam, op.cit.,
letter of Theodore to Rassam rec. Jan. 8, 1867, Vol. II, pp.
234-5). Rassam wrote a letter about the artisans such as the
King requested, and sent it to the King for his approval, fully
expecting that it would not reach England as quickly as his reports would reach Merewether. He also received a draft of a
letter which Theodore proposed to send to Victoria which was
far from complimentary (ibid., Vol. II, pp. 236-7). (By April
15 Magdala was cut off from all communications with Theodore
by revolts nearby, and the captives heard nothing more from
the King until he was on his way to their prison in January, 1868.)

When Merewether was informed of this state of affairs he
forwarded the information to London, on February 15, 1867.
He believed that the only recourse short of war was a threatening letter to Theodore; he felt that Theodore's position was so
insecure that such a threat would incite more revolts. This
letter should be backed up by a military force. He well described
Theodore's position, "Abyssinia is wearied of Him." Therefore he felt that Theodore only desired the artisans so that they
could build him armaments which would enable the King to re-
assert his power over the rebels (FO 1/19, Merewether [Aden]
-FO 2/15/67).

In December, 1866, Theodore had suppressed a revolt in
Gondar with such brutality and severity that he even destroyed
the churches. This, in the eyes of the Abyssinian to whom the
church was sanctuary, was the worst atrocity which could be
committed. As this news had spread around the country, Theodore's position had become steadily weaker. Merewether, informed of the increasingly rebellious state of the country, wrote
in March a semi-official letter to Lord Stanley giving his opinion
as to the situation. He believed that Theodore would never

release Rassam and only wished to get more English under his control to force Britain to intervene on his side in the revolts as payment for the release of the captives. The situation was all in Britain's favor, and Merewether believed that if a proclamation were made that a punitive force was to rescue the prisoners and then leave the country, rewarding those who helped the captives, the British could get almost unanimous support and the captives would be protected. He warned, however, that such intelligence would have to be made public at the beginning as Bardel, now high in the King's favor, was receiving French, Turkish and Egyptian newspapers. He suggested that Sir Robert Napier command the force, to be made up chiefly of Sepoys, and that Mr. Fitzgerald of the Bombay Government be the political head of the expedition. He also advised sending the artisans home at once (FO 1/19, semi-official [so marked] Merewether-Lord Stanley 3/4/67). Lord Stanley commented, "Read the Enclosed you will see that Merewether is bent on fighting. I do not think that I shall have to decide this question" (FO 1/19, Minute 3/22/67, attached to Merewether-Stanley 3/4/67). Hammond, of the Foreign Office, agreed with Merewether about the artisans, felt that a letter should be sent from Victoria saying that she could no longer communicate with Theodore and suggested that a rumor be spread from India regarding preparations for an expedition (FO 1/19, Minute by Hammond 3/22/67 on Merewether-Stanley 3/4/67). Hertslet, asked to check on possible expenses of a military expedition, reported that the Persian War in 1857, a rather similar proposition, had cost £2,125,000, mostly for transportation (FO 1/19, Minute by Hertslet 3/22/67 on Merewether-Stanley 3/4/67). Hammond's suggestion, equivalent to the breaking of diplomatic relations between two civilized countries, is interesting because it indicates the Foreign Office's continuing view of Theodore as a civilized monarch with a regular government which was amenable to reason, rather than as an absolute despot dependent solely on force for his power.

On receipt of an answer to his letter to Theodore (see p. 315), Flaad left for Debra Tabor early in March, 1867; the road was temporarily open (FO 1/19, Stanton-FO 3/15/67). Merewether, again at Massawa, continued to press for action as further information on the poor condition of the captives reached him (FO 1/19, Merewether-Stanley 3/28/67). A reply to Merewether was drafted (but not sent) on April 7 informing him that the

government was not yet ready to go to extremities, requesting
him to sell or return the presents after three months, and advising him that the War Office and the India Office were being
consulted as to further steps. It was also proposed to send an
ultimatum to Theodore (FO 1/19, draft FO-Merewether 4/7/67).

On April 20 the Foreign Office forwarded an outline of the
Abyssinian situation to the War Office asking for Sir John Pak-
ington's consideration and stating, "The time had therefore arrived when it is needful for H. M. Gov. to consider what further
steps it may be at once possible & advisable to take in order to
vindicate the honor of the Crown and protect her many subjects
from further harm" (FO 1/19, FO-WO 4/20/67). The same
day the India Office was informed of the seriousness of the situation with the information that Brigadier Sir William Coghlan
"has reluctantly come to the conclusion that it is inevitable"
that force must be used. It was further suggested that the information of the preliminary steps taken in forming the expedition might induce Theodore to release the captives (FO 1/19,
FO-IO 4/20/67). Meanwhile a letter to Theodore had been prepared informing him that the presents were to be returned to
Europe three months after the dispatch of this letter from Massawa unless the prisoners had been released, and that the British Government would hold no further communications with him
(FO 1/19 Stanley-Theodore 4/10/67). This was enclosed in a
letter to Merewether similar to the draft of April 7, with the
additional information that the Foreign Office was already in
communication with the War and India Offices on further steps
(FO 1/19, FO-Merewether 4/20/67). At the same time Merewether was instructed in a separate letter to return the artisans
to England (FO 1/19 Merewether-FO 5/11/67) and the Resident,
who had returned to Aden, proceeded on May 14 to Massawa
with the ultimatum (FO 1/19, Merewether-FO 5/14/67).

Another attempt to bring religious pressure on Theodore
was being made at this time from Constantinople. On December 29, 1866, Lord Lyons, Ambassador to the Sublime Porte,
was instructed to see if he could get the help of the Armenian
Patriarch in freeing the captives (FO 1/18, FO-Lyons, 12/29/
66). The Patriarch was willing to do what he could and was prepared to send Bishop Saliah with a message and appropriate
presents (FO 1/19, Moore [Jerusalem]-FO 4/3/67). The Patriarch wrote Theodore promising to protect the Abyssinian pilgrims and prepared a complete set of vestments as presents (FO

1/19, Moore-FO 4/13/67). Bishop Saliah arrived at Cairo on
April 22 (FO 1/19, Stanton-FO 4/22/67). There is no further
information of any kind on this mission until after Theodore's
death, but on June 24 the Foreign Office was still awaiting the
result of this attempt to rescue the captives before deciding to
use force (FO 1/19, FO-WO 6/24/67). There is little evidence
that Theodore was particularly interested in the state of the
Abyssinian Church in Jerusalem. Although at first a religious
man, he had completely broken with the Abuna at the time of
Cameron's arrest, when that dignitary intervened on behalf of
the Consul. The Abuna's position had been insecure ever since
the visit to Abyssinia of the Coptic Patriarch in 1856-1857. It
is very probable that the mistreatment of the Abyssinian pilgrims at Jerusalem weighed on the conscience of members of
the Foreign Office staff as Britain had assumed an unofficial
guardianship over these Christians. This, combined with the
generally religious attitude of the mid-Victorian period, probably led the Foreign Office to believe that Theodore was more
influenced by religion than was the case. Certainly the missionary background of the majority of the captives and the religious
character of the groups pressing for their release emphasized
this aspect of the problem too strongly. It is surprising that
after Rassam's failure to get any aid from the Abuna who was
in prison the Foreign Office should then proceed to get the Patriarch of the church, which had been chiefly responsible for
the persecution of the Abyssinians, to intercede with Theodore.
For the sake of the captives it is probably just as well that this
mission never reached Theodore; it would probably have aroused
the King's suspicions further and given him another grudge
against them.

The Foreign Office letter to the India Office of April 20
brought a reply on May 10. Sir Stafford Northcote, Secretary
of State for India, was of the opinion "that the main question as
to whether there shall be any ultimate resort to force, to effect
their [the prisoners] release is one the responsibility of deter-
mining which rests with Her Majesties Secty. of State for Foreign Affairs." However, if Lord Stanley and Government wished
to use force "Sir Stafford Northcote considers that no time
should be lost in making preparations for that purpose.... He
must stipulate that the revenues of India are not to be subject
to any portion of the Expenditure which may be incurred for an
object in which that country has no direct interest" (FO 1/19,

IO-FO 5/10/67).   The subject was referred to India where Sir
H. M. Durand, in charge of the military department, criticized
the lack of data.   He was opposed to any Egyptian participation
and questioned the advisability of withdrawing troops immediately after an expedition without leaving an organized government (FO 1/19, Memo by Sir H. M. Durand [Simla] 6/10/67).
Sir W. R. Mansfield, Commander in Chief of the Indian Army,
commenting on this memo, felt that such an expedition would
imply at least a two-year occupation of the country. He believed
that lack of water would make Aden a poor base and agreed that
neither the Egyptian nor Turkish governments should in any way
be mixed up in the affair (FO 1/19, Memo by Sir W. A. Mansfield
on above, 6/14/67).

The War Office, apparently seeking more information, was
informed by the Foreign Office on June 24 that there was no intention of using force until the results of the ultimatum and the
letter of the Armenian Patriarch had been determined.   However, the Foreign Office advised the War Office to find out
(1) the size of the force necessary, its composition and commander; (2) the length of time necessary to prepare the expedition assuming its base to be Bombay; (3) transport requirements;
(4) where landings could be made avoiding Egyptian territory if
possible; (5) problems of commissariat; (6) amount of reserves
necessary; (7) the preliminary steps required for all this and
the length of time necessary for these preliminaries (FO 1/19,
FO-WO 6/24/67).

The War Office replied to the Foreign Office by sending a
copy of a letter to the India Office suggesting that the force
should be organized with Bombay as a base.   They recommended
Coghlan for command and the Reverend Badger as political officer, and advised that they, with an interpreter and medical
commissariat and Quartermaster officers, proceed immediately to Massawa (FO 1/20, WO-FO 7/2/67, encl. WO-IO 7/2/67).

The Foreign Office also consulted Sir Samuel Baker who
had finished his trip to the sources of the Nile in 1866 and had
probably as good a knowledge of the Sudan as any Englishman.
He recommended Khartoum and Kassala as the best bases
against Abyssinia, since in his opinion the route from Massawa
to Magdala was too difficult for the movement of supplies necessary for an army. He suggested three alternatives: (1) an
alliance with Egypt which might scare Theodore into releasing
the prisoners as it would stir up a revolt against him, Egypt to

receive the disputed provinces as a reward; (2) an independent
British force, or (3) a mixed force of Indian and Egyptian troops
to be paid by the British. He felt that Abyssinia should foot the
cost of the expedition and be occupied as a security for this payment (FO 1/20, Sir Samuel Baker-Stanley 7/13/67).

This report was evidently subject to considerable discussion. While there is no evidence as to the time the reports
from Simla (see p. 320) were received, it does not seem possible that they could have arrived before Baker's report. Therefore the conclusions reached by Murray in his Minute of July 15
must have been influenced only by the information at his disposal in the files of the Foreign Office, and consultation with
officials in London.

Murray commented that the chief feature of Sir Samuel's
proposal was the use of Egyptian troops which could be gotten
very easily. On the other hand he felt that great consideration
should be given to what an Egyptian official had said to him:
"What is thought of the power and prestige of England when
British Officials are allowed with impunity to be imprisoned
and maltreated by an African despot." British officials in the
area seemed to feel that Britain alone should act, he added;
aside from questions of prestige and honor the use of Egyptian
troops or the passage of British troops through neutral territory would make undue complications with the other powers.
The route from Tajura was the best from the viewpoint of avoiding international complications, but if that route turned out to
be impossible, Egyptian cooperation on the Massawa route
would be necessary. Murray commented on Sir Samuel's unfavorable reaction to the route from Massawa. "Now what he said
about moving troops from Massawa on Magdala is in accord
with what we have elsewhere heard, namely that we may encounter difficulties, but he knows nothing of that route and only
speaks from hearsay" (FO 1/20, Minute by Murray 7/15/67 on
Sir S. Baker-Stanley 7/13/67).

The three main trade routes into Abyssinia from the coast
have already been mentioned: (1) the best-known and most familiar, from Massawa to Adowa, Axsum, Gondar and thence to
Debra Tabor to the east of Lake Tana; (2) the route from Tajura
to Shoa; and (3) the route from Berbera to Harar. Magdala,
the fortress chosen by Theodore as his hideout and citadel, lay
near the edge of the mountains just west of the coastal plain,
surrounded by the roughest country in Abyssinia. It was 200

miles south of Adowa and 150 miles north of Shoa. The shortest
way to Magdala was unquestionably from Tajura. However, this
route meant the use of a port which was hardly adequate for the
transport vessels used in that day; a hundred-and-fifty-mile
trip through the coastal plain, one of the most inhospitable areas
in the world, hot, fever-ridden, almost waterless and inhabited
by unfriendly tribes; uncivilized even by Abyssinian standards;
and a short and very steep approach to the highlands of Abyssinia. Since the Berbera-Harar route was too far south, only
the northern route was a reasonable one. This route was dominated by Massawa, an outpost of the Turkish Empire. This port,
together with all the area of the western Red Sea coast and the
mythical claim to Abyssinia, had been transferred in 1866 from
the jurisdiction of the Pashalik of Jidda (directly responsible to
the Porte) to the authority of the Khedive of Egypt. As the British had studiously avoided any reference to or admission of the
sovereignty of the Ottoman Empire in this area, the problem did
not come up until Egyptian and Turkish expansion in the early
1870's. But the Egyptians certainly had de facto authority over
Massawa by the actual presente of a garrison there. Therefore
permission would have to be obtained for the use of this northern route. There is no evidence that any European had ever
been to Magdala before the captives were sent there, and its
surroundings were certainly unknown. Mr. Beke who, whatever
his other faults was a competent geographer, said of Magdala,
"Its position is very incorrectly marked in the few maps in
which its name appears at all; and though it cannot be absolutely
determined... I believe I am not far wrong in placing it in lat.
11° 30' N and long. 39° 10' E. of Greenwish" (Beke, op. cit.,
p. 143). This was a very accurate estimate.

    Sir Samuel Baker's report was forwarded to the War and
the India Offices. The original draft of the letter transmitting
the report contained a discussion of the question of using Egyptian forces, but as this was cancelled in the final letter one can
only assume that the Foreign Office had definitely decided
against such a course (FO 1/20, FO-WO and FO-IO 7/16/67).

    At Massawa, Merewether received letters on May 23 from
the captives, including one from Dr. Blanc which presented the
clearest and most concise statement of the imprisonment.
Merewether suggested that this letter be published. Murray concurred in this opinion stating that it would serve as an excellent
counter to the agitation of Beke in the Times and Bulwer in the

Pall Mall Gazette for the use of an Egyptian force against Theodore (FO 1/19, Merewether-Stanley 5/24/67 and Minutes by
Murray-Stanley 6/20/67). Stanley concurred if it did not commit the government to the use of force.

Dr. Blanc reported that in February, 1867, five more Europeans had been imprisoned for planning to escape from Debra
Tabor: Steiger and Brandeis of the German missionaries;
Schiller and Essler, two of the European artisans; and Makerer,
one of Cameron's servants who had entered the King's service.
Their plans had been betrayed by Bardel. This event had been
rumored in March (FO 1/19, Merewether-Stanley 3/30/67) but
was not confirmed until May by Rassam (FO 1/20, Rassam-
Merewether 5/3/67 in Merewether-Stanley 6/15/67). These
prisoners stayed with the King until his arrival in Magdala in
January, 1868 (Rassam, op. cit., Vol. II, p. 261).

On July 11, 1867, Merewether reported the result of the
Flaad mission. Flaad had arrived on April 25 at Debra Tabor
and was given a stormy reception by Theodore. When told that
there would be no friendship with England until the captives
were released, Theodore said, "Let them come, I will beat
them." Flaad tried to reason with the King but Theodore said
that he had no fear. If he had not chained Rassam, he would not
have had artisans sent (he thought they were at Massawa), and
if he had not chained Cameron he would not have received an
answer to his letter to the Queen. A few days later he told Flaad
that he would release Rassam and the prisoners if a sign of
friendship were sent but the missionary discounted this promise
(FO 1/20, Merewether-Stanley 7/11/67). Merewether's letter
was received on August 13 and was immediately sent to the
printers to be prepared for circulation to the cabinet. Murray
commented:

> The King had duly received the final letter on the
> sixteenth of April in which he was told 'Her Majesty
> requires, for the last time, by her Secty. of State, that
> the prisoners should be made over to her & she trusts
> that Y. M. will be sufficiently well advised to comply
> with her demand, rather than forfeit the friendship. . . .
> The Queen is still disposed to entertain for you.'
> He sent the messenger back without answer, there-
> fore there is nothing left but immediate action.

Murray added that Merewether, who had been ordered to Bombay, would be in India to hear the result of the decision. Lord Stanley commented, "This must be brought before the cabinet, Circulate the papers at once" (FO 1/20, Minute by Murray 8/13/67 on Merewether-Stanley 7/11/67). The cabinet immediately decided to send the expedition; on August 17 the India Office informed the Foreign Office that Sir Robert Napier would be put in command as Merewether's rank (that of Colonel) was not high enough for such a post (FO 1/20, IO-FO 8/17/67).

Certainly there could have been no other decision. Popular opinion was behind such a move and, leaving out any humanitarian motives regarding the saving of the prisoners, British prestige had reached a new low in the East due to the ineffectiveness of their negotiations with Theodore.

XIX. PUBLIC OPINION AND THE CAPTIVES

One question has probably repeatedly occurred to the reader of this volume: Why are there no references to contemporary opinion in the foregoing pages? The answer is simple; there was no contemporary opinion on the Red Sea area. The British capture of Aden in 1839 passed virtually unnoticed in the public press, overshadowed as it was by news from the Afghan campaign. Except for a strong criticism of the actions of the British seizure of Aden published in Blackwoods Magazine in April, 1843, nothing appeared except in the more technical journals. The reports of the officers conducting surveys on the Red Sea and similar reports which were of geographical interest were published in the Journal of the Royal Geographical Society and an occasional article of military interest appeared in the United Service Journal, but these publications are too specialized to be considered as either contributing to public information or reflecting public opinion.

As for Arabia in general and the Yemen in particular, little was published, and most of what did appear was lost in obscurity in spite of the value of Playfair's history of the Yemen or Wellsted's volumes. From the time of Neibuhr until the 1860's when Burton and Palgrave published their travels, the only books which caused any popular interest were the works of John Lewis Burckhardt, NOTES ON THE BEDOUINS AND WAHABYS (London, Colburn and Bentley, 1831, 2 vols.) and TRAVELS IN ARABIA (London, Colburn, 1829, 2 vols.). Even in the latter part of the century the public had little interest in the Arabian peninsula. Burton's PERSONAL NARRATIVE OF A PILGRIMAGE TO EL MEDINA AND MECCA was a popular work, as was Palgrave's TRAVELS IN EASTERN ARABIA, but C. M. Doughty's volumes, ARABIA DESERTA, of much greater value historically and as literature, vanished into obscurity only to be rescued by the attention focused on it by T. E. Lawrence in THE SEVEN PILLARS OF WISDOM. The British public in particular and Europe in general was just not interested in Arabia. Publishing houses and magazine and newspaper editors are in business primarily to make money, and their success is closely related to their ability to give the public what it is interested in. The serious editor or publisher has the power to lead public opinion to

a certain extent, but that power is very limited unless either
human interest or national interest is present in the new subject
to a marked degree.   There was good reason for the public
apathy towards the territory on the eastern shore of the Red Sea.
Economically the Red Sea was, until the opening of the Suez
Canal, entirely removed from Europe.   After the opening of the
canal it was merely a highway and to the traveler a very unpleasant highway, in fact a hell hole to which the heat of the Indian
Ocean provided in contrast the feeling of coolness and refresh-
ment.   Diplomatically it was of such strategic and religious importance that it was better to let the weak Ottoman Empire occupy it than to allow any outside Christian power to expand its influence there.   And perhaps most important of all, it was almost
entirely Muslim.   This fact served to prevent any missionary
activity in the peninsula outside of Aden, for it must be remembered that while the Turkish Empire tolerated missionaries,
their activities were confined to non-Muslims.   If they should
turn their attention to the Muslim population, they were quickly
and effectively removed.   To the missionary-minded British
public, therefore, Arabia was of no interest, and to the com-
mercially-minded portion of the population, the port of Aden
controlled a large share of the only valuable trade of the peninsula.   Modern public interest in Arabia originated in the exploits of one man, T. E. Lawrence, but in spite of this unreliable
and romantic figure, public interest lies far behind the growing
political and economic importance of the area.

     The situation on the western shore of the Red Sea was far
different.   If Arabia existed in the mind of the Englishman as a
definite geographic area nicely defined on the map by its surrounding waters, Abyssinia was an unknown spot, sort of south
of Egypt.   But it was reputedly Christian and therefore must be
an island of civilization surrounded by a sea of Muslim and
heathens.   Furthermore, it was located in the continent of Africa which seemed to have an appalling fascination for the nineteenth century western European.   Added to this the Portuguese
in the fifteenth century had ascribed the Prester John legend to
Abyssinia, although the best efforts of modern scholars seem
to indicate that this tradition originated from some Nestorian
Christian kingdom in central Asia.   As previously mentioned,
the variety of products coming from Central Africa over the
trade route via Harar to the coast gave entirely too favorable
an impression of the riches of Abyssinia.   Taken all in all,

Abyssinia presented all the elements necessary to intrigue the European mind of the nineteenth century: first, it was Christian; second, it was in Africa; third, it had a legendary tradition; fourth, it offered possibilities for profitable trade; and fifth, it was unknown. It is not surprising then that first England, then Italy, and then France and then Italy again should have become involved at considerable expense and effort in an area which even at the present day has yet to return any profit to anyone on the investments made therein.

If an Englishman in 1840 entered a library to find out something of the nature of the Yemen, he would have found only two or three authors available to him, Neibuhr, Burckhardt, and possibly Wellsted. If, however, he desired to be informed on Abyssinia he would find, besides the translations from the Jesuits such as Dr. Johnson's translation of Father Lobo or Ludolphus' history of Ethiopia based on the Jesuit fathers, the works of Bruce, Valentia, Salt, Pearce in English, the new French book by Combes and Tamisier, and Rüppel's REISE IN ABYSSINIEN in German.

At the time the Indian Government was preparing the Harris expedition to Shoa, the Frenchman Rochet d'Hericourt was already in that country, and two Englishmen, Charles Tileston Beke and Charles Johnston were planning to make independent journeys into Abyssinia. Two young Frenchmen traveling under British passports, the d'Abbadie brothers, also entered into this field of exploration. The reasons that attracted all these men to Shoa are explained in Chapter VII. Out of these various expeditions came the first public controversy on Abyssinia and also the beginning of the rivalries which became so bitter in the 1860's.

Major Harris was the first of these explorers to break into print in England. His expedition had begun with considerable publicity and his negotiation of a trade treaty with the King of Shoa had become widely known. Therefore his HIGHLANDS OF ETHIOPIA was an anticlimax when it appeared, for Harris glossed over the complete failure of his expedition in a meaningless flow of words which contributed little new information either to the story of the expedition or to the knowledge of the country. The book was received very unfavorably. The review in the Edinburgh Review of July, 1844, is of considerable importance as it stresses for the first time in modern times the old wives' tale that the Nile could be diverted and Egypt starved.

At almost the same time Charles Johnston publiched his TRAV-
ELS IN SOUTHERN ABYSSINIA (London, Madden, 1844, 2 vols.),
attacking the Harris expedition and pointing out its complete
failure. Beke also published a pamphlet entitled "A Statement
of facts relative to the Transactions between the writer and the
late British Political Mission to the Court of Shoa in Abessinia"
which attacked the expedition and especially Harris' leadership.

In view of Beke's character, which has been amply described elsewhere, it would be easy to say that he was motivated in this case merely by jealousy and that Johnston suffered
from the same complaint. However, this was not true. Harris'
leadership was thoroughly incompetent and his handling of the
Abyssinians was almost fatal to his expedition. Both Beke and
Johnston had pulled him out of some pretty serious difficulties
and both had loaned him money when his supply of Maria Theresa thalers had run out. At the time of the publication of Harris'
book, they were having a hard time trying to collect their just
debts from the Indian Government due to Harris' obstinate refusal to admit that he had had to ask for their aid.

But all three men had over-emphasized one fact, the influence of the French in Shoa. The controversy therefore had
three results, all of which had a bearing on later events: first,
an exaggeration of French influence throughout Abyssinia, a
theme which Beke continued to harp on; second, popularization
of the old wives' tale by Beke that the Nile could be diverted
and Egypt starved; and third, a great increase in Beke's antagonism to Palmerston in particular and the Liberal party in general, which had started in the 1830's when Beke was in Germany.
To the public, Beke became one of the leading authorities on
Abyssinia. His reputation was increased by his lengthy controversy with the brothers d'Abbadie whose explorations proved
Beke's theories false. Beke, however, was English and the
d'Abbadies were French, so it is not hard to see which one of
the disputants would be backed by the British public.

After this controversy, events in Abyssinia were not of a
nature to attract public notice for a considerable period of time.
Meanwhile two books appeared which were chiefly of interest to
missionary circles, Bishop Samuel Gobat's journal, and the
journals of the missionaries William Isenberg and J. L. Krapf.
In France, Rochet's FIRST VOYAGE was published in 1841,
his SECOND VOYAGE in 1846, Ferret and Galinier's VOYAGE
EN ABYSSINIE in 1847-1848 and Lefebvre's VOYAGE EN

ABYSSINIE in 1845-1854. The 1850's added little more; Mansfield Parkyns LIFE IN ABYSSINIA was the chief contribution.
However, most of these above mentioned volumes related to
Tigré and Gondar rather than Shoa where feuds among the Dankali tribesmen had closed off all access to the province. This
fact resulted in probably the most popular work of the period,
although it does not bear on Abyssinia proper. This was Burton's FIRST FOOTSTEPS IN EAST AFRICA, an account of his
exploratory trip of the route to Shoa via Harar, a route which
avoided the unpleasant Dankali country.

It was unfortunate that the Foreign Office had never adopted
the policy of the Bombay Government, the publication of dispatches of geographical importance, for in Plowden, the Consul
at Massawa, it had by far the ablest of all the explorers and observers in Abyssinia. The publication of his general reports
might well have changed public opinion in the 1860's.

The Englishman of the early 1860's then had available to
him a considerable literature on Abyssinia from which he could
gain a fairly good idea of the country. His interest was heightened by Central African explorations, the slave trade, and the
attempts to establish mission stations throughout Africa. But
above all, Abyssinia was forced on his attention by French ex-
pansionist activity in that direction in the period following the
Crimean War. Beke, then living in Mauritius, put himself
forward again as an authority on Abyssinia in letters to the
Times and published a pamphlet entitled "Letters on the Commerce & Politics of Abyssinia addressed to the Foreign Office
and Board of Trade." His rather brazen attempts first to get
the backing of the Bombay Government in a grandiose trading
scheme and then to get the Foreign Office to appoint him instead
of Cameron as consul to Abyssinia resulted in failure and
served to add to his hatred of the government.

By 1863, public attention was drawn to the area by a pro-
spectus issued for a contemplated "Egyptian Commercial &
Trading Co." to be backed by £20,000,000 capital, its purpose
being to develop cotton in the Sudan to replace the source of
supply cut off by the American Civil War. This company was
to be underwritten by the international bankers of Europe and
included such familiar names as Fruhling and Goschen of London, Oppenheim Neveu & Cie of Alexandria and others later
notorious for their part in the bankruptcy of Egypt. Reports of
the discovery of coal in the area, later proved groundless, were

also prevalent. Thus commercial interest was beginning to supplement the previous attention drawn to Abyssinia by the romantic attractions of the Christian legend of Prester John, the ro-
mance of unknown Africa, and the possibilities of missionary
activity.

The first reports of trouble at Theodore's court reached
London in February, 1864. In March the Foreign Office received the first confirmation of the imprisonment of Mr. Stern
which had occurred in October, 1863. By the end of April, 1864,
this information had become public property but created no very
great stir as it was still largely based on rumor. As the year
wore on further information was published, but the Rassam mission seemed to promise an end to the question and the government did not come under attack. However, Rassam's prolonged
stay in Massawa plus added information coming out of Abyssinia
began to turn public attention to the captives. The government,
following a policy outlined by Mr. Haussmann, refused to release any accurate information for fear that unfavorable opinion
might reach Theodore and thus react on the captives. That this
policy was wise at the beginning of the Rassam mission seems
rather obvious but as time wore on and it seemed that Rassam
would fail, rumors multiplied. With what was leaking out
through Egyptian and continental sources, it seems incredible
that Layard and Lord Russell were such inept politicians as to
persist in this secrecy, for in doing so they were simply pushing the whole matter into politics. Missionary circles were
naturally the first to become aroused, and on December 1,
1864, Christian Work published a letter from J. L. Krapf
calling for more drastic measures.

In India the Bombay Gazette of January 3, 1865, attacked
the government policy violently and gave credence to the rumor
that Theodore wished to marry Victoria, ending with the following statement: "At any rate it is clear that no good end can be
gained by the further stay of Mr. Rassam and his colleagues at
Massawa; where they are not in a position to employ either
force or persuasion" (1/3/65 in FO 1/15). The rumored desire
of Theodore to marry Victoria was picked up by the English
papers, and formed part of the fiction which surrounded the
whole Abyssinian affair.

One of the London papers, the Pall Mall Gazette, was
strongly conservative, and therefore anti-government. Some-
how, through a leak either in Alexandria or in the Foreign Office,

it obtained a copy of a dispatch which Colquhoun had sent on
February 12, enclosing an interview with a Coptic priest just
returned from Abyssinia. The priest reported that Theodore
wished to be assured England should ask no reparations if the
prisoners were freed. The interview, thus of considerable importance, was summarized in the Pall Mall Gazette of February 23, 1865, among "Occasional Notes," a column which appeared daily. The Foreign Office, adhering to their policy of
secrecy, wrote a strongly worded letter to Colquhoun to discover where the leak had occurred and apparently tried to put
pressure on the Pall Mall Gazette to suppress such information
(FO 1/16, FO-Colquhoun 2/27/65).

     A year later, in reporting the news of the release of the
captives on April 7, 1866 (this was the report which was issued
by the Foreign Office when Rassam's mission appeared to be
complete, before the captives and Rassam's party were sent to
Magdala), the Pall Mall Gazette claimed that it had originated
the whole agitation on behalf of the captives. Assuming this
claim to be correct, and there is no evidence to disprove it,
the editors of this paper worked quietly behind the parliamentary
scene until on March 30, 1865, they published a long leading
article beginning, "It is somewhat strange that the long captivity
of several of our countrymen in Abyssinia had hitherto created
so little public interest, and it is therefore satisfactory to learn
that the subject is at length to be brought under the notice of
Parliament" (3/30/65). The article then gave an accurate summary of the history of the incident obviously prepared from information supplied by someone who had access to the official
files, and concluded by taxing the government for its failure to
answer Theodore's letter.

     The Pall Mall Gazette had brought up a perfect issue. It
was a superb human interest story. It had universal appeal:
the civilized Englishmen held captive by the arrogant Emperor
and missionaries being abused by a native prince in a far-off
romanticized land with no apparent means of rescue. In addition, it served the political leanings of the paper; it made a
political issue against the Liberal government. As the story
developed it also brought up subsidiary issues relating to secrecy, freedom of the press, etc. It was a "natural," and besides
serving humanitarian and political purposes, it incidentally increased the circulation of the Pall Mall Gazette, the ultimate
object of all newspapers.

Public interest, of course, should be reflected in Parliament. The first mention of the captives was made in Commons
on June 3, 1864, and was answered by Layard with the statement that the government was doing all it could. The question
had attracted no attention at that time but the Pall Mall Gazette's
publicity stirred Parliament again. On April 24, 1865, Layard
was again questioned in Commons and refused to give any information, as such information might injure the captives if and
when Theodore heard about it. Three days later Lord Chelmesford, president of the Jewish Society, questioned Lord Russell
in the House of Lords. Lord Russell stated that the government was doing all that it could do under the circumstances and
concluded by requesting that the House not ask for the papers
"because a great deal of the information in the possession of the
Government came from persons who would be exposed to danger
if it were published" (London Times, 4/17/65).

The Pall Mall Gazette attacked both these statements and
deplored the sending of an "Asiatic Gentleman" like Rassam to
try to get the release of the captives. The Gazette followed this
by an article on May 10 quoting from the Literary Christian of
March 25 attacking the action of the Basle missionaries (the
artisans who were in Theodore's favor). This article also included the rumor of Theodore's offer to marry Victoria as a
contributing factor to the situation. This brought a violent
denial from Mr. Badger, of Aden fame, which was published a
couple of days later. No other papers apparently had joined the
campaign as yet, but the pressure was growing.

On May 23, 1865, in the House of Lords, Lord Chelmesford
moved for the placing of the papers in the case before Parliament (i. e. , the preparation of a Blue Book on the case). After
a heated debate with Earl Russell the question was put. Then
ensued a long and undignified wrangle on rules and the right of
certain members to vote. (Apparently procedures common to
all parliamentary bodies were used; corridors were searched
for all members to come in to vote; the government, rightly
fearful of losing the question, endeavored to prevent the vote by
working all the parliamentary rules, including an appeal from
the ruling of the chair, a classic delaying tactic.) Finally Lord
Chelmesford's motion was carried by a vote of forty-three to
forty-two. The Gazette in a leading article praised the vote as
removing the secrecy from the whole matter but the Times, taking cognizance of the question for the first time in a leading

article, sarcastically attacked the wrangle over rules, supported
Russell's policy, and accused Cameron of being wholly to blame
for his predicament by leaving his post at Massawa and going
to the interior.

After the debate in the House of Lords, Russell instructed
the Foreign Office to prepare the presentation of the letters regarding the imprisonment of the captives. These papers were
thoroughly censored and contained only those which supported
the government's contention that Cameron had violated his orders: (1) the instructions to Cameron; (2) Cameron's letter regarding Theodore's proposed embassy to England and the reply
of the Foreign Office; (3) Theodore's letter; (4) Cameron's report on Bogos; (5) the orders to Cameron to return to Massawa;
(6) the date of the answer by the Queen to Theodore's letter but
not the letter; (7) a list of presents to be sent to Theodore; and
(8) all offers of assistance which had been made to the Foreign
Office (FO 1/15. Order for the Presentation to Parliament of
letters and papers relating to the Imprisonment of British Subjects, 5/23/65). That such a collection of papers would throw
little light on the question and would arouse controversy should
have been obvious to anyone, but the Foreign Office was so imbued with the idea of secrecy and so fearful of the distortion of
information which might reach Theodore that they persisted in
following this course.

But before these papers were made public, Layard, who
was not a very able politician or a very tactful man, in a debate
in Commons on June 8 accused the Pall Mall Gazette, with the
connivance of certain officials of the Foreign Office, of publishing confidential material. The Gazette naturally defended itself,
for it was completely innocent of such a charge, as Layard admitted on June 30. The Gazette and the Foreign Office got the
information from the same source in Egypt. The net result of
such an argument led, as always occurs in discussions of freedom of the press, to an increase in public interest in the question.

The Blue Book appeared about June 20, 1865, and was immediately criticized by opposition papers for its almost complete lack of information. The Gazette pointed out the offers of
assistance and the refusal of the Foreign Office to employ some
of the Englishmen who volunteered in the place of Rassam (PMG
6/21/65). On June 30 a debate in Commons ensued on the subject of the papers. The debate was long and acrimonious, and
Layard's refusal to back up his charges with specific information

did not help his case. The papers naturally followed the party lines, the Gazette attacking the government and the Times supporting it. This debate was followed by one in the House of Lords on July 4 in which Earl Russell, although defending himself more ably and tactfully than Layard, emerged the loser. However, these arguments accomplished nothing as Parliament was about to adjourn for the summer.

The Gazette's attitude has already been made clear. The story had human and political interest, was a proper occasion for moral indignation, and had distinct possibilities of increasing circulation. The question remains why the government acted as it did. As in the case of the Gazette, motives were mixed. There was a real feeling on the part of Foreign Office officials that secrecy was necessary to ensure any success for Rassam's mission. They knew that Theodore's dislike of Stern's and Rosenthal's criticism of him was partly responsible for their imprisonment. They also knew that through certain Frenchmen he was in touch with what appeared in the European press. This fact was well-shown the next year when Theodore could discuss intelligently with Rassam the tactics of the armies in the American Civil War. The policy of secrecy was probably justified, but it was never ably defended in public debate. Their other motives were less praiseworthy. The accusation against Cameron was completely unjustified, especially as Murray and Herstlet in the Foreign Office had carefully checked the documents and reported to Earl Russell on April 1 that he had not violated his instructions, and that the direction to him to return to Massawa had not been received by him until conditions made it impossible for him to obey (FO 1/15, Minute by Murray & Hertslet 4/1/65). However, Cameron made a good political scapegoat who was not present to defend himself, to cover up the inexcusable failure to reply to Theodore's letter; and Russell and Layard were politicians — with a general election pending in 1866, they had to think of votes. They were therefore interested in covering up the errors of the government, to avoid any opening for the opposition. The attacks on Rassam's mission and his ability caused Layard to see red, as Rassam was his personal protégé, and his emotions did not help him to maintain composure in debate. Thus in 1865 the Abyssinian captives had become a hot political issue.

A study of the magazines of the 1860's provides an interesting commentary on magazine publishing of the period. Today

our magazines provide a great deal of background material for
contemporary news, and often they supply interpretations and
commentaries of considerable value. In the 1860's this sort of
material was completely lacking and comment on the captives
and their plight was limited among the magazines to the Illustrated London News, primarily a news magazine, and articles
in certain missionary journals, which were professionally interested in the problem. In fact, the only magazine articles on
the whole Abyssinian question were written after the campaign
of 1868 and consisted of eyewitness accounts. It would seem
that British magazine editors of this period did not consider
themselves molders of public opinion.

The events which followed the closing of Parliament in
1865 served to quiet the controversy. The false report of the
release of the prisoners in September, followed by Rassam's
movements into the interior, calmed public opinion. By absence
of criticism the public appeared to endorse the government policy. The Foreign Office continued to be secretive. The absurd
Rassam-Palgrave-Beke mix-up did not reach the public until it
was too late to be news, but the Foreign Office did release the
essence of Rassam's dispatches reporting his progress. Beke's
abortive expedition was thoroughly covered in the Times by the
publication of his own letters by his agent Julius Reuter (letter
in the Times 3/29/66 by Reuter calling attention to a misinter-
pretation of one of Beke's letters). The only reflection of the
question in Parliament occurred in February, 1866, when Lord
Chelmesford in the House of Lords on February 5 questioned
Lord Clarendon on the problem and put in his usual attack on
Rassam as not being an "English gentleman. "

The Pall Mall Gazette did not let the matter drop, however,
and besides releasing virtually the same news items as the
Times provided some interesting commentary. An article on
September 11, 1865, pointed out the wide variation in interpretation of the affair by the papers, especially regarding Cameron,
who was accused by the Times of getting into trouble by following his orders too closely, while the Telegraph believed his
fault lay in not obeying his orders to the letter. The cause for
this confusion was the fragmentary manner in which the Parliamentary Blue Book was prepared. None of Cameron's replies
was included so that the dates on which he received his instructions could not be determined.

News from Rassam that the captives had been released was

received in April, 1866. The Times offered no editorial comment although it ran this news as a special bulletin next to its
leading articles. The Gazette, however, printed on April 7 a
leading article commenting on the good news and ending up with
an editorial pat on its own back by laying the success of the mission to "the beneficial operation of a watchful press on languid
and perverse officials" (PMG 4/7/66, leading article).

The next outburst in Parliament occurred in August, 1866,
when Stanley, now Foreign Minister, was questioned in Commons regarding Flaad's presence in England. However, other
events, the Reform Bill, the German-Austrian War, etc., had
so seized the public imagination that the question of the captives
had become of minor political importance. The captives were
still news, all information about them was published as news
items, but the Pall Mall Gazette alone kept needling the government for action.

In early 1867, the feud between Beke and the Foreign Office
officials which started with the refusal of the Foreign Office to
sanction his trip to Abyssinia in 1866 broke into public print.
Rassam, as mentioned, was the personal protégé of Henry Layard, who, as Parliamentary Undersecretary for Foreign Affairs
in the Palmerston and Russell cabinets, had been in charge of
the whole Abyssinian question for the Foreign Office. Layard
was not tactful nor was he one to take any attack lying down.
Beke was, of course, a vindictive and egotistical man who at
times seems to have been unbalanced in his egotism. Apparently
private discussion of the failure of the Rassam mission had resulted in the opinion that Beke's interference was largely responsible for the plight of the captives, who by this time had
been moved to Magdala. Since the time of Beke's accusations
against Palgrave in September, 1865, the Foreign Office had
considered him persona non grata and had not bothered to answer his numerous and often unbalanced letters. Beke had been
carrying on two other controversies, one through the Journal
of the Royal Geographical Society with the d'Abbadie brothers
on purely geographical questions, chiefly regarding the sources
of the Nile, thus giving Beke an opportunity to air his opinion
that the Nile could be diverted, the other through the Athenaeum
magazine where he was expounding on Abyssinian politics against
several opponents. This was not really a controversy, since
the opposition was very light, but it served to encourage Beke
to expound his theories on the failure of British policy against

the French in the Red Sea area. The files of the Foreign Office indicate that Beke was willing at any time to have an audience for a controversy with Layard, but apparently he had been unable to get anyone to print his effusions.

The winter and spring of 1867 had produced little news from Abyssinia except routine reports on the health of the captives. The Pall Mall Gazette had little to help its campaign. On February 19, a long summary of the Rassam mission was published, but brought little new information except a defense of the Conservative government's policy. This, in retrospect, is rather amusing, as they were doing very little that was different from the preceding Liberal government which had initiated the Rassam expedition. In the course of this article several slurring remarks were made concerning Beke's part in the failure of the expedition. Beke hastened to reply on February 26, and he included very uncomplimentary remarks regarding Layard. The controversy was on. It served a very useful purpose as it kept the Abyssinian question before the readers of the Gazette during a period of almost no news.

The situation changed with the news in May of the failure of Flaad to get any agreement with Theodore. It was rapidly becoming apparent that force would have to be used. In April the Foreign Office had begun communications with the War Office suggesting such a possibility (FO 1/19, FO-WO 4/20/67) but nothing had appeared in print except for a general comment on the subject from Lord Stanley.

In June the Pall Mall Gazette took up the battle again. The timing of this whole incident raises a serious question of historical interpretation. What did the British newspaper editors in the nineteenth century consider was the function of "letters to the editor"? Was not this section of the paper even then used by the editors as an instrument to form public opinion even to the extent of "planting" anonymous letters to help any controversy along? The evidence speaks for itself. On June 11, the Gazette carried a letter from Sir Henry Bulwer, former British Ambassador to the Sublime Porte, at this time retired and living in France, urging the use of force to release the captives. A letter from such a distinguished Englishman carried considerable weight. Was it really happenstance that it was written at this time or, as seems more probable, was his opinion privately requested by the editor of the Gazette? The Foreign Office files show that this letter focused their attention more closely

on the question of using force (FO 1/19, Memo, Murray to Stanley 6/20/67), and resulted in another request to the War Office
for more detailed plans to be made for a possible expedition
(FO 1/19, FO-WO 6/24/67).

The Gazette used this letter as the basis for an extremely
well-planned and well-timed campaign to bring the issue to a
head. A flood of anonymous letters followed it. On June 15 a
letter signed "Common Sense" disagreed with Bulwer. Three
days later, June 18, one "Anglo Indian" backed "Common
Sense." The next day, the nineteenth, "Indicus" took Bulwer's
side to be replied to by "Common Sense" on the twentieth. On
June 26 a long article was published entitled the "History of
the Abyssinian Difficulty" in which the Gazette took credit for
starting the move to help the captives. The next day two letters
appeared in favor of a military expedition and on June 28 the
Gazette published a leading article urging the use of a relief
expedition as well as a letter attacking Theodore. The timing
was too perfect to be wholly fortuitous and the use of so many
anonymous letters can only make one suspicious that they were
inspired. The campaign served its purpose; it aroused public
opinion in favor of an expedition. In August the cabinet decided
on the expedition, the Gazette having laid the groundwork of
publicity.

On examining the evidence, one can only conclude that the
whole campaign of the Gazette at this time was deliberately
planned, unquestionably with the full approval of certain elements
in the Conservative party. Its purpose was obvious, as shown
by later events. The cabinet decision in August to send an expedition was not publicly announced, but news of it leaked out
and the Gazette published several leading articles in September
in favor of the cabinet's decision. The official announcement
came in November when Parliament was called into special
session for the purpose, among other things, of appropriating
money to finance the expedition. An article in the Gazette of
November 27 summarized the attitude of the other London papers. The Post, the Telegraph, and Standard supported the
government and the expedition; the Times, Star, and News opposed it. The opposition was not well-supported. When debate
on the appropriation opened in Commons, attacks were made
on the government for not informing Parliament of its decision
to undertake the expedition. This opposition was feeble, however, and the appropriations were carried by a heavy majority
in both houses.

From then on the expedition was public property. Every paper had war correspondents; every armchair strategist in England, and there were lots of them, had an audience. From November, 1867, until the announcement of its successful conclusion on April 27, 1868, "The Expedition" dominated the news. The Times brought out a special "Victory Edition" on April 27, and the next day, at the conclusion of its long leading articles on the campaign, summed up the high moral attitude of the whole undertaking (which had perhaps represented the greatest influence of Victorian morality on foreign policy) in these words: "It has been, in short, a modern Crusade, but a Crusade sullied by no incidents of which England need be ashamed, and not stultified by the foundation of a mock kingdom of Jerusalem, only to be maintained by fresh expeditions" (London Times, leading article 4/28/68).

XX. THE EXPEDITION AND THE DEATH OF THEODORE

While the decision to send a military force to rescue the prisoners relieved the Foreign Office of much of its responsibility, there still remained a great deal of political work to be done. All details for the expedition were turned over to the India Office which had complete charge of the preparation of the military force. The campaign was to be based at Bombay and conducted by troops of the Indian Army. It is 2,065 nautical miles by sea from Bombay to Massawa and 960 miles from Suez to that port. Nothing can emphasize more completely the revolutionary character of the Suez Canal than the fact that the contemplated expedition had to be sent from a base 10,000 miles by sea from England and 2,000 miles from the objective of the expedition. In 1867 Abyssinia was one of the remote places on the earth; two years later, with the opening of the Suez Canal, it lay next to one of the greatest of the world's trade routes. Under these circumstances all decisions except those of general policy had to be made in India, and all responsibility had to rest there.

Even before the cabinet's final determination to use force, the India Office had informed the Foreign Office that orders had been sent to India to send officers to the Red Sea to make a thorough inquiry into routes into Abyssinia (FO 1/20, IO-FO 7/27/67). By August 13, 1867, the day of the cabinet's decision, the India Office reported that officers had been dispatched to the Red Sea and that the expedition could proceed by January if sufficient mules for transport could be obtained (FO 1/20, IO-FO 8/13/67). On being informed that the cabinet had decided to use force, the India Office instructed Bombay that a peremptory demand would be made on Theodore backed up by an expedition under the leadership of Lieutenant General Sir Robert Napier with Brigadier Sir Charles Stavely as second-in-command. Funds for the expedition were to be advanced from the revenues of India but were to be repaid by the Treasury (FO 1/20, IO-Bombay 8/16/67).

Lord Stanley, the Foreign Minister, informed Merewether that the whole question had been handed over to the India Office (FO 1/20, Stanley-Merewether 8/19/67). Reade, Acting Consul General at Alexandria in Stanton's absence, was instructed to request permission from the Khedive to have the expedition pass through Egyptian territory and to allow the use of Massawa, if necessary, assuring his highness that Britain had no designs of conquest (FO 1/20, FO-Reade [Alexandria] 8/19/67). Barron, chargé d'affaires at Constantinople, was requested to ask the cooperation of the Porte in furthering the progress of the proposed expedition (FO 1/20, FO-Barron [Constantinople] 8/22/67), and permission to use the overland route for transmission dispatches from Suez to Baghdad and thence to Bombay via the Persian Gulf if necessary. At the same time, Alison in Teheran was instructed to ask the assistance of the Persian Government in the use of the overland telegraph route through Persia (FO 1/20, FO-Alison [Teheran] 8/22/67).

The War Office requested the assistance of the consuls in the Mediterranean area in the purchase of mules for the expedition, which were to be collected at Alexandria, shipped overland to Suez, and thence by sea to the port of debarkation (FO 1/20, WO-FO 8/27/67, 8/29/67 and 9/2/67). There is a great deal on mules and other transport beasts in the Abyssinian files of the Foreign Office, some of which might be of interest to a military historian. These purchases did lead to a minor diplomatic crisis with Spain where efforts were made to hire muleteers. The Spanish Government, overly suspicious, believed that Britain was trying to recruit soldiers in Spain. However, this misunderstanding was soon straightened out (FO 1/20, West [Madrid]-FO 9/27/67 and 10/17/67).

Consul Reade reported from Alexandria that the Viceroy had given permission for British forces to pass through Egyptian territory and had dispatched officers to Massawa to aid the expedition in every way. The Viceroy also placed all Egyptian war vessels in the Red Sea at the disposition of the British in case of need (FO 1/21, cable, Reade-FO 9/2/67). The Consul had been requested to find out how far construction had proceeded on the proposed Cairo-Suakin telegraph line and to ascertain if the English Government could finish the line (FO 1/29, FO-Reade tel. 8/29/67). Reade replied that the line had proceeded only as far as Wadi Halfa and that twelve months' construction lay ahead (FO 1/20, Reade-FO tel. 8/21/67). Permission was granted the British Government to continue the construction, previously delayed because of the destruction of the wooden poles by termites (FO 1/21, Reade-FO 8/21/67). There is no evidence that this plan was followed up. Inquiries as to the use of other telegraph facilities in Asia Minor were made but none of the lines was found reliable.

Permission for the use of the eastern shore of the Red Sea in case of necessity was obtained from the Sharif of Mecca with the consent of the Porte (FO 1/21, Reade-FO 9/3/67). Ismail, on his return to his capital from Constantinople, offered to send an envoy to Theodore, at the same time requesting information as to what would happen if the captives were released (FO 1/22, cable-Reade-FO 10/7/67). This offer was accepted by the British Government and Reade was instructed to tell his highness that the government would not relax its preparation but "if the prisoners are released no further steps would be taken against the king" (FO 1/22, cable-FO-Reade 10/10/67 and letter same date). The Khedive forwarded a letter to Theodore by a Coptic priest. It was a very able letter, giving Theodore excellent advice and composed in very good French verse (FO 1/23, Reade-FO 10/25/67). Its transmission was stopped at the request of the India Office as it was felt that the impression that Egypt and England were acting in concert would greatly confuse the issue within Abyssinia (FO 1/23, IO-FO 12/31/67).

Certain other details fell to the Foreign Office, the most important of which was money for the use of the expedition in Abyssinia. The only coin recognized in the area was the Maria Theresa thaler dated 1780. Coinage of this was stopped in 1858 by the coinage convention between Austria and the German states and the supply was exhausted. However, arrangements were made to have the imperial mint in Vienna coin a supply with the British Government supplying the silver (FO 1/21, Valentine [Venice]-FO 8/29/67 and Bloomfield [Vienna]-FO 9/1/67).

As news of the expedition became known, there was pressure from all sides for permission to go with the military force. Volunteers were easily discouraged, but requests from foreign governments for observers were something else again. Finally, the Foreign Office had to send a message to all the foreign ambassadors and ministers at London informing them that because of the nature of the expedition, the rough country, and the lack of transport it would be impossible to grant the usual courtesies to foreign officers, and consequently other nations would have to be limited to one observer or at the most, two, from each country (FO 1/22, Message fo Foreign Ministers in London 10/19/67). The Prussian Embassy requested permission for the German scientist Gerhard Rohlfs to accompany the expedition

(FO 1/23, Bernstorff-FO 11/12/67). This communication was passed on to the India Office with the advice that the request be refused, but the India Office apparently decided to let him go along (FO 1/23-FO-IO 11/22/67). It was unfortunate, as he caused some later complications by looting Theodore's crown from the King's treasure room at Magdala. In 1872 the British had considerable difficulty in reclaiming the crown from the Berlin Museum so that it could be returned to its proper owner, the Emperor of Abyssinia.

The India Office, preparing the expedition, wrote the Foreign Office on September 9 requesting that formal intimation be sent to Theodore that all further proceedings would be in the hands of Sir Robert Napier (FO 1/21, IO-FO 9/9/67). To this the Foreign Office replied that it was preparing a letter to Theodore demanding the release of the captives and advising him that this demand was being backed up by Sir Robert Napier and a military force (FO 1/21, FO-IO 9/9/67).

Five days later the India Office requested formal instructions for the commanding general. Sir Stafford Northcote wished principally for definite political instructions as to Napier's actions in event the prisoners were not released. He felt that the military force was large enough so that any military operations would be of short duration and the country could be quickly evacuated. He suggested that Napier be instructed to proclaim the object of the expedition at the earliest opportunity "to indicate the dignity of the British Govt. by procuring the release of Mr. Rassam and his suite, and of Consul Cameron.... and also; 1. The free egress from Abyssinia of all other Europeans who may be detained by King Theodore... against their will together with, 2. The satisfaction for the insult offered to the British nation in the persons of H. M. Consul.... It should also be made generally known that H. M. Govt. would greatly deprecate any necessity for a British Force remaining in Abyssinia" (FO 1/21, IO-FO 9/13/67).

Hammond felt that there were several problems involved. First, assuming the release of Rassam and Cameron, should operations continue in order to release first their fellow prisoners of whatever nationality, second those Europeans who had been voluntarily in Theodore's service and only recently met his displeasure (Steiger, Brandeis, etc.), and third, what should be considered as satisfaction for these insults. He believed any proclamation should state that no injury was intended to the

people of Abyssinia, that everyone helping the British would be
protected and none molested except those who "attempt to im-
pede the army by arrows, removal of cattle & subsistence or
afford information, aid or support to a hostile force." To this
is added in another hand "It may be well to add that the king will
be held responsible for any further injury to the captives."
Hammond starred the word "responsible" and noted, "What does
this mean? Is Theodore to be hanged if he puts the Captives or
any of them to death and is he to be tried or executed without
trial? And is the murder of any captive of whatever nationality
to be a ground for execution?" (FO 1/21, Notes by Hammond
and other on IO-FO 9/13/67).

By September 19, the Foreign Office had prepared instructions for Napier, to be followed insofar as possible under the
conditions he might face. He was informed that the first object
of the expedition was the release of Rassam, Cameron, and
their suites. In addition there were two other classes of Europeans with whom he had to deal: other captives of whatever
nationality, called by the Foreign Office the second class; and
artisans in the employ of Theodore who had been imprisoned,
called the third class. As the government was not insisting on
pecuniary or territorial compensation all efforts should be made
to release the second class. The release of the first class was
"one of international right," the release of the second class
"can only be pressed on grounds of general humanity." Only in
event that the release of the second class would cause a prolonged occupation of Abyssinia should Napier desist. The third
class had no claim on Her Majesty's government, as none of
these prisoners was of British nationality and there was no evidence that any foreign nation had asked the British to intercede
for their nationals. However, they should be given a chance
for escape; "a general demand for the release of all Europeans
including citizens of the United States if there be any who desire
to leave the country should be made but not pushed."

Upon his arrival on the coast, Napier was instructed by the
Foreign Office to forward a prepared ultimatum to Theodore
(see below). If this was rejected and the King continued to mis-
treat his prisoners or should kill them, he was to be held personally responsible if he should fall into the hands of the army.
In any event, he should be taken to Bombay if captured. Napier
was told to take advantage of any assistance and even to encourage it with "pecuniary inducements" but he was "not sent to

overthrow one ruler and set up another in order to extend British territory or increase British influences," and he "must not make future entangling committments. " On the grounds of humanity the government would like to see the people contented and prosperous "but they do not feel it incumbent on them to set up or support any form of government or any particular ruler... in a country in which they have really no particular British interests to promote. " Napier was further advised to give the fullest possible circulation to the information that the British had no intention of occupying any part of Abyssinia and would cause no injury to those who did not oppose the expedition. He was instructed to emphasize that those who helped the expedition would be liberally paid and those who resisted would bring severe retribution upon themselves (FO 1/21, FO-IO 9/19/67).

The ultimatum began by stating that Theodore had disregarded all appeals for release of the captives. It continued, "The Queen can no longer endure such conduct on the part of your Majesty and Her Majesty had therefore given instructions that a military force under the command of Lt. Gen. Sir Robert Napier K. C. B. should without delay enter into your dominions and obtain from you by force a concession which you have hitherto withheld from friendly representations. " After stating that Theodore alone was responsible for the result of his conduct, the letter said "That this course of action is irrevocable determined on and that the only means of preserving your country from war and your own power from overthrow, will be found in the delivery to the Commander of the British invading army of all Europeans in your keeping" (FO 1/21, FO-Theodore 9/19/27). This letter was prepared in quadruplicate and Napier was instructed to send it to Theodore by four separate messengers (FO 1/21, IO-FO 9/20/67, enclosing instructions to Aden).

To anyone who has studied the history of imperialism, the instructions to Napier might indicate that Britain would take the opportunity to extend its influence in this area. However, as shall be seen, these instructions meant exactly what they said, and present a phenomenon unique in the history of European imperialism. A large and expensive expeditionary force had been prepared for the purpose of releasing a few persons from imprisonment, without any demands of any kind for pecuniary or territorial indemnity and with explicit instructions not to extend British territory or increase British influence. It is doubtful that this could have occured at any other time than in the 1860's or have originated in any other minds than those of the mid-Victorian English. Napier's orders expressed the ideals of mid-Victorian morality in its best sense, without the mental reservations so often made and without the opportunism so often present.

The India Office meanwhile was obtaining all possible information on Abyssinia and enlisted the services of Mr. Krapf as chief Amharic interpreter (FO 1/21, IO-FO 9/18/67 and 9/28/67). When Hammond doubted the wisdom of this choice Lord Stanley commented "I suppose there was no one better to be got" (FO 1/21, Minute on IO-FO 9/26/67). They also obtained the services of Mr. Haussman and a Mr. Dufton who had been in Plowden's employ when he was in Abyssinia.

In India preparations were progressing. Merewether at Poonah wrote Murray on September 3, 1867, that he was planning to leave with the advance party on the tenth of that month, to reconnoitre and fix the landing place, probably in Annesley Bay. He informed Murray that the force was to consist of between eleven and twelve thousand men of whom only six thousand would go to the interior due to the very limited transport facilities (FO 1/22 Merewether [Poonah]-Murray 9/3/67). On October 19 the India Office sent to the Foreign Office five dispatches on the military preparations (FO 1/22, IO-FO 10/19/67). Murray noted "These letters show that nothing, apparently, has been left undone to assure the success of the expedition" (FO 1/22, Minute by Murray on IO-FO 10/19/67). The first and most important work was the establishment and marking of a channel from Aden to Massawa. This was not a regular steamship run and while steamers frequently went between these ports, they were either naval vessels assigned to occasional patrols of the Red Sea or regular P. & O. steamers. In either case, their captains were familiar with the treacherous Red Sea waters. H. M. S. "Star" was assigned to the survey work and was aided by four sloops of war in installing temporary buoys and beacons to aid in navigation of these difficult waters. Thirty thousand tons of coal were assembled at Bombay and another 20,000 at Aden, in addition to the normal supplies at those ports. Ten transports averaging 2,200 tons each were assigned to carry troops, and three steamers averaging 2,300 tons were equipped as hospital ships. Every effort was being made to assemble as many mules as possible, not exceeding 7,000, at Suez by the end of November. Arms consisted of 4,000 Snider

rifles, 1,000 carbines, 2,500,000 rounds of ammunition for these
light arms, 12 seven-pounder mountain guns with 500 rounds
for each gun and 300 six-pound war rockets (FO 1/22, Bombay
[Military]-IO 9/3/67). Instructions were issued that these
preparations were not to interfere with regular troop movements
(FO 1/22 Bombay [Military]-IO 9/16/67). Two or three scien-
tists were to go with the expedition and it is interesting to note
that a photographic unit of one non-commissioned officer and
six men from the Royal Engineers was to accompany the expedition (FO 1/22, Bombay [Military]-IO 9/30/67). The first portion of the troops sailed for Annesley Bay on October 16, the
remainder on November 2 (FO 1/22, Bombay [Military]-IO
10/18/67).

In Abyssinia, little happened to alleviate the boredom of the
captives. Theodore's influence was rapidly waning as revolts
became more general. Captain Blanc said in a letter of June 30,
"For our own liberty, for the good name of England for the
safety of the whiteman [sic] in future days, − an army must be
marched into this country and the lost prestige restored" (FO
1/21, Blanc-Merewether 6/30/67). Letters from Rassam describe the rising tide of revolt and the growing strength of two
rebels, Wagshum Gobaze and Menelik of Shoa. The latter wrote
a letter to Queen Victoria in which he requested friendship with
England and apologized for the actions of his grandfather (Sahle
Selassie) in the unfriendly treatment of the Harris expedition in
1843 (FO 1/20, Menelik-Victoria without date, received approximately 7/25/67). A letter of friendship was prepared and forwarded to Merewether on August 19 (FO 1/20, Victoria-Menelik
8/19/67). Merewether forwarded it with some presents purchased originally for Theodore on September 28, but felt
that it would do little good (FO 1/22, Merewether-Stanley
9/28/67).

The captives had little hope that any of the rebels could capture Magdala; the site of the town made it impregnable to Abyssinian arms. Rassam wrote on July 27 that Menelik was planning an attack on the stronghold but put little hope in his success.
He felt that if the captives should fall into Menelik's hands they
would be released, but if Wagshum Gobaze were to "rescue"
them they would simply be held for ransom. He added "I fear
if England does not get us out by force of arms we shall have to
spend many an August in this wretched State" (FO 1/22, Abbott
[Aden]-Stanley 9/11/67, enclosing Rassam-Merewether 7/27/67).

Luckily the prisoners remained in good health.   Magdala had a
decent water supply and its altitude, about 8,000 feet, made it
free from fever.

Merewether arrived at Annesley Bay at the end of September, 1867, with the advance expedition, and began exploring for
a suitable base.   Zula on Annesley Bay was set up as the port
of debarkation, and Senafe was chosen as a base in the highlands.
Senafe lies fifty-two miles southwest of Annesley Bay, with a
gradual ascent to it from the coastal plains.   The advance bri-
gade was encamped there by December 7 and already various
chiefs had appeared asking for friendship (FO 1/23, cable,
Stanton-FO 12/17/67).   Stanton was ordered to Senafe but before
he left for the encampment certain difficulties arose with the
Khedive.

Ismail, apparently with the object of capitalizing on the
prestige of the expedition and possibly for the purpose of territorial acquisitions after its withdrawal, began heavily re-enforcing his troops along the Abyssinian frontier and at Massawa.
This action, combined with the news of his letter to Theodore
(see p. 342), gave rise to rumors in Abyssinia that Egypt was
joining the expedition in concert with the English, thus bringing
into the affair the element of Christian-Muslim rivalry which
the Indian Government was trying to avoid.   It also greatly increased the difficulty of obtaining supplies in the area, since the
two forces were bidding against each other in the open market.
Stanton reported, after an interview on December 1, that Fuad,
Ismail's Minister of Foreign Affairs, was being informed that
England planned to occupy Abyssinia permanently and use it as
a base to occupy Egypt (FO 1/23, Stanton-FO 12/6/67).   Stanton was instructed to inform Fuad that England had no intention
of occupying either Abyssinia or Egypt (FO 1/23, FO-Stanton
2/19/67).   Reade, taking over as Acting Consul General in
Stanton's absence with the expedition, had considerable discussion with His Highness and finally convinced him to withdraw
some of these troops, the number of which, Stanton said after
investigation, was greatly exaggerated (FO 1/23, Stanton-FO
1/16/68).

In accordance with his orders, Sir Robert Napier had issued
the following proclamation on October 26, 1867 (Rassam, op.
cit., Vol. II, p. 255):

It is known to you that Theodore, King of Abyssinia detains in Captivity the British Consul Cameron, the British Envoy Rassam, and many others, in violation of the laws of all civilized nations.

All friendly persuasion having failed to obtain their release, my Sovereign has commended me to lead an army to liberate them.

All who befriend the prisoners, or assist in their liberation shall be well rewarded, but those who may injure them shall be severely punished.

When the time shall arrive for the march of a British Army through your country, bear in mind, people of Abyssinia, that the Queen of England has no unfriendly feeling towards you, and no design against your country or your liberty.

Your religious establishments, your persons, and property shall be carefully protected.

All supplies required for my soldiers shall be paid for; no peaceable inhabitants shall be molested.

The sole object for which the British force has been sent to Abyssinia is the liberation of Her Majesty's servant and others unjustly detained as captives, and as soon as that object is effected it will be withdrawn.

There is no intention to occupy permanently any portion of the Abyssinian territory, or to interfere with the Government of the Country.

R. Napier Lieutenant-General

Commander in Chief, Bombay Army

Theodore, hearing of the proclamation on December 2, began his march from Debra Tabor to Magdala. Rassam states that the King just smiled when he saw the proclamation but did not show it to anyone (Rassam, op. cit., Vol. II, p. 254). On January 4, 1868, direct communications between Magdala and the King were reopened for the first time since the middle of April, 1867. Meanwhile Rassam in Magdala had organized a system of communications to the coast by means of couriers between certain stations, similar to the famous pony express of the American west. This had worked very successfully especially in getting information to the British expeditionary force,

but with the King's approach, it was, of necessity, stopped (ibid.,
Vol. II, pp. 247-48 & FO 1/24, Stanton-FO 12/28/67), to be
replaced by a slower and more uncertain roundabout route. On
January 26, the captives were joined by five more European
prisoners and 108 Abyssinian political prisoners, including
some of the most influential chiefs in the country.

Sir Robert Napier had also prepared and sent an ultimatum
to Theodore demanding the release of the prisoners. Through
friends, the message reached Rassam on February 8. The captives read it and discussed its implications, and on the advice
of Abyssinians decided that it should be destroyed as it would
infuriate Theodore and imperil their lives (ibid., Vol. II, pp.
265-66 & FO 1/24, Rassam-Stanley, 2/11/67). Theodore, approaching Magdala slowly, was again threatened by a revolt,
and all communications with the fortress were cut off from February 18 until March 4.

Stanton reported on January 11 from Senafe that a road had
been finished to Adigrat and that advance units were progressing
to that spot. A supply system was soon organized and was working effectively as far as Adigrat, which became the jumping-off
place for the expedition.

The captives at Magdala were thus between two forces and
it was uncertain which would get there first. By March 18 the
reconnoitering units of the British were at Kosso Amba two
days' journey away, Theodore at Dalanta ten miles away. That
same day Rassam was freed from his chains but remained a
prisoner (ibid., Vol. II, pp. 273-77). Theodore entered the
fortress of Magdala on March 27. By March 30 the British main
force had reached Ashangi, about seventy-five miles away, and
Theodore had begun perfecting his defenses. Rassam was able
to get the remaining captives unchained on April 2. The envoy
took this opportunity to endeavor to get Theodore to open communications with Napier, but the King refused, saying that he
had had the fetters struck off out of courtesy to Rassam, not out
of fear of the British.

By April 9, the British were in sight of Magdala on its high
plateau. That afternoon, Theodore, in an insane rage, slaughtered 197 of his political prisoners, only 35 of whom had committed any crime other than incurring the royal displeasure.
The next day Napier wrote to Theodore asking the release of the
prisoners. Theodore, at the approach of the British advance
guard, attacked them. In a sharp skirmish Theodore's troops

took a sound beating. The King decided that night that he would ask Rassam to reconcile him with the British, sending Flaad and Prideaux with Abyssinians of high rank to the British camp. Napier then wrote to Theodore (Rassam, op. cit. , Vol. II, pp. 319-20):

> Your Majesty has fought like a brave man, and has been overcome by the superior power of the British Army.
> It is my desire that no more blood may be shed. If, therefore, your Majesty will submit to the Queen of England, and bring all the Europeans now in your Majesty's hands and deliver them safely, this day, in the British Camp, I guarantee honourable treatment for yourself, and all the members of your Majesty's family.

Theodore, in a conciliatory mood when he initiated these negotiations, flew into a rage on the receipt of this letter and replied by an angry and rather incoherent dispatch. However, by four that afternoon Theodore ordered the prisoners to go to the British camp together with the artisans. Rassam had some bad moments when Theodore ordered him to a final interview; Theodore, however, was quite calm. The captives reached the British camp where they were cordially received.

Then ensued one of the strangest episodes of the entire campaign. On Easter Sunday, April 12, Theodore sent Napier a letter apologizing for his previous letter and stating that he had tried to commit suicide as a result of his defeat. He added his willingness to release all the Europeans including the artisans, who had not all gone to the British camp, but requested that artisans be left in Abyssinia "as I am a lover of the mechanical arts" (ibid. , Vol. II, pp. 326-27). He also offered a present of sheep and cows, in Abyssinia an offer of peace and friendship. Rassam had the letter translated for Napier and then specifically asked the Commander in Chief for his reply to the offer of cattle. Rassam states that Napier said "I accept them" (ibid. , Vol. II, pp. 326-27). Late that afternoon all the remaining Europeans, their families and possessions, and all the property of the released captives, were sent to the British camp.

Theodore immediately dispatched all his cattle, 1,000 cows and 500 sheep, to the British camp, believing peace had been made, but the British refused them. Theodore then prepared his defenses and retired with as many followers as would go with

him from his camp on the plateau below the fortress into the
fortress itself. The soldiers who refused to go up immediately
surrendered to the British. As Theodore was preparing his
final defenses he saw some British cavalry nearby. The King
and twelve others rushed the cavalry, but after one of his men
was wounded, retired to the fortress. The first British artillery fire and rockets on the morning of the thirteenth caused
most of the defenders to surrender. With five men Theodore
opened fire on the storming party. Two of his men were killed,
and Theodore retired alone to the second gate of the citadel
where he drew a pistol and shot himself. The fortress was captured at four-thirty in the afternoon of April 13.

There is no satisfactory explanation of this incident. Napier's acceptance of Theodore's offer of cattle had certainly
led the King to believe that his offer of peace had been accepted.
Rassam does not state that he explained the full meaning of the
offer of cattle to Napier although he assumes that Napier realized its significance. It is probable that Napier was not fully
aware of its significance, and after accepting the cattle had
realized that he would have to take Theodore to Bombay which
would have been a violation of this peace offer. Two years
later he stated that he couldn't remember the incident distinctly
and said that he thought acceptance of sheep or cattle accompanying the letter simply meant that the letter was accepted.
Merewether did not believe that Napier accepted the gift but just
nodded his head, and that only when the cattle arrived had Napier understood the significance of the gesture. Merewether
then goes into an elaborate and rather ingenious explanation
which whitewashes both Rassam and Napier but does not make
sense (FO 1/29, IO-FO 4/3/69 encl. Napier-Bombay 2/11/69,
and Rassam-IO 3/27/69). Rassam in reply repeated the statement in his book and report, and produced evidence from Munzinger to back him up. A great deal of discussion of Theodore's
suicide ensued later in London. Regardless of the apparent bad
faith shown by Napier, which was certainly not intentional on
his part, Theodore would probably have committed suicide anyhow. At Rassam's last interview on April 11 with the King he
had said to Rassam "I want you to bear this in mind — that unless you befriend me, I shall either kill myself or become a
monk" (Rassam, op. cit. , Vol. II, pp. 323-24). Theodore certainly had no idea that if he came to terms he would be made a
prisoner himself, although Napier had been ordered to take him

to Bombay. In Napier's letter of April 11, he stated "I guarantee honourable treatment for yourself and all members of your
family" and Rassam commented on the occasion when the captives were preparing to go to the British camp, "Had the idea
ever occurred to him [Theodore] that he would be required to
surrender himself a prisoner, he would assuredly have had us
cut to pieces rather than give us up" (ibid. , Vol. II, p. 321).
If Napier had accepted his cattle and then made Theodore a
prisoner as he was ordered, Theodore would undoubtedly have
killed himself and then the British commander would have been
really open to a charge of bad faith.

   After the fall of the fortress, it was cleared of the Abyssinian captives as rapidly as possible and the remainder of the
garrison was ordered off the rock. On April 17 the fortress
was destroyed by the British. Theodore was buried in a family
vault near Ababa and the native prisoners and the garrison sent
to their homes. Napier decided to take Prince 'Alamayo, Theodore's only legitimate son according to Abyssinian canon law,
to England. Rassam escorted him to Zula on Annesley Bay and
then began his homeward trip with the rest of the former captives, except for Cameron who was too sick to travel. The captives reached Britain on June 22, 1868, five years after some
of them had been imprisoned.

   News of the fall of Magdala reached England on April 25
(EO 1/25, cable, Stanton-FO 4/25/68). On receiving the news,
Hammond telegraphed it to the Queen and the Prince of Wales
and released it to the papers (FO 1/25, Minute by Hammond on
cable, Stanton-FO 4/25/68).

   The military aspects of the expedition are very well cov-
ered by the official history (Markham, C. R. , HISTORY OF
THE ABYSSINIAN EXPEDITION, London, Macmillan, 1869),
the volumes by Major T. J. Holland and Captain H. M. Hozier
(RECORD OF THE EXPEDITION TO ABYSSINIA, London, H. M.
Stationery Office, 1870, 3 vols.) and Captain Hozier's work
THE BRITISH EXPEDITION TO ABYSSINIA (London, Macmillan,
1869). It was popularized in a volume by G. A. Henty entitled
THE MARCH TO MAGDALA.

   Militarily speaking the expedition is of interest only from
the viewpoint of logistics. The transportation and maintenance
of between five and six thousand men for a campaign which was
conducted about 250 miles from the advance base in Adigrat, in
wild, rough, and almost roadless country, was remarkable

considering the primitive means of transportation available.
For both the British and the Abyssinians the campaign was virtually bloodless. It can probably be best summed up in a remark of Cameron, formerly an Indian Army officer, in a letter
to Hertslet of December 19, 1867: "The expedition will be a
monster picnic party for the Indian Army" (FO 1/23, Cameron-
Hertslet, 12/19/67).

The expedition did make complications, however, in an unforeseen manner. The European nations, particularly France,
and the Italian states were fearful of the spread of eastern dis-
eases, especially cholera, into their port cities. Strict quarantine regulations had been established by various nations in
the Mediterranean. While control was fairly easy to maintain
at Suez during most of the year, the annual pilgrimage to Mecca
with its gathering of pilgrims from all over the Muslim world
from Morocco to the Philippines and from the Cape of Good
Hope to Mongolia was a period of continual worry. The movement of large numbers of troops from India, where cholera was
endemic, to the Red Sea, where it was fairly well suppressed,
was an additional danger, coming as it did at the time of the
annual pilgrimage. On February 4, Stanton reported from
Senafe that cholera had broken out on a transport coming from
Bengal to Annesley Bay. Efforts were made to stop the ship at
Aden, since an outbreak of cholera in the Red Sea would cut off
direct communications with England due to the quarantine regulations (FO 1/24, Stanton-FO tel. 2/4/68).

The rumors of these two incidents caused the French Ambassador to London, de la Tour d'Auvergne, to file a formal
protest with the Foreign Office against having the sick and
wounded evacuated via Suez during the pilgrimage season (FO
1/25, de la Tour d'Auvergne-FO 3/19/68). The India Office,
to whom the matter was referred, told the Foreign Office that
all quarantine regulations would be observed for any men in-
valided home via Suez (FO 1/25, IO-FO 3/26/68). Stanton, now
back at Alexandria, reported that the French and Italian members of the Sanitary Board in Egypt were trying to obstruct the
expedition in every way by insisting on a five-day quarantine
(FO 1/25, Stanton-FO 4/18/68). Stanton was very probably un-
fair in imputing political motives to these men. The countries
which they represented, with their large Mediterranean trade,
had good and sufficient reasons to insist on such a quarantine
without having to include any political considerations. The

Foreign Office, however, instructed Lyons in Paris and Paget in Florence to protest the actions of the representatives of these respective governments on the quarantine regulations (FO 1/26, FO-Lyons [Paris] 5/2/68 and FO-Paget [Florence] 5/8/68). The Italian Government readily acceded to this request (FO 1/26, Paget-FO 5/19/68) but the French Government refused until more information was available (FO 1/26, Lyons-FO 5/14/68). Stanton solved the whole problem by arranging for sealed quarantine trains from quay to quay so that the returning troops could come directly home (FO 1/26 Stanton 5/22/68).

The Foreign Office files on Abyssinia and the blue books on the same subject are filled with letters offering aid, making suggestions for releasing the captives or dealing with minor diplomatic matters caused by the expedition. Most of these make amusing reading but are of little interest to the historian. Those concerning the Beke-Layard-Rassam argument belong properly in a discussion of public opinion in relation to the whole problem of the captives. One small incident of a diplomatic nature is of interest to the historian for the light it throws on English-Prussian relations two years before the outbreak of the Franco-Prussian war. Colonel Walker, British military attaché at Berlin, requested the Foreign Office for fuller information on the expedition as it would help him to get more military information in Prussia (FO 1/24, Col. Walker [Berlin]-FO 1/4/68). This was passed on to the War Office with the recommendation that fuller information would produce a "good effect" in Prussia especially regarding "military improvements emanating from England" (FO 1/24, FO-WO 1/13/68).

The tangled web of 200 years of chaotic Abyssinian politics produced one European claimant to the throne of Abyssinia, a Mr. Henry Bridgetower, living in Rome. He claimed descent from the rightful heir to the Abyssinian throne through his mother's family. His ancestor, he said, had come from Abyssinia in the middle of the eighteenth century and had been a favorite of George III. He wrote to Lord Stanley after the expedition had been announced, requesting to be proclaimed Emperor of Abyssinia (FO 1/21, Henry Bridgetower [Rome]-Stanley, 9/13/67). One could easily dismiss this man as another crackpot or adventurer but he gave unimpeachable references, and a quick check by the Foreign Office led them to believe his story was legitimate. He was therefore informed that the British had no interest in interfering with the succession of the throne in Abyssinia (FO 1/21, Stanley-Bridgetower 9/18/67).

356   CHAPTER XX

While the Foreign Office thought that everyone involved had
been safely rescued from Abyssinia, it received rather a shock
when Elliot, then Ambassador at the Porte, on May 2, 1868,
requested information regarding Bishop Saliah and the other
Armenian ecclesiastics who had gone to Abyssinia in April,
1867, with a letter from the Armenian Patriarch (FO 1/26, Elliot-FO 5/2/68). Munzinger in Massawa was put on the trail
and in November reported through Stanton that they were at
Wagshum Gobaze's camp in Gondar and were completely without
funds (FO 1/26, Stanton-FO 11/5/68). The question of what to
do about these poor emissaries was turned over to the India Office, which replied on February 27, 1869, that they had no idea
how to release the Armenians and had no funds to send them
(FO 1/29, IO-FO 2/27/69). What happened to them no one
knows.

Rassam and his companions reached London on June 22,
1868, Napier and his staff about two weeks later. Thus the expedition ended. The captives were freed and British prestige
was restored. But the Abyssinian affair was far from closed.
In true English fashion, the whole question of the captives and
the conduct of the expedition was rehashed in the newspapers
until the opening of the Franco-Prussian war.

XXI. ADEN AND ARABIA 1863-1867

Early in 1863 Brigadier Coghlan returned to England and
was replaced by Colonel William Merewether. Aden was again
fortunate in having another very able man appointed as Resident.
The new Resident was a different type of man from either of his
predecessors. Haines had been a genius at dealing with the
Arabs and by necessity had had to do all his administrative work
personally. Coghlan, while not Haines' equal in intelligence,
showed a different type of ability in surrounding himself with
very able advisers, synthesizing and using their advice with
remarkable success. In their dispatches both these men reveal
themselves as definite and sometimes unorthodox characters.
Their successor was a considerably more orthodox person. He
came to the position as a much younger man, and his work can
be characterized by its remarkable intelligence and energy.
It is unfortunate that his later career in the India Office was
terminated by his early death, for he was a man of great ability,
without the often unorthodox characteristics of brilliance that
made an Englishman great in the East and made him distrusted
in the conservative atmosphere of London.

Merewether found Aden and its environs quiet. While none
of the tribal feuds was settled, at least for the time being an
uneasy balance of power existed. In February, 1864, he paid
a state visit to Lahej which was peaceful and friendly. Merewether's chief accomplishment was to induce the old Sultan to
grow more vegetables and potatoes, both essential to the growing port of Aden. On the same trip he was able to make headway in straightening out the conflicting claims to Little Aden
which were holding up the purchase of that peninsula. He reported persistent rumors that the French were still trying to
negotiate for the purchase of that land as well as Ras 'Umeira
farther west (IO-LAM, Merewether-London 2/18/64). Heavy
rains in February, 1864, filled Aden's reservoirs and relieved
the continual anxiety over the water supply for the next six
months (IO-LAM, Merewether-Bombay 3/11/64). In June,
Merewether visited Mukalla and Shihr to deliver copies of the
slave trade treaty arranged by Coghlan and signed by the Viceroy of India on June 29, 1863. He found Mukalla greatly damaged by a cyclone in May which had sunk at least 150 ships on

its course from Socotra to the Arabian coast. He was unable to
land at Shihr because of rough weather (IO-LAM, Merewether-
London 6/17/64).

In August, 1864, a plague of locusts destroyed the grain
crop in the hinterland of Aden. While no immediate danger of
a serious shortage was present, the loss of the crop served to
destroy the uneasy peace between the tribes, with consequent
raids on supplies approaching Aden (IO-LAM, Merewether-London 8/18/64, 9/18/64, 9/26/64). The Resident, anticipating a
shortage, investigated the possibility of importing grain from
the Yemen or the Hedjaz but found that famine conditions there
were as dangerous as around Aden. The Somali coast offered
no assistance as no grain was grown there for export (IO-LAM,
Merewether-London, 10/6/64).

In November, 1864, the Sultan of Lahej requested an interview with the Resident. He presented two problems: first, the
hostile attacks of the old Fadhli Sultan, Ahmed ibn Abd Allah,
who was now over ninety years old; and second, the suffering
of the people of Lahej from the continued lack of grain. Formerly the Abdali had been the most powerful tribe near Aden,
but in recent years the old Fadhli Sultan had strengthened his
position by achieving a much better discipline among his followers than that which existed among the Abdali. Further, the
Abdali were weakened by the loss of their grain crop and an epidemic which had greatly reduced their herds of cattle. To
counteract this new power of the Fadhli, the Sultan of Lahej
suggested an alliance with the 'Aulaqi tribe to attack the Fadhli
if necessary. Merewether agreed to this and pointed out that
the Lahej Sultan's country could be rich if internal unity and
peace would allow the proper development of agriculture. The
alliance of the two tribes temporarily restored the balance of
power, and heavy rains in the interior somewhat alleviated the
grain shortage by helping other crops (IO-LAM, Merewether-
London 11/17/64, 12/3/64).

The Fadhli continued to cause some disturbances, but active hostilities did not break out. However, Merewether's
actions were disapproved by Bombay in a letter of January 5,
1865, as the government was opposed to aiding one tribe in attacking another. This statement of policy was certainly new,
although Merewether had brought it on himself. Haines and
Coghlan had often followed the same tactics as the new Resident,
in fact that was the only way they had kept the peace, but

Merewether was too frank about his motives in his reports. The Resident stated in reply that he had no intention of meddling except to preserve the peace. He went on to explain fully the situation, and complained that he was tired of treating Ahmed ibn Abdullah in a "liberal manner." He reviewed the old Sultan's lengthy and imposing list of crimes and insults to the British and to the other tribes. He further pointed out that the increase in the size of Aden had made the question of daily supplies of greater and greater importance and that Aden could ill afford to have the roads closed even for a couple of days. He again beseeched the Bombay Government to allow the establishment of an Aden troop of horse which had been authorized in 1855 and then after its organization diverted to the Persian War. The camel corps organized in its stead had proved a failure, as the Indian cameleers were no match for the Arabs. He asked for permission to organize a troop of 100 irregular cavalry with a small Arab auxiliary which could protect adequately the roads near Aden (IO-LAM, Merewether-London, encl. Bombay-Aden 1/4/65 and Merewether-Bombay 1/28/65).

The roads were disturbed occasionally during the next six months, but a patrol of Abdali subsidized indirectly by the British maintained relative quiet. A sharp skirmish in April, 1865, resulted in a defeat for the Fadhli at the hands of the Abdali.

However, a much more serious difficulty soon arose. In the interior, already half-starved for lack of grain, a serious epidemic of cholera broke out. This resulted in the abandonment of the patrols and allowed the Fadhli Sultan a free hand again. He thereupon plundered two buggalows, one of which was from India. Merewether's hands were completely tied. His only available ship was being used to carry communications to the Rassam mission in Abyssinia and he had no cavalry to make a rapid raid into Fadhli territory. His requests for grain from India were also unanswered. It was obvious that if peace were not restored and established so that agriculture could be revived on a permanent basis, Aden would be forced to draw on India for much of her supplies (IO-LAM, Merewether-London 6/17/65).

In the reply to the report of Merewether was enclosed a letter from the government of India to the Bombay Government rejecting Merewether's appeal for irregular cavalry as it would be likely to embroil the British in reprisals if its patrols should kill any tribesmen. It also contained a severe rebuke to

Merewether and disavowed his policy of inciting one tribe against another (IO-LAM, Merewether-London 6/17/65 encl. Govt. of India [Simla]-Bombay Govt. 5/5/65). Merewether, unabashed by this rebuff, asked that the whole problem be reconsidered, pointing out how the cost of a troop of irregular horse would save money, as the cost of rations alone for the garrison had risen almost one hundred per cent since May, 1860, due to the unsettled state of the local agriculture. Local misrule had resulted in imports from the hinterland being limited almost entirely to wood and fodder. He felt that such a troop would be able to keep the peace in an area 100 miles around, and backed his statement by a private letter from Brigadier Coghlan. Merewether concluded by asking that the Indian Government place confidence in him not to misuse such a force (IO-LAM, Merewether-Bombay 6/24/65).

The cholera epidemic spread to the Fadhli country, enforcing a temporary peace, but Aden was now facing a water shortage. The Resident recommended that an aqueduct be built from the springs at Sheikh 'Othman four miles away to give a more dependable water supply, and to save money by stopping the expense of having the water carried to the city by camels and donkeys (IO-LAM, Merewether-London 7/2/65). The grain situation worsened as a new plague of locusts destroyed the young crop. However, the Bombay Government had refused his earlier request for grain as it was against, in principle, distributing grain free to the population, an idea which Merewether pointed out he had never considered. Three Aden merchants were willing to underwrite the venture, take all risks, and sell the grain at cost to the needy. They had further expressed their intention to turn over any profit which might be made to the Famine Relief Fund. Aden, Merewether said, was completely stripped of grain except for the garrison, and supplies of rice, jowaree and wheat were essential. In order to keep the poor from being completely destitute Merewether was employing them on public works projects. Conditions in the Yemen and the Hedjaz were even worse, and at Hodeida and other ports the Turks had been forced to place guards at all provision ships to prevent rioting (IO-LAM, Merewether-London 7/17/65, 8/1/65). Conditions remained serious during August, although the cholera epidemic had run its course. Not until September 5, 1865, did the first shipload of grain arrive from India, almost a year after the Resident had warned that a famine was imminent and five months after he had reported that the situation was acute. Aden was still the poor relation of the Bombay Government.

The passing of the cholera epidemic and the relief of the famine started the old Fadhli chief on new depredations. He attacked a kafila half a mile inside British ground on the isthmus and committed another act of piracy on a buggalow. Merewether's patience was exhausted. He stated that the policy of paying chiefs to keep the peace was a failure, after twenty-six years, and that a show of force was absolutely necessary. The Resident suggested that Ahmed ibn Abdullah's capital at 'Asala, forty miles away, be seized and held for ransom (IO-LAM, Merewether-Bombay 9/18/65). However, the Bombay Government in reply to his earlier request for a reconsideration of the problem, stated that the Viceroy of India still refused to allow the establishment of a troop of cavalry but suggested that the Sultan of Lahej be supplied with some funds to keep up the patrol of the roads. Merewether replied that he thought this policy would also fail but said he would try it (IO-LAM, Bombay-Merewether, 8/21/65, Merewether-Bombay 10/17/65).

The Sultan of Lahej agreed to this plan but was very dubious of its success. In November, 1865, the Fadhli were reported collecting for a raid which was made on December 11 on a kafila at Sheikh 'Othman. After this raid they were preparing to attack the Abdali country in order to destroy the crops there, an event which would have been a serious blow to Aden as well as to the Abdali. Merewether, disregarding instructions from Bombay, decided to act on his own, and called on Brigadier General Raines, the commandant, to prepare an expedition. On December 20, 1865, a British force moved to cut the Fadhli off from Abdali country. This force, consisting of four hundred men and four howitzers, caught the Fadhli completely by surprise at the small village of Bir Said. The fight lasted five hours and resulted in the complete rout of the Arabs. Merewether planned to follow this up with a march on 'Asala and Shuqra, backed up by H. M. S. "Victoria" then stationed at Aden. He concluded by hoping that the Bombay Government would approve this course (IO-LAM, Merewether-Bombay 12/18/65, 12/21/65).

The British force was increased to over 500 men and was joined by Sultan Fadhl of the Abdali and about 1,500 men. The march began on December 26. By the twenty-ninth the expedition

had caught up with part of the Fadhli force and a light skirmish
ensued. Then Merewether awaited the decision of the old Sultan to surrender (IO-LAM, Merewether-Bombay 12/31/65).
No surrender came and on January 2 'Asala was occupied. The
fortifications of the town were destroyed as were those at Alk-
hore, a neighboring village, and the force returned to Jowala,
receiving the submission of some of the Fadhli. Jowala, which
properly belonged to the Yafa tribe, was returned to them.
The "Victoria" found Shuqra abandoned and the plundered buggalows unseaworthy. Merewether decided that the Fadhli had
had enough punishment and the expedition returned to Aden on
January 9, 1866 (IO-LAM, Merewether-Bombay 1/9/66).

It must have given the Resident considerable amusement
to receive, shortly after this expedition, a letter from Bombay
enclosing a dispatch from the India Office to Aden instructing
him to blockade the Fadhli ports until a final decision should
be reached regarding what action ought to be taken, but still refusing a troop of cavalry, adding that the question would be reconsidered if the Bombay Government insisted. The policy of
non-interference with the tribes was reiterated and insisted
upon and again the suggestion of a camel corps was raised (IO-
LAM, Bombay-Merewether encl. Govt. of India-Bombay
12/9/65).

Merewether replied that the insolent attitude of the Fadhli
allowed no delay and Aden could not risk another famine. He
stated that the policy of non-interference could not be followed
if Aden were to live. As for the Fadhli chief, he was "simply
a highway robber and should be treated as such by us." He reported that the Fadhli tribe was torn with dissension as a result
of the expedition (IO-LAM, Merewether-Bombay 1/16/66).
This tribe continued to argue among themselves on the question
of getting back into favor with the British. Merewether met
their tentative peace feelers by insisting on his original terms:
surrender, reparations, and a hostage. The part of the tribe
still loyal to Ahmed ibn Abdullah began to stir up the countryside again and committed another act of piracy at Shuqra. On
March 15, Merewether landed four hundred men and two guns
at that port, recovered the buggalow, and destroyed the town,
the only casualties being two bullocks who could not be induced
to get back on the ship (IO-LAM, Merewether-Bombay 3/17/66,
and FO 78/3186. Stanton-FO 3/26/66).

This action resulted in the secession of the Yafa tribe under

their leader, Abdullah ibn Nasir, from their alliance with the
Fadhli, this tribe now allying itself with the Abdali. Ahmed ibn
Abdullah continued his intrigues and in September, 1866, sent
a messenger to Achmet Pasha, the Turkish governor at Hodeida, offering his allegiance to Turkey in return for aid against
the British. Goodfellow, Acting Resident in Merewether's absence in England, countered by sending an envoy to the Pasha,
giving him full information on the matter (IO-LAM, Goodfellow-
Bombay 10/2/66).

Merewether, returning to Aden from England in December,
found that the campaign against the Fadhli had had very beneficial results as the Abdali were cultivating their abandoned
fields and the prospects for a big crop were excellent. He also
found that the aqueduct from Sheikh 'Othman was nearing completion, which was a relief to the settlement as no rain had
fallen at Aden in nineteen months (IO-LAM, Merewether-Bombay 12/27/66). The old Fadhli chief was stubborn, but in May
of 1867 finally gave in. He agreed to maintain peace and friendship with the British, to protect all merchants and travelers,
and to have one of his sons or a blood relative reside in Aden
to do the business of his tribe. On May 28 peace between the
British and the Fadhli Sultan was finally proclaimed. The old
Sultan, life-long enemy of the British, stuck to his terms and
for the remainder of his life was loyal to Aden. He died in 1870
at the reputed age of nearly one hundred (IO-LAM, Russell-
Bombay 2/11/70).

That French interest in Zeila had been revived was evident
when Merewether was informed in October, 1864, that mail had
arrived addressed to M. Monge, French Consul at Zeila. This
gentleman arrived within a week and proceeded in a French
schooner loaded with arms and powder to Zeila to trade with the
natives (IO-LAM, Merewether-Bombay 10/3/64, 10/19/64).
A French transport, "L'Orne," arrived at Aden in November
and nearly caused an international crisis when some of the officers, out to do the town, started a riot in the red light district,
ending only when two of them were locked up in jail. An investigation was made and apologies were soon forthcoming from
both the police and the French (FO 78/3186, IO-FO 1/10/65,
1/26/65). The incident is of importance only as an indication of
the continued tense rivalry between France and England in the
area. The French frigate, "Junon," arrived at Aden in January, 1865, after visiting Obock and Zeila with very good reports

of both places (FO 78/3186, IO-FO 1/26/65). The French
steamer, "Surcouf," appeared about this time and remained
stationed in the area for about a year. It proceeded to Zeila in
February, picked up M. Monge and investigated a reported coal
deposit between Obock and Tajura on land belonging to the chief
of Raheita. It then returned to Zeila and its commander demanded $20,000 indemnity for the death of M. Lambert in 1859.
Abu Bakr, the governor, said he had paid yearly installments
to Ali Pasha, governor of the Yemen, who was his superior.
The "Surcouf" then proceeded to Hodeida where Ali Pasha stated
that he had no orders to give the French any money and that all
moneys from Zeila were part of the government revenue. While
the "Surcouf" was at Hodeida, Achmet Pasha replaced Ali as
governor and continued to deny any indemnity to the French
(IO-LAM, Merewether-Bombay 2/18/65).

Merewether, taking no chances, sent H. M. S. "Pantaloon"
to investigate Obock. Its commander took a very different view
of this port from the French and said that it was virtually
worthless as a harbor or as a place for a settlement. He found
Tajura a poor anchorage for large vessels. The natives at
Obock, however, reported that the Turks had informed them
that Obock had been purchased by the French, giving some indication that the purchase had official Turkish approval (IO-
LAM, Merewether-Bombay 3/22/65). Later trips to Obock by
the "Surcouf" rather discouraged the French officers who reported the summer heat unbearable even off shore. However,
in August a colonel of the French engineers arrived to inspect
the site for possible fortifications (IO-LAM, Merewether-Bombay 8/31/65). On his return the "Surcouf" remained in the
Aden area until February, 1866, when she returned to Ile de
France. No further French moves in the area were apparent
until the opening of the Suez Canal put an entirely different aspect on the whole Red Sea.

In the Yemen and Arabia little happened except for the continued desultory warfare between the Turkish establishments
on the coast and the Asiri. A gathering of a tribal group to attack Hodeida was dispersed by an outbreak of smallpox, but
when the Turks tried to take advantage of this epidemic to seize
one of the Asiri strongholds at Jayn, they suffered a severe defeat (IO-LAM, Merewether-Bombay 1/1/64, 3/11/64). The replacement of Ali Pasha by Achmet Pasha in February, 1865, as

governor of the Yemen made little difference there, but the
famine and the cholera epidemic which spread through the Yemen enforced an uneasy peace. Not until early in 1867 was this
peace broken, when the Asiri again attacked the Turks, with the
usual result — the Turks were driven from the country areas
into the towns which the Asiri were unable to enter except by
treachery (FO 78/3186 Stanton-FO 5/2/67). Turkish misrule
and chaotic conditions inside the country had reduced the once
rich Yemen to a land which was barely capable of supporting itself. Thanks to Turkish intrigue and the weaknesses of the
Imam himself, the Imamate had become merely an empty title,
and no government except that of a tribal nature existed in the
interior. Certain of the tribes bordering on the Aden hinterland continued to be prosperous, as they could export their products through Aden and thus avoid the tariffs, arbitrary levys,
and bribes necessary to trade through the Turkish-controlled
ports of Hodeida, Loheia and Mocha. In the 1850's, the Porte
had provided an army large enough at least to make an effort to
conquer and hold the country. They had succeeded in being able
to capture more or less what they wished, but had shown themselves not strong enough to hold their conquests. In the 1860's
they were able to occupy the ports and nothing more. The reasons for this are not hard to find. They lie imbedded in the
method of government followed by the Porte in Arabia as well
as in other outlying provinces so well described by Captain
Haines in his dispatch of June 13, 1849. (See pp. 149-50.)

    When the Porte took over the Yemen from Muhammad Ali
in 1840, the country was relatively prosperous, although still
depressed in comparison with its prosperity in the seventeenth
century. Its coffee monopoly had been broken effectively by the
plantations in the Dutch East Indies and in the West Indies, but
the office of governor was still a profitable one to hold; the income of the Pashalik yielded enough revenue to maintain a good-
sized army and still fill the governor's pocket. It was therefore easy to get native Arabs to act as governors. Having a
good-sized army, and wishing to increase their revenues further, the governors set out to conquer the cities on the chief
trade routes and gain for themselves the revenues of these towns.
They had no difficulty in conquering almost any place they wished
but they did not have enough strength to maintain garrisons able
to cope with the natural independence of the Arab and the

religious antagonism incurred by the Sunnite Turks trying to
rule the Zaidi Yemeni. The prosperity of the country gradually
declined with the collapse of the Imamate of San'a and the return
to tribal rule in the interior; each tribe now exacted a transport
duty on goods which passed through its territory. By 1848 it
had become no longer profitable for native Arabs to rule the
territory since costs were higher than income; as a result Pashas were assigned from Constantinople. Declining revenues
caused by chaotic inland conditions resulted in cutting the costs
of administration by cutting the size of the army, and thus a
vicious circle of lowered revenues and less stable government
was begun. The influence of the free port at Aden had some
bearing on this situation. While it certainly made no difference
to Hodeida and Loheia, it did greatly affect the port of Mocha
which was the outlet for the southern Yemen. The routes to
Mocha were easier than those to Aden, but misgovernment
forced the traders and the coffee caravans to make the more difficult overland journey. By the 1860's the Yemen had reached
its lowest state of depression. When the crop failures of 1864
and 1865 and the cholera epidemic of the latter year spread over
the country, the Yemen was no longer the Arabia Felix of former years.

The Somali coast was little better off. Tribal rivalries
had reduced the great Berbera fair to a shadow of its former
self. The countryside still provided meat for Aden, but its other trade had disappeared. The coast, however, was now safe
for shipwrecked sailors, and the tribes on the eastern end of the
coast near Cape Guardafui remained loyal to the British.

Coal was reported existing both near Tajura and near Sheikh
Said on the Arabian coast. Samples from both places were obtained and forwarded to England. Merewether, in forwarding
the samples from the Dankali country behind Tajura, called it
"material supposed to be coal" (IO-LAM, Merewether-London
2/29/64) and the sample from Arabia was still worse. Such reports created considerable interest in London but no steps were
taken to further the investigations after the samples were seen.
The Viceroy of Egypt did, however, send an expedition early in
1866 to investigate, but this group was discouraged by Merewether's report on the samples and returned to Egypt (IO-LAM,
Merewether-Bombay 1/17/66).

The area for which the government of Aden was responsible
was never defined on paper, but it covered roughly the so-called

Gulf of Aden and ran from the Kuria Muria Islands off the South
Arabian coast to Socotra off Cape Guardafui. The two ports of
the Hadramaut, Mukalla and Shihr were thus under the watchful
eye of the Resident. In November, 1865, Goodfellow, Acting
Resident at Aden, reported that Shihr had been captured on
October 21 by the Sultan of the Ka'aiti (a branch of the Yafa
tribe), Ghalib ibn Mahsin al-Qashri (IO-LA, Goodfellow-Bombay 11/2/65). Aside from the potential value of these two ports
to a foreign power for use as a base, this territory was mixed
up in Indian politics, as the Nizam of Hyderabad employed the
Hadrami as his personal guards. As a result, high officials in
the Nizam's court had considerable interests in the area. Actually the rightful ruler of Shihr was the chief of the Kathiri, in
the employ of the Nizam (FO-LA, Merewether-Bombay 12/27/
65). The troubled state of affairs continued in this area for a
long time and was later seized on by the Turks as a pretext for
interference and expansion. The feud between the two tribes
arose from the repudiation of a debt by the Kathiri Sultan. It
persisted until the 1930's when the British intervened to bring
peace.

Of course Aden was the key to all communications with
Abyssinia and considerable time and effort were spent on the
Abyssinian problem by Merewether, not only because of governmental reasons, but because of his personal relationships with
the members of the Rassam mission, all of whom were officials
at Aden.

The period from 1863 through 1866 marked the lowest point
in the decline of the Red Sea area. The only trade in the area
which prospered was the slave trade, driven north by British
efforts at suppression in the Zanzibar area, and flourishing because of the inability of the British to reach a satisfactory treaty
with the Ottoman Empire on its suppression. British prestige
was at its lowest, but there was no other European country to
challenge it. Aside from Ottoman misgovernment, the chief
factors in this situation were, first, a complete lack of interest
in imperial problems throughout Europe and, second, the American Civil War. The first of these factors will be discussed elsewhere, the second deserves comment here.

Proper trade figures for Aden are extremely difficult to
find and are unreliable; they do not differentiate between imports necessary for the maintenance of the garrison, the P. & O.
coaling station, and other facilities of a port of call, and those

which were due to trade alone. We have the figures for 1857-
1859, and these show that trade with the United States was considerable, in fact a large enough factor to make the difference
between the prosperity of Aden and depression, as in 1859 they
amounted to about eight per cent of Aden's exports. We have
no figures for the 1860's but in THE EXPLOITATION OF EAST
AFRICA Reginald Coupland gives the figures for Zanzibar in
this period. As Zanzibar is part of the same economic area,
these figures can be taken as an indication of the effect of the
Civil War on Aden. In 1859, thirty-five American ships called
at Zanzibar; in 1866 only five called at that port (Coupland, R.,
THE EXPLOITATION OF EAST AFRICA 1856-1890, London,
Faber & Faber, 1939, pp. 77-8). The loss of this trade was entirely due to the Civil War and certainly added its influence to
the decline of the Red Sea area.

    In January, 1867, British prestige had all but vanished.
Aden, while now a large city, was ill-prepared to combat the
outside influences which were bound to appear when the Suez
Canal was finished. It was only through fate, which delivered
a few missionaries and a tactless consul into the clutches of a
capricious and disillusioned Abyssinian monarch, that Aden
was prepared to meet the challenge of the opening of the Suez
Canal. It is incredible but true that after the occupation of
Perim in 1857 there is absolutely no mention of the canal project in any of the documents bearing on Aden, Abyssinia, or any
other place in the Red Sea. It seems impossible to believe that
the Indian Government did not consider the military and economic implications of this project, but if they did, they never
confided the results of their deliberations to any officials in
the area.

XXII. ADEN 1866-1869

In April, 1866, Rassam and his party were imprisoned,
and Flaad was sent by Theodore on his mission to England.
Flaad returned to Massawa in November and forwarded Victoria's letter to the King. Merewether, returning from leave in
England in December, went to Massawa to facilitate communications with the captives. By the spring of 1867 all of Aden's
energies were concentrated on the Abyssinian affair. The decision of August 17, 1867, to send an expedition to Abyssinia
served to change the whole aspect of the settlement. Aden,
serving as an advance base for the shipment of supplies to the
expedition, proved for the first time in the eyes of the Indian
Government its unique military and naval value, which was to
be gradually enhanced with the opening of the Suez Canal.

As the canal neared completion, only three countries gave
any indication of understanding its great imperial importance.
Two of them, Egypt and the Ottoman Empire, the powers most
immediately affected by the canal, began to make preparations
for expansion. The third power, Italy, at first merely toyed
with the idea.

The claims of the Ottoman Empire to the Red Sea area were
based on the conquests of Selim I, in 1517, which were perpetu-
ated in the titles of the Sultan. Thus the Porte laid claim to
both shores of the Red Sea, Abyssinia, and all of Arabia. These
claims had been disregarded throughout the years by both the
Foreign Office and the India Board, later the India Office. The
apparent though unstated British policy throughout the period
from 1825 to 1870 was to avoid, if possible, bringing up the
question of sovereignty. The Ottoman Empire, therefore, had
a weak de jure claim to sovereignty of the area to Bab-el-Mandeb and Zeila. However, by physical occupation, the Porte had
de facto claims only to the following places, on the west coast:
Q'usier, Suakin, Massawa (the island only), and Zeila (through
its dependency on Mocha); on the east coast: Yambu', Jidda,
Mecca, Medina, Ta'if, al-Qunfidha, Loheia, Hodeida, and
Mocha. In some spots on the east coast Turkish occupation went
a short distance inland, but their chief claims lay in the occupation of the ports themselves. On the west coast there was no
question as to the Egyptian occupation of the Sudan for which

Q'useir and Suakin were the chief ports, although during the
early 1860's Suakin was occupied by Turkish, not Egyptian,
troops. The strange legal relationship of the Viceroy of Egypt
and the Porte is well known. By the 1860's the two governments
were for all practical purposes separate, although the legal
questions of sovereignty involved in their relationship made a
convenient excuse for delay and procrastination.

The interior of the area was largely a governmental vacuum.
Abyssinia in 1867 was actually a group of feudal states in continual turmoil. The Red Sea coast from Massawa to Zeila was
largely unoccupied except by minor Dankali tribes in a state of
constant warfare. The Somali coast from Zeila to Cape Guardafui was tribal in organization. Near Berbera it was in a state
of chaos; further to the east the tribes were fairly stable. In
the Hedjaz, tribes still controlled the hinterland except for
Mecca, Medina, and Ta'if. To the south, the strongest single
influence lay with the large Asiri tribal confederation, nomadic
in character and a sworn enemy of any organized government
unless they could be bought off. Conditions in the Yemen were
chaotic, with each city independent, although certain claims of
sovereignty still remained with the title of Imam of San'a, who
was entirely too weak to enforce them. To the east of Aden,
the Hadramaut was entirely independent and Muscat in Oman
contained the only relatively settled native government in the
peninsula under Sultans Seyyid Thwain and Seyyid Salim, who
ruled under the paternal eye of the Indian Government.

European claims in the area, aside from the settled and
occupied city of Aden and the island of Perim, were largely tenuous and of legal value only. In 1840 the British had purchased
two islands off Tajura, Musa and Aibat. Neither of these islands was ever occupied, and the title to Aibat was dubious, to
say the least. The British had certain other territorial concessions for lighthouses and cable stations, but these could
scarcely be called territorial claims, although the concessions
on the island of Kamaran led to the British supervision of that
island when it became a quarantine station for the pilgrim traffic to Jidda. It should be noted that the occupation of this island
was always an international public health measure and could
scarcely be classified as imperialistic. To the east of Aden,
the British controlled the Kuria Muria Islands purchased from
Sultan Said of Muscat for the guano reportedly found there. (For
a full treatment of this incident see Coupland, Reginald, EAST

AFRICA AND ITS INVADERS, Oxford, Clarendon Press, 1938, pp. 524-45.)

The French also had certain claims in the area. The earliest of these was the purchase in 1840 by a French company of the port of Edd (Ayd) halfway between Massawa and Assab Bay. This was apparently considered a private venture, as the title to the territory was offered to the British in 1850. In 1859 the French expedition under Comte Russel acquired the island of Dissei in Annesley Bay, and in 1862 another French expedition under M. Schaeffer purchased Obock, a purchase defined by the treaty of March 11, 1862, between the government of Napoleon III and the local chiefs. A definite attempt to exploit this last purchase occurred in 1864-1865, but because the climate was discouraging, the project was temporarily abandoned.

In 1867 the only potential bases for any territorial expansion were Suakin, Massawa, Jidda, Hodeida and Aden. The remaining ports were too undeveloped for any important use. Suez, of course, existed as the gateway to the area from Europe, but this port was international in character and was so essentially a part of international trade that it could hardly serve as a base for imperialistic expansion without causing a serious diplomatic crisis.

In a firman of May 27, 1866, the ports of Suakin and Massawa, formerly under the control of the Ottoman Pashalik of Jidda, were transferred to the control of the Viceroy of Egypt, Ismail Pasha. In the same year, the Ka'aiti tribe in the Hadramaut occupied the port of Shihr and threatened Mukalla, and in 1867 the British cabinet determined on the expedition to Abyssinia. These three unrelated incidents paved the way for the first phase of modern imperialism in the Red Sea area from 1867-1877, a conflict which involved the two countries territorially adjacent to the area and the nation which held the predominant influence there. Two other European countries which later became involved in the area, France and Italy, made their first tentative imperialistic steps during this ten year period.

The Abyssinian expedition resulted in a fundamental change in the attitude of the Indian Government towards the settlement of Aden. Lieutenant Colonel H. F. Jacob in his book KINGS OF ARABIA makes the statement that beginning in 1854 Aden was throttled in its economic development by the concept that the settlement was merely a military post (op. cit., pp. 62-66). Technically this statement might be called correct on the basis

of Outram's appointment as Resident to replace Haines and the
appointment of officers of the Indian Army as residents and political officers. Practically, however, there is plenty of evidence to show that Aden was considered primarily as a coaling
station and communication outpost of the Bombay Government.
Its military importance was largely disregarded except when
some other rival appeared in the area, as the French did in
1860. In 1867 Sir W. A. Mansfield of the Indian Government
stated that Aden would not be a reliable base as it had too little
water (FO 1/19, Minute Sir W. A. Mansfield on proposed Abyssinian Expedition 6/14/67). On the basis of the prolonged
drought of 1865-1867 this was a correct assumption, although
the situation had been fairly well taken care of by the installation of condensers to purify salt water which turned out a safe
but not very palatable substitute for fresh water. However, the
lack of appreciation of Aden's military possibilities was due to
ignorance and probably personal dislike rather than any reasoned
arguments. Certainly every high official in India had visited
Aden on his way to or from England. The settlement, though
healthy, was unbearably hot, and in that period the hinterland
and the cooler hills to the north were not open to visits by Europeans as they are today, when a trip to Lahej can give a certain
amount of relief from the unbearable heat. The story exists of
an American tourist on a world cruise who, after visiting Aden,
remarked "If I had a house in Aden, I would sell it and buy one
in hell. It would be much cooler." To the average official,
Aden must have been a lonely and unpleasant outpost of the Empire, a necessary stopping place which one wished to leave as
soon as possible. To those officials who lived in Aden, however,
the place was relatively comfortable compared to the other Red
Sea ports and the Persian Gulf.

The Abyssinian expedition served to show Aden's usefulness
to officials of India and especially the officers of the Indian Army. Aden was one of the main bases of the expedition and became the communications center for the army. Most of the
reports from Aden in 1867-1868 were concerned with the technical details of the operation of this base, and the expedition
left Aden with an augmented garrison, better harbor facilities,
and, at long last, a troop of irregular horse. Although the Foreign Office stood by its idealistic instructions to Napier and rejected his plans for the re-establishment of an English consulate in Abyssinia to develop the results of the expedition, the

Indian Government more realistically took advantage of the development of Aden's strength, and maintained the military power which had accrued by force of necessity. After 1868, Colonel
Jacob is correct, Aden became primarily a military outpost.

In November, 1865, disturbances in the Hadramaut had
been reported to Aden. These disturbances continued. The con-
test between the Nakeeb of the Kathiri of Mukalla, and the
Ka'aiti tribe who had occupied Shihr, came to no final decision
because of the almost equal strength of the two parties. In
August, 1867, Merewether reported the arrival at Aden from
Jidda of a Turkish corvette, the "Azmeer," loaded with soldiers
bound for Mukalla, with the object of making the Nakeeb of Mukalla and the Ka'aiti submit to the Turkish Government by agreeing to fly the Turkish flag and pay a small tribute to the Porte.
As far as Merewether could find out, this expedition was undertaken by the authorities at Jidda without any authorization from
the Porte. The Resident countered this Turkish move by sending letters to the chiefs advising them to refuse the demands of
the Porte. He pointed out to the Bombay Government that the
Porte had no claims of any kind to this territory [actually they
had never had a claim – at the greatest extent of Selim's conquests the Hadramaut had never been occupied, although at that
time the chiefs there may have paid tribute to the Turks]; that
any attempt by the Turks to establish themselves at the south
coast of Arabia was unjustified; and that protests should be made
to Constantinople. He further added that he was powerless to
take effective measures as he had no warships stationed at
Aden (IO, LA Merewether-Bombay 8/10/67).

Reports from this expedition were received shortly. The
"Azmeer," after difficulties due to unfavorable winds, reached
Mukalla. The Nakeeb and the agent of the Ka'aiti were informed
that the whole Arab peninsula belonged to the Porte, which did
not allow her subjects to quarrel with each other. The Turks
were informed by the Nakeeb that there was no quarrel between
them, the Ka'aiti had simply taken part of the Nakeeb's territory
and he was trying to get it back. The Turkish agent demanded
that Shihr be abandoned by both sides as it was the cause of this
"misunderstanding" and should be occupied by Turkish troops.
The Turks were put off by the Nakeeb, who said that nothing
could be done until after the annual pilgrimage. Both Arab
groups then requested the British that they be placed under British protection (IO, LA, Abbott [Acting Res.]-Bombay 9/17/67).

Enclosed with this information was a copy of the letter of the
Sharif of Mecca to the Nakeeb stating that other countries wished
the Arabian sea coast and were about to seize the land (IO, LA,
encl. in Abbott-Bombay 9/17/67. Sharif of Mecca-Nakeeb of
Mukalla, N. D.). Merewether was confident that the Sharif
was merely trying to fish in troubled waters for his own advantage and was acting without authority from the Porte, but felt
that the Foreign Office should intervene (IO, LAM, Vol. 147.
Merewether-Bombay 9/20/67). The Bombay Government requested the Resident at Aden to investigate the rights of Turkish sovereignty (IO, LAM, Bombay-Russell 1/24/68). Brigadier Russell, who had replaced Merewether when the latter was
assigned to the Abyssinia Expedition, replied that the families
of the present rulers had been in control of the Hadramaut for
at least 200 years, although previously it had been ruled at
times by the Imam of San'a. He concluded by saying "Turkey
has no rule to the east of Aden and it is highly desirable that
she should not have" (IO-LAM, Russell-Bombay 2/20/68). Although the conflict between the Nakeeb of Mukalla and the Ka'aiti
tribe continued, the Turks did not interfere again in the area.

This Turkish expedition cannot be explained as simply as
Merewether assumed that it could. Another element entered
into the picture, and it is very surprising that neither the Foreign Office nor the India Office realized its importance. There
was plenty of evidence of the expansion of Egyptian rule to the
south, but official British interest was so concentrated on the
Abyssinian affair that every other interest seemed to be excluded. Theodore had a well-grounded fear of Egyptian expansion into Abyssinian territory. While no expansion had taken
place along the border, the tribal raids, one of which Plowden
had settled years before, appeared more frequently and were
apparently of a more official character. Furthermore Britain
had lost her official observer in the Sudan when Petherick returned to England in 1864. He was the merchant in Khartoum
who had served as unpaid British Consul. He was not replaced.
Cameron was, of course, imprisoned in Gondar, and those officials who were from time to time in Massawa were much more
interested in the Abyssinian captives than in Egyptian politics.
The firman Ismail Pasha received dated May 27, 1866, gave
him, among the rights, that of hereditary rule over Suakin and
Massawa. This transfer was shortly followed by reports of
troop concentrations on the Abyssinian border, a rumor which

was denied by Ismail. Any further designs which Ismail may have had were countered by the British expedition to Abyssinia.

Alternate plans for the Abyssinian expedition have been mentioned, especially that suggested by Sir Samuel Baker for the use of Egyptian troops. While the Foreign Office rejected such ideas on a religious basis and quite properly so, the flat rejection of these ideas by the Indian Government was probably made because of a desire to prevent the expansion of another power in the area. Ismail's offers of assistance and his re-enforcing of troops in Massawa and elsewhere have also been mentioned. In 1867 Djaafer Pasha, governor of the Sudan, made a survey of the Red Sea (Sabry, Mohammed, L'EMPIRE EGYPTIENNE SOUS ISMAIL 1863-1879, Paris, Guenther, 1933, p. 391) and Abd-El-Kader Pasha was appointed to take charge of the Kaymakamate of Massawa with the title "gouverneur des cotes orientales d'Afrique" (ibid., p. 391). Djaafer Pasha stopped at Aden on August 19, 1867. Abbott, Acting Resident, discovered that he had raised the Egyptian flag at Edd, and Obock, where the local Sultan denied having sold land to France. It was reported that he (Djaafer Pasha) was proceeding to Zeila, Tajura, and Berbera to establish Egyptian sovereignty over the area (IO, LA, Abbott-Bombay 8/24/67). In the midst of the preparations for the Abyssinian campaign no particular notice was taken of this expedition, especially as it was not accompanied by any troops. This was unfortunate as Djaafer's visits became the legal basis for later Egyptian claims in the area.

If the British had no idea of Ismail's intentions, the Sharif of Mecca knew them. In November, 1866, Stanton at Alexandria was informed by a Mr. Hollas, who was acting British agent at Jidda, that certain persons implicated in the massacre of 1858 and banished from that place had been allowed to return. Hollas, an acting agent without consular status, could make no protest, and Stanton suggested that Lord Lyons in Constantinople protest to the Porte (FO 78/1925, Stanton-FO 11/12/66). Lord Lyons and the French chargé d'affaires made such a protest, and the Porte issued a vizierial letter to the governor of Jidda ordering the removal of these criminals (FO 78/1926, Minute without date on Stanton-FO 11/12/66). Conditions in Jidda remained disturbed and Stanton, fearful of a repetition of the 1858 incident, sent Mr. Sandison, the chief dragoman of the Embassy at Constantinople, as special consular agent to the Arabian port (FO 78/1976, Stanton-FO 3/11/67). Here he was able to straighten

out the affair amicably; he found out a great deal about the condition of the Hedjaz and Yemen although his contemplated trip
to Ta'iz had to be abandoned because of disturbed conditions
there.

Sandison found ample evidence of Egyptian intrigues against
the Turkish authority in Arabia. Ismail was encouraging the
leaders of the Asiri to reconquer the three northern provinces
of the Yemen. Not knowing this, the Sharif of Mecca, governor
of the Hedjaz, appealed to Ismail for aid in putting down this
revolt, with the result that Ismail tried, through influence in
Constantinople, to get the Sharif deposed and to obtain the cession of Arabia to Egypt. Sandison felt that such a cession would
obligate Egypt to use at least 30,000 men in controlling the provinces of the Hedjaz and the Yemen, while the Sharif, on friendly
terms with the Emir of the Nejd, and with his great religious
prestige, was able to control the area with little trouble or effort and at the same time maintain a just and stable government.
Sandison estimated that there were about 10,000 Indian subjects
in the Hedjaz and the Yemen who were receiving no proper protection of their interests by either the British or Indian Governments, and he recommended the re-establishment of a regular
consulate at Jidda and the sending of a mission to the Sharif to
arrive at an understanding with him against further Egyptian intrigues (FO 78/1977, Reade-FO 7/14/87 and Sandison [Jidda]-
Read 6/7/67). Such good advice fell on deaf ears in London,
and Sandison was ordered to return to Constantinople, leaving
a Banyan merchant as British agent at Jidda (FO 78/1977,
Reade-FO 8/12/67). There is nothing to show that this information was ever transmitted to the India Office, which was vital-
ly involved, and it is apparent that Sandison's reports were
disregarded at the Foreign Office.

It can be seen then that Merewether's assumption that the
Turkish expedition to Mukalla was just fishing in troubled waters
was incorrect. It was unquestionably undertaken deliberately
by the Sharif as a counter to Djaafer Pasha's trip and the "other countries who wished the Arabian seacoast." In his letter
to the Nakeeb was a reference to the Egyptian designs on the
Somali coast which, for all he knew, might be extended to the
Arabian coast of the Gulf of Aden.

One European power cast a longing eye at the Red Sea. The
newly created kingdom of Italy probably realized the potentialities of the Suez Canal more fully than any other European

country. The opening of the canal would put Italy, of all the
Western European countries, closest to the East and would revive her trade in the Eastern Mediterranean, which had all but
disappeared. On December 14, 1867, Paget, British Minister
at Florence, informed the Foreign Office that the Italian Government was considering establishing a penal colony on the
shore of the Red Sea, in the neighborhood if not in the territory
of Abyssinia. However, in view of the Abyssinian expedition,
the Italian Government, which wished to do nothing which might
injure the successful release of the captives, agreed to make
no moves until the expedition was over. Paget believed that the
penal colony, while probably necessary, was only a blind for
the establishment of an Italian outpost in the area (FO 1/23,
Paget-FO 12/14/67). [For the early Italian interests in the
Red Sea area see Woolbert, Robert G, "The Purchase of Assab
by Italy," in McKay, Donald C. , ESSAYS IN THE HISTORY OF
MODERN EUROPE, New York, Harpers, 1936, pp. 114-129.]

By 1868, then, the Egyptians, the Turks, and the Italians
had indicated an interest in the Red Sea. Of these three, the
Foreign Office seemed to take only the Italian interests seriously. The India Office had not informed the Foreign Office of
the Turkish expedition to Mukalla, and the Foreign Office had
not forwarded Sandison's report to the India Office, although it
contained information vital to the protection of 10,000 Indians,
residing in the Hedjaz and the Yemen. Furthermore, the Foreign Office had not replaced Petherick as Consul at Khartoum,
Jidda was without a competent observer as consul, and the
Foreign Office, fed up with all things Abyssinian, was in 1868
to refuse to re-establish a consulate at Massawa. With the
opening of the Suez Canal but a year-and-a-half away, only Aden
was left to observe actions in the area. One cannot conclude
that the British cabinets of the 1860's were imperialistically
inclined.

In 1868, French commercial interests revived their activities in the Red Sea. In October, Major General Russell, the
Resident, reported that two Frenchmen, Mas and Poli, both
traders, had purchased a small harbor called Sheikh Said from
Sheikh Ali Tabet of the Haqmi tribe. This spot was located on
the Arab shore of the Red Sea directly opposite the island of
Perim; investigation showed that $40,000 was the agreed pur-
chase price with $2,000 paid down as a deposit. General Rus-
sell doubted that the Haqmi tribe had title to the land, which he

believed belonged to the Subahi (IO, LA, Russell-Bombay 10/ 15/68 and 10/23/68). Subsequently M. Poilex, a former engineer on the construction of the Suez Canal, informed Russell that the purchase was a purely private venture. General Russell commented, "It is evident that the British government cannot occupy every port in the neighborhood that a foreign nation may wish to annex but it does appear undesirable that a foreign power should occupy a port in such close vicinity to Perim" (IO, LA, Russell-Bombay 10/30/68).

H. M. S. "Dryad," Captain Colombe commanding, was sent to investigate both shores of the Red Sea in the vicinity of Perim. He reported that Aden should have no anxiety over Sheikh Said as it was an open roadstead and that the only neighboring harbor capable of development was Assab Bay, about thirty-five miles north of Perim on the African shore. However, the value of Assab Bay was very limited unless good fresh water was readily obtainable. General Russell felt that the British should occupy this port: "I submit the subject for consideration and await instructions — From the appearance of the bay in the chart I should imagine it would be desirable to secure it" (IO, LA, Russell-Bombay 11/10/68 enclosing survey of Assab Bay). A report from Lieutenant Dalmahoy in command at Perim reported Sheikh Said to be merely a landing place for cattle and sheep from the African shore, with only one brackish well. Militarily it was of little value as it could not command the ship channel between the Arabian shore and Perim (IO, LA, Colombe-Russell 11/8/68).

General Russell, wishing further information on the area, sent H. M. S. "Star," Captain de Kantzow commanding, to make further inspections, particularly at Assab Bay. De Kantzow examined not only the bay but explored the hinterland, and his report was not as encouraging as that of Colombe. He found the bay excellent as a harbor of refuge, but the hinterland was low, swampy, and barren. The nearest village was two miles inland, occupied by a poverty-stricken tribe which existed by exporting a few goats and chickens to Mocha. The shore was shallow, requiring long piers to be built for any development as a harbor. The nearest fresh water was a mile-and-a-half from shore. There were no natural sites for fortifications and the islands in the harbor were devoid of all vegetation, and were waterless. Due to the swampy nature of the ground, port and coal storage facilities would, in Captain de Kantzow's opinion, be prohibitively expensive to build. He concluded "The Bay, I believe (except as a harbor of refuge) would be quite unsuitable to the wants of a foreign government; and a place very unlikely to be occupied by any nation, its possession even by a foreign power could only be a nominal inconvenience to us and would not seriously operate against us as an obstruction to the passage or free navigation of the Red Sea" (IO, LA, Russell-Bombay 1/15/69 encl. de Kantzow-Russell 1/11/69).

The French Government had not forgotten the Lambert affair. In August, 1868, a French vessel appeared at Jidda bearing new demands for the payment of $20,000 damages, payable from the revenue of the Yemen, which the Porte had granted in 1862 as a result of Lambert's death. The commander of the French vessel and the French Vice-consul proceeded to Ta'if to interview the Sharif and almost touched off a riot in that city by displaying the French flag and shooting off a salute on August 15, the Fête Napoleon. Only by the exertions of the brother of the Grand Sharif was the crowd calmed without serious trouble (FO 78/2039, Stanton-FO 11/1/68 encl. Raby [Agent at Jidda]-Stanton 10/23/68). As a result, the Frenchmen were delighted to leave without pressing their claim.

In Aden itself, changes of policy had taken place. In a dispatch of October 30, General Russell stated that because of an attack of scurvy the Aden troop (the irregular horse) were being sent to the more healthy territory around Lahej, concluding, "Such a movement of the troop in the territory of our Allies will have a beneficial affect" (IO, LA, Russell-Bombay 10/30/68). This was certainly a great change from the days of the earlier Residents when the army and the Europeans were not allowed outside the walls of the settlement. In December, General Russell noted that Lord Napier and Lord Mayo stopped at Aden and made an extended examination of the fortifications and aqueduct, showing an official interest in the settlement previously unheard of (IO, LA, Russell-Bombay 12/11/68).

While the Abyssinian expedition was going on, the tribes lived at peace with Aden but not among themselves. A tribal conflict in July, 1868, between the Abdali and the Haushabi resulted in a victory for the former. In the peace settlement, the Haushabi ceded the town of Zaida on the border of their territory to Lahej. This town had been the cause of the conflict, as the Haushabi had diverted the water of a stream which ran through the town into their territory, to the detriment of the farmers

living in the neighboring portion of Lahej. The Haushabi soon
regretted this cession and sought the aid of other tribes, in order to retake the town. General Russell wrote to the chief to
desist, but felt that this would do little good. He appealed to
the Bombay Government to drop the policy of non-interference
with the tribes, as Aden was too dependent on Lahej for water
and supplies to allow the Abdali country to be plundered (IO,
LA, Russell-Bombay 11/19/68). This situation was further complicated by the recommendation of the settlement's chief engineer that water from Zaida be partially diverted to Aden to increase the water supply of the rapidly growing city, a report
which had been concurred in by Lord Napier and Lord Mayo on
their visit to Aden (IO, LA, Russell-Bombay 12/18/68). By diplomacy and intrigue the question was temporarily settled, but
the basic conflict between the two tribes remained, to be exploited in 1872 by the Turkish forces attempting to conquer all
of the Yemen.

    In April, 1869, General Russell completed the process of
unscrambling the rival claims to Little Aden, a work which
Coghlan had begun in 1863 and Merewether had continued. These
claims were settled for $30,000 and the deeds forwarded to
Bombay (IO, LA, Russell-Bombay 4/5/69). Some minor claims
remained to be straightened out, but by September 19 the British flag was officially raised over the peninsula, which was then
incorporated as a part of the settlement (IO, LA, Goodfellow
[Acting Resident]-Bombay 9/22/69). The value of this acquisition was purely protective. In the hands of another power, it
would have been a very serious threat to Aden; in the hands of
the British it was valuable for defense purposes only. (Today
it is the site of the Anglo-Iranian oil refinery.)

    The Somali coast remained in its usual state of turbulence,
a condition which had existed since Shermarkee's death in 1861.
The fairs at Berbera were unsuccessful, but Aden continued to
be able to draw upon the area for fresh meat. General Russell's
efforts to settle the dispute there met with apparent success in
1869 (IO, LA, Russell-Bombay 4/3/69) but the peace was only
temporary.

    The French made two other attempts to obtain sites in the
Aden area. The French Consul at Aden tried unsuccessfully to
negotiate with the Somali chiefs for possession of Ainterad and
Karin, east of Bulhar on the Somali coast (IO, LA, Russell-
Bombay 4/24/69). Both these places were mere open roadsteads

and of no great value. The Nakeeb of Mukalla came to Aden in
May, 1869, to ask for British protection, as the French had appeared on the Hadramaut coast and were intriguing with his enemy the Ka'aiti (IO, LA, Goodfellow [Acting Resident-Bombay
6/15/69). As there is no other evidence to confirm this report,
the Nakeeb may well have been using the fact of a visit of a
French war vessel on that coast as an excuse to gain British
protection and help against his enemy.

The French traders who were interested in Sheikh Said had
been unable to obtain a firman from the Porte recognizing their
purchase of this spot (IO, LA, Goodfellow-Bombay 5/28/69).
However, two Frenchmen went to Sheikh Said in May, 1869, to
conclude the transaction. Further investigation indicated that
the Pasha of the Yemen planned to counter this move by occupying Sheikh Said with Turkish troops (IO, LA, Goodfellow-Bombay 10/16/69). The establishment of any port in this area,
General Russell felt, would damage seriously Aden's trade with
the hinterland, which, with the disappearance of Mocha as an
important port, now approached a monopoly (IO, LA, Russell-
Bombay 12/31/69). In the light of the previous reports on
Sheikh Said, it is hard to justify General Russell's pessimism,
as the place was almost useless as a harbor.

To complete the picture of the area prior to the opening of
the Suez Canal, it is necessary to consider what happened in
Abyssinia after the withdrawal of the British expeditionary force.

When all the leaders of the expedition had returned to England, the India Office on July 15, 1868, recommended to the
Foreign Office the appointment of the Swiss, Werner Munzinger,
as consul at Massawa (FO 1/26, IO-FO 7/15/68). This gentleman had been of the greatest aid to the British, had acted as
Rassam's agent in Massawa, and had accompanied the expedition to Magdala as technical adviser. His knowledge of the
country was amazingly complete and his abilities were unques-
tioned. Lord Napier called at the Foreign Office on August 4,
1868, to discuss the question with Murray. Murray took the
initiative in the conversation, pointing out that there was no reason for a consulate at Massawa as there was no trade there, and
experience had shown that politically such a consulate had involved Britain in a war. Napier replied that the withdrawal of
a British agent would be the signal for the encroachment of
Egypt on Abyssinia, which was, after all, the only Christian
country in Africa. He felt a consul should be only an observer

and not go up into Abyssinia, but he admitted that there was only
a small trade, carried on almost entirely by Indian merchants.
Napier believed that any agent should be an agent of the Indian
Government, as the Consul General in Egypt was too far away
to evaluate properly dispatches from Massawa. He further felt
that all agents on the coasts of Africa and Arabia in the area
should be responsible to the Resident at Aden. He stated that
General Russell, the Resident, was very able and that Munzinger
was the best possible man for the post. Murray replied that
strictly speaking the post was not vacant, as Cameron still held
the position, and that no decision could be reached until Rassam's full report was available (FO 1/26, Murray-Minute dated
8/4/68). Lord Stanley noted on this Minute that he would see
Lord Napier on August 8 (FO 1/26, Murray-Minute 8/4/68,
note by Stanley 8/6/68). Napier apparently had no more success
with Stanley than he had had with Murray, as the Foreign Office
informed the India Office that "in so far as imperial interests
are concerned," it was not necessary to have a consul at Massawa and no successor to Cameron would be appointed, but that
the Foreign Office would not object if the India Office wished to
have an agent at that port (FO 1/26, FO-IO 8/6/68).

Napier's request, while reasonable in our eyes, was really
revolutionary to the Foreign Office. In the first place, he proposed a change in the traditional spheres of control of the Foreign Office and the India Office, giving the India Office jurisdiction over the whole Red Sea area while its responsibility had
formerly been limited to the Yemen, due to its ancient factory
at Mocha. The Foreign Office had maintained the consulates at
Massawa and Jidda. Secondly, he proposed that the consul, a
post which carried with it diplomatic immunities, etc., be
placed under the jurisdiction of the India Office, thus granting
certain prerogatives of the diplomatic service to an India Office
employee. The counter offer of the Foreign Office, not to object to the appointment of an agent of the India Office, meant
the appointment of an official who lacked the prestige and immunities of a consul and who would depend for his influence
largely on the prestige enjoyed by the Indian Government in the
area at the moment. Unquestionably the Foreign Office felt that
such an arrangement would deprive them of their prerogatives,
and the India Office unquestionably realized the futility of having
an agent at Massawa who lacked the status and immunities of
a consul. Therefore nothing was done, although Munzinger acted

as an unofficial agent for the Resident at Aden for a considerable time, as well as being a source of information for the Consul General at Alexandria.

Munzinger, who had apparently been promised the position of consul by Napier, suffered a loss in prestige when the consulate was closed. This information resulted in immediate violations of the trade agreement of 1838 by the imposition of increased landing and import fees by the Egyptian officials. Goodfellow, Acting Resident in Aden, complained through the India Office to the Foreign Office without effect (FO 1/29, IO-FO 12/9/69 encl. dispatches from Aden to Bombay). Lord Clarendon, the new Foreign Minister, on receipt of this dispatch, repeated Stanley's decision but felt that Munzinger should be rewarded for his work (FO 1/29, Minute by Clarendon on IO-FO 12/9/68). It was therefore decided to pay Munzinger the salary of consul up to June 30, 1869, and award him the order of Companion of the Bath (FO 1/29, FO-IO 12/17/69 & IO-FO 12/23/69).

In accordance with his instructions but against his better judgment, Lord Napier had left Abyssinia without attempting to form any stable government. Consequently the country was in a chaotic condition. With familiar repetition, two leaders arose above the rest, Kassa in Tigré and Wagshum Gobaze in Gondar, Shoa as usual being by its geographical location removed from the scene of conflict. In Shoa, Menelik continued to consolidate his rule. Munzinger, in Massawa, reported in February, 1869, that Kassa, who was probably the stronger, had sent to Egypt for a new Abuna (IO, LA, Russell-Bombay 2/11/69). Both Gobaze and Menelik sent letters of friendship to Queen Victoria. On Napier's and Rassam's advice a civil reply was given to them advising them to consult with the British Government through the Resident at Aden. In addition, it was decided to send a similar letter to Kassa so that any charges of favoritism could be avoided (FO 1/28, IO-FO 11/5/69, FO-IO 12/21/69).

On the eve of the opening of the Suez Canal, Britain therefore had only one reliable source of information in the area, the Resident at Aden. Thanks to the foresight of the India Office, the settlement had become much stronger than in 1866. The Egyptians were well established at Massawa, and Ismail's plans for expansion southward were taking definite form, for in April, 1869, Stanton reported that Sir Samuel Baker had been appointed to head an expedition to the lake regions of the White Nile to suppress the slave trade and open commerce in the area (FO 78/

2092, Stanton-FO 4/2/69). The Turkish action regarding the
French purchase of Sheikh Saïd indicated that the Porte would
not allow further settlements in the area which it claimed. The
Italians and the French had indicated their interest in the area,
with Italian designs centering on Assab Bay. The British Foreign Office, however, was in no position to counter any of this
as it had closed the Massawa consulate and was represented
merely by a native agent in Jidda.

XXIII. ADEN 1870-1872

The Suez Canal was opened on November 17, 1869. In one day, the Red Sea, economically a backwater of the Indian Ocean, in spite of the mail and passenger traffic to India, became one of the main sea routes of the world. The great success of the canal was due in large part to the development of the steamship. In the eighteenth century, with the decline of the coffee trade from the Yemen and the domination of the spice trade by the Europeans, Aden had declined to insignificance. Its major economic importance had been as a trans-shipping port, where cargoes were transferred from the larger Arab vessels to the small buggalows capable of navigating the treacherous Red Sea. It was the development of the early steamship which had made Aden important again as a coaling station for the East India Company's steamers in the 1840's. These steamers used mechanical propulsion as an auxiliary to their sails. In the treacherous and reef-strewn Red Sea, steam gave them a factor of safety for year-round travel, hitherto available to sailing vessels only during certain months when favorable winds prevailed. In evaluating the importance of the Suez Canal, one must fully account for the development of steamships. The 1850's saw the invention of the screw propeller to replace the clumsy and undependable paddle wheel, but the greatest development came in the early 1860's with the practical application of the compound engine to steam navigation, resulting in increased power, fuel saving, and greater dependability. It was no longer necessary to use steam only as an auxiliary to sail because of the excessive fuel consumption of the primitive engines. The monsoons had met their master.

De Lesseps' plan in 1857 for a canal through the Isthmus of Suez was based on vision, but the success of such a project was largely a gamble. When it was completed in 1869 its success was automatically assured by technological developments far beyond its planner's imagination. The timing of the opening of the canal was fortuitous and its effect on the course of history was far beyond the concept of any of the men of the period.

European imperialism of the eighteenth century might well be described by saying that the mercantilist theory was being carried to its logical conclusions by a small group of men in

England, France, and Holland who would make tremendous profits by its success. Nineteenth century imperialism was due to
other influences. As far as England is concerned, and she was
the dominant imperialistic country, several factors enter in.
First, while the English came out of the Napoleonic wars as
the dominant imperial nation of the world, the Treaty of Vienna
did return to France many of its imperial outposts, not enough
to threaten British power, but enough to continue Anglo-French
rivalry. Second, the Napoleonic wars produced one unforeseen
result, unrealized by people at the time and still without proper
evaulation by historians: the economic potential of France,
England's only possible rival in the Industrial Revolution, had
been destroyed, and Great Britain had been given a twenty-year
start on the rest of Europe. Third, the gradual broadening
base of British government with the passage of the Reform Bill
in 1832 and the Reform Act of 1867 spread interest in the Empire to many people outside of the small groups of exporters
and importers.

The mercantile groups of the eighteenth century who profited by imperial interests were joined in the 1830's by the new
manufacturers, interested primarily in the selling of their
mass-produced goods, particularly cotton materials, throughout the world. They were the group who benefited politically
by the Reform Act of 1832, and their participation in government was felt almost immediately. With their influence the
East India Company reached the height of aggressive expansion
in the 1830's. The news of the disastrous Afghan campaign of
1838 resulted in a wave of anti-imperialism in England, already
strained by a major economic depression. Economic and social
troubles in England in the period of transition from 1840 to 1870
from an agricultural to an industrial economy, combined with
the new standards of morality led by the example of Queen Victoria and resulting largely from the degeneration of eighteenth-
century romanticism into mid-Victorian sentimentality, diverted
attention from the Empire. England was so far ahead in the industrial race that her products dominated the world market and
did not need to be pushed. New capital, which in the eighteenth
century was often put into mercantile ventures, was ploughed
back into industry. Popular support of imperialism, already
at a low ebb, was not increased by the army scandals of the
Crimean War and the news of the India Mutiny, a result of the
general inefficiency of the East India Company. Imperial

outposts lacked funds for their proper operation, and official
interest in their welfare was negligible, as in the case of Aden.
That the Empire survived was due largely to the acts of individuals, men in England such as Palmerston and men in the colonies and the Indian controlled outposts who, like Haines, Coghlan, and Merewether, made the most of what little they had.

Paradoxically, the interest of the English people in the
world was greatly broadened. British trade increased rapidly.
This period of transition marked the establishment of many of
the great British steamship lines: the Cunard Line was established in 1840; Royal Mail Steam Packet Company to the West
Indies in 1839; Elder Dempster to the west coast of Africa in
1852; British India Steam Navigation Company in the Far East
in 1855; the famous Peninsular and Oriental established in 1835
with service to the Mediterranean, incorporated in 1840, with
service extended from Suez to India via Aden in 1842; the Union
Steamship Company, later the Castle Line, established in 1853,
extending its service to South Africa in 1858; the White Star
Line, established in 1867. The maintenance of regular and dependable mail and passenger service was a great factor in
broadening the interests of the English people. A very important additional element which influenced the politically important
classes in England was a by-product of the Victorian standards
of morality. This period marks the expansion of the great missionary movement which, by the 1880's, was to flood the world
with missionaries and bring about the familiar pattern of the
missionary followed by the trader, with resulting imperial
interest.

Technical developments served greatly to speed up communications, and thus bring remote parts of the world closer to
England. The invention of the telegraph, the laying of subma-
rine cables, some successful, some not, the development of
regular mail and passenger services by sea and land, and the
continued improvement of ships and railroads prepared the way
for a new resurgence of interest in imperial affairs. Last, but
far from least, England began to lose its pre-eminent leadership in industry before the rising competition of the Industrial
Revolution on the continent and in the United States, compelling
her to consider controlling her markets through occupation
rather than through her superior products.

In 1869, conditions were favorable in England for a new era
of imperialism. Excess capital had been invested in foreign

countries and new means of communications were developing.
The people were psychologically ready for such a movement
and economic factors justified the new course. That neither the
people of England nor their leaders realized this is shown by the
Abyssinian campaign and the lack of preparedness for the effects
of the opening of the Suez Canal.

The results of the opening of the canal were quickly seen
in Aden. Scarcely six weeks after the opening ceremonies, on
January 12, 1870, General Russell reported that Prussian,
Dutch, Spanish, French, and Austrian warships were at Aden.
The French gunboat "Bruat" and the Austrian ship "Narenta"
he understood were to be stationed at the settlement for a year,
and rumor said that the Austrians had purchased Assab Bay
and that French plans for the occupation of Sheikh Said were
progressing rapidly. Under these circumstances, he asked that
a naval vessel, preferably an ironclad, be stationed permanently at Aden and that the defenses be re-enforced by large caliber
guns capable of answering the fire of war vessels (IO, LA, Russell-Bombay 1/12/70).

The first real threat to English predominance in the area
came from none of these nations. Since the capture of Aden in
1839, the British had not had to face any real rival in the Red
Sea. French interests had been largely unofficial in appearance and were not backed up by any large display of force. As
a result of the visit of the various European warships and the
rumors which these visits incurred, Russell sent the steamer
"Sind," a troop transport, to inspect the Gulf of Aden and the
lower part of the Red Sea (IO, LA, Russell-Bombay 1/12/70).
Shortly after its departure the Egyptian warship "Khartoum"
put in at Aden and then proceeded to Berbera (IO, LA, Russell-
Bombay 2/11/70). This news alarmed Russell, who had had
previous intimation that the Egyptians might occupy the port and
had dispatched a confidential native agent there on December 24,
1869 (FO 78/3186, IO-FO 1/5/70 encl. Russell-Bombay 12/6/
69 and 12/24/69, also in IO, LA, 1870).

The "Sind" reported that troops under Djemal Bey had
landed at Berbera with two guns and that the Bey had told the
tribes he had come to settle their disputes. The tribes swal-
lowed this, especially after the Bey landed a brass band and had
a big parade which made a great impression on the Somalis.
Fearful that the Egyptians would be able to obtain the submission
of Berbera and Bulhar, Russell requested again that a British

warship be stationed at Aden. Meanwhile he ordered the "Sind" to return to Berbera after it had carried out the regular replacement of the Perim garrison, and searched the Aden records to find out what claims of sovereignty might exist to the coast (FO 78/3186, IO-FO 8/5/70 encl. Russell-Bombay 2/25/70, also in IO, LA, 1870). Russell sent on the "Sind" another confidential agent from Aden. The agent was landed at Bulhar and on March 14 his camp was attacked by a rival tribe. In the general melee that followed several tribesmen were killed. The captain of the "Sind," Commander Westbrook, held a "durbar" with the Somalis and managed to restore order (FO 78/3186, IO-FO 8/5/70 encl. Russell-Bombay 3/18/70).

Luckily H. M. S. "Teazer" arrived at Aden and was sent to Berbera and Bulhar at the end of March. She arrived at Berbera on April 4 and found the "Khartoum" and the "Sind" both at anchor. The Turkish flag was flying over the port and the Bey, by the judicious use of bribes, was trying to induce the tribes to submit to the Egyptians. The Egyptians, except for the show of force in the parade mentioned above, had not occupied the town or gone ashore except for such peaceful purposes as were required by a ship anchored in the harbor. No bonds or written documents had been signed between the Egyptians and the Somalis, but Captain Blowfield, commander of the "Teazer," found sufficient evidence to lead him to believe that the confidential agent of General Russell had been attacked on orders of the Egyptians. It was reported that the "Khartoum" was to leave when the fair was over, to be replaced by another vessel carrying a civil pasha and troops who were to occupy the site. Captain Blowfield had a friendly talk with Djemal Bey who said that the Turkish flag had been given to the town five years before [Djemel Bey probably meant three years before at the time of the visit of Djaafer Pasha] and the whole area was part of Turkish territory. The Bey further stated that he had no authority to purchase any territory, but as commander of the Red Sea squadron was merely "looking after Egyptian interests." He added that personally he was sick of the constant quarrels of the Somali tribes and would be glad to leave (FO 78/3186, IO-FO 8/5/70 encl. Russell-Bombay 4/8/70, also in IO, LA, 1870).

The "Khartoum" left for Aden to refuel at the end of March. Meanwhile the Mukalla-Shihr feud had broken out again. As a result of these two incidents General Russell again requested diplomatic action to confine the Turks to the Red Sea, and prevent expansion into the Gulf of Aden (FO 78/3186, IO-FO 8/5/70 encl. Russell-Bombay 3/31/70). The Foreign Department of the government of Bombay informed the Political Department that a protest had been made by H. M. Ambassador to the Porte on this subject in October, 1869, and added, "His Excellency in Council further desires me to point out that the principle which the Resident appears to advocate... that where British traders go, the political interference of the British government is to follow, is a dangerous one and is not acquiesced in by the Supreme Council" (FO 78/3186, IO-FO 8/7/70, For. Dept. -Pol. Dept. [Bombay] 5/17/70). It is very difficult to understand how Russell's dispatches could be interpreted in such a fashion. He was urging that aggressions be prevented, first in the case of the Hadramaut because of political repercussions in India, and second, in the case of Berbera, because its independence was essential to Aden's welfare as the main source of meat for the settlement. The interpretation put on the affairs by the governor could only be reached by a man who was suspicious of any possible implications of imperialism in the actions of his subordinates.

Meanwhile Russell wrote to Djemal Bey requesting fuller information on his actions. He was informed that the Somali coast was under the authority of the Sultan (FO 78/3186, IO-FO 8/5/70 encl. Russell-Bombay 4/21/70). Russell replied to Djemal asking him to do nothing until the governments involved could straighten out the matter (FO 78/3186, Stanton-FO 6/3/70). The Foreign Office reviewed the question of sovereignty, and came to the conclusion that Turkish sovereignty in the area did not exist inasmuch as the British had made treaties direct with the tribes (FO 78/3186, Memo on Sovereignty by Hertslet, 7/18/70). This was forwarded to the India Office, which replied that it concurred and was advising the Resident not to appoint a British Resident at Berbera as he wished to do. Merewether, now in the India Office, did not concur, however, and advocated a British Resident, preferably a European at Berbera during the fair, and a ship stationed at Aden to back him up. He emphasized the importance of Berbera to Aden and noted that trade at the fair had been constantly growing in spite of unsettled conditions (FO 78/3186, IO-FO 8/5/70).

In August the English learned that Momtaz Pasha had been appointed as governor of the African coast from Suez to Cape Guardafui and was reported to have left Suez to call at the

various ports in his territory. This news caused Russell again
to ask for the appointment of a British agent at Berbera, suggesting Munzinger as the best man available. To back this up
he enclosed a report of the trade between Aden and Berbera
and Aden and Bulhar (IO, LA, Russell-Bombay 8/25/70): (figures
given in rupees)

Aden and Bulhar

Year	Imports from Bulhar	Exports Aden-Bulhar
1867-1868	25,2836	38,9494
1868-1869	45,7067	32,0537
1869-1870	30,6406	33,2335

Aden and Berbera

	Imports from Berbera	Exports Aden-Berbera
1867-1868	38,6387	25,7740
1868-1869	29,2272	23,8405
1869-1870	20,8627	8,2818

These figures show that the trade was extensive and also show
that the rivalry of the tribes at Berbera had made Bulhar the
more important trading center in spite of its poor port facilities.

Russell's fears of Egyptian action were heightened by the
receipt of a letter from Munzinger at Massawa reporting that
Egyptian troops were gathering at that port for the occupation of
Berbera (IO, LA, Russell-Bombay 9/15/70 encl. Munzinger-
Russell 8/21/70). However, nothing developed until the next
season of the fair began. Russell's requests were, as usual,
disregarded both in India and at home.

Closer to Aden, the French again pressed their claims to
Sheikh Said, although it was very difficult to tell whether the
French Government was interested in the place or whether it
was purely a trading venture. The French were also making

inquiries in other directions, none of which materialized into
anything of importance (IO, LA, Russell-Bombay 1/22/70). In
February, Russell received a letter from the Pasha of the Yemen protesting against French actions at Sheikh Said and informing the Resident that the Porte had definitely refused to
grant permission for the sale of this site as it was part of the
Ottoman Empire (IO, LA, Russell-Bombay 2/11/70). The official rejection by the Porte of the purchase apparently caused
the French Government to lose interest in the development of
Sheikh Said, as the French Consul informed Russell that the
naval authorities considered the harbor there valueless (IO,
LA, Russell-Bombay 5/13/70). However, the commercial interests involved persisted and in May the French steamer "Afrique," belonging to Fraescinet Père & Fils Cie., landed two
Europeans, an interpreter, and a large supply of stores there,
in behalf of three trading companies which had taken over all
previous rights which had been acquired by the French (IO, LA,
Russell-Bombay 5/20/70).

     The Turkish government countered this move by establish-
ing a lazaretto (quarantine station) at Sheikh Said, with the excellent excuse of a serious cholera epidemic in Zanzibar; Su-
leiman Bey with 400 troops was dispatched from Hodeida to
Sheikh Said for this purpose (IO, LA, Russell-Bombay 6/18/70).
The Turks soon arrived and both parties amicably continued
their preparation for forming a settlement. The French were
reported attempting to cut a canal to a salt lake to establish
safe harbor facilities, and claimed an area thirty-six miles
long and six miles deep around the cape opposite Perim. Russell felt that the establishment of a harbor there might seriously
injure the coffee trade at Aden (IO-LA Russell-Bombay 6/24/
70 and 6/30/70).

     Whatever French plans were, the outbreak of the Franco-
Prussian war in July halted any serious exploitation of Sheikh
Said. The merchants remaining there continued to develop the
place under the watchful eye of a garrison of 150 Turks. What
trade they could obtain was subject to interference by the Subahi
tribes, and the French seemed to be unable to reach a satisfactory agreement with the tribes to keep the roads open (IO, LA,
Russell-Bombay 10/7/70). In October, Russell himself visited
the site and found that the French establishment consisted of a
few tents, but that neither party had fortifications of any kind
(IO, LA, Russell-Bombay 10/22/70). It did not prosper as a

trading post, and after a northeast storm had driven several
French ships on the rocks in February, 1871, the place was
abandoned.

The opening of the Suez Canal had revived Italian interest
in Assab Bay. In March, Paget at Florence reported that local newspapers stated that an Italian frigate was being sent to
establish a penal settlement in the Red Sea. He could get no official confirmation of this except a statement that an Italian
steamship line was being formed to go from Genoa to the Far
East via Suez, and that they wished a coaling station on the Red
Sea (FO 78/3186 & 78/2138, Paget-FO 3/2/70). In May, Russell reported that an Italian company was negotiating for the
purchase of Assab Bay, but so far had not had success (IO, LA,
Russell-Bombay 5/5/70, 5/20/70). Stanton at Alexandria reported that a small party of Italians had proceeded to Massawa
ostensibly for scientific purposes (FO 78/2138, Stanton-FO
4/13/70). An article from Le Canal de Suez, Journal Maritime
et Commercial of May 12, 1870, reporting the acquisition of an
island in Assab Bay by Maison Rubattino of Genoa in November,
1869, and the arrival of an expedition there under Professor
Sapeto, caused Stanton to make inquiries of the Egyptian government. He was informed that the sale was not sanctioned by the
government and that the Italian consul general knew nothing of
it. The Egyptian government assured Stanton that while they
were willing to grant reasonable concessions they refused to
cede any territory to another power (FO 78/2139, Stanton-FO
5/25/70). Egyptian troops were sent to Assab and removed the
Italian flag which had been raised there by the departing expedition. Russell commented, "The Turks and the Egyptians are
very jealous of any land within the Red Sea being taken by Foreigners, – their actions in the case of Sheikh Seyd (Said) and
Assab evinces this" (IO, LA, Russell-Bombay 7/22/70).

Around Aden the tribes were relatively quiet. In February,
the Sultan of Lahej went on a three-month trip to India with
Goodfellow as an interpreter and official companion (IO, LA,
Russell-Bombay 2/19/70). By this time also cable communications had been definitely established between Aden and India and
a new cable was being laid up the Red Sea by the "Great Eastern."

However, some tribes in the hinterland threatened trouble
in September by extorting tribute from Lahej. Taking advantage
of the smoldering Abdali-Haushabi dispute over Zaida, the
tribesmen of the interior had little difficulty in getting the

Haushabi as allies. The dispute, Russell discovered, centered
around the transit dues levied by the Abdali. Inasmuch as the
transit dues were sanctioned and fixed by treaty between the
British and Lahej, it seemed that little could be done (IO, LA,
Russell-Bombay 12/2/70, 12/10/70).

Major General C. W. Tremenheere succeeded Russell as
Resident in December, 1870. It was a wise choice, as the new
Resident had been stationed at Aden for a considerable length
of time as commander of the garrison, and was thoroughly familiar with all the details of the settlement. He proceeded to
get an eight-months' truce between the tribes and advised the
Bombay Government that the only solution for the quarrel lay
in increasing the Lahej Sultan's pension in return for abolition
of the transit dues, an increase which he felt would be paid for
by a consequent reduction in costs of supplies from the interior
(IO, LA, Tremenheere-Bombay 12/31/70). The death of the
leader of the interior tribesmen in January, 1871, followed in
two months by the death of his successor, caused internal strife
in the tribes which removed a threat to the peace, but the question of transit dues came up in another place. The Subahi to
the west caused disturbances on the roads in April, 1871, and
the Aden troop was sent to capture the Subahi chief. A skirmish
ensued in which several Arabs were killed. The chief was not
captured but the threat of force caused his voluntary appearance
at Aden on May 1 (IO, LA, Tremenheere-Bombay 4/7/71,
4/14/71 & 5/4/71).

An investigation convinced the Resident that the whole system of the relations with the tribes had to be changed. The
general policy of dealing with the tribes had been established by
the treaty of 1849 between the government of India and the Sultan of Lahej. In it, the Sultan of Lahej was paid a stipend to
keep the roads open. This meant, in fact, that the Sultan was
responsible for the actions of the other chiefs, and Haines,
Coghlan, and Merewether had cleared all their tribal questions
through him. As long as the Resident was bound by a strict interpretation of the non-interference policy of the Indian Government such a plan was necessary, and as long as the Abdali remained the predominant tribe in the area, it was effective.
However, the dominant position of this tribe was destroyed by
the famine of 1864-1865, the cholera epidemic of 1865, and an
epidemic among the cattle at the same time which destroyed
much of the wealth of the tribe. Furthermore, the changes

brought by the use of Aden in the Abyssinian campaign gave the
Residents a freedom of movement in the countryside which enabled them to exert direct control on the other tribes through
the use of the Aden Troop. Tremenheere's actions in the Subahi affair, in which he dealt directly with the Subahi chief, convinced him that the policy of dealing through the Sultan of Lahej
was a primary cause of disturbances on the roads. The Resident had no difficulty in reaching an agreement with the Subahi
in which they guaranteed to keep the roads open for a subsidy
of $95 a month. At the same time he reached an agreement with
the Atifi, a sub-tribe living on the coast, to protect shipwrecks
from Ras Imran to Bab-el-Mandeb (IO, LA, Tremenheere-
Bombay 5/4/71 & 5/18/71). He then made a similar arrangement with the Lower 'Aulaqi, who controlled another section of
the coast to the east of Aden (IO-LA, Tremenheere-Bombay
6/2/71). These arrangements led the government of Bombay
to request the Resident on June 29 to re-examine the whole question and estimate the concessions which could be obtained from
the Sultan of Lahej in a new treaty, suggesting five points which
ought to be gained if possible: (1) concessions enabling the
settlement to further its supply of fresh provisions; (2) concessions to construct water works on the Sultan's territory; (3)
permission to quarter troops in his territory during certain portions of the year when heat made Aden unbearable; (4) an engagement "not to permit any European power to acquire a footing in his territory without the consent of the British Government"; and (5) the abandonment of the transit dues (IO, LA,
Bombay-Tremenheere 6/29/71).

     Although the Bombay Government did not call it that, these
requests, if granted, would have constituted a virtual protectorate over Lahej. The first concession envisaged an increased
use of Aden due to the more frequent calls for supplies by ships
using the Suez Canal route. The reason for the second concession was obvious; either it did not rain in Aden, as in the period
from 1864-1866 or else, as on May 28, 1870, it rained so severely that a rainfall of between 7.30 and 8.65 inches was recorded in five hours, collapsing many houses and destroying
part of the Sheikh 'Othman aqueduct (IO, LA, Russell-Bombay
6/3/70). The last concession was obviously necessary, as previous events have shown. The third and fourth concessions
indicated a wholly new policy on the part of the Bombay Government. Aden was, as said before, generally healthy, although it

could be unbearably hot. Europeans did not seem to suffer any
ill results from the climate. Why then this sudden concern for
the comfort of the troops? The Turkish-Asiri quarrel had not
as yet developed into a threat to Aden. One can only believe
that the facts of the French effort at Sheikh Said, Egyptian interest in the Somali coast, and a rising European interest in the
Red Sea area caused the Bombay Government to believe that the
hinterland should be in some way secured to protect the settlement. The excuse given certainly appeared innocent, and in
view of Aden's notorious heat, reasonable. The fourth point
was obviously designed to prevent a possible occurrence similar
to the Sheikh Said incident. The Bombay Government probably
did not realize what would result from the adoption of this fourth
point, although any perusal of the documents relative to the purchase of Little Aden should have shown them the conflicting
claims of the tribes. The policy expressed by the Bombay Government on this point would have led to a continued expansion
of the protectorate until a national frontier or a strongly established government was reached.

Tremenheere's reaction to this request was not encouraging.
Regarding the first point, he did not feel that supplies could be
increased very much, for when cattle, sheep, etc., could not
be obtained from the Somali coast, contractors grazed imported
animals near Aden, the local cattle having been wiped out by the
murrain of 1865-1868. The hinterland did supply fowls, vegetables, eggs, and fruit. All these were taxed two per cent ad
valorem as agreed in the treaty of 1849. Tremenheere believed
that the abolition of the transit dues would do more than anything else to encourage an increase in these products, since the
dues were unpopular and, in some cases, against the religion of
the chiefs. Actually there had been no shortage of provisions
in recent years. On the second point, Tremenheere felt that
the Sultan would gladly grant increased water facilities in return
for an increase in his stipend. However, the position of assistant to the executive engineer of the settlement was, and had
been, vacant, and consequently there was no one who could work
on such a development. The Resident could not see much sense
to the third point. He thought the climate of Aden was quite
pleasant, and as the country of Lahej was rather flat he did not
believe it would be much cooler there. (Actually Tremenheere
was wrong on this; later visitors often have remarked on the relief from Aden's heat given by a trip to Lahej.) He was convinced

that the Sultan would be very glad to have troops stationed in his territory, but that he certainly would not cede any land to the British for this purpose or be disposed to allow his country to be administered by a British officer. As to the fourth point, the Sultan only owned six miles of shallow and useless seacoast which he would be perfectly willing to sell or lease to the British. Tremenheere did feel that the fifth point was most essential to the welfare of Aden and expressed a willingness to undertake negotiations immediately (IO, LA, Tremenheere-Bombay 8/25/71). In Arabia such negotiations took months and even years. Before anything could be arranged, the settlement and the tribes found themselves involved in a fight for their independence.

In 1867, Stanton had sent Sandison to Jidda to investigate the return to that port of certain criminals involved in the massacre of 1858. Sandison had reported Ismail's intrigues with the Asiri against the Turks in the Yemen. In November, 1870, word reached Russell that the Asiri, reportedly 30,000 strong, were approaching Hodeida, much to the alarm of the Banyan merchants there (IO, LA, Russell-Bombay 11/4/70). The situation was so serious that Ali Pasha of the Yemen asked Russell for a gun, 150 rifles, 2,500 pounds of powder and a ship. Russell, while sympathetic, did not feel he could comply with this request without special permission (IO, LA, Russell-Bombay 11/19/70 encl. Ali Pasha-Russell N. D.). The Asiri were gathered near Abu 'Arish, nominally a Turkish possession, but the Pasha, distrustful of the governor of that town, had retired towards Hodeida (IO, LA, Russell-Bombay 11/25/70).

However, when he heard of the capture of Abu 'Arish, Russell on his own responsibility shipped the Pasha 2,500 pounds of powder. He felt that the British should send a ship to Hodeida as the merchants were preparing to abandon the port, but his only available vessel was the transport "Sind" which was unarmed and therefore unable to defend herself against an attack. Russell expected that the Asiri would capture Hodeida as the Pasha had few troops and the Arabs of the town were antagonistic to Turkish rule (IO, LA, Russell-Bombay 12/2/70). Attacks by the tribes on December 2 and 3 compelled Russell to send the "Sind" to Hodeida to aid refugees and also to bring some arms to help the Pasha. Westbrook, captain of the "Sind," reported the attacks repulsed with a loss to the Asiri of some 400 men, the Turks losing only 30 out of a garrison of 1,800

(IO, LA, Tremenheere-Bombay 12/24/70 encl. Westbrook-
Tremenheere 12/23/70).

Rumors of the attack reached Alexandria early in December. Stanton immediately sought an interview with Ismail, who
denied any knowledge of the disturbance, saying that he had received a letter from the Emir of the Asiri that any reports of
disturbances in the Yemen were without foundation. When Stanton asked His Highness if he had any knowledge of the report
that the Porte was dispatching 10,000 troops to re-enforce the
Sharif of Mecca, Ismail replied that it would be better for the
Sultan to send a confidential agent to find out what the trouble
was all about (FO 78/3186, Stanton-FO 12/2/70). Elliot at
Constantinople reported that the Sultan was sending 15,000 men,
2 corvettes, and 3 gunboats to put down the revolt. Because of
the tense political crisis between the Porte and Ismail, Constantinople was afraid to entrust such an action to the Viceroy,
as they had three years previously in a similar but less important revolt (FO 78/3186, Elliot-FO 12/16/70). While there is
no positive proof that Ismail was connected with this affair, one
cannot help but agree with Aali Pasha, then Ottoman Grand
Vizier, when, in conference with Elliot on December 28, he
told the British Ambassador that he believed the whole thing
was the result of the Viceroy's plotting with the leader of the
Asiri and the Sharif of Mecca (FO 78/3186, Elliot-FO 12/28/70).

In the light of Sandison's reports of 1867 a conclusion such
as that reached by Aali Pasha seems entirely probable. In an
interview with Ismail on December 20, Stanton found the Viceroy very upset that he had not been called on to provide troops
to put down the revolt (FO 78/3186, Stanton-FO 12/20/70).
Things had apparently not worked out quite as he had planned.

The incident is very interesting for the light it throws on
Turkish-Egyptian relations in the Red Sea area. When he was
in danger, the Pasha of the Yemen did not turn for help to the
Egyptians, well established with considerable numbers of men
and supplies at Massawa, but requested help from the Resident
at Aden with whom he personally was not on very good terms.
When re-enforcements were sent they were Turkish troops
from Constantinople, not Egyptians from much nearer bases.
One rather amusing sidelight on the oriental character is shown
by the difference between Ali Pasha's report of the attack on
Hodeida to Constantinople and Westbrooke's report to the Resident at Aden. Westbrook, on the scene very shortly after the

attack, described it as fierce, but indicated that the port was at
no time in serious danger. Ali told Constantinople that he had
been driven from the city and that by a fierce counter-attack
he had recaptured the town (FO 78/3186, Elliott-FO 12/23/70
encl. Ali Pasha [Hodeida]-Constantinople N. D.).

As a result of the attack on Hodeida, and unquestionably to
prevent Ismail from stirring up further trouble in Arabia, the
Porte decided to pacify the whole area whether the Asiri sued
for peace or not (FO 78/3186, Elliot-FO 12/23/70). This decision was to lead to serious consequences for the British at
Aden.

Tremenheere received news that Muhammad Redif Pasha
with 4,000 troops and 2 warships had left Constantinople for the
Yemen (IO, LA, Tremenheere-Bombay 1/7/71). Two weeks
later he reported the arrival of Ahmed Pasha and 6,000 men at
Hodeida and the arrival of Redif Pasha at Jidda on his way to
disembark at El-Qunfidha. Redif Pasha had issued a proclamation dated January 8, 1871, announcing the intention of capturing
and punishing the chief of the Asiri for his revolt. Meanwhile
Ali Pasha had captured Bajil, twenty-five miles northeast of
Hodeida, and exacted a penalty of $10,000 from the chief of the
town, Hamud ibn Ali Homeida, for helping the Asiri. The garrisons at Mocha and Sheikh Said were both re-enforced. Tremenheere commented "Although the operations of the Turks
are ostensibly directed against the Asseeries only, considerable
alarm exists as to the real object of so many troops being landed
in Yemen, and their movements are being watched with much
distrust and suspicion by all the tribes in the province" (IO,
LA, Tremenheere-Bombay 1/27/71). In March the Asiri offered
to submit to the Turks, but this offer was turned down and the
Turks demanded complete surrender (IO, LA, Tremenheere-
Bombay 3/24/71). In May, reliable information reached Aden
that the chief of the Asiri had been captured at his capital (IO,
LA, Tremenheere-Bombay 5/11/71). The Turks spent the remainder of the year cleaning up Asiri country, establishing
local governments favorable to them, and placing their own ap-
pointees at key places. The news came in February that 8,000
Turkish infantry and 1,000 cavalry, with guns in proportion,
had landed at Hodeida and were awaiting the arrival of Ahmed
Muktar Pasha before proceeding against San'a. The Imam of
the Yemen Mahsin was an incompetent man, lacking funds and
forces, and in continual difficulties with his subjects; he could

consequently not be expected to put up much opposition. Tremenheere asked the Bombay Government to get the views of the
British government on this contemplated extension of Turkish
power "as the progress of the Turks in the neighborhood cannot
fail to have considerable influence on the position of this settlement both politically and commercially" (IO, LA, Tremenheere
-Bombay 2/8/72).

The Turks captured San'a on April 24, 1872. Tremenheere
believed that this would be followed by a rapid conquest of the
coffee-growing region, and an attempt by the Turks to occupy
all of the country as far as Aden, an action which would seriously threaten Aden's trade with the Red Sea ports. The tribes
were naturally apprehensive, especially the Sultan of Lahej,
who had everything to fear and nothing to hope for from a Turkish occupation. Tremenheere, still awaiting the views of the
home government, was seriously concerned about the danger
(IO, LA, Tremenheere-Bombay 5/7/72). The Imam of San'a,
now made their agent by the Turks, wrote to the Sultan of Lahej
advising him to submit to the Turks. Tremenheere advised
Fadhl to pay no attention to any letters unless they came from
the Turkish commander (IO, LA, Tremenheere-Bombay 5/21/72).

The Turks, turning southward from San'a, found themselves
blocked by the stiff defense of the town of Qa'taba in the hills of
the coffee country. Their military progress was held up there
but their political pressure continued. Brigadier General J.W.
Schneider, who succeeded Tremenheere as Resident in July,
1872, found all the surrounding tribes in receipt of demands
for submission to the Sultan. The only tribe which appeared at
all receptive to this demand was the Haushabi, the enemies of
the Abdali in whose breasts the loss of the springs at Zaida still
rankled.

In September, 1872, the Resident reported that the Mushir
(Turkish civil governor) had distributed percentages of the revenues of the Yemen, estimated at $400,000 a year, to the prin-
cipal chiefs in the country, thereby ensuring their allegiance.
But the Turks were still held up by the stubborn resistance of
Qa'taba, which marked the southern limit of their power (FO
78/2753, IO-FO 2/12/73 encl. Schneider-news letter 9/12/72).

The Sultan of Lahej visited Schneider on October 24 and
asked if the British would back him up if he refused to submit
to the Turks. Schneider told the Sultan to reply to the Turks
"in a friendly and courteous strain and state that he is an ally

and stipendiary of the British Govt.: that treaty obligations exist between him and that govt.: that a copy of the Mushire's communication would be forwarded through the Resident to the Govt. and that he the Sultan, did not desire to act without its wishes being known to him." Schneider felt that nothing would lower British prestige more than allowing "the forcible incorporation of the neighboring states into the Turkish Empire, states which have for years looked on us as the arbiter of their acts and who have been made to feel that we have been hitherto all powerful." The Resident feared that the practical result of Turkish aggression would be the cutting off of Aden's supplies. Schneider requested that Palmerston's policy be followed and the Turks kept out of the Tehama by diplomatic means (IO, LA, Schneider-Bombay 10/26/72).

In November, Sultan Ali ibn Mani of the Haushabi visited the Mushir, returning on the nineteenth bearing a letter to Sultan Fadhl from the Mushir urging him to submit. Qa'taba surrendered early in December (FO 78/2753, Aden news letter, 12/14/72).

Tremenheere had asked for information from the home government in February, 1872, and repeated that request in May. Schneider had laid the matter in the hands of the Bombay Government in October. No action was taken in the affair. Fate, however, seemed to favor the settlement. At the end of December, Sir Bartle Frere arrived in Aden on his way to investigate the conditions of the slave trade at Zanzibar. When the situation was explained to him, his protests to Grenville and Elliot made things move rapidly, if not effectively, in London and in Constantinople.

XXIV.   THE TURKISH CRISIS 1873

The Foreign Office in London actually knew nothing of the actions of the Turks in the Yemen.   None of Schneider's or Tremenheere's reports had been forwarded from the India Office.   The activities of the Turks in Arabia had been casually mentioned in a few dispatches from Alexandria, but these references were entirely to Turkish actions against the Asiri, miles away from Aden.   British interests in the Ottoman Empire were partly concerned with Ismail's dealings with the Porte and the Gladstone government's sympathy with the growing reform movement in Turkey, which promised to solve some of the Balkan irritations, especially in Bulgaria.   But chiefly the British were employing their energies in countering Russian intrigues in Constantinople.

On January 1, 1873, Sir Henry Elliot, the British Ambassador, was summoned to an audience with the Sultan, who requested assurances that British troops had been withdrawn from Lahej, as the Russian Ambassador had informed him that troops were still there and were preparing an expedition into Turkish territory (FO 78/2753, cable Elliot-FO 1/1/73).   This fabrication threw the Foreign Office into confusion.   There were no British troops in Lahej and in fact at the moment no Turkish troops near there.   However, neither Elliot nor the Foreign Office was in a position to know this.   The India Office promptly got together what information they had and forwarded it to the Foreign Office with the request that the latter have Elliot put a stop to further Turkish aggression (FO 78/2753, IO-FO 1/6/73).

Action also came from other quarters.   Sir Bartle Frere, on his way to Zanzibar to negotiate a new slave trade treaty, arrived at Aden on December 31, 1872.   Frere had to a certain extent been forewarned about the situation.   While in Paris he had had a conversation with Comte M. de Remusant (French Foreign Minister) and Server Pasha (Turkish Ambassador to France) in which Turkish claims to the entire Arabian peninsula had been discussed.   What had alarmed him as a result of this conversation was the possibility of Turkish aggression on Oman and the Hadramaut coast which Frere believed should be put immediately under British protection, as Turkish sovereignty to the area would lose many of the gains already made in suppressing the slave trade (FO 78/3186, Frere [Cairo] -FO 12/24/72).

Two days after his arrival at Aden, Frere wrote a private letter to Sir Henry Elliot, explaining to him the gravity of the situation at the settlement. On January 2, news had reached Schneider that the Sultan of Lahej had been peremptorily summoned to San'a to submit to the Mushir Ahmed Muktar Pasha. The situation, Frere explained, had been reported fully by the Resident on October 26, 1872, with a request for instructions which he had never received. Frere pointed out that all the Turks needed to do to starve Aden out was merely to occupy Lahej, not to commit any overt acts of aggression. The only excuse of the Mushir for his interference in the affairs of a tribe which was a British ally was that "the Sultan has resumed his rights divine to this country, where no Turk has been for generations," constituting an unjustifiable aggression by a supposedly friendly country. The Haushabi tribe, at feud with Lahej, had submitted to the Turks after waiting some months for definite word of British intentions. "Before Telegrams were invented any British Official could act on his own responsibility and would. Now his hands are tied by the necessity of obeying express instructions not to act without orders." Frere concluded by saying that Turkish actions threatened the whole life-line to the East. "If nothing is done and the Turks are allowed to take the low country of Lahej, Aden might just as well be given up" (FO 78/2753, Frere-Elliot [private] 1/2/73).

Schneider, still waiting for an answer to his letter of October 26, 1872, was presented with the outright request of the Sultan of Lahej for British protection, and wired London this information on January 3, 1873 (FO 78/2753, cable Schneider-IO 1/3/73). Frere also wired the India Office on January 5 "Turkish moves against Tribes very serious, unless stopped garrison will be starved or expense of commissariat quadrupled" (FO 78/2753, cable Frere-IO 1/5/73). Merivale in the India Office forwarded these wires to the Foreign Office, together with a telegram from the Duke of Argyle on vacation at Inverary which read, "Send telegram of Frere to Foreign Office. Protest should be made to Porte." Merivale requested action "to induce the Turkish authorities to abstain from starving our poor people at Aden in order to punish their own mal-contents" (FO 78/2753, IO-FO 1/6/73).

Frere's approach to the Foreign Office and the India Office

and Merivale's approach to the Foreign Office are noteworthy.
Frere's letter to Elliot is a factual exposition of the situation
written without sentiment. In order to bring home his point to
the Gladstone government, however, he felt it necessary in his
letter to Grenville to drag in the slave trade, although Aden
could never do much about it, as vessels under the Turkish flag
could not be boarded, and even if they could have been, Aden
did not have any warships stationed there to carry on a patrol.
To emphasize the gravity of the situation to the India Office,
Frere in his telegram of January 5 stated "expenses of commissariat quadrupled," playing up the continual desire to save
money which was characteristic of that Office. Merivale's request to the Foreign Office "to induce the Turkish authorities
to abstain from starving our poor people" was certainly calculated to enlist the sympathy of the sentimental Gladstone. Thus
a very small group of documents throws a very interesting sidelight on the Liberal ministry.

    Frere and Schneider must have wired duplicates of their
telegrams to India, for the Viceroy cabled the India Office on
January 6 that they had instructed the Resident to call on the
Pasha "to suspend all demonstrations or actions against chiefs
or tribes around Aden with whom we have political relations
pending instructions from his government." The Resident was
to tell the Pasha that "such (demonstrations) are likely to raise
serious questions between England and the Ottoman Porte and
if persevered in will be regarded as an unfriendly act on Pasha's
part towards Great Britain. Should Pasha persevere I have desired resident to suggest by telegraph whether any and what
moral and material support can be given to Lahej Sultan to enable him to hold his own until question is diplomatically settled"
(FO 78/2753, cable Foreign Secretary, Calcutta-Political Secretary Bombay 1/6/73). The Viceroy then requested the Foreign Office to refer to Palmerston's dispatch of May 24, 1838,
regarding Turkish authority beyond the mouth of the Red Sea,
and ended by instructing the India Office to have the Foreign
Office inform the Porte of this dispatch and ask the Porte "to
issue immediate instructions to restrain Pasha from course he
had adopted." With this telegram was forwarded a copy of Palmerston's dispatch. This dispatch is quoted in full on p. 60
together with the circumstances that were responsible for it.
However, it is worth repeating, as from 1838 on it had been the
keystone of Indian policy in southwestern Arabia.

Muhammad Ali had undertaken the conquest of the Yemen, and his efforts threatened to prevent the British from establishing a coaling station at Aden for the new line of steamships from Suez to Bombay. At that time the Bombay Government was negotiating for the peaceful acquisition of certain rights at that port. The dispatch to Campbell, then Consul General at Alexandria, read as follows (FO 78/2753, IO-FO 1/8/73, encl. Cable, Viceroy [Calcutta] IO 1/6/73 and copy of Palmerston-Campbell 5/24/38):

> I have to instruct you to remind Boghos Bey of the declaration already made by H. M. Govt. through you as reported in your dispatch No. 31 of last year, that Great Britain could not see with indifference any attempt made by Muhammad Ali to invade or conquer the country lying at and beyond the mouth of the Red Sea.
> With respect to the occupation of the Yemen by Egyptian troops, you will say that the British Govt. have no desire that such occupation should continue, but, on the contrary, would be better pleased by any overt act which would show that the Pasha is engaged in improving the administration of the Provinces confided to his Govt. instead of employing the energies of his mind and the resources of the country he governs in aggressive expeditions against neighboring districts.

It is the painful duty of an historian to record examples of incompetence which sometimes border on crass stupidity. Some unknown Foreign Office official appended the following Minute to the dispatch from the India Office: "Ld. Palmerston's dispatches only referred to Muhammad Ali's encroachments" (FO 78/2753, unsigned Minute on IO-FO 1/8/73). Actually, with just a change in names, Palmerston's dispatch was just as pertinent in 1873 as it had been in 1838. However, Grenville was not Palmerston.

But what of the Viceroy's telegram? What he wished the Foreign Office to do is clear, but his wording was that of an order, not a request. But were his instructions to Schneider as clear? Was the Resident empowered to grant British protection to the Sultan of Lahej, and if he were, was he sanctioned to back up this protection by force? The Viceroy had instructed him to deliver an ultimatum to Ahmed Muktar Pasha. To refuse

this ultimatum would constitute an "unfriendly act" on the part
of the Pasha, diplomatically very strong words. Certainly the
words "moral and material support" indicated a willingness on
the part of the Indian Government to go to war over the issue,
but Schneider was left dependent on instructions from India.
And what was the position of the Foreign Office in its relations
with the Ottoman Empire? It was bound to continue its support
of the Porte against the Russians, and to support Constantinople
against any internal weakening of its position by Ismail's ambitions, while at the same time another part of the British government, a very powerful state in itself, with its own army,
was ready to make war on the Porte in self-protection. Conflict of interests between the two offices have been apparent before, and proper liaison between them did not exist, as the situation in the Yemen rather dramatically proves. With proper
liaison, the situation could easily have been handled long before
it had reached the explosive point. It was now an acute crisis
because of indifference on the part of the India Office, combined
with mutual jealousy and distrust between two divisions of the
British government.

On January 11, the Foreign Office instructed Elliot by telegraph to inform the Porte that the Sultan of Lahej was apprehensive of the hostile movements of Turkish forces, and further
to inform them that "Any such movement would be viewed in a
serious light by Her Majesty's Government as calculated to
interfere with the British territory of Aden." Elliot was to inquire as to whether or not the movements near Aden were sanctioned by the Porte and "in any case request the Porte to send
immediate orders to its authorities to suspend hostile operations in that quarter against any of the Arab chiefs which, as
calculated to disturb the position we hold in Aden, would certainly produce a bad impression in England no less than in India"
(FO 78/2753, cable FO-Elliot 1/11/73, copy to IO).

Elliot replied on January 13 with the following telegram:
"No operations have been or will be commenced against the Lahej without orders from the Porte, which will do nothing without
consulting Her Majesty's Government.

"Lahej is considered here as forming a part of the Yemen
and the Governor of that province reports that the chiefs having
attacked and plundered a neighboring chieftain who recognized
the Sultan's authority, his aggression ought not to pass unnoticed"
(FO 78/2753, cable Elliot-FO 1/13/73).

This telegram was amplified by letter, which read in part, "Lahej or Lash is regarded by the Porte as forming part of the territory of the Yemen... having lately been [underlining done at FO] reduced to more complete submission to the authority of the Sultan." The Porte accused the Sultan of Lahej of plundering a neighboring chief and refusing to submit, but "most scrupulous respect was being shown for British territory" as the Porte had no idea of conquering beyond the Red Sea. Elliot asked what had been the previous position of this chief. Khalil Pasha replied that "the report of the governor of the Yemen had only just then been received and he was not yet very fully acquainted with all the particulars" (FO 78/2753, Elliot-FO 1/13/73).

On receipt of this the Foreign Office prepared a printed memo summarizing Palmerston's correspondence with Muhammad Ali on the subject, and the documents relative to the establishment of the settlement of Aden. It also reviewed possible Turkish claims to sovereignty based on von Hammer's excellent history of the Ottoman Empire, conclusively proving no Turkis claim existed after their retirement in 1633 (FO 78/2753, Memo on Yemen, Printed for the Foreign Office, January, 1873). This memo and Schneider's dispatch of October 26, 1872, were forwarded to Elliot with a covering letter which told him to inform the Porte "Her Majesty's Government would view seriously any proceedings calculated to disturb the country in the neighborhood of that place (Aden)" (FO 78/2753, FO-Elliot 1/23/73).

This second note was slightly stiffer than the first one, and certainly should have made plain to the Porte that the British were concerned with the tribes as well as with Aden itself.

The Duke of Argyle, in a letter to Hammond of the Foreign Office dated January 25, indicated that he was not at all satisfied with the result of Elliot's first protest, feeling that "to this Turkey replies 'oh it is nothing at all these tribes and territories are already ours (part of Yemen a province of Turkey) and we are only punishing some depredations made by one chief upon another.'

"Well — But if we admit this as satisfactory we are giving up all that Frere and others are contending for." While he did not know the historical Turkish claims over the tribes, Frere had denied them. He continued, "However, they have been practically independent and we have established relations with

them for very practical and important reasons. We must not
therefore accept without protest a reply which asserts the very
dominion we object to – and merely assures us that they are taking no new steps.

"Will you look into this matter. What I am afraid of is a
seeming acquiescence in a reply which may involve the whole
question in dispute" (FO 78/2753, Argyle-Hammond 1/25/73).

In view of Argyle's protest, new instructions were drafted
to Elliot which were approved by the Queen, Gladstone, and Argyle and telegraphed in cypher on January 30, 1873. The instructions stated that the Pasha's language was satisfactory as regarded any new operations, but that it was not satisfactory in the
"assumption of the right of the Porte to call upon these chieftains to make professions of obedience to the Porte, on the
ground that the territory of the Yemen is subject to the authority
of the Porte, even though this assumption was qualified by the
assurance of the most scrupulous respect being shown for British territory." Elliot was instructed to point out to Khalil Pasha that it was not a question of British territory "but that the
Sultan of Lahej and other Arab chiefs in friendly relations with
the British government at Aden, should not be molested or interfered with by Turkish authorities on the alleged ground that
the Province of Yemen belongs to the Porte and that those chiefs
... are subjects of the Porte." Whatever claims the Porte had
lapsed in 1633. "Her Majesty's government have, however, no
desire to discuss that question [sovereignty] generally; but they
cannot, as matters stand, but intimate through you to the Porte
... (as was done to Muhammad Ali in 1838) that Her Majesty's
government wish that the independence of the native chiefs in the
vicinity of Aden be respected and that any attempt to subvert
their authority would not be viewed with indifference by Her Majesty's government" (FO 78/2753, FO-Elliot tel. 1/30/73).

Argyle had won his point; the use of the terminology "would
not be viewed with indifference," made this note almost as
strong as a direct ultimatum. It could not be brushed off by polite words or oriental procrastination.

The Porte, however, found itself in a difficult position.
Khalil Pasha suggested to Elliot, on February 3, that the Sultan
of Lahej make a nominal submission without tribute or services
being required. Elliot assured him that there was no probability of such an arrangement being obtained and pointed out the
agreement with Muhammad Ali that the mountains were the

boundary of the Yemen. Elliot, after the interview, felt that
the Porte did not wish to give offence to the British but were
trying to find a way to back out of the embarrassing position in
which Ahmed Muktar Pasha had placed them. Elliot believed
that Khalil Pasha was fearful of serious consequences to Turkish authority in the surrounding territory if, after having demanded submission and backed this demand by a show of force,
the Turks should suddenly withdraw their demands (FO 78/2753,
Elliot-FO 2/3/73). Negotiations proceeded in Constantinople,
and on February 12 Elliot wired the following information:
"Vizerial orders founded upon an Imperial rescript have been
forwarded to the Governor General of the Yemen to abstain from
attacking or interfering with the Ruler of Lahej and directing
him to leave matters in their former position" (FO 78/2753,
cable, Elliot-FO 2/14/73).

The Foreign Office believed that this vizierial order could
stop further difficulties, but what did it actually do? It served
to settle a dispute based on conditions which existed two months
previously. While Schneider's authority was limited and he
was tied by cable to Bombay and London, Ahmed Muktar Pasha
was on his own. As far as communications were concerned he
was as far from Constantinople as Haines was from London in
the 1840's. A message to him could go by cable only as far as
Suez; from there it would go by coastal vessel to Hodeida and
by horseback up to San'a. Therefore, Constantinople, acting
in good faith, could not know the exact situation in the Yemen
and what information they would get would unquestionably be
colored by oriental exaggeration, as illustrated so well by the
difference in the versions of Westbrook and Ali Pasha on the
Asiri attack on Hodeida in 1871. Also, as was customary with
most Pashas far from home, Ahmed Muktar probably did not
feel the authority of Constantinople too strongly.

At Aden things had not gone smoothly. The dispute between
Mukalla and Shihr on the Hadramaut coast had never been settled, and in December the Turkish authorities called on the
Sheikh of Shihr to submit. He was instructed by the Indian Government to disregard this request, but it was more difficult to
hold off the Turks when two Turkish steamers appeared off the
coast, and the Sheikh renewed his request made four years previously for British protection (FO 78/2753, IO-FO 2/12/73).

Schneider, his position strengthened by the Viceroy's orders
of January 6, called on the Haushabi Sultan to explain his

submission to the Turks. The Haushabi Sultan professed a willingness to be guided by the British, but said that he had submitted under the threat of Turkish occupation of his territory,
and confirmed Turkish intrigues which were aimed at disturbing
the tribal governments. Schneider forwarded the ultimatum of
the Viceroy to Ahmed Muktar Pasha on January 8. This ultimatum seemed to halt the Pasha temporarily, but his intrigues
continued (FO 78/2753, IO-FO 2/12/73).

In India, preparations were made to establish a protectorate over all the tribes with which the British had treaties. In
March, a tentative draft of the arrangement was forwarded from
the India Office to the Foreign Office for Grenville's concurrence
(FO 78/2753, IO-FO 3/14/73). Hammond commented that the
question of Lahej had been satisfactorily settled, but the plan of
the Indian Government involved a much more sweeping demand
on the Porte. "I confess," he went on, "before making it, I
think we ought to have some positive proof that we have the right
on our side. The demand practically involves a recognition of
a British Protectorate over some independent districts in Arabia.
The Porte may not have sovereign rights in this quarter but are
we entitled to expect any ourselves" (FO 78/2753, Minute by
Hammond on IO-FO 3/14/73, 3/16/73). The India Office was,
therefore, requested to produce proof of British rights in this
area (FO 78/2753, FO-IO 3/24/73).

Muktar Pasha's intrigues finally discovered the weakest
point in intertribal relations. The Haushabi had always regretted
the cession of Zaida to the Abdali in 1868. Although Russell had
tried to compromise this settlement in 1870 by returning a small
part of the land around the village to the Haushabi, Zaida itself
had remained part of the domain of the Sultan of Lahej. On May 5
Schneider reported that the Haushabi Sultan, Ali ibn Mani had
been ordered to San'a. Here the civil governor of Ta'iz appointed him as chief of the Haushabi territory at a salary of $50
a month. He returned to his territory with the assurance from
Ahmed Muktar Pasha that Turkish troops would be sent to protect his territory (FO 78/2753, IO-FO 5/12/73 encl. cable Aden
-Ft. Williams 5/5/73).

Almost at the same time, the Foreign Office received from
the government of India their justification of the contemplated
protectorate over the tribes. The Indian Government considered
that two questions were involved, first, the British rights regarding the alleged claims of the Porte, second, the British

rights regarding the chiefs themselves. In answer to the first point, the Indian Government wrote as follows:

"1st. That the Chiefs are and for the last century have been independent of Turkish influence and control. 2nd. That the British government has as a matter of fact already entered into Treaty relations with these chiefs without reference to Turkey or any other foreign power and may conclude fresh engagements with them if deemed expedient. 3rd. That the recent proceedings of the Turkish officials have been so prejudicial to British interests at Aden as to afford good ground for such arrangements being concluded with the chiefs as may be deemed best fitted to present repetitions of the evils. To such arrangements for the peace and security of our settlement no objection can reasonably be offered. 4th. That the chief of the largest and most important tribe, the Abdalies has distinctly claimed British assistance and asked for protection. 5th. That while the chiefs have been independent of Turkey they have not been so of the British government, which for some years has paid them stipends and has frequently interfered to settle their tribal quarrels. They have come to look on the Resident at Aden as their friend and adviser in all their difficulties. The question is therefore somewhat a domestic one."

As to the question of the rights of the British government with the chiefs themselves, the Indian Government stated: "While we consider ourselves free to impose any measures upon the chiefs which we may deem essential for the safety of our Aden possessions, it is far from our intentions to have recourse to any forcible measures. We propose to secure the objects we have in view with the consent of the chiefs and by negotiation with them."

The Indian Government then discussed the extent of protection which they contemplated. "1st. in regard to the territorial limits of the protectorate and 2nd. as to the precise degree of such protection.

"In the former respect, we are of the opinion that the protection of the British government should extend to all the tribes marginally noted. [In the margin were inscribed "1. The Abdalee [Lahej] 2. The Foodhlee. 3. The Akrabee. 4. The Houshebee. 5. The Alowee. 6. The Ameer. 7. The Soubahee. 8. The Yaf-aee. 9. The Owlakee (with whom treaties have been, at various times, concluded).]

"As to the degree of protection, we consider that it will be

sufficient 1st to require the chiefs to abstain from political intercourse with Foreign Powers without the consent of the British government and to refer all disputes with foreign powers or
with each other to the British government for settlement and
2nd on our part to engage to defend them against unprovoked aggression by foreign powers" (FO 78/2753 encl. in Govt. of India
[Ft. William]-IO 4/12/73, IO-FO 5/11/73).

In view of the information contained in the report from Aden
and this document just quoted, Elliot was instructed on May 15
to inform the Porte that the instructions and assurances of
Turkish non-interference be extended to the whole province, as
the Turks were still interfering in tribal affairs. He was to
call the attention of the Porte to the new aggression in Haushabi
territory, and was further instructed that he was to use the arguments put forth in the above statement "as the ground for your
insistence with the Turkish Government against interference
with the Arab tribes enumerated by the Governor General" (FO
78/2753, FO-Elliot 5/15/73).

Before Elliot had had an opportunity to carry out his instructions, news came from Aden that the Turks had billeted
twelve soldiers in a house belonging to the Haushabi Sultan near
Saida on the border of Lahej (FO 78/2753, cable Schneider-
Ft. William 5/21/73 in IO-FO 5/22/73). Elliot was instructed
to press the Porte for the immediate removal of these troops
(FO 78/2753, cable FO-Elliot 5/23/73).

The results which Elliot obtained could hardly be called
satisfactory. On June 1 he wired that the Porte would issue an
order for the withdrawal of the troops from the Haushabi Sultan's home and that the "Porte will officially notify its intention
of abstaining from molesting any of the Tribes who have treaties
with England. Even with communicating this resolution they
propose to make certain reservations of their rights with the
particulars of which I am not yet acquainted" (FO 78/2753,
cable Elliot-FO 6/1/73).

In London, both the Foreign Office and the India Office were
becoming thoroughly confused because of the time lag between
the receipt of cables from India and the arrival of mail from
both India and Aden. Brief telegraphic information had not given
the full story, and the situation in Aden was much more serious than it had appeared. Furthermore, the India Office was
not giving the Foreign Office all the information that it had
available.

What had happened at Aden was not clear until late in June. On May 5, Aden informed London that the Mushir had interpreted Constantinople's order to apply to Lahej only, and was continuing pressure on other tribes (FO 78/2753, Schneider-London 5/5/73, encl. in IO-FO 6/17/73). Under threat of force the Amiri tribe had submitted to the Turks who had imposed an eight per cent duty on imports from Aden to Amiri territory, and duty of two-and-a-half per cent on exports to Aden. This revenue had been farmed out to the uncle of the Amiri Sultan for $222 a month. The Sultan was to be paid a stipend of $40 a month and give a hostage who was to reside in Ta'iz. The Resident, powerless to do anything, advised the Amiri Sultan to agree temporarily to these terms (FO 78/2753, Schneider-Bombay 5/12/73 encl. in IO-FO 6/17/73). The Bombay Government, acting on earlier information regarding the defection of the Haushabi Sultan, instructed Schneider on May 11 to stop his stipend. Ali ibn Mani replied that if his stipend were stopped he would close the roads (FO 78/2753, Schneider-Bombay 5/18/73).

The Turks renewed their intrigues in Lahej, instigating the Abdali Sultan's uncle and some disaffected minor sheikhs to revolt. Schneider pointed out the impossibility of a situation which allowed any petty sheikh to defy the Aden government and be backed up in his defiance by Turkish troops (FO 78/2753, Schneider-London 5/26/73). The next day, May 27, the situation took a critical turn when Schneider wired the India Office that the Civil Governor of Ta'iz had departed on a reconnaissance of the Subahi, Amiri, and Haushabi country with three regiments. Such a reconnaissance in force, so close to Aden, would have a disastrous effect on the tribes, and Schneider sought permission to send troops to Lahej to support the Sultan if necessary (FO 78/2753, cable Schneider-IO 5/27/73). In this critical situation the Viceroy informed the Duke of Argyle, Secretary of State for India, that he would leave the question of ordering of troops to Lahej to the India Office in London (FO 78/2753, cable Viceroy-Argyle 5/29/73). This information was transmitted to the Foreign Office with the comment by Kaye of the India Council that the Turks did not appear to be acting in good faith (FO 78/2753, Kaye [IO]-Hammond 5/30/73).

That the Porte realized the seriousness of the situation was apparent when Elliot in Constantinople wired, on June 6, that a new governor general had been dispatched to the Yemen with instructions not to molest the tribes. He had departed June 5, but as there was no telegraph to Hodeida the instructions would be delayed until he arrived (FO 78/2753, cable Elliot-FO 6/6/73).

For a second time the situation seemed to be settled. However, in the Yemen there appeared to be no relaxation of Turkish aggression. The Sultan of the Amiri, returning from a visit to Aden, was summoned to Qa'taba, imprisoned by the Turks, and was replaced as Sultan by his uncle (FO 78/2753, Schneider -Bombay 6/6/73 encl. in IO-FO 7/11/73). The Subahi tribe attacked the expedition of the Governor of Ta'iz on the border of their territory and were severely defeated, losing one of their leading chiefs (FO 78/2753, Aden-IO 6/18/73). The new Governor General, Ahmed Ayub Pasha, arrived in June to replace Ahmed Muktar, Purtu Pasha became the deputy to the Governor General, and Muhammad Pasha the governor of the province of Ta'iz (FO 78/2753, Aden-IO 6/25/73). Instead of easing the situation, these replacements caused it to become more critical. Four hundred Turkish troops moved into Haushabi territory, and eight hundred into Subahi territory (FO 78/2753, cable Aden-IO 6/27/73). However, these troops were almost immediately withdrawn to Amiri country, where they seized the fort of the Sultan (FO 78/2753, Schneider-Bombay 7/2/73). Schneider waited for proof of good faith on the part of the new Turkish officials, but by the end of July his patience was nearly exhausted when the troops in the Haushabi territory were re-enforced by thirty Arab irregulars (FO 78/2753, cable Schneider-IO 7/30/73). These continued aggressions, coupled with other disturbances in the East in the Nejd, Kashgar, and Yennan led the Duke of Argyle to request Grenville to inform his officials to investigate whether these disturbances were connected in any way (FO 78/2753, IO-FO 8/9/73).

In 1871, Midhat Pasha, then governor of the Baghdad Pashalik, had been ordered to occupy the Nejd in northeastern Arabia. Lacking sufficient force to occupy the interior oases, he had been able to set up a government friendly to the Ottoman Empire in most of the area. In Kashgar, the westernmost province of Chinese Turkestan, the Chinese Muslims had revolted in 1862. Under their General Yakoub Khan, they were threatening other provinces of Chinese Turkestan in the early 1870's. The revolt was suppressed and Chinese authority re-established in 1877. In Yennan province, bordering on Burma, a Muslim rebellion occurred in 1856, and the province remained independent under Muslim rulers until 1872, when the revolt was suppressed by the Chinese.

Ever since the Indian Mutiny, the Government of India had been alarmed at the effect of successful Muslim revolts or aggressions on the large Muhammadan population of India. Yakoub Khan's exploits in Kashgar had attracted the attention of the entire Muslim world, and the India Office was interested in seeing if there was any connection between these various manifestations of Muslim independence.

In August, Schneider reported that the Amiri Sultan was still a prisoner, and that the Turks continued to interfere in Subahi affairs (FO 78/2753, Schneider-IO 8/9/73). This was shortly followed by the reception of a letter by Sultan Fadhl of Lahej from Ahmed Ayub Pasha threatening him with the occupation of this territory if he did not submit. Schneider immediately wrote the new Ottoman Governor General that he was acting in violation of his orders; that his predecessor had admitted that he had been instructed to respect the independence of the Abdali. He also pointed out that contrary to orders the Turks still occupied Haushabi territory (FO 78/2753, Schneider-Bombay 8/21/73). On October 10 Schneider received a reply from Ahmed Ayub that the Haushabi district was part of the territory of the province of Ta'iz, and that he categorically refused to withdraw his troops (FO 78/2753, cable Schneider-IO 10/10/73 encl. in IO-FO 10/10/73).

Due again to the time difference between mail and telegraphic communication, neither the India Office nor the Foreign Office had nearly as clear a picture of events as described above. In the Foreign Office files the dispatches are arranged as to date of receipt, and the dates of the forwarding letters from the India Office indicate that the dispatches were not received in chronological order. At certain times, both offices might easily have been led to believe that the situation was clearing up.

On September 5, however, the Viceroy appealed to Argyle "to urge Her Majesty's Government to demand from the Porte the immediate release of Ameer Ali bin Mookbil and the abstinence of non-interference in the affairs of his tribe" (FO 78/2753, IO-FO 9/5/73). The Foreign Office prepared a memo on this chief from what little was in the files, and had it forwarded to Elliot.

On hearing from the India Office of Ahmed Ayub Pasha's refusal to evacuate the Haushabi district, the Foreign Office prepared copies of all the correspondence and forwarded it to Elliot with instructions to request the Porte to issue "even more stringent orders" (FO 78/2753, FO-Elliot 10/13/73).

Meanwhile, in Constantinople, the Porte had submitted to Elliot an explanation of its actions in the Yemen. Reschid Pasha informed Elliot on July 15 that the only basis for any fears of the British government was the isolated incident of the Haushabi Sultan. The Turkish government did not believe it was the proper moment to invalidate "l'independance seculaire" of the nine tribes and the country of the Hadramaut. The Porte had ordered that the Haushabi question be settled, and reported that the Turks were on good terms with all the neighboring chiefs in the Yemen, due to proximity and the common bonds of religion. Reschid stated that when Ottoman ships visited Mukalla and Shihr it was only for commerce, as the needs of the population were augmented by the increasing civilization brought by the Turks. Reschid concluded with a description of the civilizing effect of the Turkish occupation of the Yemen of which he was sure the British government would approve (FO 78/2753, Reschid Pasha-Elliot 7/15/73). This did not indicate a very submissive attitude on the part of the Porte, nor bode too well for the success of Elliot's next protest. The instructions to Elliot had, however, been dispatched by mail on October 13, and as mail took from seven to twelve days to arrive, he did not have time to act until events at Aden took an even more serious turn.

Procrastination in the Foreign Office contributed greatly to this coming crisis. In March, 1873, the India Office had requested the opinion of the Foreign Office on setting up a protectorate at Aden. The Foreign Office request for further information as to the rights involved in the matter had been answered by dispatch from the Government of India of April 11, received on May 12. This dispatch had been filed away without action. On October 13 the India Office forwarded a letter from the Viceroy asking for a decision (FO 78/2753, IO-FO 10/13/73 encl. Small-IO 8/11/73).

Lord Tenterden, Assistant Under Secretary of Foreign Affairs, after reviewing the situation, wrote "This is a very serious matter. If we protect these tribes we must see to their good behaviour & sooner or later shall have to govern them altogether & annex them. I presume you will consult Mr. Gladstone before deciding." Grenville noted "I suggest to Mr. Gladstone that we should make another representation to the Porte, telling them that such a measure has been proposed but before taking it into consideration we think it right to make another representation to them of the absolute neglect of their bonafide carrying out of their assurances" (FO 78/2753, Minutes by Tenterden and Grenville on IO-FO 10/13/73, 10/14/73). The same day the Foreign Office received from the India Office a cable from the Viceroy reading "May I give orders to protect Lahej and stipendiary chiefs if necessary and enter into treaty proposed in dispatch of August 11" (FO 78/2753, cable Viceroy-IO 10/13/73 encl. in IO-FO 10/14/73). This confused Tenterden completely. "I haven't gotten to the bottom of this," he wrote. "There seems to be a correspondence with Constantinople which has caused the Governor General to be changed." He then appended a list of treaties and expressed his uncertainty as to which treaty was referred to (FO 78/2753, Minute by Tenterden 10/15/73 on cable Viceroy-IO 10/13/73).

Lord Tenterden was an able man and he had all the justification in the world for his confusion: first, because the British had never demanded the replacement of the Governor General of the Yemen, the Turks had done it of their own accord for their own purposes; second, because neither the Foreign Office nor the India Office had ever received any draft of the proposed treaty although the dispatch from the Government of India on April 11 had amply covered its main points.

But incidents in Lahej answered the first part of the Viceroy's request. A group of Abdali followers of the Sultan's brother, Abdullah, raided a village in Lahej and were beaten off about October 16. The sheikhs of the tribe mediated the dispute and hostages were given for good behavior. However, twenty-five Turkish soldiers entered Lahej territory and occupied Abdullah's house and demanded hostages from the Sultan. On his refusal to submit, the Turks demanded the right to occupy Zaida as the governor of Ta'iz had ordered them to do. Schneider ordered the Turks to withdraw from Lahej territory, and advised Bombay that if his order was refused it would be necessary to use force (FO 78/2753, IO-FO 10/24/73 encl. cable Aden-IO 10/20/73). Two days later Schneider wired London and Bombay that the Turkish officer refused to leave as he was protecting Abdullah, who was an Ottoman subject. Schneider requested that Constantinople give a telegraphic order via Aden to the Governor of Ta'iz to withdraw the troops (FO 78/2753, cable Aden-London 10/22/73). The Viceroy of India, tired of futile diplomacy, ordered Schneider to send troops to protect the Sultan of Lahej but not to attack the Turks. He stated further

to London, "early orders urgently required" (FO 78/2753, Viceroy-IO 10/23/73).

As to the second part of the request regarding the establishment of a protectorate, Gladstone definitely turned it down.
After stating that he concurred with Grenville's opinion that a
further protest be made to the Porte, he went on, "There is
every imaginable objection to the proposed protectorate. It involves the most indefinite obligation. It binds us to support
those whose conduct to others we have no control. It threatens
to impair and that chronically our good understanding with Turkey which is so necessary to the peace of the East. Nothing
but absolute necessity can warrant our interference and then
only within the limits moral and local, to which that necessity
extends. What we are fairly entitled to ask is that Turkey shall
commit no act of aggression against these chieftains and that,
we have every reason to believe, we can obtain from our general experience in Constantinople.

"It would be unpardonable to make another Gold Coast out
of this" (FO 78/2753, Minute by Gladstone, 10/11/73). (Gladstone's mention of the Gold Coast refers to the Ashanti War of
1873 which resulted from a rather indefinite protectorate established over a tribe which the Ashanti considered as their tributary.) This decision was transmitted privately to the Duke of
Argyle (FO 78/2753, Grenville-Argyle [private] 10/19/73) but,
probably due to the events mentioned above, the India Office
was not officially advised that any decision had been made.

Under the circumstances, the Foreign Office took the only
course available and wired Elliot "Resident at Aden says Turkish officer declines to remove troops from Lahej country.
There under orders of acting Governor of Ta'iz to protect Abdullah Sultan's brother. Tell Porte astonishment of H. M. G.
at failure of Turkish Govt. to carry out their assurances and
press for immediate instructions by telegraph to new governor
to withdraw troops from Houshebee country and Lahej" (FO 78/
2753, cable FO-Elliot 10/25/73).

On receipt of these telegraphic orders, Locock, who was
chargé d'affaires in Constantinople in Elliot's absence, presented the protest to the Foreign Minister through Pisani, the
British Dragoman. The Turkish reply consisted of a copy of
a report on the state of affairs by Ayub Pasha, the Governor
General, and a promise to take up the matter at the next cabinet
meeting (FO 78/2753, Locock-FO 10/31/73).

The report of Ayub Pasha, dated August 6, is worthy of close scrutiny. He stated that his investigation showed that the Subahi had submitted of their own free will, so that there was no need for the Turks to use force there. The Haushabi had also submitted willingly, so that there was no need for troops in Haushabi country except for the fact that the Sultan of Lahej had become their enemy through refusal to submit to the Porte, and had commenced a system of persecution and encroachment against this tribe. Therefore the Haushabi had petitioned the Turks to protect them. Furthermore the Sultan of Lahej had usurped Haushabi lands near Zaida, so the Governor General had ordered Sultan Fadhl of the Abdali to submit or abandon that territory. As far as he could find, the only relation the British had with the tribes was a slight gift of money. Therefore, the Governor could not understand the real motive of the pretensions advanced by the British Embassy. Fadhl's brothers, Abdullah ibn Mahsin and Abdul Kerim ibn Mahsin, had "spontaneously and influenced solely by their zeal for Islamism, formally enrolled themselves as Turkish subjects and, up to the present time, had been firm and faithful in their allegiance to the Porte. But in consequence of the insults and persecutions of their brother, Sheikh Fazyl [Fadhl] who had violently seized their lands and property, and encroached on their legal rights for a long time past, they have petitioned for redress and protection" (FO 78/2753, Gov. Gen. Yemen [Ayub Pasha]-Constantinople 8/6/73; translated at Embassy in Constantinople, encl. in Lacock-FO 10/31/73). An official of the Foreign Office, ignorant, on the whole, of the history and situation of Aden, commented "There is a dispute among the tribes in which one side seeks Turkish, the other British support" (FO 78/2753, Minute on Lacock-FO 10/11/73).

From Aden, Schneider reported that pursuant to the Viceroy's order, he had dispatched infantry, artillery, and sappers to the number of 328 under Colonel MacKenzie to support the Sultan on October 27, after sending fifty men of the Aden Horse there on October 24. Schneider himself was leaving to take command (FO 78/2753, cable, Aden-IO 10/27/73). On November 3, Schneider reported, Turkish re-enforcements arrived at Abdullah's house in Lahej and at Shuha in Haushabi territory (FO 78/2753, cable, Aden-IO 11/3/73).

On November 13, the India Office forwarded to the Foreign Office dispatches received by mail from Aden, giving much fuller details of the whole affair and bringing out a new fact which was unquestionably adding to Ayub Pasha's irritation. Turkish soldiers had been deserting in considerable numbers and fleeing to Aden. From there they went to Mukalla and Shihr in order to avoid Turkish territory. Ayub demanded the return of these deserters, and Schneider informed him that there was no treaty between Britain and the Porte which called for the delivery of army deserters (FO 78/2753, Aden-Bombay 10/8/73). In the letter forwarding these dispatches, the India Office informed the Foreign Office that the state of affairs was very unsatisfactory. "If the Government of the Sultan cannot be persuaded by efforts of diplomacy to adhere to its promises so frequently made, and to fulfill them at once, more active measures should be taken" (FO 78/2753, IO-FO 11/13/73).

Burgin, in the Foreign Office, commented "H. M. G. have decided it appears, not to extend British protection to these tribes. (But this has not been as yet made known to the India Office)" (FO 78/2753, Minute by Burgin 11/13/73).

The Foreign Office wired Elliot to press for an answer to his protest of October 27, and he replied on November 15 by wire, "Porte promises order sent at once for evacuation of Houshebi country and engages that orders shall be executed" (FO 78/2753, cables, Elliot-FO 11/15/73 and FO-Elliot, 11/14/73).

Tenterden, meanwhile, prepared a review of the whole crisis, noting that nothing had been said about the release of the Amiri chief nor had Argyle made any reply to Gladstone's note. He concluded, "The whole matter requires the consideration of the Cabinet as to the next step to be taken" (FO 78/2753, Memo by Tenterden 11/14/73).

Elliot confirmed his telegram of November 15 enclosing a translation of the orders sent to Ahmed Ayub Pasha. "Understand troops and police sent into Houshebi country, You have acted under misapprehension, instructed to withdraw immediately those troops and Fatisieh [police] which have been sent to Lahej." As Tenterden commented, "This doesn't quite agree with the telegram received which said Lahej and Houshebee" (FO 78/2753, Elliot-FO 11/16/73 & Minute by Tenterden N. D.).

Tenterden's opinion was confirmed by a telegram from Aden of November 18. The Governor General of the Yemen had sent an officer to request the Resident to help in making peace between Abdullah and his brother, Sultan Fadhl. After Schneider had insisted that he and Fadhl demanded Abdullah's complete submission, the Turkish officer Izzul Effendi, admitted that orders had been received not to interfere with Lahej, but these did not cover the Haushabi or other chiefs. Schneider commented, "Resident sees nothing but discreditable subterfuge in conduct of Turkish authorities and trusts there is a limit to forbearance of British Government" (FO 78/2753, cable Schneider-IO 11/18/73). This telegram was transmitted to Elliot.

The Porte now assumed the diplomatic offensive. Reschid Pasha wired Musurus Pasha, Turkish Ambassador in London, protesting against the sending of 500 British troops to Lahej, which the Porte attributed to the duplicity of the Sultan of Lahej which "had blinded the eyes of the British Government to exact situation for Sir H. Elliot has already received assurances that the imperial government will not occupy or has not thought of occupying the district." Musurus was instructed to assure Grenville categorically that the Turkish troops were withdrawn (FO 78/2753, cable, Reschid-Musurus 11/26/73). Musurus was reminded that previous promises of the Porte had not been fulfilled but that after the matter was settled there would probably be no need for British troops to remain in Lahej, although the final decision would remain with the India Office. This information and a copy of Reschid's telegram was forwarded to Elliot (FO 78/2753, FO-Elliot 11/27/73).

The value of the Porte's categorical assurance was proved by a telegram from Aden on December 2, reporting not only the continued presence of Turkish troops, but the rumored departure of re-enforcements from Ta'iz. Schneider considered that the continued disregard of orders by the Governor General would leave force as the only remedy for the situation, and requested that re-enforcements for Aden be held in readiness (FO 78/2753, cable, Schneider-London 12/2/73).

In transmitting this letter to the Foreign Office, the India Office asked Grenville what further diplomatic steps he contemplated. The covering letter concluded, "I am further to state that in the opinion of the Secretary of State for India, the time seems to have almost come when the Turkish forces should be summoned to retire, and when, on refusal, that retirement should be enforced by the troops under the command of the Resident." A Minute attached reads "Ld. Grenville says on this − wait" (FO 78/2753, IO-FO 12/2/73 & Minute). The India Office backed this up by a memorandum from Sir Bartle Frere, in which he pointed out the necessity of getting the Turks away from the tribes around Aden. He had advocated that Aden be supported by troops with orders to act, accompanied by naval action at Hodeida, the Turkish base of supplies. He believed Elliot should insist on precise and clear orders which would prevent any evasion or delay and which would be carried to Hodeida by a naval force "to insure immediate attention and an early reply." Mukalla should also be protected by a small naval vessel. A Minute appended read, "seen by Ld. Grenville, Do you want anything done on this?" "Not at present. G) (FO 78/2750, Memo by Sir Bartle Frere 12/2/73 & Minute).

While tempers were rising in the India Office, the crisis at Aden suddenly ended. On December 6, Schneider wired, "Turkish troops have evacuated Lahej and Shuha, country cleared of Turks between Lahej and Ta'iz. Reenforcements not required to be held in readiness" (FO 78/2753, cable, Schneider-London 12/6/73). This news was followed next day by the information that Abdullah and the other Lahej rebels had given up. Their forts had been occupied by British troops which would soon destroy them. Schneider promised to deal with Ali ibn Mani, the Haushabi Sultan, at an early date (FO 78/2753, cable, Schneider-IO 12/7/73). Elliot was, of course, immediately informed of these facts (FO 78/2753, cable, FO-Elliot 12/9/73).

In Constantinople, Elliot had pointed out the obscurity of the order issued on November 16, insisting that such an order should apply to all nine tribes. Reschid had countered with a proposal "that as the tribes recognize the Sultan as their Khaliph, the Porte should issue a firman granting them an autonomy and assimilating them to Egypt and Tunis" (Egypt and Tunis, while technically Turkish territories, enjoyed complete independence with their own armies, monetary system, and foreign service). Elliot replied that he doubted very much if the British government would consider such a proposal, as "such a firman implied a right of Sovereignty on the part of the Porte which they will not be disposed to admit" and that the safest course was to leave the tribes unmolested (FO 78/2753, Elliot-FO 11/29/73). As a result of this conversation, Elliot informed Reschid that if the new orders were not executed he believed that the British government "Would think it necessary to adopt measures for the protection of the threatened district" (FO 78/2753, Elliot-FO 12/2/73). He wired London to allow about a week for orders to reach San'a as they had to go by messenger

from Aden, concluding, "The Porte appears convinced that their
late instructions will be at once executed and they know that it
is only thus that a conflict can be avoided" (FO 78/2753, cable,
Elliot-FO 12/5/73).

To Elliot, the key to the whole crisis appeared on December 5 when he was informed that the Russian Ambassador had
complained to the Grand Vizier that the British had no right to
interfere with the Arab tribes and that the Porte was acting in-
judiciously in listening to their remonstrances. The Grand
Vizier had replied that the Porte had no authority over the trib
in alliance with the British government, and that the cabinet
"having ascertained the blunder committed by the Governor General of the Yemen...had considered it their duty to direct him
forth with to evacuate these territories" (FO 78/2753, cable
Elliot-FO 12/5/73).

This information put a wholly new light on the situation,
and Elliot did a little discreet investigation. He found out that
the interference with the tribes had been due entirely to the
Minister of War, who, with the Minister of Marine, was intriguing with the Russian Ambassador to cause the fall of the
Grand Vizier and the Foreign Minister Reschid Pasha. The
Minister of War was trying to use the withdrawal of troops to
his own advantage as indicating the weakness of the Grand Vizier's policies. In a cabinet meeting of December 14 he had
stated, using very violent language, "That he considered that
the proceedings of the British troops in taking the Houshebi
sultan's [sic] brother prisoner to Aden and blowing up his fortress was an act of hostility towards Turkey and an encroachment on the Ottoman Empire" (FO 78/2753, Elliot-FO 12/15/
73). However, the Grand Vizier's actions were approved by
the Sultan, who was warned to say nothing about it to General
Ignatiev, the Russian Ambassador, who was about to leave for
home (FO 78/2753, Elliot-FO 12/25/73).

Elliot had an interview with the Sultan on January 4 in which
the Sultan said that he had "no disposition to complain of the
actions of the British government in Lahej." The secure approaches to the Holy Places was, he said, an essential point
for him, but beyond those limits he blamed the profitless expeditions that had been made without his authority. He hoped to
be able to recall the army (FO 78/2754, cable, Elliot-FO 1/4/74).

As a result of this interview, Reschid informed Elliot that
the Sultan requested definite and clear orders be sent to the

Governor General of the Yemen to do nothing to give the slightest offense to England (FO 78/2753, Elliot-FO 1/6/74). Under these circumstances, Elliot was convinced that there was no intentional bad faith on the part of the Grand Vizier Muhammad Nubin or of the Foreign Minister Reschid Pasha.

The explanation offered to Elliot satisfied the Ambassador and the Foreign Office as to the cause of the trouble. Russian intrigues were, however, not a cause but merely a symptom of the real cause which lies deeply imbedded in the history of the Ottoman Empire in the nineteenth century.

Ottoman civilization was essentially a product of the sixteenth century. In 1789, with the accession of Selim III as Sultan, the Empire obtained its first ruler who had had personal contact with Western ideas. Fully aware of the weakness of Ottoman government, he attempted to impose from above reforms based on western concepts. The attempt failed, and eventually led to the assassination of Selim; but among a small group the idea of reforms based on western ideas persisted. The reformers made little headway until the appearance of Stratford Canning, the great Elchi, as English Ambassador to the Porte.

Stratford Canning, backed by Palmerston, used his tremendous influence to support the reform group. This support was not only political but also educational, and in the 1850's a group of young intellectuals trained either in Europe or by European instructors began to appear as minor officials in Turkish departments of government. These young men, imbued with the spirit of the eighteenth century French philosophes, carried reform into literature and thence into new governmental ideas, with a twofold result, a Turkish literary renaissance and the development of a new political group, the "Young Turks." Their program was rather hazy, but it did involve one revolutionary concept, the limitation of the absolute power of the Sultan. On this point, in the 1860's, they broke with their patrons, the reforming Grand Viziers Fuad and Ali, and were expelled from the Empire. From European centers, they bombarded the small literate group in the Empire with their propaganda and made considerable headway with a vague program of reform. One aspect of this program was a revival of national feeling; in fact, the "Young Turks" were essentially nationalistic, and it was on this basis that they made their greatest appeal.

The facts of the reform program and the "Young Turks" are

well-known and easy to verify. The reaction to this movement
by the conservative element is much less clear. The obvious
measure of banishment undertaken by Fuad Pasha was relaxed
with the death of Ali Pasha in 1871, and the "Young Turks"
were allowed to return by a government which was ultra-conser-
vative and anti-reform. Why? In the writer's opinion, based
on evidence from the British documents and other contemporary
events, the ultra-conservatives, or if you wish "Old Turks,"
believed that they had developed a nationalistic program which
appealed to the natural conservatism of the literate Turks and
provided a more effective outlet for national feeling. It was,
in essence, the re-establishment of the Sultan's position as
Calif as dominant power in the Muslim world, a concept developed to its full by Abdul Hamid in the eighties and nineties.
This was implemented practically by a two-pronged attempt to
reconquer all of Arabia, for in conjunction with the reconquest
of the Yemen undertaken in 1871, Midhat Pasha, then Pasha of
Baghdad, was ordered to reconquer the Nejd. The califate concept is adequately shown in the next chapter in an amazing note
delivered to the British Foreign Office on January 28, 1874
(see p. 429). In addition to its internal political significance,
such a program effectively prevented the Sultan's rival, Ismail,
Khedive of Egypt, from following Muhammad Ali's pattern of
establishing an Arab Empire, a nightmare continually present
in the official Turkish mind since 1833.

When the "Old Turks" came into power on the death of Ali
Pasha in 1871, they had to have the support of at least one great
power in the continual diplomatic turmoil of Constantinople.
British influence was low under the inept foreign policy followed
by the Gladstone government. Furthermore, the "Old Turks"
realized that they could get little sympathy from the country
which had so ardently aided the reformers. French influence,
which had predominated during the 1860's, had evaporated following the defeat of that Empire in the Franco-Prussian War.
The new German Empire had as yet to become involved in Near
Eastern affairs, leaving Russia as the only great power in a position to support the "Old Turks." In addition, the Russians
were the only one of the great powers which at that time was
willing to use bribery at the Porte, and the "Old Guard" group
in power were about as venal a group of politicians as ever
graced the government of the Ottoman Empire. In this way, Russian influence became predominant, and thus the explanation to
Elliot of the cause of the Yemen crisis was in part correct.

XXV. THE SOVEREIGNTY QUESTION 1874

Although the Turks had withdrawn to Ta'iz, there were several questions still to be settled. The Indian Government knew
exactly what it wanted, non-interference with the tribes and complete freedom of action in the hinterland of Aden. The Foreign
Office, however, had to base its policy on the larger policy of
relations with the whole Ottoman Empire. And the fundamental
problem involved with the Porte was the countering of Russian
influence there. Elliot's analysis of the forces behind the Yemen
dispute indicated, therefore, that some compromise would have
to be reached in order to allow the Porte to save face. Such a
compromise was necessary because at all costs a crisis must
be avoided within the Turkish government. Outright refusal to
compromise could easily prejudice the Grand Vizier's position.
If he fell, he could probably be replaced by one of his pro-Rus-
sian colleagues. A closer liaison between the Foreign Office
and the India Office might have shortened greatly the lengthy
negotiations which followed the withdrawal of the Turks.

When the Porte had withdrawn its forces from Lahej, it assumed that the British would do likewise. In fact, that was the
only way in which the Turks could maintain their prestige in the
southern Yemen. If both parties withdrew at approximately the
same time it would be obvious that it was done by agreement; if
the British remained it would appear that the Turks had suffered
a real diplomatic defeat. Therefore, Reschid wired Musurus
in London on December 11 to ask the Foreign Office when British troops were to be withdrawn. The Foreign Office, unable to
give any assurances, requested the India Office for information
(FO 78/2753, cable, Reschid-Musurus 12/11/73, & FO-IO 12/
11/73). The whole question was further broadened by a request
for information by Musurus as to the status of Abdullah, the
brother of the Lahej Sultan. The India Office only knew what it
had received from Aden in the Resident's telegram of December 7, i.e., that Abdullah was a British prisoner. Grenville
noted, "How does this matter stand? Have the Turks any ground
for interferring in the matter of Abdoola?" (FO 78/2753, FO-IO
12/18/73, IO-FO 12/23/73 and Grenville's Minute thereon).

The India Office informed the Foreign Office on December 23
that the field force had been returned to Aden but that the Aden

troop had remained at Lahej. As to the request for complete evacuation, the India Office commented that it "cannot admit the right of the Porte to make any such request as that above indicated since the relations of the British Government with the tribes around Aden are independent of Turkey, whom we do not admit to have any locus standi there" (FO 78/2753, IO-FO 12/ 23/73 and cable, Schneider-IO 12/20/73).

Musurus requested that Abdullah and his family be sent to Constantinople as they were Turkish subjects who had been attacked by the British. The Foreign Office, on the meagre information of a telegram from Aden, told him that they had surrendered, they had not been attacked (FO 78/2753, Memo on Musurus' request 12/27/73). To throw light on the problem of Abdullah, on the obscurity surrounding the withdrawal of the troops, and to clarify a very confused report that the Haushabi had been heavily punished by the Turks, the Foreign Office requested the India Office for a full explanation (FO 78/2753, FO-IO 12/18/73). Sanderson, of the Foreign Office staff, personally took this request over to the India Office and had an interview with Sir John Kaye, secretary of the India Council, who could give him no real answer to any of the problems, but promised to cable Aden for information, advising Sanderson that Elliot should make no statements. Sanderson concluded his memorandum, "He [Kaye] was very wrath at Gen. Ignatiev's interference and anxious that the General or whoever mentioned his authority should be told that Russia had nothing whatever to do with the matter" (FO 78/2754, Memorandum of interview by Sanderson 1/2/74). In Constantinople, to add fuel to the flames, the Minister of War circulated a report that the brothers of the Haushabi Sultan (sic — this should be Lahej) had been shot (FO 78/2754, cable Elliot-FO 1/6/74). This rumor the Foreign Office answered quickly by assuring Elliot that no one had been shot by the British (FO 78/2754 cable, FO-Elliot 1/9/74).

Meanwhile Schneider, at Aden, complicated the situation by cabling the India Office requesting the release of the son of the Alawi chief who was reported to be a prisoner at Qa'taba (FO 78/2754, Tel. Schneider-IO 1/6/74).

It was becoming obvious that nothing could be done intelligently until the Aden mail arrived with full reports on the situation. These reports arrived on January 12, and were forwarded to the Foreign Office together with an outright rejection of Reschid's proposal for the issuance of a firman granting Lahej and

the Haushabi independence similar to Egypt and Tunis (see p.
422), (FO 78/2754, IO-FO 1/12/74).

Schneider described in detail his actions after the Turkish
withdrawal. On December 5 he had written to Abdullah, reviewing his acts of unfaithfulness to the British government especially in asking the Turks for aid after accepting the mediation of
the Abdali sheikhs in his dispute with the Sultan and giving hostages for good behavior. Schneider demanded his absolute submission by four o'clock in the afternoon and the surrender of his
forts to British troops. After attempts at negotiation, Abdullah
surrendered, and his forts, too well built to be destroyed by
anything but heavy artillery, were dismantled. Schneider felt
that British prestige had been restored, as he, in the eyes of
the tribes, had compelled the Turks to withdraw, and without
using any apparent force inflicted a severe punishment on a
chief who was a constant rebel (FO 78/2754, Schneider-Bombay
12/7/73). Abdullah's punishment scared Ali ibn Mani, the
Haushabi Sultan, so much that he fled the country. Schneider
was trying to get him to return so that the Zaida problem could
be settled and a lasting peace restored between the Abdali and
Haushabi (FO 78/2754, Schneider-Bombay 12/10/73). He enclosed a summary of the Zaida question which he hoped could
be settled if Ali ibn Mani would return.

As a result of the above information, Musurus Pasha was
informed orally that the relatives of its Lahej Sultan could not
be released to Constantinople (FO 78/2754, Memo FO 1/19/74).

Further dispatches from Aden arrived on January 23.
Schneider had finally gotten in touch with Ali ibn Mani and sent
him a safe conduct to Aden. Captain Hunter and thirty of the
Aden troop went to Raha, his capital, to escort him to the settlement. There they found the village deserted. Schneider then
requested the Haushabi sheikhs to meet with him. The Resident
made a compromise settlement in which the Sultan of Lahej retained control of the water at Zaida, but released enough of it
to allow the Haushabi to irrigate their fields. After this the
field force returned to Aden on December 20 and the Aden troop
retired to its usual base, Khor Maksar, just outside the settlement (FO 78/2754, Schneider-Bombay 12/23/73, encl. in IO-
FO 1/23/74).

In the light of all this information, the problems between
Aden and the Turks might seem quite simple. The British held
Abdullah, a rebel against his brother, who the Porte claimed

was a Turkish subject, and the Turks held the Amiri Sultan,
and the son of the Alawi sheikh, as hostages, the first at San'a,
the second at Qa'taba. But the Porte, now taking the diplomatic
initiative, proceeded to toss a bombshell into the negotiations.

On January 28, 1874, Musurus presented a lengthy note
while discussing the situation with Grenville. After reviewing
the Turkish version of the Abdullah affair, again charging the
English with attacking him before his arrest, Musurus claimed
a divergence in the assurances given by Grenville to him and
by Elliot to Reschid. Elliot had, he said, made no claim to possession of the territory, but had simply requested that the British be allowed to safeguard their treaties with certain chiefs.
However, in seizing the person of Abdullah and destroying his
forts, the English Resident "avoir fait acte d'autorité sur un
territoire que la Sublime Porte n'a jamais entendu abandonner
a une Puissance Etrangère, et a méconnu aussi les conditions
de l'accord intervenu entre les deux Gouvernements pour le
maintain de Status quo. . . . En effet, le Gouvernements pour
de sa Majesté Britannique ne devait pas ignorer que comme
d'autres provinces de l'Arabie, celle de Yemen, dont les territoires de Havachib [Haushabi] et de Lahej font partie intégrante,
appartient depuis des siècles a l'Empire Ottoman par droit de
conquête autant que par droit de souveraineté legitime et
que l'object de las présence actuelle d'une armée Imperiale en
Yemen n'est pas un envahissement, mais l'exercise d'un droit
incontestable." He went on to say that the purpose of the army
in the Yemen was to prepare the way for the administrative reforms established in the European provinces. (There, reforms
had the wholehearted backing of the British government, as
their application to local and provincial affairs should remove
many of the complaints of the populace and strengthen the Ottoman Empire against outside influences and propaganda.) Musurus stated that anything to do with Arabia was a delicate question with the Porte. "Que l'arabie est le berceau de l'Islamisme,
que Sa Majesté Imperiale le Sultan est le successeur de Pro-
phete et le chef du Khaliphate universel, et que, comme tel et
comme possesseur des villes Saintes, il a des droits à exercer
surtoute le Peninsule Arabique et des devoirs a remplir envers
les Musulmans en général et ses sujets en particulair." These
considerations made anything which might injure the Sultan's
dignity and prestige in Arabia of the greatest importance.
Therefore the Porte requested Abdullah be sent to Constantinople,

as he had made submission to the Porte, and his imprisonment at Aden was contrary to civil and international law. The Porte, on the other hand, was willing to give assurances that they would keep him away from Lahej in the event that he was handed over to their jurisdiction (FO 78/2754, Musurus-Grenville 1/28/74).

Tenterden, on receiving this note, commented "This note raises a very serious question indeed. In it the Turkish Government advance a claim as hereditary right to the whole of the Yemen and to all the country of Arabia challenging not only the independence of the tribes near Aden but our title to the possession of Aden itself.... We have always reserved the question of right in the present Lahej case and it is strange that the Turks shd. not themselves see the danger of raising it.

"There can be no doubt that the India Office will advise (and as it appears to me justly) a repudiation of Turkish claims to sovereignty and an absolute refusal which this claim provokes to render up the prisoners.

"The India Office should be asked for observations and the Yemen memo (which was prepared in 1855) completed up to date.

"Sir H. Elliot will be here soon & can advise as to the answer to be sent" (FO 78/2754, Minute by Tenterden 1/31/74 on Musurus-Grenville 1/28/74).

This note certainly did raise very serious questions. Looking at the situation theoretically, it involved not only Aden, but Muscat, Bahrein, the Hadramaut and, due to Turkish sovereignty over Egyptian territory, the whole question of sovereignty on the western shore of the Red Sea. Practically, the Turks were in no position seriously to threaten Muscat or the Hadramaut. Bahrein is outside the scope of this volume, but a serious situation was arising there in connection with the Turkish attempt to reconquer the Nejd. As to the western shore of the Red Sea, it is necessary to review what had been happening there in order to understand the factors which compelled the British government to abandon Palmerston's policy regarding the area and to establish a new one which, they believed, was better adapted to the changing conditions.

The Egyptian survey of Berbera conducted in 1867 by Djaafer Pasha has been mentioned, and the visit of the Egyptian warship "Khartoum" to Berbera during the trading season of 1869-1870. At that time, the Resident at Aden had proposed the installation of a British agent at Berbera during the time of the fair, and had recommended the appointment of Mr. Munzinger (IO, LA, Russell-Bombay 8/28/70). But no action was ever taken on this matter. Momtaz Pasha had been appointed governor of all the African coast to Cape Guardafui in June, 1870, but the Egyptians did not immediately press the question. In January, 1871, Tremenheere, then Resident at Aden, informed Bombay that the tribes at Berbera had referred a dispute to him for settlement (IO, LA, Tremenheere-Bombay 1/13/71). A dispute at Bandar Muraiah caused the Resident to blockade that port for a short time during the same month (IO, LA, Tremenheere-Bombay 1/20/71). However, in February the Egyptians again appeared at Berbera and Bulhar. This time Momtaz Pasha arrived on the Egyptian warship "Senaar." After staying four days at Bulhar, where $2,000 worth of presents were distributed to the elders of the tribe in return for permission to hoist the Egyptian flag, the Pasha proceeded to Berbera. Here he disembarked 150 Arabian soldiers and distributed $7,000 to the elders. He remained eight days and then departed, leaving two soldiers, one with each of the main tribes, at that port. Tremenheere commented that the fair was almost over, so that he did not expect any further interference before next October when the fair would begin again. By that time he hoped to have instructions from his government on what action to take. He reiterated the importance of the Berbera trade to Aden and concluded by saying that, if the Egyptians had a valid claim, the British should appoint either Munzinger or Captain Miles as agent during the fair season to maintain English interests (IO, LA, Tremenheere-Bombay 3/9/71). It was obvious that the Egyptians intended to maintain their claims to this area, which they had incorporated as part of the government of Massawa. However, affairs were not proceeding smoothly at that port, and the growing Egyptian-Abyssinian dispute prevented any occupation of the Somali coast in force. During the trading seasons of 1871-1872 and 1872-1873, the Egyptians confined themselves to similar short annual visits to Bulhar and Berbera. The Resident at Aden, having received no instructions, could do nothing but observe. There was no interference with the trade of Aden nor any large display of force.

However, the question of sovereignty was placed in the lap of the Foreign Office by Ismail in September, 1873. He had an interview with Vivian, who was Acting Consul General during Stanton's leave, in which he stated that the French were

proposing to press their claim to their purchases near Zeila,
bought, as Ismail said, from Sheikh Ahmed about ten years previously. Ismail denied the right of Sheikh Ahmed to make this
sale as the land belonged to Egypt. He requested the British
who, he said, had purchased an island opposite the French purchase, to give up their claims to him, for if they did so and
thus recognized his sovereignty he would be able to induce the
French and the Italians to give up their claims. Vivian commented to Ismail that he thought the French were too weak to
press any such ambitious designs as the occupation of Zeila.
Ismail concluded by asking for the appointment of a British consul at Massawa (FO 78/3187 Vivian-FO 7/22/73 copy in FO
78/2284). It is difficult to determine exactly to what spot Ismail was referring. He apparently meant Obock, acquired by
Schaeffer in 1862. The British claims were to islands off Tajura. Both claims were a considerable distance from Zeila,
which had always been a dependency of Mocha and thus of the
Porte. Munzinger, then in Cairo, recently appointed as Governor of Massawa by the Egyptian government, prepared a
memorandum for Vivian on Abyssinia and the Red Sea coast.
He stated that Zeila and Tajura were still in possession of the
Turks as part of the Pashalik of the Yemen, but that the Egyptians claimed Berbera and the Somali coast to Guardafui (FO
78/2284, Vivian-FO 10/18/73).

This report coincided with the receipt of news from Schneider at Aden that the Egyptian corvette "Arkha" had landed
fifty men at Berbera. The Resident, fearful of a diminution of
supplies, especially in view of the Turkish crisis in Lahej, instructed the "Dalhousie" to remain at Berbera and observe the
actions of the Egyptians. He reported that Egyptian interests
at the Somali port had caused a sharp rise in the prices of commodities at the fair (FO 78/2187, Schneider-Bombay 9/2/73).

Vivian's dispatches regarding French aspirations was sent
to the India Office and to Elliot. The India Office forwarded
them to the Viceroy, with the comment that Ismail was apparently trying to increase his prestige at the expense of the French
and English; considerable alarm was shown because they thought
that Little Aden was referred to (FO 78/3187, IO-FO 10/27/73
encl. letter to Viceroy 10/27/73).

Elliot took a different view of the matter. He felt that the
best safeguard to British interests in the Red Sea would be to
encourage the sovereignty of Ismail and the Porte over all of it.

He was of the opinion that if the question of sovereignty lay between the Viceroy and independent tribes, as was apparently the case, the Viceroy was much to be preferred unless the British wished to establish a post of their own. Ismail's occupation would help destroy the slave trade there (Zeila was the port of embarkation for Galla slaves) and would provide a stable government. As to Vivian's comment that the French were too weak to accomplish very much, Elliot stated, "Their agents in the East seem nervously anxious to prove that notwithstanding the late reverses, France has no intention of abandoning the position formerly occupied, or of allowing it to be thought that her influence was diminished" (FO 78/8187, Elliot-FO 11/13/73).

Dashwood, in the Foreign Office, reviewing the correspondence, felt that two questions were involved; first, whether or not the British would be willing to cede to Ismail the islands at Tajura, and second, whether Egyptian sovereignty extended to Berbera or only as far as Zeila.

Further reports from Aden indicated that the "Arkha" had left Berbera in October and that the fair had returned to its normal quarrelsome atmosphere, proving that Egyptian sovereignty could only be enforced by the actual occupation of the port by Egyptian troops (FO 78/3187, Schneider-Bombay 10/22/73).

A memorandum on the dispatches prepared in the Foreign Office brought up three important points. First, the British purchased the islands off Tajura while the chiefs were independent, the French made their purchases at Obock after the Egyptians had stated their claim to the coast in 1848. Second, the French would not necessarily give up their claims if the British did. Third, Aden had treaty rights with the chiefs on the Somali coast and it would appear inconsistent to take a strong stand against the Turks at Aden and be easy on Egyptian claims on the Somali coast (FO 78/3187, Memorandum by Hertslet 1/18/74). Tenterden noted "It seems best to let matters slide for a while. Complete memo and send to Mr. Gladstone" (FO 78/3187, Minute by Tenterden, 1/21/74).

The Government of India showed no such restraint. After stating the inconsistency of taking vigorous steps against the Turks and giving in to Ismail, it advised the Foreign Office to instruct the Consul General at Alexandria "to represent to the Khedive that H. M. Govt. view these proceedings with much dissatisfaction and are anxious to adopt such measures as shall

secure the Somalis from all interference" (FO 78/3187, IO-FO
1/17/74).

Sanderson commented, "It might be convenient to Aden that
the Turks should not hold sway in Berbera but that could scarcely be a sufficient grounds for disputing their right to do so."
He pointed out the great difference in treaty relations, the Aden
tribes being paid stipends, the Somali tribes agreeing merely
to commercial advantages. He felt that Britain's only reserva-
tion should be to object to any steps that would interfere with
freedom of intercourse between Aden and the tribes. Tenterden
and Gladstone concurred in his views (FO 78/3187, Memo by
Sanderson 1/19/74 on IO-FO 1/17/74).

The Egyptians did not, however, wait for the next trading
season to put in an appearance. Schneider, informed of Egyptian pretensions to the whole coast, sent H. M. S. "Kwantung,"
with Captain Prideaux on board, to inspect the coast. He arrived at Berbera on November 20 and found the Egyptian corvette "Saika" in harbor. Its captain informed him that Egypt
looked on the occupation as a fait accompli and planned to send
fifteen to sixteen hundred men to occupy the place as soon as an
adequate water supply was obtained. Pending that time, two or
three hundred men would be sent to form an occupation force.
Ainterad and Bulhar were reported to have submitted to the
Egyptians, and the whole coast had been placed under Munzinger
Bey's governorship. The "Kwantung" then proceeded to Zeila
which was governed by old Abu Bakr, Shermarkee's one-time
enemy, who was under the control of the Pasha of the Yemen.
Prideaux found a flourishing trade in Galla slaves going on.
These Gallas were mostly girls who were famed for their beauty
and value as concubines, and were either captured in raids by
the Shoa Christians or else sold into slavery by their parents.
Brought to the coast by the Harar trade route to Zeila, they
were transferred overland to Raheita, crossing from there to
Fazeka on the Arabian coast in small boats, and thence overland to Hodeida. Abu Bakr received a transit duty of from $.75
to $1.00 for every slave, and as no other duties were charged
on other goods and the taxes were farmed out for $3,000 a year,
the trade was considerable. Prideaux found 100 slaves awaiting
shipment, and was informed that four cargoes had been shipped
in two months. The Pasha at Hodeida, he felt sure, connived at
the trade, as it was the chief source of revenue of the port of
Zeila. Proceeding to Tajura, Prideaux found a similar situation,

although the volume of slaves was smaller, the Shoa-Tajura
trade route being more difficult to traverse, as Harris and Beke
had found out years before. Tajura was also under the Turkish
flag, and was governed by Muhammad ibn Muhammad (FO 78/
3187, Schneider-London 12/4/73 encl. Prideaux-Schneider 11/
26/73). The arrival of this dispatch was followed almost immediately by the information that Munzinger had arrived at Berbera to receive the submission of the sheikhs (FO 78/3187,
cable Schneider-London 1/6/74).

Dashwood commented that the British should keep hands off
Berbera and not protest, but should advise Turkey to cede Berbera and Tajura to Egypt so that the slave trade there could be
suppressed. Tenterden noted that a memorandum on the whole
matter was being printed for discussion by the cabinet. He felt
that some agreement should be reached with the India Office, a
policy established, and then both offices should adhere to this
policy (FO 78/3185; Minutes by Dashwood and Tenterden 1/29/74).

Munzinger's arrival at Berbera was confirmed by a letter
from Aden in which Schneider reported a conversation between
a French officer and the Bey, in which Munzinger advised the
Frenchman that Egypt was preparing to occupy the coast to
Cape Guardafui and rebuild an old aqueduct to Berbera to give
a dependable water supply (FO 78/3187, Schneider-London
12/31/73).

In May, the India Office was still waiting for a decision on
the Somali coast problem. They enclosed with their request
further dispatches from Aden which informed them that the
Egyptians had sent an expedition inland to open up trade with
Harar over the route explored by Burton in 1854. A census of
trade in Berbera was being taken, and merchants were being
induced to build permanent warehouses and shops there. The
Resident also reported that he had reliable information that the
Egyptians were planning to extend their occupation to Mogadisco
and Brava on the Indian Ocean portion of the Somali coast (FO
78/3187, IO-FO 5/12/74 encl. Schneider-IO 3/20/74).

It seems strange that Kirk, British Consul at Zanzibar,
was not informed of the Egyptian intentions as expressed in this
dispatch. Mogadisco was definitely part of the Sultan of Zanzibar's territory, and with any proper coordination in the Foreign
Office this information should have been sent to him. But Coupland, in his excellent volume THE EXPLOITATION OF EAST
AFRICA, gives the impression that the Sultan and Kirk were

both taken by surprise by McKillop's expedition of autumn, 1875. While Coupland is undoubtedly correct in believing that the extension of McKillop's instructions to occupy the coast to Formosa Bay rather than stopping at the mouth of the Juba was a sudden change in plan, there is every reason to believe that Ismail had always planned to occupy all the Somali coast to the Juba. As will be seen later (p. 486), Ismail's primary motive was control of commerce. Ismail's interest in the suppression of the slave trade, which the Foreign Office officials in London accepted so readily, as apparently Coupland also had, was simply an excuse to make his aggressions more palatable.

The situation at Berbera, combined with developments in the negotiations with the Porte resulting from the Aden-Yemen crisis, made some decision necessary, and it was decided to hold a meeting of permanent Foreign Office and India Office officials on June 2, 1874, to discuss the whole question of British policy in the Red Sea and Gulf of Aden. In order fully to understand the problems involved, it is necessary to review Anglo-Turkish negotiations on the Yemen crisis which followed the delivery of Musurus' note on January 28.

The Foreign Office acknowledged Musurus Pasha's letter on February 2, informing him that the Government was considering a reply, and forwarded copies of the letter both to Locock, chargé d'affaires at the Porte in Elliot's absence, and to the India Office for observations. The India Office replied quickly and decisively that it could not depart from its previous position "viz that the Sultan had no rights in that part of the world, such as to enable him to interfere in the internal affairs of the various chiefs around Aden with whom we have concluded engagements" (FO 78/2754, IO-FO 2/10/74).

This information was communicated to Musurus while Locock, in Constantinople, was being pressed to obtain the release of the Amiri Sultan and the son of the Alawi chief. Locock wired on March 3 that the Porte had made the release of the son of the Alawi chief conditional on Abdullah's release (FO 78/2754, cable Locock-FO 3/5/74). At this point the negotiations became very confused, not only because of oriental evasion as practiced at Constantinople, but also because neither Locock, Musurus nor Reschid knew much about the tribes around Aden. (Their lack of knowledge was not helped by the fact that the British used the Arab names for the tribes, while the Turks used Turkish equivalents. Tenterden was able to follow developments, but from his comments on some of the dispatches, his patience must have been nearly exhausted on several occasiona.) In view of this Turkish proposal, Burgin went to the India Office to discover Abdullah's status. There he was informed that the whole matter had been turned over to the Viceroy, who had instructed Schneider to try to make a reconciliation between Abdullah and his brother Fadhl, the Sultan of Lahej (FO 78/2754, note by Burgin 3/6/74). Tenterden was definitely opposed to the exchange proposed by the Porte, but Lord Derby, who had replaced Grenville when the Disraeli cabinet came into office in February, thought that such a proposition would be reasonable if the claims of the Ottoman Sultan to Aden, Muscat, etc., were distinctly denied (FO 78/2754, Minutes by Derby and Tenterden on Locock FO 3/3/74).

Locock's dispatch covering his telegram explained the new Turkish attitude. Midhat Pasha, the Grand Vizier, had lost his influence and had been replaced by the former Seraskier or Minister of War who had been responsible for the Yemen crisis. The new Grand Vizier had acquired extensive influence, and Locock commented, "it may require a considerable display of firmness to prevent his employing it [his influence] to the injury of the position which we now hold among the independent tribes" (FO 78/2754, Schneider-IO 1/31/74 encl. in IO-FO 3/7/74).

The attitude of the new Grand Vizier was well shown in a dispatch sent from Reschid to Musurus protesting the detention of Abdullah. Purporting to be a report from the Governor General of the Yemen, it rehashed and amplified all the accusations against the tribal chiefs which the Porte had put forward the year before, added a few new ones, and ended with a demand that Lahej be placed under the government of Ta'iz (FO 78/2754, Reschid-Musurus 2/25/74).

The India Office forwarded, on March 10, a letter from the Viceroy requesting permission to negotiate new treaties to prevent a recurrence of the Lahej incident (in other words, to establish a protectorate over the tribes), a project with which Lord Salisbury, who had replaced Argyle as Secretary of State for India, heartily concurred. Dispatches from Aden, also enclosed, showed that the prestige of the British had been fully restored and the tribes were more than friendly (FO 78/2754, IO-FO 3/10/74).

The Porte continued to press for Abdullah's release as a condition for the release of Salim ibn Saif. However, two incidents occurred which greatly weakened the Turkish case. First, word reached London that the Turks had invaded Amiri territory and occupied the town of Dhala, the Sultan's capital, which controlled the main trade route from the Yemen to Aden, the circumstances being very similar to the tactics employed earlier with the Haushabi Sultan. In this case, however, Ali ibn Mukbil was able to escape to Aden and tell his story (FO 78/2754, Schneider-IO 2/12/74 encl. in IO-FO 3/14/74). Second, reliable information reached London that Salim ibn Saif was held in chains in a dungeon at Qa'taba while Abdullah was living in luxury at Aden (FO 78/2754, tel. FO-Locock 3/16/74).

On being presented with this information, Reschid became very conciliatory, as did the Grand Vizier. On March 20, Reschid informed Locock that a vizierial order was being sent to release Salim and to withdraw the troops from Dhala (FO 78/2754, cable Locock-FO 3/20/74). Locock also reported that a general had been sent to investigate the conduct of the Governor General of the Yemen, "some of whose actions aside from those of which H. M. Govt. have complained, haven't given satisfaction" (FO 78/2754, Locock-FO 3/20/74).

The India Office, at the request of the Foreign Office, had wired Aden to find out if there were any objections to releasing Abdullah on condition that he leave the Yemen (FO 78/2754, cable IO-Schneider 3/11/74). That gentleman, having refused reconciliation with his brother, had no desire to leave Aden, and threw himself on the mercy of the British government (FO 78/2755, cable Schneider-IO 4/19/74).

A month passed and Selim ibn Saif was not released; in fact, the Turkish officials in the Yemen were now asking that he be ransomed. Nor did it seem that the Turks had any inclination to remove their troops from Dhala; Ali ibn Mukbil, the Amiri Sultan, reported that, in addition to occupying the town, the Turks had collected $2,700 in revenues (FO 78/2755, cables Schneider-IO 4/19/74 & 4/21/74).

Under pressure from Locock, Reschid sent Musurus a copy of the order to the Governor General which was found to be conditional in nature (FO 78/2755, cable Reschid-Musurus 4/21/74). Lord Derby noted, "The conditional order for release is at variance with the assurances made to Mr. Locock that it should be absolute" (FO 78/2755, Minute by Derby 2/44/74 on above). A new protest was made which brought results, as Salim ibn Saif was released on May 3. The number of Turks at

at Dhala, however, had been increased to a considerable force
(FO 78/2755, cable Schneider-IO 5/3/74).

During these conversations the Turks again raised the question of the sovereignty of Arabia. In March, Hertslet finished
compiling an extensive memorandum entitled "Memorandum on
the Turkish Claims to Sovereignty over the Eastern Shore of the
Red Sea and the whole of Arabia and on the Egyptian claim to
the whole Western Shore of the Same Sea including the African
Coast from Suez to Cape Guardafui." This memorandum contained a summary of all documents pertaining to any question
of sovereignty in the area which were in the possession of the
Foreign Office. As all this information has been used elsewhere
in this volume, amplified by the India Office records, there is
no reason to review the evidence here. However, Hertslet's
conclusions are extremely valuable, as they were used as a
basis for British policy in the Aden area not only in this dispute
with the Turks, but again in a similar dispute in 1902. In 1874,
the situation was as follows: (1) the French had tried to get
footholds on the west shore of the Red Sea at Dissei, Anfile,
Edd, and Obock without success; (2) in the Lambert case, the
French recognized the sovereignty of the Porte over Zeila;
(3) the Turks had reasserted their sovereignty in 1862 over
Disseh, Anfile, and Edd; (4) the Italians had tried to establish
themselves at Assab Bay without success; (5) the Americans
had tried to establish a factory on the south coast of Arabia in
1835. (This was a rumor picked up by Mackenzie in 1837. It
refers undoubtedly to the visit of American war vessels to the
area which culminated in the American commercial treaty with
Zanzibar of 1833; see Coupland, EAST AFRICA AND ITS IN-
VADERS, pp. 372-75 for the proper explanation); (6) since January, 1838, the British had occupied Aden and Perim, and had
treaties with the nine tribes and the chiefs of Zeila, Tajura,
and Berbera, acknowledging the independence of these chieftains;
(7) the English acquired Musa and Aibat off Zeila and Tajura
but never occupied them; (8) the British refused to acknowledge
any Turkish claims east of Bab-el-Mandeb; (9) Palmerston in
1839 refused to acknowledge Turkish claims to the interior of
Arabia; (10) the British never recognized the Egyptian claim to
any of the African coast outside the Straits even as far as Zeila,
much less to Cape Guardafui, which was probably a step to
claiming the Somali coast to Ras el Khyle (mouth of the Juba
River); (11) Berbera was always independent and as such was
important to Aden as a source of grain (sic) and cattle.

The Turks now claimed the whole of Arabia, and Egypt was
advancing a claim to the African coast to Guardafui, asking the
British to give up their claims to Musa and Aibat and the French
to give up their pretensions to Obock. The basic question
raised was whether or not it was better for Turkey and Egypt to
claim the whole coast, or to leave the coast open for French,
German, and Italian settlements. If the Porte was allowed to
claim all of Arabia as part of the religious pretensions to the
Califate, they "could claim half of the world and the Pope could
claim a large portion of the remaining half." On the west shore
of the Red Sea the tribes would be compelled to recognize Turkey, Egypt, or Abyssinia if they did not wish to be occupied by
a European power, as they were completely defenseless. The
Somali tribes, Hertslet pointed out, were essentially a pastoral
and commercial people, but the constant feuding of the past
twenty-five years had caused them to turn to slave trading as
the most profitable pursuit. The lack of naval vessels in the
Red Sea following the abolition of the Indian Navy had served to
increase this trade, especially between Zeila and the Arabian
coast. However, the position of Aden and the neighboring tribes
should be maintained as essential to the commerce of the entire
East. With this condition, Hertslet felt that allowing Turkish
and Egyptian occupation of the Red Sea coast could prove beneficial to the British. (FO 78/3187 Printed confidential Memorandum by E. Hertslet, "Memorandum on the Turkish claims to
Sovereignty over the Eastern Shores of the Red Sea, the Whole
of Arabia; and on the Egyptian claim to whole Western Shore
of the same Sea including the African Coast from Suez to Cape
Guardafui" Printed for the Foreign Office, March 10, 1874,
64 pp. signed at end "E. Hertslet, Foreign Office, March 5,
1874. ")
        This memorandum was summarized by Elliot, on leave in
London, and Tenterden into a long dispatch to Locock. The
draft was then slightly revised by the India Office and finally
greatly reduced by the omission of historical detail. With slight
alterations it was printed separately in 1902 during the dispute
which led to the final delimitation of the boundaries of the Aden
Protectorate in 1904.
        The dispatch first summarized this memorandum, and then
mentioned the Turkish pretensions to the whole of Arabia, "to
which the Sultan is assumed to be entitled in virtue of the ancient
dominion of the Kalifate. " After denying any rights of the Porte

to land beyond the mouth of the Red Sea, backing this denial up
by quotations from earlier correspondence, the dispatch went
on "It is with some surprise that H. M. Govt. have found an attempt made to raise an obsolete pretension to the possessions
of the Kalifate & arguments advanced in support of it appealing
to national and religious sympathies, which, if carried to their
logical conclusions would have an effect on the integrity of the
Turkish Empire which H. M. Govt. can scarcely suppose the
Govt. of the Porte to have sufficiently contemplated." The dispatch then quoted a passage from the Proclamation of the Governor General of the Yemen, of August 29, 1872. (This had
been forwarded from Aden in the original Arabic with a summary
prepared by Captain Hunter and had been translated in the Foreign Office for the purpose of this dispatch.) "We write you
this letter after our arrival by command of our Lord the Sultan
of Al-Islam, the desert follower of the religion of the two Holy
Cities, the Monarch of the Kingdom of the East & West may his
magnificence be perpetual & may the moment of his glory be
raised aloft & the full moon of his life, in the Land of Yemen,
to resuscitate the Kingdom which his ancestors the Sultan's
founded by the revival of religion & the promulgation of the Or-
dinances of the Chief of the Prophets." The dispatch then gives
the following good advice: "The Govt. of the Porte must be
aware that the Sultan is not the only sovereign who claims to be
head of a church & that appeals of this nature to religious sympathies have never been wanting when it has been desired, by
those who would gladly see the dismemberment of the Turkish
Empire to excite the Christian populations in the Principalities
and other parts of the Ottoman dominions to throw them off their
allegiance to the Porte." (This was an obvious reference to
Russian intrigues among the Balkan Christians.) The original
dispatch instructed Locock to read the note to Reschid and leave
a copy with him but as telegraphic advices had reached London
that the whole affair was nearly settled, the ending was changed
and Locock was advised that the note was for his information
only (FO 78/2755, FO-Locock 4/30/74).

It is apparent from this dispatch that the Foreign Office and
the India Office had agreed on a policy, as far as Arabia was
concerned, when a joint meeting of the two Offices was held on
June 2. However, the two Offices were still far apart on the
question of sovereignty on the African coast. It should be noted
that there was a personal element involved in the Egyptian

question. Munzinger Bey, as Governor of Massawa, would have
jurisdiction over any Egyptian acquisitions. Munzinger was well-
known to officials in the area as well as to those in London. He
was frankly pro-British, and was a man highly respected by all
who knew him. His personal prestige unquestionably influenced
the final decisions regarding Egyptian sovereignty.

At the meeting of the permanent officials held at the Foreign
Office on June 2, Sir Henry Rawlinson, Sir Louis Mallet, Colonel Pelley, Mr. Aitcheson and Major Burn represented the India
Office, and Lord Tenterden and Mr. Bourke represented the Foreign Office. The question of sovereignty of the whole of Arabia
and the Red Sea was discussed and the following conclusions
reached:

> 1. Bahrein. The independence of this island must be
> insisted on but the British were not to give protection
> to Bahreinites in Turkish territory.
>
> 2. Aden. The status quo was to be maintained and the
> boundaries of the nine tribes established, the informa-
> tion to be sent to Constantinople.
>
> 3. Berbera. This question should be treated in the
> light of all the treaty rights along the coast. The India
> Office was to prepare a memorandum of these treaty
> rights and indicate those rights on which the British
> wished to lay stress. This memorandum was to be re-
> viewed by the Foreign Office and then sent to Stanton in
> Alexandria.

Tenterden, who had been sorely tried by lack of liaison between
the Foreign Office and the India Office, proposed that Aden be
transferred to a colonial status (as it was in 1937), and that consulates in the Persian Gulf and Zanzibar be transferred from
control of the India Office to the Foreign Office. Aitcheson stated
that while the India Office would like more of the expense of
these posts borne by the Home Government, the India Office
could not concur in this move. After some discussion, Tenterden stated that the problem was a cabinet matter anyway and
should be decided by them.

Derby, on reviewing the minutes of the meeting, wrote, "I
agree in what has been proposed by this conference" (FO 78/
3187. Minutes of meeting in FO 6/2/74, by Tenterden & Derby,
Minute thereon 6/3/74).

What was accomplished by this meeting? The question of
Bahrein is outside the scope of this volume; however, a conflict
of policy in this area was resolved and a definite policy agreed
on. In the case of Aden, both Offices had come to see the situation in much the same light before the conference. The agreement reached simply removed possible causes of misunderstanding which might result from conflicting interests. The decision
on Berbera, while indefinite, had resulted in a considerable
victory for the Foreign Office, as the India Office had consented
to have the question open for discussion, and had dropped its
definite policy of no expansion of Egyptian interests beyond the
mouth of the Red Sea. Tenterden's proposal as to the change in
status of Aden and the consulates is of great interest, although
nothing came of it. The history of the Red Sea area shows the
difficulties inherent in the territorial division of consulates, etc.,
between the two Offices. When Palmerston was the dominant
figure in British foreign affairs, this conflict was not very apparent, as he simply overrode the protests of the Company, and
later of the India Office, if they conflicted with the basic policies
which he had laid down. Because of the difficulties of communication, Palmerston's system, of giving officials a broad policy
and letting them have more or less a free hand in working out
details, worked extremely well. The development of the telegraph and the cable changed all this, as Frere so well pointed
out in his dispatch from Aden in January, 1873. The strings
were now pulled from London. The official on the spot had his
hands tied by telegraph wires, and yet the offices in London still
continued in their old habits of leisurely communications. Napier's proposal in 1868, after the Abyssinian campaign, to establish consulates in the Red Sea under the jurisdiction of the
India Office, was an attempt to make some sense out of the conflicting division of authority in the region. Napier had been on
the receiving end of the confusion resulting from this anachron-
istic division of authority. His proposal had gotten nowhere because the Foreign Office would not give up its prerogatives.
Now Lord Tenterden, who had come up against the same confusion, this time at London, presented a Foreign Office version
of the same idea.

In 1868, before the opening of the Suez Canal, Napier unquestionably had the right solution, but six years later Tenterden's
proposal was much more in line with international conditions as
they were developing with the opening of the canal. No historian

can deal with the documents relating to the Near East in the
1870's without being impressed with Tenterden's knowledge of
conditions and his grasp of the policies which should be applied
in the area. If British diplomacy in the Near Eastern crises of
the 1870's can be said to be successful, and it certainly was,
the credit belongs to Tenterden, not the various Ministers of
Foreign Affairs. But, if Napier's proposal was unsuccessful in
1868 because of the inherent conservatism of the Foreign Office
in refusing to give up its prerogatives, Tenterden was equally
unsuccessful in 1874 because of a similar refusal of the India
Office to surrender any of its traditional power.

XXVI. THE YEMEN CRISIS 1874-1876

The release of Selim ibn Saif left only two points of conflict between the Turks and the British at Aden; first, the Turkish desire to obtain Abdullah's release, which had now become a question of prestige and face for them, and second, the question of the occupation of Dhala in the Amiri country.

Abdullah's release, while not of great importance, has amusing aspects. This brother of the Sultan of Lahej had no desire to leave Aden where he was comfortably housed at the expense of the British government. When Locock informed Reschid of this fact on May 4, 1874, Reschid showed much disappointment that Turkish concessions had no visible practical results (FO 78/2755, Locock-FO 5/5/74). Musurus, instructed by telegraph, visited Derby on May 8, and at Derby's request wrote a note to him requesting Abdullah's release to the Governor General of the Yemen, and giving assurances that he would be kept away from the vicinity of Aden (FO 78/2755, Musurus-Derby 5/8/74 & Minute by Derby 5/8/74). This note was referred to the India Office.

The mails from Aden brought full details of Schneider's efforts to effect a reconciliation between Abdullah and his brother, Sultan Fadhl. It was obvious to the Resident that a reconciliation was impossible, but when he suggested that the sheikh would have to leave the Yemen and go to either the Hedjaz or Istanbul, Abdullah threw himself on the mercy of the British government. This raised a considerable problem, as Abdullah was not the only one involved; he had with him in Aden his mother, two sisters, four wives, nine children, his son Fadhl with two wives and two children, and a brother, Abdul Kerim ibn Mahsin, with three wives and five children, making twenty-eight persons in all besides servants who were living at the expense of the British government. Schneider felt that to allow them to return to Lahej without a reconciliation was out of the question, but it was obvious that something had to be done with them, as their exile in Aden was burdening the settlement with a heavy expense (FO 78/2755, Schneider-IO 4/9/74 encl. in IO-FO 5/12/74).

The India Office finally agreed to release Abdullah unconditionally with the warning that if he caused trouble again he

would be severely punished. However, the India Office refused
to turn him over to the Turks, as such an action "might be construed into an admission of the right of the Porte to interfere in
the affairs of the tribes around Aden" (FO 78/2755, IO-FO 6/
11/74). When news of this release reached Constantinople,
Musurus was instructed to thank Derby for Abdullah's release
but to express disagreement with the principles involved (FO
78/2755, Musurus-Derby, N. D.). The Foreign Office prepared
a note to Elliot to tell him that they considered the case closed,
but on second thought it seemed better to disregard all future
requests of the Porte to reopen the question of interference with
Lahej, and the note was cancelled (FO 78/2755, first draft of a
note to Elliot without date [approx. 7/30/74]). Later requests
of the Porte to reopen the question were disregarded, and eventually the Turks dropped the matter. Abdullah remained in
Aden for a while and later moved to Mocha.

The question of Dhala was not as easily settled. Of the
nine tribes around Aden, the Amiri lay the farthest away, occupying territory north of Lahej in the foothills of the mountains.
Their country formed the northern border of the British sphere
of influence agreed on by Muhammad Ali in 1838 (FO 78/343,
Campbell-FO 9/1/38). Dhala was the traditional capital of this
tribe; it lay on the northern boundary of their territory, sixty-
five miles north of Aden, but only seventeen miles south of
Qa'taba, an indisputable Turkish possession. As has been seen,
all the tribal boundaries were at best rather indefinite, so some
conflict was bound to ensue in this area. Furthermore, the
sixty-five miles from Aden to Dhala was a different affair from
the eighteen to twenty miles from Aden to Lahej. Not only was
it more difficult to keep track of events there, but any military
operations in that area posed a very different problem of supply
from operations at nearby Lahej. Turkish officials in the area
were perfectly well aware of these facts. They also were aware
of the orders they had received from Constantinople which mentioned in general the tribes around Aden, but specifically had
designated only the Haushabi and Abdali (Lahej). As Dhala was
not only the capital of the Amiri country, but also lay on the
main caravan route from San'a to Aden, it enjoyed considerable
revenue, and was thus a tempting prize safely removed from
British power at Aden, and of a questionable enough status so
that orders could be misinterpreted, especially when they were
conditional in nature.

Of all the tribes around Aden, the Amiri had been the most consistently friendly to the British. They were far enough removed from the settlement not to have any particular reason to come in conflict with Aden, and they had profited immensely from the increased caravan trade which had been diverted from Mocha. Furthermore, they had had less intratribal disturbances than most of the other tribes and were consequently more uniformly prosperous.

When the Turks first interfered with this tribe, their chief, Ali ibn Mukbil, had been made a prisoner, but he was released when the Turks withdrew from Lahej in December, 1873. Shortly after this the Turks had occupied his capital, Dhala, and refused to leave. Repeated protests had proved futile. In April, 1874, the small Turkish force was suddenly increased to over 700 men, who seized Ali ibn Mukbil's house at Dhala and plundered the town, the Amiri Sultan fleeing for his life into the mountains (FO 78/2755, Schneider-IO 4/10/74). The situation was made more serious almost immediately by the murder of Muhammad Musaed, a brother of Ali ibn Mukbil, and the appointment of his son as chief of the Amiri tribe (FO 78/2755, cable, Schneider-IO 5/14/74). The India Office pressed the Foreign Office to obtain orders from the Porte stopping this interference with the tribe, and Locock was so instructed (FO 78/2755, FO-Locock 5/23/74).

Elliot, who had returned to Constantinople, had an interview with Aarifi Pasha, the new Minister of Foreign Affairs, and Reschid, on June 8. From his report of the interview it is apparent that he was brutally frank in expressing the opinion of the British government on Turkish evasion and the issuance of obscure orders from the Porte. He did find, however, that there was a real confusion in the localities in question, as the Turkish name for Dhala, Zhali, was identical with the Turkish name for a small village in the Haushabi country (FO 78/2755, Elliot-FO 6/9/74).

Elliot did obtain new instructions but, as he commented, they were vague as usual (FO 78/2755, Elliot-FO 6/18/74). These instructions had an unforeseen result. Ali ibn Mukbil was visited by the Mufti of Ta'iz who offered to reinstate him as the Amiri chief if he would submit to the Porte, an obvious compromise to save the prestige of the Turks. On Ali's refusal to submit, the Mufti reaffirmed his appointment of a rival as Amiri chief, and then withdrew all the regular Turkish army men and officials to Qa'taba, but left the Turkish irregulars as police in Dhala (FO 78/2755, Schneider-IO 6/29/74). Further evidence showed that orders had been issued not to molest Ali ibn Mukbil personally, but the usurper was still supported and the revenues of the Amiri country taken by the Turks (FO 78/2755, Schneider-Bombay 7/21/74). In transmitting this letter to the Foreign Office, Lord Salisbury stated, "Repeated instances of aggressive action on the part of the Turkish authorities should be made the subject of renewed & most urgent representation on the part of Her Majesty's Ambassador at the Sublime Porte" (FO 78/2755, IO-FO 9/2/74).

The Sultan of Lahej, Fadhl, had died on July 5 and was succeeded by his nephew, Fadhl ibn Ali, who had succeeded in 1863 but because of his extreme youth had then abdicated in favor of his uncle. Ali ibn Mukbil visited Lahej to present his condolences to the new Sultan, giving Schneider an opportunity to discuss personally the whole Dhala situation with him. After his conversations, Schneider felt that Turkish influence in the Amiri tribe was dependent on force alone and that a complete withdrawal of Turkish troops would soon restore the country to normal (FO 78/2755, Schneider-Bombay 7/29/74). Further Turkish aggressions led to a request by Mr. Butler of the India Office in a private letter to Sanderson for a new and stiffer protest to the Porte (FO 78/2755, Butler-Sanderson private 9/8/74). A very stiff protest was drafted, but was cancelled when Butler, again in a private letter, asked that it be held up pending the receipt of mail dispatches (FO 78/2755, Butler-Sanderson, private 9/14/74).

The cancellation of this protest brought about a very strange situation, which led to the complete breakdown of liaison between the India Office and the Foreign Office at a very critical point. Tenterden, who had been on vacation, returned to the Foreign Office on October 1 and tried to find out the reason for the cancellation of the request of the India Office, but without success (FO 78/2755, Minute by Tenterden and others 10/1/74). No word of any kind was received from the India Office for two months, when suddenly a telegraphic protest from Aden regarding continued aggressions at Dhala was sent to the Foreign Office (FO 78/2755, cable, Schneider-London 11/13). Meanwhile, Elliot had forwarded a report from the Governor General of the Yemen protesting British actions at Lahej (FO 78/2755, Elliot-FO 10/17/74). This was sent to the India Office for comment, where it remained for nearly a month. Tenterden tried to straighten the matter out, but found the inter-departmental situation too involved. He commented, "These papers should not be delayed longer, they contain important information regarding the doings of the Turks in the Ameer country who if allowed to get a firm footing in that district will not be easy to turn out later. ... Doesn't the present telegram (which by the way hasn't been officially communicated) authorize us to go ahead? Private communication between the India Office and the Foreign Office should stop" (FO 78/2755, Minute by Tenterden 11/19/74). The arrival of copies of letters from Aden (the originals had been apparently lost in transmission) threw the question into complete confusion. These were again transmitted privately, with a statement that the political department of the India Office was in process of reorganization and showed utter confusion in the dates of letters which had reached Schneider from Ali ibn Mukbil. Tenterden commented, "This business has got into a dreadful mess as I foretold it would when the papers were sent to me in the country from the system of unofficial communications from the India Office" (FO 78/2755, Minute by Tenterden 11/22/74). It took another month for Tenterden to get things straightened out and receive official copies of all the correspondence. On December 24, 1874, a new protest was forwarded to Elliot reporting the continued aggressions of the Turks and the evasiveness of their officials in the Yemen (FO 78/2755, FO-Elliot 12/24/74).

Meanwhile, another disturbance had occurred in the Gulf of Aden which gave the British much concern. Reference has frequently been made to the disturbed state of affairs in the Hadramaut, where a lengthy and sporadic struggle had been going on between the Kathiri and Ka'aiti tribes. The Kathiri had been the traditional overlords of the area for several generations, and controlled Mukalla and Shihr, the two ports of the country. They had provided men for the personal bodyguard of the Nizam of Hyderabad, and one of these had risen to the position of Jemadar, or Lieutenant, in the Nizam's personal guard, and had obtained considerable influence and wealth in Hyderabad. This wealth he began using in the 1860's to prevent the Ka'aiti from pressing their claim to a repayment of a debt from the Kathiri. As the two parties in the dispute had virtually equal resources and military strength, the struggle dragged on and on, never seriously disturbing the country, but providing an excellent

opportunity for intrigue by outside powers, an opening which the
Turks had previously tried to exploit to their advantage.

In February, 1874, the Ka'aiti, Sultan Nawaz, sent two buggalows filled with soldiers to attack Mukalla. The Nakeeb of
Mukalla, Omar ibn Saleh, countered this move by capturing
these ships in a naval battle. On hearing of this, the Government of India, concerned naturally with the Kathiri's connections
in Hyderabad, instructed Schneider not to interfere and to maintain strict neutrality, as the Government of India considered
that a state of war existed between the two tribes (FO 78/2755,
Schneider-Bombay 6/6/74). This would have just been another
incident in the Ka'aiti-Kathiri struggle except for the fact that
Mahsin ibn Abdullah, the Jemadar at the court of the Nizam,
wrote to the Imam of Muscat, Seyyid Turki, begging him to interfere on the side of the Kathiri (FO 78/2755, Political Agent
[Muscat]-Political Resident [Persian Gulf] 3/5/74). Information reached India that the Ka'aiti had countered by asking the
Governor General of the Yemen for aid. Under the circumstances
the India Office requested the Foreign Office to prevent Turkish
interference in this dispute (FO 78/2755, IO-FO 6/29/74). Instructions to Elliot were so prepared, and the Foreign Office
was surprised and pleased when Elliot wired on July 9 that the
Grand Vizier had told him that there would be no interference
by the Turks, and that he hoped that there would be none by the
British from Aden (FO 78/2755, cable, Elliot-FO 7/9/74).

In October, Schneider paid a visit to the area in H. M. S.
"Kwantung" and was well received in all the ports. He talked to
both the Kathiri and Ka'aiti leaders, but could find no interference by the Turks. As usual, both chiefs asked for British protection as they had previously, and as usual the Resident had to
answer evasively. He stopped at other minor ports on the south
coast of Arabia, and was impressed with the reception he got
and the favorable disposition of all the tribes towards the British (FO 78/2755, Schneider-Bombay 11/13/74). The importance
of this incident lay in the willingness of the Porte to agree not
to interfere in the quarrel, a considerable retreat from the
Turkish pretensions put forth earlier in the year to sovereignty
over all of Arabia. The reason for this attitude is not hard to
find. The Turks had bitten off more than they could chew in the
Yemen. They had never been able to occupy the territory without a large force; the natural independence of the tribes and the
religious differences between the Zaidi Yemenites and Sunnite

Turks made any ordinary civil rule impossible. From 1873 to
the World War, the Turks could make their occupation good only
by force, and their experience was in no way different from that
of Ibrahim Pasha the younger in the early nineteenth century,
or that of the Turks in the sixteenth and early seventeenth centuries. Furthermore, the Bulgarian troubles were beginning,
and the growing crisis in the Balkans made further extension of
power an unwise diffusion of available Turkish forces.

A new development in the Yemen again threatened to bring
undue complications. On January 2, Schneider informed Bombay that the Turks wished to establish a telegraph line from
Ta'iz to Aden, and had appointed a Turkish official to come to
Aden as telegraph agent. He explained that they already had
two telegraph lines in the Yemen, one from Hodeida to San'a
and another from Hodeida to Ta'iz. The Turkish agent at Aden
had acted for the Porte for the receipt and transmission of messages which were sent overland to Ta'iz or San'a, or by sea to
Hodeida, after having been received by cable at Aden. Schneider
believed such a telegraph line would create undue complications:
first, because the sheikhs would expect an annual subsidy for
allowing the line to pass through their territory; second, if there
were any damage or injury to a Turkish subject or Turkish property, the question of punishment would bring a conflict in authority between the Turks and the British; third, such a project
would employ Turkish officials for construction and maintenance
and Zaptyes (native police) for protection, and their presence
would certainly be construed by the tribes as a recognition by
the British of the sovereign rights of the Sultan; fourth, the proposal would certainly be opposed by the Sultan of Lahej and
would be very distasteful to him (FO 78/2756, Schneider-Bombay 1/2/75 and Schneider-IO 1/19/75).

This information, which did not reach the Foreign Office
until March 10, was not available to the Foreign Office when,
on January 4, Musurus Pasha visited Tenterden and presented
a very menacing note from Aarifi Pasha, the Minister of Foreign Affairs. This note began by informing the British that the
Governor General of the Yemen reported difficulties and em-
barrassments which the turbulent tribes near Lahej, who were
under British protection, put in the way of Turkish attempts to
construct a telegraph line from Ta'iz to Aden, which had to traverse Lahej. He further complained of the continual annoyances caused by Ali ibn Mukbil and his adherents. The note

then concluded: "Il est évident que, si ces individuels contin-
uaient leurs méfaits, les Autorités Imperiales se verraient ob-
ligées d'avoir recours a la force" (FO 78/2756, cable Aarifi
Pasha-Musurus 1/4/75). Tenterden noted, "This is a very
menacing communication and should meet with a decided answer
but query India Office for opinion as to instructions which should
be sent to Sir H. Elliot in Reply" (FO 78/2756, Minute by Tenterden N.D.). This note was transmitted to the India Office and
on March 10 that office sent the Foreign Office the reply from
the Indian Government and the dispatches from Aden mentioned
above covering the question. The Indian Government stated,
"We are of the opinion that it would not be advisable to consent
to the proposal of the Porte unless the arrangement were pre-
ceeded by an absolute and formal abandonment by the Turkish
government of the position which it still continues in an indirect
way to advance with respect to the nine tribes around Aden."
The Indian Government made it clear that in case of such an understanding it would not object to the construction of such a telegraph line but they "should certainly be disposed to object to
the stationing of Turkish troops in the country for such a purpose" (FO 78/2756, Govt. of India-IO 2/5/75).

The India Office divided its opinion on the question into two
parts: first, the question of Dhala, and second, the general
question of the telegraph line. Dhala, of course, did not concern
the proposed telegraph line as it would not pass through Amiri
country. Lord Salisbury recommended that Sir Henry Elliot in
this question deny "the position assumed by the Turkish Government." On the question of the telegraph line, Lord Salisbury
felt that Elliot should discourage construction in every possible
legitimate manner. Lord Salisbury felt that "The Porte is bound
to ask formal permission...to construct such a line through
those states." However, if the Foreign Office felt it inadvisable
to oppose the construction of such a line, the India Office proposed that it be constructed by a British agency from funds supplied by the Ottoman Government, "and that a small subsidy be
paid to the tribes for its protection. Such subsidy being dis-
bursed by the Aden Resident and recovered annually from the
Turkish Government." In such an event, a formal convention
would have to be reached between the two governments (FO 78/
2754, IO-FO 3/10/75).

The position taken by the India Office was certainly reasonable and fair. The correspondence was forwarded to Elliot at

Constantinople with the following instructions signed by both
Derby and Disraeli: "Your Excellency will take no decisive
steps in opposition to the proposed telegraph until more precise
information is obtained as to what the Porte proposes to do particularly as to the arrangements for the protection of the line,
but you will take an opportunity of again drawing attention to the
interference in the affairs of Dhala & Endeavour to come to a
proper understanding with the Porte on the General Question"
(FO 78/2756, FO-Elliot 3/1/75).

In Constantinople, Safvet Pasha had replaced Aarifi Pasha
as Foreign Minister. When Elliot protested against the continued interference in Dhala, he stated that he knew nothing about
it, as it had happened before he had become Foreign Minister.
The Grand Vizier, Midhat Pasha, professed complete ignorance
on what was going on, "with which," Elliot commented, "I am
disposed to credit him, although it is true that in those distant
provinces the Governors General are allowed great latitude in
their proceedings and do not always keep the Porte informed
upon that." The Grand Vizier proposed that the question be held
in abeyance until the arrival in Constantinople of Redouf Pasha,
who was to be the new Governor General of the Yemen. Elliot
felt that this course was advisable, as he had confidence in Redouf (FO 78/2756, Elliot-FO 3/31/75). Redouf, however, did
not go to the Yemen, but remained as Minister of Marine at
Constantinople, and the depredations of the Amiri district continued. Diplomatically the matter lay dormant, awaiting the
appointment of a new Governor General.

In June, 1875, Elliot was informed of a rumor that Ismail
was going to receive authority from the Sultan to have his own
diplomatic representations at the foreign courts, and receive
the concession for the administration of the Yemen, for a payment to the Porte of Ł1,000,000. Elliot believed that he was referring to the advance payment only. Essaed Pasha added that
whatever the concessions were, they would not come while he
was Grand Vizier. Safvet declared with "every appearance of
dismay" that the making over of the Yemen to the Viceroy
"would be the first step to the end of the califate." Elliot demurred, saying that he could see little difference, since the
Sultan would retain sovereignty over any provinces of the Viceroy. Safvet replied that it would lead to serious consequences,
and reminded Elliot that on the previous occasion of such an offer,
(in 1872) had probably led to the dismissal of Mahmud Nedim

Pasha as Grand Vizier for having suggested it to the Sultan.
Elliot advised the Foreign Office that if such a concession were
carried out it would be beneficial to Britain's interests, since
the Viceroy "would be more careful than the Pashas have shown
themselves to avoid giving cause for complaint." He believed,
however, that such a course would cause great discontent among
the Muslim subjects of the Sultan (FO 78/2756, Elliot-FO
6/20/75).

There is no question but that Ismail wished the Yemen in
order to complete his concept of a great African Empire, but it
is difficult to see how, in view of the chaotic condition of his
finances in 1875, he could afford to put up the price which Elliot
mentioned. Less than six months later he was compelled to
sell Egypt's greatest financial asset, the Suez Canal shares, to
keep his government solvent, and 1875 marks the year when he
refinanced several of his former loans at a terrific cost to the
Egyptian treasury. What effect such a transfer would have on
Aden is not difficult to foresee. Ostensibly, the settlement
would have been benefited, as the Egyptians would unquestionably have recognized British domination over the tribes and all
interference would have ceased. However, in the long run,
Aden would have suffered more loss than gain. There was little
difference between Ismail's economic policy in his African Empire and the system of monopolies practiced by Muhammad Ali
and so hated by Palmerston. However, Ismail's plans for the
control of the Yemen never were fulfilled.

If the Foreign Office was willing to await the appointment
of a new Governor General for the settlement of the question of
Dhala, the Indian Government had slightly different ideas. On
May 4, 1875, the Government of India requested Schneider to
inform them of measures which could be taken to expel the Turks
by force. Schneider reported that no Turkish regulars were at
Dhala, which was occupied by only a few Zaptyes (native police);
the main Turkish force was at Qa'taba, headquarters for raids
into Amiri country. The distance to Dhala was seventy-eight
miles, of which the first fifty-eight were mapped and well-known
to the British. The Turks did not have large forces in the area,
about 300 men at Qa'taba and 1,200 at Ta'iz, which lay on the
left flank of the route to Dhala, about forty miles to the northwest. In addition, a sizeable number of Turkish troops were
continually on the move in the interior of the Yemen, so that any
move against Dhala would have to be made with sufficient force

to handle a possible armed clash; the distance was too great to allow a withdrawal after the move had been started. Schneider recommended a striking force of two regiments with sappers and mountain guns, and a considerable force in Lahej territory to protect the left flank against an attack from Ta'iz. The time was propitious; the Turks were involved with rebellious tribes north of San'a, and could not afford to send re-enforcements from there without risking a tribal attack on their rear. The most opportune time was in October when the garrison relief arrived, and the relief and garrison could be combined. Two warships would be necessary to protect the settlement from any attempts by the Turks to take action from the sea. Schneider concluded by stating that, in his opinion, the threat of force alone would compel the Turks to withdraw from the Amiri country although the temptation to meddle with this border tribe was very great (FO 78/2756, IO-FO 6/24/75, encl. Schneider-Bombay 5/26/75). This dispatch was transmitted to Tenterden unofficially on June 24, and caused him considerable alarm. He transmitted the document to Derby who noted: "What Gen. Schneider proposes is really a war on Turkey....we are always ready to remonstrate when necessary with the Porte. The difficulty has been to know what is doing" (FO 78/2756, Minute by Derby 6/27/75). Tenterden wrote Colonel Burne at the India Office unofficially, requesting him to caution Schneider to take no steps without the sanction of the home government (FO 78/2756, Tenterden-Burne [unofficial] 7/2/75).

It is not hard to understand that Schneider's patience was wearing rather thin. After all, the Foreign Office had been protesting to the Porte for two-and-a-half years, and the only effective action had been taken after the British field force had moved into Lahej in November, 1873. To the Foreign Office, however, the situation which had appeared so important two years before, had been overshadowed by other developments in the Balkans which might threaten the integrity of the Ottoman Empire. In addition, the information which they had was rather vague, and disturbances eighty miles removed from the settlement did not have the urgency of the presence of Turkish forces in Lahej only a few miles from Aden's fortifications.

Elliot, in Constantinople, did have a certain success in obtaining new instructions to the Pasha of the Yemen ordering the withdrawal of troops and Zaptyes if Dhala was found to be in the Amiri country (FO 78/2756, Elliot-FO 7/14/75). This new order was important – not because it was carried out, which, as usual, it was not, but because it placed the whole controversy on a totally different plane. It removed the conflict from the high level of questions of sovereignty, religious pretensions, and national honor, and placed it where it belonged, in the category of an ordinary boundary dispute which could be settled by compromise and good will.

Some of the reason for this change in tone may be found in an interesting report to Schneider from a confidential source in Hodeida (the confidential source was a Banyan merchant, the son of Abdul Russool, Britain's friend and agent in Mocha in the 1840's). The information was sent in reply to a query from the Resident as to the truth of a rumor that Mocha had been made a free port. This was not true, Schneider's informant stated, as such a move would cause a terrific loss of revenue to the other ports of the Yemen. He then described the organization of the Yemen. It had been made into four districts, one in the Asiri country, one around Hodeida, one with San'a as a capital, and one with Ta'iz as the seat of administration. The Turks had an occupying force of thirteen regiments of Turkish regulars and four regiments of Zaptyes. The Zaptyes acted as police, and were distributed throughout each district in small numbers backed by relatively large regular garrisons in the larger towns. The San'a and Asiri districts contained the largest garrisons (a natural distribution as these two districts contained the most rebellious population, San'a being the center of the Zaidi sect in the Yemen and the Asiri country containing the always dangerous tribal confederation of that name). The total number of troops probably did not exceed 15,000 men. (FO 78/2756, Schneider-IO 7/15/75 encl. translation of letter rec. from Hodeida on 7/10/75. The writer's name is not given in the translation.)

That the Turks had learned a great deal since their abortive attempts at conquest in the 1840's is obvious. Thirty years before they had attempted to rule the Yemen by the occupation of a few strong points, the establishment of wholly Turkish rule in these places, and the use of subsidies to keep the country quiet. This, of course, was the method employed by the British at Aden. They had the same difficulties that beset the early Residents, but while Haines, Coghlan and Merewether succeeded in overcoming these difficulties, the Turkish officials lacked the ability of the British, and most of all lacked adequate garrisons to back up their diplomacy. Their use of native police in the

1870's softened somewhat the explosive qualities which so often
resulted from the direct impact of Turkish officials on Yemeni
sheikhs, and further gave them a reliable intelligence network
which they had not had before. It is also obvious that they made
much greater use of local Arabs as minor officials than in the
1840's, which was another factor in their success. Unquestionably the improvement in weapons made the work of the Turks
easier. While the Turkish army was probably not provided in
the 1870's with as modern weapons as the British forces at
Aden, they did have considerably more effective weapons than
in the 1840's, while the Arabs were largely armed with the same
type of arms they had had in the 1840's, that is, matchlocks
and flintlocks.

     That the new vizierial letter on Dhala marked a new phase
in Turkish claims in Arabia was confirmed by Turkish actions
in a new resurgence of the disturbances in the Hadramaut. In
May, Elliot forwarded information from Safvet Pasha concerning an attack planned on the Ka'aiti at Shihr by Ghalib Khissain,
Jemedar of the Nizam of Hyderabad. Safvet requested that the
British at Aden do all in their power to keep peace between the
two tribes, recognizing the position of the British in relation to
this coast. Safvet feared a planned attack by sea which the
Turks felt would disturb the trade of Turkish and Arab vessels
under Turkish protection in this area. He was, in other words,
asking for British protection for legitimate Turkish trade, a
far cry from the previous claims of sovereignty in the area (FO
78/2756, Elliot-FO 5/15/75). This request was turned over to
the India Office for investigation.

     Since the disturbances of the previous year, the Indian Gov-
ernment had been trying through its Resident at Hyderabad to
get to the bottom of the financing of certain purchases of steamships in India. These investigations had proved fruitless (FO
78/2756, C. B. Sanders [Hyderabad]-Aitchison [Govt. of India]
10/30/74 and 6/14/74). Incidents in Aden in April had caused
considerable concern. Each party in the Hadramaut was reported to have blockaded the other's port, and buggalows bound
from India for Mukalla and Aden had been plundered near Shihr.
On receipt of this news, H. M. S. "Vulture" had been sent to
stop this apparent piracy, shortly followed by Captain Prideaux
on the "Kwantung" to investigate the situation. Prideaux could
find no sign of legitimate blockade at either Mukalla or Shihr,
but found that both parties had anchorages, the Kathiri at Bandar

Broom fifty miles from Shihr, and the Ka'iti at Shubar roadstead thirty miles from Mukalla. The commander of the Ka'iti
"naively observed to Capt. Prideaux that if he had invested Mukalla in such a manner as to constitute an effective blockade,
the fort would have fired at his Dhows." Therefore he stopped
all vessels in his neighborhood on the chance that some of them
might be going to Mukalla. Prideaux pointed out to him that this
was piracy rather than legitimate blockade, and restitution was
made to the owners of three plundered buggalows. The purchase
of a steamer in Italy had been reported, and Prideaux observed
that if the party allied to the Nizam should win, as seemed likely, the British might be faced with a neighbor allied with a powerful Indian native state. Schneider, on receiving Prideaux's
report, suggested that both sides be forbidden to maintain hostile fleets and use Aden for the purchase of stores (FO 78/2756,
Schneider-Bombay 4/26/75). The situation was greatly complicated by the fact that the Jemadar, who had been supporting the
Kathiri tribe, suddenly switched his allegiance to the Ka'aiti
because of the failure of the Nakeeb of Mukalla to live up to certain concessions and payments promised the Jemadar for his
aid. It had become obvious that the Jemadar, with his Indian
connections, had become the most powerful influence on the
Hadramaut coast.

Schneider's proposal that the use of Aden be denied both
sides of the conflict was overruled by the Indian Government
when they received information from the Resident of Hyderabad
that all parties involved in that state were outside of British
protection or influence, and that such interference would only
upset relations between the Indian Government and the Nizam
(FO 78/2756, IO-FO 8/21/75 encl. Sanders-IO 8/5/75). This
information was forwarded to Elliot for transmission to the
Porte (FO 78/2756, FO-Elliot 8/30/75). The problems raised
by the experiment of the Jemadar ended quickly and suddenly
when the steamer which he had purchased in Italy suddenly appeared at Aden in August to claim protection of the British government through the Italian consul. So many violations of Admiralty law had been involved in the purchase of the vessel —
arrears of pay for the crew and violation of contract (the crew
had been hired for legitimate commerce, not warfare) — that the
Jemadar would have to spend several years paying up the claims
involved rather than using his money to achieve his ambitions
in the Hadramaut. In reporting this incident Schneider concluded

"The Jemadar seems well punished for his attempts to outwit the British government" (FO 78/2756, Schneider-Bombay 8/28/75 encl. in IO-FO 10/9/75).

The appearance at Aden of a new telegraphic agent for the Turkish government caused Schneider and the India Office some concern about a possible resurgence of the whole question of a telegraph line from Aden to Ta'iz, but inquiries by Elliot at the Office of Director of Telegraphs in Constantinople assured him that the building of such a line was contemplated only at some future date (FO 78/2756, Elliot-FO 10/15/75).

As Balkan affairs assumed the character of a crisis in 1876, rumors naturally flew around Europe. One of these rumors, that Russian interests in the guise of an American trading company were purchasing French claims to Sheikh Said, is of itself of no importance. However, Schneider was asked to investigate the situation at the roadstead. Schneider obtained copies of the original purchase agreements. They showed that the original concession had later been sold to another French trading company but that only a first installment of $2,000 out of a promised $80,000 had been paid, and that had been in 1868. The Turks had continued to keep a small detachment of troops at the Bandar, but the houses which the French had built were still closed and were rapidly falling into ruin. The local sheikh, Schneider reported, had twice tried to sell the site to the British at Aden, as everyone concerned had agreed that, through failure to live up to the contract, the French agreement was void (FO 78/2756, Schneider-Bombay 4/22/76). In fact, the French never did put forth any claim, and there is every reason to believe that the project was a private one whose only chance of success rested in interesting the French Admiralty in the spot as a coaling station. When this was turned down in 1869, the attempt was doomed to failure, as no important overland trade routes ended near the place.

In August, 1875, the Dhala question again plagued the Foreign Office. On August 14, the India Office complained that the vizierial letter of the year before had been "very imperfectly carried out," and that attempts were being made to include at least a part of the Amiri country in the Yemen. Salisbury thought that the proceedings of the authorities in the Yemen "should no longer be allowed to pass unnoticed." It was requested that Elliot press for the withdrawal of all Turkish officials, troops, and Zaptyes, and for the restoration of Ali ibn

Mukbil as sheikh of the tribe. The request went on, "At the
same time it might be expedient to suggest...that her Majesty's
Govt. cannot be expected to be satisfied for an indefinite time
with constantly renewing remonstrances to which no kind of attention is paid" (FO 78/2756, IO-FO 8/14/76). A Minute to this
note read, "It could not require much provocation on the part
of the Turks to create a serious outbreak in the Yemen, and in
the present state of affairs in Bulgaria the Turkish Authorities
if well advised wd abstain from all proceedings of a nature likely to give offense to the Arabs" (FO 78/2756, Minute attached
to above). A protest to the Porte was prepared for Elliot and
approved by Lord Beaconsfield (FO 78/2756, FO-Elliot 7/26/
76). New orders were issued, and the Turks really did withdraw from Dhala, allowing Ali ibn Mukbil to return to his capital. There remained, however, a real and legitimate boundary
dispute, and after considerable negotiation all parties concerned
agreed in March, 1877, to have the Resident at Aden settle the
matter directly with the Turkish officials on the spot. This work
was taken up and the boundaries tentatively agreed on shortly
afterwards (FO 78/2756 various dispatches). [Note: in 1958,
this boundary was still in dispute between the Yemen and the
British.]

Thus ended the first real threat to Aden by a foreign power
as distinct from tribal activity, and the first phase of the uneasy
control of the Yemen by the Turks which lasted through the
first World War.

XXVII. SOMALI COAST 1874-1875

After the meeting between permanent officials of the Foreign Office and India Office on June 2, 1874, considerable discussion ensued as to the exact policy to be followed regarding Berbera. However, before trying to understand what this discussion involved, it is necessary to know what had been happening in Abyssinian-Egyptian relations since 1869, because the Egyptian Government considered expansion to the south as an integral part of their relations with Abyssinia.

Events in Abyssinia have already been mentioned, as well as the decision of the Foreign Office to send equal presents to the three leading rulers, Kassa of Tigré, Gobaze of Gondar, and Menelik of Shoa. Early in 1869 a new character entered the scene. In January, the Foreign Office received a letter signed "Lt. Col. Kirkham," notifying them of this gentleman's acceptance of the command of Kassa's army, and requesting the opinion of the British government on Abyssinian affairs "to enable him to carry out any views that the Government might entrust him with" (FO 1/29, IO-FO 1/7/69). As the gentleman could not be discovered in any India Army list, information was requested from the War Office. Lieutenant Colonel C. G. Gordon (Chinese Gordon) happened to be at the War Office at the time, and reported that he knew Kirkham well. Kirkham had been steward to Admiral Keppel, former Commander in China, and a steward with the P. & O. He had entered the service in 1862 for two years, served at Amoy in the Chinese Imperial forces, run a hotel in Tientsin for a short while, and had finally gone to Abyssinia with the British as a sutler (a camp follower who sells extra provisions to the troops). Gordon had had a high opinion of him, but because Kirkham had received a severe head wound in 1864, Gordon felt, "he is no longer the same man and I should be averse to recommend him in any way" (FO 1/29, Col. C. G. Gordon [WO]-FO 1/27/69). The Foreign Office therefore sent him a letter stating that the government had no views on Abyssinia to communicate to him, and that no official cognizance could be taken of his actions.

Kirkham's influence with Kassa was undiminished by this rebuff, and showed itself in October, 1870, when Stanton informed the Foreign Office that two envoys from Kassa had

arrived at Suez on their way to England with presents for the
Queen, with sufficient funds to defray their traveling expenses
and the information that King and Co., a British mercantile
firm, had been appointed as Kassa's commercial agent (FO 1/
28, Stanton-FO 10/7/70 IO-FO 10/10/70). However, the envoys, who had been guests of the Viceroy of Egypt, expected to
become guests of the British government on arrival in London,
an expense which neither the Foreign Office would pay out of
their funds nor the India Office out of theirs. There remained
certain Imperial funds, but the Treasury refused to sanction the
use of these funds for the purpose. Meanwhile, the two envoys
remained in Cairo, knowing full well, as did the Foreign Office,
that they would probably lose their heads if they didn't get to
England.

Stanley, Vice-consul in Cairo, succeeded in inducing the
envoys to send their presents to England; he suggested that, as
the presents were worth Ł1,500, presents to an equal amount
should be sent to Kassa, who had expressed a desire for a bat-
tery of mountain guns and some rockets (FO 1/28, Stanton-FO,
1/13/71).

The Foreign Office, anxious to avoid another Theodore incident, discussed this question at length. It was decided to send
Kassa a letter from the Queen, and also a letter from Grenville
explaining why it was not necessary for the envoys to come to
England. Presents to an equal value were also to be forwarded
(FO 1/28, Minutes by J. B. B. 2/4/71, Hammond & Grenville
3/10/71). Funds for these presents were asked from the Treasury, which refused to grant the request. An acrimonious correspondence with the Treasury ensued while the poor envoys
remained in Cairo. This correspondence lasted for a year.
Meanwhile Kassa and Kirkham informed the Foreign Office that
Gobaze had been defeated in August, 1871, and that Kassa ruled
all of Abyssinia except Shoa (FO 1/29, Stanton-FO 9/15/71).

The correspondence came to Tenterden's attention when he
took office early in 1872. He commented, "These Savage Princes
are, I have no doubt, as punctilious as other people. Theodore
certainly was. It is a strong measure to leave a letter unanswered for several months" (FO 1/28, Minute by Tenterden
1/9/72).

Things moved faster after Tenterden began to handle the
question, and in June presents were at Aden for Prideaux to
take to Massawa and there meet the envoys (FO 11/28,

Tremenheere-IO 6/15/72). The envoys and the presents were
dispatched to Tigré with Munzinger Bey's help. Meanwhile
Prideaux had an opportunity to assess the situation in Abyssinia.
He found that the country was at peace at the moment. Kassa,
who was crowned Emperor with the throne name Johannes, in
February, had returned from an expedition against the Gallas,
but his real power was limited to the province of Tigré, the
other chiefs recognizing merely his overlordship. Prideaux,
who of course knew the country well, remarked that Kassa's
character had changed for the worse since he had become Emperor. He had expelled the Roman Catholic missionaries, and
treated the Europeans in his service very badly. Munzinger,
since becoming Governor of Massawa, had done much to improve his area. Cotton had been introduced with great success
at Tokar, near Suakin, and attempts were being made to found
a settlement there and improve the water supply for irrigation.
The Sudan telegraph system was almost finished, connecting
Berber (on the Nile), Khartoum, Kasa'a, Suakin, and Massawa.
Massawa itself had had a boom as a result of the British expedition, and was a vastly improved town. Munzinger had reformed
the system of taxation and enforced it with even justice to all
the peoples, so that revenue of the province had increased to
Ł50,000 annually (FO 1/28, Tremenheere-IO 7/1/72 encl. Pri-
deaux-Tremenheere 6/28/72).

That Johannes intended to carry on relations with England
soon became obvious. Kirkham was reported on his way to
England in September, 1872, with letters for the Queen (FO 1/
28, Schneider-IO 9/28/72). His arrival in London was followed
by a request from King & Co. that Henry S. King be recognized
as Johannes' consul in London (FO 1/29, King & Co. -FO 11/15
72). Kirkham, in London, also requested the return of a certain book taken from Magdala by the expedition in 1868. This
book was the Fetha Negast, or law digest, of Ethiopia and was
the official copy of this work. The British Museum readily acceded to the request, and it was given to Kirkham to take back
with him. [Note: Colonel Leo J. Query, United States Army
Attaché in Ethiopia from 1950 to 1952, stated that the Fetha
Negast is still in use in rural Ethiopia and has strongly influenced the present-day Ethiopian legal code. He adds, "I have
seen cases where the Supreme Court has used the Fetha Negast
instead of the Statutory Code, e.g., in the trial of the conspira-
tors against the regime in 1951. "]

Kirkham also brought to the attention of the Foreign Office
Johannes' claims as to Ismail's aggressions on his land. Bogos
was, as usual, the disputed spot, but the Egyptian occupation
of Anfile threatened the salt beds inland which were essential
to Abyssinia's welfare (FO 1/27B, Kirkham-Grenville 10/31/
72). Grenville replied that the Foreign Office was not familiar
with these details but had requested Stanton to investigate the
matter at Alexandria (FO 1/27B, Grenville-Kirkham 11/7/72).

Reports of an invasion of Abyssinia had been prevalent in
Alexandria since June, 1872, and had been denied by the Egyptian government. When Stanton received orders to investigate
the matter, in November, he immediately proceeded to question
Sharif Pasha, the Egyptian Foreign Minister (FO 78/2229, FO-
Stanton 11/7/72). Sharif claimed that the whole affair was due
to the refusal of the Abyssinians to recognize the Egyptian claim
to Bogos, which, he said, Muhammad Ali had conquered in 1842.
Stanton then saw Ismail, who put forth the same claim and said
that he was ready to invade Abyssinia to establish his boundary
(FO 78/2229, Stanton-FO 11/30/72). After further negotiation,
Ismail was persuaded to withhold further action, especially as
the French Consul General joined Stanton in his protests (FO
78/2229, Stanton-FO 1/27/72).

Munzinger reported that the French Consul at Massawa had
used this protest to Ismail as a lever to get Johannes to accept
a new Roman Catholic mission in Tigré (FO 78/2229, Stanton-
FO 12/21/72). Frere, on his way to Zanzibar, made some investigations of his own, and came to the conclusion that French
influence in Abyssinia was not in the best interests of anybody;
the Frenchmen in the country could only be classified as arms
smugglers and adventurers (FO 78/2283, Frere [private letter]
1/11/73).

A new disturbance, a raid by the Abyssinians into the Taka
province, upset Ismail considerably, but he stated that he
would not attack the Abyssinians (FO 78/2283 cable, Stanton-
FO 3/4/73). As usual, all activity ceased during the rainy season. In May, Tenterden reviewed the situation. Acting on the
assumption that Abyssinia was a sovereign nation, the British
had interchanged views with the French Government which had
joined in a protest to the Porte. As a result of the Abyssinian
raids, Ismail had seized the province, or rather area, called
Hamasein as a guarantee against further aggressions, and had
given Johannes three months to make reparations for the raids.

Stanton had protested to Ismail against this action, stating that
the British government viewed this in "a very serious light,"
and a similar protest had been made in Constantinople.

The peculiar relationship of Egypt and the Ottoman Empire
now showed itself in its most elusive form. The Porte, interested
in seeing that Ismail's energies were used up on the western
shore of the Red Sea rather than in Arabia, stated that Ismail
had freedom of action in the area. Nubar Pasha, Egyptian Grand
Vizier in Alexandria, told Stanton that Egypt could not act without the consent of the Porte, thus placing the blame on Constantinople. Munzinger, the local governor, thought that the whole
episode was greatly exaggerated by rumors in Egypt. Tenterden
felt that it was primarily a local border dispute with which Johannes had nothing to do and over which he had no control (FO
1/27B, Memo by Tenterden 5/19/73).

Meanwhile, Ismail's plans for an empire in Africa were
taking shape. Sir Samuel Baker had established himself at
Gondoroko on the White Nile, completely flanking Abyssinia on
the west. Egyptian expansion on the shore of the Red Sea, already tentatively carried as far as Berbera, showed Ismail's
intent to flank Abyssinia on the east. If these two flanking movements could be linked as McKillop and Gordon tried to do in
1875, Ismail would dominate the whole northeast corner of Africa, and even if Abyssinia were not conquered, she would be
completely controlled economically. It was a grandiose plan for
an empire, the first of those plans to which the African continent was to be subject in the period from 1870 to 1914. Of all
the plans it was probably the most sensible, as Ismail, if he had
had the funds to carry it out and then develop the country, would
have acquired a compact and potentially profitable empire.
Furthermore, in contrast to the outright imperialism prevalent
a few years later, Ismail went about establishing his empire
with a humanitarian excuse, the suppression of the slave trade.

There can be no doubt that Ismail was sincere in disliking
the slave trade. However, it is very doubtful that he was so
foolish as to expend the great sums of money involved in his African expansion just for this humanitarian purpose. That the
period of his imperialistic desires should have coincided with
the revival of interest in the suppression of the slave trade following the Civil War in the United States was lucky for him, and
he made the most of his opportunities. Abolition of slavery in
the United States ended the slave trade from the west coast of

Africa. Attention therefore was concentrated on the east coast.
Early in 1873 Sir Bartle Frere had visited Zanzibar and while
immediately unsuccessful in his mission, a new treaty abolishing the trade was signed shortly after his departure. However,
the trade had never been suppressed in the Red Sea, the Gulf of
Aden, nor overland through the Sudan. Ismail had fairly effectively stopped the overland route northwards, and Sir Samuel
Baker's expedition had certainly curtailed the trade in central
Africa, but it continued to flourish on the coast. In fact, as
other routes were cut off, the trade increased at the mouth of
the Red Sea. It was difficult for large patrol craft to navigate
these waters; worst of all, it was openly encouraged by Turkish
officials who were far enough removed from Constantinople to
feel themselves free to disregard any firmans sent them. Therefore, in British eyes, Ismail remained the only hope for the
suppression of this trade.

If the British should prove willing to allow the Egyptians to
control the western shore of the Red Sea, how would this affect
Abyssinia? The Abyssinians also claimed the western shore of
the Red Sea from Annesley Bay at least as far south as Edd.
This claim was largely mythical, and was comparable to the
tenuous Turkish claim to all of Abyssinia. Certainly no European power would consider such a claim valid. The Abyssinians
also claimed Bogos, Hamasein, and Metemma, a part of Sennar.
However, they exercised no real sovereignty over these provinces, which were occupied by various small tribes, and the only
validity in their claim might come from the fact that these tribes
were Abyssinian Christians rather than Muslims. Previously,
on more than one occasion, the British had intervened on behalf
of these peoples. However, if Ismail aimed to establish effective government in the Sudan, he would have to incorporate
these territories into that country in order to reach the natural
frontier of the Ethiopian highlands, the actual boundary of effective Abyssinian rule. Otherwise Ismail would be faced with
continual border disputes resulting in friction, punitive expeditions, and a large outlay of money and men for border defenses,
for if history has proved nothing else, it does prove that no
organized government can peacefully exist bordering on tribal
rule unless some natural and defensible boundary is reached.
Ismail and Munzinger were fully aware of this fact, and the British representatives in Egypt became convinced of it also.

In Alexandria, the Egyptians took one step to diminish these

border disturbances by prohibiting the passage of arms through
Egyptian territory to Abyssinia, excepting, of course, small
arms for sporting purposes (FO 78/2283, Stanton-FO 7/19/73).
Ismail followed this up with a proposal to abolish the slave trade
and gradually outlaw slavery in Egypt. Vivian, who was acting
for Stanton during his absence in England, had a long interview
with Ismail on August 22, in which the Viceroy stated the essen-
tials of his plan. Aside from the outright abolition of the slave
trade, slavery in Egypt was to be abolished by first, register-
ing all transactions in slaves sold from Egypt for export; second,
prohibiting the importation of slaves; third, by making all children born of slaves in Egypt automatically free men. Vivian
felt that Ismail was absolutely sincere in this plan and would
carry it out to the best of his ability (FO 78/2284, Vivian-FO
8/22/73).

This was followed by Ismail's wish to appoint Colonel Gordon to command of the Sudan to replace Sir Samuel Baker, with
headquarters in Ismailia, and to provide Gordon with full powers to suppress the slave trade (FO 78/2284, cable, Vivian-FO
8/30/73). The Foreign Office had no objection to this, but said
that all negotiations would have to be conducted with the War
Office (FO 78/2784, FO-Vivian 9/29/73). Ismail then proposed
to the British to give up their two islands off Zeila and Tajura
in return for the abolition of French claims to Obock (see pp.
432-33, 439, 469, 478, 492-93).

Hertslet's memorandum on the claims of sovereignty on the
coast has been mentioned. This memorandum did not cover
the Abyssinian-Egyptian problem. A memorandum on this problem was prepared in Egypt and was discussed in a statement
attached to a dispatch from Vivian, dated October 18, 1873.
Prepared by Vivian with Munzinger's aid, it is a document of
great interest. The Abyssinians claimed Bogos, Ailat, Agade,
Baghi, Tora, Zula, and Anfile, the Somali country, the Shankalla country, and Metemma. Ailat, Agade, Baghi, Tora, and
Zula were all in the neighborhood of Annesley Bay and had been
to a certain extent controlled by the Turks since 1820 and in no
way controlled by the Abyssinians. Bogos had been in continual
dispute, but the tribes had requested Munzinger to take them
under his protection to prevent constant raids. As the district
lay across the only route from Massawa to the interior of the
Sudan, its control was of considerable importance to the Egyptians. Anfile had not been occupied by the Abyssinians for 250

CHAPTER XXVII

years, separated as it was by wild and inhospitable country
from the Abyssinian highlands. Abyssinian claims to the Somali
and Galla or Shankalla countries was traditional, but effective
control had been lacking since the sixteenth century or earlier.
Metemma had been a part of Abyssinia under Theodore, but
since his death there had been no effective government there,
and the people of Metemma had appealed for Egyptian protection
in 1871 to prevent their country from being laid waste by warring feudal chieftains. The revenue from Bogos, Metemma,
and the coastal villages amounted to about $95,000 plus an addi-
tional $60,000 collected as a tax on salt. The report concluded
with an account of the government of the Massawa area. The
city had prospered under Munzinger, and its trade in 1872
amounted to more than £400,000, of which half was British and
Banyan. Munzinger governed his provinces through five classes
of officials, an assistant governor, a military officer, local
merchants, muftis, and the leading local sheikhs. Justice was
apparently well-handled and the whole government was fairly
effective, a total of 3,000 troops controlling between one and
two million partially civilized tribesmen so well that the slave
trade had practically disappeared (FO 78/2284, Vivian-FO 10/
18/73).

Reports of further border disturbances came throughout
the winter, but Ismail controlled his ambitions at the request of
Vivian and Stanton. In June, 1874, the Reverend Mr. Flaad,
who had returned to Abyssinia in 1869, revisited England. He
had an interview with Stanton at Alexandria. He gave such an
unfavorable report of Johannes and his intolerant attitude both
towards Europeans and the Egyptian government that Tenterden
again reviewed the entire Abyssinian question. He concluded,
"The Less we have to do with these Abyssinian-Egyptian disputes the better." Lord Derby, on reviewing the papers, went
even farther, instructing Tenterden "Keep absolutely clear of
them in the future" (FO 78/2342 Stanton-FO 6/17/24 and Minutes by Tenterden and Derby 6/27/74).

If Ismail's imperial designs in central Africa had been sanctioned by the British approval of Sir Samuel Baker's appointment, they were further approved by the release of Gordon from
active military duty by the War Office in order to accept the
position of Governor of the Sudan. Derby's decision to keep a
hands-off policy on Abyssinian-Egyptian disputes gave Ismail a
free hand not only on the northern frontier, but also in the Galla
country and the interior of Somaliland, a fact of primary

importance to him if he was to develop effectively his central
African territories. There remained only a decision on the
question of the control of the coastline beyond Bab-el-Mandeb.

The Foreign Office-India Office meeting of June 2, 1874,
had been called, among other reasons, for the purpose of reaching some agreement as to the policy to be followed on the Somali coast. At that meeting it had been agreed that the India Office
was to supply a memorandum on treaty rights on the coast, with
emphasis on those rights which the India Office considered important.

The first request from the India Office was to drop the question of the return of the islands in the Gulf of Zeila unless Ismail brought up the question. The Foreign Office concurred in
this and so instructed Stanton at Alexandria (FO 78/2187, IO-
FO 7/4/74 & FO Stanton 6/19/74).

On August 7, the Foreign Office received a long memorandum on the treaties with the Somali tribes together with memoranda by Sir Bartle Frere and General Tremenheere on the
situation. The memorandum on the treaties simply listed them,
emphasizing the anti-slave trade portions and those clauses
which forbade the chiefs to make treaties with other powers
without British consent (FO 78/3187, IO-FO 8/7/74).

Tremenheere's memo dealt largely with the dependence of
Aden on the Somali coast for supplies, pointing out that while
each small port on the coast was unimportant in itself, the aggre-
gate trade was essential to Aden's welfare. His statement that
the relation of the Somali tribes to Aden was similar to that of
the Arab tribes to the settlement was certainly far from the
truth in actual fact, although the wording of the treaties was
rather similar. He recommended that if Egypt were to be allowed to control the area, the British should insist on two points:
first, the right to have a British agent at Berbera; second, the
insistence that all ports east of Bab-el-Mandeb be free ports
(FO 78/3187, Memo by Tremenheere 7/13/74).

Sir Bartle Frere's memorandum, dated June 27, clearly
showed the viewpoint of the India Office on the matter. It was
extensively annotated by Lord Tenterden, whose comments
point up the fundamental disagreement between the two offices.
Frere broke the question up into three aspects: first, how
Egyptian occupation would affect the military and political position of Aden; second, how it would affect the Indian subjects
trading on the Somali coast; and third, how it would affect the
slave trade.

In discussing the first point, Frere emphasized Aden's importance as a communications center. Occupation of neighboring territories by the Turks or Egyptians would not, he felt, affect the military power of Aden, nor would it affect the trade of the settlement to any great extent as this could largely be protected against the monopolistic tendencies of the Turks and Egyptians by enforcing existing commercial treaties.

However, the Banyans would suffer considerably from such an occupation. Under the tribal government of the areas involved no single chief was strong enough to bully them, nor could any chief afford to do without them or the revenue they brought in import and export taxes. With a central government, independent of purely local taxes for its finances, controlling the area, these industrious Indians would probably not fare as well.

Frere's concern for the Indian trader marks a very new departure in the policy of the Indian Government. Since the early 1840's no concern had been shown for the welfare of these traders. The Residents at Aden had felt themselves responsible for the Banyans, but had had no means at their disposal to aid them, especially after the Indian Navy was dissolved. Protests by the Resident regarding violations of the commercial treaties seldom went any further than the archives of the Bombay Government unless there was actual danger to life and limb. Frere's interest in these people had been awakened by his mission to Zanzibar (see Coupland, THE EXPLOITATION OF EAST AFRICA, pp. 200-201). As Aden had been neglected until Napier's experience with the expedition to Abyssinia, so the Banyans were neglected until Frere's experience in Zanzibar.

As for the slave trade, Frere was very dubious of the effects of Egyptian and Turkish occupation, as he felt that however sincere Ismail or the Porte were in their intentions, their distant officials felt free to act as they saw fit. He then discussed European attempts to acquire territory in the area, pointing out how effectively the Aden authorities had counteracted French attempts, on which Tenterden noted: "This is scarcely correct. French own islands at Obock." Frere then mentioned recent Italian attempts to occupy Socotra, asking the permission of the Indian Government, which had been refused, with the note "Why we should object, we really didn't know at the time and had we been asked our reasons we should have been puzzled to give them. Now if we let in the Egyptians we shall not be able to

object to other European nations." Tenterden disagreed with
this viewpoint, writing, "I don't see this, Egyptians are actually in possession of some places & their flag is the one which
naturally claims to fly over others. It is just the opposite, the
only way to keep the other nations out is to let the Egyptians
place the country under the guarantee of the Ottoman Empire."
Frere then went on, "We cannot long keep a neutral zone of
savagedom around us; and, if we do not go on extending our own
empire & ruling the nations we annex & civilize, we ought not
to object to other nations extending their own limits & with them
the bounds of civilization." But apparently he did not feel that
the Egyptians were civilized unless they could be bound to an
anti-slave trade treaty and free trade with moderate customs
duties. He felt that if they were to make these acquisitions into
new slave-hunting territories and set up monopolies in the manner of Muhammad Ali, Palmerston's policy of exclusion should
be adhered to. He then noted the increase in slave trade at
Zeila and Tajura under Turkish control, but vitiated his whole
argument by quoting probably the most fantastic slave trade
story ever to grace an official document.

This story, based, Frere said, on information provided by
a German traveler named Hildebrandt and the Austrian Consul
at Aden, was as follows: The Chief of Tajura wished to present
sixteen Galla slaves to Ismail's mother, and he shipped them
on an Egyptian steamer to Suez. The captain of the steamer,
afraid of Ismail's anti-slave trade edicts and afraid not to deliver the slaves, listed them as objets d'art for the Vienna exposition and smuggled them through the customs at Suez in water tanks. Tenterden noted, "I think this story must have originally been told to the Marines, it is too good to be true."
Actually, by using this illustration, Frere contradicted his own
argument, for if the Turks at Tajura traded in slaves, it was
obvious that Ismail did not and Egyptian control would thus
serve to stop, not aid, the trade (FO 78/3187, Memo by Frere,
6/27/74).

In the letter transmitting these memoranda, the India Office
made the statement that Lord Salisbury was "not disposed to
any extension of Egyptian power beyond Bab-el-Mandeb" (FO
78/3187, IO-FO 8/7/74). Tenterden, after reading all the enclosures, noted, "Most unsatisfactory letter from the I.O. It
appears to be a result of differences of opinion in the council.
Instead of a letter which can be sent to Stanton, the I.O. draws

up an abstract of treaties." He noted the clauses in the Zeila
and Tajura treaties prohibiting them from entering into agreements with other nations, and questioned whether the India Office had raised any protest at the time of the Egyptian occupation of these ports. As to containing the Egyptians within Bab-
el-Mandeb, Tenterden said, "There is no good in futile protests. It is best either to let the matter slide or arrive at a
friendly understanding next year (1875) when the commercial
treaty is being discussed" (FO 78/3187, Memo by Tenterden
8/12/74 and IO-FO 8/7/74). All the material was forwarded
to Stanton for his information (FO 78/3187, FO-Stanton
8/20/74).

This material, especially Frere's memorandum, showed
considerable muddled thinking on the part of the India Council.
One of the first things that strikes one is the lack of real knowledge of the difference between the governments of Turkey and
Egypt. Whatever Ismail's faults and ambitions might be, he
was trying to run his government in a responsible manner, and
any study of the documents relating to Egyptian affairs shows a
minimum of subterfuge and delay. His use of Europeans as officials helped considerably in this, and he had much more real
control in his distant provinces than the Porte ever had had. A
second feature is the insistence of the India Office on retaining
a status quo which they themselves had never made any real
effort to maintain. Of course Turkish aggressions around Aden
had brought this position to the fore, and unquestionably they
were chiefly interested in protecting the settlement from further difficulties while the Turks still threatened in the Yemen.
The third feature is, of course, the emphasis on the suppression of the slave trade, which was omnipresent in all discussions of eastern Africa in the 1870's.

The Foreign Office replied to the India Office in the sense
of Tenterden's note, requiring information as to whether or not
the India Office had protested the Turkish occupation of Zeila
and Tajura about 1864. The India Office was advised that the
Foreign Office saw only two alternatives: first, to leave everything alone; or, second, to try to regulate the present situation
as the Turks already had occupied Zeila and Tajura for a considerable time (FO 78/3187, FO-IO 8/21/74).

Stanton, in Alexandria, after reviewing the material from
the India Office, advised the Foreign Office that an Egyptian occupation of the Somali coast would be more favorable to Aden

than the existing situation, first, because the duties levied by
the Commercial Treaty with the Porte were more favorable than
those allowed the local sheikhs by treaty, and second, that the
Egyptians would really make an effort to suppress the slave
trade, while it was obvious that the local chieftains, all treaties
to the contrary, had not done so. He felt that Egyptian sovereignty should be granted with provision for free trade at all
ports as it would serve to exclude foreign powers (FO 78/3187,
Stanton-FO 9/15/74). Both Tenterden and Derby agreed with
Stanton and decided to reopen the question with the India Office.
However, the India Office had referred the whole matter to the
Indian Government for its opinions, so negotiations temporarily
ceased.

As so often happened in the nineteenth century, while policy
was being discussed events took place in the area which made
such discussions academic. In November, 1874, a telegram
was received from Aden that the Egyptians had closed the port
of Bulhar, and that the Egyptian Pasha at Berbera had refused
to open it when ordered to do so by the captain of H. M. S. "Vulture" (FO 78/3187, cable, Aden-IO 11/22/74). Later details
indicated that Redwan Pasha had taken the action which should
have been taken by the British years before if trade was really
to prosper on the Somali coast.

To understand what he had done it is necessary to repeat
some of the earlier history of the coast. Of the two chief ports,
Berbera and Bulhar, Berbera was a port in the real sense of
the word, with a well-protected harbor, and it had traditionally
been the site of the annual fair. Bulhar, forty miles to the west,
was an open roadstead offering protection against the winter
monsoon, but very vulnerable to winds from any other direction.
There were two tribes here – the Ayal Ahmeds occupied Berbera
and the Ayal Yunis occupied Bulhar. There had always been
some rivalry between these tribes, but the Ayal Ahmeds had
dominated the area until the later 1840's. At this time Ali Shermarkee, unofficial British agent at Zeila, the political boss of
the coast, for there is no other term to describe his great unofficial influence, threw his support to the Ayal Yunis at Bulhar
in order to control the trade of the fair for the good of his own
pocketbook. Haines had chastised him verbally, but had limited
his punishment to that, as Shermarkee's influence on the coast
was entirely too valuable to the British to be lost, especially in
view of possible French intrigues. From then on the fair was

divided between the two ports and constant rivalries changed the basic trade of the fair. Where formerly the fair constituted the end of the Harar trade route from central Africa and served as a market place for products of that area, these rivalries diminished that trade to the vanishing point, and substituted instead a trade in local agricultural products. As Aden grew, the demand for these products, ghee or clarified butter, grain, sheep, etc., greatly increased, so that the total business transacted also grew in volume although the basic reason for the fair had disappeared. Almost annually the British had tried to settle the tribal rivalry by negotiation but without success. Redwan Pasha had merely taken the logical step for restoring the proper balance of trade on the coast. In doing this, however, he had shut off the Bulhar trade from Aden with a consequent reduction in available food supplies.

Captain Hunter, investigating the situation, reported that the Egyptians had indisputably made good their occupation of the coast, but that he could not find any truth in the rumors that the Egyptians had deliberately cut off the export of certain agricultural products, chiefly ghee, to Aden. In transmitting the report, the India Office requested a copy of the commercial treaty with Turkey to see whether or not it was being violated.

Tenterden, feeling the time ripe to force a decision on the question of sovereignty, noted, "The I.O. have allowed this question to drift on, by their impracticable position on it until the Egyptians are getting firmly established" (FO 78/3187, IO-FO 12/21/74 encl. Aden-IO 11/23/74 and Tenterden's Minute).

Stanton was directed to inquire into the matter, and reported that Ismail was sending McKillop to investigate and that Redwan had reported that the natives wished to use Berbera but were being prevented by the Ayal Yunis at Bulhar (FO 78/3187, Stanton-FO 12/26/74). Stanton followed this by forwarding to the Foreign Office Ismail's orders to McKillop to investigate the matter and to reconcile the differences between the Pasha and the Resident at Aden. These instructions were simple, direct, and clear, without any of the oriental evasiveness characteristic of those instructions issued from Constantinople to the Governor General of the Yemen (FO 78/3188, Stanton-FO 1/28/75).

Schneider, at Aden, received letters from the tribes at Bulhar protesting against the blockade and reporting a case of piracy at el-Darad. In view of this piracy, Schneider wished to blockade this port about forty miles east of Berbera and bombard it if necessary, attributing this outrage to the Egyptians. The India Office had passed this on to the Foreign Office to ask their permission to blockade. This was just what Tenterden had been waiting for (FO 78/3188, IO-FO 2/13/75 and Aden-IO 1/7/75 and Tenterden's Minute). He therefore wrote the India Office that the sovereignty question must be settled first, before considering a blockade or bombardment (FO 78/3188, FO-IO 2/20/75). McKillop, by this time in the Gulf of Aden, quickly settled the piracy case and reported back to Alexandria the facts as he found them. He agreed with Redwan Pasha that Berbera was the only adequate port, and felt that while the closing of Bulhar might temporarily have caused inconvenience to the settlement, the chief causes of shortages lay in virtual famine in the Yemen resulting from Turkish activities there (FO 78/3188, Stanton-FO 3/17/75). While Schneider in Aden still held to the policy of exclusion as shown in a letter to Stanton of February 22 (FO 78/3188, Stanton-FO 3/18/75), the India Office was coming round to the viewpoint of the Foreign Office.

On March 23, 1875, the India Office requested a clarification of the Somali coast question. They suggested a friendly convention with Ismail dealing with British treaty rights in Somali ports, especially with reference to the importation of cattle to Aden and a prohibition of monopolies. They expressed a willingness to give up British claims to the two islands off Zeila and Tajura in return for considerations from the Egyptians; and, last of all, they proposed permission of the Foreign Office to make an agreement with the Sultan of Qishn not to transfer Socotra to another power nor to permit any foreign concessions there without British permission (FO 78/3188, IO-FO 3/23/75). Derby and Tenterden agreed on Socotra and prepared to consult Stanton and Elliot in other problems involved (FO 78/3188, Notes by Derby & Tenterden on IO-FO 3/23/75).

The India Office hastened to give the Foreign Office details on the island of Socotra (FO 78/3188, IO-FO 3/31/75). A large island lying off Cape Guardafui, its geographical position is such that it appeared to dominate the African approaches to the Gulf of Aden and the Red Sea, serving as an effective naval base for control of the whole area. The Arabs of the south coast of Arabia were primarily sea-faring peoples, and the colonization and control of the coast of East Africa by the Omani is well-known. Another tribe, the Maharah, living in the Hadramaut, east of the Ka'aiti and Kathiri of Mukalla and Shihr, had controlled Socotra since the seventeenth century. The sovereignty of Socotra therefore rested with the Sultan or Sheikh of Qishn, the capital of the Maharah tribe. When the use of the Red Sea as a steamship route to India was first considered in 1833, the Bombay Government decided to purchase Socotra as a coaling station. Captain Daniel Ross I. N. negotiated with the Sultan of Qishn in that year and received permission to land and to store coal on the island but got no permanent concession.

In 1834, Commander Haines in the I. N. brig "Palinurus" was empowered to purchase the island for a sum not to exceed $10,000. The government of India, anticipating no difficulty in obtaining the island, sent Indian troops to occupy the port there and appointed Captain Bagley as Commander (IO-BSC 1835, Bombay-Bagley 12/24/34). The negotiations with the Sultan fell through, however. The Arabs were very reluctant to sell the island, although they expressed a willingness to lease a coaling station to the British if such a lease did not prejudice their title to the island (IO-BSC 1835 various reports). Such a lease might well have been concluded, but the climate of the island was found to be very bad for the troops and they were withdrawn in November, 1835.

Lieutenant J. R. Wellsted was one of the officers accompanying Haines on the "Palinurus." In his book, TRAVELS TO THE CITY OF THE CALIPHS ETC. (London, Colburn, 1840, 2 vols.), Wellsted has included a very detailed and important description of the island and also covered the negotiations in detail. Although the Indian Government had dropped the plan to use Socotra as a coaling station and turned their attention to Aden, the Arabs at Qishn, tempted by the money involved, offered to "farm" the island to the British in 1837 (IO-BSC 1838, Sheikh Ali ibn Saad ibn Wazir-Bombay Govt. 12/8/37). This offer was turned down in light of the experience of 1835, and no further overtures were made toward the acquisition of Socotra.

Rumors of French intrigues about Socotra led Haines to send Cruttenden to investigate the place in 1847 when on a tour of the Somali coast (IO-BSC 1847, Haines-Bombay 2/9/47). Cruttenden found the island almost completely depopulated as a result of three years of fever and famine. Almost no buildings were left intact on the island, although Cruttenden found about a hundred tons of coal left from 1835 (IO-BSC 1847, Cruttenden-Haines 4/20/47). Rumors of interest in the island by European countries continued; the most reliable was the interest shown by Austrian representatives of the Lloyd Trestrino steamship line in 1870, shortly after the opening of the Suez Canal. The Slave Trade Committee in London had proposed in 1860 the use of Socotra for a spot for the liberation of slaves captured from slavers off the Somali coast, but nothing had come of this proposal. In 1871, the Italian Government had asked the India Office for permission to purchase the island, as mentioned in Frere's memorandum of June 27, 1874, but permission was denied.

Now the India Office wished to negotiate for the island in view of Ismail's expansion towards Cape Guardafui. The island was of no value to the British, but its occupation by another power could prove very embarrassing, therefore this step was a preventive measure to protect Aden just as Salisbury's agreement with the Sheikh of Kuwait in 1899 was to protect British interests in the Persian Gulf at the time Germany was pushing the Berlin-to-Baghdad Railway. Negotiations, at first hindered by the opposition of the government of India, were opened, and on January 23, 1876, a treaty was signed with the Sultan of Qishn in which the Sultan agreed not to sell or alienate Socotra to any foreign power in return for an annual stipend from the Indian Government. The Sultan was paid $3,000 for signing the treaty and received a stipend of $360 a month. In order to avoid confusion in case of the Sultan's death, all possible heirs also signed the treaty (FO 78/3189, IO-FO 2/24/76, Admiralty-FO 3/7/76 and IO-FO 4/8/76).

The India Office was still hesitant regarding the Somali coast, as was shown in a memorandum prepared in April, 1875. However, the Foreign Office received independent information from the Admiralty that the Egyptians were living up to the commercial treaty in their handling of trade at Bulhar and Berbera, which confirmed Stanton's investigations in Egypt (FO 78/3188, Admiralty-FO 3/23/75 and Stanton-FO 4/23/75). Full details from Aden, including depositions of merchants at Bulhar, arrived at this time. These depositions were so contrary in character and so obviously unreliable that Schneider's case against the Egyptians was completely destroyed (FO 78/3188, IO-FO 4/26/75).

In order to arrange for a convention recognizing Ismail's rights to the Somali coast, it was necessary to deal with the Porte as well as with Ismail. In May a draft was prepared for Sir Henry Elliot, offering the extension of sovereignty to Cape

Guardafui, the cession of British rights to the islands in the
Gulf of Zeila, conditional on the French cession of Obock to the
Egyptians, in return for which no foreign power was to be allowed to hold any position on the coast. The first draft instructed Elliot to tie these negotiations in with the demand for the
recognition of the independence of the nine tribes around Aden,
but it was later decided to omit this as it would confuse the issue
(FO 78/3188, Draft to Elliot, May, 1875). Schneider continued
to fight against this move and bombarded the India Office with
lengthy memoranda from the files at Aden which, however, received little sympathy at the Foreign Office.

Negotiations between Ismail and the Porte proceeded
smoothly, and on July 7, the Porte authorized Ismail to take
over the administration of Zeila for the payment of a yearly
tribute of $15,000 (FO 78/3188, Elliot-FO 7/5/75 and Cookson
[Alexandria]-FO 7/7/75). This tribute was really staggering
in view of Prideaux's statement in 1873 that the taxes at Zeila
were farmed out at $3,000 a year. The cession of the islands,
however, was not as easy, and on the advice of both Stanton and
Elliot the matter was temporarily dropped (FO 78/3188, Elliot-
FO 7/19/75 and Stanton-FO 7/5/75).

On November 10, 1875, Stanton was instructed to begin
negotiations on a convention covering the sovereignty of the Somali coast. These instructions were initialled by Derby and
Disraeli. The terms offered by the British were as follows:
(1) the sovereignty of the Ottoman Empire was to be extended to
Cape Guardafui; (2) the British were to give up their islands if
the French gave up claims to Obock, and Ismail was to guarantee to alienate none of this territory to another power; (3)
Berbera and Bulhar were to be open ports, and no monopolies
were to be allowed at any port; (4) Ismail was to make every effort to suppress the slave trade in Somali country and the surrounding waters; (5) the British reserved the right to station
British agents on the Somali coast if they wished (FO 78/3188,
FO-Stanton 11/10/75). The same instructions were sent to
Elliot with the advice that these terms applied to the Somali
coast alone. He was further advised to bring up the question of
the nine tribes at Aden only if the opportunity offered, and not
to press the issue (FO 78/3188, FO-Elliot, 11/10/75, two dispatches same date).

XXVIII. THE END OF AN EMPIRE AND
THE SOMALI COAST CONVENTION

In recent years, there has been a growing school of historians who have been writing what is called "diplomatic history."
The publication of the German and French documents from 1870
to 1914 gave a great impetus to this school, who found readily
available in these documents the subject for much research.
Use of these documents has led many of these historians to believe that the Chancelleries of Europe laid down the policies
followed in imperial affairs, and has contributed to a cynical
attitude towards diplomacy and diplomatic maneuvering. In the
hands of a capable historian, diplomatic history is very valuable.
However, it too often results in very misleading studies in
which diplomacy is entirely separated from the events responsible for the decisions made by the Foreign Offices involved
and leads to conclusions which, while they may have a legitimate
de jure basis, bear absolutely no relation to the de facto situations.
    A superb example of the fallacy of diplomatic history is
shown in the negotiations which led up to the signing of the Somali Coast Convention in 1877. A policy had been laid down by
the Foreign Office, followed by negotiations on the diplomatic
level, and a treaty was concluded which events had made almost
completely meaningless, for during the period Ismail had acquired and lost the first modern African empire.
    As has been apparent, military operations could only take
place in the Abyssinian-Red Sea area between September and
May, since summer is the rainy season and entirely too hot and
humid for much exertion. Such conditions did not prevail in all
of Central Africa, however. During the summer of 1874, Gordon turned his attention to Kordofan and Darfur in the western
Sudan where the slave trade had become a menace to the rest
of the upper Sudan.   After a lengthy campaign, Darfur was annexed to the Sudan and the slave trade suppressed, for the time
being, at least (FO 78/2342, Stanton-FO 8/27/74, 11/5/75, 11/
21/74 & 12/10/74). Communications were opened between Darfur and Gordon's headquarters at Gondoroko via Fashoda. At
the same time, an exploring force under Lieutenant Colonel
Chaillé-Long, an American officer formerly of the Confederate
Army, reached the capital of King Mtesa of Uganda on Lake

Victoria Nyanza and explored the lake. There Long discovered that the trade route to Zanzibar was closed, and opened a new overland route northward to Gondoroko (FO 78/2342, Stanton-FO 11/13/74). Thus Gordon had really brought the Egyptian Empire in contact with the sphere of influence of the only other important power in eastern Africa, Zanzibar. Reginald Coupland's two excellent volumes on Zanzibar clearly show the nature of this influence. The Sultan of Zanzibar had no real power away from the coast, but his prestige had great influence inland almost as far as the lakes.

As for the rest of the Empire, the year 1874-1875 marked a period of preparation. We have seen how the Egyptians were consolidating their position at Berbera, trying to expand the port and make a permanent settlement there. The cession of Zeila and Tajura to Ismail gave him a further base of operations and actual control of the last of the routes to Abyssinia. At the end of the rainy season of 1875, in August, Ismail's African Empire was in potential control of all of northeast Central Africa. In the Sudan he controlled the provinces of Sennar, Kordofan, Darfur, Bahr-el-Gazal and the new province of Equatorial Africa centered on Gondoroko. The Nile was his to Lake Albert, and exploration had reached to Lake Victoria. On the east along the Red Sea he controlled all the routes into Abyssinia: the northernmost route Massawa-Keren-Kassala-Metemma leading into Gondar; the Tigré route from Massawa as far as Senafe; the Zeila end of the route to Shoa and the Berbera end of the route to Harar. In short, he controlled the entire White Nile basin and had a strangle hold on the area around the Blue Nile, a very impressive achievement by any standards, ancient or modern. The cost to Ismail of this Empire must have been considerable. For his sovereignty of the Suakin, Massawa areas plus certain other perquisites, he was reputed to have paid the Porte £1,000,000. The cost of the Baker and Gordon expeditions must have been tremendous, but appear to have been fully paid for by the revenues of the Sudan. By 1875 Ismail's finances were in a very serious state.

What, then, led him to undertake the conquests implied in his actions in the autumn of 1875? According to Munzinger's description, the province of Massawa was capable of paying for itself and its protection. While Ismail had failed to reach a commercial agreement with Johannes in 1872, he so controlled the routes into northern Abyssinia that he benefited from all trade going there. The newly acquired Zeila area was insulated from its nearest strong neighbor, Shoa, by a stretch of wild and desolate country occupied by the relatively weak Dankali tribes whose constant feuds had made the route almost unusable. However, a gradual control over the route by the establishment of a series of posts would have been more effective in opening trade than any attempt to conquer the tribes. At Berbera, there was no sense in controlling the hinterland as trade flowed freely to the annual fair. The only excuse for the conquests planned for the season of 1875-1876 lay in a well-thought-out scheme of empire which unfortunately suffered from geographical ignorance. The key and center of the whole plan centered on Gordon's position at Gondoroko and the control of central African trade. What real knowledge of central African geography did Ismail, or for that matter any European, have at that time? From Lake Victoria it was 780 miles to Formosa Bay, 810 miles to the mouth of the Juba Riber, and almost 950 miles to Harar as the crow flies. All this area was unexplored except for the Formosa Bay route to the interior, which was well known as far as Mt. Kenya. How far did geographic knowledge go along the coast? Burton had penetrated to Harar, and there was certainly enough trade between that city and Berbera so that the geography was fairly well known. Since the time of Beke, Harris, and Rochet d'Hericourt, there had been no contact between Shoa and Zeila, and so little was really known about that route. Northern Abyssinia was of course well known to many individuals.

In September, 1875, Stanton informed the Foreign Office that there was serious danger of a clash near Massawa (FO 78/2404, Stanton-FO 9/11/75). An Egyptian expeditionary force was under the command of a Colonel Arendrup, a Swedish officer of great ability, who, it was reported, was faced with an army of 30,000 Abyssinians, six hours' march from Massawa (FO 78/2404, Stanton-FO 9/27/75). Such an army had gathered only because Ismail had greatly increased his garrison at Massawa to form this expeditionary force. In October, Arendrup moved forward into Abyssinia and established his headquarters at Godofellassy, halfway between Massawa and Adowa (FO 78/2405, Stanton-FO 11/14/75). A battle followed almost immediately, resulting in a complete defeat for the Egyptians, who lost two thousand dead and ten guns; the Egyptians were saved from complete annihilation by the failure of the Abyssinians to

to follow up their victory. Ismail then dispatched 12,000 men
under Ratib Pasha and General Loring (a former Confederate
officer) with instructions to defeat the Abyssinians and seize
Adowa (FO 78/2405, Stanton-FO 11/27/75). Ismail stated that
he only wished to settle the border disputes and had no designs
on Abyssinia. The Foreign Office in London, afraid that Ismail
really wished to conquer the country, advised Stanton to tell the
Viceroy that such designs would be politically and financially
fatal to him. Stanton again received assurances that Ismail had
no designs on Abyssinia and reported that he had already spent
between Ł500,000 and Ł1,000,000 on the expedition (FO 78/2403,
FO-Stanton 12/14/75; and FO 78/2404, Stanton-FO 12/29/75).

The new expedition arrived in December and moved into
Hamasein province and in March a "victory" over the Abyssinians was reported after five days of fighting (FO 78/2501, Stanton-FO 3/13/76). Later reports indicated that this was a
victory only because the Abyssinians finally withdrew. Egyptian
losses were very severe. The soldiers conducted themselves
very badly, so badly in fact that the whole re-enforcing army
was withdrawn and the sole result of this "victory" was that the
Egyptians captured in the first battle were able to be ransomed
(FO 78/2502-3-4, Stanton-FO 5/6/76, 5/13/76, Cookson-FO
6/2/76, 8/7/76, Vivian-FO 11/3/76).

Ismail had received title to Zeila in August, 1875. In the
fall of that year Munzinger Bey was dispatched with 450 troops
to explore the hinterland to the borders of Shoa. We have no
copies of Munzinger's orders, but he was unquestionably to
make contacts with Menelik and if possible arrange for him to
attack Johannes from the rear. Ismail had several times told
Stanton that he wished to intrigue with Menelik against Johannes
as he could deal with Menelik as one ruler to another, while
Johannes refused to have any dealings at all with the Egyptians.
Munzinger penetrated the wild Dankali country to the vicinity of
Aussa on the Hawash River. Here, on November 15, 1875, he
was ambushed by Dankali tribesmen. Half the Egyptian force
was killed, including Munzinger, and the remainder barely es-
caped to the coast (FO 78/3188, cable Bombay-IO 11/26/75).
Thus ended disastrously the second of Ismail's imperial schemes.
Where did Munzinger start his expedition? Loring says that he
started from Anfile and Sabry takes this as the truth (Sabry,
Mohammed, L'EMPIRE EGYPTIENNE SOUS ISMAIL, Paris,
Guenther, 1933, p. 428). But a glance at the map would make

this statement hardly credible. He must have started from
Zeila or Tajura.

The major effort, however, was centered around Somaliland. Stanton reported in November that the Amir of Harar had
submitted to an army under Raouf Pasha and that the Egyptians
were well-established in the largest city in the Galla country,
thereby opening up the trade route from Harar to Zeila and Berbera, and, according to Nubar Pasha, providing an outlet for
the products of an estimated million-and-a-half people, products
such as myrrh, incense, and good coffee (FO 78/2405, Stanton-
FO 11/11/75). With the news of this success, the Viceroy
decided to send two exploring parties from Harar, one to go inland to the source of the Juba River and follow it to its mouth,
the other to the source of the Blue Nile. McKillop Pasha was
reported cruising off Formosa Bay and the mouth of the Juba
River, and Stanton ventured the guess that Ismail contemplated
making the Juba River the southern boundary of his empire (FO
78/3188, Stanton-FO 11/11/75).

The expeditions from Harar never materialized. Raouf Pasha had obtained the submission of the Amirs but not the submission of the Galla tribes. Raouf had no more success in dealing with these independent people than any of the Abyssinian
monarchs had had, and he was soon tied up in Harar with tribal
rebellions.

The news of Ismail's ambitious program disturbed Stanton
exceedingly and he discussed the matter with Nubar Pasha in
November of 1875. Nubar confirmed these reports, stating that
Ismail laid claim to all Somali territory to the mouth of the Juba River and in addition had instructed McKillop to take possession, if possible, of Formosa Bay with a view to opening an outlet to the lake region of Equatorial Africa. McKillop was to
establish posts at the mouth of the Juba and Formosa Bay, and
push forward detachments from the coast to Lake Victoria Nyanza to meet Gordon, who had strongly recommended this step.
On hearing this, Stanton warned Nubar that Ismail was grasping
too much and that he might well get into trouble with other powers (FO 78/3188, Stanton-FO 11/14/75). On receipt of this,
Tenterden noted "1. Since this dispatch sent, H.H. forces defeated & Pasha killed [referring to Munzinger]. 2. England
has bought Suez Canal shares. Should dispatch be written or
should allow the failure of the expedition to preach its own moral.
Objection to dispatch, might annoy H.H. by interfering too much

after our bargain. Have Cave mention it?" (Sir Stephen Cave was sent to Egypt to investigate Ismail's financial position immediately after Disraeli's purchase of the Suez Canal shares in November, 1875.) Derby advised the latter course (FO 78/3188, Memo by Tenterden on Stanton-FO 11/14/75).

Probably the most ambitious scheme of Ismail centered around the acquisition of a port in East Africa from which a trade route could be opened to the Equatorial province. Coupland in THE EXPLOITATION OF EAST AFRICA discusses this attempt very fully (pp. 271-99), so that it is necessary only to summarize the facts here. This idea was not a new one with Ismail. In 1871, Colonel Purdy had been ordered to proceed from Mombasa inland to Lake Victoria between Mounts Kenya and Kilimanjaro (Sabry, op. cit., p. 396), but the scheme had been cancelled. In the fall of 1875 McKillop was ordered to proceed to the mouth of the Juba River, an order later changed to instruct him to go to Formosa Bay. Chaillé-Long, one of Gordon's officers, had been sent from the Sudan to lead an expedition to meet Gordon coming down from Lake Victoria. Such a plan was, of course, bound to conflict with the sovereignty of the Sultan of Zanzibar who had garrisons in the following ports north of Formosa Bay: Warsheik, Mogadishu, Merka, Barawa and Kismayo north of the mouth of the Juba River, and Lamu and Kipini on Formosa Bay. Coupland assumes that Ismail was cognizant of these sovereignty claims. He may have been, but it is doubtful whether he was aware of the fact that these were de facto occupations of these ports, and it is very dubious if he was fully aware of the British policy towards the Sultan of Zanzibar. At any rate, McKillop seized Barawa in the middle of November and proceeded to Kismayo after an unsuccessful attempt to land at Lamu. Coupland fully describes the furor this created in Zanzibar. Immediate pressure put on Ismail by the British resulted in McKillop being ordered to return to Suez, which he did, leaving Kismayo on January 20, 1876.

There is only one factor missing from Coupland's description. Stanton heard of the McKillop expedition on November 11, and received information from Nubar Pasha on the fourteenth that Ismail intended to lay claim to all the Somali territory and gain posts at the mouth of the Juba River and on Formosa Bay with the object of opening communications with Gordon at Lake Victoria (FO 78/3188, Stanton-FO 11/14/75). Tenterden's note quoted above indicates the lack of liaison between the various sections within the Foreign Office. Tenterden, in charge of Near Eastern Affairs, looked upon the plan purely in relation to its effect on Egyptian internal affairs, i. e., the effect of this expedition on the shaky finances of the country. The information was not passed on to Wilde, head of the East African section, so that Kirk, Consul in Zanzibar, could be informed, nor was any protest made in Egypt at the time about the encroachment on the sovereignty of the Sultan of Zanzibar. The failure of the Munzinger expedition was to be allowed "to preach its own moral." There was a dangerous lack of liaison in the Foreign Office; Tenterden was not at fault, but Derby should have caught the implications. Stanton had done so when he told Nubar that such a plan might get him into trouble with a foreign power.

Kirk, on finding out the facts of the case, cabled the information to the Foreign Office; Stanton, after making a protest as instructed by cable on December 3, was able to cable on December 5 that Ismail would desist from occupying Zanzibar territory, His Highness explaining that he was suppressing the slave trade. This was followed by a detailed account of Nubar's explanation of the incident. He attributed it to Gordon, lumping the Harar and Zanzibar schemes together as a means of opening up the area to commerce and suppressing the slave trade. Nubar stated that Ismail did not know the extent of the claims of the Sultan of Zanzibar (a statement which may well have been true) and McKillop had been ordered to return to Berbera (FO 78/3188, Stanton-FO 12/9/75). This dispatch did go to Wilde, who commented that it was unfortunate that Ismail had not informed the British of his intentions, as he believed Gordon's idea was a good one, and that Ismail should be assisted in getting a port on the east coast. He believed that it would be an excellent idea to get the whole coast under a strong power so as to suppress effectively the slave trade (FO 78/3188, Minute by Wilde 12/27/75 on Stanton-FO 12/9/75). As shown in Coupland, Kirk was able to forestall any Egyptian claims to the coast, and the McKillop expedition accomplished nothing for Ismail.

It can be said truthfully that the winter of 1875-1876 marked the end of Ismail's imperial dream. The expeditions of that winter, undertaken at terrific cost, had gained him only a tenuous hold on the area around Harar, and even this imperial acquisition was to become a liability. The only coherent discussion of Ismail's empire is in Sabry's volume (op. cit., pp. 375-

552). As is the case throughout his volume, Sabry is so violently pro-Egyptian that his work is almost useless. He consistently plays up Ismail's civilizing tendencies, his suppression of
the slave trade, the contribution of his expeditions to geographical information, and stresses many minor details of little historical importance. He pretends to prove that Ismail's conquests
were made against British opposition, and that Britain was
responsible for the failure of the Egyptian plans. Under these
circumstances a summary of Ismail's empire and his imperial
achievements is not out of place.

The imperial dream of Ismail was extremely intelligent in
scope and planning. It failed for two reasons, first, a lack of
what in military affairs would be termed proper intelligence due
to the complete ignorance of the nature of the country and the
peoples involved; and, second, to the failure of the Egyptian
troops to perform the work assigned to them.

Ismail's plans have been fairly well described. There is
no question but that he had been planning his acquisition from
1865 on. The whole plan was centered around the fundamental
change to be wrought in the Red Sea with the opening of the Suez
Canal, a change which Ismail fully realized would convert the
Red Sea from a backwater of the Indian Ocean into a main highway of the world. There is enough evidence to indicate that the
original concept included the Egyptian occupation of Arabia or
at least the Yemen. This venture, apparently first planned by
intrigue, later proposed by purchase, failed because of Turkish fear of Ismail's power, a fear based on memories of Muhammad Ali's conquests. To what extent religious aspects were
involved is problematic, but there is considerable evidence to
show that the Turkish expansions in Arabia were at least partially religious in character, motivated, one can guess, by the
need felt in Constantinople by the conservative group, or Old
Turks, to counter the influence of the Young Turk party by
building up the importance of the Sultan's empty title of Calif.

If Ismail could not obtain Arabia, the western shore of the
Red Sea was obtainable, and the Western Sudan and the sources
of the Nile were his for the taking. These areas were governmental vacuums, the only European power having any interest
in them was Great Britain. Ismail's primary motive in gaining
an empire in these parts was unquestionably to establish commercial monopolies on the profitable ivory trade, and other
natural products. He greatly overestimated the value of

Abyssinian trade and the wealth of the country; what little trade there was had to be concentrated in only three places because natural obstacles limited the trade routes. These same conditions applied to the Upper Sudan and Equatorial Africa. Trade concentrated in a few places gave indications of much greater natural wealth than actually existed, as Coupland shows in his two volumes on Zanzibar. Certainly the actual trade could not justify Ismail's great expenditures, which he estimated at over Ł1,000,000 in about seven years. On a long-term basis of development it is probable that the conquests could have been made to pay for themselves, but it is doubtful if Ismail had this concept.

Ismail was fully aware of British antipathy to the establishment of monopolies, an antipathy which more than anything else was at the bottom of Palmerston's often unreasoning antagonism to Muhammad Ali. He therefore justified his conquests on the basis of suppressing the slave trade, capitalizing on the revival of interest in this subject in Britain resulting in part from the American Civil War and the emancipation of the slaves, and in part from the moral and religious revival in England which we call Victorianism. That Ismail used humanitarianism as a cloak for imperial aggression should not imply that he was not sincere in his desire to suppress this odious trade. Stanton, Vivian, and Kirk, all of whom were probably in the best position to know, were completely convinced of his sincerity while at the same time recognizing his primary motives. But Ismail did not stop here. He made his interest more convincing by appointing men in charge of his imperial expansion who had the confidence of the British and who bore the highest character. As his two commanders in Central Africa, Sir Samuel Baker and Colonel Gordon, were intensely interested in the suppression of the slave trade, how could the Foreign Office object to their actions? On the Red Sea coast, Ismail's appointment of Werner Munzinger unquestionably aided him in obtaining the consent of the British government in his imperial designs. Exactly what Munzinger's position was, is very hard for the historian to define. He was called Governor of Massawa, but seemed to have been chiefly a "front man" for Ismail. The British Foreign Office apparently believed that he had control of all the Red Sea coast, but there is little evidence that his power existed beyong the province of Massawa, although he always seemed to appear at the right place at the right time to make an impression.

McKillop Pasha too was held in considerable esteem by all the
English officials, except Kirk who described the expedition to
the Juba as "a filibustering expedition, organized by the Khedive
and commanded by English adventurers, worthy of the palmy
days of the buccaneers" (Coupland, EXPLOITATION OF EAST
AFRICA, p. 283, quoting Kirk [private letter]-F. T. Carnegy
2/10/76).

To Ismail's clever emphasis on his anti-slavery policies,
and his judicious appointment and use of unimpeachable European leaders, was added the growing realization of the British
Foreign Office of the true meaning of the opening of the Suez
Canal on Britain's private lake, the Red Sea. Lord Tenterden
was the only British official who really seemed to understand
these implications, and he almost single-handedly fought for
Ismail's empire. He was responsible for giving Ismail a free
hand with Abyssinia, and he was responsible for opening the
discussions leading to the Somali coast treaty which gave Ismail
a free hand in that area. Tenterden's policy was undoubtedly
correct in the larger view of British interests, but he certainly
did not expect that the new freedom given the Viceroy would
bring such sudden and unexpected results. As the Egyptian imperial program first undertaken in 1869 had progressed logical-
ly and sensibly, how was anyone to know that Ismail was to
throw all cautions to the winds and undertake such grandiose
plans in one period of six months?

The answer is not hard to find, although, like the answer
to many historical problems, it is hard to prove. It is not the
purpose of this study to go into the tangled financial affairs of
Egypt. However, the year 1875 marked the end of any real
financial independence on the part of Ismail. Almost every type
of revenue was earmarked in some way for one of the Viceroy's
many loans except the revenues which might come from his potential empire. He had, over the years, developed at considerable expense a modern army trained by foreign officers, many
from the United States. He had, at great expense, developed a
navy of considerable strength. He had virtually been given the
go-ahead signal by the British, although he was over-extending
their good will in East Africa. If he could succeed in his imperial plans, he could acquire an empire free of debt, whose
revenues were entirely his. The chance was well worth taking,
and Ismail was a born gambler. It was not in the power of any
man living at that time to realize that there was no possible

chance of success under the most favorable conditions. Its almost complete failure unquestionably hastened Ismail's financial collapse, the second Abyssinian expedition of 1876 alone costing him close to Ł1,000,000. The contrast between Ismail's former restrained and sensible imperial expansion and the sudden burst of activity in 1875-1876 shows that it must be considered as the gamble of a desperate man. Whether or not the financing of this expansion contributed to the necessity of selling Egypt's birthright, the Suez Canal shares, it is very difficult to say; however, it is certainly a large factor to be considered in any study of the Khedive's tangled finances.

A historian has a very distinct advantage over the contemporary commentator. He has a chance to weigh evidence and to see in perspective the implication of events. To his contemporaries, Ismail's defeat in Abyssinia did not appear as such. The first reports reaching Alexandria on March 13 reported the lengthy engagement as a victory (FO 78/2501, Stanton-FO 3/13/76), and the first real indications of the true nature of the battle were not available until May when the first troops began to return to Egypt (FO 78/2503, Stanton-FO 5/13/76 and Cookson [chargé d'affaires]-FO 6/13/76). Not until Major Dye and General Loring, two American officers who were in the battle, published their volumes in the 1880's did the true story appear (Dye, William E., MOSLEM EGYPT AND CHRISTIAN ABYSSINIA, New York, Attain & Prout, 1880, and Loring, General W. W., A CONFEDERATE SOLDIER IN EGYPT, New York, Dodd-Mead, 1884). These two accounts supplement each other very adequately. Dye, a field officer, saw more of the melee of the battle; Loring, a staff officer, describes the tactics or rather tactical chaos of the battle more fully. Both lay the blame for the defeat on the lack of staff coordination and the mutual jealousy of the Egyptian officers rather than on the fighting qualities of the troops, a marked variation from Sharif Pasha's official explanation of lack of discipline given to Vivian in October of 1876 (FO 78/2503, Vivian-FO 10/20/76). From the above it is obvious that Ismail was able to suppress information about the nature of the battle from Europeans and to retain his imperial prestige.

The defeat, however, had repercussions in another direction. The Foreign Office, alert to the whole Near Eastern picture, heard disquieting rumors of anti-Christian activities in Egypt. Such activities, coupled with the already strong anti-

Christian feeling in the Balkans due to the Bosnian and Bulgarian crises, were alarming (FO 78/2499, FO-Cookson 5/25/76). Cookson could find no trustworthy rumors of organized anti-Christian activity, but stated that the Abyssinians' unhappy habit of mutilating their prisoners was not kindly received by the Egyptian population; this, coupled with the terrifically heavy taxation due to the foreign debt, had created a situation which might cause a revolt against Ismail. [Note: Such mutilation is an historical myth. Mutilation of prisoners was not practiced by the Amharic Ethiopians, but only by Dankali and Jam-Jam tribesmen. As nineteenth century Abyssinian armies were not noted for discipline, and as they nearly always contained some tribal elements, individual cases of emasculation of prisoners did occur. The practice was not nearly as widespread as rumors from the Egyptian-Abyssinian campaign of 1876 or the battle of Adowa in 1892 made it appear.] The army, Ismail's sole means of suppressing a revolt, was also near mutiny, a result of the demoralizing effect of the Abyssinian campaign, and also because they had not been paid for several months (FO 78/2503, Cookson-FO 6/3/76).

In Harar the situation of Raouf Pasha remained serious until March. One relief expedition met defeat at Sheikh Surbain twenty-one miles from that city (FO 78/3189, IO-FO 2/24/76 encl. Aden-IO 1/14/76 and 1/20/76). A second expedition, however, was successful, and the Egyptians were able to open communications with Menelik in Shoa. Schneider reported that the Egyptians had about 2,600 men in the Berbera-Harar area and were proceeding with the construction of docks and permanent buildings at the site of the fair (FO 78/3189, IO-FO 4/11/76 encl. Aden-IO 3/1/76). Work was being carried on at Zeila and Tajura by Egyptian troops, but after Munzinger's defeat at Aussa, the straight route to Shoa had been abandoned and the more roundabout but much safer road via Harar substituted, a wise decision in view of the experience of travelers in the early 1840's [this route via Harar later became the route of the Djibouti-Addis Abbaba Railroad] (FO 78/3189, IO-FO 6/9/76 encl. Aden-London 4/17/76). However, Redwan Pasha at Berbera mistreated some Somalis, creating a rather difficult situation which, combined with Egyptian plans to levy an export duty of one per cent and an import duty of seven or eight per cent at the next fair, threatened to create a serious crisis (FO 78/3189, IO-FO 7/19/76 encl. Aden-IO 6/3/76).

It was announced in Alexandria that Gordon had annexed the territory around Lakes Albert and Victoria and the Somerset River in Equatorial Africa. This was a rather broad claim for an expedition which was largely exploratory in nature (FO 78/2502, Stanton-FO 6/6/76). In October, Gordon requested that Ismail replace him in Equatorial Africa as he was overworked (FO 78/2503, Vivian-FO 10/31/76). He left Colonel Prout in charge of the Equatorial provinces and returned to England, to be recalled by Ismail as Governor of the Sudan in February, 1877. The political questions involved in his retirement and re-appointment belong properly to a study of the Sudan and Equatorial Africa. What does concern this study is that one of his first duties on his reappointment as governor was the establishment of peace between Abyssinia and Egypt.

On Gordon's return to Egypt in 1877, he proceeded almost at once to Massawa, where conditions had continued to be serious. In December, 1876, Captain Wharton, in command of a British war vessel which had been stationed at that port to protect the Banyan merchants, reported a small advance guard of Egyptians about twenty miles inland from Annesley Bay and a force of about 1,500 men at Massawa itself (FO 78/2631, Vivian-FO 1/18/79). Continued border raids had resulted in minor Egyptian defeats and a change of commanders; Ratib's replacement by Osman Pasha had not improved matters. Abyssinia remained closed to travelers by the border warfare. The presence of certain Englishmen in Massawa had given considerable concern to the British. "General" Kirkham had arrived in that port after having been captured in January, 1876. He had been well taken care of but had died at the home of General Loring, an American officer, from a combination of dysentery and drunkenness (FO 78/2503, Cookson-FO 7/28/76). Two adventurers, Houghton and Barlow, were also there, supposedly on a hunting expedition but chiefly interested in getting through to join Johannes' army. As they had connections with European newspapers, they were a constant source of unfounded rumors concerning the slave trade and Abyssinia, at first aimed at Ismail and later at the British. These rumors caused considerable trouble and continued to do so until peace was obtained. They approached such serious proportions that on March 22, 1877, Vivian wrote the Foreign Office that they were damaging the influence of England in Egypt. He commented, "It is no business of mine to defend His Highness' character and I do not

doubt that much still goes on that is inconsistent with the strict
fulfillment of the Khedive's promises respecting the purchase
and sale of slaves; but in common fairness such acts as the appointment of Col. Gordon with independent powers to the government of all the Soudan provinces, the dispatch of an expedition
to the Red Sea to put down the Slave Trade and the readiness
His Highness is showing to engage himself by an anti-slave
trade convention with Her Majesty's Government ought at least
to be recognized as giving him some title to public confidence
and allowed to weigh against vague rumours founded upon travelers' tales or gossip or perhaps even less innocent motives"
(FO 78/2631, Vivian-FO 3/23/77).

 Gordon, arriving to clean up this mess, found that in typical Abyssinian fashion Menelik had taken advantage of Johannes'
involvement with the Egyptians to invade his territories in Gondar in alliance with Walad-el-Michael, a rebel in that province.
This event speeded Gordon's negotiations, as the new threat in
his rear convinced Johannes that peace with Egypt was the best
policy. In April, Gordon went up to Senhait to make peace on
the following terms: (1) an armistice; (2) Johannes to have his
ancient frontiers; (3) Johannes to be allowed free trade and free
passage of envoys to foreign countries through Egyptian territory; (4) Johannes to be allowed to import fifty pounds of powder, ten muskets and five thousand percussion caps free of duty
each year; (5) Ismail to sanction the appointment of a Coptic
bishop from Cairo as Abuna; (6) Johannes to be allowed an agent
at Massawa; (7) Walad-el-Michael to be kept away from Abyssinian territory (he had been living in the Sudan); (FO 78/2632,
Vivian-FO 4/7/77). These terms were agreed on, but Johannes
left to attack Menelik before the final draft could be signed (FO
78/2633, Vivian-FO 7/24/77). But it did not really matter,
turbulent Abyssinian politics were producing a new Emperor in
Menelik, a far great man than any of his predecessors. Johannes has at least one claim to historical fame, however inferior he was as an Emperor, even by Abyssinian standards –
he did defeat the first attempt to form a modern African empire.

 In spite of Ismail's failure to establish his empire in Abyssinia, the British persisted in their attempt to settle the question of sovereignty of the Somali coast. The plan to give up the
British claims to the islands off Zeila and Tajura was soon
dropped when Stanton reported in December, 1875, that the
French had reasserted their claim to Obock (FO 78/3188, Stanton

-FO 12/11/75). Elliot in Constantinople also objected to raising the question of the islands with the Porte, on the grounds
that it made the whole problem too involved. He further pointed
out that the question of hereditary sovereignty had already been
settled in a previous firman; in his opinion a convention with the
Porte was not necessary in this instance (FO 78/3189, Elliot-
FO 1/2/76). McKillop's expedition to the east coast of Africa,
the Cave mission to Egypt, and affairs in Abyssinia, distracted
attention from this area; negotiations did not begin again until
Stanton was instructed at the end of March, 1876, to proceed
with discussions, leaving out the question of French and English
claims, but including a clause which would prevent any further
alienation of territory in this quarter (FO 78/2189, FO-Stanton
3/22/76). Stanton then had a conversation with Ismail on April
6 in which the Viceroy stated that he was already occupying Ras
Hafun, more than one hundred miles south of Cape Guardafui,
which had never been claimed by anyone. He demurred at making Zeila a free port as he had to pay the Porte $15,000 a year
in lieu of customs duties. Ismail questioned his ability to suppress the slave trade unless he could control all of the Somali
country, and suggested that therefore it might be well to discuss, at the same time, the boundary between his territory and
that of the Sultan of Zanzibar (FO 78/3189, Stanton-FO 4/7/76).
The question lay dead until July when Cookson, acting chargé
d'affaires at Alexandria, again brought it up with Sharif Pasha,
who claimed the mouth of the Juba as the boundary, pointing out
the impossibility of controlling the slave trade unless Brava
(Barawa) was controlled by the Egyptians. Sharif added that
the conditions the British attached to the recognition of sovereignty, the free ports and the slave trade obligations, certainly
justified the extension of the Egyptian sovereignty to the Juba.
Sharif agreed to make Berbera and Bulhar free ports, but wished
to retain the customs house arrangements at Zeila and Tajura
(FO 78/3189, Cookson-FO 8/8/76).

In London, Wilde felt that the Egyptian claim would be considered an unprovoked aggression by the Sultan of Zanzibar.
He further believed that an Egyptian occupation of this area
would divert the profitable trade built up by the Banyan merchants into the Viceroy's hands. To this Sanderson agreed.
Lord Derby pointed out that Britain could not take land from
Zanzibar and give it to Egypt, and that the two countries should
settle the dispute themselves. Tenterden agreed with all this

and added that Vivian, who was about to go to Egypt as Consul General would "have to be pretty stiff about the matter as the Khedive has started haggling" (FO 78/3189, Minutes by Wilde, Sanderson, Derby and Tenterden on Cookson-FO 8/8/76). The India Office agreed in large part with these observations, suggesting that Ismail's sovereignty be limited to Cape Guardafui but be recognized beyond this point if he could come to an amicable agreement with the Sultan of Zanzibar. As to the ports, they were satisfied if Berbera and Bulhar were free ports, and arrangements at Zeila and Tajura were made to give British merchants rights similar to those enjoyed in the existing treaties with those ports (FO 78/3189, IO-FO 11/13/76). Ismail's "haggling" continued until the India Office informed the Foreign Office that the British at Aden would treat the Somali tribes as independent unless Ismail agreed on the Guardafui boundary (FO 78/3189, IO-FO 1/27/77 embodied in FO-Vivian 2/8/77).

At this threat, Ismail capitulated, requesting merely that the British would use their good offices to get him a boundary between his territory and that of the Sultan of Zanzibar (FO 78/3189, Vivian-FO 2/21/77). However the Egyptians demanded higher duties at Zeila and Tajura than the five per cent which the treaties required. Vivian pointed out that it was impossible for the British to agree to this, and suggested that if the Egyptians would come to terms with Abyssinia, trade at these ports would improve to such an extent that the five per cent duty would be profitable. In reporting this conversation, Vivian suggested that the Foreign Office might consider extending the boundary beyond Guardafui to Ras Hafun eighty miles south. Wilde noted that Ras Hafun was out of the territory of the Sultan of Zanzibar and might be granted as the southern boundary. Tenterden added, "Yes, but must not let the matter dawdle" (FO 78/3189, Vivian-FO 3/4/77 & Minutes by Wilde & Tenterden).

An excellent memorandum on the coast was obtained from the Admiralty who suggested the tenth parallel north as the boundary (FO 78/3189, Admiralty-FO 4/2/77). This was agreed to by the India Office, who also approved a draft of the treaty (FO 78/3189, IO-FO 4/10/77 and 6/21/77). The draft of the treaty was forwarded to Vivian on July 4, and after slight modifications signed on September 7, 1877. It provided: (1) Bulhar and Berbera were to be free ports without monopolies, and a duty of five per cent was to be levied at Tajura, Zeila and other ports, the British being entitled to most favored nation treatment;

(2) the Khedive engaged for himself and his successors that no portion of the territory formally incorporated in the Ottoman Empire would ever be ceded to a foreign power; (3) the British were to be allowed consuls in the territory; (4) the Khedive undertook to suppress the slave trade as far as Berbera, but from Berbera to Ras Hafun he only undertook to do his best until his authority would be regularly established, consenting that British cruisers employed in suppressing the slave trade should have full rights along the coast; (5) the agreement was to go in force as soon as the Porte placed this territory under the hereditary administration of the Khedive (FO 78/3189, FO-Vivian 7/4/77 text in Hertslet, Sir Edward, Treaties and Conventions, Etc., [Commercial Treaties] London, Butterworths, 1893, Vol. 18, pp. 359-61). Together with this treaty, negotiations had proceeded between England and France on the one hand and Egypt on the other, to install lighthouses in the area. Such negotiations are of no particular interest as the Egyptian treasury was too bankrupt to undertake any of the terms agreed upon.

This treaty was a meaningless victory for Ismail. Except for constituting a de jure recognition of the de facto occupation of Berbera and Zeila and Tajura, its meaning was destroyed on the day the Abyssinians defeated the Egyptians in 1876. From that time on, Ismail's African empire was a sham. Vivian summed the situation up very ably in commenting on Gordon's difficulties with Zobeir Pasha in 1877: "The moral that I draw from Gordon's story is that the conquests made by the Egyptians in the interior of Africa have brought no better government nor greater happiness to the natives; on the contrary their position is in every respect rendered worse instead of better under the misrule of Egyptian Officials who from timidity, want of energy and even more corrupt motives connive at gross oppression and slave hunting. I entirely acquit the Khedive of any encouragement of these practices...but none of his officers are to be trusted...I doubt if it is in the interests of humanity that the extension of Egyptian rule should be encouraged" (FO 78/2634, Vivian-FO 9/11/77).

Thus the promise of a great empire ended. It was begun on a firm foundation, but lack of finances and rapid overexpansion brought about its downfall. The hollow shell of the empire remained, the Equatorial provinces, Darfur, Massawa, Zeila, the province of Harar, to disintegrate slowly and in many cases to become the prey of European imperialism.

XXIX. CONCLUSION

The year 1877 marks the ending of the period of exclusive British dominance over the Red Sea area. This dominance was bound to fail, challenged as it was by the totally new conditions in the area resulting from the opening of the Suez Canal. The Foreign Office, becoming aware of the changes which the Canal was to bring about, had encouraged the comparatively weak Ottoman Empire and Egyptian Khedivate to occupy the area as a preventive to colonization by other European powers. The India Office, on the contrary, had refused to look facts in the face, and fought a losing battle for the maintenance of British, or rather Indian, dominance.

Actually neither the British nor the Indian governments had any vital interest there aside from Aden and its dependence on food from the Somali coast. The preservation of Indian dominance would have required an expenditure of moneys for naval patrol alone which would not have been justified by any positive advantage, and would, in the long run, have unnecessarily antagonized the French and the Italians in their imperialistic ambitions.

The occupation of Aden in 1839 was an answer to economic necessity, the need of a coaling station for the steamship route to India. Whether it had any moral justification is immaterial; in actual fact it hurt very few people and aided a great many.

In 1837 Captain MacKenzie wrote, "It seems to be a law of nature that the civilized nations shall conquer and possess the countries in a state of barbarism and by such means however unjustifiable it may appear at first sight extend the blessings of knowledge, industry and commerce among people hitherto sunk in the most gloomy depths of superstitious ignorance" (FO 78/3185 Report of Capt. MacKenzie 1/6/37; see also pp. 51-54). While to the modern mind this statement may seem preposterously conceived, there was a great deal of truth in it. Aden was a center of stability in the chaos of South Arabian politics and saved what little prosperity was left in that once prosperous area.

It is the present fashion to decry imperialism and colonialism, particularly in the underdeveloped countries of this world. A Nehru and a Nasser feel that the development of their countries has been stifled by the selfish interests of the imperial powers.

In actual fact, they owe a tremendous debt to their former rulers
for having given them the minimum prosperity and training in
the technical fields necessary for them to survive in our modern
complex world. Where imperialism failed, and is failing where
it persists today, is in the psychological field. It is unable to
give its subject people self-respect.

If the hinterland of Aden had been economically useful, the
occupation of Aden might have led to the British occupation of
all of southwest Arabia. The situation was similar to that in
India or around Singapore which led to the British control of all
of India and of the Straits Settlement (Malaya). The Bombay
Presidency was well aware of this, as is evidenced by repeated
injunctions to the Resident not to get involved in affairs of the
interior, even to the extent of not permitting him to avenge murders, insults and attacks.

Yet at the same time, the Resident was enjoined to enforce
the policy of exclusion of European powers from the area, a
policy which was modified after the opening of the Suez Canal to
accept Ottoman and particularly Egyptian expansion by tacit
consent.

Yet even in this situation, British imperial interest had to
be protected. This led to the development, particularly on the
shores of Arabia, to what this author would like to call "passive
imperialism." It was in essence the denial of an area to any
other imperial power, without any intent of its exploitation on
behalf of the British Empire. While that development is later
than the period of this study, the beginning of the idea is apparent during the Yemen Crisis of 1873-1877 (FO 78/2753, enclosure in IO-FO 5/11/73; see Chapters XXIV, XXVI). It was implemented beginning in the 1880's by creating protectorates
whereby the British government handled the foreign affairs of
an area while the local ruler, in return, agreed not to grant any
rights within his territory to another country without the consent
of the British government. By 1914 these treaties covered the
southern and eastern shore of the Arabian peninsula, from Aden
to Bahrein, with a similar agreement with Kuwait to prevent
that port from being used as the terminus of the German-fi-
nanced Berlin-to-Baghdad railroad.

Having established passive imperialism, the British implemented it by doing nothing unless a crisis of catastrophic proportions impended, as with the Omani attacks on Muscat in 1915,
or the threatened starvation of the Hadramaut in the 1920's, the

result of an intensification of the long-standing feud between the Ka'iti and the Kathiri described in this study.

The practical effect of this policy is well described by H. St. John Phillby (SHEBA'S DAUGHTERS, London, Methuen and Co., 1939, pp. 222-238). In effect, any penetration of these areas even by exploration-minded Britishers was rigidly controlled. These areas were, in fact, cut off from the rest of the world. While the exploited areas of imperialism at least received material benefits from the exploitation, these areas were allowed to stagnate; what little prosperity they had was destroyed by interminable tribal feuds, and their exportable products were made obsolete by technical advances. It has only been since the end of the second World War that any interest has been displayed in developing the protectorates, and that has been largely the result of the discovery of the Arabian oil fields. Actual and projected exploration for oil requires a far larger measure of internal security than the previous policy of non-interference could provide.

Passive imperialism probably had its origins in the intense, almost unthinking, rivalry between the British and the French manifest throughout this entire study. There is the possibly apocryphal story of the British general in the Crimean War who began his daily communique as follows: "We and our enemies the French successfully attacked the Russian position...." Anglo-French rivalry was entirely responsible for the British interest in Abyssinia from the abortive Harris expedition to the appointment of Cameron as consul, an appointment which was to lead directly to the Abyssinian expedition.

French and English relations on the west coast of the Red Sea during the period of the study illustrate clearly the method of imperial expansion during the eighteenth and early nineteenth centuries. A ship here, a man there, like a gigantic chess game. It was essentially adapted to naval activity and to the domination of an island group or shoreline where the sea could provide fairly rapid communication, support, and, if necessary, way of retreat. When applied to a large land mass among relatively primitive peoples it could prove disastrous (or very expensive) as in the case of Cameron and some of Ismail's African adventures. The classic case is the disastrous Afghan affair of 1839-1842 which, while outside the scope of this volume, had indirect influence on the Red Sea area, ending quickly any ideas of further British expansion there.

Looking backwards, it seems incredible that apparently no discussions occurred in India or in London on the political and military implications of the opening of the Suez Canal in 1869. While such discussions may have occurred (the file of the Bombay Secret and Political Proceedings breaks off in 1858 and does not resume again until the 1890's in the India Office), the implication is that either they did not, or else the Bombay Government did not see fit to inform the Resident at Aden of the results of their discussions. Possibly this question was not considered important in other European capitals either, inasmuch as the only two powers to take immediate advantage of the opening of the canal were the two powers which already had sovereignty in the area, the Ottoman Empire and Egypt.

Yet the political and military implications of the opening of the canal were tremendous, as is shown in the complexities of planning and operating the Abyssinian expedition in 1866-1867. This whole expedition was mounted and supplied from Bombay except for the mules. How they reached Abyssinia from the Mediterranean and Spain is not apparent from the documents; they may have gone around Africa. Yet before we judge the lack of foresight of the European statesman too hastily, it should be pointed out that the Suez Canal might well not have been success-ful except for some contemporary developments in steamship design whose implication the most advanced statesman could hardly have foreseen: the invention of the reciprocal engine which drastically cut fuel consumption per ton-mile, the efficient application of the screw propeller which dispensed with the un-wieldly paddle housings and greatly improved hull design, and the increased use of steel for ships which broke through the max-imum length for a ship dictated by the use of wood.

To the historian one of the interesting aspects of this study is the light it throws on British imperial expansion, the East India Company and its successor the India Office, and their re-lationship to the Foreign Office. We live in an age of complexity and rapid change. In the period of this study, 1800-1878, the speed of change was slower but the new problems presented must have been just as complex to the official involved. In re-constructing events from historical sources, one essential fact must be understood. Until the last few years of the period of this study, officials in Bombay, or in London, had little, if any, control of events. Communications were primitive and the of-ficials concerned with the imperial and foreign policy were often dealing with events which had happened long before. Put simply, the man on the spot was responsible for decision and action, the chancelleries of Europe were concerned chiefly with picking up the pieces.

The year 1800 marks the end of an imperial era, the period of the freewheeling private trading companies, the East India Company and the Levant Company. The Levant Company, with extensive extraterritorial rights in the Ottoman Empire, had been to all intents and purposes the British diplomatic agency at Istanbul. With its demise in 1802 the Foreign Office fell heir to the Levant Company's diplomatic position in this area.

The East India Company had grown during the eighteenth century from a group of private traders with a trading monopoly into what was to all intents and purposes a privately run major nation, conducting its own foreign affairs, issuing its own currency, and maintaining a private army and navy. Parliament recognized this duality of purpose when the new East India Company charter was voted in 1813, and deprived the Company of its trading monopoly. At the same time the Company was deprived of its agency in Egypt, established in the late eighteenth century in an attempt to use the Red Sea route for dispatches, and the Foreign Office soon established a consulate there. Thus it created the division of interest in the Red Sea area, the Foreign Office responsible for Egypt, the Holy Cities and northern Abyssinia, Tigré and Gondar, the East India Company (and its successor the India Office) responsible for southern Arabia, the Gulf of Aden, and Shoa and Harar in Abyssinia.

One of the most striking aspects of working in the India Office documents is the informality or, rather, lack of clarity in the responsibilities of the various levels of government involved. Yet during the period up to 1850, at any rate, the line of authority between the East India Company and the Foreign Office seemed clear and concise. This was probably the result of two factors: first, during the Napoleonic struggle, the Foreign Office adopted a policy which treated the boundaries of the Ottoman Empire, Iran and Afghanistan from the Adriatic to Pamir mountains, as one unit, considering any hostile act along this lengthy line in relation to all other activities hostile or friendly in the area; second, Palmerston, who thoroughly understood the principle, apparently dominated the East India Company directorate, and, by force of his personality, made the two branches of government work smoothly together. This unity of purpose was of major importance during the crisis with Muhammad Ali in the 1830's when Palmerston adopted, with the cooperation of the East India Company, a policy of containment establishing the mouth of the Red Sea, Bahrein in the Persian Gulf and Baghdad as the limiting spots where an attack by Muhammad Ali's forces would be considered as aggression against the British Empire.

With the end of the Egyptian crisis, cooperation between the H. E. I. C. and the Foreign Office became unimportant in the Red Sea area which was dominated rather by the sporadic Anglo-French rivalry. The Crimean War and the Sepoy Rebellion scarcely affected the Red Sea area, and yet both incidents provided in the documents indications of the effect of one event and what led up to the other. Admittedly these are impressions gained from peripheral events, but they deserve to be brought forward. The territorial expansion of the East India Company, culminating in the disastrous Afghan Campaign of 1839-1842, left the Company over-expanded and financially weakened at a period when depression and retrenchment were taking place in Great Britain. The over-expansion, in addition, strained the rather primitive governmental structure to the utmost, as did the lack of funds. This is manifested in the documents by indecision, interminable discussion, timorousness, and the development of personal and service backbiting and rivalries. Certainly if there can be any basic cause for the Sepoy Rebellion, it was due to inefficiency and consequent acts of omission on the part of the East India Company rather than any overt acts on its part.

A contributing factor must have been the Crimean War, which lowered British prestige in the Ottoman Empire and throughout the East in two ways: first, the British appeared to the Muslims to be at their beck and call; and second, the very indecisive nature of the campaign and its unimaginative planning lowered the prestige of British arms in Eastern eyes. The scandals surrounding the British military effort in the Crimea have often been taken as a turning point in internal British history. Certainly the Crimean War and the subsequent Sepoy Rebellion provided as great a turning point in imperial history.

The establishment of the India Office as a regular governmental agency with a Secretary of cabinet rank was reflected in the Red Sea area by a clearer and more concise relationship among the different levels of government. However, the same officials remained in the India Service, with the same tendency towards independent action which was manifest under the Company, and the same policies persisted.

Meanwhile the Foreign Office, with its system unchanged, was suffering from a major revolution in communications. In his best days, the genius of Palmerston manifested itself in his understanding of the basic problems of foreign relations, his ability to outline the objectives of his policy in broad directives, and his judgment in selecting an able man, sometimes one whom he personally disliked, who had the discretion, technical understanding, and force of character to carry out these directives.

The development of, first, the telegraph, and then the cable, created a revolution in diplomacy which must have been as confusing to the Chancellors of Europe as to the diplomats themselves. Where wire communication existed, decisions formerly made by an ambassador were made in London. And yet the new methods were very imperfect tools, since telegrams and cables were inordinately brief, probably to save money, and at times, as during the Yemen crisis, were partially incomprehensible until regular mail dispatches arrived. Meanwhile, where wire communications did not exist, the old system was followed.

The whole series of misunderstandings and inefficient handling of the incidents which led up to the Abyssinian expedition provided a superb example of the problem of communications. The original incident was largely a result of primitive communications which prevented Cameron from receiving his instructions. Yet the expedition itself a few years later had the benefit of wire communications from Aden to handle its problems.

Perhaps more startling was the ability of the British to communicate with Aden by wire during the Yemen crisis while the Turkish commander received his orders by primitive means, thus, in a sense, leaving the protagonists with totally different orders although a modus vivendi had been arrived at in London and Istanbul.

The Yemen crisis provides a wonderful example of lack of coordination between the India Office and the Foreign Office, not only in routine day-to-day affairs, but in major policy as well. A situation in which the Foreign Office was bending every effort to counter Russian intrigue in Istanbul while forces of the Ottoman and Indian armies were drawn up face to face at Lahej in South Arabia can only be described in Sir William Gilbert's

words, "A paradox, a paradox, a most ingenious paradox."
Even after the immediate crisis was resolved, its ancillary effects required lengthy negotiation, not between London and
Istanbul, but rather between the Foreign and India Offices,
each acting with the appearance of separate governments. It
required a meeting of the offices on the highest level to finally
solve the immediate problem of the Red Sea area and change a
basic policy, born of military necessity during the Napoleonic
invasion of Egypt, nurtured by the economic necessity of the
nascent steamship trade, and coming of age under the containment policy caused by an ambitious Middle Eastern leader.
And as has been so often the case in the past hundred years,
the solution was overtaken by events and was, in effect, meaningless.

BIBLIOGRAPHY*

This bibliography is not intended to be exhaustive. It is rather a list of the works which either actually are quoted or have been found useful as a background for the history of the Red Sea area. An exhaustive bibliography would have been much larger. For instance, a list of the various articles written by Charles T. Beke would easily extend to more than two pages, but the four titles selected contain all of Dr. Beke's ideas.

At various times the author has had available to him the resources of the Widener Library at Harvard, the Sterling Memorial Library at Yale, and the British Museum, India Office Library, and the Public Records Office in London. No attempt has been made to indicate which titles are available in which library, but it should be noted that most of the books published in India and at Aden are available at the India Office Library alone.

Chapter I is based on the following:

Browne, Edward G., LITERARY HISTORY OF PERSIA, Cambridge, University Press, 1928, Vol. I, TO 1000 A. D.

Budge, E. A. Wallis, HISTORY OF ETHIOPIA, NUBIA AND ABYSSINIA, London, Methuen & Co., 1928, 2 vols.

Kamerer, Albert, LA MER ROUGE, L'ABYSSINIE ET L'ARABIE DEPUIS L'ANTIQUITE, Le Caire, L'Imprimerie de l'Institute Français d'Archéologie orientale, pour la Société royale de géographie d'Egypte, 1929-1935. (Memoires de la Société Royale de géographie d'Egypte. T. XV-XVI.)

Playfair, Robert L., HISTORY OF ARABIA FELIX OR YEMEN, Bombay, printed for the Government, 1859, in the series Selections from the Records of the Bombay Government, New Series number XLIX

Rostovtzeff, Mekhail I., CARAVAN CITIES, Oxford, Clarendon Press, 1932

*Some books are not included in the bibliography even though they are cited in the text.

Rostovtzeff, Mekhail I. , THE SOCIAL AND ECONOMIC
    HISTORY OF THE ROMAN EMPIRE, Oxford, Clarendon
    Press, 1926.
Sanceau, Elaine, LAND OF PRESTER JOHN, New York, Knopf,
    1944.
Schoff, Wilfred H. , PERIPLUS OF THE ERYTHRAEAN SEA,
    New York, Longmans Green, 1912.
Vincent, William, COMMERCE AND NAVIGATION OF THE
    ANCIENTS IN THE INDIAN OCEAN (translation of PERI-
    PLUS MARIS ERYTHRAEI), London, Cadell and Davies,
    1807, 2 vols.

Chapter II is based on the following:

Charles-Roux, Francois, LES ORIGINES DE L'EXPEDITION
    D'EGYPTE, Paris, Plon-Nourrit et Cie. , 1910.
CAMBRIDGE HISTORY OF INDIA (Dodwell, H. H. , ed.), Vol. V,
    BRITISH INDIA 1497-1858, Cambridge, University Press,
    1929.
Head, Captain C. F. , EASTERN AND EGYPTIAN SCENERY,
    RUINS, &c. , London, Smith Elder & Co. , 1833. This con-
    tains an excellent economic analysis of the Red Sea route
    entitled "Steam Navigation from England to India."
Hoskins, Halford L. , BRITISH ROUTES TO INDIA, New York,
    Longmans Green, 1928.
Mengin, Felix, HISTOIRE DE L'EGYPTE 1823-1838, Paris,
    1839, containing a detailed account of the Arabian campaigns
    by M. Jomard.
Playfair, Robert Lambert, op. cit. This author used all the
    British voyages bearing on the Red Sea published before
    1859 and also the early voyages and log books in the East
    India House (now the India Office) which have since been
    published.
Sabry, Mohammed, L'EMPIRE EGYPTIEN SOUS MEHEMET
    ALI ET LA QUESTION D'ORIENT 1811-1849, Paris,
    Guenther, 1930.

Chapter XIX is based on the following:

The Pall Mall Gazette, London, 1864-1868.
PARLIAMENTARY DEBATES (commonly known as Hansard),
    third series (Hodgskin, Thomas, ed.), Vols. 178-192
    (1865-1868).

Chapter XIX (continued)

The Times, London, 1864-1868.

Documentary Sources

India Office

Bombay Government:

> Egypt, No. 7, contains dispatches from Red Sea area,
> 1820-1827.
> Bombay Political and Secret Consultations 1820-1837.
> Bombay Secret Consultations (a continuation of the above),
> 1837-1857.
> Bombay Secret Letters and Enclosures, 1857-1859.
> Bombay Secret Enclosures, 1859-1869.
> Letters from Aden and Muscat, 1864-1866.
> Letters from Aden, 1866-1872.

From 1872-1877 practically every dispatch from Aden appears
in copies in Foreign Office files.

Public Records Office

Foreign Office files:

> Abyssinia FO 1/1-FO 1/29, 1808-1879.
> Turkey FL 78/, Reports of the Consul and later Consul General in Egypt from 1825-1878. The volume numbers
> are too numerous to record.
> Turkey FO 78/1333, The island of Perim 1856-1857.
> Turkey FO 78/1785, The Lighthouses in the Red Sea, 1859-
> 1863; also refers to Perim.
> Turkey FO 78/1488, Jeddah Massacre, Commissioners
> Captain Pullen and Mr. Walne, 1858-1859.
> Turkey FO 78/2753 - FO 78/2756 - Yemen, Sovereignty
> Question 1873-1877.
> Turkey FO 78/3185 - FO 78/3189 - Egypt, Claims to
> Sovereignty in the Red Sea, Africa and Arabia, 1827-
> 1877.
> Slave Trade FO 84/ various volumes; of little value for the

Red Sea area as almost all documents are published
in annual Slave Trade Blue Books.
Many documents appear in both India Office and Foreign Office
files. Where they do, both sources are cited, providing an
interesting commentary on the degree of liaison between the
two offices.

Published Documents

Various Blue Books on Abyssinia, Aden, Yemen and Shoa:

These are of little value as most of the important political
material has been censored from the documents. They are
cited only when the censorship has an important effect on
public knowledge.

Travels:

The East India Company made it a policy to publish reports
containing geographical information in the Journal of the
Royal Geographical Society or the Journal of the Asiatic
Society of Bengal. These reports were usually censored
in that all political information was excluded.

Barker, Lieutenant W. C., "Report on the probable geo-
    graphical position of Harar," JRGS, Vol. XII, 1842
——————————————— , "On Eastern Africa," JRGS,
    Vol. XVIII, 1848
Cruttenden, Lieutenant C. J., "A Memoir on the Western
    or Edoor Tribe of the Somali Coast," JRGS, Vol. XIX,
    1849
——————————————— , "Note on the Myjertheyn
    Somalis," JASB, Vol. XIII, Part 1, 1844
Graham, Captain A. B., "A report on the Produce of Shoa,"
    JASB, Vol. XIII, Part 1, 1844
——————————————— , "Report on the manners etc. of
    the People of Shoa," JASB, Vol. XII, Part 2, 1843
Haines, Captain Stafford B., "Memoirs on the South and
    East Coast of Arabia," JRGS, Vol. XI, 1845
——————————————— ,"Memoir to accompany a chart
    of the entrance to the Red Sea," JRGS, Vol. IX, 1839
——————————————— , "An Account of an excursion

in Hadramaut by Adolphe Baron von Wrede," JRGS,
Vol. XIV, 1844

Kirk, Assistant Surgeon R. , "Report on the route from
Tajura to Ankobar," JRGS, Vol. XII, 1842

Wilkins, Lieutenant H. St. C. , "Extracts from a Report on
attempts made to supply Aden with water," Journal of
the Bombay Branch of the Royal Asiatic Society,
Vol. V, 1857

Official Publications Based on Documents

Aitchison, C. V. , COLLECTION OF TREATIES, ENGAGE-
MENTS AND SUNNUDS RELATING TO INDIA AND
NEIGHBORING COUNTRIES, Calcutta, Government Press,
1929-1933, 14 vols. Volume XI contains treaties and
historical summaries relative to the Red Sea area

Forrest, George W. , SELECTIONS FROM THE TRAVELS AND
JOURNALS PRESERVED IN THE BOMBAY SECRETARIAT,
Bombay, Government Central Press, 1906

Great Britain: Admiralty, Naval Staff, Naval Intelligence
Division, HANDBOOK OF ARABIA (I. D. 1128) Vol. I,
London, H. M. Stationery Office, 1920; (Vol. II not for
public sale; Vol. I partially censored)

Hunter, Major F. M. , AN ACCOUNT OF THE BRITISH SETTLE-
MENT AT ADEN, London, 1877

——————————— , and Sealey, Captain C. W. H. , AN
ACCOUNT OF THE ARAB TRIBES IN THE VICINITY OF
ADEN, Bombay, Government Central Press, 1886

King, Lieutenant J. S. , A DESCRIPTIVE AND HISTORICAL
ACCOUNT OF THE BRITISH OUTPOST OF PERIM, Bombay, Government Central Press, 1877. Selections from
the Records of the Bombay Government, new series, CXLIX

Low, Charles R. , HISTORY OF THE INDIAN NAVY 1613-1863,
London, Bentley, 1877, 2 vols. Prepared, with official
sanction, from the Records of the Indian Navy preserved
in the India Office in London

Playfair, Captain Robert L. , A HISTORY OF ARABIA FELIX
OR YEMEN, Bombay, Government Central Press, 1859.
Selections from the Records of the Bombay Government,
new series, XLIX

——————————— , AN ACCOUNT OF ADEN, reprinted
in the HISTORY OF ARABIA FELIX, Aden, Jail Press, 1859

Playfair, Captain Robert L. , A MEMOIR ON THE ANCIENT
    RESERVOIRS LATELY DISCOVERED AND NOW IN THE
    COURSE OF RESTORATION AT ADEN, Aden, Jail Press,
    1857
Tremenheere, Major General C. W. , REPORT ON THE VARI-
    OUS ARAB TRIBES IN THE NEIGHBOURHOOD OF ADEN,
    Calcutta, Foreign Department Press, 1872; written by
    Captain W. F. Prideaux and incorporated in toto in Hunter
    and Sealey, ACCOUNT OF THE ARAB TRIBES, vide supra

                          Printed Material

                          Bibliographies

Fumagalli, G. , BIBLIOGRAPHIA ETHIOPICA, Florence,
    Hoepli, 1893
Gay, Jean, BIBLIOGRAPHIE DES OUVRAGES RELATIFS A
    L'AFRICA ET L'ARABIA, San Remo, J. Gay et fils, 1875

                          Other Material

d'Abbadie, Arnauld, DOUZE ANS DANS LE HAUTE ETHIOPIE,
    Paris, Hachette, 1862, Vol. I (all published)
Allen's Indian Mail, editorial on death of Captain S. B. Haines,
    London, August 6, 1860, p. 1
Angoulvant, G. & Vigneras, Sylvain, DJEBOUTI, MER ROUGE
    ET ABYSSINIE, Paris, Libraire Africaine et Colonial,
    1902
Asiatic Journal, "Account of Aden" (unsigned), Vol. XXVIII,
    April, 1839
Beke, Charles T. , THE BRITISH CAPTIVES IN ABYSSINIA,
    London, Longmans, 1867, second ed. (the first edition is
    a brief pamphlet)
————————— , "On the Countries south of Abyssinia, "
    JRGS, Vol. XIII, 1843
————————— , THE FRENCH AND ENGLISH IN THE RED
    SEA, London, 1862
————————— , "A Statement of facts relative to the Trans-
    actions between the writer and the late British Political
    Mission to the Court of Shoa in Abessinia, " London,
    Madden, 1846, second ed.

Beke, (Mrs.) Emily (Alston), SUMMARY OF THE LATE DR.
BEKE'S PUBLISHED WORKS AND OF HIS INADEQUATELY
REQUITED PUBLIC SERVICES, Tunbridge Wells, Baldwin,
1876
Blackwoods Magazine, "The Occupation of Aden" (unsigned),
Vol. LIII, April, 1843
Blanc, Henry, A NARRATIVE OF CAPTIVITY IN ABYSSINIA,
London, Smith, 1868
Bruce, James, TRAVELS TO DISCOVER THE SOURCES OF
THE NILE, 1768-73, Dublin, Sleater, 1790, 6 vols.
Budge, Sir E. A. Wallis, A HISTORY OF ETHIOPIA, London,
Methuen, 1928, 2 vols.
Burckhardt, John Lewis, NOTES ON THE BEDOUINS AND
WAHABYS, London, Colburn and Bentley, 1831, 2 vols.
——————————————, TRAVELS IN ARABIA, London, Col-
burn, 1829, 2 vols.
——————————————, TRAVELS IN NUBIA, London, Col-
burn, 1819, 2 vols.
Burton, Richard F., FIRST FOOTSTEPS IN EAST AFRICA,
London, Longmans, 1856
——————————————, "Narrative of a Trip to Harar," JRGS,
Vol. XXV, 1855
Chaillé-Long, Charles, MY LIFE ON FOUR CONTINENTS,
London, Hutchison, 1912
Combes, Eduard, & Tamisier, M., UN VOYAGE EN ABYS-
SINIE, Paris, Dessart, 1838, 4 vols.
Coupland, Reginald, EAST AFRICA AND ITS INVADERS,
Oxford, Clarendon Press, 1938
——————————————, THE EXPLOITATION OF EAST AFRICA
1856-90, London, Faber & Faber, 1939
de la Rocque, Jean, A VOYAGE TO ARABIA THE HAPPY,
London, Strahan, 1726
Dodwell, Henry H., THE FOUNDER OF MODERN EGYPT,
Cambridge, University Press, 1931
Dufton, Henry, NARRATIVE OF A JOURNEY THROUGH ABYS-
SINIA, London, Chapman and Hall, 1867, second ed.
Dye, William E., MOSLEM EGYPT AND CHRISTIAN ABYS-
SINIA, New York, Attain & Prout, 1880
Exupere de Prats de Mollo, P., ADEN ET LE GOLFE D'ADEN,
Letters, Tours, Maine, 1871
——————————————————————, "Voyage a Aden et sur la Cote
Orientale d'Afrique," Revue de Monde Catholique,

August 10, 25, September 10, 1868, Vol. VII

Ferret, Pierre Victoire, Galinier, Joseph-Germaine, VOYAGE EN ABYSSINIE, Paris, Paulin, 1847, 2 vols.

Foreign Quarterly Review, "French and English Rivalry in East Africa" (unsigned; the ideas are those of Beke, but it is not written in his characteristic style), April, 1844, Vol. XXXIII

Foster, Captain R. , "Short topographical and General Description of Aden," Transactions of the Bombay Geographical Society, 1838-1839, Vol. II

Gobat, Samuel, JOURNAL OF THREE YEARS RESIDENCE IN ABYSSINIA, New York, Dodd, 1850

Goldsmid, Colonel Sir Frederick J. , TELEGRAPH & TRAVEL, London, Macmillan, 1874

Guillain, M. , DOCUMENTS SUR L'HISTOIRE... DE MADEGAS-CAR, Paris, Imprimerie Royale, 1845

Hall, John James, LIFE AND CORRESPONDENCE OF HENRY SALT, London, Bentley, 1834, 2 vols.

Harris, Major W. Cornwallis, THE HIGHLANDS OF ETHIOPIA, London, Longmans, 1844, 2 vols.

Henty, George A. , MARCH TO MAGDALA, London, Tinsley, 1868

Von Heuglin, Martin Theodore, REISE NACH ABESSINIEN, Jena, Costenoble, 1868

Holland, Major Treven J. & Hozier, Captain Henry M. , RECORD OF THE EXPEDITION TO ABYSSINIA, London, W. Clowes & Sons, 1870, 3 vols.

Hoskins, Halford L. , BRITISH ROUTES TO INDIA, Philadelphia, Longmans Green, 1928

Hotten, John Camden, editor, ABYSSINIA AND ITS PEOPLE OR LIFE IN THE LAND OF PRESTER JOHN, London, John Camden Hotten, 1868

Hozier, Captain Henry M. , THE BRITISH EXPEDITION TO ABYSSINIA, London, Macmillan, 1869

Irwin, Eyles, A SERIES OF ADVENTURES IN THE COURSE OF A VOYAGE UP THE RED SEA, London, Dodsley, 1780

Isenberg, William & Krapf, J. Lewis, JOURNALS, London, Seeley, Burnside & Seeley, 1843

Jacob, Lieutenant Colonel Harold F. , KINGS OF ARABIA, London, Mills & Boon, 1923

Johnston, Charles, TRAVELS IN SOUTHERN ABYSSINIA, London, Madden, 1844, 2 vols.

Kammerer, M. Albert, "La Mer Rouge, L'Abyssinie et
    L'Arabie depuis L'antiquite," Societe Royale de Geographie
    d'Egypte, Le Caire, 1929, Vols. I & II
Krapf, J. Lewis, TRAVELS, RESEARCHES AND MISSIONARY
    LABOURS, London, Trubner, 1860
(Le Blanc, Vincent), White, Vincent, THE WORLD SURVEYED,
    trans. Brooke, Francis, London, Starkey, 1660
Lefebvre, Theophile, VOYAGE EN ABYSSINIE... 1839-1843,
    Paris, Bertrand, 1845-1854, 6 vols. and 3 vols. atlas
Lejean, Guillaume, THEODORE II, LE NOUVEL EMPEREUR
    D'ABYSSINIE, Paris, Amyot, N. D. (1865)
Loring, General W. W., A CONFEDERATE SOLDIER IN EGYPT,
    New York, Dodd, Mead, 1884
Malcolmson, J. P., "An Account of Aden," Journal of the Royal
    Asiatic Society, 1846, Vol. VIII
Markham, Clements R., HISTORY OF THE ABYSSINIAN EX-
    PEDITION, London, Macmillan, 1869
Martineau, John, LIFE AND CORRESPONDENCE OF SIR
    BARTLE FRERE, London, Murray, 1895, 2 vols.
Mengin, Felix, HISTOIRE DE L'EGYPT 1823-1838, Paris,
    Firmin Didot, 1839. (Contains Jomard, M., "Arabie," a
    description of Mehemet Ali's campaigns in Arabia.)
Miles, Samuel B., "Report on a portion of the African Coast"
    (Somali), TRANSACTIONS OF THE BOMBAY GEOGRAPH-
    ICAL SOCIETY 1873-4, Vol. XIX reprinted in JRGS,
    Vol. XLII
——————————, "Journal of a Trip with Munzinger,"
    TRANSACTIONS OF THE BOMBAY GEOGRAPHICAL
    SOCIETY, 1873-4, Vol. XIX reprinted in JRGS, Vol. XLI
Mookerji, Radhakumuda, INDIA SHIPPING, Bombay, etc.,
    Longmans Green, 1912
Niebuhr, Karsten, DESCRIPTION DE L'ARABIE, trans.
    Monrier, Ferdinand-Louis, Amsterdam & Utrecht,
    S. J. Bualde, 1774
NOUVELLES ANNALES DES VOYAGES, 1838, Vol. LXXVIII,
    review of UN VOYAGE EN ABYSSINIE by Combes &
    Tamisier, pp. 293 ff
"Officer in the Queen's Army," anonymous, A HISTORICAL
    AND STATISTICAL SKETCH OF ADEN IN ARABIA FELIX,
    Madras, Twigg, 1848
Oliver, Samuel Passfield, MADAGASCAR, London, Macmillan,
    1886, 2 vols.

Parkyns, Mansfield, LIFE IN ABYSSINIA, London, Murray,
    1853, 2 vols.
Pavic, Th. M. , "La Mer Rouge et le Golfe Persique," Revue
    de deux Mondes, 1844
Pearce, Nathaniel (Halls, J.J. , editor), LIFE AND ADVEN-
    TURES OF NATHANIEL PEARCE, London, Colburn &
    Bentley, 1831, 2 vols.
Playfair, Sir Robert Lambert, "Reminiscences," CHAMBERS
    JOURNAL, sixth series, Vol. II monthly from December,
    1898 through November, 1899
Plowden, Walter Chichele (Plowden, Trevor C. , editor),
    TRAVELS IN ABYSSINIA, London, Longmans, 1868
Poilet, J. B. (editor), LES MISSION CATHOLIQUES FRAN-
    ÇAISES AUX XIX SIECLE; Vol. II, ABYSSINIE, INDE,
    INDO-CHINE, Paris, Armand Colin, N. D. (c. 1900)
Rambaud, Alfred (editor), LA FRANCE COLONIALE, Paris,
    Armand Colin, 1895, seventh ed.
Rassam, Hormudz, NARRATIVE OF THE BRITISH MISSION
    TO THEODORE, London, Murray, 1869, 2 vols.
Robinson, Arthur E. , "Egyptian-Abyssinian War 1874-6,"
    Journal of the African Society, 1927, Vol. XXVI
Rochet d'Hericourt, Charles E. , VOYAGE SUR LA COTE
    ORIENTALE DE LA MER ROUGE DANS LE PAYS D'ADEL
    ET LE ROYAUME DE SHOA, Paris, Bertrand, 1841
    ————————————————————— ,SECOND VOYAGE SUR LES
    DEUX RIVES DE LA MER ROUGE...ET LA ROYAUME
    DE SHOA, Paris, Bertrand, 1846
Rüppel, Eduard, REISE IN ABYSSINIEN, Frankfurt-am-Main,
    Schmerber, 1838, 2 vols.
Russel, Captain Comte Stanislaus Jules Marie (Charmes,
    Gabriel, ed.), UNE MISSION EN ABYSSINIE ET DANS LA
    MER ROUGE, Paris, Plon, 1884
Sabry, Mohammed, L'EMPIRE EGYPTIENNE SOUS ISMAIL
    1863-1879, Paris, Guenther, 1933
    ————————————————— , L'EMPIRE EGYPTIENNE SOUS MEHEMET
    ALI ET LA QUESTION D'ORIENT, 1811-1849, Paris,
    Guenther, 1930
Salt, Henry, VOYAGE TO ABYSSINIA, London, Rivington, 1814
Sammarco, Angelo, HISTOIRE DE L'EGYPTE MODERNE,
    Tome III, "Regne du Khedive Ismail," Le Caire, Societe
    Royale de Geographie d'Egypte, 1937
Schoff, Wilfrid H. (trans. and ed.), PERIPLUS OF THE

ERYTHRAEAN SEA, New York, Longmans, 1912

Shepherd, A. F., CAMPAIGN IN ABYSSINIA, Bombay, 1868

Stern, Henry A. (Purday, C. H., editor), ABYSSINIAN CAP-
TIVES, RECENT INTELLIGENCE, London, privately
printed, N. D. (1866)

——————————, CAPTIVE MISSIONARY, London, Cassell
(1869)

——————————, "Journal of a trip to Sana," Jewish Intelligence, 1857, Vol. XXIII; in Missionary Intelligence section,
April, May, and August, 1857

——————————, WANDERINGS AMONG THE FALASHAS IN
ABYSSINIA, London, Wirthkerim, 1862

United Service Journal, 1840, part II, May, "A Descriptive
and Historical Notice of Aden lately captured by the British" (unsigned)

Valentia, Lord (later Mountnorris, Lord), VOYAGES AND
TRAVELS TO INDIA, CEYLON, THE RED SEA, ABYS-
SINIA AND EGYPT IN THE YEARS 1802, 1803, 1804, 1805
and 1806, London, Miller, 1809, 3 vols.

Vincent, William (trans. and ed.), PERIPLUS OF THE
ERYTHRAEAN SEA, London, Cadell & Davies, 1800, 2 vols.

Walda Maryam, Alaqa (trans. Mondon-Vidailhet, C.),
CHRONIQUE DE THEODORE II, Paris, 1904 (the complete
work from 1853-1868)

——————————, (trans. Weld-Blundell, H.), "History
of King Theodore," Journal of the African Society, Vol. VI,
1907 (contains only latter part of the Chronicle from 1863-
1868)

Wellsted, Lieutenant J. R., TRAVELS TO THE CITY OF THE
CALIPHS, ETC., London, Colburn, 1840, 2 vols.

——————————, TRAVELS IN ARABIA, London,
Murray, 1837, 2 vols.

Newspapers

Allen's Indian Mail, 1843-1855
Pall Mall Gazette, 1864-1868
The Times, London, 1864-1868

521

Armament (cont'd)
gun powder, 272; Turk vs.
Arabs (1870's), 457. See also
Theodore and artisans (who
made arms)
Armenian Patriarch, 318-20, 356.
For Abyssinian-Armenian
church controversy, see Jeru-
salem
Arrah Selassie, Ras of Tigré, 171
Arthur, Governor, 107. See also
Bombay, Govt of
Artisans. See Gaffat; Theodore
and artisans; Schiller and Ess-
ler
Asala, Fadhli village, 155, 361-
362
Ashangi, 350
Ashfa, 301
Asir country in Arabia, 4-5, 36,
38; government, 46; route of
approach, 46
Asiri confederation, 44-6, 52, 55,
61, 75; and Sharif Husain of
Abu 'Arish, 100, 102; as mili-
tary force, 105, 141; and Turks,
218-19, 364, 376, 396-99, 402,
456. See also Mecca
Assab Bay, 6, 245, 377-79, 384,
388, 393
Assal, Lake, 122
Atbara River, 6
Athenaeum magazine, 336
Atifi, 395
'Aulaqi, 84, 208-10, 216, 358,
411; Upper 'A., 66, 209; Lower
'A., 66
Aussa, 482
Austria, 58, 255
Austrian ship, "Narenta," 388
Avanchers, Leon des, 238
Awamir, 74
Axum, 33, 166, 247, 275, 321;
Axumite kingdom, 16-17
Ayal Ahmed, 147, 214, 473; Habr
Owuls, subtribe, 214, 254
Ayal Yunis, 147, 473-74
Ayrton, Consul at Cairo, 288

Bab-el-Mandeb, 4, 20, 24, 32,
64, 67, 97, 113-14, 223, 242,
258, 270, 272, 369
Badger, George Percy, 207, 209,
252, 285-86, 289, 320, 332
Baghdad, 11-14, 52, 209, 341;
object of Muhammad Ali's campaign, 54, 62; B. Pashalik,
414. See also Rawlinson
Baghi, 467
Bahrein Island, 54, 61-2, 430,
442-43
Bahr-el-Gazal, Sudan province,
480
Baird, General, 32
Bajil, 399
Baker, Sir Samuel, 480, 487; consulted on Abyssinian expedition,
320-22, 375; head, expedition
to White Nile region, 383; officer for Ismail, 465-68
Balkania (Yalkama; modern Balkis), Queen. See Sheba, Queen
of
Bandar Broom, 457-58
Bandar Muraiah, 431
Banyans (B. merchants), 25-6,
29, 34, 41, 45, 103, 105, 107;
Br. protection of at Berbera,
113, 144, 148; at Massawa,
115, 169, 174, 178, 182, 468,
491; at Hodeida, 216, 397; at
San'a, 261; at Jidda, 376; under Egyptian occupation, 470;
on Somali coast, 493
Barakat, family of, 26
Barawa. See Brava
Barber, Consul at Alexandria,
41-2
Barclay, David, Colonial Office,
175
Bardel, follower of Cameron,
305-06, 308, 312-13, 317, 323
Barker, Lieutenant: sent to Ta-
jura, 122 (see also Moresby);
and routes for expedition to
Shoa, 132
Barlow. See Houghton

522

544